BUILDING IN BIG BROTHER

BUILDING IN BIG BROTHER

The Cryptographic Policy Debate

Edited by

Lance J. Hoffman

*Institute for Computer and Telecommunications Systems Policy and
Department of Electrical Engineering and Computer Science
School of Engineering and Applied Science
The George Washington University*

Springer-Verlag

New York   Berlin   Heidelberg   London   Paris
Tokyo   Hong Kong   Barcelona   Budapest

Lance J. Hoffman
Dept. of Electrical Engineering and Computer Science
The George Washington University
Washington, DC 20052 USA

Library of Congress Cataloging-in-Publication Data
Building in big brother : the cryptographic policy debate / edited by
    Lance J. Hoffman.
        p.   cm.
     Includes bibliographical references.
     ISBN 0-387-94441-9
     1. Computer security.   2. Cryptography.   I. Hoffman, Lance J.
QA76.9.A25B85   1995
363.2'52--dc20   95-3758

Printed on acid-free paper.

Production managed by Impressions, a division of Edwards Brothers, Inc. and supervised by Karen Phillips; manufacturing supervised by Jacqui Ashri.
Typeset by Impressions, a division of Edwards Brothers, Inc.
Printed and bound by R.R. Donnelley & Sons, Harrisonburg, VA.
Printed in the United States of America.

9 8 7 6 5 4 3 2 1

ISBN 0-387-94441-9   Springer-Verlag New York Berlin Heidelberg

To Nina

Preface

The announcement of the Clipper chip by the U.S. Government in April 1993 set off a frenzy of discussions about cryptography policy in the technological community. The shock waves from it ultimately included front page treatment in The New York Times, repeated questions to the Vice President, creation of several new newsgroups on the Internet, and some very productive public discussions about striking the balance between national security, law enforcement, and civil liberties.

We still don't have good answers for some of the questions that have been raised. As the Global Information Infrastructure is being built, we are writing portions of the Constitution for Cyberspace. I've been fortunate to have a front row seat and to share much of this with my students.

The original reading and selection of materials was made by the first cohort of students* in The George Washington University Accelerated Master of Science Program in Telecommunications and Computers at the Ashburn, Virginia campus. They worked many long hours—reading, debating, and selecting materials for this book. In addition, Bob Patton spent a great deal of time scanning and editing the material. Nestor Torres prepared the index. And Harish Nalinakshan provided an enormous amount of technical and administrative assistance and kept the project on track as new developments took place in the debate and new papers and legislation reflected these.

As with most readings books, some of the selections cover similar material. We have tried to hold this duplication to an acceptable level. The original source of each article is noted with the article itself. In a few cases, previously unpublished material is making its debut in these pages.

By bringing together the most significant policy and technological viewpoints in one place, we hope to move the debate along and to arrive at a rational cryptographic policy to support the developing Global Information Infrastructure.

Lance J. Hoffman
Washington, D.C.
November 1994

---

* Amjad (Jim) Arnous, Raleigh Baker, Cameron Craig Berry, Edward Paul Black, Christopher Bondi, Dan Byrne, John Morgan Day, Bruce Fleming, Raul Fumagali, Michael George, Lester Gregory, Lawrence Guidry, Michael Hassien, Leroy Jeter, Kim Lawson-Jenkins, Ralph Leyrer, John McRae, Richard Mendelowitz, Husni (Al) Naja, Suparak Pathammavong, Everett Ray, Randall Root, Marie Wai Tai, Farley Warner, Jr., Jack Wiiki.

Contents

Contributors

Betsy Anderson	*The White House*
Diana Arrington	*The George Washington University*
David M. Balenson	*Trusted Information Systems, Inc.*
Stewart A. Baker	*National Security Agency (now with Steptoe & Johnson)*
John Perry Barlow	*Electronic Frontier Foundation*
Donna Berkelhammer	*The George Washington University*
David S. Bernstein	*Infosecurity News*
Matt Blaze	*AT&T Bell Laboratories*
Ernest F. Brickell	*Sandia National Laboratories*
Clint Brooks	*National Security Agency*
Todd Buchholz	*The White House*
William Bulkeley	*The Wall Street Journal*
James Chandler	*National Intellectual Property Law Institute*
Scott Charney	*U.S. Department of Justice*
Larry E. Christensen	*U.S. Department of Commerce*
Dorothy E. Denning	*Georgetown University*
Whitfield Diffie	*Sun Microsystems, Inc.*
Rebecca Duncan	*Datapro Information Services Group*
Carl M. Ellison	*Trusted Information Systems, Inc.*
Louis J. Freeh	*Federal Bureau of Investigation*
A. Michael Froomkin	*University of Miami*
G. T. Gangemi, Sr.	*Wang Laboratories*
James Gattuso	*Office of the Vice President*
David Gelernter	*Yale University*
Lamarris Gill	*The George Washington University*
Albert Gore	*Vice President, United States of America*
John M. Harmon	*U.S. Department of Justice*
Martha Harris	*U.S. Department of State*
Stephen T. Kent	*BBN Communications Corp.*
Steven B. Lipner	*Trusted Information Systems, Inc.*
Susan Landau	*University of Massachusetts*
Anthony Lauck	*Digital Equipment Corp.*
Kim Lawson-Jenkins	*Motorola Cellular Group*
Ron Levy	*U.S. Treasury Department*
Steven Levy	*Author and Journalist*
David P. Maher	*AT&T*
David McIntosh	*Office of the Vice President*
Silvio Micali	*Massachusetts Institute of Technology*
Douglas Miller	*Software Publishers Association*
David Naccache	*Thomson Consumer Electronics R&D, France*
Peter Neumann	*SRI International*
Deborah Russell	*O'Reilly & Associates, Inc.*
David Sobel	*Electronic Privacy Information Center*

CONTRIBUTORS

Sebastiaan von Solms	*Rand Afrikaans University*
Bruce Sterling	*Author and Journalist*
Walter Tuchman	*Amperif Corporation*
Geoffrey W. Turner	*SRI International*
Stephen T. Walker	*Trusted Information Systems, Inc.*
Philip Zimmermann	*Boulder Software Engineering*

INTRODUCTION

As the information superhighway develops, the United States government is increasingly concerned with communication, privacy, and security. This is not a new area for government concern; indeed, it has been around since before the French revolution when governments were, even then, worried about accountability of authors and publication of seditious materials. In recent months, three interwoven initiatives have been prominent: the so-called "digital telephony improvement initiative," the Clipper chip key escrow encryption initiative, and modifications to the Export Administration Act.

The digital telephony initiative is an effort by the government to maintain some capability to wiretap in cases where advances in telecommunications technology could (or have already) outrun law enforcement's ability to intercept communications in order to enforce laws and protect national security. A law enacted in late 1994 requires telecommunications carriers to ensure that they possess the capability and capacity to enable the government to isolate and intercept, pursuant to authorization by a court, call-identifying information and the contents of a communication. This law is significantly more narrow than the original Bush and Clinton Administration proposals. Most importantly, the requirements apply only to carriers who engage in "the transmission of switching of wire or electronic communications as a common carrier for hire". They do not apply to information service providers (the Internet, AOL, Prodigy, etc.), to private networks, or to PBXs.

In addition, the law has some important new privacy protections, including the prohibition of remote monitoring. Law enforcement cannot require a carrier to install a port which can be activated by a law enforcement officer. All taps must be conducted with the intervention of the carrier (as is the case under current law). The warrant requirements under current law have not been changed.

The law authorizes $500 million to be paid by the government to carriers for upgrades of existing features and services within the first 4 years after its passage.

The Clipper chip is a Government attempt to protect American communications against industrial espionage and other compromises while at the same time maintaining the existing capability of law enforcement and national security agencies to eavesdrop, with a court order, on suspect communications. When law enforcement or national security agencies are interested in a person's communications, they obtain a warrant from the appropriate issuing authority. They then fax a notification that they have this to two independent government agencies (currently the National Institute of Standards and Technology and the Automated Systems Division of the Department of the Treasury), who then each give up half of the digital key necessary to decrypt the conversation. When the two half-keys are joined to form the entire key, law enforcement officials can then obtain the unit key for the given chip used in the communicating telephone and use it to decrypt the conversation (assuming that telephone has used the Clipper chip in the first place).

This so-called "escrowed encryption standard" is urged but voluntary in the federal government. The Administration, after looking into potential violations of the First, Fourth, and Fifth Amendments of the Bill of Rights, decided not to make it mandatory for private persons. Nevertheless, it clearly hopes that almost everybody will use this system. A number of civil libertarians and outside observers remain concerned that it will become mandatory in the future and the response to this initiative has been almost uniformly negative in non-governmental circles.

No one has seriously suggested that the algorithm is insecure (although a method of using it which negates any value to law enforcement because of a minor design flaw has made the front page of *The New York Times*). But many do not completely trust the key escrow agents. Many suggestions have been made such as adding a third escrow agent from the private sector, adding one from the Judiciary, letting users pick whichever escrow agents they want, having software manufacturers serve as the escrow agents, etc. Only recently have some of these started to be considered by the Administration.

Clipper's encryption algorithm, "Skipjack", fits into Capstone, the U.S. government's long-term project to develop a set of standards for publicly available cryptography for use in voice and data communications. In one scenario, the government itself and all private companies doing electronic business with the government would be required to use Capstone, which could all be contained on a single computer chip. This would provide economies of scale but would also force users who wanted "government-proof" communications to superencrypt using other commercially available algorithms.

There is a large and growing collection of encryption software and hardware available. The July 1994 Software Publishers Association study shows well over 800 products, of which roughly half are manufactured overseas. There is an increasing fear that more and more American sales are being lost because American software cannot provide the same sort of good encryption that is provided in other countries (since it is illegal to export really good encryption from the United States). Indeed, one vendor has actually set up a completely independent cryptographic development lab overseas from which crypto products are imported into the United States (but can't be re-sent out again). Only recently have export controls been loosened a bit so traveling business executives can at least take their laptops overseas and encrypt information using the Data Encryption Standard (the standard used for banking and financial transactions) without violating U.S. export laws. Nevertheless, there is a movement afoot to abandon many export controls on encryption, arguing that the economic needs outweigh the national security needs.

This collection of readings presents the best writings to date on these issues. The first part contains material to provide readers with an overview of current technology trends in cryptography. The next part deals with current U.S. Government policy and the often vehement reactions to it. The last part presents papers dealing with three aspects of cryptography policy: law enforcement, civil liberties, and export controls.

PART I

BACKGROUND

CHAPTER 1

CRYPTOGRAPHY (FROM JULIUS CAESAR THROUGH PUBLIC KEY CRYPTOSYSTEMS)

METHODS TO KEEP SECRETS SECRET

Encryption has been used from the days of Julius Caesar, and has now become indispensable for the storage and transmission of sensitive information in computer and communications systems. This chapter presents an introduction to encryption and a number of encryption schemes.

The first three readings give an overview of cryptography and of some modern cryptgraphic schemes. First, Gangemi and Russell provide a comprehensive definition of encryption and then give a history of encryption starting with the Caesar Cipher, progressing to the use of the Enigma machine in World War II, and ending with a brief introduction of some more modern forms of encryption (e. g., public key encryption). Following this, an excerpt from a Datapro Information Services Group report focuses specifically on encryption methods for computer networks. It describes link and end-to-end encryption and various key management techniques. Then, "Answers to Frequently Asked Questions About Today's Cryptography" from RSA Laboratories covers a range of encryption topics from key management to factoring and from patents to encryption standards. It also discusses various algorithms.

The next excerpt from the Association for Computing Machinery's report on U. S. cryptography policy reviews the last twenty years in cryptography, identifying key policy and technology development players and issues.

Those who think implementing cryptography policy is easy need only look to the comprehensive and well-written work of Kent to start to appreciate how complex that task is. It is the first of several readings which end this chapter and provide descriptions of some widely used cryptographic algorithms: Internet Privacy Enhanced Mail, cellular phone system encryption algorithms, the Digital Signature Standard (DSS), the Secure Hash Standard (SHS), and Pretty Good Privacy (PGP).

Kent provides an overview of the proposed Internet Privacy Enhanced Mail (IPEM) as defined in various RFC[1] documents describing basic services; messaging environment; use of cryptographic algorithms; message processing steps; message integrity and originator authentication; message encryption/decryption; encoding; delivery; verification; Internet public key certification system; and policy issues. He also discusses IPEM's relationship to the OSI Security Reference Model, the CCITT Message Handling Service (MHS; X.400), CCITT security (CCITT recommendation X.509), the recently adopted Multipurpose Internet Mail Extensions (MIME; RFC 1341), and SMTP (RFC 821).

Lawson-Jenkins then lays out security and privacy concerns in wireless communications, describing various security measures that have been adopted in Europe and comparing them to methods in the U.S. She describes call establishment procedures for wireless communications using various standards, but does not give details on the cellular algorithms used.

Next, the NIST standard Digital Signature Algorithm (DSA) is given, including specifics of parameter definition and of signature generation and verification. Additional information on parameter generation, algorithm validation, and random number generation is not included in these excerpts, but is available from NIST.

Then, the Secure Hash Algorithm (SHA), required for use with the DSS, is described. This produces a 160-bit hash value from a variable-sized input. It is structurally similar to Message Digest 4 and 5 (MD4,

---

[1] Requests for Comment (RFCs) are the official archival publications of the Internet and include protocol standards, experimental protocol descriptions, policy statements, and various informational documents. RFCs are available on-line at various sites and in hardcopy format from SRI International in Menlo Park, California.

MD5), but may be more secure given the longer message digest being produced.

Finally, Pretty Good Privacy (PGP), "public key encryption for the masses," is described. PGP employs public key cryptography and strong algorithms for authentication and message transmission, currently combining the International Data Encryption Algorithm (IDEA) and the DES algorithm. I've chosen to excerpt a lot from the PGP manual, because PGP, much more than any of the other algorithms, is somewhat ideological as well as technological. The history of PGP is also covered in Bulkeley's article on pages 400–405.

Encryption*

Deborah Russell and G. T. Gangemi, Sr.

Encryption is a method of information protection that dates back 4000 years, an ancient art that's taken on new significance in the modern computer age. It's a particularly effective way to protect sensitive information—for example, passwords—that's stored in a computer system, as well as information that's being transmitted over communications lines.

Through the ages, encryption has protected communications while they were being transmitted through a hostile environment—usually one involving war or diplomacy. Hundreds or even thousands of years ago, this might have meant encrypting a letter from a battlefield general to the home front; encryption protected the communication in case the soldier carrying the letter was captured. In modern times, this might mean encrypting an electronic mail message containing sensitive information (of military, corporate, or personal importance) transmitted across a network; encryption protects the information in case an intruder taps into the network.

Information that's encrypted remains secure even when it's transmitted over a network that doesn't provide strong security—in fact, even if the information is publicly available. In most versions of the UNIX operating system, for example, the file containing user passwords stores those password in encrypted form. Encryption protects these passwords so effectively that, except in quite secure systems, the password file is publicly readable. Anybody can read it, but nobody can understand the passwords in it.

Because encryption has historically been an expensive method of computer security (expensive in terms of product cost as well as computer time needed to encrypt), it has most often been used to protect only classified or particularly sensitive information—for example, military information, intelligence information, information about funds transfers, and information about the passwords in a computer system. Encryption is now becoming a more popular and inexpensive method of protecting both communications and sensitive stored data. For ex-

---

* *Computer Security Basics*; pp. 165—179. O'Reilly & Associates, Inc., Sebastopol, California, 1991.

ample, the nationwide Internet network recently began offering an encryption service to its users. As awareness of encryption benefits grows, as more penalties are introduced for failing to protect information, and as encryption technology becomes more accessible and affordable, encryption is more likely to be used as a matter of course to protect data — whether it's classified information being transmitted over a network, or ordinary user data stored on an office computer system.

This chapter describes basic encryption techniques and how they're used to protect data. Chapter 8[1], *Communications and Network Security*, discusses communications security (of which encryption is an important part) and networking concepts, and elaborates on how encryption fits into overall communications security.

Cryptography is a complex topic. This chapter provides an introduction to basic encryption techniques, but it doesn't try to describe the mathematical basis of encryption algorithms or explore all the complexities of the topic. For detailed information, an excellent reference is Dorothy Denning's *Cryptography and Data Security*.[2]

SOME HISTORY

The earliest ciphers date back to early Egyptian days—around 2000 B.C., when funeral messages consisting of modified hieroglyphs were carved into stone—not to keep the messages a secret, but to increase their mystery. In The Codebreakers,[3] David Kahn's definitive work on codes and those who have broken them through the centuries, Kahn traces the history of cryptography from ancient Egypt to India, Mesopotamia, Babylon, Greece, and into Western civilization and eventually the dawn of the computer age.

From the Spartans to Julius Caesar, from the Old Testament ciphers to the Papal plotters of the Fourteenth Century, from Mary, Queen of Scots to Abraham Lincoln's Civil War ciphers, cryptography has been a part of war, diplomacy, and politics. Mary, Queen of Scots, for example, lost her life in the sixteenth century because an encrypted message she sent from prison was intercepted and deciphered. During the Revolutionary War, Benedict Arnold used a codebook cipher to communicate with the British. Throughout history, governments and individuals have protected secret communications by encoding them. The development of ciphers and ciphering devices over the centuries

---

[1] Of the book *Computer Security Basics*

[2] Dorothy E. R. Denning, *Cryptography and Data Security*, Addison-Wesley, Reading (MA), 1983.

[3] David Kahn, *The Codebreakers*, Macmillan Company, New York (NY), 1972.

has culminated in the complex computer-based codes, algorithms, and machines of modern times.

The protection of communications has always been particularly critical in times of war and political strife. The development of modern cryptography owes much to the research conducted under the pressures of World War II, and particularly to the breaking of the Enigma machine.[4]

The Enigma machine was originally developed in Germany by an electrical engineer, Arthur Scherbius, during World War I. He offered an early version of the machine to the German navy and foreign office as early as 1918. The machine was originally rejected, but after some additional security enhancements were made to the commercial model, the German navy began using Enigma machines early in 1926.

The Enigma machine (shown in Figure 1) worked as follows: An operator typed the original text of the first letter of the message to be encrypted on the machine's keyboard-like set of buttons. The battery-powered machine encrypted the letter and, using a flashlight-type bulb, illuminated a substitute letter on a glass screen. What was special about the Enigma machine was a set of wheels known as rotors. Made of rubber or some other nonconducting material, the rotors contained electrical contacts which were wired in such a way that turning the rotors would change the correspondence between letters. Before the encryption began, the operator would set these rotors to an initial position. When the operator typed the first character—"A", for example, the machine might illuminate a light corresponding to "P". The operator would then copy the letter "P" onto an encryption worksheet, would advance the rotors, and would enter the next letter. With the new rotor settings, the correspondence between letters would change. An "A" might now be translated to an "X". This process would continue until the entire message was encrypted. The encrypted message could now be transmitted by radio to its destination, usually a U-boat in the Atlantic.

At the other end of the communication, the operator trying to decrypt a message coded by the Enigma machine would need another, identically built Enigma machine and would also need to know the original settings of the rotors.

The first breakthrough in solving the Enigma codes came from Poland. In the late 1920s, the Poles formed a cryptanalysis unit that began to work on breaking the German codes. Marian Rejewski and two other mathematicians cracked some of the early Enigma messages.

---

[4] For a full and fascinating discussion of the Enigma machine and the breaking of its codes, see David Kahn's *Seizing the Enigma*, Houghton Mifflin, Boston (MA), 1991.

In the early 1930s in France, a German named Hans-Thilo Schmidt offered French intelligence some information about setting the Enigma keys. The French cryptanalysts didn't have the resources to take advantage of this information and the British also rejected the information as being insufficient. The French offered the information to Poland, where Rejewski used it to make additional brilliant advances in cracking the Enigma codes.

After the fall of Poland in 1939, the Poles passed their information on to the French and the British. As the Germans continued to change keys and to modify the design of the Enigma machine, the British built on the Polish solution. Under the direction of mathematician Alan Turing, and with the help of Enigma documents captured from U-boats sunk during the remainder of the war, the highly secret "Ultra" project began to decrypt German naval messages on a regular and timely basis. In the early 1940s, Americans—some of them from IBM—made their own contributions, based on knowledge they'd gained reconstructing Japanese diplomatic cipher machines through the "Purple" project in the U.S.

In the decades since World War II, the use of computers to break codes has transformed the codebreaking game and has contributed greatly to the use of cryptography in military and intelligence applications, as well as in systems used in everyday computer systems.

WHAT IS ENCRYPTION?

Encryption (sometimes called *enciphering*) transforms original information, called *plaintext* or *cleartext*, into transformed information, called *ciphertext*, *codetext*, or simply *cipher*, which usually has the appearance of random, unintelligible data. The transformed information, in its encrypted form, is called the *cryptogram*.

Encryption is reversible. After transmission, when the information has reached its destination, the inverse operation (*decryption*, sometimes called *deciphering*) transforms the ciphertext back to the original plaintext.

The technique or rules selected for encryption—known as the *encryption algorithm*—determines how simple or how complex the process of transformation will be. Most encryption techniques utilize rather simple mathematical formulas that are applied a number of times in different combinations. Most also use a secret value called a key to encrypt and decrypt the text. The key is a kind of password, usually known only to the sender and the recipient of encrypted information. The encryption algorithm mathematically applies the key, which is usually a long string of numbers, to the information being encrypted or decrypted.

Unlike a regular password, a key doesn't directly give you access to information. Instead, it's used by the algorithm to transform information in a particular way. With the key, information that's been locked (encrypted) by the key can readily be transformed; without the key, that information is inaccessible. The examples shown later in this chapter will help make encryption keys more understandable.

The study of encryption and decryption is called *cryptography*, from the Greek *kryptos* meaning "hidden," and *graphia*, meaning "writing."

The process of trying to decrypt encrypted information without the key (to "break" an encrypted message) is called *cryptanalysis*.

The type of encryption algorithm, the secrecy of the key, and a number of other characteristics together form what's called the strength of the encryption; cryptographic strength determines how hard it is to break an encrypted message.

An important consideration in assessing the strength of any encryption algorithm is not whether it can be broken (given sufficient pairs of plaintext and ciphertext, any secret message—except one encoded with a so-called "one-time pad," described later in this chapter—can theoretically be decrypted) but how likely it is that decryption can be performed in a reasonable amount of time. A message that can be broken, but only with a network of supercomputers grinding away for decades, is very safe indeed.

Remember that a poorly chosen, or improperly protected, encryption key opens the door to an intruder, just as a shared or stolen password does. If an intruder gets access to an encryption key, even the strongest encryption algorithm won't protect your data.

Figure 2 shows simple encryption and decryption.

WHY ENCRYPTION?

Encryption provides security in three of the four security categories introduced in Chapter 1, *Introduction*. (Encryption is not a particularly effective way to achieve the fourth category, availability.)

FIGURE 2.
Simple Encryption and Decryption

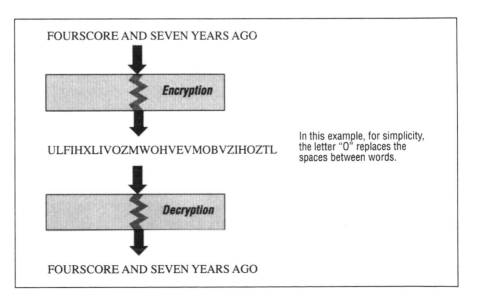

FOURSCORE AND SEVEN YEARS AGO

Encryption

ULFIHXLIVOZMWOHVEVMOBVZIHOZTL

In this example, for simplicity, the letter "O" replaces the spaces between words.

Decryption

FOURSCORE AND SEVEN YEARS AGO

Secrecy or Confidentiality. Encryption is very good at keeping information a secret. Even if someone is able to steal your computer or to access an encrypted file, that person will find it extremely difficult to figure out what's in the file.

Accuracy or Integrity. Encryption is also very good at ensuring the accuracy or the integrity of information. In addition to keeping information secret, certain types of encryption algorithms protect against forgery or tampering. This type of processing detects even the slightest change—malicious or inadvertent—in the information. While military, intelligence, and many corporate users care a lot about secrecy, financial institutions are more concerned about accuracy: making sure that a decimal point or a zero hasn't slipped, or that an electronic embezzler hasn't rounded off a few transactions here and there. Integrity checking is also a way that network users can ensure that their communications have not been affected by viruses or other penetrations.

Authenticity. Encryption is also very good at making sure that your information is authentic. Certain encryption techniques let you confirm absolutely who sent a particular piece of information. This is extremely important to financial or legal transactions. An authentication technique that's becoming a popular encryption tool is a digital signature. A digital signature is unique for every transaction and can't be forged. (Digital signatures are described later in this chapter.)

Transposition and Substitution Ciphers

There are two basic types of encryption ciphers:

Transposition: *Transposition ciphers* (sometimes called permutation ciphers) rearrange the order of the bits, characters, or blocks of characters that are being encrypted or decrypted.

Substitution: *Substitution ciphers* replace the actual bits, characters, or blocks of characters with substitutes (for example, one letter replaces another letter).

With a very simple transposition cipher (shown in Figure 3), the letters of the original text (the plaintext) are scrambled. With this type of cipher, the original letters of the plaintext are preserved; only their positions change.

With a very simple substitution cipher (two variations are shown in Figure 4), the letters of the plaintext are replaced with other letters, numbers, or symbols. With this type of cipher, the original positions of the letters of the plaintext are preserved, but the letters themselves change.

More about Transposition

In *The Codebreakers*, David Kahn recounts the development of a number of early transposition and substitution ciphers in ancient civiliza-

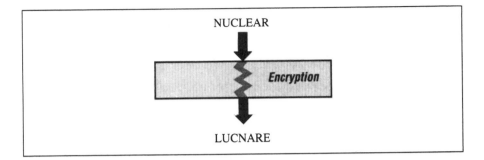

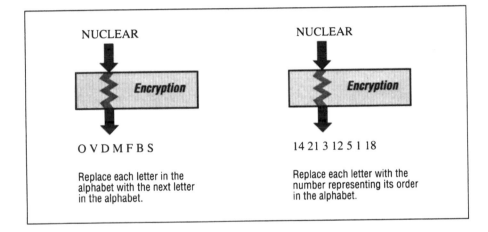

tions. In the fifth century B.C., the Spartans used a particularly interesting type of transposition cipher. During the Peloponnesian War, Spartan rulers encoded official messages by writing them on a long strip of parchment wound in a spiral around a wooden staff called a skytale. A message written in this fashion could be deciphered only by an official Spartan reader who had been given a baton of identical diameter. Thucydides, Plutarch, and Xenophon all have written about the use of this early cryptographic device.

Figure 5 shows another example of a transposition cipher.

MORE ABOUT SUBSTITUTION

Although earlier substitution ciphers existed, Julius Caesar's military use of such a cipher was the first clearly documented case. Caesar's cipher, shown in Figure 6, was a simple form of encryption in which each letter of an original message is replaced with the letter three places beyond it in the alphabet.

FIGURE 5.
Another Transposition Cipher

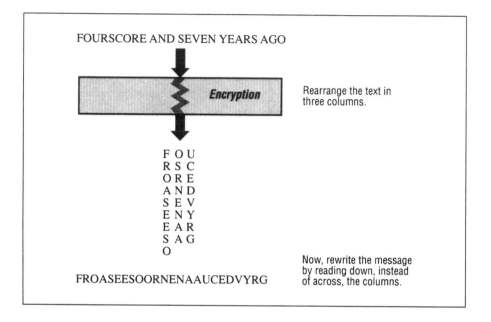

FIGURE 6.
The Caesar Substitution Cipher

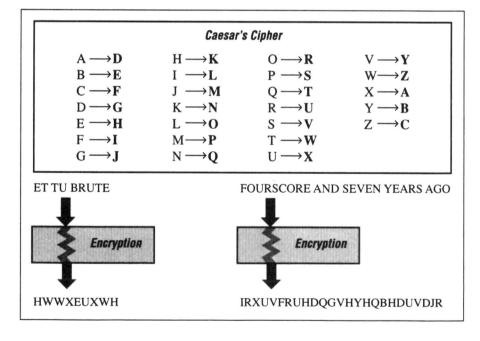

The cipher used in Edward Allen Poe's short story, "The Gold Bug," is a good example of a substitution cipher. Another example from literature is the cipher used in Sir Arthur Conan Doyle's Sherlock Holmes tale, "The Adventure of the Dancing Men."

Usually, cipher alphabets are much more complex than these examples. Sometimes an alphabet will have multiple substitutes for a letter, sometimes the alphabet will include substitutes that mean nothing, and sometimes several alphabets are used in rotation or combination.

The Enigma machine described earlier in this chapter used substitution to encrypt communications.

CRYPTOGRAPHIC KEYS: PRIVATE AND PUBLIC

More complex ciphers do not use simple substitutions or transpositions. Instead, they use a secret key to control a long sequence of complicated substitutions and transpositions. The operation of the algorithm upon the original information and the key produces the cipher "alphabet" that encrypts the information.

Modern cryptographic systems fall into two general categories (identified by the types of keys they use): private key and public key systems:

Private Key Cryptography

Private key (sometimes called symmetric key, secret key, or single key) systems use a single key. That key is used both to encrypt and to decrypt information. A separate key is needed for each pair of users who exchange messages, and both sides of the encryption transaction must keep the key secret. The security of the encryption method is completely dependent on how well the key is protected. The Data Encryption Standard (DES) algorithm, described later in this chapter, is a private key algorithm.

Public Key Cryptography

Public key (sometimes called asymmetric key or two key) systems use two keys: a public key and a private key. Within a group of users—for example, within a computer network—each user has both a public key and a private key. A user must keep his private key a secret, but the public key is publicly known; public keys may even be listed in directories of electronic mail addresses.

Public and private keys are mathematically related. If you encrypt a message with your private key, the recipient of the message can decrypt it with your public key. Similarly, anyone can send anyone else an encrypted message, simply by encrypting the message with the recipient's public key; the sender doesn't need to know the recipient's private key. When you receive an encrypted message, you, and only

FIGURE 7.
A Simple
Example of
Private Key
Encryption/
Decryption

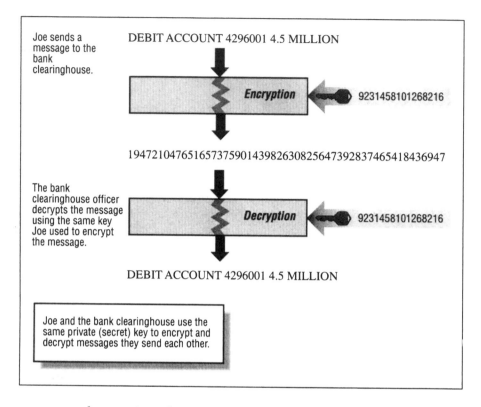

you, can decrypt it with your private key. The RSA cryptographic algorithm, described later in this chapter, is an example of a public key algorithm.

In addition to providing an encryption facility, some public key systems provide an authentication feature which ensures that when the recipient decrypts your message he knows it comes from you and no one else.

In Figures 7 and 8, a banker named Joe uses his private key (known only to him) to encrypt a message. When the message is sent to the bank clearinghouse, the clearinghouse officer applies Joe's public key (known to everyone within the bank). Because decryption produces an intelligible message, the officer knows that only Joe could have created the message, and proceeds to follow Joe's instructions.

KEY MANAGEMENT AND DISTRIBUTION

A major problem with encryption as a security method is that the distribution, storage, and eventual disposal of keys introduces an expensive and onerous administrative burden. Historically, cryptographic

FIGURE 8.
A Simple
Example of
Public Key
Encryption/
Decryption

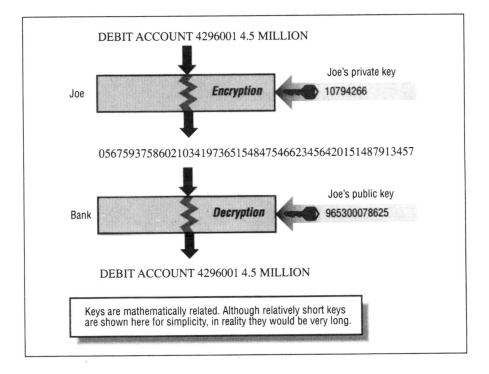

keys were delivered by escorted couriers carrying keys or key books in secure boxes. In some cases, this is still the way it's done. With most modern high-security cryptographic products, government agencies do the actual key distribution, delivering the keys on magnetic media to individual sites. Another approach is to distribute a master key, which is then used to generate additional session keys. A site must follow strictly enforced procedures for protecting and monitoring the use of the key, and there must be a way to change keys. Even with all of these restrictions, there's always a chance that the key will be stolen or compromised.

Of course, if a key is lost, there's another problem. Because deciphering encrypted information depends on the availability of the key, the encrypted information will be lost forever if you can't locate the key.

The difficulty of key distribution, storage, and disposal has limited the wide-scale usability of many cryptographic products in the past. Automated key variable distribution is problematic because it's difficult to keep the keys secure while they're being distributed, but this approach is finally becoming more widely used. The Department of Defense-sponsored Secure Telephone Unit (STU-III) project is an example of a system that uses automated key distribution.

Standards for key management have been developed by the government and by such organizations as ISO, ANSI, and the American Banking Association (ABA); see "Encryption in Banking and Financial Applications" later in this chapter for some relevant publications.

ONE-TIME PAD

One approach, known as a one-time pad or a one-time cipher key, can be proven mathematically to be foolproof. As its name indicates, the pad is used only once, and the key must be destroyed after a single use.

With a one-time cipher, you create two copies of a pad containing a set of completely random numbers. (These are numbers produced by a secure random number generator, possibly one based on some physical source of randomness. Sometimes, one-time pads are based on the process of nuclear radioactive decay.) The set contains at least as many numbers as the number of characters in your message. The sender of the message gets one copy of the pad; the recipient gets the other. On a computer system, one way to encrypt or decrypt a one-time message is to use a mathematical function called an exclusive OR, or XOR. When the sender XORs the message with the first copy of the pad, the process creates the encrypted message. When the recipient XORs the encrypted message with the second copy of the pad, the process recreates the original message, as shown in Figure 9.

One-time pads are sometimes used to encrypt important diplomatic communications, but they're not practical for most communications because of the difficulty of distribution. (For each possible pair of users who might wish to communicate, a key has to be generated and distributed to those users; the key must be longer than all the messages they might wish to exchange.)

FIGURE 9.
A One-time Pad

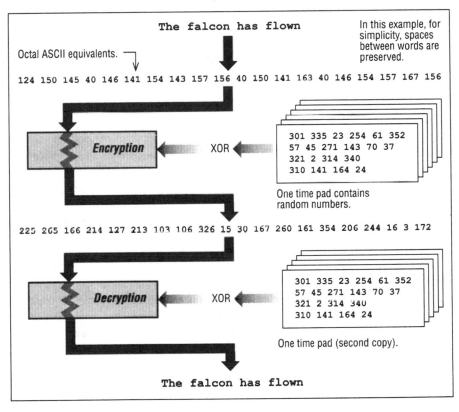

The falcon has flown

In this example, for simplicity, spaces between words are preserved.

Octal ASCII equivalents.

124 150 145 40 146 141 154 143 157 156 40 150 141 163 40 146 154 157 167 156

Encryption ← XOR ←

```
301 335 23 254 61 352
57 45 271 143 70 37
321 2 314 340
310 141 164 24
```

One time pad contains random numbers.

225 265 166 214 127 213 103 106 326 15 30 167 260 161 354 206 244 16 3 172

Decryption ← XOR ←

```
301 335 23 254 61 352
57 45 271 143 70 37
321 2 314 340
310 141 164 24
```

One time pad (second copy).

The falcon has flown

## 2

Data Encryption Devices: Overview Technology Analysis*

Rebecca J. Duncan, Datapro Information Services Group

The two most widely used methods of protecting transmitted data are cryptographic systems and network access control systems. Encryption scrambles plaintext requiring a key to decrypt or unscramble the data. Network access control systems control access to a system by dialing back a user at an assigned telephone number or requiring the user to go through an authentication process to identify him or herself.

Encryption systems include both data encryption hardware devices and software packages. Many hardware-based encryptors are simple microprocessor-based "black boxes" that electronically encode data at the sending end and decode data at the receiving end. Several effective software packages are also available and run as application programs on the user's resident mainframe, midrange, or microcomputer system.

Hardware encryption devices provide certain advantages over software resident on a user's applications processor. For example, the installation of encryption hardware has a minimal effect on the user's existing computer system. Also, an encryption process employing hardware is virtually immune to unauthorized, undetected alteration. Software, on the other hand, is susceptible to programmer modification.

Computer data lends itself to encryption because of the logic used in the encryption algorithms. These algorithms are much too complex to attempt to execute manually, but when reduced to a microelectronic chip or software routine, the processing time on the computer is negligible. Most U.S.-based manufacturers of encryption equipment use the U.S. government-approved Data Encryption Standard (DES)—described later in this report—as the means to protect data. Other vendors, however, have developed their own proprietary encryption codes.

* Datapro Reports on Computer Security; Copyright 1993 McGraw-Hill, Incorporated. Datapro Information Services Group, Delran NJ 08075 USA.

TECHNOLOGY HIGHLIGHTS

Network Access Control Systems

Network Access Control Systems identify network users and authorize or deny access according to prescribed guidelines. The best-known technology is callback—a device calls the user back at a predetermined, preprogrammed telephone number to confirm proper access. A callback system accepts an incoming call from a remote terminal or telephone user, records the number from which the call was made, and hangs up. The system then checks the number against an authorized list and, if it is valid, dials the authorized user and connects to the resources requested.

Message Authentication

Message Authentication essentially allows users to determine whether a received message is identical to the one that was transmitted from the originating point. It checks whether errors were introduced by accident or design and that no messages have disappeared and no new ones have been introduced. Authentication provides integrity but not confidentiality. It simply proves that the message originated from its proper source and that the source is authorized to issue the instructions that were received.

Message authentication secures electronic funds transfers (EFTs). In message authentication, the system detects modifications, identifies the message originator, and authenticates data verification. In addition to EFT, message authentication is used to validate letters of credit, security transfers, loan agreements, and foreign exchanges.

Message authentication requires that both sender and receiver have additional hardware to perform calculations and comparisons. The sheer number of nodes which may be required to implement authentication is creating a sizable industry segment that work with the government on development, standards, and supplying equipment.

TECHNOLOGY BASICS

This report deals specifically with data encryption devices that convert intelligent data at the sender's end to an unintelligible form for transmission and then reconvert the data to the original form at the receiver's end. This conversion is called encipherment or encryption. The reconversion at the receiving end is known as decipherment or decryption. The information in its original form is called plaintext or cleartext; the enciphered form, ciphertext.

On-Line Encryption

Data encryptors may work on line or off line, although this report focuses on on-line devices. On-line encryption is applied during communications over either leased or dial-up telephone lines. An encryption device resides between the host or front-end processor and the modem or between the terminal and the modem. Data is then encrypted immediately before it is placed on the transmission line and is decrypted immediately after passing through the modem at the receiving end. Basically, there are two types of on-line encryption approaches: end-to-end and link.

End-to-End Encryption

End-to-End encryption: Although a very secure method of encryption (because the data is disguised throughout its path), end-to-end encryption is the most difficult to implement. It requires that the decoding and encoding devices be synchronized, a sometimes difficult task because of variable delays. In its favor, end-to-end involves encrypting the data only once, at the source terminal prior to transmission, and not decrypting it until it has reached its destination. Thus, only two encryption/decryption devices are necessary—each is placed between the device sending or receiving the information and its respective modem or multiplexer. The data link header, which contains routing and other information, is left in cleartext. End-to-end encryption is most useful for transferring bulk information, such as data files and records, where the destination need not be kept secret. This method is not transparent to the hardware—the device must detect start/stop text instructions and/or be sensitive to the data communications procedures. (See Figure 1.)

Link Encryption

Link Encryption: Link encryption is a multiple-encryption method that is performed by sending the data through s series of switches (nodes) before it reaches its destination. Link Encryption is desirable if the source and destination of the information need to be secret; the header need not be kept in cleartext. The devices are transparent to the data on the line, and the data does not affect the processors at both ends. It is, however, more expensive than end-to-end encryption because a device is needed at each of the nodes.

FIGURE 1. *End-to-End Versus Link Encryption*

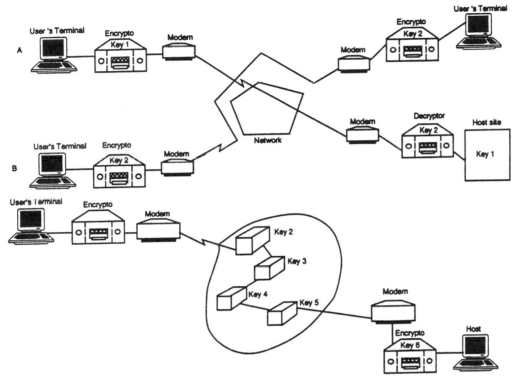

The figure above is of an end-to-end encryption scheme. The message is encrypted at the point of origination and then decrypted at the recipient's site. In line A, the communication occurred on a regular phone line; on line B, it occurred on a leased line. The figure below is a simple link scheme. The message is encrypted and decrypted a prescribed number of times before it reaches its destination, where it is ultimately decrypted.

OFF-LINE ENCRYPTION

Off-line encryption is performed by entering plaintext into a keyboard device, which encrypts it and stores the ciphertext in a medium. The coded message can then be transmitted by means of any terminal that accepts the storage medium. The principal application for off-line encryption is storing confidential archival files. Protection of the key presents a problem, however, if the key is to be stored for long periods of time. In such cases, the key itself should be encrypted with another key not resident in any part of the system.

Other types of off-line encryption devices include handheld and other portable devices containing some type of display and semiconductor memory. These are particularly useful for executives and other corporate personnel who receive and must record confidential information while away from the office.

Hand-held encryptors require a device at each end of the communications line, each programmed with the same key. A person enters cleartext information which is converted into ciphertext within the unit. The ciphertext is then transmitted via telephone or message service to the person at the other end. When the information is received, it is keyed into the recipient's unit, and a readout in cleartext is produced. Other available portable encryptors are typewriter size or smaller. With this type of unit, information is encrypted and either stored in internal memory or presented as hard copy ciphertext for decryption at a later date.

An increasingly popular off-line encryption method uses microcomputers equipped with expansion boards that encrypt files or programs and prepare them for communication.

Some off-line devices not included in this report are used to encrypt large databases that do not require remote transmission. These are for extended storage of confidential records; for example, bank customer information.

FEDERAL STANDARD 1027

In 1982, the General Services Administration published a standard for all hardware cryptographic devices used by the United States government and military services. Federal Standard 1027, titled *Telecommunications: Inter-operability and Security Requirements for use of the Data Encryption Standard, in the Physical Layer of Data Communications*, specifies the minimum security characteristics required to implement the DES algorithm in a telecommunications environment. To qualify for certification under FS 1027, vendors must submit their products to the National Security Agency (NSA) for tests. The criteria include provisions for the following:

- The device must transmit only ciphertext. Plaintext bypass may be an option, but its operation must be clearly marked.
- The device must generate an alarm immediately if any disturbance in the cryptosystem is detected.
- The device's key variables must not be disclosed or modified.
- The device must have a fail-safe provision to ensure that a breakdown will not occur in the encryption process.
- The device must be installed securely to prevent theft, unauthorized use, or modification.

Devices endorsed under FS 1027 must employ DES, but certification includes much more than the encryption functions. Specific physical concerns such as locks, mountings, key entry and transport, alarms, tests, and indicators are essential to certification. FS 1027 does not permit keys to be internally generated by the encryption device. Users must enter keys manually or with a KOI-18 key loader, which requires a nine-pin, synchronous, serial interface. A special key is required to open a physical lock to initiate key entry and entry of the initializing key variable. In accordance with this standard, certain internal function tests and diagnostics must be performed.

KEY MANAGEMENT

The success of an encryption system hinges upon its key management. Key management comprises the generation, distribution, entry and destruction of key settings. Electronic and physical measures are used to safeguard the settings. Key settings are referred to as the secret code, the key variable, the crypto key, or the key fill. While it is common in cryptography for the encryption algorithm to be common knowledge, transmission security is achieved through the safeguarding of the keys. For example, the DES algorithm is a published formula (FIPS Publication 46) within the public domain. Distribution and handling of the keys is controlled and remains secret, ensuring the encryption system operates properly.

Keys are required to encrypt and decrypt data. Depending on the information being transmitted, the user may determine that the keys need to be changed monthly, weekly, daily, or after each transmission. The keys themselves can be generated electronically or manually. Electronically generated keys may be distributed physically in key fill devices—an expensive method requiring designated personnel or a carrier service—or encrypted and transmitted to remote ciphering devices. Usually, manual key entry is performed through the front panel of the device via switches, key pads, or key modules. The keys are stored in memory and often erased from view. Finally, keys are destroyed after they have been used. Key fill devices have erase functions as well for key destruction after use.

The ability to send end-to-end communications requires that both parties have the same type of equipment and use the same key at the time of transmission. Before a transmission is sent, a validation process or "handshake" occurs whereby one machine identifies itself to the other. A link is established, and then the information is encrypted and set down the line. The receiving device takes the information and either decrypts it or stores it until retrieved. In end-to-end encryption, users must keep a record of each other's keys to guard against improper access. Several options for key management are available.

Central Key Management Facility

Each user is given a long-term private key which allows him or her to interact with the central site. When a user needs to transmit an encrypted message to another in the network, communication is set up with the central facility. Instead of each user having to employ a unique key, the central facility generates a random, short-term key just for that connection. This type of system is expensive compared to some of the other methods of implementation.

In some networks, an identical set of codes is distributed to each user station by the key management facility, with each code being usable for a specific 24-hour period. One station is designated as the network control station and is tasked to manage communications between the stations in the network (see Figure 2).

Public Key Systems

This method employs one community or "public" key that is shared by all users in the network to encrypt electronic communications. De-

FIGURE 2. *Centralized Key Management*

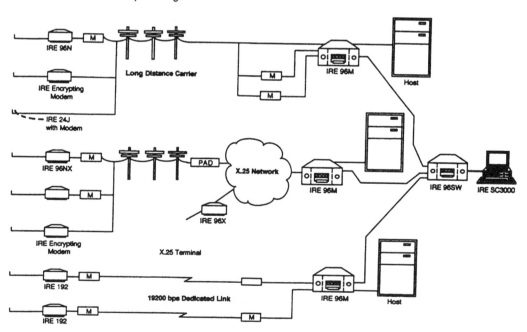

Information Resource Engineering's (IRE) SC3000 Key Management System provides centralized key management for IRE encryptors at remote geographic locations distributed among many networks.

cryption is accomplished by a "private" key that is different for each user.

The procedure is based on *trapdoor functions*, which means that certain computations are easy to do in a forward direction (find a three-digit number's cube) but difficult in reverse (find a ten-digit number's root). Thus, the encoder could send a complex message to a decoder equipped with the inverse. Where the encoded details could otherwise take millions of years to decode, the decryption key does it in seconds. Public key systems are also being used for electronic mail signature verification.

Remote Key Loading

Some vendors have designed key management methods that allow users to downline load keys from a central encryptor to remote slave devices. Downline loading of keys is applicable only for commercial devices; FS 1027 does not permit it. In automatic key management, the keys are generated and monitored by the device.

Traditionally, keys are distributed by registered mail or through messengers who transport the actual keys or key loaders. Downline loading of keys eliminates much of the operating cost associated with traditional key management.

Very similar to downline loading is *public key management*. Public key cryptography is an asymmetric key method for encryption information. Developed by Diffie and Hellman, the key is automatically generated and transported downline. Based on a mathematical formula, the public key permits the construction of a shared common secret key which can be exchanged using messages that do not need to be kept secret.

WHAT IS DES?

Born in the 1970s, the Data Encryption Standard (DES) was the result of a request by the U.S. National Bureau of Standards (NBS—now the National Institute of Standards and Technology, NIST) for an algorithm to be used for encrypting digital information. Several algorithms were submitted for evaluation. One algorithm would be chosen to be the government standard. The winner was Lucifer, an algorithm developed by IBM, which was transformed into what is now DES. A complex algorithm, DES employs a key consisting of 56 bits, plus 8 parity bits, and presents over 72 quadrillion possible key combinations. It provides a high degree of security at a modest link cost. With frequent key changes, the algorithm satisfactorily renders confidential information inaccessible.

Surrounded by controversy—then and now—the DES standard was (and still is) considered by many to be an adequate deterrent to computer crime. Some experts, however, contend that the adoption of this particular standard was a mistake, claiming that advances in technology make it possible to break the DES by "brute force," i.e., a computer can be programmed to attempt every possible combination until the correct key us discovered. Supporters of DES, however, claim that even the latest generation vector computer would take 2,284 years to break the code, operating at one try per microsecond.

Nevertheless, opponents continue to maintain that the construction of special chips and the decreasing cost of computer equipment makes brute force code breaking potentially cost-effective. In fact, some critics claim that a special decoding machine with thousands of parallel processors could break the code within a day. DES supporters respond that the algorithm could be applied twice, thus doubling the key size to 112 bits. That size key, according to them, would take centuries to break. Through it all, IBM defends the 56-bit key because it is complex enough to provide ample security and small enough to fit on a chip. Thus DES has persisted, surviving a flurry of speculation that government support would not continue past 1988. In fact, DES continues to be supported by the government and appears to be alive and well. If anything, the battle is moving away from getting rid of DES to a struggle to allow other algorithms to be recognized by the government along with DES.

DES VS. PROPRIETARY ALGORITHMS

Though DES provides an important standard for data encryption, it is by no means the only method of encrypting data. Some of the same companies that sell DES products also sell encryption products using proprietary algorithms. Some use public key algorithms (most notably RSA). Others use proprietary algorithms so they can sell their products abroad without government approval. Though some buyers believe that a proprietary algorithm provides greater protection against unauthorized encryption than DES does, no proprietary algorithm has been tested as thoroughly as DES. Proprietary encryption algorithms have other drawbacks, too: the buyer depends heavily on a single supplier and can communicate only with other encryption devices from that supplier. If the supplier goes out of business, the buyer could be left without support.

3

Answers to Frequently Asked Questions about Today's Cryptography*

RSA Laboratories

WHAT IS ENCRYPTION?

Encryption is the transformation of data into a form unreadable by anyone without a secret decryption key. Its purpose is to ensure privacy by keeping the information hidden from anyone for whom it is not intended, even those who can see the encrypted data. For example, one may wish to encrypt files on a hard disk to prevent an intruder from reading them.

In a multi-user setting, encryption allows secure communication over an insecure channel. The general scenario is as follows: Alice wishes to send a message to Bob so that no one else besides Bob can read it. Alice encrypts the message, which is called the plaintext, with an encryption key; the encrypted message, called the ciphertext, is sent to Bob. Bob decrypts the ciphertext with the decryption key and reads the message. An attacker, Charlie, may either try to obtain the secret key or to recover the plaintext without using the secret key. In a secure cryptosystem, the plaintext cannot be recovered from the ciphertext except by using the decryption key. In a symmetric cryptosystem, a single key serves as both the encryption and decryption keys.

Cryptography has been around for millennia; see Kahn [5] for a good history of cryptography; see Rivest [11] and Brassard [1] for an introduction to modern cryptography.

WHAT IS AUTHENTICATION? WHAT IS A DIGITAL SIGNATURE?

Authentication in a digital setting is a process whereby the receiver of a digital message can be confident of the identity of the sender and/or the integrity of the message. Authentication protocols can be based on either conventional secret-key cryptosystems like DES or on public-key

* Excerpted from "FAQ", RSA Laboratories, Redwood City, California; Revision 2.0, October 5, 1993; Copyright RSA Laboratories.

systems like RSA; authentication in public-key systems uses digital signatures.

In this document, authentication will generally refer to the use of digital signatures, which play a function for digital documents similar to that played by handwritten signatures for printed documents: the signature is an unforgeable piece of data asserting that a named person wrote or otherwise agreed to the document to which the signature is attached. The recipient, as well as a third party, can verify both that the document did indeed originate from the person whose signature is attached and that the document has not been altered since it was signed. A secure digital signature system thus consists of two parts: a method of signing a document such that forgery is infeasible, and a method of verifying that a signature was actually generated by whomever it represents. Furthermore, secure digital signatures cannot be repudiated; i.e., the signer of a document cannot later disown it by claiming it was forged.

Unlike encryption, digital signatures are a recent development, the need for which has arisen with the proliferation of digital communications.

WHAT IS PUBLIC-KEY CRYPTOGRAPHY?

Traditional cryptography is based on the sender and receiver of a message knowing and using the same secret key: the sender uses the secret key to encrypt the message, and the receiver uses the same secret key to decrypt the message. This method is known as secret-key cryptography. The main problem is getting the sender and receiver to agree on the secret key without anyone else finding out. If they are in separate physical locations, they must trust a courier, or a phone system, or some other transmission system to not disclose the secret key being communicated. Anyone who overhears or intercepts the key in transit can later read all messages encrypted using that key. The generation, transmission and storage of keys is called key management; all cryptosystems must deal with key management issues. Secret-key cryptography often has difficulty providing secure key management.

Public-key cryptography was invented in 1976 by Whitfield Diffie and Martin Hellman [3] in order to solve the key management problem. In the new system, each person gets a pair of keys, called the public key and the private key. Each person's public key is published while the private key is kept secret. The need for sender and receiver to share secret information is eliminated: all communications involve only public keys, and no private key is ever transmitted or shared. No longer is it necessary to trust some communications channel to be secure against eavesdropping or betrayal. Anyone can send a confidential message just using public information, but it can only be decrypted with a private key that is in the sole possession of the intended recipient. Furthermore, public-key cryptography can be used for authentication (digital signatures) as well as for privacy (encryption).

Here's how it works for encryption: when Alice wishes to send a message to Bob, she looks up Bob's public key in a directory, uses it to encrypt the message and sends it off. Bob then uses his private key to decrypt the message and read it. No one listening in can decrypt the message. Anyone can send an encrypted message to Bob but only Bob can read it. Clearly, one requirement is that no one can figure out the private key from the corresponding public key.

Here's how it works for authentication: Alice, to sign a message, does a computation involving both her private key and the message itself; the output is called the digital signature and is attached to the message, which is then sent. Bob, to verify the signature, does some computation involving the message, the purported signature, and Alice's public key. If the results properly hold in a simple mathematical relation, the signature is verified as genuine; otherwise, the signature may be fraudulent or the message altered, and they are discarded.

A good history of public-key cryptography, by one of its inventors, is given by Diffie [2].

WHAT ARE THE ADVANTAGES AND DISADVANTAGES OF PUBLIC-KEY CRYPTOGRAPHY OVER SECRET-KEY CRYPTOGRAPHY?

The primary advantage of public-key cryptography is increased security: the private keys do not ever need to transmitted or revealed to anyone. In a secret-key system, by contrast, there is always a chance that an enemy could discover the secret key while it is being transmitted.

Another major advantage of public-key systems is that they can provide a method for digital signatures. Authentication via secret-key systems requires the sharing of some secret and sometimes requires trust of a third party as well. A sender can then repudiate a previously signed message by claiming that the shared secret was somehow compromised by one of the parties sharing the secret. For example, the Kerberos secret-key authentication system [15] involves a central database that keeps copies of the secret keys of all users; a Kerberos-authenticated message would most likely not be held legally binding, since an attack on the database would allow widespread forgery. Public-key authentication, on the other hand, prevents this type of repudiation; each user has sole responsibility for protecting his or her private key. This property of public-key authentication is often called non-repudiation.

Furthermore, digitally signed messages can be proved authentic to a third party, such as a judge, thus allowing such messages to be legally binding. Secret-key authentication systems such as Kerberos were designed to authenticate access to network resources, rather than to authenticate documents, a task which is better achieved via digital signatures.

A disadvantage of using public-key cryptography for encryption is speed: there are popular secret-key encryption methods which are significantly faster than any currently available public-key encryption method. But public-key cryptography can share the burden-with secret-key cryptography to get the best of both worlds.

For encryption, the best solution is to combine public- and secret-key systems in order to get both the security advantages of public-key systems and the speed advantages of secret-key systems. The public-key system can be used to encrypt a secret key which is then used to encrypt the bulk of a file or message. Public-key cryptography is not meant to replace secret-key cryptography, but rather to supplement it, to make it more secure. The first use of public-key techniques was for secure key exchange in an otherwise secret-key system [3]; this is still one of its primary functions.

Secret-key cryptography remains extremely important and is the subject of much ongoing study and research.

IS CRYPTOGRAPHY PATENTABLE IN THE U.S.?

Cryptographic systems are patentable. Many secret-key cryptosystems have been patented, including DES. The basic ideas of public-key cryptography are contained in U.S. Patent 4,200,770, by M. Hellman, W. Diffie, and R. Merkle, issued 4/29/80 and in U.S. Patent 4,218,582, by M. Hellman and R. Merkle, issued 8/19/80; similar patents have been issued throughout the world. The exclusive licensing rights to both patents are held by Public Key Partners (PKP), of Sunnyvale, California, which also holds the rights to the RSA patent. Usually all of these public-key patents are licensed together.

All legal challenges to public-key patents have been settled before judgment. In a recent case, for example, PKP brought suit against the TRW Corporation which was using public-key cryptography (the El Gamal system) without a license; TRW claimed it did not need to license. In June 1992 a settlement was reached in which TRW agreed to license to the patents.

Some patent applications for cryptosystems have been blocked by intervention by the NSA or other intelligence or defense agencies, under the authority of the Invention Secrecy Act of 1940 and the National Security Act of 1947; see Landau [6] for some recent cases related to cryptography.

RSA

What Is RSA?

RSA is a public-key cryptosystem for both encryption and authentication; it was invented in 1977 by Ron Rivest, Adi Shamir, and Leonard Adleman [12]. It works as follows: take two large primes, p and q, and find their product $n = pq$; n is called the *modulus*. Choose a number, e, less than n and relatively prime to $(p\text{-}1)(q\text{-}1)$, and find its inverse, d mod $(p\text{-}1)(q\text{-}1)$, which means that $ed = 1$ mod $(p\text{-}1)(q\text{-}1)$; e and d are called the *public* and *private exponents*, respectively. The *public key* is the pair (n,e); the *private key* is d. The factors p and q must be kept secret, or destroyed.

It is difficult (presumably) to obtain the private key d from the public key (n,e). If one could factor n into p and q, however, then one could obtain the private key d. Thus the entire security of RSA is predicated on the assumption that factoring is difficult; an easy factoring method would "break" RSA.

Here is how RSA can be used for privacy and authentication (in practice, actual use is slightly different):

RSA privacy (encryption): suppose Alice wants to send a private message, m, to Bob. Alice creates the ciphertext c by exponentiating: $c = m^e$ mod n, where e and n are Bob's public key. To decrypt, Bob also exponentiates: $m = c^d$ mod n, and recovers the original message m; the relationship between e and d ensures that Bob correctly recovers m. Since only Bob knows d, only Bob can decrypt.

RSA authentication: suppose Alice wants to send a signed document m to Bob. Alice creates a digital signature s by exponentiating: $s = m^d$ mod n, where d and n belong to Alice's key pair. She sends s and m to Bob. To verify the signature, Bob exponentiates and checks that the message m is recovered: $m = s^e$ mod n, where e and n belong to Alice's public key.

Thus encryption and authentication take place without any sharing of private keys: each person uses only other people's public keys and his or her own private key. Anyone can send an encrypted message or verify a signed message, using only public keys, but only someone in possession of the correct private key can decrypt or sign a message.

DES

What Is DES?

DES is the Data Encryption Standard, an encryption block cipher defined and endorsed by the U.S. government in 1977 as an official standard; the details can be found in the official FIPS publication [9]. It was originally developed at IBM. DES has been extensively studied over the last 15 years and is the most well-known and widely used cryptosystem in the world.

DES is a secret-key, symmetric cryptosystem: when used for communication, both sender and receiver must know the same secret key, which is used both to encrypt and decrypt the message. DES can also be used for single-user encryption, such as to store files on a hard disk in encrypted form. In a multi-user environment, secure key distribution may be difficult; public-key cryptography was invented to solve this problem. DES operates on 64-bit blocks with a 56-bit key. It was designed to be implemented in hardware, and its operation is relatively fast. It works well for bulk encryption, that is, for encrypting a large set of data.

NIST has recertified DES as an official U.S. government encryption standard every five years; DES was last recertified in 1993, by default. NIST has indicated, however, that it may not recertify DES again.

What Is DSS?

DSS is the proposed Digital Signature Standard, which specifies a Digital Signature Algorithm (DSA), and is a part of the U.S. government's Capstone project. It was selected by NIST, in cooperation with the NSA, to be the digital authentication standard of the U.S. government; whether the government should in fact adopt it as the official standard is still under debate.

DSS is based on the discrete log problem and derives from cryptosystems proposed by Schnorr [13] and El Gamal [4]. It is for authentication only. For a detailed description of DSS, see [10] or [8]. [See p. 84 in this book—Ed.]

DSS has, for the most part, been looked upon unfavorably by the computer industry, much of which had hoped the government would choose the RSA algorithm as the official standard; RSA is the most widely used authentication algorithm. Several articles in the press, such as [7], discuss the industry dissatisfaction with DSS. Criticism of DSS has focused on a few main issues: it lacks key exchange capability; the underlying cryptosystem is too recent and has been subject to too little scrutiny for users to be confident of its strength; verification of signatures with DSS is too slow; the existence of a second authentication standard will cause hardship to computer hardware and software vendors, who have already standardized on RSA; and that the process by which NIST chose DSS was too secretive and arbitrary, with too much influence wielded by NSA. Other criticisms were addressed by NIST by modifying the original proposal. A more detailed discussion of the various criticisms can be found in [8], and a detailed response by NIST can be found in [14].

In the DSS system, signature generation is faster than signature verification, whereas in the RSA system, signature verification is faster than signature generation (if the public and private exponents are chosen for this property, which is the usual case). NIST claims that it is an advantage of DSS that signing is faster, but many people in cryptography think that it is better for verification to be the faster operation.

1. G. Brassard. Modern Cryptology. Volume 325 of Lecture Notes in Computer Science, Springer-Verlag, New York, 1989.

2. W. Diffie. The first ten years of public-key cryptography. Proceedings of the IEEE, 76:560–577, 1988.

3. W. Diffie and M.E. Hellman. New directions in cryptography. IEEE Transactions on Information Theory, IT-22:644–654, 1976.

4. T. El Gamal. A public-key cryptosystem and a signature scheme based on discrete logarithms. IEEE Transactions on Information Theory, IT-31:469–472, 1985.

5. D. Kahn. The Codebreakers. Macmillan Co., New York, 1967.

6. S. Landau. Zero knowledge and the Department of Defense. Notices of the American Mathematical Society, 35:5–12, 1988.

7. E. Messmer. NIST stumbles on proposal for public-key encryption. Network World, 9(30), July 27, 1992.

8. National Institute of Standards and Technology (NIST). The Digital Signature Standard, proposal and discussion. Communications of the ACM, 35(7):36–54, July 1992.

9. National Institute of Standards and Technology (NIST). FIPS Publication 46–1: Data Encryption Standard. January 22, 1988. Originally issued by National Bureau of Standards.

10. National Institute of Standards and Technology (NIST). Publication XX: Announcement and Specifications for a Digital Signature Standard (DSS). August 19, 1992.

11. R.L. Rivest, Cryptography. In J. van Leeuwen, editor, Handbook of Theoretical Computer Science, MIT Pres/Elsevier, Amsterdam, 1990.

12. R.L. Rivest, A. Shamir, and L. Adleman. A method for obtaining digital signatures and public-key cryptosystems. Communications of the ACM, 21(2):120–126, February 1978.

13. C.P. Schnorr. Efficient identification and signatures for smart cards. In Advances in Cryptology—Crypto '89, pages 239–251, Springer-Verlag, New York, 1990.

14. M.E. Smid and D.K. Branstad. Response to comments on the NIST proposed Digital Signature Standard. In Advances in Cryptology—Crypto '92, Springer-Verlag, New York, 1993.

15. J.G. Steiner, B.C. Neuman, and J.I. Schiller. Kerberos: as authentication service for open network systems. In Usenix Conference Proceedings, pages 191–202, Dallas, Texas, February 1988.

4

Cryptography in Public: A Brief History*

*Susan Landau, Stephen Kent, Clint Brooks, Scott Charney,
Dorothy Denning, Whitfield Diffie, Anthony Lauck, Douglas Miller,
Peter Neumann, David Sobel*
Association for Computing Machinery, U.S. Public Policy Committee

Cryptography is being debated in public—again. The particular confluence of events—the worldwide availability of strong cryptosystems (including DES and RSA), the accessibility of computer networks, and the Escrowed Encryption Standard—is new, but as cryptography has evolved from a military tool to a corporate product, many policy issues have been discussed and resolved. Reinventing the wheel is poor engineering; it is even worse in public policy. The current discussion of cryptography needs to be placed in context.

The overriding conflict is the same as it has been for two decades: Who should make the policy decisions for civilian cryptography? Before commercial and academic groups became active in developing cryptography, the area "belonged" to the National Security Agency. Twenty years ago, conflicts over control of cryptography arose. In 1987, Congress passed the Computer Security Act, legislating that decisions about civilian computer security (including cryptography) would be made by a civilian agency. Seven years later Computer Professionals for Social Responsibility (CPSR) and various industrial organizations believe the NSA dominates civilian cryptography policy, a charge members of the defense agency dispute. This chapter presents a brief review of the last twenty years of cryptography in the public domain. The story has several strands, which we have separated into sections: (i) The Government's Standard: DES; (ii) Cryptography Research in the late 1970s: The Emerging Conflict; (iii) The Mid-Eighties: the Computer Security Act; (iv) the Digital Signature Standard; and (v) Securing the Communications Infrastructure: Digital Telephony and EES.

THE GOVERNMENT'S STANDARD: DES

Our history begins in the mid-seventies. The Federal government sparked the encryption controversy when in 1975, the National Bureau

---

of Standards (NBS) proposed a Data Encryption Standard (DES). What the Bureau published in the Federal Register was an IBM design with changes recommended by the NSA, including a shorter key length (56 bits).

A public comment period followed. Concern centered on whether the key length left the algorithm vulnerable to attack and whether the algorithm contained a trapdoor. Finally in 1977, DES (with a 56-bit key) was issued as a Federal Information Processing Standard (FIPS); the standard has been subject to a review every five years. It was re-certified in December 1993.

Only recently—nineteen years after DES was introduced—have any attacks short of exhaustive search threatened the security of the algorithm [Mats, BiSh]. As discussed in Chapter 1 [of the original paper—Ed.], DES is used in a broad array of applications.

CRYPTOGRAPHY RESEARCH IN THE LATE 1970s: THE EMERGING CONFLICT

In the mid-seventies Whitfield Diffie and Martin Hellman at Stanford were wrestling with two problems:

- Key distribution: In the absence of a secure method to exchange information, how do two distant parties exchange keys?
- Digital signatures: Could a method be devised so as to provide the recipient of an electronic message a way of demonstrating that the communication had come from a particular person?

This led to public-key cryptography and the RSA algorithm (described in Chapter 1).

The RSA algorithm attracted interest from a number of circles. Ronald Rivest planned to present the work at an IEEE conference in Ithaca, New York. Before the conference, the authors received a letter from one "J. A. Meyer," who warned that since foreign nationals would be present at the scientific meeting, publication of the result was a potential violation of the International Traffic in Arms Regulations.

On lawyers' advice, the MIT scientists halted distribution of their paper so that the matter could be reviewed. Meyer was identified as an employee of NSA; the Agency promptly disavowed his letter. Rivest presented the paper. The scientists resumed distribution, and the furor died down for the moment.

The following year brought a new incident and greater apprehensions. This time NSA involvement was official. The Agency requested a secrecy order on a patent application submitted by George Davida, a professor at the University of Wisconsin; this meant that Davida could not publish or discuss his research. After Davida and the University of Wisconsin chancellor publicly protested, the secrecy order was lifted.

In 1979, the director of the NSA went public with the Agency's concerns. In a speech at the Armed Forces Communications and Electronics Association Admiral Bobby Inman warned that open publication of cryptography research was harmful to national security. NSA would seek statutory authority limiting publication of cryptographic research unless a satisfactory solution could be found.

The American Council on Education formed a study group that recommended a two-year experiment in prepublication review by NSA of all cryptography research [PCSG]. Review would be voluntary and prompt. Despite the voluntary nature of the review, there was anxiety in the academic cryptography community that this process would have a chilling effect on the emerging field.

Meanwhile there was action on a third front: funding. Two agencies were responsible for funding cryptography research: NSA and the National Science Foundation (NSF), the organization responsible for support of "basic" research. When Adleman submitted a research proposal to the NSF in the spring of 1980, the situation came to a head. NSA offered to fund the cryptographic portions of the grant; NSF declined. (NSF policy is to refuse to support work with alternative funding sources.) Adleman feared that NSA's requirement of prior review of research could lead to classification of his work. An agreement was reached at the White House: both agencies would fund work in cryptography.

Fourteen years later, the two-year experiment in prepublication review continues. However, researchers' fears about prior restraint and impounded research have eased. There have been times when an author, on NSA request, did not publish; there have been NSA suggestions for "minor" changes in some papers [Land, pg. 11]. But the requests have been few; the academic community has not felt imposed upon by the prepublication reviews. On one occasion, NSA apparently aided the academic community in lifting a secrecy order placed on a patent application. Shamir was one of the researchers involved, and he thanked "the NSA . . . who were extremely helpful behind the scenes . . ." [Land, pg. 12]. As far as the research community has been concerned, it is fair to say that there have been no long-term chilling effects.

THE MID-EIGHTIES: THE COMPUTER SECURITY ACT

The concerns of the 1970s—government interference in the development of publicly available cryptography—seemed to have been laid to rest. Then in September 1984, President Reagan issued National Security Decision Directive (NSDD-145), establishing the safeguarding of sensitive but unclassified information in communications and computer systems as Federal policy. NSDD-145 stipulated a Defense Department management structure to implement the policy: the NSA, the National Security Council, and the Department of Defense. There were many objections to this plan, from a variety of constituencies. Congress protested the expansion of Presidential authority to policy-making without legislative participation. From the ACLU to Mead Data Central, a broad array of industrial and civil liberty organizations objected to Department of Defense control of unclassified information in the civilian sector [USHR-87].

Congress responded. In 1987 it passed the Computer Security Act (CSA), which:

> . . . assign[s] to the National Bureau of Standards responsibility for developing standards and guidelines to assure cost-effective security and privacy of sensitive information in Federal computer systems, drawing on the technical advice and assistance (including work products) of the National Security Agency, where appropriate.

Civilian computing standards were to be set by a civilian agency. NSA was placed in an advisory role. The legislative history of the Act makes that desire clear:

> The key question during the hearings was: Should a military intelligence agency, NSA, or a civilian agency, NBS, be in charge of the government's computer standards program? The activities of NSA . . . reinforced the view of the Committee and many others that NSA is the wrong agency to be put in charge of this important program [USHR-87, pg.19].
>
> Since work on technical security standards represents virtually all of the research effort being done today, NSA would take over virtually the entire computer standards from the Bureau of Standards. By putting NSA in charge of developing technical security guidelines (software, hardware, communications), NBS would be left with the responsibility for only administrative and physical security measures—which have generally been done years ago. NBS, in effect, would on the surface be given the responsibility for the computer standards program with little to say about the most important part of the program—the technical guidelines developed by NSA [USHR-87, pg.95].

The House was specifically concerned that cryptography be allowed to develop in the public sector:

> . . . NSA's secretiveness resulted in an inappropriate approach when it attempted to deal with national policy issues such as the issue of public cryptography. Historically, this science has been the exclusive domain of government, and in this country it is one of NSA's primary missions. However, with the advent of modern computers and communications, there has been in recent years considerable interest in cryptography, particularly by the business community, which is interested in keeping its proprietary

information from competitors. As a result of the emerging need to protect information, the academic community has done research work in the field. NSA has made numerous attempts to either stop such work or to make sure it has control over the work by funding it, pre-publication reviews or other methods [USHR-87, pg.21].

During the debate on the Act, Director of the Office of Management and Budget, Jim Miller, had told the Government Operations Committee how the legislation would be implemented:

> Computer security standards, like other computer standards, will be developed in accordance with established NBS procedures. In this regard the technical security guidelines provided by NSA to NBS will be treated as advisory and subject to appropriate NBS review [USHR-87, pg. 37].

The implementation of the Act has been controversial. The National Institute of Standards and Technology (NIST, formerly NBS) and NSA signed a Memorandum of Understanding (MOU) to implement the Act, outlining areas of necessary agency interaction. As part of this, they established a Technical Working Group "to review and analyze issues of mutual interest pertinent to protection of systems that process sensitive or other unclassified information." The MOU also states:

> The NIST and the NSA shall ensure the Technical Working Group reviews prior to public disclosure all matters regarding technical systems security techniques to be developed for use in protecting sensitive information in federal computer systems to ensure they are consistent with the national security of the United States.

In this document, NIST and NSA were acknowledging that the public development or promulgation of technical security standards regarding cryptography could present a serious possibility of harm to national security. Critics of the MOU, including CPSR, contended that Congress, cognizant of the national security considerations, had nonetheless sought to restrict NSA's ability to dictate the selection of security standards for unclassified information standards. These critics contend that this and other aspects of the MOU violate the intent of Congress. In the next two sections of this chapter, we examine several Federal initiatives in cryptography, two of which had a large NSA role.

DIGITAL SIGNATURE STANDARD

As noted in Chapter 1 [of the original paper—Ed.], cryptography performs a variety of functions: "[It] can help prevent penetration from the outside. It can protect the privacy of users of the system so that only authorized participants can comprehend communications. It can ensure integrity of the communications. It can increase assurance that the received messages are genuine."

Digital signatures facilitate electronic funds transfer, commitment of computer resources, and signing of documents. Without that electronic establishment of authenticity, how can you establish the validity of a signature on an electronic contract? It was no surprise that NIST should decide to establish a digital-signature standard; the one the agency chose was.

RSA Data Security was established in 1981; by 1991 the list of purchasers of its digital-signature technology included Apple, AT&T, DEC, IBM, Lotus, Microsoft, Northern Telecom, Novell, Sun, and Word-Perfect. RSA had been accepted as a standard by several standards organizations;[1] it was fast on its way to becoming the defacto digital-signature standard.

In establishing a standard for digital signatures, NIST's criteria were somewhat different from that of the computer industry. In particular, the government wanted to avoid the possibility that the digital-signature standard could be used for confidentiality. It was also important that the standard be nonproprietary. NIST proposed the Digital Signature Standard (DSS) [NIST-XX] as a FIPS. There was great consternation—and not only at RSA Data Security. It was immediately apparent that DSS could not interoperate with digital signatures already in use.

Although NIST announced that DSS would be patented by the government and would be available free of charge, patent problems arose immediately. The government agency had chosen an algorithm that was based on unpatented work of an independent researcher, Tahir El Gamal. David Kravitz, an employee of NSA, filed a patent application for the Digital Signature Algorithm; this was subsequently awarded [Krav].

To its chagrin, NIST discovered that Claus Schnorr, a German mathematician, had already received U.S. and German patents for a similar algorithm [Schn-89, Schn-90b]. Public Key Partners (PKP) acquired Schnorr's patent rights. PKP offered the government free use of the algorithm in exchange for exclusive rights to Kravitz's algorithm. Under the PKP proposal, DSS users outside the Federal government would have to pay for use of the DSS algorithm. Following public opposition, the government declined the offer.

There were other objections to DSS, most notably that NIST was promulgating a weak standard. NIST proposed a key size of 512 bits.

---

[1] RSA is listed by International Standards Organization standard 9796 as a compatible cryptographic algorithm. RSA is part of the Society for Worldwide Interbank Financial Transactions (SWIFT) standard, and the ANSI X9.31 standard for the U.S. banking industry. It forms part of the Internet Privacy Enhanced Mail (PEM) standard.

Earlier work on the algorithm had suggested that 512 bits "appear[ed] to offer only marginal security" [LaOd, BFS]. Scientists complained that restricting the key size unnecessarily constrained flexibility, and that improvements in algorithms could quickly render the NIST standard obsolete. A flexible key size would not have that difficulty. These issues were similar to ones raised when DES was proposed.

There were also differences from the DES situation, and these raised concern. For DSS, there had been no public request for proposals, and NSA had designed the algorithm. CPSR and members of industry and academia asserted that NIST's reliance on NSA was directly contrary to the Computer Security Act. These concerns were noted by Representative Jack Brooks, who had served as Chairman of the House Government Operations Committee during the passage of the Computer Security Act:

> [u]nder the Computer Security Act of 1987, the Department of Commerce [through NIST] has primary responsibility for establishing computer security standards including those dealing with cryptography. However, many in industry are concerned that in spite of the Act, the NSA continues to control the Commerce Department's work in this area. For example, Commerce (at the urging of the National Security Agency) has proposed a "digital signature standard" (DSS) that has been severely criticized by the computer and telecommunications industry [USHR-92, pg.2].

DSS was proposed in 1991. Public concerns resulted in modifications, including a flexible key size (key sizes from 512 to 1024 bits are permitted, in jumps of 64 bits). Problems with the patent have slowed the process, but on May 19, 1994, the government adopted DSS as a Federal Standard [FIPS-186], announcing that the "Department of Commerce is not aware of patents that would be infringed by this standard" [NIST-186]. James Bidzos, President of both PKP and RSA Data Security Inc., believes otherwise, "We disagree. There are a number of patents that we believe cover DSS."

SECURING THE COMMUNICATIONS INFRASTRUCTURE: DIGITAL TELEPHONY AND EES

As the phone system has moved to a digital system, another issue arises. Encryption affects the government's ability to comprehend an intercepted signal, but the government is also concerned about its ability to intercept the signal. For this reason we include a discussion of the FBI's "Digital Telephony" proposal in this chapter.

As a result of increasing standardization of telephone switching practices, modern communication systems can provide much more information about each call, revealing in real time where the call came from even when it originates a long way away. But advanced communications systems, including such improvements as cellular telephones and call forwarding, can also present problems to law enforcement. The FBI was concerned about the ability of service providers to locate a call and, at law enforcement's behest, install a tap. In 1992, the Bureau prepared a legislative proposal.

At the time, the FBI was responding more to a problem the Bureau saw coming than to one that had hit full force. A Washington Post story of April 30, 1992 reported that "FBI officials said they have not yet fumbled a criminal probe due to the inability to tap a phone . . ." [Mint]. The FBI contended that there were numerous cases where court orders had not been sought, executed, or fully carried out by law-enforcement agencies because of technological problems [DGBBBRGM, pg. 26]. However, Freedom of Information Act litigation initiated by CPSR in April 1992 produced no evidence of technical difficulties preventing the FBI from executing wiretaps as of December 1992.

Major members of the computer and communications industries, including AT&T, Digital Equipment, Lotus, Microsoft, and Sun, strongly opposed the 1992 proposal. The Electronic Frontier Foundation helped coordinate this opposition. Industry was particularly concerned that the proposal was too broad, covering operators of private branch exchanges and computer networks. Industry feared that it would have to foot the bill. The General Accounting Office briefed Congress, and expressed concern that alternatives to the Digital Telephony proposal had not been fully explored [GAO-92]. The U.S. General Services Administration characterized the proposed legislation as unnecessary and potentially harmful to the nation's competitiveness [GSA-92]. There were no Congressional sponsors for the proposal.

In 1994, the FBI has prepared a revised proposal that limits the scope to common carriers and allocates $500 million to cover their costs. Carriers would have three years to comply; after that, failure to fulfill a wiretap order could result in a fine of up to ten thousand dollars a day. The revised proposal, the "Digital Telephony and Communications Privacy Improvements Act of 1994," was submitted to Congress in March 1994.

On February 17, 1994, FBI Director Louis Freeh reiterated the agency's concerns in a speech to the Executives' Club of Chicago: "Development of technology is moving so rapidly that several hundred court-authorized surveillances already have been prevented by new technological impediments with advanced communications equipment." In testimony to Congress on March 18, 1994, Freeh reported that a 1993 informal survey of federal, state and local law-enforcement agencies revealed 91 instances of recent court orders for electronic surveillance that could not be fully implemented [Freeh, pg 33]. The problems were due to a variety of causes, including 29 cases of special calling features (such as call forwarding), and 30 cases involving difficulties with cellular phones (including the inability of the carriers to provide dialed number information). Under questioning by Senator Leahy, Freeh answered that the FBI had not encountered court-authorized wiretap orders the Bureau could not execute due to digital telephony. However, in his prepared testimony Freeh cited two examples where wiretaps could not be executed due to digital telephony [Freeh, pg. 34].

While wiretapping can procure signals, secure telephones can render those signals useless to the wiretapper. Secure telephones using advanced key management are widespread in the national security community. Although voice-encryption systems for the commercial market have been a staple of companies such as Gretag and Crypto AG in Switzerland and Datotek and TCC in the U.S., only in 1992 was the first mass market device for secure voice encryption brought forth by a major corporation. AT&T announced the Model 3600 Telephone Security Device, which employed a DES chip for encryption.

The Department of Justice had been concerned about just such a development, and a federal initiative had been underway to preempt it. In April 1993 the President announced the key-escrow initiative: the "Clipper" chip and its associated key escrow scheme, while AT&T announced a telephone privacy device that uses the device. This proposed standard raises a number of questions about cryptography within telecommunications. In the next chapter [of the original paper—Ed.] we discuss the Escrowed Encryption Standard.

[BFS]   Beth, T., Frisch, M. and Simmons, G. (Eds.), 1992, Public Key Cryptography: State of the Art and Future Directions, Lecture Notes in Computer Science, No. 578, Springer-Verlag, 1992.

[BiSh]   Biham, E. and Shamir, A., 1993, Differential Cryptanalysis of the Data Encryption Standard, Springer-Verlag 1993.

[DGBBBRBM] Denning, D., Godwin, M., Bayse, W., Rotenberg, M., Branscomb, L., Branscomb, A., Rivest, R., Grosso, A. and Marx, G., 1993, "To Tap or Not to Tap," Communications of the ACM, Vol. 36(3), March 1993 , pp. 24–44.

[Freeh]   Freeh, L., 1994, Written Statement before the Subcommittee on Technology and the Law of the Committee of the Judiciary, United States Senate and the Subcommittee on Civil and Constitutional Rights of the Committee on the Judiciary, House of Representatives, March 18, 1994, Washington, DC.

[GSA]   General Services Administration, 1992, Offices of Congressional Affairs, Memo of May 5, 1992, in The Third CPSR Cryptography and Privacy Conference Source Book, June 7, 1993, Washington, DC.

[Krav]   Kravitz, D., Digital Signature Algorithm, U.S. Patent Number 5231668, applied for July 26, 1991, received July 27, 1993.

[Land]   Landau, S., 1988, "Zero Knowledge and the Department of Defense," Notices of the American Mathematical Society (Special Article Series), Vol. 35, No. 1 (1988), pp.5–12.

[LaOd]   LaMacchia, B. and Odlyzko, A., 1991, Computation of Discrete Logarithms in Prime Fields, in Design, Codes, and Cryptography, Vol. 1, 1991, pp. 47–62.

[Mats]   Matsui, M., 1993, "Linear Cryptanalysis of DES Cipher," in Proceedings Eurocrypt 1993.

[Mint]   Mintz, J., 1992, "Intelligence Community in Breach with Business," Washington Post, April 30, 1992, Sec. A.

[NIST-XX]   National Institute of Standards and Technology, 1991, Publication XX: Announcement and Specifications for a Digital Signature Standard (DSS), August 19, 1991, Washington, DC.

[NIST-186]   National Institute of Standards and Technology, 1994, Federal Information Processing Standards Publication 186: Digital Signature Standard (DSS), May 19, 1994, Washington, DC.

[PCSG]   Public Cryptography Study Group, 1981, Report of the Public Cryptography Study Group, American Council on Education, February 1981.

[Schn-89]   Schnorr, C., Procedures for the Identification of Participants as well as the Generation and Verification of Electronic Signatures in a Digital Exchange System, German Patent Number 9010348.1, patent applied for February 24, 1989, patent received August 29, 1990.

[Schn-90a]   Schnorr, C., 1989, "Efficient Identification and Signatures for Smart Cards," in Advances in Cryptology—Crypto '89, Springer-Verlag, New York, 1990, pp. 239–251.

[Schn-90b]   Schnorr, C., Method for Identifying Subscribers and for Generating and Verifying Electronic Signatures in a Data Exchange System, U.S. Patent Number 4995082, patent applied for February 23, 1990, patent received February 19, 1991.

[USHR-87]   House Report 100–153, 1987, Part 2, the Committee on Government Operations' Report on the Computer Security Act of 1987, Washington, DC.

[USHR-92]   Hearing before the House Judiciary Subcommittee on Economic and Commercial Law, May 7, 1992, Washington, DC.

## 5

Internet Privacy Enhanced Mail*

Stephen T. Kent

The primary focus of the effort to develop and deploy Internet Privacy Enhanced Mail (PEM) is the provision of security for email users in the Internet community. The PEM effort began in 1985 as an activity of the Privacy and Security Research Group (PSRG) [15] under the auspices of the Internet Architecture Board (IAB).[1] The effort has yielded a series of specifications of which the most recent set, Requests for Comment (RFCs) 1421–1424 are proposed Internet standards [1, 11, 14, 16]. These RFCs are products of the PEM Working Group within the Internet Engineering Task Force, a subsidiary group of the IAB. For the purposes of this article, the Internet community is interpreted to include those users who employ the email protocols defined by Requests for Comment (RFCs) RFC 821 and RFC 822. (RFCs are the official archival publications of the Internet. All protocol standards are published as RFCs, but not all RFCs are protocol standards. For example, some RFCs are merely informational, others describe experimental protocols, and others constitute policy statements. RFCs are available on-line at various sites and in hardcopy format from SRI International).

SECURITY SERVICES

A variety of security services for email users are provided in PEM: confidentiality, data origin authentication, connectionless integrity, and, with the algorithm suite currently specified, support for nonrepudiation with proof of origin. These services, defined by the OSI security reference model [10], are bundled into two groups: all messages proc-

---

* Communications of the ACM; August 1993/Vol.36, No.8, pp. 48–60. Copyright 1993, Association for Computing Machinery, Inc. Reprinted by permission.

[1] The PSRG was formed in 1985 and is one of several groups pursuing various research topics in the context of the Internet. Other groups have been created to explore topics such as end-to-end protocols, multimedia teleconferencing and information location services. In 1985 the IAB acronym represented "Internet Activities Board" and its role included approval of Internet protocol standards. In 1992 the IAB and its subsidiary organizations became part of the Internet Society, and the IAB now focuses on architectural planning for the Internet.

essed through PEM incorporate the authenticity, integrity and nonre-pudiation support facilities, whereas confidentiality is an optional security service.

In the email context, the confidentiality service protects the contents of a message against unauthorized disclosure (i.e., disclosure to other than the recipients specified by the message originator). Thus the message is protected against attacks such as wiretapping during transit and against accidental misdelivery by the message system. This service is especially important for many users given the ease with which email (and other data) transmitted on most local area networks (LANs) can be intercepted by network maintainers and users. The confidentiality service also protects messages while they are stored in a user's mailbox (e.g., on a disk in a computer), if the user elects to retain the messages in confidentiality-protected form.

The data origin authentication service permits the recipient of a message to reliably determine the identity of the originator of the message. (In the case of a forwarded message, this service reliability identifies the forwarder, not the original sender, of the message.) This service counters a serious deficiency in current email systems, where it is often quite easy to forge the identity of the sender of a message. The recipient of a forged message might be misled into taking inappropriate actions or might wrongly attribute libelous comments.

The connectionless integrity service provides the recipient with assurance that the received message content is identical to the content sent by the originator. This service protects against attacks in which the message content is modified while in transit. The service is deemed "connectionless" because it does not attempt to impose any ordering among received messages. Although authentication and integrity services are described here as independent, they are usually provided in tandem. Receipt of a message that is guaranteed to be intact, but whose sender is unknown, is not a useful combination.

Support for nonrepudiation[2] in PEM allows a message to be forwarded to a third party, who can verify the identity of the originator (not just the identity of the message forwarder) and can verify that the message has not been altered, even by the original recipient. In existing network email systems, the recipient of a forwarded message has no good means to verify the identity of the "original" sender or the integrity of the forwarded message. A more significant use of this service is in support of electronic commerce, where PEM-protected messages

---

[2] A full implementation of a nonrepudiation with proof of origin service, will require an extensive infrastructure establishing semantic and legal conventions for interpretation of "signed" documents. Message processing in PEM and the certification hierarchy described later are important parts of this service, but do not provide a complete nonrepudiation service.

could be used in a number of ways, including securing transmission of purchase orders and providing receipts.

THE PEM MESSAGING ENVIRONMENT

As previously noted, PEM is intended for use in conjunction with existing email systems, primarily Internet email. Figure 1 illustrates how PEM fits into existing mail system architectures. Several representative email components and their interactions are illustrated in this figure. In this example, messages are prepared on a multiuser computer, in which each user has an individual mailbox and an individual instance of a User Agent (UA), the software employed for message submission and reception. This multiuser computer also includes a Message Transfer Agent (MTA),[3] software that acts as the interface to the rest of the messaging world—it is the interface through which all messages exiting this computer are transmitted and all messages arriving at this computer are received.

Another MTA, an intermediate mail relay executing on a computer dedicated to this function (an email server), is included to represent the (common) case where the sender and recipient are served by different MTAs operated by different administrative authorities. Only a single recipient is illustrated in this figure, even though many messages are sent to multiple recipients. This recipient is located on a single-user personal computer or workstation, but his mailbox is maintained at the MTA.

Many messaging systems assume that a user's mailbox is continuously available for delivery of incoming messages. If a user switches off his computer overnight, on weekends or holidays, this model would be violated and a message originator might receive an error indication from the MTA. Hence desktop computer users often maintain mailboxes on server computers that provide continuous availability. Such users retrieve messages from a server using the Post Office Protocol [19] and read them on their desktop computers. Messages are protected while stored in these (remote) mailboxes under PEM, exposing them only when they are being read on the user's personal computer.

To maximize compatibility with existing email systems, PEM is designed to be transparent to MTAs, so the existing email transport infrastructure can be used to transfer PEM messages. Privacy En-

---

[3] The concepts of UAs and MTAs are taken from international email standards, i.e., X.400 [4], but apply equally well to messaging in general. In the TCP/IP protocol suite, MTAs are represented by Simple Mail Transfer Protocol (SMTP) processes that route and relay mail traffic. User Agents are represented by processes which implement RFC 822 message processing.

FIGURE 1.
Privacy
Enhanced Mail
environment

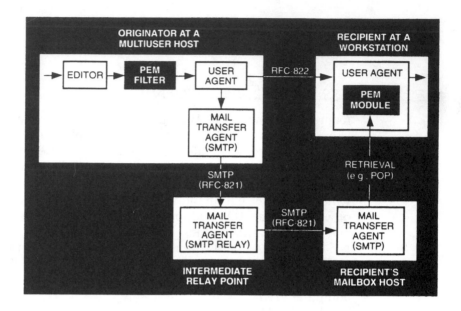

hanced Mail also is designed to be minimally intrusive to UAs. For example, it is possible to implement PEM in a fashion that entails no changes to the UA. One can implement PEM as a filter applied to a file created using an editor, but before input to a UA. Although minimally intrusive, this approach tends to provide an awkward user interface (UI), unless a substantial amount of mechanism from the UA is replicated in the PEM filter. For example, the user might be required to supply recipient identifiers twice, once for PEM processing and once for email addressing. In Figure 1 the message originator employs the filter approach to PEM implementation.

To provide a more "user-friendly" interface for PEM, it is usually necessary to integrate PEM into the UA. When PEM processing is integrated into a UA, the UA provides additional UI facilities to allow selection of security services and integrate with key management facilities. For example, a message originator might identify recipients using either email addresses or local aliases, and the integrated UA would automatically translate these into the cryptographically authenticated identifiers used within PEM. In Figure 1 the recipient employs an integrated PEM-UA. Both implementation options are purely local matters, invisible outside of the computers on which they appear.

Privacy Enhanced Mail is oriented primarily toward use in the Internet email environment, as characterized by two Internet standards: RFC-822 [6] and SMTP [17]. The former standard defines the syntax of messages and the semantics of message headers. The latter standard defines a protocol for transport of messages. Work is now under way to extend PEM for use with the recently adopted Multipurpose Internet Mail Extensions (MIME) [2], a move that will marry email security and multimedia email capabilities. Although designed primarily for use with Internet email protocols, PEM can be employed in a wider range of messaging environments. For example, the NIST Open System Implementors Workshop Security Working Group has defined an X.400 body part to carry PEM messages. This paves the way for email gateways that connect SMTP and X.400 messaging systems to pass PEM-protected messages. A character-encoding scheme is also used in PEM to maximize the likelihood that PEM-processed messages can successfully transit mail gateways that link Internet email to other email systems (e.g., BITNET, and UUNET), many of which do not provide completely transparent forwarding of message contents.

CRYPTOGRAPHIC ALGORITHMS USED IN PEM

In providing the security services described in the preceding paragraphs, PEM makes use of a variety of cryptographic algorithms (see "Cryptographic Concepts and Terminology" sidebar). These algorithms provide for message integrity, message encryption, and distribution of the cryptographic keys used to encipher messages. If public-key cryptoalgorithms are employed for key management, then additional algorithms must be specified.

The base PEM standards do not require the use of specific algorithms for any of these purposes, but rather provide facilities to identify which algorithms are employed on a per-message and per-recipient basis. A separate standard within the PEM series (RFC 1423) identifies a suite of algorithms for use with PEM. In the future, other algorithm suites may be defined, extending PEM through the issuance of additional RFCs. By grouping algorithms into suites, PEM attempts to avoid combinatorial growth as new algorithm options are added. Such growth would likely result in diminished interoperability.

In addition to the specification of message-processing facilities, the PEM standards provide for a public-key certification infrastructure. Although PEM allows for the use of either secret-key or public-key cryptoalgorithms for key distribution, the standards encourage the use of public-key cryptography because of its ability to support a very large, distributed user community. The specific approach to public-key cryptography adopted for PEM is based on the use of certificates, as defined in CCITT Recommendation X.509 [4] and as adopted by ISO for both directory and messaging security (see sidebar on Public-Key Certificates).

The PEM standards establish a specific framework for a public key certification system for several reasons. Although PEM makes use of

X.509 certificates, the international standards do not provide a semantic context in which to interpret certificates. Recommendation X.509 embodies a degree of generality that, if fully exploited, could result in extremely complex certification relationships. The certification system developed for PEM imposes conventions that make certification relationships straightforward and allow users to readily evaluate a certificate associated with another PEM user. Another advantage of establishing this certification framework is that it can be employed in conjunction with security facilities in other protocols, for example, X.500 and X.400. The same certificates used for PEM can be employed with these other applications in support of security services.

PEM PROCESSING: MESSAGE SUBMISSION

The overall flow of data for PEM message submission processing is illustrated in Figure 2. There are two sources of data input to PEM for message submission processing: message header data and message content. The message header information will be carried in the (external) email header of the final, processed PEM message. This data largely bypasses PEM processing, with the possible exception that the Subject field, if present and deemed sensitive, might be omitted or a benign Subject might be substituted (e.g., "Encrypted Message"). A sensitive Subject field can be enclosed within the PEM-protected content,

FIGURE 2. Privacy Enhanced Mail submission processing overview

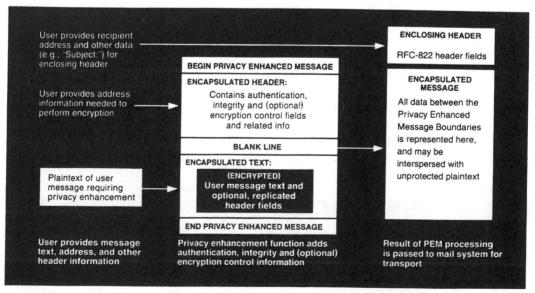

affording it confidentiality. Only one portion of the header data, namely recipient identifiers (e.g., mailbox addresses), is required to control PEM processing. If the (optional) confidentiality service is selected by the message originator, these recipient identifiers are used to control message encipherment.

Cryptographic Concepts and Terminology

Privacy Enhanced Mail uses cryptographic algorithms (cryptoalgorithms or ciphers) to provide a variety of security services. Knowledge of cryptoalgorithms is not critical to understanding how PEM works but understanding the terminology used with such algorithms is helpful. Figure A depicts a graphic framework for the discussion that follows.

A cryptoalgorithm is used to transform data through an **encryption** process. The input to this process is called **plaintext** and the output is called **ciphertext**. The encryption is inverted by a **decryption** process which accepts ciphertext as input and yields plaintext. In both cases the process is controlled by a **key** which is a parameter to the process. In a symmetric (secret-key) cipher the same key is used to encrypt and decrypt data. In Figure A, KEY-1 and KEY-2 would be identical.) That key is kept secret and is shared by a transmitter and a receiver. Symmetric ciphers typically exhibit good performance and are used to encrypt user data. Privacy Enhanced Mail uses symmetric ciphers to encrypt messages.

In an asymmetric (public-key) cryptoalgorithm a pair of distinct, but mathematically related keys are used for encryption and decryption. One key is kept private and is known only to its owner whereas the other key is made publicly known hence the term "public-key cryptography." (In Figure A, KEY-1 and KEY-2 would be distinct and either could be the public or private key.) Data encrypted with a user's private key can be decrypted using his public key and vice versa. In the general model of public-key cryptography. Since the performance of asymmetric ciphers generally is not as good as that of symmetric ciphers, the former usually are not used to encipher user data directly. Instead, the asymmetry of public-key ciphers is often exploited to distribute symmetric keys and for digital signatures.

A **digital signature** is often effected using public-key cryptography and a (one-way) **hash function**, as illustrated in Figure B. The hash function is used to compute

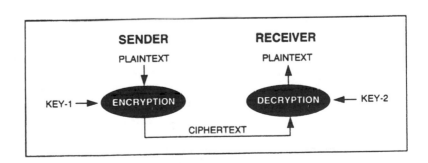

Figure A.
Cryptoalgorithm example

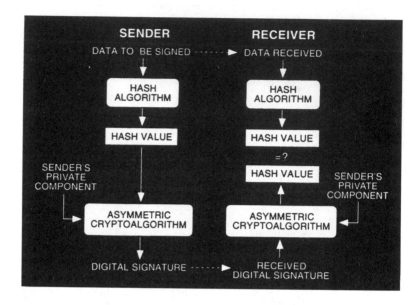

a value that is a complex function of the data to be signed. A property of a good one-way hash function is that it is computationally infeasible to construct two distinct messages yielding the same hash value, making it a "fingerprint" of the data. A user digitally signs data by encrypting the hash value of the data using his private component. Using an algorithm such as RSA, the signature on (purportedly) signed data is validated, by any user, in a three-step process. The validator computes the hash value of the data, transforms the hash that arrived with the (purportedly) signed data using the signer's public component, and compares the results. A match indicates a valid digital signature.

Privacy Enhanced Mail makes use of public-key ciphers to encrypt the symmetric key used to encrypt a message and to digitally sign a message.

Public Key Certificates: The X.509 Way

A public-key certificate is a data structure used to securely bind a public key to attributes. The attributes can consist of identification information, for example, a name, or authorization information (e.g., permission to use a resource). A standard for identification certificates is contained within the international standards for directories. An X.509 certificate binds a public key to a directory name and identifies the entity who vouches for the binding. The whole data structure is digitally signed in approximately the same fashion as a PEM message is signed (the canonicalization rules are different). Figure C illustrates the certificate format as specified by X.509, with sample field values.

The **version** field differentiates among successive versions of the certificate format. The initial value identifies the 1988 version, the version adopted by PEM. The **serial number** field uniquely identifies this certificate among those issued by the same entity.

FIGURE C.
The X.509
Certificate
format

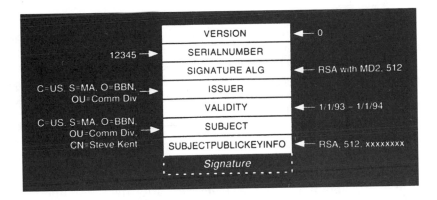

It provides a convenient shorthand means of uniquely identifying a certificate relative to an issuer. The **signature alg** field identifies the digital signature algorithm used to sign this certificate. The **issuer** field holds the (distinguished) name of the entity that vouches for the binding between the **subject** name and the public key contained in the certificate (see the following subsection on distinguished names). The **subject** and **issuer** distinguished names illustrated here represent the author and his employer. The **validity** field specifies the start and end times and dates that delimit the interval over which the certificate is valid, in much the same way as many credit cards are marked. The public key alluded to earlier, along with an identifier to specify the algorithm and any parameters required by the algorithm, are contained in the **subjectPublicKeyinfo** field.

As noted previously, the signature alg field specifies the algorithms and any parameters required to verify the digital signature applied to the certificate. Both a one-way hash function and a public-key signature algorithm will be specified (e.g., the RSA public key algorithm and the MD2 hash algorithm in this example). This signature is applied by the issuer (using his private component) and appended after these other certificate fields. Appended to the certificate is a data structure that reproduces the algorithm identifiers and parameters needed to verify this signature (using the public component of the issuer).

One "validates" a certificate by verifying the signature applied by the issuer of the certificate, as described in the previous section "Cryptographic Concepts and Terminology." This use of certificates transforms the problem of acquiring the public key associated with a user into one of acquiring the public key of the issuer of the user's certificate. This issuer also will have a certificate, and thus the process of certificate validation is recursive and implicitly defines a (directed) certification graph. The validation algorithm must conclude at some point, however, implying that the user holds a public key obtained through some out-of-band, integrity-secure channel (not through an untrusted network).

A certificate, like a credit card, does not remain valid forever. It naturally expires when the validity interval passes, or it may be revoked ("hot-listed") by the issuer if the binding between the subject and the subject public key is no longer valid. This revocation of the binding may result from a number of possibilities: the subject's name changes, (e.g., due to a job change or a move) or because the subject's private component is feared compromised. A Certificate Revocation List (CRL) to facilitate dissemination of revoked certificate information is defined in X.509. A CRL is a data structure, signed by an issuer, consisting of the issuer's name, the date the CRL is generated, and a sequence of pairs, each consisting of a certificate serial number and the date when that certificate was revoked. Thus, as part of validating a certificate, one must also check that the certificate is not hot-listed by its issuer, that the issuer's certificate is not hot-listed by its issuer, and so forth. Privacy Enhanced Mail makes use of a CRL format that differs slightly from X.509; the PEM version adds a date indicating the next scheduled CRL generation and simplifies the format of the serial number and date list.

In Internet email, the header data is separated from the message content by a blank line. In a PEM-processed message, an explicit boundary marker is inserted after the blank line to identify the beginning of PEM processing. Following this boundary marker is a collection of PEM header data, used by each recipient to validate message integrity and authenticity, and to decipher an enciphered message. Following this PEM header data is another blank line. The message text itself, augmented by any header fields that are replicated to afford them PEM protection, becomes the encapsulated content of the PEM-processed message, following the (second) blank line. Finally, a complementary PEM boundary message marks the end of the PEM message-processing area.

Three types of PEM messages are defined to provide different combinations of security services for different messaging contexts: MIC-CLEAR, MIC-ONLY, and ENCRYPTED.[4] A MIC-CLEAR message employs a cryptographic message integrity code (MIC) to check the integrity and authenticity of the message, but no confidentiality is provided and the encoding step is omitted to permit viewing by recipients who have not implemented PEM. A MIC-CLEAR message can be sent to a mailing list that contains a mixture of PEM and nonPEM users, all of whom will be able to "read" the message, but only the PEM users will be able to verify the message integrity and authenticity.

A MIC-ONLY message offers the same security services as MIC-CLEAR, but applies an optional encoding. This encoding helps ensure that the PEM-processed message can pass through a variety of email gateways without being transformed in a fashion that would invalidate the integrity and authenticity checks. An ENCRYPTED message adds the confidentiality service to integrity and authenticity. This message type also uses the encoding transformation described for MIC-ONLY, since otherwise the (binary) output of the encryption processing would be unable to transit many email systems (which were designed to transfer text, not binary data).

---

[4] A fourth message type, CRL, is defined for dissemination of certificate revocation lists. This message type is intended for use by PEM administrators, not end users, and thus is not addressed in this article.

SUBMISSION PROCESSING

Submission processing in PEM involves three major transformation steps: canonicalization, computation of the message integrity code (MIC) and optional message encryption, followed by optional 6-bit encoding. These steps are illustrated in Figure 3. Since the encryption and encoding constitute optional processing steps, a field indicating the PEM processing options (Proc-Type) appears at the beginning of each PEM message. This is the first field of the PEM header, which contains the data needed by each recipient to verify the integrity and authenticity of a received message (and to decrypt a confidential message). Data generated during the second and third transformation steps are later assembled to form the PEM header. Figure 4 contains a sample ENCRYPTED PEM message to illustrate the elements of a PEM header.

CANONICALIZATION

The first step in PEM submission processing is the canonicalization of the message content. Canonicalization involves transforming the message content from the "native" representation for the computer from which the message is submitted, into a network standard representation. Many email systems designed to operate in a heterogeneous computer environment employ this step to avoid the need for each computer to implement a pairwise translation for every other computer with which it may communicate. For example, on some computers each line of text in a file is terminated by an ASCII newline character, on other computers a carriage return and a line feed are employed, and others may employ some form of (non-ASCII) record mark.

FIGURE 3.

Privacy Enhanced Mail submission processing steps

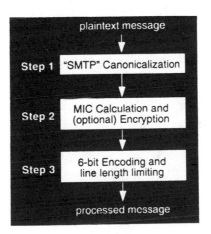

The canonicalization step must be performed as part of PEM processing, prior to when the email system would normally perform the equivalent step. Any change to the message content after the PEM integrity service has been applied would cause the integrity check performed by a recipient to fail, hence PEM must apply this transformation before the normal email processing. Also, if the message content is enciphered for confidentiality, it would be impossible for the normal email canonicalization to take place, i.e., the message content would be just as unintelligible to this email software as it would be to a potential eavesdropper.

The specific canonicalization transformation used in PEM is specified by a parameter in the Content-Domain field of the PEM header, permitting different transformations to be specified for use in different messaging environments. A Content-Domain value of "RFC822" specifies use of the same canonicalization employed by the Internet Simple Mail Transfer Protocol (SMTP) for unprotected email, as Figure 4 illustrates. Other transforms can be defined for use with PEM in other messaging contexts, e.g., ASN.1 [5] for use with X.400 messaging. However, only one canonicalized format can be specified per submitted message. Thus if the recipients of a single message were to span multiple messaging system types, multiple message submissions would be required to accommodate their distinct, canonical message formats.

MESSAGE INTEGRITY AND ORIGINATOR AUTHENTICATION

The second step in PEM message processing begins with the calculation of the message integrity code (MIC). Here too, PEM treats the choice of the MIC algorithm as a parameter that can differ among user communities or evolve as better MIC algorithms are developed.

PEM requires the use of a very strong form of MIC algorithm, a one-way hash function, whenever messages are addressed to multiple recipients. Users are strongly encouraged to use this sort of function in all cases. The need for a one-way hash function stems from a desire to prevent "insider spoofing." A message addressed to both User-B and User-C from User-A might be tampered with by User-B and then sent to User-C. If a less secure form of MIC algorithm were employed, e.g., the DES Message Authentication Code [8], this sort of insider spoofing would be undetectable by User-C, i.e., he would believe the message modified by User-B was sent (intact) by User-A.

The MIC is calculated on the canonicalized version of the message to permit verification in the heterogeneous computing environment previously described. The specific algorithm employed to compute the MIC for a message is specified in the MIC-Info field of the PEM header. The sample PEM message in Figure 4 uses the RSA MD5 one-way hash

FIGURE 4. *Encrypted PEM message example from RFC 1421*

```
----- BEGIN PRIVACY-ENHANCED MESSAGE -----
Proc-Type: 4,ENCRYPTED
Content-Domain: RFC822
DEK-Info: DES-CBC,BFF968AA74691AC1
Originator-Certificate:
    MIIBlTCCAScCAWUwDQYJKoZIhvcNAQECBQAwUTELMAkGA1UEBhMCVVMxIDAeBgNV
    BAoTF1JTQSBEYXRhIFN1Y3VyaXR5LCBJbmMuMQ8wDQYDVQQLEwZCZXRhIDExDzAN
    BgNVBAsTBk5PVEFSWTAeFwOSMTA5MDQxODM4MTdaFW05MZA5MDMxODM4MTZaMEUx
    CzAJBgNVBAYTA1VTMSAwHgYDVQQKExdSU0EgRGFOYSBTZWN1cm1OeSwgSW5jLjEU
    MEIGA1UEAxMLVGVzdCBVc2VyIDEwWTAKBgRVCAEBAgICAANLADBIAkEAwHZH17i+
    yJcqDtjJCow-TdBJrdAiLAnSC+CnnjOJELyuQiBgkGrgIh3j8/xOfM+YrsyFlu3F
    LZPVtzlndhYFJQIDAQABMAOGCSaGSIb3DQEBAgUAAlkACKrOPqphJYwlj+YPtcIq
    iWlFPuN5jJ79Khfg~ASFxskYkEMjRNZV/HZDZQEhtVaU~Jxfzs2wfX5byMp2X3U,'
    5XUXGx7qusDgHQGs,Jk9W8CWlfuSWUgN4w==
Key-Info: RSA,
    I3rRIGXUGWAF8js5wC-RTkdhO34PTHdRZY9TuvmO3M+NM7fx6qc5udixps2LngO+
    wGrtiUm/ovtKdin-6ZQ aQ==
Issuer-Certificate:
    MIIB3DCCAUgCAQowDQYJKoZIhvcNAQECBQAwTzELMAkGA1UEBhMCVVMxIDAeBgNV
    BAoTF1JTQSBEYXRhIFN1Y3VyaXR5LCBJbmMuMQ8wDQYDVQQLEwZCZXRhIDExDTA~
    BgNVBAsTBFRMQOEwHhcNOTEwOTAxMDgwMDAwWhcNOTIwOTAxMDclQTU5WjBRMQsw
    CQYDVQQGEwJVUzEgMB4GA1UEChMXU1NBIERhdGEgU2VjdXJpdHksIEluYy4xDzAN
    BgNVBAsTBkJldGEgMTEPMAOGA1UECxMGTk9UQVJZMHAwCgYEVQgBAQICArwDYgAw
    XwJYCsnp61QCxYykNlODwutF/jMJ3kL+3PjYyHowk+~'9rLg6X65B/LD4bJHtO5XW
    cqAz/7R7XhjYCmOPcqbdzoACZtIlETrKrcJiDYoP+DkZ8klgCk7hQHpbIwIDAQAB
    MAOGCSqGSIb3DQEBAgUAA38AAICPv4f9Gx/tY4+p+4DB7MV+tKZnvBoy8zgoMGOx
    dD2jMZ/3HsyWKWgSFOeH/AJB3qr9zosG47pyMnTf3aSy2nB07CMxpUWRBcXUpE+x
    EREZd9++320fGBIXaialnOgVUnOOzSYgugiQO77nJLDUjOhQehCizEs5wUJ35a5h
MIC-Info: RSA-MD5,RSA,
    UdFJR8u/TIGhfH65ieewe210W4tooa3vZCvVNGBZirf/7nrgzWDABz8w9NsXSexv
    AjRFbHoNPzBuxwmOAFeAOHJszL4yBvhG
Recipient-ID-Asymmetric:
    MFExCzAJBgNVBAYTA1VTMSAwHgYDVQQKExdSU0EgRGFOYSBTZWN1cm1OeSwgSW5j
    LjEPMAOGA1UECxMGQmVOYSAxMQ8wDQYDVQQLEwZOTlRBUlk=,
    66
Key-Info: RSA,
    06BSlww9CTyHPtS3bMLD+LOhejdvX6QvlHK2ds2s~PEaXhX8EhvVphHYTjwekdWv
    7xOz3Jx2vTAhOYHMcqqCjA==

qeWlj/YJ2Uf5ng9yznPbtDOmYloSwIuV9FRYx+gzY+8iXd/NQrXHfi6/MhPfPF3d
jIqCJAxvld2xgqQimUzoSla4r7kQQ5c/Iua4LqKeq3ciFzEv/MbZhA==
-----END PRIVACY-ENHANCED MESSAGE-----
```

function [18] as the MIC algorithm. To provide data origin authentication and message integrity, and to support nonrepudiation with proof of origin, the MIC must be protected in a fashion that binds it to the message originator. In the example seen in Figure 4, which uses asymmetric cryptography, the MIC is protected using the private component of the originator's public-key pair. This effects a digital signature on the message, which can be verified by any user, as described in the message delivery processing section. The MIC-Info field contains the MIC value and also specifies the means used to protect the MIC (e.g., RSA encryption is employed in Figure 4).

To facilitate the ability of a recipient to establish the binding between the MIC value and the identity of the message originator, the PEM header contains a field that purports to identify the originator. Figure 4 illustrates one means of providing this identification when using asymmetric cryptography (i.e., the Originator-Certificate field). This field conveys the public-key certificate of the originator, which will be used by a recipient in verifying the integrity of the MIC value. The figure also illustrates the inclusion of multiple Issuer-Certificate fields in the PEM header. Implementations of PEM provide the originator with an ability to include, automatically, all the certificates that a recipient may require to validate the MIC value, the details of which are discussed in the context of delivery processing.

Finally, the transformation of the MIC value using the originator's public key does not protect against disclosure of this value. It is not possible to work backward from a MIC value to determine the content of a message; thus even if a message is encrypted to provide confidentiality one might not feel a need to encrypt the MIC value. However, an attacker might make educated guesses about the message content and test these guesses against the (signed) MIC value in the PEM header. Therefore, if the message is encrypted using PEM, the MIC value is also encrypted (using the same key employed to encrypt the message content) to protect against this attack. Also, since the value of the MIC (before or after encryption) is usually binary, it may not be possible to transmit it using a messaging system that deals only with text. Thus the MIC value can be encoded for transmission, and the encoding technique is implied by the messaging system context (e.g., for Internet email the same 6-bit encoding is employed for this field as is applied to the message content).

ENCRYPTION

The second PEM processing step also provides message encryption, if selected by the originator. This processing is performed only if the PEM header specifies a Proc-Type value of "ENCRYPTED." Any padding required by the message encryption algorithm is applied to the canonicalized plaintext before encryption.[5] A message encipherment key, to be used exclusively to encrypt this one message, is generated by the originator. The data encryption algorithm employed in PEM, and its mode of use, is not fixed but is another parameter, specified in the DEK-Info field of the PEM header. If the encryption algorithm requires any parameters, these are also specified in this field. The canonical (padded as required) message text is then encrypted using the per-message key. The example PEM message shown in Figure 4 uses the Data Encryption Standard (DES) [9] in cipher block chaining (CBC) mode [7] for encipherment. This mode of the DES requires an 8-byte, (pseudo) random "initialization vector" for cryptographic synchronization, and this value is included as a parameter in the DEK-Info in the sample message.

As described in the preceding paragraphs, a PEM message is encrypted exactly once, irrespective of the number of recipients. Only one copy of this encrypted message is submitted to the message transfer system, and copies of this message are delivered to user mailboxes just as is done for regular, non-PEM messages. Effecting this multicast message encryption capability requires a key distribution technique that differs from those commonly employed for point-to-point communication [12]. Using asymmetric cryptography for key distribution, one copy of the message key is encrypted using the public component of the public-key pair for each recipient.[6] In this way, each copy of the message key is protected in a fashion that makes it decipherable by exactly one recipient.

Each encrypted message key copy is placed in a Key-Info field, following an identifier for the public-key algorithm used to encrypt the copy of the message key. Each Key-Info field is preceded by a Recipient-ID-Asymmetric field that identifies the recipient, by the X.500 distinguished name of his certificate issuer and certificate serial number, a combination that uniquely identifies the recipient.[7] Each pair of these PEM header fields provides the information required for a recipient to decrypt a message. If different recipients employ different key distribution algorithms, this is naturally accommodated by this pairing of

---

[5] Any padding applied for encryption is removed as part of the decryption process performed by each recipient, so the padding does not affect the MIC computation and it does not appear in the message content presented to the user.

[6] If symmetric cryptography is employed for key distribution, the same general approach is employed. A different, symmetric cryptographic key is shared by each originator-recipient pair and that key is used to encrypt the message key on a per-recipient basis.

[7] The use of the recipient's distinguished name, rather than a mailbox name, permits a recipient to receive email on multiple computers with different local account and mailbox names, while retaining a single cryptographically authenticated identity.

per-recipient fields. In Figure 4, RSA is employed as the public-key encryption algorithm and it is identified in the Key-Info field.

ENCODING FOR TRANSMISSION

The third (final) processing step renders ENCRYPTED or MIC-ONLY message into a character set suitable for transmission through a messaging system and across various messaging system boundaries. As noted earlier, the specific transformation employed here is another parameter of PEM processing and can vary for different messaging system environments. The encoding step initially specified transforms the (optionally encrypted) message text into a restricted 6-bit alphabet, plus line-length constraints, that make the encoding compatible with SMTP canonicalization and with most email gateways that link the Internet to other messaging systems. If the message has been encrypted, this encoding serves to transform the 8-bit (binary) ciphertext into a form that can be transmitted using SMTP and other message transfer protocols, many of which require messages to consist of only 7-bit ASCII. As previously noted, MIC-CLEAR messages are not subject to any portion of the third processing step.

Even if the message has not been encrypted, this encoding step ensures, with high probability, that the canonicalized version of the message (produced in step 1) will not be altered benignly in transit, for example, as a side effect of transiting an email gateway. A change to as little as one bit of the message content would cause the MIC check to fail at a destination, hence the need to ensure the PEM-processed message text can be transmitted without modification. Because MIC-CLEAR messages are not encoded, they are susceptible to this type of benign gateway manipulation, with increased risk of failing the MIC check at recipients who perform PEM processing. The provision of the MIC-CLEAR message type in PEM thus represents an explicit trade-off of immunity to benign transport manipulation versus flexibility in sending mail to mixed user communities.

PEM PROCESSING: MESSAGE DELIVERY

On receipt of what appears to be a PEM-protected message, the recipient PEM software first scans to find the PEM message boundary, then parses the PEM header to identify the version of PEM that was employed, and the message type, which determines the processing steps that will be performed by the recipient. Our sample message uses version 4 of PEM and is ENCRYPTED.

DECODING AND DECRYPTION

For a message of type ENCRYPTED or MIC-ONLY, the first step is the inversion of any encoding step applied by the originator (e.g., converting the 6-bit encoding back into the ciphertext or canonical plaintext form). The decoding performed is determined by the message system context.

If the message is ENCRYPTED, the recipient scans the PEM header to locate the Recipient-ID-Asymmetric field that uniquely identifies him. The recipient then examines the Key-Info field immediately following this ID field. The first parameter of this field specifies the cryptographic algorithm used to encipher the message key, and the second field contains the enciphered key.[8] In the asymmetric cryptographic context, the recipient uses the private component of his public-key pair to decrypt the second field, yielding the message key.

The DEK-Info field, which appears earlier in the PEM header, specifies the algorithm, mode, and any parameters necessary for decryption. In the sample message, this field specifies that each recipient would use the decrypted message key in conjunction with the DES, in CBC mode, with the initialization vector included in the DEK-Info field. The recipient can now use the message key, as indicated by the Key-Info field, to decrypt the message text. After decryption, the message content is now at the same processing status as a MIC-ONLY or MIC-CLEAR[9] message. Thus the following discussion applies to those message types as well.

VERIFYING MESSAGE INTEGRITY AND AUTHENTICITY

The recipient parses the MIC-Info field, to determine the MIC algorithm and signature algorithm identified for this message. The recipient computes the MIC on the canonical form of the message and saves the value for later comparison. In an asymmetric cryptographic context, the recipient must acquire the public component of the originator, to decrypt the signed MIC value and perform the comparison. If the comparison succeeds, the integrity of the message is verified. This verification step applies to all three message forms. Additionally, the recipient must verify the binding of an originator identity with this component, in support of originator authentication.

---

[8] This second field will generally be encoded, since the encrypted key is a binary value, and thus must be decoded before it can be decrypted.

[9] A MIC-CLEAR message actually requires a processing step unique to that message type. The step is the recanonicalization of the message insofar as lines are delimited by a carriage return and a line feed, versus a local representation of delimited lines.

In principle, this identification requires validating a sequence of public-key certificates that terminates with the certificate of the originator. As noted in a previous subsection "Message Integrity and Originator Authentication," PEM provides a facility that enables the originator to include (in the PEM header) all the certificates required for any recipient to verify the originator's identity and to acquire his public component. However, not all PEM messages will necessarily carry these certificates (e.g., because of space overhead). In practice, caching of certificates by UAs is expected to short-circuit the process of certificate validation in many instances, and to supply certificates when they are not all included in the PEM header.

Finally, after verifying message integrity and authenticity, the canonical form of the message is translated into a local representation apropos for the recipient's system and is displayed for the user. The recipient's PEM UA informs him that message integrity has been verified and it displays the authenticated originator identity. This displayed identity should include both the originator's name from his certificate (or a local alias assigned by the recipient) and an indication of the policy under which that name was validated.

Note that this identity is independent of the identity contained within the message, for example, the value of the "From" field. In a graphical UI system, this integrity and authenticity notification could be effected using a window separate from that used to display the message text. Errors encountered in attempting to validate message integrity, originator authenticity, or in decrypting the message may result in informative messages or may preclude display of the message for the recipient, depending on the severity of the error and on local security policy.

MESSAGE DISPOSITION

After PEM processing, the recipient may elect to store the message in decrypted, decanonicalized form, with none of the PEM headers. Alternatively, the message may be stored in canonical (but decrypted) form, along with the PEM header fields needed for signature verification (MIC-Info, Originator-ID-Asymmetric, Originator-Certificate, Issuer-Certificate). This form of storage is appropriate if the user wishes to forward a signed message to a third party for signature validation (e.g., as input to resolution of a dispute). This form of storage also provides continuing protection against modification of the message while in storage. Finally, the user may save the message in encrypted form, to additionally protect the message against disclosure while in storage.

THE INTERNET PUBLIC-KEY CERTIFICATION SYSTEM

The PEM specifications encourage use of public-key cryptography for message integrity, originator authentication, and for distribution of data encryption keys. As noted previously, PEM makes use of public-key certificates that conform to CCITT X.509 (see the Public Key Certificates sidebar). The X.509 recommendation defines an authentication framework, not only a certificate format, in which certificates play a central role. This framework is quite general and places very few constraints on the resulting certification system. At one end of the spectrum are arbitrary "mesh" certification systems in which there is no common semantic model of trust in certification (i.e., trust in certification is locally defined for each user). At the other end of the spectrum are systems in which there is a single, well-publicized and universally agreed-on certification policy. Both ends of this spectrum are accommodated under the X.509 framework.

In the Internet, a compromise approach to a certification system is adopted. This approach accommodates a wide range of certification trust policies, but imposes some policy constraints throughout the certification system to facilitate uniform certificate validation procedures. In particular, this system permits automated certificate validation with minimal user interaction, yet it ensures that users can readily interpret the results of the (automated) certification procedure. The following sections describe this certification system. PEM makes use of this Internet certification system, a concrete realization of certification that is a conformant subset of that envisioned in X.509.

CERTIFICATION AUTHORITIES

A certification authority (CA) is defined in X.509 as "an authority trusted by one or more users to create and assign certificates." As previously noted, X.509 imposes no constraints on the semantic or syntactic relationship between a certificate issuer, such as a certification authority, and a subject. Different CAs may be expected to issue certificates under different certification policies (e.g., they may strive for varying degrees of assurance in vouching for name-public-key bindings). However, X.509 makes no provisions for users to learn what policy each CA employs in issuing certificates. This makes it difficult for a user to assign semantics to the bindings effected by certification. The certification system used by PEM explicitly addresses this issue.

The Internet community has adopted a certification system that takes the form of a singly rooted tree, as illustrated in Figure 5. The root of this tree is designated the Internet PCA Registration Authority (IPRA) and it is operated under the auspices of the Internet Society, a

FIGURE 5. *Example Internet certification hierarchy*

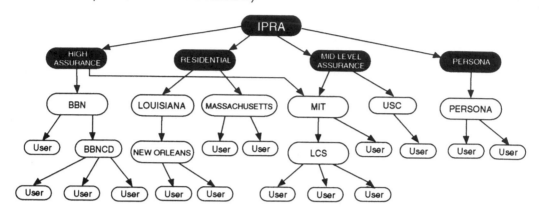

nonprofit, professional organization that promotes use of Internet technology on a worldwide basis. The **IPRA** provides a reference point from which all certificates in this certification hierarchy can be validated. The **IPRA** establishes a common policy that applies to all certificates issued under this hierarchy. The **IPRA** directly issues certificates to a second tier of entities designated Policy Certification Authorities (PCAs) which, in turn, issue certificates to CAs. CAs issue certificates to (subordinate) CAs or directly to users (individuals, organizations, organizational roles, mailing lists).

Typically a CA will be certified by one PCA, and Figure 5 illustrates this common case. However, it is valid for a single CA to be certified under multiple PCAs. In the latter case, the implication is that a single administrative entity is prepared to issue certificates under multiple disjoint policies. For each PCA under which a CA is certified, the CA certificate signed by the PCA must incorporate a different public component. This ensures that the certificates issued by the CA under each policy are readily identifiable, since each will be signed using different private components. For example, in Figure 5, MIT is certified under both the MID-LEVEL and HIGH ASSURANCE PCAs, and thus is capable of issuing certificates to faculty, staff and students based on either of the policies imposed by these PCAs. MIT would achieve this capability by having two certificates, with different public keys, each signed by the relevant PCA.

In addition to the organizational CAs shown for MIT, BBN, and USC, residential CAs also are illustrated in Figure 5. These are identified using names indicative of distinguished name formats, instead of the full distinguished names (see the sidebar entitled "What's In a (Distinguished) Name?") that would appear in their certificates.[10] For example, two residential CAs are illustrated in Figure 5, one for Louisiana and another for Massachusetts, both within the U.S. As depicted in Figure 5, below the Louisiana CA is a subordinate CA for the city of New Orleans.

COMMON POLICY HIGHLIGHTS

A common certification policy that applies to all entries certified, directly or transitively, by the IPRA is established by RFC 1422. It is intended to encompass a minimum set of essential requirements that apply to all PCAs, CAs and UAs. A critical aspect of this policy requires that each PCA file its statement of policy according to a format that is also part of the common policy. No PCA policy may contravene the IPRA common policy. Rather, a PCA specifies policy aspects not addressed by the common policy. For example, a PCA policy statement will characterize the procedures used to authenticate CAs and users certified under this policy, plus any security requirements imposed on CAs for certificate management.

Two requirements levied on PCAs by the common policy are critical but interim. When X.500 directories become very widely available these requirements will vanish. The IPRA will establish a database to facilitate detection of potential conflicts in CA and residential user distinguished names. Because many organizations and users will create their distinguished names as a result of PEM use (prior to registration with an X.500 directory server), there is a significant chance that conflicting names may be selected. There is also a requirement that each PCA provide robust access (for its users) to a global CRL database. This database is coordinated among the IPRA and the PCAs, and it will contain CRLs issued by the IPRA, all PCAs, and all CAs.

A critical aspect of the IPRA policy deals with UA processing of certificates, rather than PCA or CA issuance of certificates. The fundamental requirement is distinguished name subordination. Every PEM certificate must have the property of the subject distinguished name being subordinate to the issuer distinguished name, unless the certificate in question is issued by the IPRA or a PCA. This rule ensures the user of a "natural" certification path that can be inferred by examination of the final certificate in the path, plus display of the name of the PCA under whose policy the certificate was issued.

---

[10] The organizational CAs shown here do not contain their distinguished names due to space limitations.

The following example illustrates this rule. The CA for the author's employer might have the following distinguished name: {C = US, S = Massachusetts, L = Cambridge, O = Bolt Beranek and Newman Inc.}. This would appear in the issuer field in all certificates signed by this CA. The author's certificate would contain the following subject distinguished name: {C = US, S = Massachusetts, L = Cambridge, O = Bolt Beranek and Newman Inc., CN = Stephen T. Kent}. If this CA signed a certificate in which the subject name was {C = US, S = Virginia, L = McLean, O = Mitre Corporation, CN = Robert Shirey}, a compliant PEM UA would reject that certificate. The subject name is not subordinate to the issuer name, and hence is disallowed under the common certification policy. However, there is no subordination restriction on the relationship between a PCA and the CAs it certifies. Thus this CA can be certified by a PCA with any distinguished name.

What's In a (Distinguished) Name?

The X.500 directory standards establish a format for naming a wide range of entities: individuals, organizations, roles, devices, mailing lists, applications, and so forth. The format consists of a sequence of sets of pairs of attributes and values. The **distinguished name** (DN) of a node in this tree is formed by traversing the directory information tree (DIT) from the top to the node, concatenating the relative distinguished name of each node along the path.

The X.500 directory standards do not specify the overall structure for the DIT, but do provide examples to indicate likely forms for the DIT. Countries and organizations are expected to establish conventions that further specify the DIT structure. Typically, the nodes at the top of the tree are country names, expressed as two-character abbreviations, or international (not multinational) organizations. At the next layer in the DIT are organizations with national standing (e.g., federal government agencies and large corporations) and states or provinces. Succeeding levels include localities (cities and towns), regional organizations, units within organizations, and individuals.

Using an attribute-value notation, one might express the author's DN on a business card as {C = US, S = Massachusetts, L = Cambridge, O = Bolt Beranek and Newman Inc., CN = Stephen T. Kent}. Here "C" represents the country attribute, "S" the state or province name, "L" the locality name, "O" the organization name, and "CN" the common name of the entity (here, an individual). A number of attributes useful for constructing DNs are defined in X.520, but the directory specification also permits creation of new attributes as needed.

SAMPLE PCA POLICIES

Although none are in place at the time of writing, several PCA policies have been proposed and are being refined. One such policy would serve businesses or other organizations that require a high degree of security from their use of PEM: a "high assurance" PCA. This PCA policy is intended to provide a certification environment conducive to the conduct of electronic commerce. This PCA would execute a legal agreement with each CA and require high-quality credentials to authenticate the CA. The PCA would require the CA grant certificates to its users (e.g., employees) to use the same level of authentication it would employ in issuing ID cards. The CA would be required to issue CRLs at least monthly, but not more often than once a week.

The CA would also be required to employ highly secure technology, approved by the PCA, to generate and protect the CA's component pair and to sign all certificates issued by the CA. The PCA would employ the same technology in generating its own component pair and in signing CA certificates. The PCA would promise to protect the privacy of all information provided by the CA during registration. This level of service is expected to require that the CA pay a registration fee to the PCA.

Another candidate PCA policy that has been put forth might be termed a "mid-level assurance" PCA. Here the validation of CA credentials would be less stringent (e.g., written registration using a company letterhead might suffice). The CA would execute a very simple agreement, requiring a "good faith effort" to authenticate users. There would be no requirement to issue CRLs with any specific periodicity. Here each CA would be free to use any technology deemed appropriate to generate the CA component pair and to sign certificates. However, the PCA itself expects to employ strong security technology to generate and protect its own component pair. This PCA envisions no charge to certify CAs, but would level a charge if a CA certificate had to be placed on the PCA's CRL.

A third PCA is envisioned to support residential users, that is, users not claiming affiliation with any organization. Such users could be registered using distinguished names based on geographical attributes, for example, country, state, locality and street address. (In the U.S., a nine-digit zip code might be used in place of locality and street address data.) The user would be required to submit a notarized registration form as proof of identity. In this context, the PCA is expected to operate "virtual" CAs representing geographic areas before civil authorities are ready to offer this service. The PCA, through its virtual CA, would issue CRLs bi-weekly. User registration under this PCA is expected to entail a fee.

Finally, in support of personal privacy, a PCA has been proposed which would issue certificates that do *not* purport to express real user identities. These "persona" certificates will allow anonymous use of PEM, while providing continuity of authenticity. Thus even though one might not know the true identity of the holder of a persona certificate, one could determine if a series of messages originated under that identity were all from the same user (assuming the persona user does not share his private component). A PCA supporting persona users would ensure all certificates it issues are (globally) unique and, due to the name subordination rules cited earlier, these certificates would not be confused with certificates that do purport to convey true identities. A candidate PCA has proposed to issue persona certificates without charge, although it would charge a fee to place one of these certificates on the CRL managed by the PCA.

CONCLUSIONS

Privacy Enhanced Mail represents a major effort to provide security for an application that touches a vast number of users within the Internet and beyond. Because of the backward compatibility with existing message-transfer services and through provision of features such as MIC-CLEAR processing, PEM has been designed to accommodate gradual deployment in the Internet. The ultimate success of PEM will depend not only on the widespread availability of implementations for the range of hardware and software platforms employed throughout the Internet but also on successful establishment of the certification hierarchy that underlies asymmetric key management for PEM.

Privacy Enhanced Mail was envisioned not as a long-term goal technology for secure messaging, but as an interim step before widespread availability of secure OSI messaging (and directory) services. However, depending on the viability of X.400 and X.500 in the marketplace, PEM may become a long-term secure messaging technology rather than an interim step. In either case, PEM (or a successor) has the opportunity to become a crucial component in the evolution of the Internet, as it paves the way for various mail-based applications that would not be possible without the foundation of security services provided by PEM.

REFERENCES

1. Balenson, D. Privacy enhancement for Internet electronic mail: Part III—Algorithms, modes, and identifiers, RFC 1423, Feb. 1993.

2. Borenstein, N. and Freed, N. Multi-purpose Internet mail extensions, RFC 1341, May 1992.

3. CCITT Recommendation X.509. The Directory—Authentication framework, Nov. 1988.

4. CCITT Recommendation X.400. Data communications networks: Message handling system and service overview, Nov. 1988.

5. CCITT Recommendation X.208. Specification of abstract syntax notation one (ASN.1), Nov. 1988.

6. Crocker D. Standard for the format of ARPA Internet text messages, RFC 822, Aug. 1982.

7. Federal information processing standards publication (FIPS PUB) 81. DES modes of operation, Dec. 1980.

8. Federal information processing standards publication 113, Computer Data Authentication, May 1985.

9. Federal information processing standards publication (FIPS PUB) 46–1. Data encryption standard, Reaffirmed Jan. 1988 (supersedes FIPS PUB 46, Jan. 1977).

10. Information processing systems—Open systems interconnection—Basic reference model—Part 2: Security architecture, ISO 7498–2, Feb. 1989.

11. Kaliski, B. Privacy enhancement for Internet electronic mail: Part IV: Key certification and related services, RFC 1424, Feb. 1993.

12. Kent, S. Security requirements and protocols for a broadcast scenario, *IEEE Trans. Commun. 29*, 6 (June 1981), 778–786.

13. Kent, S. and Rossen, K. E-mail privacy for the Internet. *Bus. Commun. Rev. 20*, 1 (Jan. 1990).

14. Kent S. Privacy enhancement for Internet electronic mail: Part II—Certificate-based key management, RFC 1422, Feb. 1993.

15. Linn, J. and Kent, S. Electronic mail privacy enhancement. In *Proceedings of the Second Aerospace Computer Security Conference* (Dec. 1986).

16. Linn J. Privacy enhancement for Internet electronic mail: Part I—Message encipherment and authentication procedures, RFC 1421, Feb. 1993.

17. Postel J. Simple mail transfer protocol, RFC 821, Aug. 1982.

18. Rivest, R. The MD5 Message-Digest Algorithm, RFC 1321, MIT Laboratory for Computer Science and RSA Data Security Inc., Apr. 1992.

19. Rose, M. Post office protocol: Version 3, RFC 1225, May 1991.

6

Privacy in Today's Wireless Environment*

Kim Lawson-Jenkins
Motorola Cellular Infrastructure Group

INTRODUCTION

The dramatic growth in wireless communications technology has created new security issues related to telephony. In a wireless system, a telephone user is associated with a physical location and a particular wire pair in a telephone network. There is no such physical association when a user accesses a wireless network. That is the beauty of the system. A person can access and use resources of the system via radio frequencies. Unfortunately, radio waves are much more susceptible to intruders (eavesdroppers). Wireless systems have taken steps to ensure the privacy of the user's conversation, data, and location when the system access occurs.

OVERVIEW OF WIRELESS TECHNOLOGY

The range of products which use radio waves as the medium of data transport increases daily. Parents use baby monitors to hear a baby in another room of a home, a cordless telephone to verify the time of a PTA meeting, and alphanumeric pager to warn a teenager that the weeknight curfew has long since passed. Police departments and Wall Street investment firms were some of the early users of wireless e-mail applications. New business ventures in the former USSR and Eastern Europe are some of the biggest customers of wireless phone systems for businesses because the systems can be installed quickly and cheaply as compared to wireline telephone equipment infrastructure. Communication companies throughout the world are promoting Personal Communication Systems where users carry handset units which weigh a few ounces and can be carried in a shirt pocket, purse, or attaché case.

As the quality, size, and convenience of use of these products improve, more and more people become familiar with the products and

---

* This paper was especially written by Ms. Lawson-Jenkins for this volume.

their use becomes more common. Users think that they can use these units "just like a telephone or computer" which is connected by a telephone line cord to a wall jack. In fact, equipment manufacturers and service providers encourage this type of thinking. However, there are significant differences between the operation of wireline and wireless handsets. Users of first generation cordless telephones would routinely inadvertently hear segments of a neighbor's conversation when both neighbors had cordless telephones. Some of the more amusing discussions at European cellular standards meetings centered on a U.K. tabloid printing the text of conversation on a cellular system between a Minister of Parliament and his mistress. Even the U.S. newspapers headlined the text of recorded conversations of the British Royal family who had cellular telephones. Telecommunication engineers in the 1980's would use radio scanning equipment which could be bought from a local Radio Shack store to monitor conversations on cellular systems during their daily commutes. One of my associates would do this while commuting to and from work and would say that the monitored conversations were much better than watching Dallas or Falcon Crest on television because this was real life! While technologists in the industry have always been aware of the security issues relating to wireless systems, the general public is generally just becoming aware of these issues. As a result, the newest wireless technology, digital cellular communication, supports an array of security features which protect the privacy of cellular users.

SECURITY FEATURES IN DIGITAL CELLULAR SYSTEMS

There are four major digital cellular systems being deployed at the present time. Three of the systems are Time Division Multiple Access (TDMA) systems. The Personal Digital Cellular (PDC) system is a TDMA system developed by the Research and Development Center for Radio Systems standards organization in Japan. This system is currently being installed in Japan and some equipment manufacturers hope to use this technology in other Asian markets. The Global System for Mobiles (GSM) is a TDMA system developed by standards bodies operating under the European Telecommunications Standards Institute (ETSI). This system is being deployed in Europe and Australia. A slight variation of the GSM system, using a different, higher frequency and smaller cellsites, has been proposed for a PCS system in the U.S. The third TDMA system is the U.S. Digital Cellular (USDC) system which is being developed by the Telecommunications Industry Association. All of the TDMA systems subdivide the RF channel into fixed timeslots, which are allocated to users who share the resource of one

RF channel. Depending on the TDMA technology, an RF full rate channel can be sub-divided into 3 or 8 timeslots.

A digital alternative to TDMA is Code Division Multiple Access (CDMA) technology. This technology allows users to share the same spectrum by allocating a distinguishing code to each user of the spectrum. When a signal is sent at a certain spectrum, all users of the spectrum will receive the signal. Even though all users will receive the signal, only one user will be able to understand the signal because the signal will contain his/her allocated code. All other users, which have a different code than the one contained in the signal, will interpret the signal as "noise." The fourth type of digital cellular system, which is currently being deployed in the United States, uses CDMA technology.

All four of the digital cellular systems—GSM, PDC, USDC, and US-CDMA—support authentication, voice privacy, and signaling message encryption. In addition to these features, GSM also protects the user's identity as it is transmitted.

AUTHENTICATION AND ENCRYPTION

Authentication is the process by which a user proves to the network that he possesses a secret that was established at service initialization. All of the digital cellular technologies use a private-key method of authentication. Authentication procedures can take place any time a user accesses the system (by making or receiving a call, performing a location registration/update, or changing a supplementary service such as activating call forwarding). The authentication can be associated with the actual mobile equipment and/or with a "smart card" which the user possesses and which can be inserted in the mobile unit. The system can deny service to the user based on failure to authenticate the smart card (i.e. someone programming a smart card in an attempt to use someone else's telephone account), or the mobile equipment (i.e. someone inserted his valid smart card in a stolen mobile). Once the user has been authenticated, the privacy of the user's voice and data traffic needs to be protected by encryption. In all of the digital cellular private systems, the session key used in encryption is a by-product of authentication. While authentication is a mandatory function during most system accesses, use of encryption during a system access is optional. The cynical analysis of this situation is that authentication reduces fraud in the cellular system (and reduces revenue loss due to fraud for system operators) while encryption is seen as a value added customer service for which the system operator can charge the user.

None of the standards bodies (TIA, GSM, or RCR) release information to the general public about the specific types of authentication/encryption algorithms supported by the standards. This type of information is made available on a limited basis to equipment manufacturers and cellular system operators. However, general details about the procedures used in the network to support authentication and encryption are in the public domain. Both GSM and PDC standards documentation allow system operators to support multiple types of encryption algorithms. One specific encryption algorithm is defined in standards documentation and has to be supported by all GSM or PDC subscriber units. In addition, GSM and PDC allow the system operator to define and use encryption algorithms which are supported by the smart cards (which are supplied by the system operator to the user) and the network infrastructure. For example, the U.K. GSM cellular operator Vodaphone can offer the standard GSM encryption service to its subscribers or it can offer one of several Vodaphone defined encryption services. The Vodaphone encryption services can be marketed as additional security features offered to its subscribers, in that they offer more secure communication than the standard GSM encryption services. The GSM encryption can be offered to Vodaphone encryption subscribers that do not want to pay a premium for the Vodaphone encryption feature and to subscribers from other networks (France Telecom, German D1 system) which are temporarily operating (i.e. "roaming") in the Vodaphone system.

The encryption of signaling messages across the radio interface has limited usefulness in the PDC, USDC, and U.S. CDMA systems. While encryption will give a user voice privacy (because encryption takes place before the call is connected) and can hide some sensitive signaling information (such as a PIN entered after the call is connected), much of the important signaling information, such as the mobile station number and dialed digits, is transmitted before the encryption starts. Thus, an eavesdropper can capture this information if he/she is listening to a channel before encryption starts. Refer to Figure 1 for a diagram of call setup procedures for PDC, USDC, and U.S. CDMA systems. GSM's call setup procedure allows the mobile to initiate a call setup procedure without broadcasting sensitive information until after the mobile has been authenticated and the connection is ciphered.

GSM's Anonymity Feature

The GSM system allocates temporary mobile identity (TMSI) numbers or aliases in order to hide a user's identity. The network allocates TMSIs for the user and sends the TMSI to the user after encryption starts on a channel. The next time the mobile accesses the system, the mobile will send the TMSI to the network on the "clear channel" (a channel on which encryption has not started). Once the network has authenticated the user and encryption starts, the mobile will transmit

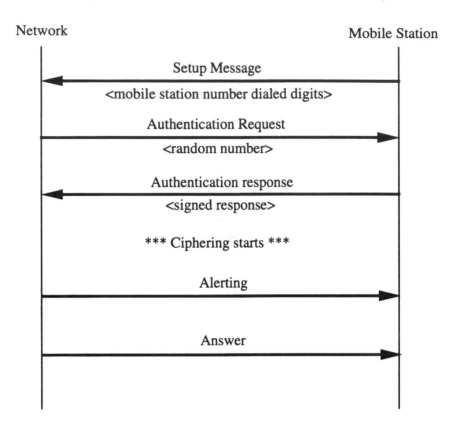

FIGURE 1.
Overview of
call setup
procedure in
PDC, USDC,
and US-CDMA

his/her mobile station number and the dialed digits. At this point, the network may also send a new TMSI to the mobile. An illustration of the call setup procedure in GSM is in Figure 2. Use of the TMSI allows the mobile to initiate a call setup procedure without broadcasting sensitive information until after the mobile has been authenticated and the connection is ciphered.

SECURITY ISSUES IN OTHER WIRELESS APPLICATIONS

As mentioned before, telecommunication bodies are currently writing specifications and working towards deploying personal communication systems. Some proposals for **PCS** suggest using public-key authentication/encryption rather than the private key methods used in today's digital cellular systems. The use of public key, however, requires heavy wireless traffic and greater computation loads as compared to the private key methods of **GSM, PDC,** and digital cellular

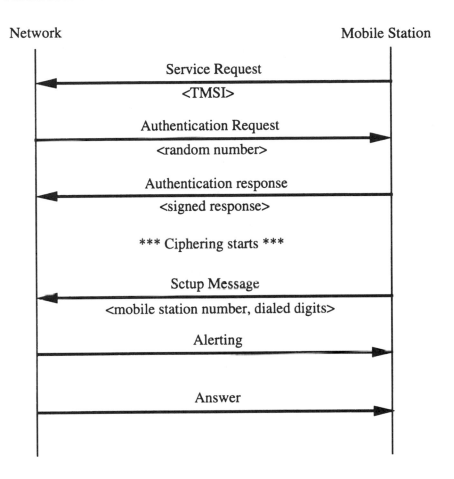

FIGURE 2.
*Overview of
call setup
procedure in
GSM*

systems in the U.S.. Just as security features were added to later-generation cordless phones, security features will have to be added to applications such as wireless microphones, wireless local loop products, dispatch services, two-way radios, etc. in order for them to gain wider acceptance among general consumers and among potential business customers.

WIRELESS SECURITY AND PRIVACY/CIVIL LIBERTY ISSUES IN THE U.S.

All of the wireless security methods detailed in this paper take place on the radio interface. Once the radio information reaches a mobile switching center, the information can be treated the same as information received at a wireline switching center. For example, calls can be monitored or traced at a mobile switching center just as they are at a wireline switching center. It can be more beneficial to monitor a call at the base station rather than at the switching center if it is desired to receive faster, more precise. real time information about the location of the mobile. However, there are different issues if the calls are monitored or traced using the radio equipment (which is commonly called a base station) as the U.S. standards are defined today.

In the U.S., a mobile user can use a voice privacy feature by making a request from the mobile or by having the network automatically providing this service for his/her calls. An indication is sent from the network to the mobile to indicate that the feature has been activated (i.e. encryption has started) or to indicate that the feature has been turned off or is not available at the base station. If the network monitors the call at the switching center and gives call trace information to a third party (which can include law enforcement agencies), does the user still receive an indication that the voice privacy feature is active? Technically, the feature is active because the conversation is encrypted between the mobile station and the base. However, having the call monitored at the switching center will certainly give the user an inaccurate perception about the privacy of the conversation.

Besides the user privacy issue, there are issues related to whether companies will be able to provide wireless security services to their customers. It was mentioned previously that wireless security standards outside the U.S., such as PDC and GSM, allow a system operator to offer network-defined encryption services to its customers, in addition to the encryption services specifically defined by the PDC and GSM standards. The U.S. digital cellular standards for TDMA and CDMA systems currently do not allow companies to offer their own "private brand" of encryption to their customers. By not encouraging companies to offer these types of services and by limiting the export of this type of technology for U.S. companies, U.S. companies could be disadvantaged in competing internationally.

CONCLUSIONS

One of the goals of today's cellular systems and future personal communication systems is that the security of these systems will be comparable to or will exceed the security found in competing wireline systems. Wireless standard bodies have written system specifications with this goal in mind and up to recently they have been successful in meeting this goal. However, just as the technology constantly changes, so do the efforts of individuals who attempt to compromise the security aspects of the latest technology. High speed computers and the fact that radio signals can always be intercepted (if not always deciphered) will always push wireless technologists to continue to develop innovative ways of providing security features to their customers. Government intervention in issues relating to how and in what manner companies may provide privacy features to wireless customers will have to be addressed as the technology continues to develop.

ACKNOWLEDGMENTS

In preparing this paper, I received valuable input from Dan Brown, an engineer at Motorola Corporate Research and Development Lab, Professor Lance Hoffman of George Washington University, and Lawrence Guidry, a fellow graduate student at George Washington University. Their comments were very much appreciated.

REFERENCES

European Telecommunications Standards Institute, "Technical Specification GSM 03.20, Security Related Network Functions," January 1993.

Electronic Industries Association, EIA Interim Standard IS-54, Rev B, "Dual Mode Mobile-Base Station Compatibility Standard," 1992.

Research and Development Center for Radio Systems (RCR), "Digital Cellular Telecommunications System RCR Standard," version 27B, December 1992.

Federal Information Processing Standards Publication 186 (1994 May 19): Specifications for the Digital Signature Standard (DSS)*

U.S. Department of Commerce, Technology Administration
National Institute of Standards and Technology

INTRODUCTION

This publication prescribes the Digital Signature Algorithm (DSA) for digital signature generation and verification. Additional information is provided in Appendices 1 through 5. [not included in this book, available from NIST—Ed.]

GENERAL

When a message is received, the recipient may desire to verify that the message has not been altered in transit. Furthermore, the recipient may wish to be certain of the originator's identity. Both of these services can be provided by the DSA. A digital signature is an electronic analogue of a written signature in that the digital signature can be used in proving to the recipient or a third party that the message was, in fact, signed by the originator. Digital signatures may also be generated for stored data and programs so that the integrity of the data and programs may be verified at any later time.

This publication prescribes the DSA for digital signature generation and verification. In addition, the criteria for the public and private keys required by the algorithm are provided.

USE OF THE DSA ALGORITHM

The DSA is used by a *signatory* to generate a digital signature on data and by a verifier to verify the authenticity of the signature. Each signatory has a public and private key. The private key is used in the

---

* Computer Systems Laboratory, National Institute of Standards and Technology, Gaithersburg, MD 20899.

signature generation process and the public key is used in the signature verification process. For both signature generation and verification, the data which is referred to as a message, M, is reduced by means of the Secure Hash Algorithm (SHA) specified in FIPS 180. [See p. 87—Ed.] An adversary, who does not know the private key of the signatory, cannot generate the correct signature of the signatory. In other words, signatures cannot be forged. However, by using the signatory's public key, anyone can verify a correctly signed message.

A means of associating public and private key pairs to the corresponding users is required. That is, there must be a binding of a user's identity and the user's public key. This binding may be certified by a mutually trusted party. For example, a certifying authority could sign credentials containing a user's public key and identity to form a certificate. Systems for certifying credentials and distributing certificates are beyond the scope of this standard. NIST intends to publish separate document(s) on certifying credentials and distributing certificates.

DSA PARAMETERS

The DSA makes use of the following parameters:

1. p = a prime modulus, where $2^{L-1} < p < 2^L$ for $512 \leq L \leq 1024$ and L a multiple of 64
2. q = a prime divisor of p − 1, where $2^{159} < q < 2^{160}$
3. g = $h^{(p-1)/q}$ mod p, where h is any integer with $1 < h < p - 1$ such that $h^{(p-1)/q}$ mod p > 1 (g has order q mod p)
4. x = a randomly or pseudorandomly generated integer with $0 < x < q$
5. y = g^x mod p
6. k = a randomly or pseudorandomly generated integer with $0 < k < q$

The integers p, q, and g can be public and can be common to a group of users. A user's private and public keys are x and y, respectively. They are normally fixed for a period of time. Parameters x and k are used for signature generation only, and must be kept secret. Parameter k must be regenerated for each signature.

Parameters p and q shall be generated as specified in Appendix 2, or using other FIPS approved security methods. Parameters x and k shall be generated as specified in Appendix 3, or using other FIPS approved security methods.

SIGNATURE GENERATION

The signature of a message M is the pair of numbers r and s computed according to the equations below:

$$r = (g^k \bmod p) \bmod q \qquad \text{and}$$
$$s = (k^{-1}(SHA(M) + xr)) \bmod q.$$

In the above, k^{-1} is the multiplicative inverse of k, mod q; i.e., $(k^{-1}k) \bmod q = 1$ and $0 < k^{-1} < q$. The value of SHA(M) is a 160-bit string output by the Secure Hash Algorithm specified in FIPS 180. For use in computing s, this string must be converted to an integer. The conversion rule is given in Appendix 2.2.

As an option, one may wish to check if $r = 0$ or $s = 0$. If either $r = 0$ or $s = 0$, a new value of k should be generated and the signature should be recalculated (it is extremely unlikely that $r = 0$ or $s = 0$ if signatures are generated properly).

The signature is transmitted along with the message to the verifier.

SIGNATURE VERIFICATION

Prior to verifying the signature in a signed message, p, q and g plus the sender's public key and identity are made available to the verifier in an authenticated manner.

Let M', r', and s' be the received versions of M, r, and s, respectively, and let y be the public key of the signatory. To verify the signature, the verifier first checks to see that $0 < r' < q$ and $0 < s' < q$; if either condition is violated the signature shall be rejected. If these two conditions are satisfied, the verifier computes

$$w = (s')^{-1} \bmod q$$
$$u1 = ((SHA(M'))w) \bmod q$$
$$u2 = ((r')w) \bmod q$$
$$v = (((g)^{u1} (y)^{u2}) \bmod p) \bmod q.$$

If $v = r'$, then the signature is verified and the verifier can have high confidence that the received message was sent by the party holding the secret key x corresponding to y. For a proof that $v = r'$ when $M' = M$, $r' = r$, and $s' = s$, see Appendix 1.

If v does not equal r', then the message may have been modified, the message may have been incorrectly signed by the signatory, or the message may have been signed by an impostor. The message should be considered invalid.

Federal Information Processing Standards Publication 180 (1993 May 11): Specifications for the Secure Hash Standard (SHS)*

U.S. Department of Commerce, Technology Administration
National Institute of Standards and Technology

INTRODUCTION

The Secure Hash Algorithm (SHA) is required for use with the Digital Signature Algorithm (DSA) as specified in the Digital Signature Standard (DSS) and whenever a secure hash algorithm is required for federal applications. For a message of length $< 2^{64}$ bits, the SHA produces a 160-bit condensed representation of the message called a message digest. The message digest is used during generation of a signature for the message. The SHA is also used to compute a message digest for the received version of the message during the process of verifying the signature. Any change to the message in transit will, with very high probability, result in a different message digest, and the signature will fail to verify.

The SHA is designed to have the following properties: it is computationally infeasible to find a message which corresponds to a given message digest, or to find two different messages which produce the same message digest.

BIT STRINGS AND INTEGERS

The following terminology related to bit strings and integers will be used:

a. A *hex digit* is an element of the set $\{0, 1, \ldots, 9, A, \ldots, F\}$. A hex digit is the representation of a 4-bit string. Examples: $7 = 0111$, $A = 1010$.

b. A *word* equals a 32-bit string which may be represented as a sequence of 8 hex digits. To convert a word to 8 hex digits each 4-bit

---

* Computer Systems Laboratory, National Institute of Standards and Technology, Gaithersburg, MD 20899. Standard here is modified as per Federal register 59 FR 35317 of 11 July 1994.

string is converted to its hex equivalent as described in (a) above. Example:

```
1010 0001 0000 0011 1111 1110 0010 0011 = A103FE23
```

c. An *integer between 0 and $2^{32}-1$ inclusive* may be represented as a word. The least significant four bits of the integer are represented by the right-most hex digit of the word representation. Example: the integer $291 = 2^8+2^5+2^1+2^0 = 256+32+2+1$ is represented by the hex word, 00000123.

If z is an integer, $0 \le z < 2^{64}$, then $z = 2^{32}x + y$ where $0 \le x < 2^{32}$ and $0 \le y < 2^{32}$. Since x and y can be represented as words X and Y, respectively, z can be represented as the pair of words (X,Y).

d. *block* = 512-bit string. A block (e.g., B) may be represented as a sequence of 16 words.

OPERATIONS ON WORDS

The following logical operators will be applied to words:

a. *Bitwise logical word operations*

$X \wedge Y$ = bitwise logical "and" of X and Y.
$X \vee Y$ = bitwise logical "inclusive-or" of X and Y.
X XOR Y = bitwise logical "exclusive-or" of X and Y.
$\sim X$ = bitwise logical "complement" of X.

Example:

```
        01101100101110011101001001111011
XOR     01100101110000010110100110110111
        --------------------------------
  =     00001001011110001011101111001100.
```

b. The *operation X + Y* is defined as follows: words X and Y represent integers x and y, where $0 \le x < 2^{32}$ and $0 \le y < 2^{32}$. For positive integers n and m, let n mod m be the remainder upon dividing n by m. Compute

$z = (x + y) \bmod 2^{32}$.

Then $0 \le z < 2^{32}$. Convert z to a word, Z, and define Z = X + Y.

c. The *circular left shift operation $S^n(X)$*, where X is a word and n is an integer with $0 \le n < 32$, is defined by

$S^n(X) = (X{<}{<}n) \vee (X{>}{>}32{-}n)$.

In the above, X<<n is obtained as follows: discard the left-most n bits of X and then pad the result with n zeroes on the right (the result will

still be 32 bits). X>>n is obtained by discarding the right-most n bits of X and then padding the result with n zeroes on the left. Thus $S^n(X)$ is equivalent to a circular shift of X by n positions to the left.

MESSAGE PADDING

The SHA is used to compute a message digest for a message or data file that is provided as input. The message or data file should be considered to be a bit string. The length of the message is the number of bits in the message (the empty message has length 0). If the number of bits in a message is a multiple of 8, for compactness we can represent the message in hex. The purpose of message padding is to make the total length of a padded message a multiple of 512. The SHA sequentially processes blocks of 512 bits when computing the message digest. The following specifies how this padding shall be performed. As a summary, a "1" followed by m "0"s followed by a 64-bit integer are appended to the end of the message to produce a padded message of length 512 × n. The 64-bit integer is 1, the length of the original message. The padded message is then processed by the SHA as n 512-bit blocks.

Suppose a message has length $l < 2^{64}$. Before it is input to the SHA, the message is padded on the right as follows:

a. "1" is appended. Example: if the original message is "01010000", this is padded to "010100001".

b. "0"s are appended. The number of "0"s will depend on the original length of the message. The last 64 bits of the last 512-bit block are reserved for the length l of the original message.

Example: Suppose the original message is the bit string

01100001 01100010 01100011 01100100 01100101.

After step (a) this gives

01100001 01100010 01100011 01100100 01100101 1.

Since $l = 40$, the number of bits in the above is 41 and 407 "0"s are appended, making the total now 448. This gives (in hex)

61626364 65800000 00000000 00000000
00000000 00000000 00000000 00000000
00000000 00000000 00000000 00000000
00000000 00000000.

c. Obtain the 2-word representation of l, the number of bits in the original message. If $l < 2^{32}$ then the first word is all zeroes. Append these two words to the padded message.

Example: Suppose the original message is as in (b). Then $l = 40$ (note that l is computed before any padding). The two-word representation of 40 is hex 00000000 00000028. Hence the final padded message is hex

```
61626364 65800000 00000000 00000000
00000000 00000000 00000000 00000000
00000000 00000000 00000000 00000000
00000000 00000000 00000000 00000028.
```

The padded message will contain 16n words for some n > 0. The padded message is regarded as a sequence of n blocks M_1, M_2, . . . , M_n, where each M_i contains 16 words and M_1 contains the first characters (or bits) of the message.

FUNCTIONS USED

A sequence of logical functions $f_0, f_1, . . . , f_{79}$ is used in the SHA. Each f_t, $0 \le t \le 79$ operates on three 32-bit words and produces a 32-bit word as output. f_t is defined as follows: for words, B, C, D,

$$f_t(B,C,D) = (B \wedge C) \vee (\sim B \wedge D) \quad (0 \le t \le 19)$$
$$f_t(B,C,D) = B \text{ XOR } C \text{ XOR } D \quad (20 \le t \le 39)$$
$$f_t(B,C,D) = (B \wedge C) \vee (B \wedge D) \vee (C \wedge D) \quad (40 \le t \le 59)$$
$$f_t(B,C,D) = B \text{ XOR } C \text{ XOR } D \quad (60 \le t \le 79)$$

CONSTANTS USED

A sequence of constant words $K_0, K_1, . . . , K_{79}$ is used in the SHA. In hex these are given by

$$K_t = \text{5A827999} \quad (0 \le t \le 19)$$
$$K_t = \text{6ED9EBA1} \quad (20 \le t \le 39)$$
$$K_t = \text{8F1BBCDC} \quad (40 \le t \le 59)$$
$$K_t = \text{CA62C1D6} \quad (60 \le t \le 79)$$

COMPUTING THE MESSAGE DIGEST

The message digest is computed using the final padded message. The computation uses two buffers, each consisting of five 32-bit words, and a sequence of eighty 32-bit words. The words of the first 5-word buffer are labeled A,B,C,D,E. The words of the second 5-word buffer are labeled H_0, H_1, H_2, H_3, H_4. The words of the 80-word sequence are labeled W_0, W_1, . . . , W_{79}. A single word buffer TEMP is also employed.

To generate the message digest, the 16-word blocks M_1, M_2, . . . , M_n defined in Section 4 are processed in order. The processing of each M_i involves 80 steps.

Before processing any blocks, the $\{H_j\}$ are initialized as follows: in hex,

H_0 = 67452301
H_1 = EFCDAB89
H_2 = 98BADCFE
H_3 = 10325476
H_4 = C3D2E1F0.

Now M_1, M_2, . . . , M_n are processed. To process M_i, we proceed as follows:

a. Divide M_i into 16 words W_0, W_1, . . . , W_{15}, where W_0 is the leftmost word.
b. For t = 16 to 79 let W_t = $S^1(W_{t-3}$ XOR W_{t-8} XOR W_{t-14} XOR $W_{t-16})$.
c. Let $A = H_0$, $B = H_1$, $C = H_2$, $D = H_3$, $E = H_4$.
d. For t = 0 to 79 do

TEMP = $S^5(A)$ + $f_t(B,C,D)$ + E + W_t + K_t;
$E = D$; $D = C$; $C = S^{30}(B)$; $B = A$; A = TEMP;

e. Let $H_0 = H_0 + A$, $H_1 = H_1 + B$, $H_2 = H_2 + C$, $H_3 = H_3 + D$, $H_4 = H_4 + E$.
After processing M_n, the message digest is the 160-bit string represented by the 5 words

H_0 H_1 H_2 H_3 H_4.

ALTERNATIVE METHOD OF COMPUTATION

The above assumes that the sequence W_0, . . . , W_{79} is implemented as an array of eighty 32-bit words. This is efficient from the standpoint of minimization of execution time, since the addresses of W_{t-3}, . . . , W_{t-16} in step (b) are easily computed. If space is at a premium, an alternative is to regard $\{W_t\}$ as a circular queue, which may be implemented using an array of sixteen 32-bit words W[0], . . . , W[15]. In this case, in hex let MASK = 0000000F. Then processing of M_i is as follows:

a. Divide M_i into 16 words W[0], . . . , W[15], where W[0] is the leftmost word.
b. Let $A = H_0$, $B = H_1$, $C = H_2$, $D = H_3$, $E = H_4$.

c. For t = 0 to 79 do

s = t $\wedge$ MASK;

if (t $\geq$ 16) W[s] = W[(s + 13) $\wedge$ MASK] XOR
W[(s + 18) $\wedge$ MASK] XOR W[(s + 12) $\wedge$ MASK] XOR W[s];

TEMP = $S^5(A)$ + $f_t(B,C,D)$ + E + W[s] + K_t;

E = D; D = C; C = $S^{30}(B)$; B = A; A = TEMP;

d. Let H_0 = H_0 + A, H_1 = H_1 + B, H_2 = H_2 + C, H_3 = H_3 + D,
H_4 = H_4 + E.

Comparison of Methods

The methods of Sections 7 and 8 yield the same message digest. Although using the method of section 8 saves sixty-four 32-bit words of storage, it is likely to lengthen execution time due to the increased complexity of the address computations for the [W[t]] in step (c). Other computation methods which give identical results may be implemented in conformance with the standard.

[Three appendices were included in the original NIST publication "for informational purposes only" and are "not required to meet the standard." These are omitted in this book but are available from NIST—Ed.]

Pretty Good Privacy: Public Key Encryption for the Masses*

Philip Zimmermann

WHY DO YOU NEED PGP?

It's personal. It's private. And it's no one's business but yours. You may be planning a political campaign, discussing your taxes, or having an illicit affair. Or you may be doing something that you feel shouldn't be illegal, but is. Whatever it is, you don't want your private electronic mail (E-mail) or confidential documents read by anyone else. There's nothing wrong with asserting your privacy. Privacy is as apple-pie as the Constitution.

Perhaps you think your E-mail is legitimate enough that encryption is unwarranted. If you really are a law abiding citizen with nothing to hide, then why don't you always send your paper mail on postcards? Why not submit to drug testing on demand? Why require a warrant for police searches of your house? Are you trying to hide something? You must be a subversive or a drug dealer if you hide your mail inside envelopes. Or maybe a paranoid nut. Do law-abiding citizens have any need to encrypt their E-mail?

What if everyone believed that law-abiding citizens should use postcards for their mail? If some brave soul tried to assert his privacy by using an envelope for his mail, it would draw suspicion. Perhaps the authorities would open his mail to see what he's hiding. Fortunately, we don't live in that kind of world, because everyone protects most of their mail with envelopes. So no one draws suspicion by asserting their privacy with an envelope. There's safety in numbers. Analogously, it would be nice if everyone routinely used encryption for all their E-mail, innocent or not, so that no one drew suspicion by asserting their E-mail privacy with encryption. Think of it as a form of solidarity.

Today, if the Government wants to violate the privacy of ordinary citizens, it has to expend a certain amount of expense and labor to intercept and steam open and read paper mail, and listen to and possibly transcribe spoken telephone conversation. This kind of labor-in-

---

* Excerpts from "PGP User's Guide", Revised 31 Aug 1994; Copyright Philip Zimmermann, Boulder, Colorado.

tensive monitoring is not practical on a large scale. This is only done in important cases when it seems worthwhile.

More and more of our private communications are being routed through electronic channels. Electronic mail is gradually replacing conventional paper mail. E-mail messages are just too easy to intercept and scan for interesting keywords. This can be done easily, routinely, automatically, and undetectably on a grand scale. International cablegrams are already scanned this way on a large scale by the NSA.

We are moving toward a future when the nation will be crisscrossed with high capacity fiber optic data networks linking together all our increasingly ubiquitous personal computers. E-mail will be the norm for everyone, not the novelty it is today. The Government will protect our E-mail with Government-designed encryption protocols. Probably most people will acquiesce to that. But perhaps some people will prefer their own protective measures.

Senate Bill 266, a 1991 omnibus anti-crime bill, had an unsettling measure buried in it. If this non-binding resolution had become real law, it would have forced manufacturers of secure communications equipment to insert special "trap doors" in their products, so that the Government can read anyone's encrypted messages. It reads: "It is the sense of Congress that providers of electronic communications services and manufacturers of electronic communications service equipment shall insure that communications systems permit the Government to obtain the plain text contents of voice, data, and other communications when appropriately authorized by law." This measure was defeated after rigorous protest from civil libertarians and industry groups.

In 1992, the FBI Digital Telephony wiretap proposal was introduced to Congress. It would require all manufacturers of communications equipment to build in special remote wiretap ports that would enable the FBI to remotely wiretap all forms of electronic communication from FBI offices. Although it never attracted any sponsors in Congress in 1992 because of citizen opposition, it was reintroduced in 1994.

Most alarming of all is the White House's bold new encryption policy initiative, under development at NSA since the start of the Bush administration, and unveiled April 16th, 1993. The centerpiece of this initiative is a Government-built encryption device, called the "Clipper" chip, containing a new classified NSA encryption algorithm. The Government is encouraging private industry to design it into all their secure communication products, like secure phones, secure FAX, etc. AT&T is now putting the Clipper into their secure voice products. The catch: At the time of manufacture, each Clipper chip will be loaded with its own unique key, and the Government gets to keep a copy, placed in escrow. Not to worry, though—the Government promises that they will use these keys to read your traffic only when duly authorized by law. Of course, to make Clipper completely effective, the next logical step would be to outlaw other forms of cryptography.

If privacy is outlawed, only outlaws will have privacy. Intelligence agencies have access to good cryptographic technology. So do the big arms and drug traffickers. So do defense contractors, oil companies, and other corporate giants. But ordinary people and grassroots political organizations mostly have not had access to affordable "military grade" public-key cryptographic technology. Until now.

PGP empowers people to take their privacy into their own hands. There's a growing social need for it. That's why I wrote it.

How It Works

It would help if you were already familiar with the concept of cryptography in general and public key cryptography in particular. Nonetheless, here are a few introductory remarks about public key cryptography.

First, some elementary terminology. Suppose I want to send you a message, but I don't want anyone but you to be able to read it. I can "encrypt", or "encipher" the message, which means I scramble it up in a hopelessly complicated way, rendering it unreadable to anyone except you, the intended recipient of the message. I supply a cryptographic "key" to encrypt the message, and you have to use the same key to decipher or "decrypt" it. At least that's how it works in conventional "single-key" cryptosystems.

In conventional cryptosystems, such as the US Federal Data Encryption Standard (DES), a single key is used for both encryption and decryption. This means that a key must be initially transmitted via secure channels so that both parties can know it before encrypted messages can be sent over insecure channels. This may be inconvenient. If you have a secure channel for exchanging keys, then why do you need cryptography in the first place?

In public key cryptosystems, everyone has two related complementary keys, a publicly revealed key and a secret key (also frequently called a private key). Each key unlocks the code that the other key makes. Knowing the public key does not help you deduce the corresponding secret key. The public key can be published and widely disseminated across a communications network. This protocol provides privacy without the need for the same kind of secure channels that a conventional cryptosystem requires.

Anyone can use a recipient's public key to encrypt a message to that person, and that recipient uses her own corresponding secret key to decrypt that message. No one but the recipient can decrypt it, because no one else has access to that secret key. Not even the person who encrypted the message can decrypt it.

Message authentication is also provided. The sender's own secret key can be used to encrypt a message, thereby "signing" it. This creates a digital signature of a message, which the recipient (or anyone else) can check by using the sender's public key to decrypt it. This proves that the sender was the true originator of the message, and that the message has not been subsequently altered by anyone else, because the sender alone possesses the secret key that made that signature. Forgery of a signed message is infeasible, and the sender cannot later disavow his signature.

These two processes can be combined to provide both privacy and authentication by first signing a message with your own secret key, then encrypting the signed message with the recipient's public key. The recipient reverses these steps by first decrypting the message with her own secret key, then checking the enclosed signature with your public key. These steps are done automatically by the recipient's software.

Because the public key encryption algorithm is much slower than conventional single-key encryption, encryption is better accomplished by using a high-quality fast conventional single-key encryption algorithm to encipher the message. This original unenciphered message is called "plaintext". In a process invisible to the user, a temporary random key, created just for this one "session", is used to conventionally encipher the plaintext file. Then the recipient's public key is used to encipher this temporary random conventional key. This public-key-enciphered conventional "session" key is sent along with the enciphered text (called "ciphertext") to the recipient. The recipient uses her own secret key to recover this temporary session key, and then uses that key to run the fast conventional single-key algorithm to decipher the large ciphertext message.

Public keys are kept in individual "key certificates" that include the key owner's user ID (which is that person's name), a timestamp of when the key pair was generated, and the actual key material. Public key certificates contain the public key material, while secret key certificates contain the secret key material. Each secret key is also encrypted with its own password, in case it gets stolen. A key file, or "key ring" contains one or more of these key certificates. Public key rings contain public key certificates, and secret key rings contain secret key certificates.

The keys are also internally referenced by a "key ID", which is an "abbreviation" of the public key (the least significant 64 bits of the large public key). When this key ID is displayed, only the lower 32 bits are shown for further brevity. While many keys may share the same user ID, for all practical purposes no two keys share the same key ID.

PGP uses "message digests" to form signatures. A message digest is a 128-bit cryptographically strong one-way hash function of the message. It is somewhat analogous to a "checksum" or CRC error checking code, in that it compactly "represents" the message and is used to detect changes in the message. Unlike a CRC, however, it is computationally infeasible for an attacker to devise a substitute message that would produce an identical message digest. The message digest gets encrypted by the secret key to form a signature.

Documents are signed by prefixing them with signature certificates, which contain the key ID of the key that was used to sign it, a secret-key-signed message digest of the document, and a timestamp of when the signature was made. The key ID is used by the receiver to look up the sender's public key to check the signature. The receiver's software automatically looks up the sender's public key and user ID in the receiver's public key ring.

Encrypted files are prefixed by the key ID of the public key used to encrypt them. The receiver uses this key ID message prefix to look up the secret key needed to decrypt the message. The receiver's software automatically looks up the necessary secret decryption key in the receiver's secret key ring.

These two types of key rings are the principal method of storing and managing public and secret keys. Rather than keep individual keys in separate key files, they are collected in key rings to facilitate the automatic lookup of keys either by key ID or by user ID. Each user keeps his own pair of key rings. An individual public key is temporarily kept in a separate file long enough to send to your friend who will then add it to her key ring.

HOW TO PROTECT PUBLIC KEYS FROM TAMPERING

In a public key cryptosystem, you don't have to protect public keys from exposure. In fact, it's better if they are widely disseminated. But it is important to protect public keys from tampering, to make sure that a public key really belongs to whom it appears to belong to. This may be the most important vulnerability of a public-key cryptosystem. Let's first look at a potential disaster, then at how to safely avoid it with PGP.

Suppose you wanted to send a private message to Alice. You download Alice's public key certificate from an electronic bulletin board system (BBS). You encrypt your letter to Alice with this public key and send it to her through the BBS's E-mail facility.

Unfortunately, unbeknownst to you or Alice, another user named Charlie has infiltrated the BBS and generated a public key of his own with Alice's user ID attached to it. He covertly substitutes his bogus key in place of Alice's real public key. You unwittingly use this bogus key belonging to Charlie instead of Alice's public key. All looks normal because this bogus key has Alice's user ID. Now Charlie can decipher the message intended for Alice because he has the matching secret key. He may even re-encrypt the deciphered message with Alice's real public key and send it on to her so that no one suspects any wrongdoing. Furthermore, he can even make apparently good signatures from Alice with this secret key because everyone will use the bogus public key to check Alice's signatures.

The only way to prevent this disaster is to prevent anyone from tampering with public keys. If you got Alice's public key directly from Alice, this is no problem. But that may be difficult if Alice is a thousand miles away, or is currently unreachable.

Perhaps you could get Alice's public key from a mutual trusted friend David who knows he has a good copy of Alice's public key. David could sign Alice's public key, vouching for the integrity of Alice's public key. David would create this signature with his own secret key.

This would create a signed public key certificate, and would show that Alice's key had not been tampered with. This requires you have a known good copy of David's public key to check his signature. Perhaps David could provide Alice with a signed copy of your public key also. David is thus serving as an "introducer" between you and Alice.

This signed public key certificate for Alice could be uploaded by David or Alice to the BBS, and you could download it later. You could then check the signature via David's public key and thus be assured that this is really Alice's public key. No impostor can fool you into accepting his own bogus key as Alice's because no one else can forge signatures made by David.

A widely trusted person could even specialize in providing this service of "introducing" users to each other by providing signatures for their public key certificates. This trusted person could be regarded as a "key server", or as a "Certifying Authority". Any public key certificates bearing the key server's signature could be trusted as truly belonging to whom they appear to belong to. All users who wanted to participate would need a known good copy of just the key server's public key, so that the key server's signatures could be verified.

A trusted centralized key server or Certifying Authority is especially appropriate for large impersonal centrally-controlled corporate or government institutions. Some institutional environments use hierarchies of Certifying Authorities.

For more decentralized grassroots "guerrilla style" environments, allowing all users to act as a trusted introducers for their friends would probably work better than a centralized key server. PGP tends to emphasize this organic decentralized non-institutional approach. It better reflects the natural way humans interact on a personal social level, and allows people to better choose who they can trust for key management.

This whole business of protecting public keys from tampering is the single most difficult problem in practical public key applications.

It is the Achilles' heel of public key cryptography, and a lot of software complexity is tied up in solving this one problem.

You should use a public key only after you are sure that it is a good public key that has not been tampered with, and actually belongs to the person it claims to. You can be sure of this if you got this public key certificate directly from its owner, or if it bears the signature of someone else that you trust, from whom you already have a good public key. Also, the user ID should have the full name of the key's owner, not just her first name.

No matter how tempted you are—and you will be tempted—never, NEVER give in to expediency and trust a public key you downloaded from a bulletin board, unless it is signed by someone you trust. That uncertified public key could have been tampered with by anyone, maybe even by the system administrator of the bulletin board.

If you are asked to sign someone else's public key certificate, make certain that it really belongs to that person named in the user ID of that public key certificate. This is because your signature on her public key certificate is a promise by you that this public key really belongs to her. Other people who trust you will accept her public key because it bears your signature. It may be ill-advised to rely on hearsay—don't sign her public key unless you have independent firsthand knowledge that it really belongs to her. Preferably, you should sign it only if you got it directly from her.

In order to sign a public key, you must be far more certain of that key's ownership than if you merely want to use that key to encrypt a message. To be convinced of a key's validity enough to use it, certifying signatures from trusted introducers should suffice. But to sign a key yourself, you should require your own independent firsthand knowledge of who owns that key. Perhaps you could call the key's owner on the phone and read the key file to her to get her to confirm that the key you have really is her key—and make sure you really are talking to the right person. See the section called "Verifying a Public Key Over the Phone" in the Special Topics volume for further details.

Bear in mind that your signature on a public key certificate does not vouch for the integrity of that person, but only vouches for the integrity (the ownership) of that person's public key. You aren't risking your credibility by signing the public key of a sociopath, if you were completely confident that the key really belonged to him. Other people would accept that key as belonging to him because you signed it (assuming they trust you), but they wouldn't trust that key's owner. Trusting a key is not the same as trusting the key's owner.

Trust is not necessarily transferable; I have a friend who I trust not to lie. He's a gullible person who trusts the President not to lie. That doesn't mean I trust the President not to lie. This is just common sense. If I trust Alice's signature on a key, and Alice trusts Charlie's signature on a key, that does not imply that I have to trust Charlie's signature on a key.

It would be a good idea to keep your own public key on hand with a collection of certifying signatures attached from a variety of "introducers", in the hopes that most people will trust at least one of the introducers who vouch for your own public key's validity. You could post your key with its attached collection of certifying signatures on various electronic bulletin boards. If you sign someone else's public key, return it to them with your signature so that they can add it to their own collection of credentials for their own public key.

PGP keeps track of which keys on your public key ring are properly certified with signatures from introducers that you trust. All you have to do is tell PGP which people you trust as introducers, and certify their keys yourself with your own ultimately trusted key. PGP can take it from there, automatically validating any other keys that have been signed by your designated introducers. And of course you may directly sign more keys yourself. More on this later.

Make sure no one else can tamper with your own public key ring. Checking a new signed public key certificate must ultimately depend on the integrity of the trusted public keys that are already on your own public key ring. Maintain physical control of your public key ring, preferably on your own personal computer rather than on a remote time-sharing system, just as you would do for your secret key. This is to protect it from tampering, not from disclosure. Keep a trusted backup copy of your public key ring and your secret key ring on write-protected media.

Since your own trusted public key is used as a final authority to directly or indirectly certify all the other keys on your key ring, it is the most important key to protect from tampering. To detect any tampering of your own ultimately-trusted public key, PGP can be set up to automatically compare your public key against a backup copy on write-protected media. For details, see the description of the "-kc" key ring check command in the Special Topics volume.

PGP generally assumes you will maintain physical security over your system and your key rings, as well as your copy of PGP itself. If an intruder can tamper with your disk, then in theory he can tamper with PGP itself, rendering moot the safeguards PGP may have to detect tampering with keys.

One somewhat complicated way to protect your own whole public key ring from tampering is to sign the whole ring with your own secret key. You could do this by making a detached signature certificate of the public key ring, by signing the ring with the "-sb" options (see the section called "Separating Signatures from Messages" in the PGP User's Guide, Special Topics volume). Unfortunately, you would still have to keep a separate trusted copy of your own public key around to check the signature you made. You couldn't rely on your own public key stored on your public key ring to check the signature you made for the whole ring, because that is part of what you're trying to check.

HOW DOES PGP KEEP TRACK OF WHICH KEYS ARE VALID?

Before you read this section, be sure to read the above section on "How to Protect Public Keys from Tampering".

PGP keeps track of which keys on your public key ring are properly certified with signatures from introducers that you trust. All you have to do is tell PGP which people you trust as introducers, and certify their keys yourself with your own ultimately trusted key. PGP can take it from there, automatically validating any other keys that have been signed by your designated introducers. And of course you may directly sign more keys yourself.

There are two entirely separate criteria PGP uses to judge a public key's usefulness—don't get them confused:

1) Does the key actually belong to whom it appears to belong? In other words, has it been certified with a trusted signature?
2) Does it belong to someone you can trust to certify other keys?

PGP can calculate the answer to the first question. To answer the second question, PGP must be explicitly told by you, the user. When you supply the answer to question 2, PGP can then calculate the answer to question 1 for other keys signed by the introducer you designated as trusted.

Keys that have been certified by a trusted introducer are deemed valid by PGP. The keys belonging to trusted introducers must themselves be certified either by you or by other trusted introducers.

PGP also allows for the possibility of you having several shades of trust for people to act as introducers. Your trust for a key's owner to act as an introducer does not just reflect your estimation of their personal integrity—it should also reflect how competent you think they are at understanding key management and using good judgment in signing keys. You can designate a person to PGP as unknown, untrusted, marginally trusted, or completely trusted to certify other public keys. This trust information is stored on your key ring with their key, but when you tell PGP to copy a key off your key ring, PGP will not copy the trust information along with the key, because your private opinions on trust are regarded as confidential.

When PGP is calculating the validity of a public key, it examines the trust level of all the attached certifying signatures. It computes a weighted score of validity—two marginally trusted signatures are deemed as credible as one fully trusted signature. PGP's skepticism is adjustable—for example, you may tune PGP to require two fully trusted signatures or three marginally trusted signatures to judge a key as valid.

Your own key is "axiomatically" valid to PGP, needing no introducer's signature to prove its validity. PGP knows which public keys are yours, by looking for the corresponding secret keys on the secret key ring. PGP also assumes you ultimately trust yourself to certify other keys.

As time goes on, you will accumulate keys from other people that you may want to designate as trusted introducers. Everyone else will each choose their own trusted introducers. And everyone will gradually accumulate and distribute with their key a collection of certifying signatures from other people, with the expectation that anyone receiving it will trust at least one or two of the signatures. This will cause the emergence of a decentralized fault-tolerant web of confidence for all public keys.

This unique grass-roots approach contrasts sharply with Government standard public key management schemes, such as Internet Privacy Enhanced Mail (PEM), which are based on centralized control and mandatory centralized trust. The standard schemes rely on a hierarchy of Certifying Authorities who dictate who you must trust. PGP's decentralized probabilistic method for determining public key legitimacy is the centerpiece of its key management architecture. PGP lets you alone choose who you trust, putting you at the top of your own private certification pyramid. PGP is for people who prefer to pack their own parachutes.

HOW TO PROTECT SECRET KEYS FROM DISCLOSURE

Protect your own secret key and your pass phrase carefully. Really, really carefully. If your secret key is ever compromised, you'd better get the word out quickly to all interested parties (good luck) before someone else uses it to make signatures in your name. For example, they could use it to sign bogus public key certificates, which could create problems for many people, especially if your signature is widely trusted. And of course, a compromise of your own secret key could expose all messages sent to you.

To protect your secret key, you can start by always keeping physical control of your secret key. Keeping it on your personal computer at home is OK, or keep it in your notebook computer that you can carry with you. If you must use an office computer that you don't always have physical control of, then keep your public and secret key rings on a write-protected removable floppy disk, and don't leave it behind when you leave the office. It wouldn't be a good idea to allow your secret key to reside on a remote timesharing computer, such as a remote dial-in Unix system. Someone could eavesdrop on your modem line and capture your pass phrase, and then obtain your actual secret key from the remote system. You should only use your secret key on a machine that you have physical control over.

Don't store your pass phrase anywhere on the computer that has your secret key file. Storing both the secret key and the pass phrase on the same computer is as dangerous as keeping your PIN in the same wallet as your Automatic Teller Machine bank card. You don't want somebody to get their hands on your disk containing both the pass phrase and the secret key file. It would be most secure if you just memorize your pass phrase and don't store it anywhere but your brain. If you feel you must write down your pass phrase, keep it well protected, perhaps even more well protected than the secret key file.

And keep backup copies of your secret key ring—remember, you have the only copy of your secret key, and losing it will render useless all the copies of your public key that you have spread throughout the world.

The decentralized non-institutional approach PGP uses to manage public keys has its benefits, but unfortunately this also means we can't rely on a single centralized list of which keys have been compromised. This makes it a bit harder to contain the damage of a secret key compromise. You just have to spread the word and hope everyone hears about it.

If the worst case happens—your secret key and pass phrase are both compromised (hopefully you will find this out somehow)—you will have to issue a "key compromise" certificate. This kind of certificate is used to warn other people to stop using your public key. You can use PGP to create such a certificate by using the "-kd" command. Then you must somehow send this compromise certificate to everyone else on the planet, or at least to all your friends and their friends, et cetera. Their own PGP software will install this key compromise certificate on their public key rings and will automatically prevent them from accidentally using your public key ever again. You can then generate a new secret/public key pair and publish the new public key. You could send out one package containing both your new public key and the key compromise certificate for your old key.

BEWARE OF SNAKE OIL

When examining a cryptographic software package, the question always remains, why should you trust this product? Even if you examined the source code yourself, not everyone has the cryptographic experience to judge the security. Even if you are an experienced cryptographer, subtle weaknesses in the algorithms could still elude you.

When I was in college in the early seventies, I devised what I believed was a brilliant encryption scheme. A simple pseudorandom number stream was added to the plaintext stream to create ciphertext. This would seemingly thwart any frequency analysis of the ciphertext, and would be uncrackable even to the most resourceful Government intelligence agencies. I felt so smug about my achievement. So cocksure.

Years later, I discovered this same scheme in several introductory cryptography texts and tutorial papers. How nice. Other cryptographers had thought of the same scheme. Unfortunately, the scheme was presented as a simple homework assignment on how to use elementary cryptanalytic techniques to trivially crack it. So much for my brilliant scheme.

From this humbling experience I learned how easy it is to fall into a false sense of security when devising an encryption algorithm. Most people don't realize how fiendishly difficult it is to devise an encryption algorithm that can withstand a prolonged and determined attack by a resourceful opponent. Many mainstream software engineers have developed equally naive encryption schemes (often even the very same encryption scheme), and some of them have been incorporated into commercial encryption software packages and sold for good money to thousands of unsuspecting users.

This is like selling automotive seat belts that look good and feel good, but snap open in even the slowest crash test. Depending on them may be worse than not wearing seat belts at all. No one suspects they are bad until a real crash. Depending on weak cryptographic software may cause you to unknowingly place sensitive information at risk. You might not otherwise have done so if you had no cryptographic software at all. Perhaps you may never even discover your data has been compromised.

Sometimes commercial packages use the Federal Data Encryption Standard (DES), a fairly good conventional algorithm recommended by the Government for commercial use (but not for classified information, oddly enough—hmmm). There are several "modes of operation" the DES can use, some of them better than others. The Government specifically recommends not using the weakest simplest mode for messages, the Electronic Codebook (ECB) mode. But they do recommend the stronger and more complex Cipher Feedback (CFB) or Cipher Block Chaining (CBC) modes.

Unfortunately, most of the commercial encryption packages I've looked at use ECB mode. When I've talked to the authors of a number of these implementations, they say they've never heard of CBC or CFB modes, and didn't know anything about the weaknesses of ECB mode.

The very fact that they haven't even learned enough cryptography to know these elementary concepts is not reassuring. And they sometimes manage their DES keys in inappropriate or insecure ways. Also, these same software packages often include a second faster encryption algorithm that can be used instead of the slower DES. The author of the package often thinks his proprietary faster algorithm is as secure as the DES, but after questioning him I usually discover that it's just a variation of my own brilliant scheme from college days. Or maybe he won't even reveal how his proprietary encryption scheme works, but assures me it's a brilliant scheme and I should trust it. I'm sure he believes that his algorithm is brilliant, but how can I know that without seeing it?

In all fairness I must point out that in most cases these terribly weak products do not come from companies that specialize in cryptographic technology.

Even the really good software packages, that use the DES in the correct modes of operation, still have problems. Standard DES uses a 56-bit key, which is too small by today's standards, and may now be easily broken by exhaustive key searches on special high-speed machines. The DES has reached the end of its useful life, and so has any software package that relies on it.

There is a company called AccessData (87 East 600 South, Orem, Utah 84058, phone 1-800-658-5199) that sells a package for $185 that cracks the built-in encryption schemes used by WordPerfect, Lotus 1-2-3, MS Excel, Symphony, Quattro Pro, Paradox, and MS Word 2.0. It doesn't simply guess passwords—it does real cryptanalysis. Some people buy it when they forget their password for their own files. Law enforcement agencies buy it too, so they can read files they seize. I talked to Eric Thompson, the author, and he said his program only takes a split second to crack them, but he put in some delay loops to slow it down so it doesn't look so easy to the customer. He also told me that the password encryption feature of PKZIP files can often be easily broken, and that his law enforcement customers already have that service regularly provided to them from another vendor.

In some ways, cryptography is like pharmaceuticals. Its integrity may be absolutely crucial. Bad penicillin looks the same as good penicillin. You can tell if your spreadsheet software is wrong, but how do you tell if your cryptography package is weak? The ciphertext produced by a weak encryption algorithm looks as good as ciphertext produced by a strong encryption algorithm. There's a lot of snake oil out there. A lot of quack cures. Unlike the patent medicine hucksters of old, these software implementors usually don't even know their stuff is snake oil. They may be good software engineers, but they usually haven't even read any of the academic literature in cryptography. But they think they can write good cryptographic software. And why not? After all, it seems intuitively easy to do so. And their software seems to work okay.

Anyone who thinks they have devised an unbreakable encryption scheme either is an incredibly rare genius or is naive and inexperienced. Unfortunately, I sometimes have to deal with would-be cryptographers who want to make "improvements" to PGP by adding encryption algorithms of their own design.

I remember a conversation with Brian Snow, a highly placed senior cryptographer with the NSA. He said he would never trust an encryption algorithm designed by someone who had not "earned their bones" by first spending a lot of time cracking codes. That did make a lot of sense. I observed that practically no one in the commercial world of cryptography qualified under this criterion. "Yes", he said with a self assured smile, "And that makes our job at NSA so much easier." A chilling thought. I didn't qualify either.

The Government has peddled snake oil too. After World War II, the US sold German Enigma ciphering machines to third world governments. But they didn't tell them that the Allies cracked the Enigma code during the war, a fact that remained classified for many years. Even today many Unix systems worldwide use the Enigma cipher for file encryption, in part because the Government has created legal obstacles against using better algorithms. They even tried to prevent the initial publication of the RSA algorithm in 1977. And they have squashed essentially all commercial efforts to develop effective secure telephones for the general public.

The principal job of the US Government's National Security Agency is to gather intelligence, principally by covertly tapping into people's private communications (see James Bamford's book, "The Puzzle Palace"). The NSA has amassed considerable skill and resources for cracking codes. When people can't get good cryptography to protect themselves, it makes NSA's job much easier. NSA also has the responsibility of approving and recommending encryption algorithms. Some critics charge that this is a conflict of interest, like putting the fox in charge of guarding the hen house. NSA has been pushing a conventional encryption algorithm that they designed, and they won't tell anybody how it works because that's classified. They want others to trust it and use it. But any cryptographer can tell you that a well-designed encryption algorithm does not have to be classified to remain secure. Only the keys should need protection. How does anyone else really know if NSA's classified algorithm is secure? It's not that hard for NSA to design an encryption algorithm that only they can crack, if no one else can review the algorithm. Are they deliberately selling snake oil?

There are three main factors that have undermined the quality of commercial cryptographic software in the US. The first is the virtually universal lack of competence of implementors of commercial encryption software (although this is starting to change since the publication of PGP). Every software engineer fancies himself a cryptographer, which has led to the proliferation of really bad crypto software. The second is the NSA deliberately and systematically suppressing all the good commercial encryption technology, by legal intimidation and economic pressure. Part of this pressure is brought to bear by stringent export controls on encryption software which, by the economics of software marketing, has the net effect of suppressing domestic encryption software. The other principle method of suppression comes from the granting all the software patents for all the public key encryption algorithms to a single company, affording a single choke point to suppress the spread of this technology. The net effect of all this is that before PGP was published, there was almost no highly secure general purpose encryption software available in the US.

I'm not as certain about the security of PGP as I once was about my brilliant encryption software from college. If I were, that would be a bad sign. But I'm pretty sure that PGP does not contain any glaring weaknesses (although it may contain bugs). The crypto algorithms were developed by people at high levels of civilian cryptographic academia, and have been individually subject to extensive peer review. Source code is available to facilitate peer review of PGP and to help dispel the fears of some users. It's reasonably well researched, and has been years in the making. And I don't work for the NSA. I hope it doesn't require too large a "leap of faith" to trust the security of PGP.

LEGAL ISSUES

For detailed information on PGP(tm) licensing, distribution, copyrights, patents, trademarks, liability limitations, and export controls, see the "Legal Issues" section in the "PGP User's Guide, Volume II: Special Topics".

PGP uses a public key algorithm claimed by U.S. patent #4,405,829. The exclusive licensing rights to this patent are held by a California company called Public Key Partners, and you may be infringing the patent if you use PGP in the USA without a license. These issues are detailed in the Volume II manual, and in the RSAREF license that comes with the freeware version of PGP. PKP has licensed others to practice the patent, including a company known as ViaCrypt, in Phoenix, Arizona. ViaCrypt sells a fully licensed version of PGP. ViaCrypt may be reached at 602-944-0773.

PGP is "guerrilla" freeware, and I don't mind if you distribute it widely. Just don't ask me to send you a copy. Instead, you can look for it yourself on many BBS systems and a number of Internet FTP sites. But before you distribute PGP, it is essential that you understand the U.S. export controls on encryption software.

## CHAPTER 2

KEY ESCROW CRYPTOSYSTEMS

KEEPING SECRETS SECRET EXCEPT WHEN . . .

Key escrow systems are those where part or all of the cryptographic keys are kept "in escrow" by third parties. The keys are released only upon proper authority to allow some person other than the original sender or receiver to read the message. The U. S. government is strongly supporting key escrow as a way to balance the needs for secrecy between communicating persons against the needs of law enforcement and national security agencies to sometimes read these encrypted communications (with proper legal authority). This chapter presents the technical aspects of the Clipper Chip, the U.S. Government's first proposed key escrow system. It also mentions how Clipper fits into other proposed government cryptosystems and then presents a more general view of key escrow cryptosystems.

Denning starts the chapter by providing the reader with some history of encryption and some specifics of the Skipjack algorithm used in the Clipper Chip. She lays out the process law enforcement officials will use to eavesdrop on a Clipper-encrypted conversation.

A non-Government review team then presents its evaluation of Clipper's Skipjack algorithm. They had only a limited time to consider brute force attacks by exhaustive search, susceptibility to shortcut attacks, and the National Security Agency's design and evaluation process. And algorithm details remain classified. Nevertheless, this interim report is the closest thing to a technical evaluation publicly available.

Blaze explains a potential problem with the Clipper chip in the generation of the Law Enforcement Access Field (LEAF), giving two methods to avoid message interception by the government. He points out that while of theoretical interest, there are more effective ways of "beating the system" (like superencryption) which are well-known. Nevertheless, this paper made front page news in the *New York Times*

(June 2, 1994), sending shock waves across some policymakers' radar screens.

A brief description of Capstone is presented next by NIST. The Capstone board has four major components: Clipper (for bulk data encryption), a digital signature algorithm, a key exchange algorithm, and a hash function. The U. S. government hopes that Capstone, since it incorporates several government standards, will be widely used in both public and private sectors.

Micali then proposes a process for building a "fair" cryptosystem that balances the needs of the Government and those of the public and private sectors. He defines a "fair" cryptosystem as one that can not be misused by criminal· organizations and guarantees citizens the same rights to privacy that currently exist under the law. His paper includes a means to make the Diffie-Hellman scheme fair, information on alternative fair public-key systems, and a proposed process to transform any public-key cryptosystem into a "fair" system. Micali has patented this process[1] and the U.S. government has negotiated a limited use license for state and federal law enforcement with him.

Walker then presents the case for software key escrow, which he believes can satisfy legitimate law enforcement requirements as well as Clipper/Capstone, and has additional advantages as well, including acceptability for use totally within private organizations. Readers wishing a more detailed examination of software key escrow are presented with "A New Approach to Software Key Escrow Encryption" by D. M. Balenson, C. M. Ellison, S. B. Lipner, and S. T. Walker. This paper proposes two designs for software key escrow systems that they believe are valid alternatives to Clipper and to hardware key escrow.

Those wish a detailed description of the safeguards and problems surrounding the official U.S. Government key escrow system can find it in D. Denning and M. Smid, "Key Escrowing Today", *IEEE Communications* magazine, September 1994. Since much of the material it contains appears elsewhere in this section, we did not include it in this book.

---

[1] U. S. patent no. 5,276,737, issued 4 January 1994.

The U.S. Key Escrow Encryption Technology*

Dorothy E. Denning

OVERVIEW

The U.S. key escrow encryption technology emerged from an effort to make strong, affordable encryption widely available in a way that would not be harmful to national security and public safety. The government has long recognized the benefits of encryption for protecting sensitive telecommunications, both in the public and private sectors, and the threat of encryption to national security when its use interferes with foreign intelligence operations. Because of this threat to national security, the U.S. government, like many other governments, restricts the export of encryption technology, although it does not restrict its use within the country (some countries, such as France, also restrict the use of encryption). More recently, the government has also acknowledged that if strong encryption becomes readily available in telephones and other communications equipment used within the country, then public safety could be seriously jeopardized since criminals would likely use the encryption products to hide their communications from law enforcement.

In order to meet all three security objectives—telecommunications security, national security, and public safety—the government designed the new technology to provide high quality encryption and at the same time a capability whereby government officials with lawful authority to intercept particular communications encrypted with the technology can gain access to those communications. The technology is based on a tamper-resistant hardware chip (originally called "Clipper") that implements an NSA-designed encryption algorithm called SKIPJACK, together with a method that allows all communications encrypted with the chip, regardless of what session key is used or how it is selected, to be decrypted through a special chip unique key and a special Law Enforcement Access Field (LEAF) transmitted with the encrypted communications.

The chip unique key is formed as the "exclusive or" (XOR) of two components, each of which is encrypted and stored in escrow with a

---

* *Computer Communications*, Butterworth-Heinemann Ltd., Linacre House, Jordan Hill, Oxford, OX2 8DP, UK. July 1994, Vol. 17, No. 7.

separate escrow agent. The key components of both escrow agents are needed to construct the chip unique key and decrypt intercepted communications. These components are released to an authorized government official only in conjunction with authorized electronic surveillance (see Section 5 and [2]) and only in accordance with procedures issued and approved by the Attorney General. The key components are transmitted to a government-controlled tamper-resistant decrypt device, where they are decrypted and combined to form the chip unique key. Upon termination of the electronic surveillance, the keys are destroyed within the decrypt device.

The escrowed encryption technology is intended to become a government standard [4] for sensitive but unclassified telecommunications, including voice, fax, and data transmitted on circuit-switched systems at rates up to 14.4 kbps or which use basic-rate ISDN or similar grade wireless service. Use of the standard outside the government is voluntary. The first product to incorporate the new chip will be the AT&T 3600 Telephone Security Device.

This article describes the **SKIPJACK** algorithm, the escrowed encryption chip, encrypting with the chip, law enforcement access, and an enhanced chip that includes algorithms for computing digital signatures and negotiating session keys. Since many details of the technology and its use either have not yet been released or are classified, we cannot give a complete or definitive description of the technology and related processes. Although we will sketch the general approach as we currently understand it, we emphasize that the description is preliminary and simplified.

THE SKIPJACK ALGORITHM

SKIPJACK is a single-key encryption algorithm that uses an 80-bit secret key to transform a 64-bit input block into a 64-bit output block. The algorithm can be used in one or more of the four operating modes defined in FIPS 81 for use with the DES: Electronic Codebook (ECB), Cipher Block Chaining (CBC), 64-bit Output Feedback (OFB), and 1, 8, 16, 32, or 64-bit Cipher Feedback (CFB). The algorithm was designed by the National Security Agency and is classified in order to prevent someone from implementing it in software or hardware without providing the law enforcement access feature, thereby taking advantage of the government's strong algorithm while rendering encrypted communications immune from lawful government surveillance.

Because the internals of the algorithm are not available for public scrutiny, the government invited outside experts in cryptography to independently evaluate the algorithm and publicly report their findings. This author was one of the reviewers, and we issued a joint report in July 1993 [1] concluding that SKIPJACK appeared to be a strong encryption algorithm and that there was no significant risk that the algorithm had "trapdoors" or could be broken by any short-cut method of attack. We also concluded that while classification was essential to protect law enforcement and national security objectives, classification did not cover up weaknesses and was not necessary to protect against a cryptanalytic attack.

With respect to a "brute force" attack by exhaustive search, we used DES as a benchmark and considered the added strength of SKIPJACK's 80-bit keys over DES's 56 bits. Since SKIPJACK keys are 24 bits longer than DES keys, there are 2^{24} times more possibilities to try. Therefore, under an assumption that the cost of processing power is halved every year and a half, it will be 1.5 * 24 = 36 years before the cost of breaking SKIPJACK by exhaustive search is comparable to the cost of breaking DES today.

Because SKIPJACK is but one component of a large, complex system and because the security of the entire system depends on all the components, we are evaluating the entire system as it becomes defined and will issue a final report when the evaluation is complete.

ESCROWED ENCRYPTION CHIPS

The SKIPJACK algorithm and method that allows for government access are implemented in a tamper-resistant escrowed encryption chip that includes the following elements:

1. the SKIPJACK encryption algorithm
2. an 80-bit *family key* (KF) that is common to all chips
3. a *chip unique identifier* (UID)
4. an 80-bit *chip unique key* (KU), which is the XOR of two 80-bit *chip unique key components* (KU1 and KU2)
5. specialized control software

These elements are programmed onto the chip after it has been manufactured. Programming takes place inside a secure facility under the control of representatives from the two escrow agents. Batches of chips are programmed in a single session.

At the start of a programming session, the representatives of the escrow agents initialize the programmer by entering parameters (random numbers) into the device as shown in Figure 1. For each chip, the two key components KU1 and KU2 are computed as a function of the initialization parameters plus the chip identifier UID. The chip unique key KU is formed as KU1 XOR KU2. The programmer places UID and KU onto the chip along with the chip-independent components.

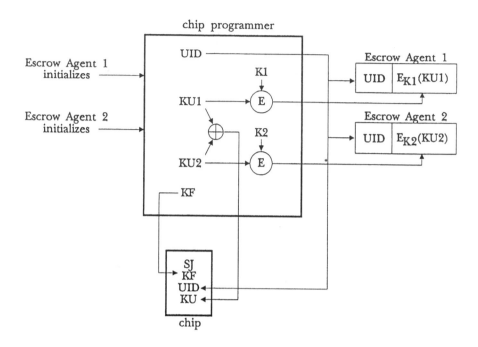

FIGURE 1.
Chip
Initialization

KU1 is then encrypted with a secret key encrypting key K1 assigned to escrow agent 1 to produce $E_{K1}(KU1)$, where $E_K(X)$ denotes the encryption of X with key K. Similarly, KU2 encrypted with a secret key K2 assigned to escrow agent 2 to produce $E_{K2}(KU2)$. The encrypted key components are each paired with the chip identifier UID and given to their respective escrow agent to store in escrow. By storing the key components in encrypted form, they are not vulnerable to theft or unauthorized release.

At the end of the programming session, the programmer is cleared so that the chip unique keys cannot be obtained or computed except by obtaining their encrypted key components from both escrow agents and using a special government decrypt device to decrypt and combine the key components (see Section 5).

The first set of escrowed encryption chips was manufactured by VLSI Technology, Inc. and programmed by Mykotronx. Mykotronx's "MYK78" chip runs at about 15 megabits per second in Electronic Codebook (ECB) mode.

ENCRYPTING WITH AN ESCROWED ENCRYPTION CHIP

In order for two persons to use the SKIPJACK algorithm to encrypt their communications, each person must have a tamper-resistant security device which contains an escrowed encryption chip. For example, each person could have an AT&T Telephone Security Device. The security device is responsible for implementing the protocols needed to establish the secure channel, including negotiation or distribution of the 80-bit secret session key KS that is used to encrypt the communications. The session key could be negotiated, for example, using the Diffie-Hellman public-key distribution method [3], which allows the two devices to compute a shared secret session key by exchanging only public values.

Once an 80-bit session key KS is established for use with an escrowed encryption chip, it is passed to the chip and an operation invoked to generate a *Law Enforcement Access Field* (LEAF) from KS and an initialization vector IV (which may be generated by the chip). The special control software encrypts KS using the chip unique key KU and then concatenates the encrypted session key with the chip identifier UID and an authenticator A. All this is encrypted using the common family key KF to produce the LEAF. The IV and LEAF are then transmitted to the receiving chip for synchronization and LEAF validation. Once synchronized, the session key is used to encrypt and decrypt messages in both directions. For voice communications, the message stream (voice) is first digitized. Figure 2 shows the transmission of the

FIGURE 2. *Escrowed Encryption System*

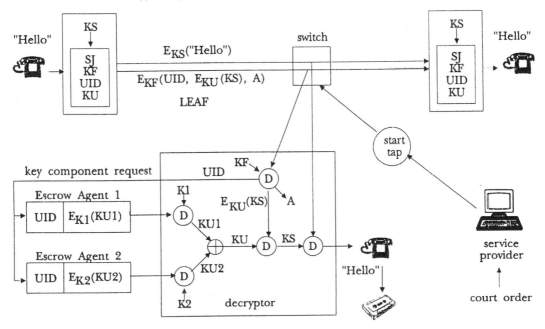

government monitoring facility

LEAF and message stream "Hello" encrypted under session key KS from a sender's security device to a receiver's device. The diagram does not show the IV.

In a two-way conversation such as a phone call, the security device of each party transmits an IV and a LEAF computed by the device's chip. However, both devices use the same session key KS to encrypt communications transmitted to the other party and to decrypt communications received from the other party.

Law Enforcement Access

U.S. law authorizes certain government officials to intercept the wire, electronic, or oral communications of a subject under criminal investigation upon obtaining a special court order. To obtain this order, the government must demonstrate that there is probable cause to believe that the subject under investigation is committing some specific, serious felony and that communications concerning the offense will be obtained through the intercepts. Before issuing a court order, a judge must review a lengthy affidavit that sets forth all the evidence and agree with the assertions contained therein. The affidavit must also demonstrate that other investigative techniques have been tried without success, that they won't work, or that they would be too dangerous. For a more detailed description of the laws and procedures for federal, state, and local electronic surveillance, see [2].

After the government has obtained a court order to intercept a particular line, the order is taken to the telecommunications service provider in order to get access to the communications associated with that line. Normally, the government leases a line from the service provider, and the service provider transmits the intercepted communications to a remote government monitoring facility over that line. If the government detects encrypted communications, the incoming line will be set up to pass through a special government-controlled decrypt device as shown in Figure 2. The decrypt device will recognize communications encrypted with a key escrow chip, extract the LEAF and IV, and decrypt the LEAF using the family key KF in order to pull out the chip identifier UID and the encrypted session key $E_{KU}(KS)$.

The chip identifier UID will be given to the escrow agents along with a request for the corresponding chip unique key components, documentation certifying that electronic surveillance has been authorized for communications encrypted or decrypted with that chip, and the serial number of the decrypt device. Upon receipt of the certification, the escrow agents will release the corresponding encrypted key components $E_{K1}(KU1)$ and $E_{K2}(KU2)$ to the government. The keys will be transmitted to the government decrypt device in such manner as to ensure that they cannot be used except with that device as authorized.

The device will decrypt the key components KU1 and KU2 using the key encrypting keys K1 and K2 respectively, compute the chip unique key KU as KU1 XOR KU2, and decrypt the session key KS. Finally, the decrypt device will decrypt the communications encrypted with KS. To accomplish all this, the device will be initialized to include the family key KF and the key encrypting keys K1 and K2.

When the escrow agents transmit the encrypted key components, they will also transmit the expiration date for the authorized surveillance. It is anticipated that the decrypt device will be designed to destroy the chip unique key and all information used to derive it on the expiration date. In the meanwhile, however, every time a new conversation starts with a new session key, the decrypt device will be able to extract and decrypt the session key from the LEAF without the need to go through the escrow agents. Thus, except for the initial delay getting the keys, intercepted communications can be decrypted in real time for the duration of the surveillance. This real-time capability is extremely important for many types of cases, for example, kidnappings and planned terrorist attacks.

Because the same session key KS is used for communications sent in both directions, the decrypt device need not extract the LEAF and obtain the chip unique key for both the caller and called in order to decrypt both ends of the conversation. Instead, it suffices to obtain the chip unique key for the chip used with the telephone associated with the subject of the electronic surveillance.

An unauthorized person wishing to listen in on someone else's communications would need to duplicate the capability of the government; that is, have access to the communications, a decrypt device, and the encrypted chip unique key components. Since a decrypt device cannot be built without knowing the classified algorithms, family key KF, and key encrypting keys K1 and K2, the adversary will almost certainly need to acquire a decrypt device from the government (e.g., by theft or bribery).

THE ENHANCED ESCROWED ENCRYPTION CHIP

Public-key methods for negotiating session keys and signing messages will be combined with the functions of the escrowed encryption chips to provide a general-purpose chip capable of implementing secure encryption, law enforcement access, and digital signatures. The enhanced chips will include:

- The SKIPJACK encryption algorithm
- The 80-bit family key (KF)

- A chip unique identifier (UID)
- An 80-bit chip unique key (KU)
- Specialized control software
- A public-key negotiation algorithm (probably Diffie-Hellman)
- The Digital Signature Algorithm (DSA) used with the DSS
- The Secure Hashing Algorithm (SHA), also used with the DSS
- A general purpose high speed exponentiation algorithm
- A random number generator that uses a pure noise source

The enhanced chips will initially be used by the Preliminary Message Security Protocol in the Defense Messaging System.

REFERENCES

1. Brickell, E. F.; Denning, D. E.; Kent, S. T.; Maher, D. P.; and Tuchman, W., "The SKIPJACK Review, Interim Report: The SKIPJACK Algorithm," July 29, 1993; available from Georgetown University, Office of Public Affairs, Washington DC or by email from denning@cs.georgetown.edu. [pp. 119–130—Ed.]

2. Delaney, D.P.; Denning, D.E.; Kaye, J.; and McDonald, A. R., "Wiretap Laws and Procedures: What Happens When the Government Taps a Line," September 23, 1993; available from Georgetown University, Department of Computer Science, Washington DC; by anonymous ftp from cpsr.org as:
cpsr/communications_privacy/wiretap/denning_wiretap_procedure.txt; or by email from denning@cs.georgetown.edu.

3. Diffie, W. and Hellman, M., "New Directions in Cryptography," *IEEE Trans. on Info. Theory*, Vol IT-22(6), Nov. 1976, pp. 644–654.

4. National Institute of Standards and Technology, "Escrowed Encryption Standard," proposed Federal Information Processing Standards Publication (FIPS PUB), 1993.

## 2

SKIPJACK Review: Interim Report*

Ernest F. Brickell, Dorothy E. Denning, Stephen T. Kent, David P. Maher, and Walter Tuchman

EXECUTIVE SUMMARY

The objective of the SKIPJACK review was to provide a mechanism whereby persons outside the government could evaluate the strength of the classified encryption algorithm used in the escrowed encryption devices and publicly report their findings. Because SKIPJACK is but one component of a large, complex system, and because the security of communications encrypted with SKIPJACK depends on the security of the system as a whole, the review was extended to encompass other components of the system. The purpose of this Interim Report is to report on our evaluation of the SKIPJACK algorithm. A later Final Report will address the broader system issues.

The results of our evaluation of the SKIPJACK algorithm are as follows:

1. Under an assumption that the cost of processing power is halved every eighteen months, it will be 36 years before the cost of breaking SKIPJACK by exhaustive search will be equal to the cost of breaking the Data Encryption Standard today. Thus, there is no significant risk that SKIPJACK will be broken by exhaustive search in the next 30–40 years.
2. There is no significant risk that SKIPJACK can be broken through a shortcut method of attack.
3. While the internal structure of SKIPJACK must be classified in order to protect law enforcement and national security objectives, the strength of SKIPJACK against a cryptanalytic attack does not depend on the secrecy of the algorithm.

BACKGROUND

On April 16, the President announced a new technology initiative aimed at providing a high level of security for sensitive, unclassified

---

* July 28, 1993. Posted to the "sci.crypt" newsgroup on August 1, 1993 by Dorothy Denning.

communications, while enabling lawfully authorized intercepts of telecommunications by law enforcement officials for criminal investigations. The initiative includes several components:

- A classified encryption/decryption algorithm called "SKIPJACK."
- Tamper-resistant cryptographic devices (e.g., electronic chips), each of which contains SKIPJACK, classified control software, a device identification number, a family key used by law enforcement, and a device unique key that unlocks the session key used to encrypt a particular communication.
- A secure facility for generating device unique keys and programming the devices with the classified algorithms, identifiers, and keys.
- Two escrow agents that each hold a component of every device unique key. When combined, those two components form the device unique key.
- A law enforcement access field (LEAF), which enables an authorized law enforcement official to recover the session key. The LEAF is created by a device at the start of an encrypted communication and contains the session key encrypted under the device unique key together with the device identifier, all encrypted under the family key.
- LEAF decoders that allow an authorized law enforcement official to extract the device identifier and encrypted session key from an intercepted LEAF. The identifier is then sent to the escrow agents, who return the components of the corresponding device unique key. Once obtained, the components are used to reconstruct the device unique key, which is then used to decrypt the session key.

This report reviews the security provided by the first component, namely the SKIPJACK algorithm. The review was performed pursuant to the President's direction that "respected experts from outside the government will be offered access to the confidential details of the algorithm to assess its capabilities and publicly report their finding." The Acting Director of the National Institute of Standards and Technology (NIST) sent letters of invitation to potential reviewers. The authors of this report accepted that invitation.

We attended an initial meeting at the Institute for Defense Analyses Supercomputing Research Center (SRC) from June 21–23. At that meeting, the designer of SKIPJACK provided a complete, detailed description of the algorithm, the rationale for each feature, and the history of the design. The head of the NSA evaluation team described the evaluation process and its results. Other NSA staff briefed us on the LEAF structure and protocols for use, generation of device keys, protection of the devices against reverse engineering, and NSA's history in the design and evaluation of encryption methods contained in SKIP-

JACK. Additional NSA and NIST staff were present at the meeting to answer our questions and provide assistance. All staff members were forthcoming in providing us with requested information.

At the June meeting, we agreed to integrate our individual evaluations into this joint report. We also agreed to reconvene at SRC from July 19–21 for further discussions and to complete a draft of the report. In the interim, we undertook independent tasks according to our individual interests and availability. Ernest Brickell specified a suite of tests for evaluating SKIPJACK. Dorothy Denning worked at NSA on the refinement and execution of these and other tests that took into account suggestions solicited from Professor Martin Hellman at Stanford University. NSA staff assisted with the programming and execution of these tests. Denning also analyzed the structure of SKIPJACK and its susceptibility to differential cryptanalysis. Stephen Kent visited NSA to explore in more detail how SKIPJACK compared with NSA encryption algorithms that he already knew and that were used to protect classified data. David Maher developed a risk assessment approach while continuing his ongoing work on the use of the encryption chip in the AT&T Telephone Security Device. Walter Tuchman investigated the anti-reverse engineering properties of the chips.

We investigated more than just SKIPJACK because the security of communications encrypted with the escrowed encryption technology depends on the security provided by all the components of the initiative, including protection of the keys stored on the devices, protection of the key components stored with the escrow agents, the security provided by the LEAF and LEAF decoder, protection of keys after they have been transmitted to law enforcement under court order, and the resistance of the devices to reverse engineering. In addition, the success of the technology initiative depends on factors besides security, for example, performance of the chips. Because some components of the escrowed encryption system, particularly the key escrow system, are still under design, we decided to issue this Interim Report on the security of the SKIPJACK algorithm and to defer our Final Report until we could complete our evaluation of the system as a whole.

OVERVIEW OF THE SKIPJACK ALGORITHM

SKIPJACK is a 64-bit "electronic codebook" algorithm that transforms a 64-bit input block into a 64-bit output block. The transformation is parameterized by an 80-bit key, and involves performing 32 steps or iterations of a complex, nonlinear function. The algorithm can be used in any one of the four operating modes defined in FIPS 81 for use with the Data Encryption Standard (DES).

The **SKIPJACK** algorithm was developed by NSA and is classified SECRET. It is representative of a family of encryption algorithms developed in 1980 as part of the NSA suite of "Type I" algorithms, suitable for protecting all levels of classified data. The specific algorithm, **SKIP-JACK**, is intended to be used with sensitive but unclassified information.

The strength of any encryption algorithm depends on its ability to withstand an attack aimed at determining either the key or the unencrypted ("plaintext") communications. There are basically two types of attack, brute-force and shortcut.

SUSCEPTIBILITY TO BRUTE FORCE ATTACK BY EXHAUSTIVE SEARCH

In a brute-force attack (also called "exhaustive search"), the adversary essentially tries all possible keys until one is found that decrypts the intercepted communications into a known or meaningful plaintext message. The resources required to perform an exhaustive search depend on the length of the keys, since the number of possible keys is directly related to key length. In particular, a key of length N bits has 2^N possibilities. **SKIPJACK** uses 80-bit keys, which means there are 2^{80} (approximately 10^{24}) or more than 1 trillion trillion possible keys.

An implementation of **SKIPJACK** optimized for a single processor on the 8-processor Cray YMP performs about 89,000 encryptions per second. At that rate, it would take more than 400 billion years to try all keys. Assuming the use of all 8 processors and aggressive vectorization, the time would be reduced to about a billion years.

A more speculative attack using a future, hypothetical, massively parallel machine with 100,000 RISC processors, each of which was capable of 100,000 encryptions per second, would still take about 4 million years. The cost of such a machine might be on the order of $50 million. In an even more speculative attack, a special purpose machine might be built using 1.2 billion $1 chips with a 1 GHz clock. If the algorithm could be pipelined so that one encryption step were performed per clock cycle, then the $1.2 billion machine could exhaust the key space in 1 year.

Another way of looking at the problem is by comparing a brute force attack on **SKIPJACK** with one on DES, which uses 56-bit keys. Given that no one has demonstrated a capability for breaking DES, DES offers a reasonable benchmark. Since **SKIPJACK** keys are 24 bits longer than DES keys, there are 2^{24} times more possibilities. Assuming that the cost of processing power is halved every eighteen months, then it will not be for another 24 * 1.5 = 36 years before the cost of breaking **SKIPJACK** is equal to the cost of breaking DES today. Given the lack of demonstrated capability for breaking DES, and the expectation that the situation will continue for at least several more years, one can reasonably expect that SKIPJACK will not be broken within the next 30–40 years.

Conclusion 1: Under an assumption that the cost of processing power is halved every eighteen months, it will be 36 years before the cost of breaking SKIPJACK by exhaustive search will be equal to the cost of breaking DES today. Thus, there is no significant risk that SKIPJACK will be broken by exhaustive search in the next 30–40 years.

SUSCEPTIBILITY TO SHORTCUT ATTACKS

In a shortcut attack, the adversary exploits some property of the encryption algorithm that enables the key or plaintext to be determined in much less time than by exhaustive search. For example, the RSA public-key encryption method is attacked by factoring a public value that is the product of two secret primes into its primes.

Most shortcut attacks use probabilistic or statistical methods that exploit a structural weakness, unintentional or intentional (i.e., a "trapdoor"), in the encryption algorithm. In order to determine whether such attacks are possible, it is necessary to thoroughly examine the structure of the algorithm and its statistical properties. In the time available for this review, it was not feasible to conduct an evaluation on the scale that NSA has conducted or that has been conducted on the DES. Such review would require many man-years of effort over a considerable time interval. Instead, we concentrated on reviewing NSA's design and evaluation process. In addition, we conducted several of our own tests.

NSA'S DESIGN AND EVALUATION PROCESS

SKIPJACK was designed using building blocks and techniques that date back more than forty years. Many of the techniques are related to work that was evaluated by some of the world's most accomplished and famous experts in combinatorics and abstract algebra. SKIPJACK's more immediate heritage dates to around 1980, and its initial design to 1987.

SKIPJACK was designed to be evaluatable, and the design and evaluation approach was the same used with algorithms that protect the country's most sensitive classified information. The specific structures included in SKIPJACK have a long evaluation history, and the cryptographic properties of those structures had many prior years of intense study before the formal process began in 1987. Thus, an arsenal of tools and data was available. This arsenal was used by dozens of adversarial evaluators whose job was to break SKIPJACK. Many spent at least a full year working on the algorithm. Besides highly experienced evaluators, SKIPJACK was subjected to cryptanalysis by less experienced evaluators who were untainted by past approaches. All known methods of attacks were explored, including differential cryptanalysis. The goal was a design that did not allow a shortcut attack.

The design underwent a sequence of iterations based on feedback from the evaluation process. These iterations eliminated properties which, even though they might not allow successful attack, were related to properties that could be indicative of vulnerabilities. The head of the NSA evaluation team confidently concluded "I believe that SKIPJACK can only be broken by brute force—there is no better way."

In summary, SKIPJACK is based on some of NSA's best technology. Considerable care went into its design and evaluation in accordance with the care given to algorithms that protect classified data.

INDEPENDENT ANALYSIS AND TESTING

Our own analysis and testing increased our confidence in the strength of SKIPJACK and its resistance to attack.

Randomness and Correlation Tests

A strong encryption algorithm will behave like a random function of the key and plaintext so that it is impossible to determine any of the key bits or plaintext bits from the ciphertext bits (except by exhaustive search). We ran two sets of tests aimed at determining whether SKIPJACK is a good pseudo random number generator. These tests were run on a Cray YMP at NSA. The results showed that SKIPJACK behaves like a random function and that ciphertext bits are not correlated with either key bits or plaintext bits. Appendix A gives more details.

Differential Cryptanalysis

Differential cryptanalysis is a powerful method of attack that exploits structural properties in an encryption algorithm. The method involves analyzing the structure of the algorithm in order to determine the effect of particular differences in plaintext pairs on the differences of their corresponding ciphertext pairs, where the differences are represented by the exclusive-or of the pair. If it is possible to exploit these differential effects in order to determine a key in less time than with exhaustive search, an encryption algorithm is said to be susceptible to differential cryptanalysis. However, an actual attack using differential cryptanalysis may require substantially more chosen plaintext than can be practically acquired.

We examined the internal structure of SKIPJACK to determine its susceptibility to differential cryptanalysis. We concluded it was not possible to perform an attack based on differential cryptanalysis in less time than with exhaustive search.

Weak Key Test

Some algorithms have "weak keys" that might permit a shortcut solution. DES has a few weak keys, which follow from a pattern of symmetry in the algorithm. We saw no pattern of symmetry in the SKIP-JACK algorithm which could lead to weak keys. We also experimentally tested the all "0" key (all 80 bits are "0") and the all "1" key to see if they were weak and found they were not.

Symmetry Under Complementation Test

The DES satisfies the property that for a given plaintext-ciphertext pair and associated key, encryption of the one's complement of the plaintext with the one's complement of the key yields the one's complement of the ciphertext. This "complementation property" shortens an attack by exhaustive search by a factor of two since half the keys can be tested by computing complements in lieu of performing a more costly encryption. We tested SKIPJACK for this property and found that it did not hold.

Comparison with Classified Algorithms

We compared the structure of SKIPJACK to that of NSA Type I algorithms used in current and near-future devices designed to protect classified data. This analysis was conducted with the close assistance of the cryptographer who developed SKIPJACK and included an in-depth discussion of design rationale for all of the algorithms involved. Based on this comparative, structural analysis of SKIPJACK against these other algorithms, and a detailed discussion of the similarities and differences between these algorithms, our confidence in the basic soundness of SKIPJACK was further increased.

Conclusion 2: There is no significant risk that SKIPJACK can be broken through a shortcut method of attack.

SECRECY OF THE ALGORITHM

The SKIPJACK algorithm is sensitive for several reasons. Disclosure of the algorithm would permit the construction of devices that fail to properly implement the LEAF, while still interoperating with legitimate SKIPJACK devices. Such devices would provide high quality cryptographic security without preserving the law enforcement access capability that distinguishes this cryptographic initiative. Additionally, the SKIPJACK algorithm is classified SECRET—NOT RELEASABLE TO FOREIGN NATIONALS. This classification reflects the high quality of the algorithm, i.e., it incorporates design techniques that are representative of algorithms used to protect classified information. Disclosure of the algorithm would permit analysis that could result in discovery of these classified design techniques, and this would be detrimental to national security.

However, while full exposure of the internal details of SKIPJACK would jeopardize law enforcement and national security objectives, it would not jeopardize the security of encrypted communications. This is because a shortcut attack is not feasible even with full knowledge of the algorithm. Indeed, our analysis of the susceptibility of SKIPJACK to a brute force or shortcut attack was based on the assumption that the algorithm was known.

Conclusion 3: While the internal structure of SKIPJACK must be classified in order to protect law enforcement and national security objectives, the strength of SKIPJACK against a cryptanalytic attack does not depend on the secrecy of the algorithm.

Appendix A

Cycle Structure Tests

The first set of tests examined the cycle structure of SKIPJACK. Fix a set of keys, K, a plaintext, m, and a function $h: M \to K$, where M is the set of all 64-bit messages. Let $f: K \to K$ be defined as $f(k) = h(SJ(k,m))$ (where $SJ(k,m)$ denotes the SKIPJACK encryption of plaintext m with key k). Let $N = |K|$. The expected cycle length of f is $\sqrt{\pi N/8}$. We chose sets of K with $N = 2^{10}, 2^{16}, 2^{24}, 2^{32}, 2^{40}, 2^{48}, 2^{56}$. For all of these N, the mean of the cycle lengths computed across all experiments was close to an expected relative error of ($1/\sqrt{j}$ for j experiments) of the expected cycle length. We did not do this test with larger sets of keys because of the time constraints.

N	# of exps	Mean cycle len	Expec cycle len	Rel Err	Expec rel err
2^{10}	5000	20.4	20.1	.019	.014
2^{16}	3000	164.7	160.4	.027	.018
2^{24}	2000	2576.6	2566.8	.004	.022
2^{32}	2000	40343.2	41068.6	.018	.022
2^{40}	1000	646604.9	657097.6	.016	.032
2^{48}	10	8,980,043	10,513,561	.145	.316
2^{56}	1	28,767,197	168,216,976	.829	1

Statistical Randomness and Correlation Tests

The second set of tests examined whether there were any correlations between the input and output of **SKIPJACK**, or between a key and the output. We also looked for nonrandomness in functions of the form $SJ(k,m) \oplus SJ(k, m \oplus h)$ and functions of the form $SJ(k,m) \oplus SJ(k \oplus h, m)$ for all h of Hamming weight 1 and 2 and for some randomly chosen h. All results were consistent with these functions behaving like random functions.

Given a set of N numbers of k-bits each, a chi-square test will test the hypothesis that this set of numbers was drawn (with replacement) from a uniform distribution on all of the 2^k, k-bit numbers. We ran the tests using a 99% confidence level. A truly random function would pass the test approximately 99% of the time. The test is not appropriate when $N/2^k$ is too small, say 5. Since it was infeasible to run the test for $k = 64$, we would pick 8 bit positions, and generate a set of $N - 10,000$ numbers, and run the test on the N numbers restricted to those 8 bit positions (thus $k = 8$). In some of the tests, we selected the 8 bits from the output of the function we were testing, and in others, we selected 4 bits from the input and 4 from the output.

Some of the tests were run on both the encryption and decryption functions of **SKIPJACK**. The notation $SJ^{-1}(k,m)$ will be used to denote the decryption function of **SKIPJACK** with key k on message m.

Test 1: Randomness test on output

In a single test: Fix k, fix mask of 8 output bits, select 10,000 random messages, run chi-square on the 10,000 outputs restricted to the mask of 8 output bits. Repeat this single test for 200 different values of k and 50 different masks, for a total of 10,000 chi-square tests. We found that .87% of the tests failed the 99% confidence level chi-square test. This is within a reasonable experimental error of the expected value of 1%.

On the decryption function, there were only .64% of the tests that failed. This was on a much smaller test set.

# k	# masks	function, $f(m)$	mask	% failed
200	50	$SJ(k,m)$	8 of $f(m)$	.87
25	50	$SJ^{-1}(k,m)$	8 of $f(m)$	.64

Test 2: Correlation test between messages and output

Single test: Fix k, fix mask of 4 message bits and 4 output bits, select 10,000 random messages, run chi-square.

# k	# masks	function, $f(m)$	mask	% failed
200	1000	$SJ(k,m)$	4 of m, 4 of $f(m)$	1.06
25	1000	$SJ^{-1}(k,m)$	4 of m, 4 of $f(m)$	1.01

Test 3: Randomness test on the xor of outputs, given a fixed xor of inputs

Single test: Fix k, fix mask of 8 output bits, select 10,000 random messages. Let X be the union of all 64 bit words of Hamming weight 1 (64 of these), all 64 bit words of Hamming weight 2 (2016 of these), and some randomly chosen 64 bit words (920 of these). Repeat this single test for all $h \in H$, 50 different masks, and 4 different values of k.

# k	# masks	# h	function, $f(m)$	mask	% failed
4	50	3000	$SJ(k,m) \oplus SJ(k,m \oplus h)$	8 of $f(m)$	.99

Test 4: Correlation test between message xors and output xors

Single test: Fix k, fix mask of 4 bits of h and 4 bits of output, select 10,000 random (m,h) pairs.

# k	# masks	function, $f(m,h)$	mask	% failed
200	1000	$SJ(k,m) \oplus SJ(k,m \oplus h)$	4 of h, 4 of $f(m,h)$	.99
25	1000	$SJ^{-1}(k,m) \oplus SJ^{-1}(k,m \oplus h)$	4 of h, 4 of $f(m,h)$	1.02

Test 5: Correlation test between messages and output xors

Single test: Fix k, fix mask of 4 bits of m and 4 bits of output xor, select 10,000 random messages. Let H be the union of all 64 bit words of Hamming weight 1 (64 of these), some of the 64 bit words of Hamming weight 2 (100 of these), and some randomly chosen 64 bit words (100 of these).

# k	# masks	# h	function, $f(m)$	mask	% failed
2	1000	264	$SJ(k,m) \oplus SJ(k,m \oplus h)$	4 of m, 4 of $f(m)$	.99

Test 6: Correlation test between keys and output

Single test: Fix m, fix mask of 4 key bits and 4 output bits, select 10,000 random keys.

# m	# masks	function, $f(k)$	mask	% failed
200	1000	$SJ(k,m)$	4 of k, 4 of $f(k)$	1.00
25	1000	$SJ^{-1}(k,m)$	4 of k, 4 of $f(k)$	1.02

Test 7: Randomness test on the xor of outputs, given a fixed xor of keys

Single test: Fix m, fix mask of 8 output bits, select 10,000 random keys. Let H be the union of all 80 bit words of Hamming weight 1 (80 of these), all 80 bit words of Hamming weight 2 (3160 of these), and some randomly chosen 80 bit words (760 of these). Repeat this single test for all $h \in H$, 50 different masks, and 2 different values of m.

# m	# masks	# h	function, $f(k)$	mask	% failed
2	50	4000	$SJ(k,m) \oplus SJ(k \oplus h,m)$	8 of $f(k)$	.99

Test 8: Correlation test between key xors and output xors

Single test: Fix m, fix mask of 4 bits of h and 4 bits of output, select 10,000 random (k,h) pairs.

# m	# masks	function, $f(k,h)$	mask	% failed
200	1000	$SJ(k,m) \oplus SJ(k \oplus h,m)$	4 of h, 4 of $f(k,h)$	1.02
25	1000	$SJ^{-1}(k,m) \oplus SJ^{-1}(k \oplus h,m)$	4 of h, 4 of $f(k,h)$	1.1

## 3

Protocol Failure in the Escrowed Encryption Standard*

Matt Blaze

ABSTRACT

The Escrowed Encryption Standard (EES) defines a US Government family of cryptographic processors, popularly known as "Clipper" chips, intended to protect unclassified government and private-sector communications and data. A basic feature of key setup between pairs of EES processors involves the exchange of a "Law Enforcement Access Field" (LEAF) that contains an encrypted copy of the current session key. The LEAF is intended to facilitate government access to the cleartext of data encrypted under the system. Several aspects of the design of the EES, which employs a classified cipher algorithm and tamper-resistant hardware, attempt to make it infeasible to deploy the system without transmitting the LEAF. We evaluated the publicly released aspects of the EES protocols as well as a prototype version of a PCMCIA-based EES device. This paper outlines various techniques that enable cryptographic communication among EES processors without transmission of the valid LEAF. We identify two classes of techniques. The simplest allow communication only between pairs of "rogue" parties. The second, more complex methods permit rogue applications to take unilateral action to interoperate with legal EES users. We conclude with techniques that could make the fielded EES architecture more robust against these failures.

INTRODUCTION AND BACKGROUND

In April 1993, the Clinton Administration announced a proposed new federal standard symmetric key encryption system for the protection of sensitive-but-unclassified government and civilian data [Mar93]. The proposal, called the Escrowed Encryption Standard (EES) [NIST94], includes several unusual features that have been the subject of consid-

---

* 2nd ACM Conference on Computer and Communications Security, Fairfax, VA, November 1994. Copyright 1994, Association for Computing Machinery, Inc. Reprinted by permission.

erable debate and controversy. The EES cipher algorithm, called "Skip-jack", is itself classified, and implementations of the cipher are available to the private sector only within tamper-resistant modules supplied by government-approved vendors. Software implementations of the cipher will not be possible. Although Skipjack, which was designed by the US National Security Agency (NSA), was reviewed by a small panel of civilian experts who were granted access to the algorithm, the cipher cannot be subjected to the degree of civilian scrutiny ordinarily given to new encryption systems.

By far the most controversial aspect of the EES system, however, is *key escrow*. As part of the crypto-synchronization process, EES devices generate and exchange a "Law Enforcement Access Field" (LEAF). This field contains a copy of the current session key and is intended to enable a government eavesdropper to recover the cleartext. The LEAF copy of the session key is encrypted with a device-unique key called the "unit key", assigned at the time the EES device is manufactured. Copies of the unit keys for all EES devices are to be held in "escrow" jointly by two federal agencies that will be charged with releasing the keys to law enforcement under certain conditions.

At present, two EES devices are being produced. The simplest, the Clipper chip (also known as the MYK-78), is essentially a drop-in replacement for a conventional DES [NBS77] chip and relies on key negotiation being handled off the chip. The other EES device, the Capstone chip (MYK-80), adds built-in support for public-key negotiation and digital signatures, with modular arithmetic functions, random number generation, and other such features. [See p. 147–148—Ed.]

The interface to the Skipjack cipher is similar to that of DES, based on a 64 bit codebook block cipher and supporting FIPS-81 [NBS80] standard modes of operation. Keys are 80 bits in length, as opposed to DES's 56 bits.

The initial application of EES is in stand-alone voice encryption telephone units, such as the AT&T Model 3600 Telephone Security Device. To facilitate computer applications such as electronic mail and file encryption, a version of the Capstone chip will also be available packaged in a standard PCMCIA card. EES PCMCIA cards can be installed easily in many commercially available laptop computers, and SCSI-based PCMCIA card readers can connect EES cards to most other computers. The government has specified a standard application interface library for communicating with the cards.

Clipper and Capstone chips are, at present, available only for use in approved products that comply with LEAF handling requirements. EES PCMCIA cards, on the other hand, are themselves a stand-alone product, and are to be made generally available "off the shelf" in the United States.

The government has stated that the goal of the EES is to make a strong cipher available for legitimate use without supplying criminals and other adversaries with a tool that can be used against American interests or to hide illegal activities from law enforcement. Thus the system is intended to be difficult to deploy without also sending a valid LEAF and thereby exposing the traffic to the possibility of government monitoring. In this paper, however, we show that it is possible to construct applications that can enjoy use of the Skipjack cipher but that do not admit law enforcement access through the LEAF. For the purposes of this paper, we consider two classes of "rogue" EES applications: those that can communicate only with other rogue systems and those that can successfully interoperate with EES "legal" systems as well. The latter category especially threatens the goals of the EES program, since such rogue applications would be operationally equivalent to their legal counterparts without being subject to government access.

LEAF Structure and Protocols

The LEAF is a 128 bit structure containing enough information for law enforcement recovery of the session key with the cooperation of the two agencies holding the unit key database. The structure contains a 32 bit unique unit identifier (the serial number of the chip that generated the LEAF), the current 80 bit session key (encrypted with the device's unit key) and a 16 bit LEAF checksum. The entire structure is encrypted with a fixed "family key" to produce the final LEAF message. All cryptographic operations employ symmetric (secret) key techniques. The family key is shared by all interoperable EES devices. The family key, the encryption modes used to encrypt the unit key and the LEAF message, and the details of the checksum are all secret. Externally, the LEAF is an opaque 128 bit package. See Figure 1.

To decrypt EES traffic, a law enforcement agency first must intercept the LEAF and the traffic itself using conventional data wiretapping technology. The LEAF is decrypted with the family key, revealing the chip serial number, the unit key-encrypted session key and the LEAF checksum. The chip serial number is provided, with appropriate authorization, to the two escrow agencies, which each return half of the unit key for the given serial number. The two half-unit keys can be combined (by bitwise exclusive-or) to produce the unit key, which the law enforcement agency can then use to decrypt the session key. This session key can then be used to decrypt the actual traffic.

The wiretapping system thus relies on the availability of the LEAF along with the encrypted traffic. To force applications to send the LEAF on the same channel as the traffic, EES devices will not decrypt data until they have received a valid LEAF for the current session key. Pre-

FIGURE 1.
LEAF Structure

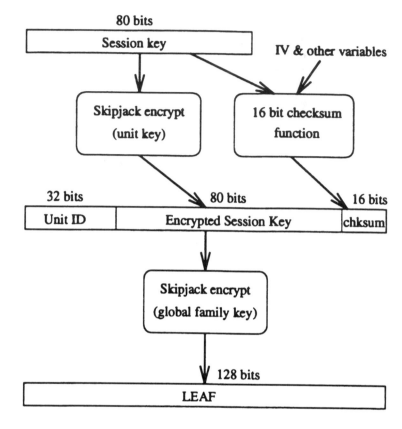

sumably, EES devices perform various integrity checks on received LEAFs prior to accepting them.

To provide a convenient application interface for LEAF management, EES devices generate and load LEAFs along with the FIPS-81 initialization vectors (IVs). The devices provide "generate IV" and "load IV" functions that operate on 192 bit fields containing an unencrypted 64 bit IV concatenated with the 128 bit encrypted LEAF. The load IV operation fails if the associated LEAF does not pass an integrity check.

Experimental Observations

Most details of the LEAF creation method, encryption modes, and data structures, beyond those mentioned above, are classified and are therefore unknown to us. In particular, the EES standard does not specify the exact mechanism that enforces the transmission of the correct LEAF. However, we were able to perform a number of simple experiments on our prototype devices to confirm and expand our knowledge of LEAF internals. All experiments were performed at the protocol level through the standard interface and did not involve cryptanalysis or direct hardware "reverse engineering." We summarize our observations below.

- LEAF integrity is verified entirely via redundancy in the checksum field. In general, attempts to load an incorrect LEAF fail. This must be due entirely to the checksum field and not through direct verification of the unit ID or encrypted session key; the receiving chip cannot confirm the correctness of the unit ID or encrypted session key fields since it does not know the unit ID or unit key of the sender. Therefore, the LEAF must be testable by the receiver based only on known information (such as the cleartext session key and IV) included in the checksum computation.
- LEAF checksum computation includes (implicitly or explicitly) the current IV. The LEAF changes whenever a new IV is generated for a given session key. Since the IV is not included directly as one of the LEAF fields, it must influence the checksum. Furthermore, the receiving device refuses to load the wrong IV for a given LEAF.
- LEAF checksum computation includes the cleartext of the current session key. Attempts to load a LEAF (and corresponding IV) from a previous session key fail. It is therefore not possible to "reuse" a LEAF generated from an old session key, even though the LEAF itself appears internally consistent.
- LEAF checksum computation includes other parts of the LEAF. Attempts to load LEAFs with a single bit inverted anywhere in the 128 bit structure fail.
- LEAF encryption diffuses its input throughout the entire 128 bit structure. The LEAF structure or encryption mode is not exactly as specified in released documents. Generating a new IV for a given session key causes changes across the entire LEAF. Recall that the EES codebook size is 64 bits, and so encryption of the LEAF involves at least two block encryptions. Since the IV affects only the checksum, and the checksum appears at the end of the LEAF in public documents, we can conclude that at least one of the following is true:
  — The LEAF is encrypted with a non-standard mode in which cleartext in "late" blocks affects the early ciphertext.
  — The LEAF is encrypted with a standard forward-chaining or stream mode but the checksum appears in the first cipherblock of the LEAF.
  — The LEAF is encrypted with a standard forward-chaining or stream mode but the current session IV is itself used to initialize it.
- The LEAF checksum is, in fact, 16 bits. A brute force search of the LEAF space for a valid LEAF requires about 2^{16} operations. See the discussion of interoperable rogue applications below.

NON-INTEROPERABLE ROGUE APPLICATIONS

First, we consider the problem of constructing a set of applications that use Skipjack to communicate among themselves without key escrow. We are free to use any method permitted by the EES processor interface without regard for standard usage. Since such applications may be restricted to communicating with other rogue systems, their general utility is somewhat limited, although they still violate the intent of the EES.

Several approaches can easily circumvent the law enforcement access mechanism, with a range of practicality and tradeoffs.

LEAF Obscuring

The simplest approach is to take steps to ensure that the eavesdropper cannot recover the LEAF or the encrypted traffic. One option is pre- or post- encryption of the traffic with another cipher. It is not clear, however, what the attacker gains from doing this, since if the second cipher is believed strong there is no need to use Skipjack in the first place, and if it is believed weak it does not protect the traffic from the government anyway.

A refinement on this approach encrypts only the LEAF. A LEAF encryption scheme could be integrated into a key exchange protocol that produces "extra" shared secret bits (such as Diffie-Hellman [DH76]). Since only 80 bits are required for the Skipjack session key, 128 of the other bits could be used as a Vernam cipher against the LEAF. Note that this scheme is not directly implementable with the EES PCMCIA card key exchange protocol, which does not permit external access to the negotiated key bits. However, an additional key exchange could be performed in software on the host processors.

Another option is to negotiate keys (and LEAFs) out-of-band or in advance. While it is not clear that there is any way EES could prevent such an attack, neither is such a scheme very useful in practical applications. Users would never be able to communicate securely without pre-negotiation or the use of a trusted channel. If a trusted channel existed, it could be just as easily used for the traffic itself. For some applications, however, such as bulk file encryption, pre-negotiated keys may be practical.

LEAF Feedback

Another possible approach is to avoid sending the LEAF altogether. Depending on the cryptographic mode this can be surprisingly simple. Recall that LEAFs are generated and loaded along with the IV. While applications cannot easily force the chip to use an externally-chosen

IV, they can easily generate a new one. Upon negotiation of a session key, the receiving side of a rogue application can simply generate a new IV/LEAF and feed it back to itself, the sender never having sent the IV/LEAF at all. This still leaves the problem of IV synchronization. Because IVs cannot be loaded without a LEAF and LEAF checksums appear to be bound to the IV, sender and receiver have no way to communicate a directly loadable IV without also communicating the corresponding LEAF. Most cryptographic modes require the sender and receiver to synchronize on the IV. This is not an insurmountable problem, however. It is possible to compose efficient implementations of each FIPS-81 cryptographic mode in terms of other modes without explicitly loading the sender's IV at the decrypting side. Let us consider "LEAF feedback" schemes for each commonly used cipher mode.

Electronic Code Book (ECB)

In ECB mode, there is no IV (or, more properly, the IV does not affect the cipher in any way). The primitive block cipher is used directly, without chaining or feedback from other blocks. LEAF feedback is therefore simple—each side generates an IV/LEAF immediately after the key is negotiated and loaded, and uses ECB mode for communication. The fact that sender and receiver generated different IVs does not matter. ECB mode is itself vulnerable to a number of well known attacks and is not considered suitable for general use.

Cipher Block Chaining (CBC)

In CBC mode encryption, the cleartext of each block is first exclusive-ORd (XOR) with the ciphertext of the previous block and then encrypted with the block cipher function. The first block is XORd against the IV. Decryption reverses the process, applying the XOR function after the ciphertext has been decrypted with the block cipher function. CBC mode is "selfsynchronizing" in that decryption can recover from missing or damaged ciphertext blocks. Since successful decryption of a block depends only on receiving the previous block's ciphertext, loss of the IV only affects the first block. LEAF feedback with a new IV, therefore, corrupts the first block but this can be easily compensated for by prefixing one "dummy" block to the message, to be discarded by the receiver.

Cipher Feed Back (CFB)

CFB mode uses the result of successive encryption through a shift register (initialized with the IV) as a keystream generator. The block encrypt function is used to generate the stream, which is XOR mixed with the datastream for both encryption and decryption. The shift register input is "fed" with the ciphertext stream from previous blocks. The stream depends entirely on the key and the previous blocks of ciphertext. CFB can be implemented based on ECB mode with an external shift register and IV. This requires one call to the EES device for each cipherblock. Experiments with this method with a prototype EES card suggest that this method carries a significant bandwidth penalty, however, since each ECB call to the card takes about 38ms and a separate call is required for each 8–64 bit block of the stream.

A more efficient implementation takes advantage of CFB's limited error propagation. CFB mode, like CBC mode, is self-synchronizing, with complete recovery from missing or damaged ciphertext once the shift register has exhausted. CFB can therefore recover from an incorrect IV. The sender can prefix a "dummy" block to the ciphertext input stream and the receiver can feed back a freshly generated, random IV and employ a bulk CFB block decrypt directly (just as with CBC mode).

Output Feed Back (OFB)

OFB mode also uses the result of successive encryption through a shift register (initialized with the IV) as a keystream generator. The block encryption function is used to generate both the encrypt and decrypt streams. Subsequent stream values are not affected by the data. Note that the entire stream depends on the key and IV and therefore requires that both sender and receiver be able to load the same IV to generate the same streams. LEAF feedback cannot therefore use OFB mode directly, since the stream will never recover from an incorrect IV. However, OFB mode can be simulated using the ECB block encrypt function and an externally implemented shift register and stream XOR mixer. The IV must still be sent to the receiver (without the LEAF, of course) to initialize the external shift register. This method carries a high performance penalty, just as with the manual implementation of CFB mode described above.

A more efficient method exists to generate an OFB stream, however, using Cipher Feed Back (CFB) mode to simulate the stream generator for large blocks. The sender generates an IV/LEAF and encrypts with OFB mode directly in the standard manner and sends only the IV to the receiver. Two passes are required on the receive side. First, the receiver generates a new IV and LEAF and encrypts a single block of all zeros with CFB mode. Now the receiver can recreate the sender's OFB keystream mask for n blocks by CFB encrypting n blocks of zeros prefixed with the block created in the previous step XORd with the real IV. The subsequent blocks, after CFB encryption, can be XORd with the ciphertext (shifted by one block) to recover the cleartext. Note that while the XOR mixing must be performed separately on the host processor, only two calls to the EES device are required to decrypt an arbitrary length ciphertext (up to the maximum block decrypt size supported by the devices).

INTEROPERABLE ROGUE APPLICATIONS

A more interesting (and useful) class of rogue applications includes those that can interoperate with "legal" peers (those that make no effort to circumvent the escrow system), still without allowing law enforcement access. Such applications have much greater utility (and are a much greater threat to the escrow system) than non-interoperable rogues, because they have all the benefits of interoperability with other EES devices without the risk of exposure to wiretapping.

In the previous section, we discussed techniques for rogue applications to communicate with one another without sending the LEAF. Such applications could be modified to adapt their behavior to send the LEAF only when communicating with a legal peer. A simple way to construct such an application is to "test the water" by sending the peer device a bogus LEAF and then, if the exchange fails (because the peer is operating legally), sending a valid LEAF. Such a "two phase" protocol is not completely satisfactory, however, because it still renders traffic vulnerable to LEAF monitoring when communicating with legal applications. Furthermore, such a protocol cannot work with non-interactive applications such as electronic mail, file encryption, fax, etc. A more general approach is to construct a LEAF field that will be accepted as valid by the receiver but that does not actually contain the encrypted session key.

Brute-Force LEAF Search

Recall that the LEAF structure contains three components: the unit serial number of the transmitter, the unit key-encrypted session key, and a 16 bit checksum, all encrypted as a block under the family key. Because the receiving chip knows only the session key, the IV, and the family key, but not the other chip's unit key or serial number, LEAF verification must be entirely on the basis of the 16 bit checksum. The checksum, which is presumably based only on the session key, IV and other LEAF data, cannot be extracted from or inserted into a LEAF without knowledge of the family key (and the encryption mode). It is therefore not possible for a rogue application to extract the checksum from a valid LEAF and re-insert into an invalid LEAF, or to damage only the encrypted session key in an otherwise-valid LEAF.

A rogue sender could simply use a different session key when generating the LEAF; this LEAF would appear internally consistent with a valid checksum but would contain the wrong session key. "Old" LEAFs are detected and rejected by the receiving chip, however, apparently by using the cleartext of the session key (rather than the unit-key encrypted session key) in the computation of the LEAF checksum.

Since the checksum is only 16 bits in length, however, another attack is possible.[2] For any session key and IV, 2^{112} of the 2^{128} possible LEAF structures will appear to have a valid checksum. Because the process of decrypting a randomly generated LEAF with the family key will tend to randomize the decrypted bits in the checksum field, any randomly generated 128 bit string will have a $1/2^{16}$ chance of appearing valid for the current session key and IV. Note that the sending chip, like the receiving chip, has a builtin LEAF-testing facility. Once a session key has been negotiated, an attacker can use the local EES device to find a valid-looking-but-invalid LEAF with an expected average of 2^{16} trials. This attack appears to be feasible in practice.

Such a randomly generated LEAF structure will be accepted as valid by the receiving chip and will enable EES communication. The traffic will not be subject to LEAF-based wiretap access, however. When the wiretapper decrypts the rogue LEAF with the family key, the checksum field will appear valid but the unit identifier and encrypted session key fields will contain only random bit strings.

Experimental Results

We measured the time to test randomly selected LEAFs on an EES PCMCIA card. All experiments were conducted with a Mykotronx prototype EES card connected through a Spyrus SCSI PCMCIA reader to a Sun Sparc-10 host running SunOS 4.1.3. We made no effort to optimize the communication with the card or library, using the standard prototype PCMCIA library and device drivers as delivered. Recall that the EES PCMCIA interface is fairly loosely-coupled to the host processor and supports a more restricted set of cryptographic operations than the basic Clipper/Capstone chips themselves. Therefore, LEAF testing operations on the PCMCIA card are inherently slower than the same operations on a more tightly coupled EES device or on a special-purpose host with a built-in EES processor. It is also possible that communication with the card can be made faster with the more tightly-coupled PCMCIA interfaces found on most laptop computers. The communication time with the card interface dominates the cost of most operations in the environment we examined; host processor speed was not a significant determining factor. We assume our results to be approximately representative of typical implementations in a worst-case environment.

Our test application required about 38ms to generate (with a pseudorandom generator) a LEAF-size bit string, send it through the

---

[2] The first observation that LEAF checksums may be vulnerable to brute-force spoofing appears have been independently made by Ken Shirriff in a posting to the "sci.crypt" Usenet group on January 27, 1994.

PCMCIA library to the EES card and check the result. Since, on average, 2^{16} random LEAFs must be generated and tested before one with a valid checksum is found, a rogue PCMCIA application can search for a valid-looking LEAF in $38 * 2^{16}$ ms, or 2,490,368 ms, which is about 42 minutes.

42 minutes obviously adds too much latency to channel setup time to be useful in real-time applications such as secure telephone calls. For less interactive applications, particularly secure electronic mail, fax and file storage systems, such a delay may be acceptable. Furthermore, the attack has almost linear speedup with parallel processing. With 60 PCMCIA cards, a valid-looking LEAF could be expected in under 45 seconds. Also, it may be reasonable to expect several orders of magnitude reduction in search time with more direct use of a Capstone or Clipper chip. Since those devices are not expected to be made available for unrestricted use outside embedded products (as the PCMCIA cards are), however, it is likely that practical implementations of this attack will be limited to applications that use the PCMCIA interface.

We implemented this attack for a simple encrypted file storage application that we built as a testbed. Other than the 30–50 minutes of latency added by the LEAF search at encryption time (which is performed "offline" from the user interface), the rogue version is functionally identical to the version that follows the approved interface. In a storage application the LEAF-search delay is almost completely transparent, since most user operation can proceed normally prior to its completion. In store-and-forward messaging applications, such as electronic mail, however, the LEAF search delays message delivery. Whether this is acceptable depends on the application; additional computing resources, in the form of EES PCMCIA cards (perhaps borrowed from nearby idle workstations) can reduce the delay. It may also be possible for messaging applications to precompute session keys and bogus LEAFs prior to their use, especially if the number of possible recipients is small. We did not implement any of these conveniences, however.

In interactive applications such as secure telephony, the search time required for LEAF forgery during call setup may render the technique impractical. Other than parallel processing with additional EES devices, there do not appear to be viable shortcuts for reducing this search time. If call setup uses a negotiated key exchange, the originator cannot generally predict the session key and therefore cannot conduct the LEAF search in advance. Neither do there appear to be shortcuts to testing an average of 2^{16} LEAF values. The formulation of the problem, in which the attacker need only discover *some* session key and corresponding LEAF, seems at first blush to admit a so-called "birthday attack" requiring only $\sqrt{2^{16}} = 2^8$ trials. However, because the LEAF checksum is cryptographically protected by the family key, there appears to be no obvious way to perform the constant-time lookup on the checksum required for each probe in such an attack.

Because no widely-deployed "official" EES PCMCIA applications existed at the time of this writing, there were no third-party supplied systems available against which we could exploit LEAF forgery techniques. We have every reason to believe, however, that building interoperable rogue versions of any noninteractive PCMCIA application that implements an open protocol would be a straightforward matter.

DISCUSSION

The EES failure modes described in this paper do not have the same semantic implications as protocol failures in the classic sense. None of the methods given here permit an attacker to discover the contents of encrypted traffic or compromise the integrity of signed messages. Nothing here affects the strength of the system from the point of view of the communicating parties; indeed, in some sense these techniques increase the security of EES-based protocols by eliminating the LEAF as a source of attack.

Instead, these methods attack an unusual aspect of EES requirements—the attempt to enforce access for a third party who is not an active participant in any part of EES-based communication. Once the system has been deployed, there is little further that the third party (the wiretapper) can do to protect its interests. In effect, the wiretapper actively participates in the protocol only by providing the narrow interface to the tamper-resistant EES module that requires that a LEAF be loaded prior to executing a decrypt operation. Our attacks thwart the wiretapper by using that interface in unexpected ways.

In considering countermeasures to these attacks, it is useful to divide the properties of the EES system into three somewhat overlapping categories:

- Fundamental. This category includes the properties of any key escrow system in a particular application domain (e.g., widely available components, FIPS-81 compatibility, identifiable LEAFs, etc.). These properties cannot be changed without affecting the applicability of the system.
- Architectural. The basic properties of the system decided upon early in the design process (e.g., the size of the LEAF field, the crypto-synchronization protocol, etc.). Changing the architecture requires re-engineering of a significant fraction of system components.
- Implementation. The characteristics of the actual EES devices and software. These can be changed by replacing or modifying the components in question.

In this paper we have focused primarily on weaknesses that are either fundamental or that arise from the EES architecture. In particular, we did not attempt to discover or exploit "bugs" in the prototype EES devices.

It is not clear that it is possible to construct an EES system that is both completely invulnerable to all kinds of exploitation as well as generally useful. Let us consider modifications to the EES interface that frustrate the various attacks.

Non-interoperable applications are particularly hard to prevent, since they are free to use the EES interface in any way they choose. LEAF feedback techniques can be discouraged by having devices recognize (and refuse to accept) locally-generated LEAFs. This would make the EES system difficult to deploy in legitimate secure storage applications, however, and such restrictions could be circumvented easily by using two devices on the receiving side, one for LEAF generation and one for decryption.

The interoperable LEAF-search method can be made less attractive by increasing the time required to check a LEAF. The ability to do this is limited by the fact that any reduction in LEAF-checking performance also degrades the performance of legal applications. EES PCMCIA cards, on which LEAFs can be feasibly searched for, already require approximately 38 ms to load an IV and LEAF. Slowing this to, say, two seconds, would noticeably increase the setup time for legitimate interactive traffic but only adds a factor of 50 to the time required by the offline rogue LEAF searcher (who could compensate with as much parallel processing as desired).

Alternatively, EES devices could limit the number of incorrect LEAFs they will accept (perhaps self-destructing after some threshold has been reached), or could impose a longer delay before returning the result of an attempt to load an invalid LEAF. These approaches are difficult to engineer reliably, however, and greatly increase the vulnerability of the system to denial-of-service attacks by an adversary who can inject noise into a receiver's datastream.

A more robust solution increases the size of the LEAF checksum to 32 or 64 bits, making exhaustive search infeasible. Since there is no "extra room" in the existing 128 bit LEAF package, any increase in checksum size would necessitate either increasing the LEAF size or reducing the size of the other LEAF fields. Increasing the size of the LEAF package to, say, 192 bits would provide room for an additional 64 bits of checksum redundancy but would would likely require significant re-engineering of many existing EES components, from the processors themselves to the protocols and applications that use them. Within the constraints of the 128 bit package, checksum size can increase only at the expense of either the unit ID or encrypted session key fields. The 32 bit unit ID field appears to be at the minimum possible size given the intended scope of the EES program (a previous version of the LEAF with a 25 bit unit ID was considered inadequate [NIST94a]). It may be possible to use bits from the encrypted session key field to increase the checksum size, at some expense in law enforcement wiretap access performance. If only 64 bits of the encrypted session key were included in the LEAF, the wiretapper could exhaustively search for the remaining 16 bits at decrypt time. Such a search, with properly optimized hardware, would likely add at most a few seconds to the decrypt time and would enable 32 bit LEAF checksums within the existing LEAF size constraints.

Finally, a more drastic approach, which thwarts non- interoperable as well as interoperable rogues, is to sharply restrict the availability of EES devices to those users and applications that are trusted not to abuse them. PCMCIA cards, being inherently portable, would need to be handled with particular care to avoid their use by unauthorized individuals. Of course, it is not at all clear that such restrictions could be made effective or consistent with the goals of the EES program, which aims to make the system widely available to the public.

CONCLUSIONS

The EES attempts to balance the seemingly conflicting goals of making widely available a strong cryptographic system while also ensuring government access to encrypted traffic. Rogue applications defeat EES by making use of the cipher without the government "back door." Whether rogues threaten the viability of the EES program depends on whether they can be easily deployed for a significant fraction of the traffic in their target application areas.

We have identified two classes of rogues. The most general, those that can take unilateral action to interoperate with legal EES systems, are potentially the most damaging to the EES program. These applications are functionally similar to their non-rogue counterparts and have all the advantages of general interoperability without the risk of wiretapping. The techniques used to implement them do carry enough of a performance penalty, however, to limit their usefulness in real-time voice telephony, which is perhaps the government's richest source of wiretap-based intelligence. The second class, those that can interoperate only with other rogue devices explicitly designed to thwart the LEAF, are also the easiest to implement and the hardest to prevent. Devices in this class are not as great a threat to the EES program as those in the former class because they do not conform to official interoperability standards. However, if the population of legal devices is substantially smaller than that of rogue devices in a particular market, lack of legal interoperability may not be a significant disadvantage.

It is worth noting that, with EES PCMCIA cards, a rogue system can be constructed with little more than a software modification to a legal system. Furthermore, while some expertise may be required to construct a rogue version of an existing system, it is likely that little or no special skill would be required to install and operate the modified software. In particular, one can imagine "patches" to defeat key escrow in EES-based systems being distributed over networks such as the Internet in much the same way that other software is distributed today. Experience with "pirate" cable TV descramblers, cellular telephone access codes, and copy-protected PC software suggests that rogue modifications to circumvent controls on widely-deployed systems tend to emerge quickly even when moderate safeguards against such modifications are present. EES PCMCIA-based systems appear to be particularly vulnerable to such abuse because the interface to the system is controlled completely in software on the user's host computer. The barriers to constructing a rogue software system are much smaller than those to modifying and deploying hardware-based rogue products, and the development and proliferation of software modifications is very difficult to regulate in the presence of open standards and communications networks.

ACKNOWLEDGMENTS

Steve Bellovin, Whitfield Diffie, Joan Feigenbaum, Peter Honeyman, Steve Kent, Jack Lacy, Tom London, Dave Maher, Andrew Odlyzko, Rob Pike, Jim Reeds, Mike Reiter and Bruce Schneier offered innumerable comments that have greatly improved this paper. The suggestion to use bits from the encrypted session key to augment the checksum size arose from discussions with Steve Bellovin. We would like to especially acknowledge the generous assistance of various individuals at NSA in providing us with prototype EES PCMCIA cards and technical data. We are particularly grateful for the spirit of openness and collegiality displayed by the members of NSA in reviewing these results.

The author remains, of course, solely responsible for any errors in this paper.

The name "Tessera" is a trademark of Tessera, Inc., which neither produced nor licensed the government supplied EES PCMCIA cards to which we refer in this paper. We know of no connection between Tessera, Inc. and the EES program. Previous references to EES PCMCIA cards as "Tessera cards" appear to have been made in error.

POSTSCRIPT

Some of the results in this paper are based on experiments conducted with pre-release prototype EES PCMCIA cards and software obtained from NSA. The production version of the EES PCMCIA system will likely exhibit different performance characteristics and have a different interface from the version we examined. The reader is cautioned to view any experimental results presented here as a "proof of concept" and not as representative of the exact performance of the final system. We understand that NSA intends to incorporate features to discourage these attacks into future versions of EES devices.

REFERENCES

[DH76]   W. Diffie and M. E. Hellman. New directions in cryptography. *IEEE Trans. on Information Theory*, November 1976.

[Mar93]   J. Markoff. Communications plan to balance government access with privacy. *New York Times*, April 16, 1993.

[NBS77]   National Bureau of Standards. Data Encryption Standard, *Federal Information Processing Standards Publication 46*, Government Printing Office, Washington, D. C., 1977.

[NBS80]   National Bureau of Standards. Data Encryption Standard Modes of Operation, *Federal Information Processing Standards Publication 81*, Government Printing Office, Washington, D.C., 1980.

[NIST94]   National Institute for Standards and Technology. Escrowed Encryption Standard, *Federal Information Processing Standards Publication 185*, U.S. Dept. of Commerce, 1994.

[NIST94a]   National Institute for Standards and Technology. *Technical Fact Sheet on Blaze Report and Key Escrow Encryption*. June 15, 1994.

CAPSTONE Chip Technology*

National Institute of Standards and Technology

CAPSTONE is an NSA developed, hardware oriented, cryptographic device that implements the same cryptographic algorithm as the CLIPPER chip. In addition, the CAPSTONE chip includes the following functions:

1. The Digital Signature Algorithm (DSA) proposed by NIST as a Federal Information Processing Standard (FIPS);
2. The Secure Hashing Algorithm (SHA) recently approved as FIPS 180;
3. A Key Exchange Algorithm based on a public key exchange;
4. A general purpose exponentiation algorithm;
5. A general purpose, random number generator which uses a pure noise source.

The Key exchange Algorithm is programmable on the chip and uses functions 1–2 and 4–5 above. Prototypes of the CAPSTONE chip are due the last week in April. The chips are expected to sell for $85.00 each (programmed). The first CAPSTONE chips are to be installed in PCMCIA electronic boards and used for the PMSP program for the security of the Defense Messaging System.

The CAPSTONE chip is big, complex and powerful. Over 850 megabytes are required by the automated design system to define the functions of the chip. VLSI Technology is fabricating the chip, and MYKOTRONX is designing and testing the chip.

1. What are the power requirements of the CAPSTONE chip? Will they fit the power requirements of battery-operated, hand held devices? *The CAPSTONE chip requires a 5 volt DC voltage source. Power ratings are currently estimated at 3.5 milliamps per MHz, i.e. at 10 Mhz and 5 volts DC, power consumed is 175 milliwatts. These estimates will be refined as data are taken into the actual chips. In comparison, the CLIPPER chip consumes approximately 150 milliwatts at 5 volts DC and 10 MHz. As you can see, both chips fall within the power requirements of hand held, battery-operated devices.*

---

* April 30, 1993. National Institute of Standards and Technology.

2. Will the CAPSTONE chip incorporate the key escrow features of the CLIPPER chip? *Yes, it will.*

3. When will CAPSTONE be announced and available? *Prototypes of the CAPSTONE chip are due the end of this month. We ask that you contact the manufacturer, Mykotronx Inc., for further information concerning the timetable for availability of CAPSTONE.*

4. Is the Department of Defense working now to incorporate CAP-STONE in the Pre-message Security Protocol? *Yes.*

5. Will CAPSTONE meet the design requirements of a PCMCIA card that combines voice and/or data communications with encryption capabilities? *Yes.*

6. Will CAPSTONE use the Digital Signature Standard? What kind of key management scheme will be employed in the CAPSTONE chip? Will CAPSTONE allow the use of RSA public-key encryption in conjunction with, or as an alternative to, the DSS? If RSA is implemented on the CAPSTONE chip, will the key escrow feature function? *CAPSTONE implements the Digital Signature Algorithm (DSA), proposed by NIST as a Federal Information Processing Standard (FIPS), to perform the digital signature functions. Key management is handled by an algorithm based on a public-key exchange technique. The CAPSTONE chip does not implement RSA.*

5

Fair Cryptosystems*

Silvio Micali

FAIR PUBLIC-KEY CRYPTOSYSTEMS

The Basic Notion

Informally speaking, and ignoring for the time-being some additional and important issues (see "Additional Important Issues"), we say that

> The goal of a Fair Public-Key Cryptosystem—Fair PKC for short—S is to guarantee a special agreed-upon party (and solely this party!) under the proper circumstances envisaged by the law (and solely under these circumstances!) to understand all messages encrypted using S, even without the users' consent and/or knowledge.

That is, the philosophy behind a Fair PKC is improving the security of the existing communication systems while keeping the legal procedures already holding and accepted by the society. In particular, we wish to design Fair PKCs so that the following proposition holds.

Proposition: Let C be a ciphertext exchanged by two users in a Fair PKC S. Then, under the proper circumstances envisaged by the law, the proper third party will either

1) find the *cleartext* of C relative to S (whenever C was obtained by encrypting a message according to S) or
2) obtain a (court-presentable) *proof* that the two users were not using S for their secret communication.

Of course, if using any other type of public-key cryptosystem were to be made *illegal*, Fair PKCs would be most effective in guaranteeing both private communication to law-obeying citizens and law enforcement. (In fact, if a criminal uses a phone utilizing a Fair PKC to plan a crime, he can still be brought to justice by court-authorized line tapping. If he, instead, illegally uses another cryptosystem, the content of his con-

* Extracted from "Fair Cryptosystems"; Laboratory for Computer Science, Massachusetts Institute of Technology, Cambridge, Mass.; MIT/LCS/TR-579.b; November 1993. An improved version of the paper is in preparation. Please contact author (by regular mail) to receive a copy.

versations will never be revealed even after a court authorization for tapping his lines, but, at least, he will be convicted for something else: his use of an unlawful cryptosystem.) Nonetheless, Fair PKCs are quite useful even without such a law.

A General Construction

We shall now present, in a very *general* way, our preferred method for constructing Fair PKCs. We shall see in "Making Fair the Diffie-Hellman Scheme" that this very general construction can be implemented in practice very efficiently for the best known PKCs.

Below, for concreteness of presentation, we shall use the *Government* for the special agreed-upon party, a *court order* for the circumstances contemplated by the law for monitoring a user's messages, and the *telephone system* for the underlying method of communication. We also assume the existence of a key-distribution center as in an ordinary PKC.

In a Fair PKC there are a fixed number of predesignated *trustees* and an arbitrary number of users. The trustees may be federal judges (as well as different entities, such as the Government, Congress, the Judiciary, a civil rights group, etc.) or computers controlled by them and especially set up for this purpose. Even if efforts have been made to choose *trustworthy* trustees, a Fair PKC does not blindly rely on their being honest. The trustees, together with the individual users and the key-distribution center, play a crucial role in deciding which encryption keys will be publicized in the system. Here is how.

Also for concreteness of exposition, assume that there are 5 trustees. Each user independently chooses his own public and private keys according to a given double-key system. Since the user himself has chosen both keys, he can be sure of their "quality" and of the privacy of his decryption key. He then breaks his private decryption key into five *special* "pieces" (i.e., he computes from his secret decryption key 5 special strings/numbers) possessing the following properties:

1) The private key can be reconstructed given knowledge of all five special pieces;
2) The private key cannot be reconstructed if one only knows (any) 4, or less, special pieces;
3) For $i = 1, \ldots ,5$, the i-th special piece can be *individually* verified to be *correct*.

Comment. Of course, given all 5 special pieces, one can verify that they are correct by checking that they indeed yield the private decryption key. The difficulty and power of property 3 consists of the fact that each special piece can be verified to be correct (i.e., that together with the other 4 special pieces yields the private key) individually; that is, without knowing the secret key at all, and without knowing the value of any of the other special pieces! (How these special pieces can be generated is explained in later sections. Below we will show how they can be used.)

The user then privately (e.g., in encrypted form) gives trustee i his own public key and the i-th piece of its associated private key. Each trustee individually inspects his received piece, and, if it is correct, *approves* the public key (e.g., signs it) and safely *stores* the piece relative to it. These approvals are given to the key-management center, either directly by the trustees, or (possibly in a single message) by the individual user who collects them from the trustees. The center, which may or may not coincide with the Government, itself approves (e.g., it itself signs) any public key *approved by all trustees*. These center-approved keys are the public keys of the Fair PKC and they are distributed and used for private communication as in an ordinary PKC.

Since the special pieces of each decryption key are privately given to the trustees, an adversary who taps a user's communication line possesses the same information as in the underlying, ordinary PKC. Thus if this is secure, so is the Fair PKC. Moreover, even if the adversary were one of the trustees himself, or even a cooperating collection of any 4 out of five of the trustees, due to property 2, he would still have the same information as in the underlying ordinary PKC. Since the possibility that an adversary corrupts 5 out of 5 federal judges is remote, the security of the resulting Fair PKC is the same as in the underlying, ordinary one.

When presented with a court order, and only in this case, the trustees will reveal to the Government the pieces of a given decryption key in their possession. This enables the Government to reconstruct the given key. Recall that, by property 3, each trustee has already verified that he was given a correct piece of the decryption key in question. Thus, the Government is *guaranteed* that, *in case of a court order*, it will be given all correct pieces of any given decryption key. By property 1, it follows that the Government will be able to reconstruct any given decryption key if necessary.

Additional Important Issues

We consider the notion of a Fair PKC given so far to be pretty basic because it does not address some additional important issues. In particular, consider the following desiderata.

Time Bounded Court-Authorized Line-Tapping
In general, courts authorize line-tappings for a prescribed amount of time only. But, in our abstract construction, once the Trustees reveal their pieces of the secret key of party X to the Government, the Gov-

ernment's ability to understand X's communications is "turned on" forever. If we wish, as we do, to improve on the *status quo* but keep our legal procedures, a mechanism must be found to "turn off" this ability at the prescribed time. By contrast, unfortunately, this important issue is totally ignored by the key-escrow proposal of the Administration.

Relying on Fewer Shares

Another important issue is the ability to rely on fewer shares in order to be able to reconstruct a secret key. So far, in fact, we have been assuming a "all-or-nothing" approach; that is, a secret key can be reconstructed given all of its special pieces, and cannot be guessed at all given all of its pieces except one. This assumes that our Trustee system will always work *perfectly*. Indeed, if a single Trustee, presented with a legitimate court order, does not contribute his own piece of X's secret key—either because he has lost it, or because the computer storing it has failed, or because of sabotage, or because he has been corrupted,—then it will totally impossible for the Government to tap X's lines. This is a serious problem: any system that assumes too much reliability from people or their computers is *insecure*. Unfortunately, this problem too is ignored by the key-escrow proposal of the Administration. However, it is possible for Fair cryptosystems to have two different thresholds α and β, $\alpha < \beta$ such that the secret key is totally unpredictable from any α or less pieces, but easily reconstructible from any β or more pieces. (Though one might always prefer setting $\beta = \alpha + 1$, in practice as we shall see in the appendix, having b<a may yield simpler algorithms for dealing with fewer shares.)

• • •

MAKING FAIR THE DIFFIE-HELLMAN SCHEME

Let us now explicit]y exhibit a Fair PKC; actually, let us show how to make Fair the popular Diffie-Hellman PKC. Though this section requires some knowledge of number theory, it illustrates that Fair PKCs can be efficient and algorithmically simple.

Recall that, a bit differently than in other systems, in Diffie-Hellman's scheme each pair of users X and Y succeeds, without any interaction, in agreeing upon a common, secret key S_{xy} to be used as a conventional single-key cryptosystem. Here is how.

The Ordinary Diffie-Hellman PKC

There are a *prime p* and a *generator* (or high-order element) *g* common to all users. User X *secretly* selects a random integer *Sx* (for "secret") in the interval *[1,p-1]* as his private key and publicly announces the integer *Px = g^{Sx} mod p* as his public key. Another user, Y, will similarly select Sy as his private key and announce $Py = g^{Sy} \bmod p$ as his public key. The value of their common and secret key is determined as $Sxy = g^{Sx \cdot Sy} \bmod p$. User X computes Sxy by raising Y's public key to his secret key mod p; user Y by raising X's public key to his secret key mod p. In fact

$$(g^{Sx})^{Sy} = g^{Sx \cdot Sy} = Sxy = g^{Sy \cdot Sx} = (g^{Sy})^{Sx} = \bmod p.$$

Notice that knowledge of a public key does not easily yield knowledge of its corresponding secret key. In fact, while it is easy, given g, p, and a, to compute $b = g^a \bmod p$, no efficient algorithm is known for computing, given b and p, the a such that $g^a = b \bmod p$ when g has high enough order. This is, in fact, the famous *discrete logarithm problem*. This problem has been used as the basis of security in many cryptosystems, and in the recently proposed U.S. standard for digital signatures. Our goal, however, is not to establish the security of the Diffie-Hellman scheme; it is proving that it can be transformed into a fair one. Again, to keep things as simple as possible we imagine that there are 5 trustees and that ALL of them should cooperate to reconstruct a secret key, that is, that ALL shares are needed to reconstruct a secret key. Relaxing this condition involves another idea and will be dealt with in section 5.

A Fair Diffie-Hellman Scheme
(All-Shares Case)

Instructions for the users

Each user X randomly chooses 5 integers $Sx1, \ldots, Sx5$ in the interval $[1, p-1]$ and lets Sx be their sum $\bmod\ p-1$. From here on, it will be understood that all operations are modulo p. He then computes the numbers

$$t1 = g^{Sx1}, \ldots, t5 = g^{Sx5} \text{ and } Px = g^{Sx}.$$

Px will be user X's public key and Sx his private key. The ti's will be referred to as the *public pieces* of Px, and the Sxi's as its *private pieces*. Notice that the product of the public pieces equals the public key Px. In fact,

$$t1 \cdot \ldots \cdot t5 = g^{Sx1} \cdot \ldots \cdot g^{Sx5} = g^{(Sx1 + \ldots + Sx5)} = g^{Sx}.$$

Let $T1, \ldots, T5$ be the five trustees. User X now gives Px and pieces $t1$ and $Sx1$ to trustee $T1$, $t2$ and $Sx2$ to $T2$, and so on. It is important that piece Sxi be privately given to trustee T_i.

Instructions for the trustees

Upon receiving public and private pieces ti and Sxi, trustee Ti verifies whether $g^{Sxi} = ti$. If so, it stores the pair (Px, Sxi), signs the pair (Px, ti), and gives the signed pair to the key-management center. (Or to user X, who will then give all of the signed public pieces at once to the key-management center.)

Instructions for the key-management center
Upon receiving all the signed public pieces, *t1* . . . *t5*, relative to a given public key *Px*, the center verifies that the product of the public pieces indeed equals *Px*. If so, it approves *Px* as a public key, and distributes it as in the original scheme (e.g., signs it and gives it to user X.)

This ends the instructions relative to the keys of the Fair PKC. The encryption and decryption instructions for any pair of users X and Y are exactly as in the Diffie and Hellman scheme (i.e., with common, secret key *Sxy*). It should be noticed that, like the ordinary Diffie-Hellman, the Fair Diffie-Hellman scheme does not require any special hardware and is actually easy to implement in software.

Why Does This Work?

First, the privacy of communication offered by the system is the same as in the Diffie and Hellman scheme. In fact, the validation of a public key *does not compromise at all* the corresponding private key. Each trustee Ti receives, as a special piece, the discrete logarithm, *Sxi*, of a *random number, ti*. This information is clearly irrelevant for computing the discrete logarithm of *Px*! The same is actually true for any 4 of the trustees taken together, since any four special pieces are independent of the private decryption key *Sx*. Also the key-management center does not possess any information relevant to the private key; that is, the discrete logarithm of *Px*. All it has are the public pieces signed by the trustees. (The public pieces simply are 5 random numbers whose product is *Px*. This type of information is irrelevant for computing the discrete logarithm of *Px*; in fact, anyone could choose four integers at random and set the fifth to be *Px* divided by the product of the first four[1]. As for a trustee's signature, this just represents the promise that *someone else* has a secret piece. As a matter of fact, even the information in the hands of the center together with any four of the trustees is irrelevant for computing the private key *Sx*.) Thus, not only is the user guaranteed that the validation procedure will not betray his private key, but he also knows that this procedure has been properly followed because he himself has computed his own keys and the pieces of his private one!

Second, if the key-management center validates the public key *Px*, then the corresponding private key is guaranteed to be reconstructible

---

[1] The result would be integral because division is modulo p.

by the Government in case of a court order. In fact, the center receives all 5 public pieces of Px, each signed by the proper trustee. These signatures testify that trustee Ti possesses the discrete logarithm of public piece ti. Since the center verifies that the product of the public pieces equals Px, it also knows that the sum of the secret pieces in storage with the trustees equals the discrete logarithm of Px; that is, user X's private key. Thus the center knows that, if a court order is issued requesting the private key of X, by summing the values received by the trustees, *the Government is guaranteed* to obtain the needed private key.

Making Fair Other PKCs

The reader who wishes to see how any PKC can be made Fair can read "How to Make Fair Any PKC" of our technical appendix. Like for all general transformations, also this one will be quite inefficient. On the other hand, "Making Fair the RSA Scheme" shows that another specific PKC, the popular RSA scheme, can be made Fair in a reasonably efficient manner. This transformation, however, requires much more knowledge of number theory, and does not possess the algorithmic simplicity of our Fair Diffie-Hellman scheme. In particular, we wish to point out that the Diffie-Hellman PKC is very convenient from a law-enforcement point of view in that, if one reconstructs the secret key of a user, he will be able to decrypt both the outgoing and the incoming encrypted messages relative to that user. By contrast, in schemes such the RSA, only the incoming message traffic becomes intelligible once a secret key becomes known. This drawback (from the law-enforcement point of view) can be removed by adding some special hand-shake protocols to the original schemes.

VARIANTS OF THE BASIC NOTION OF A FAIR PKC

As we have said, several variants of the notion of a Fair PKC are both possible and desirable. Three such variants are presented below in sufficient detail, while others are only briefly mentioned.

Time-Bounded Court-Authorized Eavesdropping

As mentioned in "Additional Important Issues," we now wish to prevent that, having received a court authorization to monitor the communications of a given user for a given interval of time, the agent doing this monitoring (say, the Police) may exceed its mandate and keep on tapping the suspected user's lines for a longer period of time. We discuss various strategies to accomplish this goal.

Multiple Public-Keys

A very simple way to ensure time-bounded court-authorized line tapping consists of having each user choose a sufficient amount of matching public and secret keys, say one per month. Each public key will then be publicized specifying the month to which it refers. Someone who wants to send user X a private message in March, will then encrypt it with X's public March key. If this level of granularity is acceptable, the court may then ask the trustees to reveal X's secret keys for a prescribed set of months.

The disadvantage of this approach is that it requires a rather large "total public key," and it may be totally impractical if a fine granularity is desired.

Tamper-Proof Chips

Simple and effective methods to ensure time-bounded court-authorized eavesdropping are possible by means of secure chips; these are special chips whose content cannot be "read from the outside," or tampered with in any way without destroying the entire chip with all its protected information. (Such chips are central to the Clipper Chip proposal.)

One such method is the following. Assume that, to monitor the communications of suspected users in response to a court order, the Police use secure chips—call them the *Polchips*—possessing an internal and thus untamperable clock as follows. Let there be a court order to tap user X's line from February to April. Then, each trustee will send the Polchip a digitally signed message consisting of his own share of user X's private key (encrypted so that only the Polchip will understand it). The Polchip can now easily compute X's secret key. Thus, if the Court sends to the Polchip a signed message consisting of, say, "decode, X, February-April", since the Polchip has an internal clock (or some other untamperable way to accurately keep track of time), it can easily decrypt all messages relative to X for the prescribed time period. Then, it will destroy X's secret key, and, in order to allow further line tapping, a new court order will be required.

A main advantage of this approach is its simplicity; it does, however, require some additional amount of trust. In fact, the citizens cannot check, but must believe, that each Polchip is manufactured so as to work as specified above.

Algorithmically-Chosen Session Keys

In the multiple public-key method described above, each user selected and properly shared with the Trustees a number of secret keys of a PKC equal to the number of possible transmission "dates" (in the above example, each possible month). Within each specified date, the same public-secret key pair was used for directly encrypting and decrypting any message sent or received by any user. Time-bounded Fair PKCs, however, can be more efficiently achieved by using public keys only to encrypt session keys, and session keys to encrypt real messages (by means of a conventional single-key system). This is, in fact, the most common and efficient way to proceed.

Session keys are usually unique to each pair of users and date of transmission. Indeed, if each minute or second is considered a different date, there may be a different session key for every transmission between two users. In fact, the date may just be any progressive number identifying the transmission, but not necessarily related to physical time.

To achieve time-bounded court-authorized line tapping, we suggest to choose session keys *algorithmically* (so that the Trustees can compute each desired session key from information received when users enter the system), but *unpredictably* (so that, though some session keys may become known—e.g., because of a given court order—the other session keys remain unknown).

The particular mechanics to exploit this approach is quite important, because not all schemes based on algorithmically selected session keys yield equally convenient time-bounded Fair PKCs.[2] An effective method is described in the technical appendix.

Relying on Fewer Shares

As mentioned above, we wish to prevent that, should a single piece of a secret key be missing, a court-authorized line tapping becomes impossible. Better said, we wish that the malicious collaboration of fewer than a prescribed number of Trustees should not enable anyone to compute even a single secret decryption key, while the honest collaboration of more than a given number (possibly different from the previous one) of Trustees should enable one to easily reconstruct a secret key.

To achieve these goals, the solution we present below increases a bit the original number of Trustees (in our case, from 5 to 15), but has the great advantage of being both conceptually and algorithmically very simple. Solutions that do not increase the number of Trustees are discussed in "Additional Methods for Relying on Fewer Shares" of our technical appendix.

---

[2] For instance, a time-bounded FAIR PKC that required the Police to contact the Trustees specifying the triplet (X,Y,D) in order to understand X's communication to Y at time D (belonging to the court-authorized time interval), might be deemed impractical. A better scheme may allow the Police to contact the Trustees only once, specifying only X, Y, and D1 and D2, in order to understand all the communications between X and Y at any date D in the time interval (D1,D2). Since, however, there may be quite many users Y to which the suspected user X talks to, also this scheme may be considered impractical.

The Share Replication Method

In this solution, each of the 5 trustees is replaced by a group of new trustees. For instance, instead of a single trustee T_1, there may be 3 trustees, $T_1^1 \ T_2^1 \ T_3^1$; each of these trustees will receive and check the same share of trustee T_1. Thus, it is going to be very unlikely that all 3 trustees will refuse to surrender their copy of the first share. This scheme is a bit "trustee-wasteful" since it requires 15 trustees while it is enough that an adversary corrupts 5 of them to defeat the scheme. (However, one should appreciate that defeating the share-replication scheme is not as easy as corrupting any 5 trustees out of 15, since it must be true that a trustee is corrupted in each group.) The scheme has, nonetheless, two strong advantages: (1) *Scalability*: denoting by n the number of trustee groups, the computational effort of the scheme grows polynomially in n, no matter what the group size is, and thus— if desired—one can choose a large value for n; (2) *Repetitiveness*: if there are n trustee groups of size k each, one should only perform n "operations," in fact, each member of a trustee group gets a "xerox copy" of the same computation.

In the final paper we shall demonstrate that both methods can be optimized, but here let us instead move on to consider a far more important problem than efficiency.

Making Trustees Oblivious

There is another issue worth discussing. Namely, a trustee requested by a court order to surrender his share of a given secret key may alert the owner of that key that his communications are going to be monitored.

A technical solution to this problem is presented in the appendix. (The idea consists of having each Trustee give the shares in his possession to the trusted center from the very beginning, but encrypted. In case of a court order, however, the center has a way of obtaining from the Trustee the decryption of the share of the suspected user without revealing to him which this share is—and thus hiding the identity of the user.)

It should, however, be realized that, while solving a potential problem, this technique may introduce new and different problems. For instance, if the Trustees do not know which user's shares they are revealing, they cannot have a serious chance to consider the evidence against that user, which, presumably, contains the user's name. Thus, the danger exists that the obliviousness of the Trustees may allow one to obtain illegally the secret key of users against which no legitimate court order has been issued.

• • •

FINAL REMARKS

Clipper Chip prevents that a diligently-designed encryption algorithm may fall in the wrong hands, and thus its wide adoption cannot directly harm national security. It may, however, harm both national security and law enforcement indirectly, by causing an unregulated public-key cryptosystem to handle the distribution of secret keys. Indeed, if the Government wants to control crime, the key-distribution infrastructure should be properly regulated. Fair PKCs may provide a technical and democratic way to regulate key distribution, but first Society must agree on the need of such a regulation. Assuming this to be the case, many other political questions await for answers: Who should the Trustees be? How many should they be? For how long should line-tapping be authorized? Answering these questions well will require a debate as public, wide, and informed as possible.

REFERENCES

[AwChGoMi]   B. Awerbuch, B. Chor, S. Goldwasser and S. Micali. Verifiable Secret Sharing and Achieving Simultaneity in the Presence of Faults. In *Proceedings of the 26th Annual IEEE Symposium of Foundations of Computer Science*. IEEE, New York, 1986, pp. 383–395.

[Be]   J. Benaloh. Secret Sharing Homomorphisms: Keeping Shares of a Secret Secret. Advances in Cryptology—Proceedings of Crypto '86. Springer Verlag, 1986.

[BeGoWi]   M. Ben-Or, S. Goldwasser, and A. Wigderson. Completeness Theorems for Fault-Tolerant Distributed Computing. In *Proceedings of the 20th ACM Symposium of Theory of Computing*. ACM, New York, 1988, pp. 1–10.

[Bl]   G. Blakley. Safeguarding Cryptographic Keys. In *AFIPS—Conference Proceedings*. NCC, New Jersey, 1979, Vol. 48 (June), pp. 313–317.

[BlMi]   M. Blum and S. Micali. How to Generate Cryptographically Strong Sequences of Pseudo-Random Bits. *Siam Journal on Computing*, 1984, vol. 13 (November), pp. 850–863. Proceeding Version: FOCS 1982

[ChCrDa]   D. Chaum, C. Crepeau, and I. Damgard. Multi-party Unconditionally Secure Protocols. In *Proceedings of the 20th ACM Symposium of Theory of Computing*. ACM, New York, 1988, pp. 11–19.

[De]   D. Denning. To Tap or Not To Tap. In *Comm. of the ACM*. March 1993, Vol. 36, No. 3, pp. 25–44.

[DiHe]   W. Diffie and M. Hellman. New Directions in Cryptography. *IEEE Trans. Inform. Theory*. IT-22, 6 (Nov. 1976), IEEE, New York, pp. 644–654.

[Fe87]   P. Feldman. A Practical Scheme for Non-Interactive verifiable Secret Sharing. In *Proceedings of the 28th Annual IEEE Symposium of Foundations of Computer Science*. IEEE, New York, 1987, pp. 427–438.

[GoMi]   S. Goldwasser and S. Micali. Probabilistic Encryption. *Journal of Computer Systems Science*. Academic Press, New York, Vol. 28 No. 2 (1984), pp. 270–299.

[GMW1]   O. Goldreich, S. Micali, and A. Wigderson. Proofs that yield Nothing but their Validity and a Methodology of Cryptographic Protocol Design. In *Proceedings of the 27th Annual IEEE Symposium of Foundations of Computer Science*, IEEE, New York, 1986, pp. 174–187.

[GMW2]   O. Goldreich, S. Micali, and A. Wigderson. How To Play ANY Mental Game or A Completeness Theorem for Protocols with Honest Majority. In *Proceedings of the 19th Annual ACM Symposium of Theory of Computing*. ACM, New York, 1987, pp. 218–229.

[LM]   T. Leighton and S. Micali. Secret-Key Distribution without public-key cryptography. Presented at *Crypto 93*, Santa Barbara, CA, August 1993. Improved manuscript available from authors.

[RaBe]   T. Rabin and M. Ben-Or. Verifiable Secret Sharing and Multiparty Protocols with Honest Majority. In *Proceedings of the 21st ACM Symposium of Theory of Computing*. ACM, New York, 1989, pp. 73–85.

[RSA]   R. Rivest, A. Shamir, and L. Adleman. A Method for Obtaining Digital Signatures and Public-Key Cryptosystems. Comm. ACM 21, 2 (Feb. 1978), pp. 120–126.

[Sh]   A. Shamir. How to Share a Secret. *Communications of the ACM*. ACM, New York, 1979, Vol. 22, No. 11 (Nov.), pp. 612–613.

Technical Appendix

How to Make Fair Any PKC

In this section we want to show how to implement concretely the general (but quite abstract) construction of page 150. Like for all things general, also this transformation is not too efficient.

Disregarding efficiency considerations, this section is devoted to the reader who, being superficially aware of concepts like "secret sharing" or "zero-knowledge," wishes to clarify what is their relationship with Fair PKCs. The reader who has never dealt with the above mentioned concepts may prefer to skip this section entirely; as for the expert in secure protocol theory, she may read just the following sketch.

A Sketch for the Expert

Cutting corners, each user should (1) come up with a pair of matching public and private keys and give the trustees his chosen public key, (2) encrypt (by a different cryptosystem, even one based on a one-way function) his chosen private key, (3) give the trustees the just computed ciphertext and a zero-knowledge proof that the corresponding "decryption" really consists of the private key corresponding to the given public key, and (4) give the trustees shares of this decryption by means of a Verifiable Secret Sharing protocol that has the property of guaranteeing that the shared secret really is what was encrypted in Step 2.

A More Informative Discussion

In expanding the above sketch for the non-expert in protocol design, we feel it is important to illustrate both similarities and differences between Fair PKCs and other related prior notions.

Secret Sharing

As independently put forward by Shamir [Sh] and Blakley [Bl], secret sharing (with parameters n,T,t) is a cryptographic scheme consisting of two phases: in phase 1, a secret value chosen by a distinguished person, the *dealer*, is put in "safe storage" with n people or computers, the *trustees*, by giving each one of them a piece of information, a *share*, of the secret value. In phase 2, when the trustees pool together the information in their possession, the secret is recovered. In a secret sharing, this storage is safe only in two senses:

1. *Redundancy*. Not all trustees need to reveal their shares in phase 2: it is enough that T of them do. (Thus the system tolerates that some of the trustees "die" or accidentally destroy the shares in their possession)
2. *Privacy*. If less than t of the trustees accidentally or even intentionally divulge the information in their possession to each other or to an outside party, the secret remains unpredictable until phase 2 occurs.

However, secret sharing suffers of a main problem: *Assumed honesty*; namely,

Secret sharing presupposes that the dealer gives the trustees correct "shares" (pieces of information) about his secret value. This is so because each trustee cannot verify that he has received a meaningful share of anything. A dishonest dealer may thus give "junk" shares in phase 1, so that, when in phase 2 the trustees pool together the shares in their possession, there is no secret to be reconstructed.

Example (Shamir). The following is a secret sharing scheme with parameters $n = 2t + 1$ and $T = t + 1$.

Let p be a prime $>n$, and let S belong to the interval $[0, p-1]$. Choose a polynomial $P(x)$ of degree t by choosing at random each of its coefficients in $[0, p-1]$, except for the last one which is taken to be equal to S, that is, $P(0) = S$. Then the n shares are so computed: $S1 = P(1), \ldots, Sn = P(n)$. *Redundancy* holds since the polynomial $P(x)$ can be interpolated from its value at any $t + 1$ distinct points. (This, in turn, allows the computation of $P(0)$ and thus of the secret.) *Privacy* holds since $P(0)$ is totally undetermined by the value of P at any t distinct points $X1 \ldots Xt$ different from 0 (in fact, any value v for $P(0)$, together with the value of P at points $X1 \ldots Xt$ uniquely determines a polynomial).

As it can be easily seen, if the dealer is dishonest, he may give each trustee a random number mod p. If this is the case, then (a) each trustee cannot tell that he has a junk share, and (b) in phase 2 there will be no secret to reconstruct. The consequence of this is that secret sharing is more useful in those occasions in which the dealer is certainly honest, for instance, because being honest is *in his own interest*. (A user that encrypts his own files with a secret key has a big interest in properly secret sharing his key with, say, a group of colleagues: if he accidentally loses it, he needs to reconstruct it!) Secret sharing alone, instead, cannot be too useful for building Fair Cryptosystems: we cannot expect that a criminal give proper shares of his secret key to some federal judges when the only purpose of his doing this is allowing the authorities, under a court order, to understand his communications!

Verifiable Secret Sharing

A closer connection exists between Fair PKCs and verifiable secret sharing (VSS) protocols. While the two concepts are not identical, a special type of VSS can be used to build Fair PKCs. As put forward by Awerbuch, Chor, Goldwasser, and Micali [CGMA], a verifiable secret sharing (VSS) scheme is a scheme that, while guaranteeing both the redundancy and the privacy property, overcomes the "honesty problem." In fact, in a VSS scheme each trustee can verify that the share given to him is genuine *without knowing at all the shares of other trustees or the secret itself*. That is, he can verify that, if T verified shares are revealed in phase 2, the original secret will be reconstructed, no matter what the dealer or dishonest trustees might do.

Example (Goldreich, Micali, and Wigderson [GMW1])

> Assume that a PKC is in place and let Ei be the public encryption function of trustee i. Then, as in Shamir's scheme, the dealer selects a random polynomial P of degree t such that P(0) = the secret, and gives each trustee the n-vector of encryptions E1(P(1)) E2(P(2)) ... En(P(n)). Trustee i will therefore properly decode P(i), but has no idea about the value of the other shares, and, consequently, whether these shares "define" a unique t-degree polynomial passing through them. The dealer thus proves to each trustee that the following sentence is true *"if you were so lucky to guess all decryption keys, you could easily verify that there exists a unique t-degree polynomial interpolating the encrypted shares."* Since easily verifying something after a lucky guess corresponds to NP, the above is an "NP sentence." Since, further, the authors show that whole of NP is in zero-knowledge, the dealer proves the correctness of the sentence, in zero knowledge, to every trustee. This guarantees each trustee that he has a legitimate share of the secret, since he has a legitimate share of P, but does not enable him (or him and any other t-1 trustees) to guess what the secret is before phase 2.

VSS and Fair PKC's

Assume that each user chooses a secret/public key pair, and then VSS shares his secret key with some federal judges. Does this constitute a Fair PKC? Not necessarily. In a VSS scheme, in fact, the secret may be *unstructured*. That each trustee can only verify that he got a genuine share of some secret value, but this value can be "anything." For instance, if the dealer promises that his secret value is a prime number, in an unstructured VSS a trustee can verify that he got a genuine share of some number, but has no assurances that this number is prime.

Unstructured VSS is not enough for Fair PKCs. In fact, the trustees should not stop at verifying that they possess a legitimate share of a "generic" secret number: they should verify that the number they have a share of actually is the decryption key of a given public key! The GMW1 scheme, as described above, is an unstructured VSS, and thus unsuitable for directly building Fair PKCs. The same is true for other VSS schemes (e.g. the ones of Ben-Or, Goldwasser and Wigderson [BeGoWi]; of Chaum, Crepeau and Damgard [ChCrDa]; and of Rabin and Ben-Or [RaBe], just to mention a few).

Some VSS schemes are *structured*, that is each trustee can further verify that the secret value of which he possesses a genuine share satisfies some additional property. What this property is depends on the VSS scheme used. For instance, Feldman proposes a VSS in which, given an RSA modulus N and an RSA ciphertext $E(m) = m^e \bmod N$ (of some cleartext message m), the trustees can verify that they do possess genuine shares of the decryption of E(m) (i.e., of m). This scheme is attractive in that it is "non-interactive," but *cannot* be used to hand out in a verifiable way shares of the decryption key of a given public key.

In fact, *the trustees have no guarantee that the decryption of E(m) actually consists of N's factorization*. In other words, the trustees can verify that they have genuine shares of the decryption (m) of a ciphertext E(m), but m is *unstructured* (with respect to N's factorization and anything else).

Constructing Fair PKCs with a Generic VSS

Can a generic VSS scheme be transformed so as to yield Fair PKCs? The answer is YES, but at a formidable cost. All of the above mentioned VSS protocols can be "structured" so that the extra properly verifiable by the trustees is that the dealer's secret actually is the decryption key of a given public key. In fact, this can be achieved as an instance of *secure function evaluation* between many parties as introduced by Goldreich, Micali, and Wigderson in a second paper [GMW2]. Such secure evaluation protocols are possible, though, more in theory than in practice in light of the complexity of the particular functions involved. In the case of the GMW1 VSS scheme, since the encryption of all the shares is publicly known, the transformation can actually be achieved by a simpler machinery: an additional zero-knowledge proof. But even in this case the computational effort involved is formidable. Essentially, one has to encode the right statement (i.e., the secret, whose proper shares are the decodings of these public ciphertexts, is the decryption key of this given public key) as a **VERY BIG** graph, 3-colorable if and only if the statement is true, and then prove, in zero-knowledge, that indeed the graph is 3-colorable. Not only are these transformations of a generic VSS to one with the right property computationally expensive, but they require **INTERACTION** (on top, if any, of the interaction required by the VSS scheme itself)! All these considerations may rule out constructing Fair PKCs this way in practice. Thus CUSTOM-TAILORED methods should be sought, whenever possible, to transform ordinary PKCs to Fair ones. This is our next goal.

Making Fair the RSA Scheme

In the previous section, we have demonstrated that any PKC can be made Fair by means of an interactive (and not so efficient) protocol for key registration. Earlier above, we have instead seen that the Diffie-Hellman scheme can be made Fair by a much simpler method, one that does not require any "talking back and forth." For completeness sake, given the popularity of the RSA scheme, I feel obliged to show here that it too can be made Fair by a non-interactive protocol. That is, I wish to show that, in order to ensure that each Trustee holds a verified piece of a user-chosen RSA secret key, it is enough that the user send a single message to each Trustee.

I wish to add, however, that our Fair RSA system, though more interesting from a mathematical point of view, does not possess the attractive simplicity of our Fair Diffie-Hellman scheme. Further, the latter scheme enjoys a big advantage from the point of view of law enforcement. Namely, in the Diffie-Hellman cryptosystem, once, in response to a court order, the secret key of a user X has been reconstructed, the Government can easily understand both the messages sent *to* X and those sent *by* X. By contrast, in the RSA scheme, if the secret key of a user X becomes known, only the messages sent to X become easily computable. To allow also the messages sent by X to become intelligible in case of a court order, one must complicate the RSA scheme by requiring a special common-key-agreement protocol prior to any encrypted conversation. An example of such a protocol is given in Subsection 8.1.3, but for now we will be content to show how to share a *standard* secret RSA key with the Trustees. Finally, let me note that our effort would be considerably simplified if we were willing to make Fair not the standard RSA scheme, but some variant exhibiting its same security.

In the basic RSA PKC, the public key consists of an integer N which is the product of two primes and one exponent e (relatively prime with f(N), where f is Euler's totient function). No matter what the exponent, the private key may always be chosen to be N's factorization. Before we show how to make a Fair PKC out of RSA we need to recall some facts from number theory.

Fact 1. Let Z_N^* denote the multiplicative group of the integers between 1 and N which are relatively prime with N. If N is the product of two primes $N = pq$ (or two prime powers: $N = p^a p^b$), then

- a number s in Z_N^* is a square mod N if and only if it has four distinct square-roots mod N: x, $-x$ mod N, y, and $-y$ mod N. (That is, $x^2 = y^2 = s$ mod N.) Moreover, for $i,j \in \{1,-1\}$, from the greatest common divisor of $ix + jy$ and N, one easily computes the factorization of N. Also,
- one in four of the numbers in Z_N^* is a square mod N.

Fact 2. On the integers in Z_N^* is defined a function easy to evaluate, the Jacobi symbol, that evaluates to either 1 or -1. The Jacobi symbol of x is denoted by (x/N). The Jacobi symbol is multiplicative; that is, $(x/N)(y/N) = (xy/N)$. If N is the product of two primes $N = pq$ (or two prime powers: $N = p^a p^b$), and p and q are congruent to 3 mod 4, then, letting x, $-x$, y, and $-y$ mod N be the four square roots of a square mod n, $(x/N) = (-x/N) = +1$ and $(y/N) = (-y/N) = -1$. Thus, because of fact 1, if one is given a Jacobi symbol 1 root and a Jacobi symbol -1 root of any square, he can easily factor N.

We are now ready to describe how the RSA cryptosystem can be made fair in a simple way. For simplicity we again assume that we have 5 trustees and that *all* of them must collaborate to reconstruct a secret key, while no 4 of them can even predict it.

A Fair RSA Scheme
(All-Shares Case)

Instructions for the user

A user chooses P and Q primes and congruent to 3 mod 4 as his private key, and N = PQ as his public key. Then he chooses, at random in $Z_N{}^*$, 5 integers whose Jacobi symbol equals 1, X_1 X_2 X_3 X_4 and X_5, and computes the values $X_i{}^2$ mod N for all i = 1, . . . ,5. (These values are called the public pieces of N, and the Xi's the private pieces.) Then, he gives each Trustee T_i the modulus N and the private piece X_i. Finally, the user computes Z, the product of the 5 public pieces and itself a square mod N; extracts a square root, Y, of Z mod N whose Jacobi symbol is -1; and sends Y to the key-management center.

Instructions for the trustees

Trustee T_i stores X_i and N, checks that X_i has Jacobi symbol 1 mod N, and if this is the case, squares X_i mod N and gives the key-management center his signature of $X_i{}^2$ mod N.

Instructions for the key-management center

The center first checks that $(-1/N) = 1$ (thereby checking that for all x: $(x/N) = (-x/N)$, which is partial evidence that N is of the right form). Upon receiving the valid signature of the public pieces of N and the Jacobi -1 value Y from the user, the center checks whether, mod N, the square of Y equals the product of the 5 public pieces. If so, the center is now guaranteed that it has a *split* of N. To make sure that it actually has the *complete factorization* of N, it must now perform the *missing procedure* (i.e., a procedure whose description we temporarily postpone) to check that N is the product of two prime powers. If this is the case, it *approves* N.

Again, it should be noticed that the Fair RSA scheme can be conveniently implemented in software.

Why Does This Work?

The reasoning behind the scheme is the following. The trustees' signatures of the $X_i{}^2$'s (mod N) guarantee the center that every trustee Ti has stored a Jacobi symbol 1 root of $X_i{}^2$ mod N. Thus, in case of a court order, all these Jacobi symbol 1 roots can be retrieved. Their product mod N will also have Jacobi symbol 1, since this function is multiplicative, and will be a root of X^2 mod N. But since the center has verified that $Y^2 = X^2$ mod N, one would have two roots X and Y of a common square mod N; moreover, Y is different from X since it has a different Jacobi symbol, and is also different from $-x$, since $(-x/N) = (x/N)$; in fact: (a) $(-1/N)$ has been checked to be 1 and (b) the Jacobi symbol is multiplicative. Possession of such square roots, by Facts 1 and 2, is equivalent to having the factorization of N, *provided that N is a product of at most two prime powers*. That's why this last property has also been checked by the center before it approved N.

The reason that 4 (or less) trustees cannot factor N with the information in their possession is similar to the one of the discrete log scheme. Namely, the information in their possession solely consists of 4 random squares and their square roots mod N. This cannot be of any help in factoring N, since anybody could randomly choose 4 integers in Z_N^* and square them mod N.

The Missing Procedure

The center can easily verify that N is not prime. It can also easily verify that N is not a prime power by checking that N is not of the form x^y, for x and y positive integers, $y > 1$. In fact, for each fixed y one can perform a binary search for x, and there are at most $\log_2(N)$ y's to check, since x must be at least 2 if $N > 1$. It is thus now sufficient to check that N is the product of at most 2 prime powers. Since no efficient algorithm is known for this task when N's factorization is not known, any such check must involve the user who chose N, since he will be the only one to know N's factorization. In the spirit of what we have done so far, we seek a verification method that is (1) *simple*, (2) *non-interactive*, and (3) *provably safe*. The key to this is the older idea of Goldwasser and Micali of counting the number of prime divisors of N by estimating the number of quadratic residues in Z_N^*. In fact, if N is the product of no more than two prime powers, at least one number in four is a square mod N, otherwise at most 1 in 8 is. Thus the user can demonstrate that N has almost two different prime divisors by computing and sending to the center a square root mod N for at least, say, 3/16 of the elements of a prescribed list of numbers that are guaranteed to be randomly chosen. This list may be taken to be part of the system. Requiring the user to give the square roots of those numbers in such a random sequence that are squares mod N does not enable the center— or anybody else for that matter—to easily factor N. To make this idea viable one would need some additional details. For instance, the trustees may be involved in choosing this public sequence so as to guarantee to all users the randomness of their elements; also the sequence should be quite long, else a user may "shop around" for a number N that, though product of—say—3 prime powers, is such that at least 3/16 of the numbers in the sequence are squares modulo it; and so on. In "practice" this idea can be put to work quite efficiently by one-way hashing the user's chosen N to a small "random" number H(N), where H is a publicly known one-way hash function, and then generating a sufficiently long sequence of integers S(N) by giving H(m) as a seed to a reasonable pseudo-random number generator. This way, the number sequence may be assumed to be random enough by everybody, since the user cannot really control the seed of the generator. Moreover, the sequence changes with N, and thus a dishonest user cannot shop around for a tricky N as he might when the sequence is chosen beforehand. Thus, the sequence chosen may be much shorter than before. If a dishonest user has chosen his N to be the product of three or more prime powers, then it would be foolish for him to hope that roughly 1/4 of the integers in the sequence are squares mod N. The scheme is of course non-interactive, since the user can compute on his own H(N), the number sequence S(N), and the square roots mod N of those elements in S(N) that are quadratic residues, and then sends the center only N and the computed square roots. Given N, the center will compute on its own the same value H(N) and thus the same sequence S(N). Then, without involving the user at all, it will check that, by squaring mod N the received square roots, it obtains a sufficiently high number of elements in S(N).

AN EFFECTIVE METHOD FOR TIME-BOUNDED EAVESDROPPING BASED ON ALGORITHMICALLY-CHOSEN SESSION KEYS.

The High-Level Mechanics of our Suggestion

In presence of a court order to tap X's lines between dates Dl and D2, no matter how many dates there may be between D1 and D2, our method allows the Trustees to easily compute and give the Police a small amount of information i = i(X,D1,D2), that makes it easy to tap X's lines in the specified time interval. The method consists of using a Fair PKC F together with a special additional step for selecting session keys for a conventional single-key cryptosystem C. In our suggested method, call it the *(F,C) method*, for any users X and Y, and any date D, there is a session key SXDY for enabling X to send a private message to Y at time D. Each user X is asked to provide the trustees not only with proper shares of his secret key in F, but also with *additional pieces of information* that enable them, should they receive a legitimate court order for tapping X between dates D1 and D2, to compute easily i(X,D1,D2) and hand it to the Police.

While the trustees can verify that they possess correct shares of X's secret key in F, we do not insist that the same holds for X's session keys. This decreased amount of verifiability is not crucial in this context for the following reasons. Assume that the Police, after receiving i(X,D1,D2) from the Trustees in response to a legitimate court order, are unable to reconstruct a session key of X during the given time interval. Then, this inability proves that X did not originally give the Trustees the proper additional pieces of information about his session keys. It is therefore quite justified that, in response to X's malicious action, the Trustees put together the verified pieces of information in their possession so as to reconstruct X's secret key in F. Consequently, from that point on, all messages sent to X via F, and in particular via the (F,C) system, will cease to be private. Moreover, the adoption of a proper "hand-shaking protocol" also ensures that the Police will understand all messages sent by X to any user who replies to him in the (F,C) system.

In sum, therefore, malicious users who want to hide their conversations from law-enforcement agents even in presence of a court order, cannot do so by taking advantage of the convenience of a nation-wide (F,C) system. They must go back to the cumbersome practice of exchanging common secret keys before hand, outside any major communication network. It is my firm opinion that the amount of illegal business privately conducted in this cumbersome way is estimated minuscule in comparison to the one that might be conducted via a nation-wide *ordinary* PKC.

The Specifics of our Suggestion

The hand-shaking protocol of our suggested (F,C) cryptosystem is the following. When X wants to initiate a secret conversation with Y at date D, she computes a secret session key SXDY and sends it to Y using the Fair PKC F (i.e., encrypts it with Y's public key in F). User Y then computes his secret session key SYDX and sends it to X after encrypting it with the received secret key SXDY (by means of the agreed-upon conventional cryptosystem C). User X then sends SYDX to Y by encrypting it with SXDY. Throughout the session, X sends messages to Y conventionally encrypted with SXDY, and Y sends messages to X via SYDX. (If anyone spots that the other disobeys the protocol the communication is automatically terminated, and an alarm signal may be generated.) Thus in our example, though X and Y will understand each other perfectly, they will not be using a common, conventional key. Notice that, if the Police knows SXDY (respectively, SYDX), it will also know SYDX (respectively, SXDY).

Assume now that the Court authorizes tapping the lines of user X from date D1 to date D2, and that a conversation occurs at a time D in the time interval [D1,D2] between X and Y. The idea is to make SXDY available to the Police in a convenient manner, because knowledge of this quantity will enable the Police to understand X's out-going and incoming messages, if the hand-shaking has been performed, independently of whether X or Y initiated the call. To make SXDY conveniently available to the Police, we make sure that it is easily computable on input SXD, a master secret key that X uses for computing his own session key at date D with every other user. For instance, SXDY = H(SXD,Y), where H is a one-way function.

Since there may be many dates D in the desired interval, however, we make sure that SXD is easily computable from a short string, i(X,D1,D2), immediately computable by the Police from the information it receives from the Trustees when they are presented with the court order "tap X from D1 to D2." For instance, in a 3-out-of-3 case, if we denote by i_j(X,D1,D2) the information received by the Police from Trustee j in response to the court order, we may set

$$i(X,D1,D2) = H(i_1(X,D1,D2), i_2(X,D1,D2), i_3(X,D1,D2)),$$

where H is a one-way (preferably hashing) function. Now, we must specify one last thing: what should i_j(X,D1,D2) consist of? Letting X_j be the value originally given to Trustee j by user X when she entered the system (i.e., X gives X_j to Trustee j together with the j-th piece of her own secret key in the FAIR PKC F), we wish that i_j(X,D1,D2) easily depend on X_j. Let us thus describe effective choices for X_j, i_j(X,D1,D2), and SXD. Assume that there are 2^d possible dates. Imagine a binary tree with 2^d leaves, whose nodes have n-bit identifiers—where n = 0, . . . ,d. Quantity i_j(X,D1,D2) is computed from X_j by storing a value at each of the nodes of our tree. The value stored at the root, node N_e (where $_e$ is the empty word), is X_j. Then a *secure* function G is evaluated on input X_j so as to yield two values, X_j0 and X_j1. The effect of G is that the value X_j is unpredictable given X_j0 and X_j1. (For instance, X_j is a random k-bit value and G is a secure pseudo-random number generator that, using X_j as a seed, outputs 2k bits: the first k will constitute value X_j0, the second k value X_j1.) Value X_j0 is then stored in the left child of the root (i.e., it is stored in node N0) and value X_j1 is stored in the right child of the root (node N1). The values of below nodes in the tree are computed using G and the value stored in their ancestor in a similar way. Let SX_jD be the value stored in leaf D (where D is a n-bit date) and SXD = H(SX_1D,SX_2D,SX_3D). If D1 < D2 are n-bit dates, say that a node N *controls* the interval [D1,D2] if every leaf in the tree that is a descendent of N belongs to [D1,D2], while no proper ancestor of N has this property. Then, if i_j(X,D1,D2) consists of the (ordered) sequence of values stored in the nodes that control [D1,D2], then

   I. i_j(X,D1,D2) is quite short (with respect to the interval [D1,D2], and
  II. For each date D in the interval [D1,D2], the value SX_jD stored in leaf D is easily computable from i_j(X,D1,D2), and
 III. The value stored at any leaf not belonging to [D1,D2] is not easily predictable from i_j(X,D1,D2).

Thus if each user X chooses her X_j values (sufficiently) randomly and (sufficiently) independently, the scheme has all the desired properties. In particular,

1. user X computes SXD very efficiently for every value of D.
2. When presented with a court order to tap the line of user X between dates D1 and D2, each Trustee j quickly computes $i_j(X,D1,D2)$. (In fact, he does not need to compute all values in the 2^n-node tree, but only those of the nodes that control [D1,D2].)
3. Having received $i_j(X,D1,D2)$ from every trustee j, the Police can, *very quickly and without further interaction with the Trustees*, compute

   (3.1) SX_jD from $i_j(X,D1,D2)$ for every date D in the specified interval (in fact, its job is even easier since the SXiD's are computed in order and intermediate results can be stored)

   (3.2) the master secret-session key SXD from the SX_jD's, and

   (3.3) the session key SXDY from SXD from any user Y talking to X in the specified time interval.

Note, however, that no message sent or received before or after the time-interval specified by the court order will be intelligible to the Police (unless a new proper court order is issued).

Additional Methods for Relying on Fewer Shares

The method described above relied on fewer shares but increased the number of necessary trustees. Here we want to show, for the case of the Fair Diffie-Hellman PKC, one can rely on the same number of Trustees, but increase the length of the messages sent by the user to the Trustees. Though this increase is exponential in the number of Trustees, the method is very effective if this number is small.

The Subset Method

Each Fair PKC described so far is based on a (properly structured, noninteractive) VSS scheme with parameters n = 5, T = 5 and t = 4. It may be preferable to have different values for our parameters; for instance, n = 5, T = 3, and t = 2. That is, any majority of the trustees can recover a secret key, while no minority of trustees can predict it at all. This is achieved as follows (and it is easily generalized to any desired values of n,T and t in which T > t). We confine ourselves to exemplifying our method in conjunction with the Diffie-Hellman scheme. The same method essentially works for the RSA case as well.

The Subset Method for the Diffie-Hellman Scheme

After choosing a secret key Sx in [1,p-1], user X computes his public key $Px = g^{Sx}$ mod p. (All computations from now on will be mod p.) User X now considers all triplets of numbers between 1 and 5: (1,2,3), (2,3,4), etc. For each triplet (a,b,c), he randomly chooses 3 integers $S1abc, \ldots, S3abc$ in the interval $[1, p-1]$ so that their sum $mod\ p$ equals Sx. Then he computes the 3 numbers

$$t1abc = g^{S1abc}, \quad t2abc = g^{S2abc}, \quad t3abc = g^{S3abc}$$

The *tiabc*'s will be referred to as *public pieces* of Px, and the *Sxiabc*'s as *private pieces*. Again, the product of the public pieces equals the public key Px. In fact,

$$t1abc \cdot t2abc \cdot t3abc = g^{S1abc} \cdot g^{S2abc} \cdot g^{S3abc} = g^{(S1abc\ +\ S2abc\ +\ S3abc)} = g^{Sx} = Px$$

User X then gives trustee Ta $t1abc$ and $S1abc$, trustee Tb $t2abc$ and $S2abc$, and trustee Tc $t3abc$ and $S3abc$, always specifying the triplet in question.

Upon receiving these quantities, trustee Ta (all other trustees do something similar) verifies that $t1abc = g^{S1abc}$, signs the value $(Px, t1abc, (a,b,c))$ and gives the signature to the key management center.

The key-management center, for each triple (a,b,c), retrieves the values $t1abc\ t2abc$ and $t3abc$ from the signed information received from trustees Ta, Tb and Tc. If the product of these three values equals Px and the signatures are valid, it approves Px as a public key.

The reason the scheme works, assuming that at most 2 trustees are bad, is that all secret pieces of a triple are needed for computing (or predicting) a secret key. Thus no secret key in the system can be retrieved by any 2 trustees. On the other hand, when after a court order, at least 3 trustees reveal all the secret pieces in their possession about a given public key, the Government has all the necessary secret pieces for at least one triple, and thus can compute easily the desired secret key.

Finally, we would like to mention that, by making better use of number theory, Ray Sidney has observed that the work of Feldman [Fe87] can be used to rely on fewer shares within the Fair Diffie-Hellman PKC without increasing exponentially the size of the messages. Describing this method does require, however, substantially more number theory. We would also like to mention that, if one allows interaction between the Trustees and the user, then by using a proper VSS protocol in the strategy discussed in "How to Make Fair Any PKC," one may transform any PKC into a Fair one relying on any fewer shares and working in polynomial time no matter how many Trustees one wishes to have.

An Effective Method for Making Trustees Oblivious

The strategy exemplified below assumes that the Trustees can communicate to the center by means of a cryptosystem satisfying a suitable algebraic property: essentially, *random self-reducibility* as introduced by Blum and Micali [BlMi]. This Trustees-center cryptosystem needs not to coincide with the underlying Fair PKC, nor to be itself Fair. To clarify this point, below we assume that the Fair PKC (for which the Trustees need to be made oblivious) is our Fair Diffie-Hellman PKC, while the cryptosystem used by the Trustees to communicate with the center is the standard RSA PKC. For simplicity, we further assume the "all-shares" case for the underlying PKC.

Oblivious and Fair Diffie-Hellman Scheme (All-Shares Case)

The Trustees' Encryption Algorithms
Since RSA itself possesses a sufficient algebraic property, let us assume that all trustees use *deterministic* RSA for receiving private messages. Thus, let N_i be the public RSA modulus of trustee T_i and e_i his encryption exponent (i.e., to send T_i a message m in encrypted form, one would send $m^{e_i} \bmod N_i$.)

Instructions for User U
User U prepares his public and secret key, respectively P_x and S_x (thus $P_x = g^{S_x} \bmod p$), as well as his public and secret pieces of the secret key, respectively t_i and S_{xi}'s (thus $P_x = t_1 \cdot t_2 \cdot \ldots \cdot t_5 \bmod p$ and $t_i = g^{S_{xi}} \bmod p$ for all i). Then he gives to the key-management center P_x, all of the t_i's and the n values $U_i = (S_{xi})^{e_i} \bmod N_i$; that is, he encrypts the i-th share with the public key of trustee T_i.
(Comment: Since the center does not know the factorization of the N_i's this is not useful information to predict S_x, nor can it verify that the decryption of the n ciphertexts are proper shares of S_x. For this, the center will seek the cooperation of the n trustees, but without informing them of the identity of the user.)

Instructions for the Center/Trustees
The center stores the values t_j's and U_j's relative to user U and then forwards U_i and t_i to trustee T_i. If every trustee T_i responds to have verified that the decryption of U_i is a proper private piece relative to t_i, the center approves P_x.

Instructions in Case of a Court Order
To lawfully reconstruct secret key S_x without leaking to a trustee the identity of the suspected user U, a judge (or another authorized representative) randomly selects a number $R_i \bmod N_i$ and computes $y_i = R_i^{e_i} \bmod N_i$. Then, he sends trustee T_i the value $z_i = U_i \cdot y_i \bmod N_i$, asking with a court order to compute and send back w_i, the e_i-th root of z_i $\bmod N_i$. Since z_i is a random number $\bmod N_i$, no matter what the value of U_i is, trustee T_i cannot guess the identity of the user U in question. Moreover, since z_i is the product of U_i and $y_i \bmod N_i$, the e_i-th root of z_i is the product $\bmod N_i$ of the e_i-th root of U_i (i.e., S_{xi}) and the e_i-th root of y_i (i.e., R_i). Thus, upon receiving w_i, the judge divides it by y_i $\bmod N_i$, thereby computing the desired S_{xi}. The product of these S_{xi}'s equals the desired S_x.

6

Software Key Escrow: A Better Solution for Law Enforcement's Needs?*

Stephen T. Walker, *Trusted Information Systems, Inc.*

SUMMARY

In a recent paper[1], Trusted Information Systems, Inc., proposed a key escrow system using public key cryptography that can be implemented entirely in software. We believe that this system can provide a level of assurance for law enforcement objectives that is equivalent to the Clipper/Capstone system. This software process is equally appropriate for telephone and computer applications, but the focus of this paper and its implications for government key escrow apply primarily to software key escrow used in computer communications applications.

We believe that variations of our software key escrow system can provide a commercial key escrow capability that will be very attractive to corporate and individual computer users to protect against loss of encrypted data. Many organizations and individuals are reluctant to encrypt important information, even though by doing so they can protect it from unauthorized disclosure to others, simply out of fear that they may forget or lose the key and thus the information. An easy-to-use key escrow system that is automatically invoked every time a file is stored or message transmitted can provide the user and his employer a great deal of confidence that encrypted data will not be lost.

We also believe that widespread use of corporate key escrow, in which corporations operate their own key escrow centers, and individual key escrow, in which bonded commercial key escrow centers provide a key retrieval capability for registered users, will better achieve the key escrow objectives of law enforcement than a government-imposed key escrow system. Widespread, voluntary use of commercial key escrow on a national or international basis may achieve all of law enforcement's key escrow objectives without the need for any government-escrowed keys.

This paper summarizes our original Clipper-equivalent software key escrow system. Variations designed to meet corporate or individual

---

* August 30, 1994.
[1] A New Approach to Software Key Escrow Encryption [pages 180 to 207—Ed.]

key escrow needs are then described. Some distinctions between key escrow of telephone and computer communications are discussed followed by an analysis of how widespread use of voluntary commercial and individual key escrow can better serve the needs of law enforcement in individual countries and internationally.

We conclude with suggestions for what is needed for this approach to succeed.

Clipper[2] Equivalent Software Key Escrow

This summary is intended to give a nontechnical overview of the software key escrow process. Those wishing more technical detail are referred to our paper cited in footnote 1.

Every time one person communicates with another using encrypted communications, either by audio via telephone or by computer data communications, an encryption key, a (hopefully) random number, is used to initialize the encryption process and make it difficult for unauthorized listeners to recover. The hardest part of encryption is making sure the intended receiver has the key without revealing it to unauthorized listeners. The next hardest part is making sure that the key is not lost so the intended sender and receiver can recover the information.

As with most escrow procedures, key escrow involves various ways of entrusting the key to a third party so that if you ever lose it, you can get it back.

The Clipper Initiative introduced the notion of key escrow for law enforcement purposes. In Clipper, if law enforcement officials have appropriate authority, through a wire tap court order or similar legal document, they can obtain from government-run key escrow centers the encryption key used for specific telephone or computer communications. The Clipper Initiative offers a hardware-based key escrow solution in combination with a very strong encryption algorithm.

In Clipper, a Law Enforcement Access Field (LEAF) containing the identity of the sending device is included along with the encrypted information being transmitted. If law enforcement officials, in the process of a legal wiretap, encounter Clipper-encrypted information, they can obtain the device key for that device from the government key escrow centers and use it to decrypt the information.

The TIS Clipper-equivalent software key escrow system, which uses the public/private key pairs of public key cryptography, provides the same capabilities to law enforcement without requiring the use of hard-

---

[2] For this paper, the term Clipper will be used to include the Clipper chip for telephone key escrow and the Capstone chip for computer communications key escrow.

ware or secret encryption algorithms. A LEAF field is attached to the encrypted message or file containing the identity of the sending program and the key used for protecting the message, itself encrypted in the public key associated with that program. Law enforcement, when properly authorized, can obtain the private key associated with that program from the government key escrow centers and then decrypt that and other messages from that sender.

Software key escrow is viewed by many as better suited to computer applications than hardware because it can be incorporated into software products without requiring the purchase and use of hardware devices. Hardware cryptography is viewed by many as superior to software encryption, but most users of mass market software products prefer the convenience and economy of software-based encryption over the potentially extra security and expense of token-based hardware approaches. For those who choose to use software cryptography, software-based key escrow is clearly preferred.

Commercial Software Key Escrow

Key escrow has significant uses other than for law enforcement purposes. If one encrypts a file or message and then forgets or loses the encryption key, the same mechanisms that are designed to keep outsiders from stealing one's data now works directly against the person they were intended to help. The second time one locks one's car keys in the car, the idea of keeping a spare key in one's wallet becomes very attractive. If one could do the equivalent with encrypted data, the biggest fear of using encryption, losing one's important data, could be greatly reduced or eliminated.

With software key escrow, a system similar to that described above can readily be added to mass market software products for use by corporations, professional groups, and individuals. After registering your "key escrow-enabled" word processor or communications application with the data retrieval center of your choice, every time you encrypt a file or message, the program will automatically add a "data retrieval field." This field contains the unique identity of the sending program and the session key encrypted in that program's unique public key. If the user or corporation is ever unable to decrypt the file or message, the data retrieval field is sent to the registered data retrieval center and the information needed for decryption is returned.

Just how widespread such commercial key escrow will become is a matter of conjecture. There are those in the electronic commerce (EC) business, among others, who believe that unless there is a widely available individual and corporate key escrow capability, users, by frequently forgetting or losing their EC keys, will cripple the effectiveness of EC. Individuals and large and small companies might make much more effective use of encryption by knowing that commercial key escrow facilities are available to ensure against loss of vital encrypted data. We believe that since commercial key escrow does provide a useful function to both individuals and corporations, this form of key escrow will see much wider use than hardware key escrow that serves primarily the purposes of the government.

Meeting Law Enforcement's Objectives with Commercial Software Key Escrow

If commercial key escrow becomes widespread, it may be possible for it to serve a useful role in meeting law enforcement's objectives as defined by the Clipper Initiative. If appropriate, the same mass market software products could produce a LEAF in addition to a commercial data retrieval field. Or it may be practical for the data retrieval field to contain the same information as that needed for a LEAF, thus allowing both requirements to be satisfied at once.

But widespread availability of commercial key escrow offers another even more attractive alternative. Since the information necessary to decrypt any file or message already exists in the commercial data recovery center, it is possible for law enforcement to achieve its key escrow objectives without the need for government escrow of any keys, at least in the case of computer communications systems (see below).

When law enforcement determines that an employee of a company may be involved in illegal activities and it is important to obtain files or papers from an employee's safe or desk, they present appropriate legal authorization to the company management and are granted access to the required papers. If law enforcement were to encounter an encrypted file or message that it believes is related to illegal activities, the data retrieval field could be used to identify the commercial data recovery center from which, having presented appropriate legal authorization, law enforcement can obtain the escrowed information needed for decryption.

If, as argued above, commercial key escrow becomes much more widely available than Clipper key escrow, this approach may provide law enforcement with a more effective tool that avoids the concerns about government escrow of private keys.

Key Escrow for Telephones vs. Computer Communications

It was noted at the beginning of this paper that while software key escrow can work for telephones as well as computer communications[3],

---

[3] Indeed, the AT&T Clipper Telephone Security Device, the only product currently using Clipper, can probably be implemented much more easily using software key escrow in the product's digital signal processor (DSP) than by interfacing to a separate Clipper chip.

commercial key escrow may be best suited to computer communications. Corporations may choose to use encrypted telephone security devices, but they are unlikely to need to escrow the keys of those devices for their own purposes. The commercial advantages of key escrow probably do not apply to point-to-point, real-time audio communications.

Since law enforcement's requirements for key escrow appear largely focused, for now at least, on telephone communications, it will probably remain necessary for the government to escrow keys of telephone security devices[4]. But since many of the major objections to the Clipper Initiative have come from its application to computer communications, removing these objections with software-oriented commercial key escrow appears to be very significant.

Reducing the International Key Escrow Problem to a Previously Solved Problem

Every discussion of the international aspects of key escrow seems to bog down in questions of which country holds which keys and how various national law enforcement entities can work together without abusing the rights of individual citizens. Software-based commercial key escrow, whereby individuals and corporations within national boundaries chose and operate their own key escrow facilities, provides a much less controversial way for international law enforcement to accomplish its goals.

Today if the US Federal Bureau of Investigation (FBI) determines that a citizen of the UK may be involved in an illegal activity, they request whatever information Scotland Yard can give them, which may include a search by Scotland Yard of that person's place of employment or personal records. In the same manner, if the FBI encountered an encrypted file or message from this individual indicating a commercial data recovery center in the UK, they could request that Scotland Yard help them decrypt the file or message, perhaps by having Scotland Yard request the key escrow information from the UK data retrieval center.

If governments are not involved in the actual escrow of keys used by private citizens, the international complexity of key escrow may be greatly reduced.

How Can All This Come About?

The following steps outline one possible path to achieving reasonably widespread software-based commercial key escrow and reducing the need for governments to escrow the encryption keys of their citizens.

---

[4] It has been observed that due to the high cost of telephone security devices with or without Clipper, there may never be a significant market for such devices and therefore little reason for an extensive telephone-only based key escrow capability.

Mass market software vendors become convinced to include good quality cryptography with software key escrow options in their products.

Corporations establish their own Corporate Data Retrieval Centers (i.e., Key Escrow Centers) for use by their employees. Bonded Commercial Data Retrieval Centers are established for individual users.

Law enforcement establishes rapid response communications capabilities with corporate and individual data retrieval centers registered within their jurisdictions.

As the need arises for corporations or individuals to retrieve information for which the encryption key is unavailable, they query the data retrieval center with which they are registered for the information needed to decrypt the information.

As the need arises for law enforcement to decrypt information suspected of being part of an illegal activity, they query, using already established legal procedures, the data retrieval center identified in the data retrieval header of the encrypted file or message for the information needed to decrypt the information. If the data retrieval center is in another jurisdiction, they use already established procedures to query the law enforcement officials of that jurisdiction for assistance.

But as has arisen so many times in the past, mass market software vendors are reluctant to include good quality cryptography in their products if they cannot export them to their foreign markets.

If governments really want widespread use of key escrow for their own purposes, they must be prepared to allow vendors who include software key escrow capabilities along with good quality cryptography to export their products. "Software key escrow-enabled" products can be configured to fail to function unless use of the product is registered with an appropriate key escrow center. In this way governments can be assured, with a very high degree of certainty, that they will, when authorized, be able to retrieve the encrypted information. If governments choose this approach while keeping current export controls on non "escrow-enabled" products, they can help ensure the success of commercial key escrow.

Some governments and some elements within some governments may have difficulty accepting this software-based commercial key escrow approach. But we feel the needs of law enforcement and other national and international interests will be better served by truly voluntary use of software-based key escrow, which the citizen chooses because it offers him or her a valuable service, rather than one that primarily serves the interests of the government itself.

7

A New Approach to Software Key Escrow Encryption*

David M. Balenson, Carl M. Ellison, Steven B. Lipner, Stephen T. Walker
Trusted Information Systems, Inc.

Summary

In August 1993, NIST announced [NIST] a cooperative program with industry to explore the possibilities of performing key escrow cryptography using software-only techniques. The purpose of that program was to determine if there were alternatives to the requirements for hardware implementation of the US government's Clipper initiative.[1]

The major deficiency ascribed to key escrow techniques when they are implemented solely in software is that they can be bypassed or subverted relatively easily and thus cannot be relied upon to meet the objectives of law enforcement that motivate the Clipper Initiative. Further, no technique has been proposed that addresses the issues associated with the implementation of a classified encryption algorithm, such as the Skipjack algorithm embodied in the Clipper chip, in a widely used software product.

Key escrow cryptography has been a controversial topic since it was proposed in 1993. We believe that it is most likely to be accepted for use outside of government if it is authorized by legislation that sets forth the circumstances under which keys may be released and the sanctions for abuse of the escrow process. Even if the policy issues associated with key escrow are resolved, however, we believe that the close coupling of key escrow with encryption hardware will remain a significant deterrent to its use. For that reason, we have explored the need for hardware support to key escrow and the possibilities of software implementation.

This paper examines the assumptions and limitations that underlie any implementation of key escrow cryptography, whether in hardware

---

* August 30, 1994.

[1] The administration's initiative has been referred to by the names of the VLSI chips that implement the key escrow concept, Clipper and Capstone, and by the name of the NIST standard that describes their function (the Escrowed Encryption Standard or EES). In this paper, we will use the phrase Clipper initiative to refer to the general program that embodies Clipper, Capstone, and potentially other future implementations that comply with the EES.

or in software. It also reviews the specific considerations that motivate the choice of hardware rather than software implementations of key escrow cryptography. It then proposes two system concepts and associated key escrow protocols that support the implementation of key escrow cryptography in software. We believe that an implementation of either concept and protocol is no more vulnerable to being bypassed or subverted than are Clipper or other hardware key escrow systems.

Background

A United States Presidential announcement on April 16, 1993 [WHITE], referred to as the "Clipper initiative," called for the development of a hardware implementation of a classified encryption algorithm called "Skipjack". The Presidential announcement characterized the Skipjack algorithm as being "significantly stronger than those currently available to the public." The hardware implementation of Skipjack would also include a capability called "key escrow" which allows the government to recover the keys used for data encryption. The integrated circuit chips which implement the Skipjack algorithm are called the "Clipper" chip and the "Capstone" chip.

The Clipper initiative (particularly the key escrow feature) attempts to preserve the ability of law enforcement and national security to intercept and exploit the contents of communications while providing law-abiding citizens with an encryption system much stronger than any now available to them. The announcement of the Clipper initiative and the subsequent discussions made it clear that, while Skipjack is a stronger encryption algorithm than the current Data Encryption Standard (DES) [NIST2], law enforcement entities considered that the proliferation of DES voice security devices would be a significant impediment to their need to preserve the ability to accomplish court-ordered wiretaps.

A great deal of resistance to the Clipper initiative was evident in the public reaction to the April 16 announcement. Objections were expressed in various forms, but the following key points stand out:

- Many people objected to the potential for loss of privacy that would result from the deployment of key escrow cryptography and the associated sharing of heretofore private cryptographic keys with government escrow agents.
- Many people raised objections to the Administration's attempt to use the buying power of government to impose as de facto standards a family of encryption products that could be defeated at will by government agencies.

- Some people objected to the introduction of a classified algorithm as the standard for the protection of unclassified information. DES is public and has had wide scrutiny in its fifteen year life. There were suggestions that Skipjack might have a defect or trap door (other than the key escrow process). These objections were not quieted by the favorable review of Skipjack by a panel of outside cryptographers.

- Many people (especially suppliers of Information Technology products) objected to the requirement for a hardware implementation because of its of cost and because of the limitations that the need to accommodate a government-designed chip imposes on overall system or product design.

In August 1993, the National Institute of Standards and Technology (NIST) announced a cooperative program [NIST] with industry to explore possible approaches to the implementation of key escrow in software products (without the need to embed dedicated hardware components such as the Clipper or Capstone chips).

There are a number of issues that intertwine in any discussion of this topic. Such issues include hardware implementation, classified encryption algorithms, and how much trust one must put in the user. It is important to unravel these factors in order to focus on finding a means to achieve a key escrow capability equivalent to that provided by the Clipper initiative, but without the need for any special purpose hardware devices or interfaces. These issues are considered below. However, before addressing these issues, it will be useful to consider key escrow.

OBJECTIVES FOR KEY ESCROW

Key escrow adds to products that implement cryptography features that allow authorized parties to retrieve the keys for encrypted communications and then decrypt the communications using such keys. Discussions of key escrow were brought into the public domain by the Clipper initiative but, as the next paragraph shows, other applications are also worth considering. In the Clipper initiative, keys for each encryption device are mathematically divided into two halves (each equal in length to the original key) and the halves are held by two separate escrow agents. Both escrow agents must cooperate (to regenerate the original key) before the communications from a given device can be decrypted. For Clipper, the escrow agents are government agencies who require assurance that the law enforcement agency requesting keys has a court order authorizing a wiretap for the communications in question. While Clipper and the systems outlined in the rest of this paper assume two escrow agents, there is no technical barrier to a system that uses three or more, if additional checks and balances are desired.

Applications of Key Escrow

A number of needs have been cited to justify key escrow cryptography. Some apply to the needs of law enforcement and national security, while others apply to the needs of individual users or organizations:

- Law enforcement and national security agencies are concerned that growing use of encrypted communications will impair their ability to use court-ordered wiretapping to solve crimes and prevent acts of terrorism. Widespread use of key escrow cryptography would preserve this ability for these agencies, while providing the public with the benefits of good quality cryptography. In the case of law enforcement and national security, government escrow agents provide access to communications when authorized by a court order.

- Some corporations have expressed a concern that careless or malicious mismanagement of keys by employees might deny the corporation access to its valuable information. Key escrow cryptography at the corporate level has been advocated as a mechanism by which such corporations might regain access to their information. In this sort of application, one might have senior management or personnel offices serve as escrow agents who would permit an employee's supervisor to gain access to his or her files or communications.

- Individuals who use encryption for their own information may forget or lose the passwords that protect their encryption keys, die or become incapacitated. Key escrow cryptography has been proposed as a safety mechanism for such individuals. In this case, an individual might select friends or attorneys as escrow agents who would allow the individual (or perhaps the executor of his or her estate) access to protected information.

- In some cases, government agencies have the authority to monitor the business communications of their employees. Such authority applies, for example, in military and national security installations where it is used to detect the misuse of classified or sensitive information. Key escrow cryptography offers such agencies the opportunity to exercise their authority to monitor even for encrypted communications. In this application, communications security officers might serve as escrow agents who would grant access to line managers or commanders.

The Clipper initiative focuses on the first of the four applications for key escrow cited above. In addition, the Clipper initiative, perhaps to offer a compromise to reluctant users, couples the introduction of key escrow with the introduction of Skipjack, a new classified encryption algorithm much stronger than the unclassified DES.

Threats Addressed and Ignored

Opponents of the Clipper initiative have argued that a key escrow encryption system such as Clipper can be defeated by sophisticated users such as organized crime, terrorist organizations, and foreign governments. Such users have the ability to write or buy their own encryption system (without key escrow) and either ignore the key escrow products altogether or encrypt first under their own system and then under the key escrow system. Other options are open to pairs of users who wish to cooperate to defeat key escrow, and some opponents of the Clipper initiative have suggested that the only way to deter such options is to forbid non-escrowed encryption by law and to enforce the law with a vigorous program of monitoring communications—an unappealing prospect to say the least.

Proponents of the Clipper initiative counter that they are well aware that pairs of cooperating users have many ways to avoid key escrow. The objective that these proponents cite is to make it difficult or impossible for a single "rogue" user to communicate securely with parties (or more precisely with escrowed encryption devices) that believe they are engaged in a communication where both communicants are faithfully following the escrow rules. The attack by Blaze [BLAZE] on the Tessera device (which incorporates a Capstone escrowed encryption chip) is of this form: it allows a single rogue user to communicate securely with users and devices that are implementing the escrow features correctly, and that are fooled into believing that the rogue user is doing likewise.

The "single rogue user" scenario constitutes a test for a key escrow system. A successful key escrow system (hardware or software) should prevent a single rogue user from exploiting the cryptography in the escrowed product, and from defeating or bypassing the product's key escrow features, while still enabling secure communication with other users (products) that believe that they and the rogue user are implementing the escrow features correctly.

The Clipper chip addresses the single rogue user by embedding the key for each individual communication in a Law Enforcement Acess Field (LEAF) that is encrypted under a secret "family" key common to all Clipper chips. The embedded information includes a checksum that is a function of the session key. A receiving Clipper chip also holds the family key; thus it can decrypt the LEAF and verify that the checksum is the correct one for the current session key (which both chips must share in private for communication to be successful and secure). The Clipper chips rely on the tamperproof hardware of the chip to protect the shared family key from disclosure.

ADVANTAGES OF HARDWARE CRYPTOGRAPHY

There are several factors that support the decision to require the use of separate hardware in the design of the key escrow products proposed as part of the Clipper initiative (the Clipper and Capstone chips). Some of these factors, discussed below, are related to the introduction of key escrow cryptography, some to the use of a classified encryption algorithm, and some to the choice of a conservative standard for the design of encryption products.

- Separate hardware provides a degree of protection for the encryption process difficult to obtain in software systems. An errant or malicious computer program can not corrupt or bypass the encryption algorithm or key management embedded in a hardware encryption device such as the Clipper or Capstone chip.
- Separate hardware also provides a degree of protection for the key escrow process difficult to obtain in software systems. While software can manipulate the externally visible parameters of the escrow process, hardware at least provides some assurance that the escrow operations are performed or verified. (Blaze's attack cited above defeats the Capstone key escrow mechanism with such manipulations, and thus emphasizes that the use of encryption hardware is not a sufficient measure to guarantee the escrow process.)
- If a classified encryption algorithm such as Skipjack is used, separate hardware that implements special protective measures may be essential to protect the design of the algorithm from disclosure.
- Cryptographic keys can be provided with a high degree of protection in a hardware device, since unencrypted keys need never appear outside the device. In contrast, it is difficult or even impossible to protect secret keys embedded in software from users with physical control of the underlying computer hardware.
- Proliferation of an encryption capability is perceived to be easier to control with respect to accounting for controlled devices and restriction of exports with hardware devices than with embedded software.

The list above makes it clear that some of the need for hardware in the Clipper initiative derives from a need to protect the classified Skipjack algorithm, some from conservative design of the encryption system, and some from a need to protect the escrow process. We defer for the moment discussion of alternatives to hardware for protecting the key escrow process and address the issues of classified algorithm and conservative design below.

Use of a Classified Data Encryption Algorithm

The Skipjack encryption algorithm that was introduced with the Clipper initiative is claimed to be much stronger than existing publicly available algorithms such as DES. Having a strong algorithm is a valuable selling point for any new encryption initiative. But, as the discussion above pointed out, protecting a classified algorithm from disclosure requires, at least at the current state of technology, a hardware implementation that embodies special measures to resist reverse engineering.

Classified encryption algorithms are often considered much stronger than those in the public domain since the algorithms used to protect government classified information are classified. But because they are not available for public review, suggestions that classified algorithms be used to protect unclassified information are suspect due to the possible existence of unknown deliberate trapdoors or unintentional flaws. While DES was initially viewed with suspicion by some, it was subject to intense public scrutiny and its principal strength now is that even after fifteen years, no serious flaw has been found.

Key escrow techniques as such do not require classified algorithms and can easily be used with publicly available algorithms such as DES [NIST2] and IDEA [LAI] or with proprietary but unclassified algorithms such as RSADSI's RC2 and RC4 [STAMM]. If a publicly available or proprietary unclassified algorithm were used in a product that embodied key escrow cryptography, it would not be necessary to have a hardware implementation to protect the encryption algorithm from disclosure (although there are other reasons for implementing key escrow cryptography in hardware, as the above list indicates).

This interdependence between hardware implementation and classified algorithm has caused considerable confusion in examining the feasibility of software key escrow approaches. If one requires a classified algorithm, one must use hardware to protect the algorithm whether one implements key escrow or not. If one chooses an unclassified public or proprietary algorithm, one is free to implement in hardware or software. The decision to implement in hardware or software is driven by other factors, such as those identified in the above list.

Until the introduction of Clipper, publicly available algorithms had been prescribed as standards for the protection of unclassified information. If key escrow techniques that work in software can be developed, they can be used with unclassified algorithms and only the relative soundness of the encryption products will remain as a reason to choose a hardware implementation. We believe that, given both options, some users will prefer the additional security offered by a hardware implementation of the Skipjack algorithm but that many who today believe that DES or other unclassified algorithms are strong enough to meet their needs (and do not want the greater strength of Skipjack) will opt for the economy and convenience of a software alternative.

Benefits and Limitations of Software Encryption

Historically, encryption systems that have been used to protect sensitive information have been implemented as separate hardware devices, usually outboard "boxes" between a computer or communications system and a communications circuit. Such devices are designed with a high level of checking for operational integrity in the face of failures or malicious attack, and with especially careful measures for the protection of cryptographic functions and keys.

Software encryption systems have historically been viewed with suspicion because of their limited ability to protect their algorithms and keys. The paragraphs above discussed the issues associated with protecting classified (or secret) encryption algorithms from disclosure. Over and above these issues is the fact that an encryption algorithm implemented in software is subject to a variety of attacks. The computer's operating system or a user can modify the code that implements the encryption algorithm to render it ineffective, steal cryptographic keys from memory, or, worst of all, cause the product to leak its cryptographic keys each time it sends or receives an encrypted message.

The principal disadvantage of using encryption hardware, and therefore the primary advantage of integrated software implementations, is cost. When encryption is implemented in hardware, whether a chip, a board or peripheral (such as the Tessera PCMCIA card) or a box, end users have to pay the price. Vendors must purchase chips and design them into devices whose costs go up because of the additional "real estate" required for the chip. End users must purchase more expensive devices with integrated encryption hardware, or must buy PCMCIA cards or similar devices and then pay the price for adding a device interface to their computing systems or dedicating an existing interface to encryption rather than a "useful" function such as that performed by a modem or disk.

A second major advantage of software implementations is simplicity of operation. Software solutions can be readily integrated into a wide variety of applications. Generally, the mass market software industry, which attempts to sell products in quantities of hundreds of thousands or millions, seeks to implement everything it can in software so as to reduce dependencies on hardware variations and configurations and to provide users with a maximum of useful product for minimum cost.

Some have argued that users do not understand the limitations of products that implement encryption in software. Such advocates of hardware encryption argue that it would be better for such users to have no encryption at all than to suffer the false sense of security that results from using software encryption and failing to understand its vulnerabilities to malicious or defective software. We believe that, in most cases, users make reasonably well informed choices, and that they should have the option of using software or hardware for encryption depending on their view of the sensitivity of the data being protected and the costs of protection. Our search for a software key escrow technique stems from the belief that, "correct" or not, many users will choose software encryption and that if key escrow is desirable, then there must (if possible) be a software key escrow system to meet the needs of such users.

CHALLENGES OF SOFTWARE KEY ESCROW

Discussions of software alternatives for implementing key escrow cryptography have surfaced a number of reasons why software implementation is impractical or inconsistent with the goals of the Clipper initiative. In this section, we consider those reasons in order to focus the discussion of our alternatives for implementing key escrow cryptography in software.

Some discussions have stressed the difficulty of protecting a classified encryption algorithm from disclosure if it is implemented in widely used software products. We concede this point. If an encryption algorithm is implemented in software, the user of that software can, with some effort, reverse engineer it and gain access to the algorithm description in order to implement it in his or her own form and for his or her own purposes, or to publish it in violation of the restrictions on classified information. We acknowledge that our approaches to software key escrow cryptography are only suitable for use with unclassified public or proprietary encryption algorithms where little or no harm will result if the algorithm is disclosed.

Other discussions of software key escrow are really about the strengths and weaknesses of software implementations of encryption. As we discussed above, we believe that users will use software encryption and that if key escrow is desirable, then there will have to be a key escrow capability that works with software encryption products.

Other arguments against software key escrow encryption are more focused than those presented above on the key escrow process itself.

- It is difficult to ensure that the key escrow software will function correctly and not be modified by the user to bypass or corrupt the escrow process[2].
- Chips that implement the Clipper initiative's Escrowed Encryption Standard (EES) [NIST3] transmit key escrow information encrypted in the Skipjack symmetric encryption algorithm under secret keys that are embedded in the Clipper or Capstone chips. It would be impossible to embed such keys in a software product without a significant risk that they would be disclosed. Such disclosure could have serious consequences for the user whose copy of the software was penetrated, and potentially for all users who shared the common "family key".

The first objection (modification by the user) is eased by the objectives of the key escrow system. If our goals are only to support interception of the communications of users who do not modify their software and to defeat "single rogue" users or applications, then there is hope of designing a viable system. This is fortunate for, in the limit, a pair of users who could modify their copies of a software product to bypass key escrow could simply write their own encrypted communications package and ignore key escrow altogether. A question remains as to how much effort a software key escrow system should expend to defeat modification by its users, and we will return to this question below.

The second objection (protection of cryptographic keys) is most readily addressed by moving from the Clipper initiative's use of a symmetric encryption algorithm to protect key escrow information to a public key (asymmetric) system. This alternative eliminates the need to protect secret keys from disclosure, but raises a challenge, that we will discuss below, regarding the features needed to defeat a single rogue user or application.

In summary, the software key escrow system that we have devised is intended to be used by users who are willing or required to use key escrow but are unwilling or cannot afford to use hardware encryption products. The Venn diagram of Figure 1 divides the population of computer and communications users by their willingness to use key escrow and their willingness to use encryption facilities implemented in hardware and software. We believe that the population of potential users

---

[2] This issue remains even with hardware solutions that allow software to control the flow of information to and from the hardware encryption device. The attack by Blaze mentioned above manipulated the software surrounding a Tessera card, not the embedded Capstone chip.

FIGURE 1.
*The Market for
Software Key
Escrow*

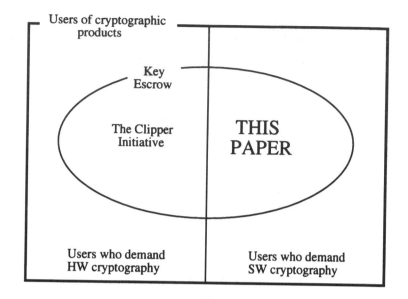

for key escrow is still to be determined, but that it is clear that there are more potential users for encryption products implemented in software than for those that require hardware.

SOFTWARE KEY ESCROW SYSTEM DESIGN

Our analysis of the issues and constraints outlined above led us to the development of two system designs for software key escrow encryption. The first attempts to mirror as closely as possible the features of systems that implement the Escrowed Encryption Standard of the Clipper initiative. The second provides an alternative set of capabilities for law enforcement decryption, and has some attractive features. We describe each system design in turn.

Both designs share a set of common features that are derived from the analyses presented above:

- Use unclassified public or proprietary encryption algorithms to perform all functions, obviating the need to protect classified algorithms.
- Use an escrow protocol based on public key cryptography to build the law enforcement access field (LEAF) that makes the user's keys available to law enforcement authorities. This choice obviates the need to include in the software products any secret keys that would be part of the escrow process.

- Design the escrow protocol so that the receiving party to a communication reconstructs the sender's LEAF to verify that the received LEAF is both valid and the correct LEAF for the current encrypted communication. This choice counters single rogue attacks such as that demonstrated on the Tessera card by Blaze.
- Consider the use of embedded digital signatures to protect the encryption and escrowing processes from tampering by the user or the underlying operating system software.

The discussions below describe the application of LEAFs built using public key cryptography, and of the concept of validating a received LEAF by reconstructing it in our two software key escrow system designs.

We have considered the use of cryptographic checksums and digital signatures to protect the escrowing software from tampering. To the extent that the primary threat to the operation of key escrow is a single rogue user, such protection apppears unnecessary, since a rogue sender will be detected by an unmodified receiver, and a rogue receiver is "too late" to prevent the transmission of a valid LEAF that can be intercepted and exploited by law enforcement. However, our design that parallels the Clipper key escrow system is susceptible to a new form of abuse by a rogue receiver (discussed below). The use of checksums and signatures may be desirable both as a way of deterring this abuse and to provide the software that implements the cryptography and key escrow process with some level of protection from tampering. We expand on the use of checksums and digital signatures in the Appendix.

The following sections present our two alternative key escrow system designs. For each, we present product manufacturing steps, the escrow protocol, the strategy for embedding the escrowing information into a software product, our approach to detecting a "rogue application", and the operation of the "law enforcement decryptor".

Key Escrow System Design and Operation: Parallelling Clipper

Our first software key escrow system parallels as closely as possible the structure of the key escrow system for Clipper and Capstone that was announced by the Administration in April, 1993 [WHITE, DENN1, DENN2]. Figure 2 depicts the overall organization and interconnection of the system. The major components of the system are a key escrow programming facility (KEPF), two (or, if desired, more) key escrow agents (KEAs), sending and receiving entities (devices in the Clipper/

FIGURE 2. *Complete Software Key Escrow System*

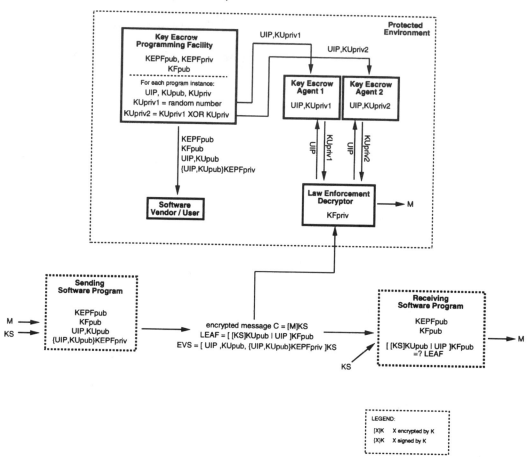

Capstone system; programs in the software system), and a law enforcement decryptor (LED).

As we mentioned above, the primary difference between this system and the Clipper/Capstone system is that this sysem uses public key cryptography in place of conventional (symmetric) cryptography to generate the law enforcement access field or LEAF. The use of public key cryptography allows software products to generate LEAFs without having to store secret keys or private keys. Only public quantities need be embedded in the software product. The product integrity features mentioned above, if used, can protect these quantities as well as the programs that use them against modification.

The paragraphs below describe the operations and interactions of the components of our system. The rationale for each aspect of the design, and the way in which the design responds to the challenges of producing an effective software key escrow system, are described along with the technical aspects of the design itself. A final subsection outlines some concerns with the attributes of this approach.

The Key Escrow Programming Facility

As shown in Figure 3, the key escrow programming facility (KEPF) is initialized with two asymmetric public/private key pairs. The first is a KEPF public/private key pair that will be used to sign and authenticate other components that are generated and distributed by the KEPF. The KEPF key pair could be generated externally and loaded into the KEPF, or generated internal to the KEPF. Controls can be applied to the generation and custody of the KEPF key pair as they are to the family and seed keys that are used by the Clipper/Capstone chip programming facility.

The second key pair used by the KEPF is a family key (KF). It is comparable to the family key used in the Clipper/Capstone system. As in the Clipper system, KF can be generated external to the KEPF. Only the public component (KFpub) is loaded into the KEPF. The corresponding private component (KFpriv) is loaded into the Law Enforcement Decryptor (LED). As with the secret family key in the Clipper/Capstone system, the private component of KF can also be split into halves and escrowed.

Generating Program Unique Parameters

On an ongoing basis, the KEPF generates unique program parameters for each program instance, just as the Clipper/Capstone programming

FIGURE 3.
Key Escrow Programming Facility

```
+-----------------------------+        
|       Key Escrow            |        +------------------------+
|   Programming Facility      |        |  Law Enforcement       |
|                             |        |     Decryptor          |
|   KEPFpub, KEPFpriv         |        |                        |
|        KFpub                |        |       KFpriv           |
|                             |        +------------------------+
|                             |
|                             |
+-----------------------------+
```

KEPFpub,KEPFpriv = key escrow programming facility key pair
KFpub = family key (public component)
KFpriv = family key (private component)

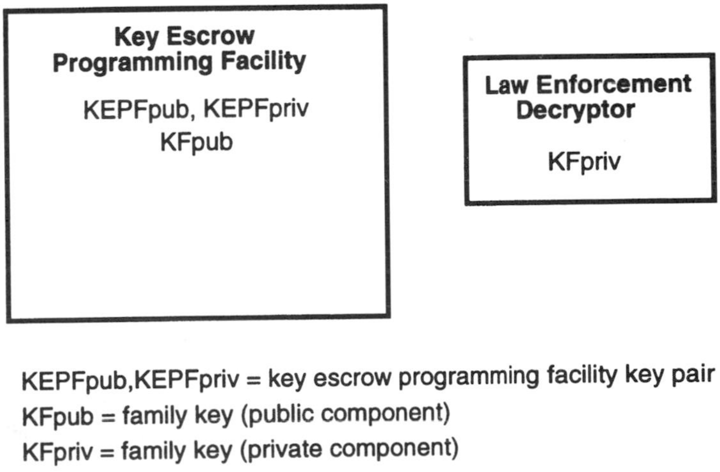

FIGURE 4. *Generating Program Unique Parameters*

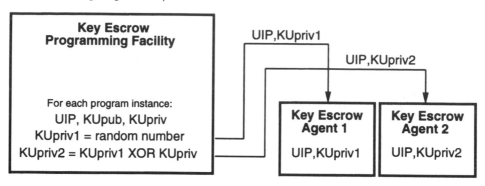

UIP = program unique identifier
KUpub,KUpriv = program unique key pair

facility programs each individual chip. In particular, as shown in Figure 4, the KEPF generates a program unique identifier (UIP) that is equivalent to the device unique identifier (UID) in the Clipper/Capstone system and a program unique key (KU) that is comparable to the device unique key used in the Clipper/Capstone system. In our system, KU is an asymmetric public/private key pair. KU can be generated within the KEPF, seeded with externally generated parameters that are loaded into the KEPF, as in the Clipper/Capstone system. The private component of KU (KUpriv) is split into halves by generating a random bit string as long as KUpriv which becomes KUpriv1 and calculating KUpriv2 as the exclusive or of KUpriv1 and KUpriv[3]. The UIP and individual private key halves are escrowed with the two escrow agents (KEAs)

The final step that the KEPF performs is to send the program unique parameters, UIP and KUpub, to the software vendor to be embedded into the software program product, as shown in Figure 5. The KEPF signs these parameters using its private key, KEPFpriv, and sends the signature along with the components. The programming facility public key (KEPFpub) and the family key public component (KFpub) are also sent to the vendor, with KFpub signed by KEPFpriv.

Generating the Software Product

If the KEPF communicates its public key to the vendor by an out-of-band (secure) channel, the vendor can reliably authenticate sets of parameters (KFpub, UIP, KUpub) received from the KEPF. As the soft-

---

[3] Other methods may be more appropriate for splitting the private key, depending on the asymmetric encryption algorithm with which the keys will be used.

ware vendor manufactures copies of its product, it embeds (Figure 6) KFpub and KEPFpub in the product code. KEPFpub and KFpub are the public keys on which the ability of the product to verify the integrity of the key escrow system depends. The vendor embeds the program unique parameters (UIP and KUpub) and the associated signatures for each program into the media for the program. While this level of customization for each copy of a software product may seem excessive, some shrink-wrap products are now sold with serial number information embedded in the product media; thus the embedding of a mod-

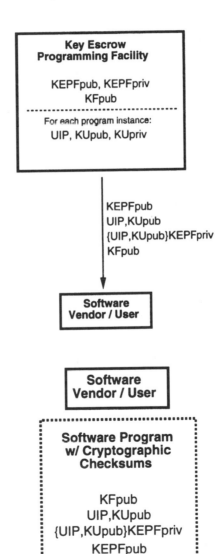

FIGURE 5.

Sending Program Parameters to Vendor/User

Key Escrow Programming Facility

KEPFpub, KEPFpriv
KFpub

- -

For each program instance:
UIP, KUpub, KUpriv

KEPFpub
UIP,KUpub
{UIP,KUpub}KEPFpriv
KFpub

Software Vendor / User

FIGURE 6.

Generating the Software Product

Software Vendor / User

Software Program w/ Cryptographic Checksums

KFpub
UIP,KUpub
{UIP,KUpub}KEPFpriv
KEPFpub

est amount of identification, key and authentication information should be feasible.

As was discussed above in the section "Challenges of Software Key Escrow", no secret keys or private keys are present within the software product. Only public keys, KEPFpub, KFpub, and KUpub are embedded in the software product.

In cases where a software product is distributed on CDROM media that is manufactured in bulk (and can not accept unique serial number or key information), or where it is installed on a shared storage device for access by multiple users, it is not feasible to embed a unique KUpub, UIP and the associated signatures for each copy of the product. In these cases, the user of the product can be required to run an installation program that retrieves KUpub and UIP over a network or communication line. The operation of the product's encryption function can be made contingent on the execution of the installation program.

Key escrow is primarily applicable to products whose function is communication, so the requirement to retrieve the unique quantities via network should not impose an undue burden on the product's user. Since the only quantities that are needed to customize the escrow software for its user are signed and public, there is no risk to retrieving them over the network. Their confidentiality is not at issue, and their integrity can be authenticated using KEPFpub which is common to all users and copies of the product and can be embedded by the vendor.

An alternative to having the product retrieve KUpub and UIP is to have the product generate KU during the initialization process and send both components (KUpub and KUpriv) to the KEPF encrypted under KEPFpub. In this variation, the KEPF would split KUpriv and distribute the halves to the escrow agents, sign KUpub, and return the signature to the product. This variation is similar to one of Micali's designs [MICALI].

Operation of the Sending Program

As shown in Figure 7, the sending program encrypts the message M using the session key KS to produce the encrypted message C (denoted

FIGURE 7. *Operation of the Sending Program*

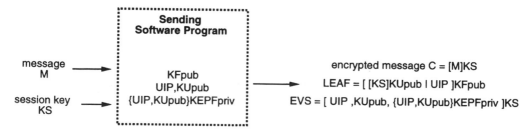

as [M]KS), and transmit the encrypted message C. The method by which sender (by convention Alice) and receiver (Bob) negotiate the session key KS is outside the scope of this paper, and independent of the operation of the key escrow system. We simply assume that Alice and Bob have a secure protocol that allows them to negotiate a shared session key.

Alice's sending program generates a LEAF by encrypting the session key under the program unique public key (calculating [KS]KUpub), concatenating the result with the program unique identifier UIP, and encrypting the concatenated values with the family public key, KFpub. The resulting LEAF is symbolized as [[KS]KUpub UIP]KFpub. This LEAF is comparable to a LEAF in the Clipper/Capstone system but encryption is accomplished using asymmetric, rather than symmetric cryptography. In addition, the LEAF generated in the software system does not include the escrow authenticator EA that is incorporated in the Clipper/Capstone system's LEAF. Replacing the Clipper/Capstone EA in the message from Alice to Bob is an escrow verification string, or EVS, that includes Alice's program unique identifier UIP, program unique public key KUpub, and the signature applied to those two quantities by the key escrow programming facility. This string is encrypted under the session key, KS, that Alice and Bob share. The use of the escrow verification string EVS is described below.

Operation of the Receiving Program

As shown in Figure 8, Bob's receiving program can decrypt the encrypted message C using the session key KS (however negotiated) to yield the original message M. However, prior to doing so, it must authenticate the LEAF to ensure that Alice's sending program has included a valid LEAF as part of the message transmission. Bob's program cannot decrypt the LEAF, since it does not have a copy of the family private key KFpriv. Instead, Bob's receiving program authenticates the LEAF by reconstructing it. It can do this because it knows all

FIGURE 8. *Operation of the Receiving Program*

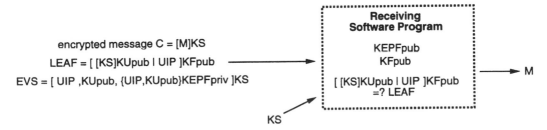

encrypted message C = [M]KS

LEAF = [[KS]KUpub I UIP]KFpub

EVS = [UIP ,KUpub, {UIP,KUpub}KEPFpriv]KS

Receiving
Software Program

KEPFpub
KFpub

[[KS]KUpub I UIP]KFpub
=? LEAF

M

KS

of the components that make up the LEAF either through communication external to the operation of the escrow sysem (KS) or because they were sent signed in the escrow verification string, EVS.

Bob's program first decrypts the escrow verification string using KS. It then verifies that the copies of Alice's program unique key $KUpub_{Alice}$ and program unique identifier UIP_{Alice} received in the escrow verification string are correct and authentic, by verifying the accompanying signature using the copy of the KEPF public key (KEPFpub) embedded in Bob's copy of the program. If the escrow verification string is authentic, Bob's program recalculates the LEAF using KS, $KUpub_{Alice}$, UIP_{Alice}, and KFpub. If the calculated LEAF is identical to the one received, it is valid and Bob's program decrypts the message.

The LEAF verification method outlined does not depend on the use of an escrow authenticator or checksum and hence the bogus LEAF checksum attacks reported by Blaze do not apply.

The use of the session key KS to encrypt the escrow verification string is not necessary to the function of verifying the LEAF. Instead, this step protects Alice's UIP and KUpub from disclosure to parties who are not in communication with her. The issues associated with protection from parties who do communicate with Alice are discussed below.

Law Enforcement Decryptor

The law enforcement decryptor or LED (Figure 9) contains the family private key KFpriv and hence, as in the Clipper/Capstone system, the LED can simply decrypt the LEAF. This operation reveals the underlying encrypted session key, $[KS]KUpub_{Alice}$, and program unique identifier, UIP_{Alice}. Given UIP_{Alice}, the LED, with the proper authorization (e.g., a court order) can obtain Alice's program unique private key components, $KUpriv1_{Alice}$ and $KUpriv2_{Alice}$ from the respective key escrow agents and combine them to form Alice's program unique key, $KUpriv_{Alice}$. With $KUpriv_{Alice}$, the LED can decrypt the session key KS. Finally, given KS, the LED can decrypt the message.

Issues and Concerns

The software key escrow system described above has a number of desirable attributes. First, it is a software system. Second, it operates with little impact on software product users. Finally, it is less susceptible to abuse by a single rogue program or user than is the case with the current Clipper/Capstone system.

The primary technical concern that has been raised about this system is that it exposes a communicating user's escrow information (UIP and KUpub) to programs controlled by other users. Thus, in our example above, Bob can modify his copy of the product to memorize or

FIGURE 9.
Law Enforcement Decryptor

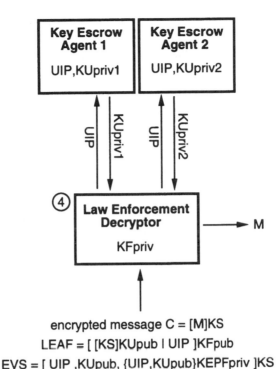

encrypted message C = [M]KS

LEAF = [[KS]KUpub I UIP]KFpub

EVS = [UIP ,KUpub, {UIP,KUpub}KEPFpriv]KS

"harvest" Alice's UIP and KUpub, and those of other parties with whom he communicates. He can then communicate with his modified program using LEAFs formed with Alice's (or other individuals') program identifiers and escrow public keys.

This abuse does not prevent the LED from decrypting Bob's communications, but it does cause the LED to withdraw Alice's, rather than Bob's private key components (KUpriv1$_{Alice}$ and KUpriv2$_{Alice}$) from the escrow agents in the event that a wiretap is initiated against Bob. Since possession of KUpriv$_{Alice}$ allows the LED to monitor all of Alice's communications (if the LED fails to erase KUpriv$_{Alice}$) many in the public would regard this as a serious exposure.

Since there is no binding in the escrow system among UIP$_{Alice}$, KUpriv1$_{Alice}$, KUpriv2$_{Alice}$ and Alice's true identity, the LED has no obvious way to get from possession of KUpriv$_{Alice}$ to Alice's true identity and the execution of a wiretap against Alice. However, a post audit of activities by the LED and escrow agents may suggest that wiretapping and decryption have been initiated against Alice rather than Bob. If a malicious party decides to harvest the escrow information (KUpub and UIP) for all parties with whom he or she communicates and then becomes the subject of a wiretap, he or she can cause the audit trails of the escrow agents to reflect a high level of apparent abuse. This apparent abuse will only come to light if an audit of the form "has Alice ever been the subject of a wiretap and decryption?" is conducted.

Use of the software integrity measures mentioned earlier and outlined in the Appendix would not provide an absolute guarantee against a rogue receiver's harvesting Kupub and UIP. However, they would require the would-be rogue receiver to first reverse engineer a legitimate copy of the receiving program and then modify it extensively while defeating the integrity measures or (more likely) to construct a completely new version of the program with "harvesting" functions embedded. The malicious user can not simply capture KUpub and UIP information external to the receiving program because that information is encrypted under KS which is only visible internal to the receiving program. On balance, it appears that, if there are adequate procedural and legal safeguards on the operation of the escrow agents and law enforcement, the additional deterrence provided by software integrity measures may be sufficient to prevent harvesting attacks from becoming a serious problem for the software key escrow system.

KEY ESCROW SYSTEM DESIGN AND OPERATION: ON-LINE ESCROW AGENTS

The key escrow protocol of the Clipper initiative has been criticized because of the fact that a device whose unique key (KU in the original Clipper scheme) has been withdrawn from the escrow agents is subject to decryption from the time of withdrawal onward. While the stated policy of the Clipper initiative is that unique keys will be erased from the law enforcement decryptor once the wiretap authorization has expired, that policy is cold comfort to individuals who find key escrow unappealing to begin with.

Our software key escrow system described above shares with the Clipper initiative the use of a device unique key (KUpriv) that is loaded into the law enforcement decryptor and that must be erased when a wiretap authorization has expired. In addition, the concern outlined above—that a malicious user with a modified software product can harvest and reuse the escrow information (UIP and KUpub) for any other user with whom he or she communicates securely—is a potential deficiency that we would prefer to eliminate.

An alternative that eliminates both of the concerns with our initial software key escrow scheme revolves around doing away with the unique key (KU, KUpub, KUpriv) and identifier (UIP) altogether. Instead, each sender splits his or her session key KS and encrypts one fragment under the public key of each escrow agent. This scheme still incorporates a LEAF and an escrow verification string (EVS), but it does away with the KEPF and simplifies the role of the vendor.

Figure 10 shows the operation of the alternative software key escrow system. There is no programming facility (KEPF). The vendor's sole role is to embed in each program instance the code that implements the key escrow functions and the public keys of two (or more) escrow agents (KEA1pub and KEA2pub).

In this scheme, when Alice wishes to send an encrypted message [M]KS to Bob, she splits KS into two halves KS1 and KS2. The LEAF for the message consists of KS1 encrypted under KEA1pub and KS2 encrypted under KEA2pub. The escrow verification string, EVS, now consists simply of KS1 followed by KS2, both encrypted under KS.

FIGURE 10. *Alternative Software Key Escrow System*

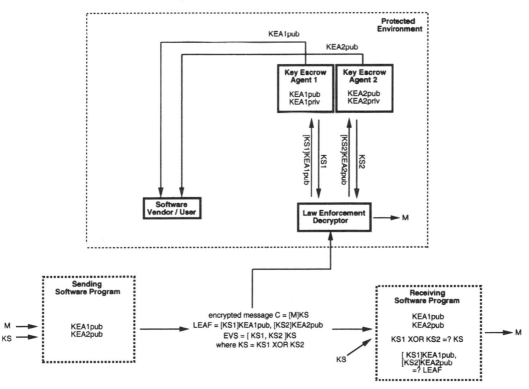

When Bob receives Alice's message, as with our previous system, he checks the escrow verification string and then recomputes the LEAF that Alice applied. In this case, checking the escrow verification string involves decrypting it using KS and then seeing that the plaintext KS1 and KS2 combine to yield KS. Since Bob has copies of KEA1pub and KEA2pub, he can easily recompute the LEAF received from Alice to to see that it corresponds to the current communication and session key KS.

When the law enforcement decryptor (LED) encounters an encrypted communication covered under a court wiretap order (or anticipates encountering one), it discloses the court order to each escrow agent. Each agent verifies the validity of the court order, records its effective dates, and generates a secret key (for a symmetric encryption algorithm) for that particular court order and issues it to the LED. Any submission of key parts for that wiretap to an escrow agent by the LED must be encrypted in the corresponding key. The escrow agents delete the secret keys on the expiration of the court order and are therefore unable to comply with any requests for keys after the expiration of the order. Since all communications with the escrow agents must be encrypted for security, this process adds no execution time to that operation.

When conducting a wiretap, the LED passes the LEAF to each of the escrow agents under the secret key for the wiretap. The agents decrypt their respective halves of the LEAF by applying KEA1priv and KEA2priv, and return KS1 and KS2 to the LED also under the secret key. The LED combines the returned KS1 and KS2 to yield KS, and decrypts the message from Alice to Bob.

Since there is no database linking a UIP to any individual targetted in a court order, the escrow agents have no choice but to trust the LED's association of an individual targetted by a court order with a specific wiretap. We may modify the protocol to include a UIP in the LEAF portions sent to the escrow agents, to enable those agents to maintain a list of program instances targetted under each court order for later auditing.

This alternative has the advantage that there is no product unique key to be disclosed to the LED. Once surveillance ceases, the LED has no further ability to decrypt Alice's communications unless it again requests the services of the escrow agents. As a side effect, there is no potential for a rogue application to trick the LED into withdrawing the unique keys of innocent users.

The potential disadvantage of this system is that it requires the escrow agents to be on-line and involved with every decryption of a new session key. Law enforcement has expressed concerns about the need for real-time decryption of intercepted communications, and we expect resistance to this system where ongoing operations are more complex and potentially slower than with Clipper or our previous system. As a practical matter, however, the escrow agents are commited to round-the-clock operation as part of the Clipper initiative. On-line computer systems at the escrow agents can be expected to respond within 0.2 seconds, provided they have hardware support for public key decryption, and reliable communications between escrow agents and LED should be easy enough to provide (and may be required even in the configuration of the Administration's Clipper initiative). Thus, this may be an alternative worth considering.

CONCLUSION

We have presented two designs for software key escrow systems that are alternatives to the hardware key escrow system proposed by the Clipper initiative. Neither system is perfect, but we believe that both offer sufficient assurance of the escrow process and resistance to abuse to be valid alternatives to the Clipper initiative as proposed.

There are serious policy concerns about key escrow encryption, and we continue to believe that these concerns should be addressed by legislation. However, we also believe that, if the United States decides that key escrow encryption is an appropriate policy to pursue, there will be a need for an alternative that can be applied by those users who wish their encryption to be implemented in software. We believe that the systems described here are two such alternatives.

ACKNOWLEDGEMENTS

The ideas in this paper have evolved over time and as a result of discussions among the authors and a number of colleagues. The members of the NIST Software Escrowed Encryption Working Group, including Dennis Branstad and Dorothy Denning, were among the first to be exposed to these ideas, along with Stuart Katzke, Lynn McNulty, and Miles Smid of NIST, and all of these people made especially valuable suggestions. Dennis Branstad helped us understand the need for LEAF verification at the receiver. Of particular value was the suggestion by Dorothy Denning that the Escrow Verification String (EVS) be encrypted under the session key shared by sender and receiver. Miles Smid made a key contribution with his early suggestion that quantities in the EVS be signed.

REFERENCES

[BLAZE]   Blaze, Matt, Protocol Failure in the Escrowed Encryption Standard, AT&T Bell Laboratories, Preliminary Draft, June 3, 1994.

[DENN1]   Denning, Dorothy, The Clipper Chip: A Technical Summary, April 21, 1993.

[DENN2]   Denning, Dorothy, and Miles Smid, Key Escrowing Today, July 13, 1994 (to appear in IEEE Communications, September, 1994).

[LAI]   Lai, X., Massey, J. L., and Murphy, S., "Markov Ciphers and Differential Cryptanalysis", Advances in Cryptology—Eurocrypt '91, D. W. Davies, Ed., pages 17–38, Springer-Verlag, Berlin, 1992

[MICALI]   Micali, Silvio, Fair Cryptosystems, MIT/LCS/TR579.b, MIT Laboratory for Computer Science, November 1993.

[NIST]   National Institute of Standards and Technology, Opportunity to Join a Cooperative Research and Development Consortium to Develop Secure Software Encryption with Integrated Cryptographic Key Escrowing Techniques, Federal Register, Notices, Volume 58, Number 162, August 24, 1993.

[NIST2]   Federal Information Processing Standard Publication (FIPS PUB) 46–2, Data Encryption Standard (DES), U. S. Department of Commerce, National Institute of Standards and Technology, Reaffirmed December 30, 1993.

[NIST3]   Federal Information Processing Standard Publication (FIPS PUB) 185, Escrowed Encryption Standard, U. S. Department of Commerce, National Institute of Standards and Technology, February 9, 1994.

[RIVEST]   Rivest, Ronald L., Adi Shamir, and Leonard M. Adleman, "A method for obtaining digital signatures and public key cryptosystems", Communications of the ACM, Volume 21, Number 2, February 1978.

[STAMM]   Stammberger, K. R., The RC2 and RC4 exportable encryption algorithms, RSA Data Security, Inc., February 12, 1993.

[WHITE]   The White House, Directive on Public Encryption Management, April 16, 1993.

Appendix: Ensuring Product Integrity

One potential objection to any software key escrow scheme is that a malicious user, in possession of the software product and in total control of the platform on which it runs, can easily modify the product's instructions and data so as to bypass the escrow feature or to send an invalid LEAF. Our approach to verifying the validity of a received LEAF (having the receiver reconstruct the LEAF) ensures that a single rogue user who has rewritten his or her sending program cannot mislead a valid receiver into believing that the sender is legitimately following the key escrow rules. In the case of a conspiracy of two rogue users who wish to use a software product but bypass its escrow features, we do not have to make it arbitrarily difficult to bypass key escrow, but merely as difficult as it is to bypass or subvert the escrow features of the Capstone chip and Tessera card or to write a new encryption package to provide the necessary security features. Blaze's work and the ready availability of encryption software from public sources worldwide make it clear that this should not be an extraordinarily difficult test to meet.

It may be that no special measures are needed to make software products that incorporate key escrow resist modification. However, we have postulated an approach to ensuring the integrity of the software product and its escrowing mechanism by building in at several points routines that calculate the message digest of the code that implements the encryption features and escrowing mechanism. These routines would verify the digest, and thus the integrity of the encryption and escrowing software, by comparing it with a digest of the same software signed by the private key of the product's vendor. In addition, these routines would verify other signed information embedded in the product. If any verification failed, then the routines would cause the product to cease to function or cease to encrypt.

In this scheme, the assurance of the integrity of the encryption and escrowing software depends on the number of places where the verification routines are embedded in the product and the difficulty of detecting and bypassing all of them. While this approach can justly be criticized as "security through obscurity", it should prove effective enough to make a key escrow product whose integrity mechanisms have been bypassed unreliable. Thus a user whose goal is to obtain a reliable software product without key escrow would be more likely to build his or her own software or obtain it through other means than to bypass the escrow mechanisms built into a software product.

While the specifics of the integrity mechanism depend on the design and structure of the software product whose integrity is being protected, some general approaches to integrating the integrity mechanism into a product appear to have wide applicability. These approaches are outlined below.

■ Build integrity checks into the product at multiple points, including product initialization (startup) code and code that will be executed during product operation. Some of the checks should be executed during the execution of common product functions and others during the execution of obscure or infrequently used functions. This approach will reduce the likelihood that an attempt to subvert the key escrow features will find and remove all checks in one or a few tries. The subversion attempt must reverse engineer and check the entire product.

- Use several different instruction sequences to perform the integrity checking function. This approach will prevent a subversion attempt from performing an automated scan of the product to find and remove all integrity checks at once. Ideally, each integrity check should be coded uniquely.

- Make the cryptographic checksums cover the code that calculates the LEAF, the code that inserts the LEAF into messages, and the code that sends the messages. This approach provides for continuous verification that the LEAF is calculated and transmitted.

- Have different integrity checks verify different areas of the product, rather than having all integrity checks verify exactly the same code and data. This approach increases the likelihood that a modification that manages to pass one integrity check will be caught by another.

- Have the integrity checks verify the signatures of all signed quantities that are built into the product. As is the case with verifying the integrity of the key escrow code, different integrity checks should verify different signatures. This approach prevents a subversion attempt from modifying data fields that are critical to the production or verification of the LEAF. The use of multiple distinct checks reduces the likelihood of a subversion attempt that finds and eliminates all signature checks at once.

- The integrity checking code will verify signatures applied by the software vendor, and the LEAF verification code will verify signatures applied by the KEPF. Embed the public keys needed to verify these signatures at several points in the product, and have different checks use different copies of the keys (either statically – each check always uses the same public key – or dynamically – each check selects a copy of the public key to use at random). This approach prevents a subversion attempt from invalidating all key escrow information by replacing one or two public keys.

The list above suggests a set of measures that would increase the difficulty of subverting the escrowing features in a software product. The facts that these measures would also increase the complexity of products that embodied them, and potentially increase the difficulty of making enhancements and reduce product reliability are matters of concern. We believe that the best approach for embedding integrity checks into a product would be to apply them en masse to an otherwise finished copy of the product, rather than to attempt to maintain them as part of the product change process. Thus the product vendor would maintain a copy of the product without embedded integrity checks, apply enhancements and bug fixes to that copy, and then add the integrity checks at a late stage before the product went to the field. Time and experience would be needed to show how pervasive the checks needed to be, and how much impact they had on product development and integrity. It appears that the basic scheme is similar to a product copy protection scheme (though without the features that users have found distasteful) and should have a similar impact on vendors.

The performance impact of the integrity checks would need to be assessed after real-world experience. It seems likely that integrity checks frequent enough to deter subversion of the key escrow process could be infrequent enough to have little impact on performance. The performance of the integrity checks would depend on the speed of the message digest and signature verification algorithms. In this context, it seems likely that RSA (which effects fast verification of signatures) would prove a better choice for integrity checks than DSA (which performs fast signature but slow verification).

## 8

International Key Escrow Encryption: Proposed Objectives and Options*

Dorothy E. Denning

This paper proposes objectives and options for international key escrow encryption. By *key escrow encryption* (or, simply *escrowed encryption*), we mean an encryption system that enables authorized government officials to decrypt particular communications through keys that are held in escrow by one or more trusted escrow agents. By *international key escrow encryption*, we mean an escrowed encryption system that can accommodate communications which cross national boundaries and the possible use of escrowed encryption products in countries other than the ones that hold the keys needed to decrypt communications encrypted with those products.

The proposed objectives and options fall into the following general areas:

1. General properties of escrowed encryption
2. The key escrow system
3. Government access and decryption
4. National controls and international and bilateral agreements

Although governments have an interest in intercepting and decrypting information both for law enforcement and national security purposes, this paper focuses on the law enforcement interests.

The ideas presented in this paper are offered for the purpose of consideration and discussion. They do not represent the policy of the U.S. government or Georgetown University.

We assume the reader has some general familiarity with cryptographic systems and with the U.S. Government's Escrowed Encryption Standard (EES) [13] and its instantiation in the Clipper and Capstone encryption chips (see, for example [5,6,7]).

GENERAL PROPERTIES OF ESCROWED ENCRYPTION

We propose the following objectives and options for any escrowed encryption system:

---

* Proc. International Cryptography Institute 1994: Global Challenges, National Intellectual Property Law Institute, Washington D.C., Sept. 22–23, 1994.

Strong Security

An escrowed encryption system should provide strong confidentiality protection for information encrypted with an escrowed encryption product, and strong assurance that such protection is achieved. Information encrypted with an escrowed encryption product should be decipherable only by the intended recipients and authorized government officials. The system should be auditable so that unauthorized use of escrowed keys can be detected.

An escrowed encryption system should provide strong protection against unauthorized disclosure of sensitive information. By strong protection, we mean there is no significant risk of a successful cryptanalytic attack against the encryption algorithm, and no significant risk that escrowed keys can be used except as authorized. With escrowed encryption, the risk of unauthorized decryption of sensitive information, whether by the government or by anyone else, should be acceptably low, including the decryption of communications intercepted prior to or following a period of authorized electronic surveillance. If unauthorized decryption does occur, it should be detectable through auditing.

The security requirements could be met through a combination of technical, operational, and legal safeguards that apply specifically to escrowed encryption or more generally to the interception of electronic communications or the seizure of stored information. Although technical safeguards often can provide a higher level of assurance against security compromises than operational or legal ones, other factors such as cost and efficiency must be taken into consideration as well.

The EES and associated key escrow system have been designed to provide strong security. The SKIPJACK encryption algorithm provides strong cryptanalytic security, and the key escrow system has extensive safeguards, including auditing, to ensure that the risk of unauthorized access to EES-encrypted communications is negligible [7].

Single Key or Public Key

Escrowed encryption technology could use single key or public key cryptography.

The EES uses a single key encryption algorithm, SKIPJACK, both for data encryption and for the key escrow functions. Silvio Micali has proposed an alternative approach to escrowed encryption based on public key cryptography, which he calls "fair public key cryptography" [12]. Some designs use a combination of both types of cryptography, for example, single key cryptography for data encryption and public key for the key escrow functions and to establish data encryption keys (e.g., session keys) [10,17].

Hardware or Software

Escrowed encryption technology could be implemented in hardware, software, or firmware.

The EES requires special tamper-resistant hardware and a secure facility for programming the Clipper chips. Currently, only one company (Mykotronx) has the capability to program the chips.

A software approach to key escrow is potentially cheaper than hardware and more readily integrated into computer-based applications such as e-mail. Trusted Information Systems has designed a software-based approach to key escrow that has many of the same characteristics of Clipper, but uses public algorithms and public key cryptography for the key escrow functions [17]. They have implemented a prototype of their design on a Sun workstation using triple-DES for data encryption and RSA to establish session keys and perform the key escrow functions.

Although a software approach may be preferred for some applications, hardware can provide greater security and integrity for algorithms and keys than is possible with software. Moreover, now that PCMCIA slots are becoming a standard feature on many computers including notebook PCs, a PCMCIA modem or Crypto Card with a Capstone chip, which provides digital signatures and key exchange in addition to escrowed encryption, could prove attractive for many applications such as electronic commerce. Indeed, the PCMCIA Crypto Card with Capstone is being used in the Defense Messaging System. The increasing popularity of smart cards and PCMCIA cards for cryptographic functions and key storage suggests that hardware approaches will flourish along with software ones.

Classified or Unclassified Algorithms

Escrowed encryption technology could use classified or unclassified algorithms. If classified algorithms are used, they must be implemented in tamper-resistant hardware. Unclassified algorithms could be proprietary or public domain.

Unclassified algorithms have the advantage of being implementable in both hardware and software. Classified algorithms must be implemented in tamper-resistant hardware since there is no known way of reliably hiding classified information in software. This is one reason that the EES specifies a hardware implementation—it uses the classified SKIPJACK encryption algorithm. Conversely, any software-based approach to key escrow must use unclassified algorithms.

Unclassified, non-proprietary algorithms have the advantage of being open to public review, which can contribute to greater public and international acceptance.

Standards and Gateways

International escrowed encryption must accommodate secure international communications. If multiple technologies and encryption algorithms are adopted as standards, trusted gateways could be established to translate communications from one standard into another.

Open, international standards for escrowed encryption are highly desirable since such standards could accommodate both domestic and international communications. Finding an approach that does not require classified technology and could be implemented in either hardware or software could greatly facilitate the adoption of such standards.

Although a single encryption algorithm and standard is desirable for interoperability, it seems likely that there will be multiple escrowed encryption standards. At the very least, if a public-domain software approach is adopted, it will co-exist with the EES. In addition, there may be application-specific standards or different national standards.

To accommodate multiple standards, trusted gateways between systems could be established in much the same way that they are established to support multiple communication protocols. For example, EES-encrypted communications could pass through a gateway where they are translated into another key escrow standard. These gateways also could be used to translate between escrowed encryption systems and unescrowed systems. Since communications passing through a gateway are, at least temporarily, in the clear, a gateway should provide a high level of assurance that those communications are not vulnerable to unauthorized disclosure.

THE KEY ESCROW SYSTEM

Escrowed Keys

The keys stored in escrow could be 1) individual data encrypting keys, 2) product unique keys, 3) user key establishment keys, or 4) master keys.

At the lowest level of granularity, individual data encrypting keys could be stored in escrow, for example, the session key for a particular conversation or a file encryption key, which may be used to encrypt all the files in a single directory [3].

The second alternative is to escrow keys that are unique to an individual product. With the EES, each individual Clipper chip has a device unique key that is stored in escrow. A similar strategy could be used with a software approach to key escrow, except that the keys would be associated with individual copies of software products rather than hardware devices. The TIS software-based key escrow system uses this strategy [17].

The third alternative is to escrow users' key establishment keys, that is, the keys used in the protocols to establish a data encryption key. Micali's fair public key cryptography follows this approach, escrowing the private key of a user's public-private key pair.

Linking the key escrow data to specific individuals may make it easier to guarantee that keys are released only to decrypt the communications of individuals named in a court order. However, it has the drawback that the escrow agents know who is under surveillance. With a product-based approach, the privacy of those under surveillance is protected. Also, by associating a key with a product, a user does not have to supply a key to the product in order to use it for encryption. For example, to use an AT&T 3600 Telephone Security Device which has an EES chip, the user simply pushes a button. This also has the advantage that if an escrowed encryption product such as a TSD is located at a site used by more than one criminal, a single key suffices to decrypt all lawfully intercepted communications encrypted with the TSD, regardless of which particular person may be using it. Another advantage to associating keys with products is that import/export controls apply to products, and a country may wish to control the import or export of products based on what country holds the keys.

The fourth alternative is to escrow "master keys" that would allow access to information encrypted by multiple products or users. This strategy obviates the need to attach keys to either products or users and the need to maintain a database of keys. However, depending on the exact protocols used, it may be more difficult to provide assurance that the master escrow key is used only to decrypt information as authorized. The KISS (Keep the Invaders (of privacy) Socially Sane) system uses the master key approach [10].

Keys Escrowed Before First Use

The key(s) used to decrypt information that has been encrypted by a particular escrowed encryption product should be escrowed before the product is used to encrypt that information.

If individual data encryption keys are escrowed, then they most likely would be escrowed at the time they are generated.

If product keys are escrowed, there are two possibilities for escrow: escrow at the time of manufacture or escrow at the time of first use. The former approach, which is used with the EES, has the advantage of ensuring that the keys are escrowed even before the products go out the door. It has the disadvantage of requiring permanent unique keys in the products and of fixing the escrow agents at the time of manufacture. An approach that delays the time of escrow to the time of first use could allow new keys to be generated and escrowed periodically. A first-use approach also would allow for greater flexibility in the selection of escrow agents. A product could be manufactured with an option for escrowing the key in one of several countries, or escrowing the key with private sector escrow agents as well as government ones.

If users' key establishment keys are escrowed, then the products that use those keys as input must have some way of recognizing whether the keys have been escrowed. This could be accomplished through some method of certification such as a public key certificate. Under Micali's proposal, users would not be able to place their public keys, which are used for key establishment and digital signatures, in the public key infrastructure unless they were escrowed [12]. This would guarantee that the public key infrastructure could not be used by criminals to evade law enforcement.

One or More Escrow Agents

A key could be escrowed in its entirety with a single escrow agent, or it could be split into two or more components, where each component is kept with a different escrow agent. If multiple agents are used, they could be set up so that all agents or only a subset of the agents is needed to provide access to an escrowed key.

If keys are split into multiple components, the splitting could be implemented in a way that requires the components of all escrow agents to recover an original key. The EES uses this approach, with a key being the XOR of two separately escrowed key components.

Alternatively, a more complex arrangement can be used that would allow particular subsets of agents to provide access to a key. For example, the escrow agents could be used with a "k out of n" threshold system, which would permit any k out of n escrow agents to participate [8,12], or with a more general access structure [1].

Single Nation Escrow

The key to an escrowed encryption product is escrowed in only one country, but can be escrowed in any country that has the authority to decrypt communications with that key. If a key is split into two or more components before escrow, all components should be escrowed in the same country.

We assume that keys are not escrowed with an international body, but that, at least potentially, they could be escrowed in any country, and not just the one where the product is manufactured or used. This would allow an escrowed encryption product to be manufactured in one country, used in a second, and have its key escrowed in a third, subject to national controls (Section 4). In practice, one would expect at least two if not all three of these to be the same. For example, an EES-based product bought and used in the U.S. would have its keys escrowed in the U.S. If the product is taken into the U.K., then its place of use would differ from its place of manufacture and key escrow. It is conceivable that an agreement could be reached with the U.K. that would allow the key to be escrowed in the U.K. If that product is then taken to Australia, we could have a situation where all three places are different.

Private Sector Key Escrow

A private sector (corporate) key escrow system could be established for the purpose of enabling organizations and individuals access to their own encrypted information. Such a system could be integrated with a government key escrow system or it could be separate.

A private sector key escrow system, sometimes referred to as "corporate key escrow," would enable organizations and individuals to escrow keys and then obtain access to those keys without a warrant. One of the concerns of many users of encryption, particularly organizations, is that encrypted information could become inaccessible if keys are accidentally lost, intentionally destroyed, or held for ransom. A corporate escrow system could help protect an organization's information assets and protect against liability problems by ensuring that keys are under the control of those accountable for the assets. Without some sort of "encryption override," an organization may suffer damages caused by "encryption anarchy" [14].

A private sector key escrow system could be separate from the one used by the government or the two could be integrated together. With a separate approach, the data and protocols could be different.

With an integrated approach, the key escrow data used for corporate access would be the same as that used for government access. Frank Sudia at Banker's Trust has proposed a design for such a system using private sector key escrow agents to support both government and corporate access [16].

TECSEC Inc. proposes that users escrow all of their data encrypting keys themselves, which would then be available to the government through a court order. Their VEIL cryptographic software tool supports this concept [15]. However, while this approach could support court-ordered access to stored files (including e-mail), it would not support wiretaps of phone conversations, which are done without the knowledge of the intercepted parties and under real-time requirements.

GOVERNMENT ACCESS AND DECRYPTION

Real-Time Access

An escrowed encryption system should allow authorized government access to information encrypted with an escrowed encryption product. Such access is to be enabled through one or more escrowed keys. For real-time communications, the system should enable initial access to the communications of a subject under investigation within two hours and real-time (5 second) access thereafter.

Real-time decryption of phone conversations is critical for many types of investigations, for example kidnapings and planned terrorist activities. Although a one-time initial delay to acquire key escrow data is acceptable, such delay for each intercepted communication would be unacceptable.

For stored information, real-time access is less critical. However, it should be possible to decrypt information in a timely manner.

Acquisition of Data Encryption Key

An authorized government official should be able to obtain the data encrypting keys for information that the official is authorized to intercept or seize, but not for other information. A data encryption key could be acquired either from the escrow agents directly, from a Law Enforcement Access Field, or by participation in the key establishment protocol.

If the data encryption key is given to the escrow agents, then it could be obtained directly from them. This would be the case with a file encryption system where the users hold their own keys or turn them over to separate escrow agents.

For communications, the data encryption key (i.e., session key) could be acquired through a *Law Enforcement Access Field (LEAF)* that is transmitted with the encrypted communications. The LEAF would contain either the session key or some other key that would provide access to the session key. To protect this key from compromise, it can be encrypted under one or more escrowed keys. This is the approach used with the EES. After a session key is established, the EES device (Clipper chip) creates a LEAF that includes the session key encrypted under the device unique key. In addition, the entire LEAF is encrypted under a common family key.

There are several options for LEAF design and law enforcement decryption depending on what keys are escrowed and the services provided by the escrow agents. If product (or user) keys are escrowed, then the logical design for the LEAF is to contain the session key encrypted under the product (user) key. The escrow agents can be set up either to release the escrowed keys to the government agency as is done with the EES, or to decrypt each individual session key on demand. The latter approach allows the escrow agents to enforce the authorization period for a wiretap, but the disadvantage of requiring participation by the escrow agents with each communication. This may cause practical problems meeting the real-time needs of law enforcement. At the very least, a reliable and secure high-speed electronic communication channel would have to be established between the escrow agents and the law enforcement decryption processor.

If the escrowed keys are master keys, then the LEAF could contain either the session key encrypted under the master key or a product (or user) key encrypted under the master key, with the session key encrypted under the product (user) key . With the former approach, the escrow agents most likely would participate in the decryption of each individual session key rather than release the master key to the law enforcement agency. However, with the latter, they could release the decrypted product (user) key to the law enforcement agency, which could then decrypt the session keys independently. The KISS system uses this approach [10]. The LEAF contains the user's private key encrypted under two master keys (one for each escrow agent). The escrow agents provide the decrypted user key to law enforcement.

For real-time, interactive communications (which excludes e-mail), an alternative to using a LEAF is to make the law enforcement agency or some other trusted third party an active participant in the protocol used by the sender and receiver to establish the session key. This would be done in such a way that the investigative agency can determine the session key, but the two parties cannot detect the participation of the agency.

Thomas Beth et al. have proposed such an approach whereby an investigative agency's key server/decrypt processor is substituted for a network key server when there is an authorized surveillance [2]. When the investigative agency's key server is in the loop, it can determine the session keys since it will have acquired the necessary escrowed keys. However, when the network key server is in the loop, it will be unable to determine the session keys since it will not have the necessary escrowed keys. The disadvantage of the approach is that it requires active, real-time participation by a third party. By comparison, the EES requires only passive interception of communications.

Beth et al.'s approach provides a technical means of strictly limiting the interval of decryption to the period of authorized surveillance. Clipper's key escrow system will prevent decryption of traffic intercepted after an authorized period of surveillance through an automatic deletion of keys in the law enforcement decryption processor, but must rely on procedural and legal safeguards to prevent the decryption of communications intercepted (illegally) prior to the authorized surveillance period. Although a technical solution is possible by adding a clock to a Clipper chip [11], the existing safeguards appear adequate and the added cost of a clock may not be justified by the potential reduction in risk.

When intercepting a conversation such as a phone call (or e-mail exchange), law enforcers need access to both sides of the conversation and not just the communications coming from the person who is the subject of the surveillance. Whether this is possible in real time will depend on the design of the escrowed encryption system. Since the subject of an investigation could have literally hundreds of such calls a day, a system that would require law enforcers to get the keys for all persons that communicate with the subject could fail to meet the real-time requirements and obstruct many investigations, particularly if the keys were held in different countries.

The EES allows real-time access to both sides of phone conversations by requiring that a common session key be used for both sides of a two-way simultaneous communication, and that both parties transmit a LEAF so that the session key can be obtained from either side of the conversation. Thus, it suffices to obtain the key escrow data of the product used by the subject of the investigation in order to listen in on all conversations involving the subject.

For electronic mail, achieving real-time access is more complex since many e-mail systems do not support the concept of a conversation. Moreover, e-mail systems that provide encryption do not require any exchanges to establish a common session key. One solution is to build into e-mail packages a capability for generating automatic "receipts" for all received messages. A receipt could carry a LEAF that contains the session key needed to decrypt the received message. Thus, once the escrowed key used by the subject of an authorized surveillance is obtained, all of that person's outgoing messages could be decrypted with information contained in the LEAFs transmitted with those messages, and all of that person's incoming messages could be decrypted with information contained in the LEAFs of the receipts for those messages.

Protection Against Interoperable Rogue Products

It should not be practical to modify or use an escrowed encryption product in a way that precludes authorized government access by circumventing the key escrow capability but allows the product to interoperate with those that correctly implement the key escrow mechanism.

An escrowed encryption product should resist practical attacks to circumvent or undermine the law enforcement access feature, for example by transmitting a null or bogus LEAF. Of particular concern are "rogue" applications that would interoperate with legitimate ones by transmitting a bogus LEAF which is accepted as valid by the receiving application but proves useless to the government. A non-interoperable application is of less concern since a person intent on avoiding government access has the option of using an alternative means of encryption when interoperability is not needed. Although an early prototype of the PCMCIA Crypto Card (formerly called Tessera), which contains a Capstone chip that implements the EES functionality, was found vulnerable to such an attack [4,7], the production devices will implement techniques that protect against the attack.

NATIONAL CONTROLS AND INTERNATIONAL AND BILATERAL AGREEMENTS

National Control of Key Escrow Technology and Keys

Each nation controls the export, import, and internal use of escrowed encryption technology. It can specify who holds the keys needed to decrypt information that is encrypted by products used within its jurisdiction and for products it exports and imports.

This requirement recognizes that nations control cryptographic technologies and can extend these controls to specify where keys may be escrowed when those keys are used within its jurisdiction, whether by citizens or non-citizens, or are associated with products that it manufactures and exports or that it imports. We do not assume that a nation necessarily can enforce whatever controls it may impose.

A national policy about key escrow technology must optimize economic and political objectives along with law enforcement and intelligence ones. Although holding keys may serve a country's law enforcement and national security interests, if a country insists on holding all the keys used within its jurisdiction, it could inhibit foreign organizations from establishing offices and conducting business within its borders out of fear of government espionage. If it insists on holding all the keys for products that it manufactures and exports, it could find few buyers for its products outside its borders, thereby diminishing its competitiveness in the global market.

Key escrow encryption offers the opportunity for less stringent export controls on products with strong encryption than for encryption products without key escrow. This can provide an incentive for companies to manufacture products with a key escrow feature.

International and Bilateral Agreements

Nations will establish international and bilateral agreements specifying provisions for assisting with criminal investigations, sharing encryption technology or manufacturing facilities, and permitting the sale and use of escrowed encryption products.

As an example, two countries or a group of countries might make an agreement that if one country is investigating a crime within its jurisdiction and needs access to communications protected by a key held by the second, then the second country will assist with the decryption under a suitable showing of probable cause. Under a mutual assistance agreement, an escrowed encryption product whose keys are held in one country could be used in another without threatening the latter's law enforcement operations.

A country holding a key needed for an investigation in another country could assist in at least three ways:

1. *Remote Decryption:* It could receive the encrypted communications, decrypt them, and return plaintext to the investigating country. All this could be done electronically, using encryption to protect the communications and for authentication.
2. *On-Site Decryption Assistance:* It could send one or more government officials to perform the decryption in the investigating country. The officials could bring with them a decrypt device loaded with the key, and return with the device when the electronic surveillance terminates.
3. *Key Transfer:* It could give the investigating country the key.

The third strategy would be feasible only if the investigating country had its own decryption capability. Even when feasible, it would not likely be used except in limited conditions since most countries would be sensitive about protecting the keys used by their citizens.

Agreements also may be reached about sharing technology or manufacturing facilities so that countries could have a common hardware standard while permitting keys to be escrowed in different countries.

National Policy Options

The following lists several options that a nation, N, could consider in establishing export and internal use controls over escrowed encryption technology and products. Import options would be similar to those governing internal use.

Export Options for Nation N
E1 Products treated like unescrowed encryption products.
E2 Products generally exportable as long as keys needed to decrypt information encrypted with those products are held by N.

E3   Products generally exportable if keys held by N, and generally exportable to another nation that would hold the keys if that other nation has established a mutual assistance agreement with N.

E4   Products exportable without constraint.

Internal Use Options for Nation N

U1   Products treated like unescrowed encryption products.

U2   Products can be used only if N holds the keys.

U3   Products can be used if keys are held by N or by any other nation that has established a mutual assistance agreement with N.

U4   Products can be used without constraint.

In some cases, these options may be the same. For example, U1 and U4 are identical in the U.S. since no controls are placed on the use of cryptography within the U.S.

Options E3 and U3 would effectively allow for free flow of escrowed encryption products between countries with mutual assistance agreements regardless of which country held the keys. Under such conditions, the users themselves might have the option of choosing which country held their keys, either by choice of product if key escrow is tied to product manufacturing or by selecting the country from a menu of options if key escrow is tied to the user or to the first use of the product.

We can analyze the advantages and disadvantages of different choices in different scenarios. For example, suppose a citizen from one country, A, has a second or temporary residence in a another country, B. Alternatively, a company based in A has an office in country B. At least in theory, the citizen or company could use an escrowed encryption product whose keys are held by either A or B. For example, they could bring in a product whose keys are escrowed in country A, or they could purchase a product in B whose keys are escrowed in B. Table I shows the advantages and disadvantages of each of the two countries holding the keys as seen from the citizen or company as well as from the two governments. Overall, it would seem preferable for country A to hold the keys since it provides better protection against potential espionage by country B.

A similar table could be constructed for other scenarios, for example, the use of a product by a citizen of country B when that product was imported from country A.

Scenarios for the Export of EES Technology

To illustrate the general framework outlined here, we consider several options for the export of the U.S. EES technology to a foreign country:

TABLE I. Advantages and disadvantages of country A and country B holding the keys for a product used by a citizen or company of A residing in B.

| | Country A holds the keys | | Country B holds the keys | |
	Advantages	Disadvantages	Advantages	Disadvantages
Perspective of citizen or company of country A	Protected from espionage by country B	Potentially subject to investigations by own country	Greater protection from own government	Vulnerable to espionage by country B
Perspective of government of Country A	Can protect its citizens from espionage by country B Facilitates investigations of own citizens			Citizens are vulnerable to espionage by country B Harder to investigate own citizens
Perspective of government of country B	Doesn't have to manage keys of non-citizens	Harder to investigate residents who are not citizens	Easier to investigate or spy on non-citizens	Must manage keys of non-citizens

1. *U.S. holds the keys:* EES products are exported to the foreign country with the U.S. holding the keys. This scenario could apply when the foreign country or organization is not concerned about the U.S. holding the keys.
2. *Foreign country escrows keys of chips manufactured in the U.S.:* The foreign country is allowed to use a U.S. chip programming facility in order to acquire the keys to chips programmed under its supervision. The chips are taken back to the foreign country and used with products in that country.
3. *Foreign country manufactures its own chips and escrows its own keys:* The U.S. shares its technology so that the foreign country can establish its own escrow programming facility and produce its own chips.

While many people have speculated that no foreign countries would be interested in devices whose keys were held in the U.S., this does not seem to be the case. Mykotronx has reported that many potential buyers in foreign countries are not concerned about the U.S. holding the keys (scenario 1); other countries, while interested in using the technology, would prefer to hold the keys (scenarios 2 and 3) [9]. In both 2 and 3, a law enforcement agreement between the U.S. and foreign government could be established in case products whose keys were escrowed in the foreign country were brought back into the U.S. or used against the U.S. Such an agreement might also be reached under scenario 1 so that the foreign government could count on assistance from the U.S. in the event the products were used to conceal criminal activity in the foreign country.

Law Enforcement Scenarios

In this section we illustrate the general principles discussed here by considering various law enforcement scenarios that might arise in the context of an international communications network that provides confidentiality protection through an international escrowed encryption system.

Suppose that a law enforcement agency in a country A, while investigating an international organized crime case, finds probable cause to believe that a Mr. X is using the network to conduct criminal activities. Table II shows several possible scenarios for the investigation. The scenarios are characterized by two attributes: the country where Mr. X is located and the country that holds the key(s) needed to decrypt communications encrypted with the product used by Mr. X. In scenarios 1–2, Mr. X is located in country A, while in scenarios 3–5, he is located in a second country B. Scenario 5 introduces a third country C as the holder of the key.

We do not show the country where the product originated. This is because it is not relevant to the investigation since we assume that the country that holds the key has the technology necessary to decrypt the communications. We also do not show the countries where individuals communicating with Mr. X are located. Their locations would be relevant if communications to X could not be decrypted except through their keys. In that case, the analysis given for the location of X could be applied, but using the countries of those communicating with X.

TABLE II. *Policy objectives for country A and country B when A initiates an investigation of a subject X and the subject is using an escrowed encryption product. IA = investigative and intercept assistance, KA = key assistance.*

Scenario	Location of Subject X	Holder of Key	Country A's Objectives	Country B's Objectives
1	A	A		
2	A	B	KA from B	
3	B	A	IA from B	KA from A
4	B	B	IA from B	
5	B	C	IA from B	KA from C

For each scenario, Table II specifies the investigative policy objectives of country A and country B. In scenarios 3–5, where Mr. X is located in B, country A needs investigative and interception assistance (IA) from B. Any additional assistance that is needed in order to decrypt the communications would be obtained by country B.

When the key is held in a country other than the one performing the intercept, then the country implementing the intercept needs key assistance (KA) from the country holding the key. For example, in scenario 2 country A needs key assistance from country B. This scenario could arise with the EES, for example, if Mr. X takes an EES product whose key is escrowed in the U.S. (country B) to the U.K. (country A) where he is under investigation. In that situation, the U.K. would need key assistance from the U.S. in order to decrypt X's communications.

Scenario 3 could arise if Mr. X takes an EES product whose key is escrowed in the U.S. (country A) to the U.K. (country B) and Mr. X is under investigation in the U.S. In that case, the U.S. needs investigative assistance from the U.K. to access the communications, and the U.K. needs key assistance from the U.S. to decrypt the communications.

In Scenario 4, the U.K. (country A) could be investigating Mr. X who is located in the U.S. (country B) and using a product whose key is escrowed in the U.S. The U.K. will need intercept assistance from the U.S., but the U.S. will have the key needed to decrypt the communications. Conversely, if EES products are exported to the U.K. with the U.K. holding the keys, scenario 4 could arise if the U.S. (country A) is investigating Mr. X who is located in the U.K. (country B). Then the U.S. will need investigative assistance from the U.K. in order to intercept the communications.

In Scenario 5, Mr. X is residing in country B and using a product whose key is held by C. In this case, country A needs investigative assistance from B, and B needs key assistance from country C. To illustrate, suppose the U.S. (country A) is conducting an investigation of Mr. X, who resides in Italy (country B) using an EES-product whose key is escrowed in the U.K. (country C). In that case, the U.S. needs investigative assistance from Italy, and Italy needs key assistance from the U.K. Alternatively, Italy (country A) could be investigating Mr. X, who is residing in the U.S. (country B) using an EES-product whose key is held by the U.K. (country C). Italy needs investigative assistance from the U.S. in order that Mr. X's communications can be intercepted, and the U.S. needs key assistance from the U.K. in order to decrypt those communications.

SUMMARY

An escrowed encryption system should provide strong cryptographic security and a high level of assurance that escrowed keys will be used only as authorized. It should allow real-time decryption by authorized government officials and resist practical attacks to circumvent or undermine the mechanisms that allow for such access.

Escrowed encryption technology could use single key or public key cryptography; be implemented in hardware, software, or firmware; and use classified or unclassified algorithm. Open standards based on public algorithms are highly desirable, especially for international communications. Although a single encryption algorithm and standard is desirable for interoperability, it seems likely that there will be multiple algorithms and standards. To accommodate these standards, trusted gateways that translate communications from one standard into another could be established.

The keys stored in escrow could be the data encryption keys, individual product keys, user key establishment keys, or master keys. They should be escrowed before they are first used.

Keys should be escrowed in only one country. They could be escrowed with a single escrow agent or be split between multiple escrow agents. A private sector key escrow system that would enable organizations and individuals to escrow keys for their own use could be established in addition to a government escrow system. The two systems might be integrated.

Each country controls export, import, and internal use of escrowed encryption technologies, and who holds the keys for products used within its jurisdiction and for products it imports and exports. International and bilateral assistance agreements could allow the flow of escrowed encryption products between countries in a way that does not jeopardize a country's law enforcement and national security objectives.

REFERENCES

1. Beth, T., Knoblock, H.-J., and Otten, M., "Verifiable Secret Sharing for Monotone Access Structures," *Proc. 1st ACM Conf. on Communication and Computer Security*, Nov. 1993.

2. Beth, T., Knoblock, H.-J., Otten, M., Simmons, G. J., and Wichmann, P., "Clipper Repair Kit—Towards Acceptable Key Escrow Systems," E.I.S.S., Karlsruhe Univ., E.I.S.S., Karlsruhe, Germany, June 24, 1994.

3. Blaze, M., "Key Management in an Encrypting File System.," AT&T Bell Laboratories.

4. Blaze, M., "Protocol Failure in the Escrowed Encryption Standard," AT&T Bell Laboratories, draft of June 3, 1994.

5. Denning, D. E., "The Clipper Encryption System," *American Scientist*, Vol. 81, July-August 1993, pp. 319–324.

6. Denning, D. E., "The U.S. Key Escrow Encryption Technology," *Computer Communications*, Vol. 17, No. 7, July 1994, Butterworth-Heinemann Ltd., Linacre House, Jordan Hill, Oxford, OX2 8DP, UK.

7. Denning, D.E. and Smid, M., "Key Escrowing Today," *IEEE Communications*, Sept. 1994.

8. Desmedt, Y., Frankel, Y., and Yung, M., "A Scientific Statement on the Clipper Chip Technology and Alternatives," 1993.

9. Droge, J., personal communication, May 1994.

10. Fortress U & T Ltd., "Keep the Invaders (of Privacy) Socially Sane—KISS," overheads of presentation, POB 844, Beer Sheva 84106, Israel, 1994.

11. Leiberich, O., private communication, June 1994.

12. Micali, S., "Fair Cryptosystems," MIT/LCS/TR-579.b, Laboratory for Computer Science, Massachusetts Institute of Technology, Cambridge, MA, November 1993.

13. National Institute for Standards and Technology, "Escrowed Encryption Standard (EES)," Federal Information Processing Standards Publication (FIPS PUB) 185, 1994.

14. Parker, D. B., "Avoid Encryption Anarchy," *Infosecurity News*, Vol. 5, No. 3., May/June 1994, pp 29,32.

15. Roberts, J. L., "Private Escrow Key Management," presentation, TECSEC Inc., Vienna, VA.

16. Sudia, F. W., "International Corporate Key Escrow," overheads of presentation, Bankers Trust Co., New York, NY, February 1994.

17. Trusted Information Systems, "Software Key Escrow," overheads of presentation, Glenwood, MD, 1994.

PART II

CURRENT GOVERNMENT POLICY

## CHAPTER 3

THE U.S. GOVERNMENT POLICY SOLUTION

KEY ESCROW CRYPTOSYSTEMS, POLICIES, PROCEDURES, AND LEGISLATION

Technological advances in communications and data security bring with them serious questions about the control of such technology, particularly if the technology is related to national defense and law-enforcement. The government has to perform a high-wire balancing act, weighing those needs against the privacy and freedom of its citizens. This section presents some of the most important documents issued by the U.S. Government as it struggles to strike an appropriate balance.

We start with a formal announcement released on February 4, 1994 by the White House. It commits to a royalty-free digital signature standard, something necessary for the Global Information Infrastructure and overdue for electronic commerce, but a cryptographic mechanism less versatile (but more friendly to law enforcement and national security interests) than another (RSA) already in common commercial use. It also announces the issuing of the Escrowed Encryption Standard while at the same time pledging to work more closely with commercial and public interest groups to develop better systems and to refine Administration policies. It announces the Administration's establishment of an interagency Working Group on Encryption and Tel-ecommunications. It announces procedures for release of escrowed keys to authorized parties, and it notes new procedures for expediting export of various encryption products (while not changing the regula-tions governing foreign sales). It reiterates the Administration's inten-tion to not restrict domestic encryption or mandate use of a particular technology.

Next, the Vice President, in a very brief statement, effectively notes that he is aware of the announcements on encryption but says almost nothing else. This probably reflects the political quagmire he would sink deeper into if he said any more about the controversial EES which the White House statement implicitly admits leaves much to be desired. On the other hand, he probably thought that he had to say something, since remaining silent would send a "disowning" message from the political architect of the National Information Infrastructure (NII).

It's interesting to note that by July 20, 1994, Vice President Gore felt comfortable explicitly noting in his letter to Representative Maria Cantwell some of the problems with Clipper and acknowledging that "the Clipper chip is an approved federal standard for telephone com-munication and not for computer networks and video networks"; that he would like a "more versatile, less expensive system" with key escrow implementable in software, firmware or hardware, or any combination thereof which "would not rely on a classified algorithm"; and that "there are many severe challenges to developing such a system" which "must permit the use of private-sector key escrow agents as one option".

Representative Cantwell had led an effort to greatly reduce export controls on cryptographic products. She had to settle, this time around, for a promise from Vice President Gore to reassess the current rela-tively strict export control licensing regime based on the results of two government studies to be carried out in 1994 and 1995.

The statement of Deputy Assistant Secretary of State for Political-Military Affairs Martha Harris of February 4, 1994 briefly announces some "reforms" in the existing controls. These changes expedite current processes without changing the substance of the regulations (see Chap-ter 7 for more detail on these). They also allow a U. S. citizen to legally carry his or her own laptop (with encryption hardware or software) out of the country on a business trip and bring it back in without obtaining an export license. One assumes this regulation was little known and even less honored.[1]

The next press release from the Attorney General's office formally identifies the two key escrow agents under current federal government

---

[1] And with good reason: a description of the pitfalls awaiting a traveler is given in Blaze, M., "My life as an international arms courier," Comp. Risks, Vol. 16, No. 73, 6 January 1995.

policy, NIST and the Automated Systems Division of the Treasury Department. It also summarizes the authorization procedures for release of encryption key components in conjunction with wiretaps pursuant to domestic crime control law and foreign intelligence surveillance. It claims that when the wiretap authorization ends, the ["decrypt"] device's ability to decrypt communications using the tapped chip will also end, though it is not clear either from the technical description in Chapter 2 or the detailed authorization procedures which immediately follow in this chapter how that can happen.

FBI director Louis Freeh said in September 1994 that if Clipper failed to gain acceptance and private encryption technologies became more widespread, he would have no choice but to press Congress to pass legislation that provided law enforcement access to *all* encrypted communications. This is the first Administration hint at a future governmental policy that could result in the banning of non-governmental, unbreakable encryption methods.

Because of concerns about these procedures, a bill[2] to regulate "voluntary encryption standards" currently under discussion on Capitol Hill is included here to provide a model for those attempting this difficult task. It provides that any encryption standard developed under the program established by this act be implementable in software, firmware, hardware, or any combination thereof.

One need not plow through the entire bill, however, since an excellent summary is provided by this chapter's final article, a release from the Electronic Privacy Information Center. They welcome this first attempt to "bring encryption standards setting under the rule of law", but propose several changes including improving citizen privacy by either creating a privacy agency or by taking away the special status for pre-issuance review of proposed encryption standards that the FBI, NSA, and the Attorney General have under this draft; providing (finally!) a proper and public risk assessment of the government's key escrow policy; and transferring key escrow responsibility from the executive branch to the judicial branch of government so that the regulators report to different persons than the regulated.

---

[2] H.R. 5199, pp. 247–256.

Statement of the Press Secretary*

The White House, Office of the Press Secretary

Last April, the Administration announced a comprehensive inter-agency review of encryption technology, to be overseen by the National Security Council. Today, the Administration is taking a number of steps to implement the recommendations resulting from that review.

Advanced encryption technology offers individuals and businesses an inexpensive and easy way to encode data and telephone conversations. Unfortunately, the same encryption technology that can help Americans protect business secrets and personal privacy can also be used by terrorists, drug dealers, and other criminals.

In the past, Federal policies on encryption have reflected primarily the needs of law enforcement and national security. The Clinton Administration has sought to balance these needs with the needs of businesses and individuals for security and privacy. That is why, today the National Institute of Standards and Technology (NIST) is committing to ensure a royalty-free, public-domain Digital Signature Standard. Over many years, NIST has been developing digital signature technology that would provide a way to verify the author and sender of an electronic message. Such technology will be critical for a wide range of business applications for the National Information Infrastructure. A digital signature standard will enable individuals to transact business electronically rather than having to exchange signed paper contracts. The Administration has determined that such technology should not be subject to private royalty payments, and it will be taking steps to ensure that royalties are not required for use of a digital signature. Had digital signatures been in widespread use, the recent security problems with the Internet would have been avoided.

Last April, the Administration released the Key Escrow chip (also known as the "Clipper Chip") that would provide Americans with secure telecommunications without compromising the ability of law enforcement agencies to carry out legally authorized wiretaps. Today, the Department of Commerce and the Department of Justice are taking steps to enable the use of such technology both in the U.S. and overseas. At the same time, the Administration is announcing its intent to work

---

* The White House, Office of the Press Secretary; February 4, 1994.

with industry to develop other key escrow products that might better meet the needs of individuals and industry, particularly the American computer and telecommunications industry. Specific steps being announced today include:

- Approval by the Commerce Secretary of the Escrowed Encryption Standard (EES) as a voluntary Federal Information Processing Standard, which will enable government agencies to purchase the Key Escrow chip for use with telephones and modems. The department's National Institute of Standards and Technology (NIST) will publish the standard.

- Publication by the Department of Justice of procedures for the release of escrowed keys and the announcement of NIST and the Automated Services Division of the Treasury Department as the escrow agents that will store the keys needed for decryption of communications using the Key Escrow chip. Nothing in these procedures will diminish the existing legal and procedural requirements that protect Americans from unauthorized wiretaps.

- New procedures to allow export of products containing the Key Escrow chip to most countries.

In addition, the Department of State will streamline export licensing procedures for encryption products that can be exported under current export regulations in order to help American companies sell their products overseas. In the past, it could take weeks for a company to obtain an export license for encryption products, and each shipment might require a separate license. The new procedures announced today will substantially reduce administrative delays and paperwork for encryption exports.

To implement the Administration's encryption policy, an interagency Working Group on Encryption and Telecommunications has been established. It will be chaired by the White House Office of Science and Technology Policy and the National Security Council and will include representatives of the Departments of Commerce, Justice, State, and Treasury as well as the FBI, the National Security Agency, the Office of Management and Budget, and the National Economic Council. This group will work with industry and public-interest groups to develop new encryption technologies and to review and refine Administration policies regarding encryption, as needed.

The Administration is expanding its efforts to work with industry to improve on the Key Escrow chip, to develop key-escrow software, and to examine alternatives to the Key Escrow chip. NIST will lead these efforts and will request additional staff and resources for this purpose.

We understand that many in industry would like to see all encryption products exportable. However, if encryption technology is made freely available worldwide, it would no doubt be used extensively by terrorists, drug dealers, and other criminals to harm Americans both in the U.S. and abroad. For this reason, the Administration will continue to restrict export of the most sophisticated encryption devices, both to preserve our own foreign intelligence gathering capability and because of the concerns of our allies who fear that strong encryption technology would inhibit their law enforcement capabilities.

At the same time, the Administration understands the benefits that encryption and related technologies can provide to users of computers and telecommunications networks. Indeed, many of the applications of the evolving National Information Infrastructure will require some form of encryption. That is why the Administration plans to work more closely with the private sector to develop new forms of encryption that can protect privacy and corporate secrets without undermining the ability of law-enforcement agencies to conduct legally authorized wiretaps. That is also why the Administration is committed to make available free of charge a Digital Signature Standard.

The Administration believes that the steps being announced today will help provide Americans with the telecommunications security they need without compromising the capability of law enforcement agencies and national intelligence agencies. Today, any American can purchase and use any type of encryption product. The Administration does not intend to change that policy. Nor do we have any intention of restricting domestic encryption or mandating the use of a particular technology.

2

*Statement of the Vice President**

The White House, Office of the Vice President

Today's announcements on encryption represent important steps in the implementation of the Administration's policy on this critical issue. Our policy is designed to provide better encryption to individuals and businesses while ensuring that the needs of law enforcement and national security are met.

Encryption is a law and order issue since it can be used by criminals to thwart wiretaps and avoid detection and prosecution. It also has huge strategic value. Encryption technology and cryptoanalysis turned the tide in the Pacific and elsewhere during World War II.

---

* The White House, Office of the Vice President; February 4, 1994.

Vice President's Letter to Representative Maria Cantwell

Albert Gore, Vice President of the United States

OFFICE OF THE VICE PRESIDENT

THE VICE PRESIDENT, WASHINGTON

July 20, 1994

The Honorable Maria Cantwell
House of Representatives
Washington, DC 20515

Dear Maria,

I write today to express my sincere appreciation of your efforts to move the national debate forward on the issue of information security and export controls. I share your strong conviction for the need to develop a comprehensive policy regarding encryption, incorporating an export policy that does not disadvantage American software companies in world markets while preserving our law enforcement and national security goals.

As you know, the Administration disagrees with you on the extent to which existing controls are harming U.S. industry in the short run and the extent to which their immediate relaxation would affect national security. For that reason we have supported a five-month Presidential study. In conducting this study, I want to assure you that the Administration will use the best available resources of the federal government. This will include the active participation of the National Economic Council and the Department of Commerce. In addition, consistent with the Senate-passed language, the first study will be completed within 150 days of passage of the Export Administration Act reauthorization bill, with the second study to be completed within one year after the completion of the first. I want to personally assure you that we will reassess our existing export controls based on the results of these studies. Moreover, all programs with encryption that can be exported today will continue to be exportable.

On the other hand, we agree that we need to take action this year to ensure that over time American companies are able to include information security features in their program in order to maintain their international competitiveness. We can achieve this by entering into a new phase of cooperation among government, industry representatives and privacy advocates with a goal of trying to develop a key escrow encryption system that will provide strong encryption, be acceptable to computer users worldwide, and address our national security needs as well.

Key escrow encryption offers a very effective way to accomplish our mutual goals. That is why the Administration adopted the key escrow encryption standard in the "Clipper Chip" to provide very secure encryption for telephone communications while preserving the ability for law enforcement and national security. But the Clipper Chip is an approved federal standard for telephone communication and not for computer networks and video networks. For that reason, we are working with industry to investigate other technologies for these applications.

The administration understands the concerns that industry has regarding the Clipper Chip. We welcome the opportunity to work with industry to design a more versatile, less expensive system. Such a key escrow scheme would be implementable in software, firmware or hardware, or any combination thereof, would not rely on a classified algorithm, would be voluntary, and would be exportable. While there are many severe challenges to developing such a system, we are committed to a diligent effort with industry and academics to achieve such a system. We welcome your offer to assist us in furthering this effort.

We also want to assure users of key escrow encryption products that they will not be subject to unauthorized electronic surveillance. As we have done with the Clipper Chip, future key escrow schemes must contain safeguards to provide for key disclosure only under legal authorization and should have audit procedures to ensure the integrity of the system. Escrow holders should be strictly liable for releasing keys without legal authorization.

We also recognize that a new key escrow encryption system must permit the use of private-sector key escrow agents as one option. It is also possible that as key escrow encryption technology spreads, companies may establish layered escrowing services for their own products. Having a number of escrow agents would give individuals and businesses more choice and flexibility in meeting their needs for secure communications.

I assure you the President and I are acutely aware of the need to balance economic and privacy needs with law enforcement and national security. This is not an easy task, I think that our approach offers the best opportunity to strike an appropriate balance. I am looking forward to working with you and others who share our interest in developing a comprehensive national policy on encryption. I am convinced that our cooperative endeavors will open new creative solutions to this critical problems.

Sincerely
 /s/
Al Gore

Encryption—Export Control Reform*

Martha Harris, Deputy Assistant Secretary of State for Political-Military Affairs

The Secretary of State is announcing today measures arising from the Administration's decision to reform export control procedures applicable to products incorporating encryption technology. These reforms are part of the Administration's effort to eliminate unnecessary controls and ensure efficient implementation. The reforms will simplify encryption product export licensing and speed the review of encryption product exports, thus helping U.S. manufacturers to compete more effectively in the global market. While there will be no changes in the types of equipment controlled by the Munitions List, we are announcing measures to expedite licensing.

Last year the President announced an initiative to encourage U.S. manufacturers and users of encryption to take advantage of a government technology (the key-escrow chip) that provides excellent security while ensuring that the Government has a means to decode the encryption when lawfully authorized, such as when executing a court-authorized warrant in connection with a criminal investigation. At the time he announced this initiative, the President directed a comprehensive review of U.S. policy regarding domestic use and export of encryption technology. The reforms we are announcing today result from that review.

The President has determined that vital U.S. national security and law enforcement interests compel maintaining appropriate control of encryption. Still, there is much that can be done to reform existing controls to ensure that they are efficiently implemented and to maintain U.S. leadership in the world market for encryption technology. Accordingly, the President has asked the Secretary of State to take immediate action to implement a number of procedural reforms. The reforms are:

■ License Reform: Under new licensing arrangements, encryption manufacturers will be able to ship their products from the United States directly to customers within approved regions without ob-

---

* United States Department of State, Washington D.C. 20520; February 4, 1994.

taining individual licenses for each end user. This will improve the ability of our manufacturers to provide expedited delivery of products, and to reduce shipping and tracking costs. It should also reduce the number of individual license requests, especially for small businesses that cannot afford international distributors.

- Rapid review of export license applications: A significant number of export license applications can be reviewed more quickly. For such exports, we have set a license turnaround goal of two working days.

- Personal use exemption: We will no longer require that U.S. citizens obtain an export license prior to taking encryption products out of the U.S. temporarily for their own personal use. In the past, this requirement caused delays and inconvenience for business travellers.

- Allow exports of key-escrow encryption: After initial review, key-escrow encryption products may now be exported to most end users. Additionally, key-escrow products will qualify for special licensing arrangements.

These reforms should have the effect of minimizing the impact of export controls on U.S. industry. The Department of State will take all appropriate actions to ensure that these reforms are implemented as quickly as possible. The Secretary of State asks that encryption product manufacturers evaluate the impact of these reforms over the next year and provide feedback both on how the reforms have worked out and on recommendations for additional procedural reforms.

The contact point for further information on these reforms is Rose Biancaniello, Office of Defense Trade Controls, Bureau of Political-Military Affairs, Department of State, (703) 875-6644.

## 5

Attorney General Makes Key Escrow Announcements*

U.S. Department of Justice, Office of the Attorney General

Attorney General Janet Reno today announced selection of the two U.S. Government entities that will hold the escrowed key components for encryption using the key-escrow encryption method. At the same time, the Attorney General made public procedures under which encryption key components will be released to government agencies for decrypting communications subject to lawful wiretaps.

Key Escrow Encryption (formerly referred to as "Clipper Chip") strikes an excellent balance between protection of communications privacy and protection of society. It permits the use in commercial telecommunications products of chips that provide extremely strong encryption, but can be decrypted, when necessary, by government agencies conducting legally authorized wiretaps. Decryption is accomplished by use of keys—80-bit binary numbers—that are unique to each individual encryption chip. Each unique key is in turn split into two components, which must be recombined in order to decrypt communications. Knowing one component does not make decryption any more feasible than not knowing either one.

The two escrow agents are the National Institute of Standards and Technology (NIST), a part of the Department of Commerce, and the Automated Systems Division of the Department of the Treasury. The two escrow agents were chosen because of their abilities to safeguard sensitive information, while at the same time being able to respond in a timely fashion when wiretaps encounter encrypted communications. In addition, NIST is responsible for establishing standards for protection of sensitive, unclassified information in Federal computer systems.

The escrow agents will act under strict procedures, which are being made public today, that will ensure the security of the key components and govern their release for use in conjunction with lawful wiretaps. They will be responsible for holding the key components: for each chip, one agent will hold one of the key components, and the second agent will hold the other. Neither will release a key component, except to a

---

* Department of Justice; February 4, 1994.

government agency with a requirement to obtain it in connection with a lawfully authorized wiretap. The system does not change the rules under which government agencies are authorized to conduct wiretaps.

When an authorized government agency encounters suspected key-escrow encryption, a written request will have to be submitted to the two escrow agents. The request will, among other things, have to identify the responsible agency and the individuals involved; certify that the agency is involved in a lawfully authorized wiretap; specify the wiretap's source of authorization and its duration; and specify the serial number of the key-escrow encryption chip being used. In every case, an attorney involved in the investigation will have to provide the escrow agents assurance that a validly authorized wiretap is being conducted.

Upon receipt of a proper request, the escrow agents will transmit their respective key components to the appropriate agency. The components will be combined within a decrypt device, which only then will be able to decrypt communications protected by key-escrow encryption. When the wiretap authorization ends, the device's ability to decrypt communications using that particular chip will also be ended.

The Department of Justice will, at the various stages of the process, take steps to monitor compliance with the procedures.

## 6

Authorization Procedures for Release of Encryption Key Components in Conjunction with Intercepts Pursuant to Title III and FISA*

U.S. Department of Justice

The following are the procedures for the release of escrowed key components in conjunction with lawfully authorized interception of communications encrypted with a key-escrow encryption method. These procedures cover all electronic surveillance conducted pursuant to Title III of the Omnibus Crime Control and Safe Streets Act of 1968, as amended (Title III), Title 18, United States Code, Section 2510 *et seq.*

1) In each case there shall be a legal authorization for the interception of wire and/or electronic communications.

2) All electronic surveillance court orders under Title III shall contain provisions authorizing after-the-fact minimization, pursuant to 18 U.S.C. 2518(5), permitting the interception and retention of coded communications, including encrypted communications.

3) In the event that federal law enforcement agents discover during the course of any lawfully authorized interception that communications encrypted with a key-escrow encryption method are being utilized, they may obtain a certification from the investigative agency conducting the investigation, or the Attorney General of the United States or designee thereof. Such certification shall:

   (a) identify the law enforcement agency or other authority conducting the interception and the person providing the certification;

   (b) certify that necessary legal authorization has been obtained to conduct electronic surveillance regarding these communications;

   (c) specify the termination date of the period for which interception has been authorized;

   (d) identify by docket number or other suitable method of specification the source of the authorization;

   (e) certify that communications covered by that authorization are being encrypted with a key-escrow encryption method;

---

* Department of Justice; February 4, 1994.

(f) specify the identifier (ID) number of the key-escrow encryption chip providing such encryption; and

(g) specify the serial (ID) number of the key-escrow decryption device that will be used by the law enforcement agency or other authority for decryption of the intercepted communications.

4) The agency conducting the interception shall submit this certification to each of the designated key component escrow agents. If the certification has been provided by an investigative agency, as soon thereafter as practicable, an attorney associated with the United States Attorney's Office supervising the investigation shall provide each of the key component escrow agents with written confirmation of the certification.

5) Upon receiving the certification from the requesting investigative agency, each key component escrow agent shall release the necessary key component to the requesting agency. The key components shall be provided in a manner that assures they cannot be used other than in conjunction with the lawfully authorized electronic surveillance for which they were requested.

6) Each of the key component escrow agents shall retain a copy of the certification of the requesting agency, as well as the subsequent confirmation of the United States Attorney's Office. In addition, the requesting agency shall retain a copy of the certification and provide copies to the following:

(a) the United States Attorney's Office supervising the investigation, and

(b) the Department of Justice, Office of Enforcement Operations.

7) Upon, or prior to, completion of the electronic surveillance phase of the investigation, the ability of the requesting agency to decrypt intercepted communications shall terminate, and the requesting agency may not retain the key components.

These procedures do not create, and are not intended to create, any substantive rights for individuals intercepted through electronic surveillance, and noncompliance with these procedures shall not provide the bases for any motion to suppress or other objection to the introduction of electronic surveillance evidence lawfully acquired.

The following are the procedures for the release of escrowed key components in conjunction with lawfully authorized interception of communications encrypted with a key-escrow encryption method. These procedures cover all electronic surveillance conducted pursuant to the Foreign Intelligence Surveillance Act (FISA), Pub. L. 95–511, which appears at Title 50 U.S. Code, Section 1801 *et seq*.

1) In each case there shall be a legal authorization for the interception of wire and/or electronic communications.

2) In the event that federal authorities discover during the course of any lawfully authorized interception that communications encrypted with a key-escrow encryption method are being utilized, they may obtain a certification from an agency authorized to participate in the conduct of the interception, or from the Attorney General of the United States or designee thereof. Such certification shall:

    (a) identify the agency participating in the conduct of the interception and the person providing the certification;

    (b) certify that necessary legal authorization has been obtained to conduct electronic surveillance regarding these communications;

    (c) specify the termination date of the period for which interception has been authorized;

    (d) identify by docket number or other suitable method of specification the source of the authorization;

    (e) certify that communications covered by that authorization are being encrypted with a key-escrow encryption method;

    (f) specify the identifier (ID) number of the key-escrow encryption chip providing such encryption; and

    (g) specify the serial (ID) number of the key-escrow decryption device that will be used by the agency participating in the conduct of the interception for decryption of the intercepted communications.

3) This certification shall be submitted to each of the designated key component escrow agents. If the certification has been provided by an agency authorized to participate in the conduct of the interception, as soon thereafter as practicable, an attorney associated with the Department of Justice, Office of Intelligence Policy and Review, shall provide each of the key component escrow agents with written confirmation of the certification.

4) Upon receiving the certification, each key component escrow agent shall release the necessary key component to the agency participating in the conduct of the interception. The key components shall be provided in a manner that assures they cannot be used other than in conjunction with the lawfully authorized electronic surveillance for which they were requested.

5) Each of the key component escrow agents shall retain a copy of the certification of the requesting agency, as well as the subsequent confirmation of the Department of Justice, Office of Intelligence Policy and Review.

6) Upon, or prior to, completion of the electronic surveillance phase of the investigation, the ability of the agency participating in the conduct of the interception to decrypt intercepted communications

shall terminate, and such agency may not retain the key components.

These procedures do not create, and are not intended to create, any substantive rights for individuals intercepted through electronic surveillance, and noncompliance with these procedures shall not provide the bases for any motion to suppress or other objection to the introduction of electronic surveillance evidence lawfully acquired.

## 7

Encryption Standards and Procedures Act of 1994*

Staff, Committee on Science, Space, and Technology, U.S. House of Representatives

103rd Congress   10/6/94
2nd Session

[H.R. 5199]

IN THE HOUSE OF REPRESENTATIVES

Mr. __Brown of California__ introduced the following bill;
which was referred to the Committee on Science, Space,
and Technology on _October 6, 1994_

A BILL

To amend the National Institute of Standards and Technology Act
to provide for the establishment and management of voluntary
encryption standards to protect the privacy and security of
electronic information, and for other purposes.

*Be it enacted by the Senate and House of Representatives of the
United States of America in Congress assembled,*

SEC. 1.   SHORT TITLE.

This Act may be cited as the 'Encryption Standards and Procedures
Act of 1994'.

SEC. 2.   FINDINGS AND PURPOSES.

(a) Findings   . - The Congress finds the following:

---

* Washington, DC 20515.

(1) Advancements in communications and information technology and the widespread use of that technology have enhanced the volume and value of domestic and international communication of electronic information as well as the ability to preserve the confidentiality, protect the privacy, and authenticate the origin, of that information.

(2) The proliferation of communications and information technology has made it increasingly difficult for the government to obtain and decipher, in a timely manner and as provided by law, electronic information that is necessary to provide for public safety and national security.

(3) The development of the Nation's information infrastructure and the realization of the full benefits of that infrastructure require that electronic information resident in, or communicated over, that infrastructure is secure, confidential, and authentic.

(4) Security, privacy, and authentication of electronic information resident in, or communicated over, the Nation's information infrastructure are enhanced with the use of encryption technology.

(5) The rights of individuals and other persons to security, privacy, and protection in their communications and in the dissemination and receipt of electronic information should be preserved and protected.

(6) The authority and ability of the government to obtain and decipher, in a timely manner and as provided by law, electronic information necessary to provide for public safety and national security should also be preserved.

(7) There is a national need to develop, adopt, and use encryption methods and procedures that advance the development of the Nation's information infrastructure and that preserve the personal rights referred to in paragraph (5) and the governmental authority and ability referred to in paragraph (6), as provided by law.

(b) Purposes . - It is the purpose of this Act -

(1) to promote the development of the Nation's information infrastructure consistent with public welfare and safety,

national security, and the privacy and protection of personal property;

(2) to encourage and facilitate the development, adoption, and use of encryption standards and procedures that provide sufficient privacy, protection, and authentication of electronic information and that reasonably satisfy the needs of government to provide for public safety and national security; and

(3) to establish Federal policy governing the development, adoption, and use of encryption standards and procedures and a Federal program to carry out that policy.

SEC. 3.   ENCRYPTION STANDARDS AND PROCEDURES.

(a) Computer System Security and Privacy Advisory Board. -

(1) Requirement of privacy expertise   . - Section 21(a)(2) of the National Institute of Standards and Technology Act (15 U.S.C. 278g-4(a)(2)) is amended by inserting '(including computer systems privacy)' after 'related disciplines'.

(2) Expanded functions   . - Section 21(b) of such Act (15 U.S.C. 278g-4(b)) is amended -

(A) by striking 'and' at the end of paragraph (2);

(B) by striking the period at the end of paragraph (3) and inserting '; and'; and

(C) by adding after paragraph (3) the following new paragraph:

'(4) to advise the Institute and the Congress on privacy issues pertaining to electronic information and on encryption standards developed under section 31(b).'.

(b) Standards and Procedures   . - The National Institute of Standards and Technology Act is further amended -

(1) by redesignating section 31 as section 32; and

(2) by inserting after section 30 the following new section 31:

'SEC. 31. ENCRYPTION STANDARDS AND PROCEDURES.

'(a) Establishment and Authority . - The Secretary, acting through the Director, shall establish an Encryption Standards and Procedures Program to carry out this section. In carrying out this section, the Secretary, acting through the Director, may (in addition to the authority provided under section 2) conduct research and development on encryption standards and procedures, make grants, and enter into contracts, cooperative agreements, joint ventures, royalty arrangements, and licensing agreements on such terms and conditions the Secretary considers appropriate.

'(b) Federal Encryption Standards . -

'(1) In general . - The Secretary, acting through the Director and after providing notice to the public and an opportunity for comment, may by regulation develop encryption standards as part of the program established under subsection (a).

'(2) Requirements . - Any encryption standard developed under paragraph (1) -

'(A) shall, to the maximum extent practicable, provide for the confidentiality, integrity, or authenticity of electronic information;

'(B) shall advance the development, and enhance the security, of the Nation's information infrastructure;

'(C) shall contribute to public safety and national security;

'(D) shall not diminish existing privacy rights of individuals and other persons;

'(E) shall preserve the functional ability of the government to decipher, in a timely manner, electronic information that has been obtained pursuant to an electronic surveillance permitted by law;

'(F) may be implemented in software, firmware, hardware, or any combination thereof; and

'(G) shall include a validation program to determine the extent to which such standards have been implemented in conformance with the requirements set forth in this paragraph.

'(3) Consultation . - Standards developed under paragraph (1) shall be developed in consultation with the heads of other appropriate Federal agencies.

'(c) Permitted Use of Standards . - The Federal Government shall make available for public use any standard established under subsection (b), except that nothing in this Act may be construed to require such use by any individual or other person.

'(d) Escrow Agents . -

'(1) Designation . - If a key escrow encryption standard is established under subsection (b), the President shall designate at least 2 Federal agencies that satisfy the qualifications referred to in paragraph (2) to act as key escrow agents for that standard.

'(2) Qualifications . - A key escrow agent designated under paragraph (1) shall be a Federal agency that -

'(A) possesses the capability, competency, and resources to administer the key escrow encryption standard, to safeguard sensitive information related to it, and to carry out the responsibilities set forth in paragraph (3) in a timely manner; and

'(B) is not a Federal agency that is authorized by law to conduct electronic surveillance.

'(3) Responsibilities . - A key escrow agent designated under paragraph (1) shall, by regulation and in consultation with the Secretary and any other key escrow agent designated under such paragraph, establish procedures and take other appropriate steps-

'(A) to safeguard the confidentiality, integrity, and availability of keys or components thereof held by the agent pursuant to this subsection;

'(B) to preserve the integrity of any key escrow encryption standard established under subsection (b) for which the agent holds the keys or components thereof;

'(C) to hold and manage the keys or components thereof consistent with the requirements of this section and the encryption standard established under subsection (b); and

'(D) to carry out the responsibilities set forth in this paragraph in the most effective and efficient manner practicable.

'(4) Authority . - A key escrow agent designated under paragraph (1) may enter into contracts, cooperative agreements, and joint ventures and take other appropriate steps to carry out its responsibilities.

'(e) Limitations on Access and Use . -

'(1) Release of key to certain agencies . - A key escrow agent designated under subsection (d) may release a key or component thereof held by the agent pursuant to that subsection only to a Federal agency that is authorized by law to conduct electronic surveillance and that is authorized to obtain and use the key or component by court order or other provision of law. An entity to whom a key or component thereof has been released under this paragraph may use the key or component thereof only in the manner and for the purpose and duration that is expressly provided for in the court order or other provision of law authorizing such release and use.

'(2) Limitation on use by private persons and foreign citizens . -

'(A) In general . - Except as provided in subparagraph (B), a person (including a person not a citizen or permanent resident of the United States) that is not an agency of the Federal Government or a State or local government shall not have access to or use keys associated with an encryption standard established under subsection (b).

'(B) Exception . - A representative of a foreign government may have access to and use a key associated with an encryption standard established under subsection (b) only if the President determines that such access and use is in the national security and foreign policy interests of the United States. The President shall prescribe the manner and conditions of any such access and use.

'(3) Limit on use by government agencies . - A government agency, instrumentality, or political subdivision thereof shall not have access to or use a key or component thereof associated with an encryption standard established under subsection (b) that is held by a key escrow agent under subsection (d) unless such access or use is authorized by this section, by court order, or by other law.

'(f) Review and Report . -

'(1) In general . - Within 2 years after the date of the enactment of this Act and at least once every 2 years thereafter, the Secretary shall conduct a hearing on the record in which all interested parties shall have an opportunity to comment on the extent to which encryption standards, procedures, and requirements established under this section have succeeded in fulfilling the purposes of this section and the manner and extent to which such standards, procedures, and requirements can be improved.

'(2) Report . - Upon completion of a hearing conducted under paragraph (1), the Secretary shall submit to the Congress a report containing a statement of the Secretary's findings pursuant to the hearing along with recommendations and a plan for correcting any deficiencies or abuses in achieving the purposes of this section that are identified as a result of the hearing.

'(g) Regulations . - Within one year after the date of the enactment of this Act, the Secretary and each key escrow agent designated by the President under subsection (d) shall, after notice to the public and opportunity for comment, issue any regulations necessary to carry out this section.

'(h) Liability . - The United States shall not be liable for any loss incurred by any individual or other person resulting from any compromise or security breach of any encryption standard established under subsection (b) or any violation of this section or any regulation or procedure established by or under this section by -

'(1) any person who is not an official or employee of the United States; or

'(2) any person who is an official or employee of the United States, unless such compromise, breach, or violation is willful.

'(i) Severability . - If any provision of this section, or the application thereof, to any person or circumstance, is held invalid, the remainder of this section, and the application thereof, to other persons or circumstances shall not be affected thereby.

'(j) Definitions . - For purposes of this section:

'(1) The term 'content', when used with respect to electronic information, includes the substance, purport, or meaning of that information.

'(2) The term 'electronic communications system' has the meaning given such term in section 2510(14) of title 18, United States Code.

'(3) The term 'encryption' means a method –

'(A) to encipher and decipher the content of electronic information to protect the privacy and security of such information; or

'(B) to verify the integrity, or authenticate the origin, of electronic information.

'(4) The term 'encryption standard' means a technical, management, physical, or administrative standard or associated guideline or procedure for conducting encryption, including key escrow encryption, to ensure or verify the integrity, authenticity, or confidentiality of electronic information that, regardless of application or purpose, is stored, processed, transmitted, or otherwise communicated domestically or internationally in any public or private electronic communications system.

'(5) The term 'key escrow encryption' means an encryption method that allows the government, pursuant to court order or other provision of law, to decipher electronic information that has been encrypted with that method by using a unique secret code or key that is, in whole or in part, held by and obtained from a key escrow agent.

'(6) The term 'key escrow agent' means an entity designated by the President under subsection (d) to hold and manage keys associated with an encryption standard established under subsection (b).

'(7) The term 'key' means a unique secret code or character string that enables a party other than the sender, holder, or intended recipient of electronic information to decipher such information that has been enciphered with a corresponding encryption standard established under subsection (b) only with such code or string.

'(8) The term 'electronic information' means the content, source, or destination of any information in any electronic form and in any medium which has not been specifically authorized by a Federal statute or an Executive Order to be kept secret in the interest of national defense or foreign policy and which is stored, processed, transmitted or otherwise communicated, domestically or internationally, in an electronic communications system, and '(A) electronic communication within the meaning of section 2510(12) of title 18, United States Code; or '(B) wire communication within the meaning of section 2510(1) of such title.

'(9) The term 'government' means the Federal Government, a State or political subdivision of a State, the District of Columbia, or a commonwealth, territory, or possession of the United States.

'(k) Authorization of Appropriations . -

'(1) In general . - From amounts otherwise authorized to be appropriated to the Secretary of Commerce for fiscal years 1995 through 1997 to carry out the programs of the Institute, the amount of $50,000,000 shall be available for such fiscal years to carry out this section. Such amount shall remain available until expended. Of such amount, $1,000,000 shall be available for the National Research Council study on national cryptography policy authorized under section 267 of the National Defense Authorization Act for Fiscal Year 1994 (10 U.S.C 421 note).

'(2) Transfer authority . - The Secretary may transfer funds appropriated pursuant to paragraph (1) to a key escrow agent other than the Secretary in amounts sufficient to cover the cost of carrying out the responsibilities of the agent under this section. Funds so transferred shall remain available until expended.'.

## 8

Comments on Encryption Standards and Procedures Act*

Electronic Privacy Information Center

The staff of the House Committee on Science, Space and Technology has circulated a draft bill to regulate the development of encryption standards. The Encryption Standards and Procedures Act would authorize the Administration to develop federal encryption standards for privacy, security, and authenticity of domestic and international electronic communications.

This memo reviews the key features of the bill, provides an assessment of the measure, and outlines recommendations for revisions of the plan.

KEY FEATURES OF ESPA

- The Secretary of Commerce will establish an Encryption Standards and Procedures Program conducted by the director of the National Institute of Standards and Technology. The Secretary will be authorized to conduct research, make grants, and enter into agreements.
- Any encryption standard put forward by the Secretary shall meet the following requirements: ensure confidentiality, integrity, or authenticity of electronic communications; advance the development of the NII; contribute to public safety and national security; preserve existing privacy rights; preserve the functional ability of government to interpret electronic information lawfully obtained; be implementable in software, firmware, or hardware.
- Standards shall be developed in consultation with the Attorney General, the FBI, the NSA, and other federal agencies. The Computer System Security and Privacy Advisory Board shall review any standard before issuance.
- Nothing in ESPA shall be construed to require the use of such standards.

---

* July 13, 1994.

- Key escrow agents may be established by the President. Each escrow agent will be a federal agency that is competent to the administer the program and is not a federal agency authorized by law to conduct electronic surveillance.
- The key escrow agent may only disclose the keys to an authorized government entity and that entity may only use the keys for the purpose expressly provided for in the court order. Foreign entities may have access to the keys if the President determines that it would be in the national security interests of the United States.
- The Secretary of Commerce shall conduct a public hearing every three years on the program and then submit a report to Congress.
- Civil penalties and injunctions may be imposed for violations of the procedures outlined.
- Regulations shall be issued one year from passage of the bill.
- The United States government shall not be liable for any loss resulting from any compromise of any standard developed under this program by any person who is not an employee of the United States or any person who is an employee and did not act willfully.
- $50 million will be authorized for the Department of Commerce for 1995 to 1997 to undertake the program. Of this $1 million will go to the National Research Counsel for a study on cryptography policy.

ASSESSMENT

Rule Of Law

ESPA attempts to bring encryption standards setting under the rule of law. This is an important development that should force government agencies to give greater weight to private parties and public opinion. It will also allow interested parties to challenge standards decisions in court. But ESPA also grants a larger role in the development of technical standards to law enforcement agencies than currently exists under the Computer Security Act. This may have the effect of limiting public say over the development of such standards and tilting recommendations toward law enforcement interests.

Oversight

The proposal requires that before a standard may be issued by the Secretary of Commerce it must be reviewed by the Computer System Security and Privacy Advisory Board. This is the 12 member panel established by the Computer Security Act of 1987 that is intended to provide public oversight of computer security policy. The board represents a cross-section of the federal government and the computer industry. It is housed within the Department of Commerce and has no special competency in privacy issues.

Key Escrow

The ESPA does not mandate a key escrow procedure but it does require that the functional ability of law enforcement to intercept communications be maintained and does establish procedures for key escrow agents. No formal study of the desirability of key escrow has yet been undertaken by the federal government and no assessment has been made of the possible risks resulting from the compromise of such a system.

There is an attempt in the selection of the escrow agents to separate the keyholders from the law enforcement agencies. However the keys would still be held by executive branch agencies rather than the judiciary. This arrangement may not comply with Constitutional requirements for the separation of powers, and no demonstrable need for such an arrangement has yet been made.

Role of Government

The act would formalize the role of the federal government in the development of encryption standards and give to the National Institute of Standards and Technology primary responsibility for developing such standards. In 1987 it was anticipated that the NIST could play such a role. Since that time, concerns have been raised about the accountability of NIST and the behind-the-scenes role of law enforcement and intelligence agencies in the development of NIST technical standards. It is not clear at this time that NIST could operate with sufficient independence. Under the measure, the NSA and the FBI would, for the first time, be granted a statutory role in the development of cryptography standards

There is also the question of whether the standards would be, as the bill proposes, truly voluntary. The government could enforce the adoption of such standards in practice through procurement procedures, practical requirements for interoperability (a private party could not communicate with a federal agency unless using the agency's encryption standard), or amendment to the ESPA.

PROPOSED CHANGES

Need for a Privacy Stakeholder

As the bill currently stands, privacy interests are greatly underrepresented. Although the bill acknowledges the need to preserve and protect the right of privacy, there is no agency in the ESPA proposal with the expertise to assess the privacy implications of new cryptography standards or to represent the privacy concerns of the general public. The bill is heavily weighted toward those agencies that routinely conduct electronic surveillance and gives special status in the development of standards to the Attorney General, the FBI, and the National Security Agency. To operate as planned, there is a clear need for an independent privacy agency that would also have the opportunity to assess the implications of any proposed encryption standard.

EPIC Recommendation #1

- A formal privacy agency should be established and this agency should be provided an opportunity to review proposed encryption standards. Such an agency should exist independently of the executive branch and Congress. In the alternative, there should be no special statutory authority for the FBI, the NSA, or the Attorney General to review proposed standards for cryptography. Absent a privacy agency with the authority to review such proposals, these agencies should be required to follow the same comment procedures available to the general public.

Strengthen Reporting Requirements

Typical reporting requirements ask agencies to report each year to Congress on the development of programs. The Attorney General is required to report annually on electronic surveillance. A similar requirement should be in place for the Department of Commerce. The Secretary should be required specifically to report on the number of times that special procedures developed by the program were deployed to execute a lawful wire intercept, and to document those instances where new technology has posed an obstacle to the conduct of lawful electronic surveillance.

EPIC Recommendation #2

- The bill should be amended so as to require that the Secretary report annually to Congress on the activities of the program. The reporting requirements should set out specific issues that the Secretary should address.

Conduct a Formal Risk Assessment

The bill attempts to control the problem of misuse of key escrow by the imposition of civil penalties. But the bill does not address the problems that may result from technical failure, negligent compromise, or subsequent change in policy.

EPIC Recommendation #3

■ The Secretary should be required in the first year to undertake a formal risk assessment of the key escrow proposal and to report to the Congress on the results of the study before any encryption standard based on key escrow is adopted. The report should be fully public and unclassified. Any subsequent encryption standard that incorporates a key escrow procedure should also require a similar public risk assessment.

Transfer Key Escrow to Judiciary

The federal constitution requires that checks and balances be preserved between the executive branch and the judiciary in the conduct of law enforcement activities. As currently proposed under the bill, the executive branch would have the authority to execute electronic surveillance and to hold keys generated by private communications. This is not a Constitutionally satisfactory escrow arrangement.

EPIC Recommendation #4

■ If a key escrow standard is adopted, the escrow responsibility should be transferred from the executive branch to the judicial branch.

Tighten Procedural Requirements

ESPA grants authority for the conduct of wire surveillance under court order and "other provisions of law" without specifying the law which permits such surveillance. Such authority should be explicitly stated. Also, the bill provides no adequate remedy for evidence unlawfully obtained as currently exists in wiretap law.

EPIC Recommendation #5

■ Tighten procedural requirements by (a) stating explicitly the legal authority for the conduct of electronic surveillance contemplated by the legislation; and (b) amending section 2518(10)(a) of the wiretap law to allow for the suppression of evidence obtained as a result of an interception not made in conformance with any standard issued pursuant to this program.

Encourage Research into the Development of Anonymous and Pseudo-Anonymous Communications

In addition to privacy and security, ESPA emphasizes the need for the development of technologies to support authenticity, but says nothing about technologies that allow for anonymous and pseudo-anonymous transactions. Such technologies will enhance privacy protection and should be encouraged by the federal government.

EPIC Recommendation #6

- NIST should encourage research, make grants, and support the development of encryption-based technologies for anonymous and pseudo-anonymous transactions.

CONCLUSION

EPIC believes that an attempt to bring the development of encryption standards under the rule of a law is a step in the right direction. However, this proposal grants far too much authority to law enforcement agencies and lacks important safeguards for privacy protection and the public interest. The proposal also assumes the need for a key escrow standard, but does not consider the potential risks to privacy and security of such a plan.

CHAPTER 4

THE POLICY DEBATE

HOW CONTROLLED A GLOBAL INFORMATION INFRASTRUCTURE DO WE WANT, AND WHO DECIDES?

This chapter details the sometimes sober, sometimes colorful debate surrounding cryptography policy—not only what that policy will be, but also who will determine it. The debate has moved from a relatively low-profile discussion among the computer and communications security and privacy elite to one with a much higher profile and a less technological, more policy-oriented bent.

Levy provides a comprehensive account of the ongoing struggle to arrive at a sensible cryptographic policy, identifying key governmental and non-governmental players and giving their positions. After it, we present first the most significant views of supporters of the Clipper initiative and then the most significant views of its opponents.

The most visible and outspoken nongovernmental Clipper supporter has been Dorothy Denning. She asserts that the Clipper Chip initiative properly balances the individual and organizational needs for secret communications with our common need for public safety and monitoring of criminal and terrorist activities. She also believes that illegal eavesdropping will be virtually impossible with this new initiative, thereby *increasing* our individual and collective privacy. Her Congressional testimony also lays out some potential future alternatives which have great international implications (since when Clipper was designed no solution to harmonizing international cryptographic standards—a necessity for an acceptable Global Information Infrastructure—was even mentioned). It's important to realize that all these alternatives are highly speculative and have downsides; all might, for various reasons, fail.

Gelernter, arguing that civilized life is a compromise, comes out in favor of the Digital Telephony and Communications Privacy Improvement Act and in favor of the Clipper chip. Gelernter is one of the few respected computer scientists besides Denning to publicly speak in favor of Clipper; he sets forth better than most (including most of the government's own spokespersons) the argument that living life is a balancing act and everything has honest costs; and he reminds us that, no matter what side we're on, we always retain the right to tell (technical, legal, national security, or other) experts to get lost or to do better.

Baker presents a comprehensive list of "fallacies" supposedly presented by opponents of Clipper and puts forth arguments to counter them. Like Denning and Gelernter, he believes that society's interests in both privacy and law enforcement must be balanced, and the Clipper chip is the best solution put forth to date. He points out another use for key escrow, intra-organizational security to protect against rogue employees. He also notes, as did Vice President Gore on page 235, that encryption wins and loses wars. Baker clearly is in the camp of those who believe, using Levy's words, that Clipper "represents the last chance to protect personal safety and national security against a developing information anarchy that fosters criminals, terrorists and foreign foes".

Clipper's opponents also have strong views and arguments. Sterling reacts to Baker's presentation as "radically unsatisfactory" and characterizes Denning as waging a "heroic and heartbreaking solo struggle against the 12 million other people with e-mail addresses". He has little respect for some of the past efforts of NSA, recalling how "Bobby Ray Inman, the legendary NSA leader, made a stab at computer entrepreneurism and rapidly sank with all hands". Sterling says he wouldn't trust Inman, and that is a good example of one thing that has made Clipper so controversial—the ongoing communications gap and lack of trust between the national security agencies and most of the computer community. In Sterling's own words, "even the Four Horsemen of Kidporn, Dope Dealers, Mafia, and Terrorists don't worry me as much as totalitarian governments".

Barlow then points out that while most expert testimony submitted to the government has opposed both Clipper and current export controls, the government decided that the arguments on the other side were more compelling. He correctly observes that the report on Clipper promised by the government in April 1993 never materialized and notes that "if you're going to initiate a process that might end freedom in America, you probably need an argument that isn't classified". He asks readers to urge Congress to reduce export controls and to boycott Clipper devices and any company involved in their production. He also voices the possibility that the Administration might "let the National

Security Agency design the rest of the National Information Infrastructure".

This is a concern shared by many. The next editorial from *Washington Technology* sees "a picture of yet another government agency filled with old Cold Warriors trying to hold on to their mortgages in the Washington suburbs." Its editorial, "Secret Agency Steps Over the Line," questions why the National Security Agency (NSA), supposedly not involved in domestic issues, has taken such an active role in advocating Clipper as a national encryption standard and effectively states that "the agency is breaking the law". And the cartoon accompanying the editorial, which gives voice to the privacy fears often stated by Clipper opponents, is priceless.

Finally, The New York Times editorial notes the legitimate concerns of government but declares the so-far-proposed solutions to be "unworkable and potentially intrusive". It seems to implicitly urge the Government to go back to the drawing board, something which—reading between the lines of the Gore letter to Cantwell earlier in this chapter—the Government may, implicitly, be doing.

The Cypherpunks vs. Uncle Sam*

Steven Levy

On a sunny spring day in Mountain View, Calif., 50 angry activists are plotting against the United States Government. They may not look subversive sitting around a conference table dressed in T-shirts and jeans and eating burritos, but they are self-proclaimed saboteurs. They are the Cypherpunks, a loose confederation of computer hackers, hardware engineers and high-tech rabble-rousers.

The precise object of their rage is the Clipper chip, officially known as the MYK-78 and not much bigger than a tooth. Just another tiny square of plastic covering a silicon thicket. A computer chip, from the outside indistinguishable from thousands of others. It seems improbable that this black Chiclet is the focal point of a battle that may determine the degree to which our civil liberties survive in the next century. But that is the shared belief in this room.

The Clipper chip has prompted what might be considered the first holy war of the information highway. Two weeks ago, the war got bloodier, as a researcher circulated a report that the chip might have a serious technical flaw. But at its heart, the issue is political not technical. The Cypherpunks consider the Clipper the lever that Big Brother is using to pry into the conversations, messages and transactions of the computer age. These high-tech Paul Reveres are trying to mobilize America against the evil portent of a "cyberspace police state," as one of their Internet Jeremiads put it. Joining them in the battle is a formidable force, including almost all of the communications and computer industries, many members of Congress and political columnists of all stripes. The anti-Clipper aggregation is an equal-opportunity club, uniting the American Civil Liberties Union and Rush Limbaugh.

The Clipper's defenders, who are largely in the Government, believe it represents the last chance to protect personal safety and national security against a developing information anarchy that fosters criminals, terrorists and foreign foes. Its adherents pose it as the answer, or at least part of the answer, to a problem created by an increasingly

---

sophisticated application of an age-old technology cryptography, the use of secret codes.

For centuries, cryptography was the domain of armies and diplomatic corps. Now it has a second purpose: protecting personal and corporate privacy. Computer technology and advanced telecommunications equipment have drawn precious business information and intimate personal communications out into the open. This phenomenon is well known to the current Prince of Wales, whose intimate cellular phone conversations were intercepted, recorded and broadcast worldwide. And corporations realize that competitors can easily intercept their telephone conversations, electronic messages and faxes. High tech has created a huge privacy gap. But miraculously, a fix has emerged: cheap, easy-to-use, virtually unbreakable encryption. Cryptography is the silver bullet by which we can hope to reclaim our privacy.

The solution, however, has one drawback: cryptography shields the law abiding and the lawless equally. Law-enforcement and intelligence agencies contend that if strong codes are widely available, their efforts to protect the public would be paralyzed. So they have come up with a compromise, a way to neutralize such encryption. That's the Clipper chip and that compromise is what the war is about.

The idea is to give the Government means to override other people's codes, according to a concept called "key escrow." Employing normal cryptography, two parties can communicate in total privacy, with both of them using a digital "key" to encrypt and decipher the conversation or message. A potential eavesdropper has no key and therefore cannot understand the conversation or read the data transmission. But with Clipper, an additional key — created at the time the equipment is manufactured — is held by the Government in escrow. With a court-approved wiretap, an agency like the F.B.I. could listen in. By adding Clipper chips to telephones, we could have a system that assures communications will be private — from everybody but the Government.

And that's what rankles Clipper's many critics. Why, they ask, should people accused of no crime have to give Government the keys to their private communications? Why shouldn't the market rather than Government determine what sort of cryptosystem wins favor? And isn't it true that the use of key escrow will make our technology so unattractive to the international marketplace that the United States will lose its edge in the lucrative telecommunications and computer fields? Clipper might clip the entire economy.

Nonetheless, on Feb. 4 the White House announced its approval of the Clipper chip, which had been under study as a Government standard since last April, and the Crypto War broke out in full force. Within a month, one civil liberties group, Computer Professionals for Social Responsibility, received 47,000 electronic missives urging a stop to

Clipper. "The war is upon us," wrote Tim May, co-founder of the Cypherpunks, in an urgent electronic dispatch soon after the announcement. "Clinton and Gore folks have shown themselves to be enthusiastic supporters of Big Brother."

And though the Clinton Administration's endorsement of Clipper as a Government standard required no Congressional approval rumblings of discontent came from both sides of the Capitol. Senator Patrick J. Leahy, the Vermont Democrat whose subcommittee has held contentious hearings on the matter, has called the plan a "misstep," charging that "the Government should not be in the business of mandating particular technologies."

Two weeks ago, an AT&T Bell Laboratories researcher revealed that he had found a serious flaw in the Clipper technology itself, enabling techno-savvy lawbreakers to bypass the security function of the chip in some applications. Besides being a bad idea, Clipper's foes now say, it doesn't even work properly.

Yet the defenders of Clipper have refused to back down, claiming that the scheme — which is, they often note, voluntary — is an essential means of stemming an increasing threat to public safety and security by strong encryption in everyday use. Even if Clipper itself has to go back to the drawing board, its Government designers will come up with something quite similar. The underlying issue remains unchanged: If something like Clipper is not implemented, writes Dorothy E. Denning, a Georgetown University computer scientist, "All communications on the information highway would be immune from lawful interception. In a world threatened by international organized crime, terrorism and rogue governments, this would be folly."

The claims from both sides sound wild, almost apocalyptic. The passion blurs the problem: Can we protect our privacy in an age of computers — without also protecting the dark forces in society?

The crypto war is the inevitable consequence of a remarkable discovery made almost 20 years ago, a breakthrough that combined with the microelectronics revolution to thrust the once-obscure field of cryptography into the mainstream of communications policy.

It began with Whitfield Diffie, a young computer scientist and cryptographer. He did not work for the Government, which was strange because in the 1960's almost all serious crypto in this country was done under Federal auspices, specifically at the Fort Meade, Md., headquarters of the supersecret National Security Agency. Though it became bigger than the C.I.A., the N.S.A. was for years unknown to Americans; the Washington Beltway joke was that the initials stood for "No Such Agency." Its working premise has always been that no information about its activities should ever be revealed. Its main mission involved cryptography, and the security agency so dominated the field that it had the power to rein in even those few experts in the field who were not on its payroll.

But Whitfield Diffie never got that message. He had been bitten by the cryptography bug at age 10 when his father, a professor, brought home the entire crypto shelf of the City College library in New York. Then he lost interest, until he arrived at M.I.T.'s Artificial Intelligence Laboratory in 1966. Two things rekindled his passion. Now trained as a mathematician, he had an affinity for the particular challenges of sophisticated crypto. Just as important, he says, "I was always concerned about individuals, an individual's privacy as opposed to Government secrecy."

Diffie, now 50, is still committed to those beliefs. When asked about his politics, he says, "I like to describe myself as an iconoclast." He is a computer security specialist for Sun Microsystems, a celebrated cryptographer and an experienced hand at Congressional testimony. But he looks like he stumbled out of a Tom Robbins novel — with blond hair that falls to his shoulders and a longish beard that seems a virtual trademark among code makers. At a Palo Alto, Calif., coffeehouse one morning, he describes, in clipped, precise cadence, how he and Martin E. Hellman, an electrical engineering professor at Stanford University, created a crypto revolution.

Diffie was dissatisfied with the security on a new time-sharing computer system being developed by M.I.T. in the 1960's. Files would be protected by passwords, but he felt that was insufficient. The system had a generic flaw. A system manager had access to all passwords. "If a subpoena was served against the system managers, they would sell you out, because they had no interest in going to jail," Diffie says. A perfect system would eliminate the need for a trusted third party.

This led Diffie to think about a more general problem in cryptography key management. Even before Julius Caesar devised a simple cipher to encode his military messages, cryptography worked by means of keys. That is, an original message (what is now called "plaintext") was encrypted by the sender into seeming gibberish (known as "ciphertext"). The receiver, using the same key, decrypted the message back unto the original plaintext. For instance, the Caesar key was the simple replacement of each letter by the letter three places down in the alphabet. If you knew the key, you could encrypt the word *help* into the nonsense word *khos;* the recipient of the message would decrypt the message back to *help.*

The problem came with protecting the key. Since anyone who knew the Caesar key would be able to understand the encoded message, it behooved the Romans to change that key as often as possible. But if you change the key, how do you inform your spies behind enemy lines? (If you tell them using the old code which may have already been cracked, your enemies will then learn the new code.) For centuries, generals and diplomats have faced that predicament. But a few years ago, it took on added urgency.

With computers and advanced telecommunications, customers outside Government were discovering a need for information security. Cryptography was the answer, but how could it be applied widely, considering the problem of keys? The best answer to date was something called a key-management repository, where two parties who wanted secrecy would go to a trusted third party who would generate a new key for the private session. But that required just what Diffie deplored — an unwanted third wheel.

"The virtue of cryptography should be that you don't have to trust anybody not directly involved with your communication," Diffie says. "Without conventional key distribution centers, which involved trusting third parties, I couldn't figure how you could build a system to secure, for instance, all the phones in the country."

When Diffie moved to Stanford University in 1969, he foresaw the rise of home computer terminals and began pondering the problem of how to use them to make transactions. "I got to thinking how you could possibly have electronic business, because signed letters of intent, contracts and all seemed so critical" he says. He devoured what literature he could find outside the National Security Agency. And in the mid-1970's, Diffie and Hellman achieved a stunning breakthrough that changed cryptography forever. They split the cryptographic key.

In their system, every user has two keys, a public one and a private one, that are unique to their owner. Whatever is scrambled by one key can be unscrambled by the other. It works like this: If I want to send a message to Whit Diffie, I first obtain his public key. (For complicated mathematical reasons, it is possible to distribute one's public key freely without compromising security; a potential enemy will have no advantage in code-cracking if he holds your public key alone.) Then I use that key to encode the message. Now it's gobbledygook and only one person in the world can decode it — Whit Diffie, who holds the other, private, key. If he wants to respond to me with a secret message, he uses my public key to encode his answer. And I decode it, using my private key.

It was an amazing solution, but even more remarkable was that this split-key system solved both of Diffie's problems, the desire to shield communications from eavesdroppers and also to provide a secure electronic identification for contracts and financial transactions done by computer. It provided the identification by the use of "digital signatures" that verify the sender much the same way that a real signature validates a check or contract.

Suddenly, the ancient limitations on cryptography had vanished. Now, perhaps before the millennium, strong cryptography could find its way to every telephone, computer and fax machine — if users wanted it. Subsequent variations on the Diffie-Hellman scheme focused on using crypto algorithms to insure the anonymity of transactions. Using these advances, it is now possible to think of replacing money with digital cash—while maintaining the comforting untraceability of bills and coins. The dark art of cryptography has become a tool of liberation.

From the moment Diffie and Hellman published their findings in 1976, the National Security Agency's crypto monopoly was effectively terminated. In short order, three M.I.T. mathematicians—Ronald L. Rivest, Adi Shamir and Leonard M. Adleman — developed a system with which to put the Diffie and Hellman findings into practice. It was known by their initials, RSA. It seemed capable of creating codes that even the N.S.A. could not break. They formed a company to sell their new system; it was only a matter of time before thousands and then millions of people began using strong encryption.

That was the National Security Agency's greatest nightmare. Every company, every citizen now had routine access to the sorts of cryptographic technology that not many years ago ranked alongside the atom bomb as a source of power. Every call, every computer message, every fax in the world could be harder to decipher than the famous German "Enigma" machine of World War II. Maybe even impossible to decipher!

The genie was out of the bottle. Next question: Could the genie be made to wear a leash and collar? Enter the Clipper chip.

When illustrating the government's need to control crypto, Jim Kallstrom, the agent in charge of the special operations division of the New York office of the F.B.I., quickly shifts the discussion to the personal "Are you married? Do you have a child? O.K., someone kidnaps one of your kids and they are holding your kid in this fortress up in the Bronx. Now, we have probable cause that your child is inside this fortress. We have a search warrant. But for some reason, we cannot get in there. They made it out of some new metal, or something, right? Nothing will cut it, right? And there are guys in there, *laughing* at us. That's what the basis of this issue really is — we've got a situation now where a technology has become so sophisticated that the whole notion of a legal process is at stake here!"

Kallstrom is a former head of the Bureau Tech Squad, involved in the bugging operation that brought John Gotti to justice. Some have described him as the F.B.I.'s answer to "Q," the gadget wizard of the James Bond tales.

"From the standpoint of law enforcement, there's a superbig threat out there — this guy is gonna build this domain in the Bronx now, because he's got a new steel door and none of the welding torches, none of the boomerangs, nothing we have is gonna blast our way in there. Sure, we want those new steel doors ourselves, to protect our banks, to protect the American corporation trade secrets, patent rights, technology. But people operating in legitimate business are not violating the laws — it becomes a different ball of wax when we have probable cause and we have to get into that domain. Do we want a digital superhighway where not only the commerce of the nation can take place but where major criminals can operate impervious to the legal process? If we don't want that, then we have to look at Clipper."

Wiretapping is among law enforcement's most cherished weapons. Only 919 Federal, state and local taps were authorized last year, but police agencies consider them essential to fighting crime. Obviously if criminals communicate using military-grade cryptosystems, wiretapping them becomes impossible.

For two years, the F.B.I. has been urging Congress to pass the proposed Digital Telephony and Communications Privacy Act, which would in essence require that new communications technologies be designed to facilitate wiretapping. Even if the bill should somehow pass, overcoming the opposition of the communications industry and civil libertarians, the extra effort and expense will be wasted if the only thing the wiretappers can hear is the hissy white noise of encrypted phone conversations and faxes. If cryptography is not controlled, wiretapping could be rendered obsolete. Louis J. Freeh, the Director of the F.B.I., surely fears that prospect. He has told Congress that preserving the ability to intercept communications legally, in the face of these technological advances, is "the No. 1 law enforcement, public safety and national security issue facing us today."

Some people criticize Clipper on the basis that truly sophisticated criminals would never use it, preferring other easily obtained systems that use high-grade cryptography. Despite Clipper, kidnappers and drug kingpins may construct Kallstrom's virtual fort in the Bronx with impunity, laughing at potential wiretappers.

The Government understands the impossibility of eradicating strong crypto. Its objective is instead to prevent unbreakable encryption from becoming routine. If that happens, even the stupidest criminal would be liberated from the threat of surveillance. But by making Clipper the standard, the Government is betting that only a tiny percentage of users would use other encryption or try to defeat the Clipper.

At a rare public appearance in March at a conference on computers and privacy, Stewart A. Baker, then general counsel of the National Security Agency, tried to explain. "The concern is not so much what happens today when people go in and buy voice scramblers," said Baker, a dapper, mustached lawyer who worked as an Education Department lawyer in the Carter Administration. "It is the prospect that in 5 years or 10 years every phone you buy that costs $75 or more will have an encrypt button on it that will interoperate with every other phone in the country and suddenly we will discover that our entire communications network is being used in ways that are profoundly antisocial. That's the real concern, I think, that Clipper addresses. If we are going to have a standardized form of encryption that is going to change the world, we should think seriously about what we are going to do when it is misused."

Not all law-enforcement experts believe that cryptography will unleash a riot of lawlessness. William R. Spernow, a Sacramento, Calif., computer crime specialist who works on a grant from the Federal Bureau of Justice Assistance, has encountered a few cases in which criminals have encrypted information unbreakably, including one involving a pedophile who encrypted the identities of his young victims. Yet Spernow sees no reason to panic. "In cases where there's encryption, the officers have been able to make the case through other investigative means," he says. "If we hustle, we can still make our cases through other kinds of police work."

But crime is only part of the problem. What happens to national security if cryptography runs free? Those who know best, officials of the National Security Agency, won't say. When the agency's director, Vice Adm. John M. McConnell testified before a Senate subcommittee on May 3, he withheld comment on this question until the public hearing was terminated and a second, classified session convened in a secure room.

Still, the effect of strong crypto on N.S.A. operations is not difficult to imagine. The agency is charged with signals intelligence and it is widely assumed that it monitors all the communications between borders and probably much of the traffic within foreign countries. (It is barred from intercepting domestic communications.) If the crypto revolution crippled N.S.A.'s ability to listen in on the world, the agency might miss out on something vital—for instance, portents of a major terrorist attack.

No compelling case has been made however, that the key-escrow system would make it easier for authorities to learn of such an attack. The National Security Agency would take the legal steps to seek the telltale keys after it had first identified those potential terrorists and wiretapped their calls, then discovered the impenetrable hiss of encryption. Even then, the keys would be useful only if the terrorists were encoding conversations with Clipper technology, the one kind the Government had the capability to decode instantly. What sort of nuclear terrorist would choose Clipper?

The Government response has been to say that potential terrorists might indeed use alternative crypto methods to converse among themselves. But if Clipper were the accepted standard, the terrorists would have to use it to communicate with outsiders — banks, suppliers and other contacts. The Government could listen in on those calls. However, the work of the Bell Labs researcher, Matthew Blaze, casts serious doubt on that contention. Blaze has uncovered a flaw in Clipper that would allow a user to bypass the security function of the chip. Anyone who tinkered with Clipper in this way could communicate in privacy with anyone else with a Clipper phone and Government wiretappers would be unable to locate the key to unscramble the conversations.

Nonetheless, it was the terrorist threat, along with national security concerns, that moved the Clinton Administration to support the key-escrow initiative. White House high-tech policy makers share a recurrent fear: one day they might be sitting before an emergency Congressional investigation after the destruction of half of Manhattan by a stolen nuclear weapon planted in the World Trade towers and trying to explain that the Government had intercepted the communications of the terrorists but could not understand them because they used strong encryption. If Clipper were enacted, they could at least say, "We tried."

Obviously the government views the crypto revolution with alarm and wants to contain it. For years, much of its efforts have focused on the use of stringent export controls. While cryptography within the United States is unrestricted, the country's export laws treat any sort of encryption as munitions, like howitzers or nuclear triggers. The National Security Agency is the final arbiter and it will approve exports of cryptosystems in computer software and electronic hardware only if the protective codes are significantly weakened.

The N.S.A. stance is under attack from American businesses losing sales to foreign competitors. Listen to D. James Bidzos, the 39-year-old president of RSA Data Security, the Redwood City, Calif., company that controls the patents for public-key cryptography: "For almost 10 years, I've been going toe to toe with these people at Fort Meade. The success of this company is the worst thing that can happen to them. To them, we're the real enemy, we're the real target."

RSA is making a pitch to become the standard in encryption; its technology has been adopted by Apple, AT&T, Lotus, Microsoft, Novell and other major manufacturers. So imagine its unhappiness that its main rival is not another private company, but the National Security Agency, designer of the key-escrow cryptosystems. The agency is a powerful and dedicated competitor.

"We have the system that they're most afraid of," Bidzos says. "If the U.S. adopted RSA as a standard, you would have a truly international, interoperable, unbreakable, easy-to-use encryption technology. And all those things together are so synergistically threatening to the N.S.A.'s interests that it's driving them into a frenzy."

The export laws put shackles on Bidzos's company while his overseas competitors have no such restraints. Cryptographic algorithms that the N.S.A. bans for export are widely published and are literally being sold on the streets of Moscow. "We did a study on the problem and located 340 foreign cryptographic products sold by foreign countries," says Douglas R. Miller, government affairs manager of the Software Publishers Association. "The only effect of export controls is to cripple our ability to compete."

The real potential losses, though, come not in the standalone encryption category, but in broader applications. Companies like Microsoft, Apple and Lotus want to put strong encryption into their products but cannot get licenses to export them. Often, software companies wind up installing a weaker brand of crypto in all their products so that they can sell a single version worldwide. This seems to be the Government's intent — to encourage "crypto lite," strong enough to protect communications from casual intruders but not from Government itself.

In the long run, however, export regulation will not solve the National Security Agency's problem. The crypto business is exploding. People are becoming more aware of the vulnerability of phone conversations, particularly wireless ones. Even the National Football League is adopting crypto technology; it will try out encrypted radio communication between coaches and quarterbacks, so rivals can't intercept last-minute audibles.

Anticipating such a boom, the N.S.A. devised a strategy for the 90's. It would concede the need for strong encryption but encourage a system with a key-escrow "back door" that provides access to communications for itself and law enforcement. The security agency had already developed a strong cryptosystem based on an algorithm called Skipjack, supposedly 16 million times stronger than the previous standard, D.E.S. (Data Encryption Standard). Now the agency's designers integrated Skipjack into a new system that uses a Law Enforcement Access Field (LEAF) that adds a signal to the message that directs a potential wiretapper to the appropriate key to decipher the message. These features were included in a chip called Capstone, which could handle not only telephone communications but computer data transfers and digital signatures.

Supposedly, this technology was designed for Government use, but in 1993 the National Security Agency had a sudden opportunity to thrust it in the marketplace. AT&T had come to the agency with a new, relatively low-cost secure-phone device called the Surity 3600 that was designed to use the nonexportable DES encryption algorithm. The N.S.A. suggested that perhaps AT&T could try something else: a stripped-down version of Capstone for telephone communications. This was the Clipper chip. As a result, AT&T got two things: an agreement that Uncle Sam would buy thousands of phones for its own use (the initial commitment was 9,000 from the F.B.I.) and the prospect that the phone would not suffer the unhappy fate of some other secure devices when considered for export. There was also the expectation that AT&T would sell a lot more phones, since private companies would need to buy Clipper-equipped devices to communicate with the Government's Clipper phones.

It was an ingenious plan for several reasons. By agreeing to buy thousands of phones, and holding out the promise that thousands, or even millions more might be sold, AT&T phones gained a price advantage that comes with volume. (The original price of the Surity 3600 was $1,195, considerably less than the previous generation of secure phones; Mykotronx, the company making the Clipper chip, says that each chip now costs $30, but in large orders could quickly go as low as $10.) That would give the phones a big push in the marketplace. But by saturating the market, Clipper had a chance to become the standard for encryption, depending on whether businesses and individuals would be willing to accept a device that had the compromise of a government controlled back door.

This compromise, of course, is the essence of Clipper. The Government recognizes the importance of keeping business secrets, intimate information and personal data hidden from most eyes and ears. But it also preserves a means of getting hold of that information after obtaining "legal authorization, normally a court order," according to a White House description.

The N.S.A. presented the idea to the Bush Administration, which took no action before the election. Then it had to convince a Democratic Administration to adopt the scheme and started briefing the Clinton people during the transition. Many in the computer industry figured that with Vice President Al Gore's enthusiastic endorsement of the high-frontier virtues of the information highway, the Administration would never adopt any proposal so tilted in favor of law enforcement and away from his allies in the information industries. They figured wrong. A little more than two months after taking office, the Clinton Administration announced the existence of the Clipper chip and directed the National Institute of Standards and Technology to consider it as a Government standard.

Clipper was something the Administration — starting with the Vice President — felt compelled to adopt, and key escrow was considered an honorable attempt to balance two painfully contradictory interests, privacy and safety.

The reaction was instant, bitter and ceaseless. The most pervasive criticisms challenged the idea that a Clipper would be, as the standard said, "voluntary." The Government's stated intent is to manipulate the marketplace so that it will adopt an otherwise unpalatable scheme and make it the standard. Existing systems have to cope with export regulations and, now, incompatibility with the new Government Clipper standard. Is it fair to call a system voluntary if the Government puts all sorts of obstacles in the way of its competitors?

Others felt that it was only a matter of time before the National Security Agency pressured the Government to require key escrow of all cryptographic devices — that Clipper was only the first step in a master plan to give Uncle Sam a key to everyone's cyberspace back door.

"That's a real fear," says Stephen T. Walker, a former N.S.A. employee who is now president of Trusted Information Systems, a company specializing in computer security products. "I don't think the Government could pull it off — it would be like prohibition, only worse. But I think they might try it."

But mostly, people were unhappy with the essence of Clipper, that the Government would escrow their keys. As Diffie notes, key escrow reintroduces the vulnerability that led him to invent public key cryptography — any system that relies on trusted third parties is, by definition, weaker than one that does not. Almost no one outside the Government likes the key-escrow idea. "We published the standard for 60 days of public comments," says F. Lynn McNulty, associate director for computer security at the National Institute of Standards and Technology. "We received 320 comments, only 2 of which were supportive."

Many people thought that in the face of such opposition, the Administration would quietly drop the Clipper proposal. They were dismayed by the Feb. 4 announcement of the adoption of Clipper as a Government standard. Administration officials knew they were alienating their natural allies in the construction of the information superhighway but felt they had no alternative. "This," said Michael R. Nelson, a White House technology official, "is the Bosnia of telecommunications."

If Clipper is the administration's techno-Bosnia, the crypto equivalent of snipers are everywhere—in industry, among privacy lobbyists and even among Christian Fundamentalists. But the most passionate foes are the Cypherpunks. They have been meeting on the second Saturday of every month at the offices of Cygnus, a Silicon Valley company, assessing new ways they might sabotage Clipper. The group was co-founded in September 1992 by Eric Hughes, a 29-year-old freelance cryptographer, and Tim May, a 42-year-old physicist who retired early and rich from the Intel company. Other Cypherpunk cells often meet simultaneously in six or seven locations around the world, but the main gathering place for Cypherpunks is the Internet, by means of an active mailing list in which members post as many as 100 electronic messages a day.

Cypherpunks share a few common premises. They assume that cryptography is a liberating tool, one that empowers individuals. They think that one of the most important uses of cryptography is to protect communications from the Government. Many of them believe that the Clipper is part of an overall initiative against cryptography that will culminate in Draconian control of the technology. And they consider it worth their time to fight, educating the general public and distributing cryptographic tools to obstruct such control.

Both Hughes and May have composed manifestos. Hughes's call to arms proclaims: "Cypherpunks write code. We know that someone has to write software to defend privacy, and since we can't get privacy unless we all do, we're going to write it."

May's document envisions a golden age in which strong cryptography belongs to all — an era of "crypto anarchism" that governments cannot control. To May, cryptography is a tool that will not only bestow privacy on people but help rearrange the economic underpinnings of society.

"Combined with emerging information markets, cryptography will create a liquid market for any and all material that can be put into words and pictures," May's document says. "And just as a seemingly minor invention like barbed wire made possible the fencing-off of vast ranches and farms, thus altering forever the concepts of land and property rights in the frontier West, so too will the seemingly minor discovery out of an arcane branch of mathematics come to be the wire clippers which dismantle the barbed wire around intellectual property."

At a recent meeting, about 50 Cypherpunks packed into the Cygnus conference room, with dozens of others participating electronically from sites as distant as Cambridge, Mass., and San Diego. The meeting stretched for six hours, with discussions of hardware encryption schemes, methods to fight an electronic technique of identity forgery called "spoofing," the operation of "remailing" services, which allow people to post electronic messages anonymously — and various ways to fight Clipper.

While the Cypherpunks came up with possible anti-Clipper slogans for posters and buttons, a bearded crypto activist in wire-rim glasses named John Gilmore was outside the conference room, showing the latest sheaf of cryptography-related Freedom of Information documents he'd dragged out of Government files. Unearthing and circulating the hidden crypto treasures of the National Security Agency is a passion of Gilmore, an early employee of Sun Microsystems who left the company a multimillionaire. The Government once threatened to charge him with a felony for copying some unclassified-and-later-reclassified N.S.A. documents from a university library. After the story hit the newspapers, the Government once again declassified the documents.

"This country was founded as an open society, and we still have the remnants of that society," Gilmore says. "Will crypto tend to open it or close it? Our Government is building some of these tools for its own use, but they are unavailable—we have paid for cryptographic breakthroughs but they're classified. I wish I could hire 10 guys—cryptographers, librarians—to try to pry cryptography out of the dark ages."

Perhaps the most admired Cypherpunk is someone who says he is ineligible because he often wears a suit. He is Philip R. Zimmermann, a 40-year-old software engineer and cryptographic consultant from Boulder, Colo., who in 1991 cobbled together a cryptography program for computer data and electronic mail. "PGP," he called it, meaning Pretty Good Privacy, and he decided to give it away. Anticipating the Cypherpunk credo, Zimmermann hoped that the appearance of free cryptography would guarantee its continued use after a possible Government ban. One of the first people receiving the program placed it on a computer attached to the Internet and within days thousands of people had PGP. Now the program has been through several updates and is becoming sort of a people's standard for public key cryptography. So far, it appears that no one has been able to crack information encoded with PGP.

Like Diffie, Zimmermann developed a boyhood interest in crypto. "When I was a kid growing up in Miami, it was just kind of cool — secret messages and all" he says. Later, "computers made it possible to do ciphers in a practical manner." He was fascinated to hear of public key cryptography and during the mid-1980's he began experimenting with a system that would work on personal computers. With the help of some colleagues, he finally devised a strong system, albeit one that used some patented material from RSA Data Security. And then he heard about the Senate bill that proposed to limit a citizen's right to use strong encryption by requiring manufacturers to include back doors in their products. Zimmermann, formerly a nuclear freeze activist, felt that one of the most valuable potential uses of cryptography was to keep messages secret *from* the Government.

Zimmermann has put some political content into the documentation for his program: "If privacy is outlawed, only outlaws will have privacy. Intelligence agencies have access to good cryptographic technology. So do the big arms and drug traffickers. So do defense contractors, oil companies, and other corporate giants. But ordinary people and grassroots political organizations mostly have not had access to affordable 'military grade' public-key cryptographic technology. Until now."

He has been told that Burmese freedom fighters learn PGP in jungle training camps on portable computers, using it to keep documents hidden from their oppressive Government. But his favorite letter comes from a person in Latvia, who informed him that his program was a favorite among one-time refuseniks in that former Soviet republic. "Let it never be," wrote his correspondent, "but if dictatorship takes over Russia, your PGP is widespread from Baltic to Far East now and will help democratic people if necessary."

Early last year, Zimmermann received a visit from two United States Customs Service agents. They wanted to know how it was that the strong encryption program PGP had found its way overseas with no export license. In the fall, he learned from his lawyer that he was a target of a grand jury investigation in San Jose, Calif. But even if the Feds should try to prosecute, they are likely to face a tough legal issue: Can it be a crime, in the process of legally distributing information in this country, to place it on an Internet computer site that is incidentally accessible to network users in other countries? There may well be a First Amendment issue here: Americans prize the right to circulate ideas, including those on software disks.

John Gilmore has discovered that Government lawyers have their own doubts about these issues. In some documents he sued to get, there are mid-1980's warnings by the Justice Department that the export controls on cryptography presented "sensitive constitutional issues." In one letter, an assistant attorney general warns that "the regulatory scheme extends too broadly into an area of protected First Amendment speech." [See also the government memo by John Harmon, pp. 537–548—Ed.]

Perhaps taking Phil Zimmermann to court would not be the Government's best method for keeping the genie in the bottle.

The Clipper program has already begun. About once a month, four couriers with security clearances travel from Washington to the Torrance, Calif., headquarters of Mykotronx, which holds the contract to make Clipper chips. They travel in pairs, two from each escrow agency, the NIST and the Treasury Department. The redundancy is a requirement of a protocol known as Two-Person Integrity, used in situations like nuclear missile launches, where the stakes are too high to rely on one person.

The couriers wait while a Sun work station performs the calculations to generate the digital cryptographic keys that will be imprinted in the Clipper chips. Then it splits the keys into two pieces, separate number chains, and writes them on two floppy disks, each holding lists of "key splits." To reconstruct the keys imprinted on the chip, and thereby decode private conversations, you would need both sets of disks.

After being backed up, the sets of disks are separated each one going with a pair of couriers. When the couriers return to their respective agencies, each set of disks is placed in a double-walled safe. The backup copies are placed in similar safes. There they wait, two stacks of floppy disks that grow each month, now holding about 20,000 key splits, the so-called back doors.

Will this number grow into the millions as the Government hopes? Ultimately the answer lies with the American public. Administration officials are confident that when the public contemplates scenarios like the Fortress in the Bronx or the Mushroom Cloud in Lower Manhattan, it will realize that allowing the Government to hold the keys is a relatively painless price to pay for safety and national security. They believe the public will eventually accept it in the same way it now views limited legal wiretapping. But so far the Administration hasn't recruited many prominent supporters. The main one is Dorothy Denning, a crypto expert who heads the computer science department at Georgetown University.

Since endorsing Clipper (and advocating passage of the Digital Telephony initiative) Denning has been savagely attacked on the computer nets. Some of the language would wither a professional wrestler. "I've seen horrible things written about me," Denning says with a nervous smile. "I try to actually now avoid looking at them, because that's not what's important to me. What's important is that we end up doing the right thing with this. It was an accumulation of factors that led me to agree with Clipper, and the two most important areas, to me, are organized crime and terrorism. I was exposed to cases where wiretaps had actually stopped crimes in the making, and I started thinking, 'if they didn't have this tool, some of these things might have happened.' You know, I hate to use the word responsibility, but I actually feel some sense of responsibility to at least state my position to the extent so that people will understand it."

The opponents of Clipper are confident that the marketplace will vote against it. "The idea that the Government holds the keys to all our locks, before anyone has even been accused of committing a crime, doesn't parse with the public" says Jerry Berman, executive director of the Electronic Frontier Foundation. "It's not America."

Senator Leahy hints that Congress might not stand for the Clinton Administration's attempt to construct the key-escrow system, at an estimated cost of $14 million dollars initially and $16 million annually. "If the Administration wants the money to set up and run the key-escrow facilities," he says, "it will need Congressional approval." Despite claims by the National Institute of Standards and Technology deputy director, Raymond G. Kammer, that some foreign governments have shown interest in the scheme, Leahy seems to agree with most American telecommunications and computer manufacturers that Clipper and subsequent escrow schemes will find no favor in the vast international marketplace, turning the United States into a cryptographic island and crippling important industries.

Leahy is also concerned about the Administration's haste. "The Administration is rushing to implement the Clipper chip program without thinking through crucial details," he says. Indeed, although the Government has been buying and using Clipper encryption devices, the process of actually getting the keys out of escrow and using them to decipher scrambled conversations has never been field tested. And there exists only a single uncompleted prototype of the device intended to do the deciphering.

Leahy is also among those who worry that, all policy issues aside, the Government's key escrow scheme might fail solely on technical issues. The Clipper and Capstone chips, while powerful enough to use on today's equipment, have not been engineered for the high speeds of the coming information highway; updates will be required. Even more serious are the potential design flaws in the unproved key-escrow scheme. Matthew Blaze's discovery that wrongdoers could foil wiretappers may be only the first indication that Clipper is unable to do the job for which it was designed. In his paper revealing the glitch, he writes, "It is not clear that it is possible to construct EES (Escrow Encryption Standard) that is both completely invulnerable to all kinds of exploitation as well as generally useful."

At bottom, many opponents of Clipper do not trust the Government. They are unimpressed by the elaborate key-escrow security arrangements outlined for Clipper. Instead, they ask questions about the process by which the Clipper was devised — how is it that the N.S.A., an intelligence agency whose mission does not ordinarily include consumer electronics design, has suddenly seized a central role in creating a national information matrix? They also complain that the Skipjack cryptographic algorithm is a classified secret, one that cryptographic professionals cannot subject to the rigorous, extended testing that has previously been used to gain universal trust for such a standard.

"You don't want to buy a set of car keys from a guy who specializes in stealing cars," says Marc Rotenberg, director of the Electronic Privacy Information Center. "The N.S.A.'s specialty is the ability to break codes, and they are saying, 'Here, take our keys, we promise you they'll work.'"

At the March conference on computers and privacy, Stewart Baker responded to this sort of criticism. "This is the revenge of people who couldn't go to Woodstock because they had too much trig homework," he said, evoking some catcalls. "It's a kind of romanticism about privacy. The problem with it is that the beneficiaries of that sort of romanticism are going to be predators. PGP, they say, is out there to protect freedom fighters in Latvia. But the fact is, the only use that has come to the attention of law enforcement agencies is a guy who was using PGP so the police could not tell what little boys he had seduced over the net. Now that's what people will use this for — it's not the only thing people will use it for, but they will use it for that — and by insisting on having a claim to privacy that is beyond social regulation, we are creating a world in which people like that will flourish and be able to do more than they can do today."

Even if Clipper flops, the Crypto War will continue. The Administration remains committed to limiting the spread of strong cryptography unless there's a back door. Recently, it has taken to asking opponents for alternatives to Clipper. One suggestion it will not embrace is inaction. "Deciding that the genie is out of the bottle and throwing our arms up is not where we're at," says a White House official.

The National Security Agency will certainly not go away. "The agency is really worried about its screens going blank" due to unbreakable encryption, says Lance J. Hoffman, a professor of computer science at George Washington University. "When that happens, the N.S.A. — said to be the largest employer in Maryland — goes belly-up. A way to prevent this is to expand its mission and to become, effectively, the one-stop shop for encryption for Government and those that do business with the Government."

Sure enough, the security agency is cooking up an entire product line of new key-escrow chips. At Fort Meade, it has already created a highspeed version of the Skipjack algorithm that outperforms both Clipper and Capstone. There is also another, more powerful encryption device in the works named Baton. As far as the agency is concerned, these developments are no more than common sense. "To say that N.S A. shouldn't be involved in this issue is to say that Government should try to solve this difficult technical and social problem with both hands tied behind its back," Stewart Baker says.

But Phil Zimmermann and the Cypherpunks aren't going away, either. Zimmermann is, among other things, soliciting funds for a PGP phone that will allow users the same sort of voice encryption provided by the Clipper chip. The difference, of course, is that in his phone there is no key escrow, no back door. If the F.B.I. initiated a wiretap on someone using Zimmermann's proposed phone, all the investigators would hear is static that they could never restore to orderly language.

What if that static shielded the murderous plans of a terrorist or kidnapper? Phil Zimmermann would feel terrible. Ultimately he has no answer. "I am worried about what might happen if unlimited security communications come about," he admits. "But I also think there are tremendous benefits. Some bad things would happen, but the trade-off would be worth it. You have to look at the big picture."

2

Testimony Before the Subcommittee on Technology, Environment, and Aviation of the Committee on Science, Space, and Technology of the U.S. House of Representatives*

Dorothy E. Denning

SUMMARY

The Clipper Chip and associated key escrow system is a technically sound approach for ensuring the security and privacy of electronic communications. Clipper's SKIPJACK encryption algorithm provides strong cryptographic security, and the key escrow system includes extensive safeguards to protect against unauthorized use of keys. The more advanced chip, Capstone, further provides all the cryptographic functionality needed for information security on the National Information Infrastructure.

Recent research suggests that the technology provides a starting point for developing an international cryptography framework that would support secure international communications while accommodating individual national cryptography policies. Such a framework would be based on standard cryptographic application interfaces and national cryptographic modules, and might support corporate key escrow. An international cryptography framework would allow U.S industry, under existing export control policies, to develop and export software applications that meet the information security needs of government, industry, and individuals.

As we move into an era of even greater electronic communications, we can and must design our telecommunications infrastructure and encryption systems to support our needs as a nation not only for secure communications, individual privacy, and economic strength, but also for law enforcement and national security. If we dismiss the intercept needs for law enforcement and national security, society could suffer severe economic and human losses resulting from a diminished capability to investigate and prosecute organized crime and terrorism, and from a diminished capability for foreign intelligence. The Clipper Chip

---

* May 3, 1994.

and Digital Telephony proposal are important steps toward meeting all of our national needs.

My name is Dorothy Denning and I am Professor and Chair of Computer Science at Georgetown University. I have been in the field of cryptography and information security for over twenty years. Before coming to Georgetown, I worked for Digital Equipment Corporation, SRI International, and Purdue University. I am author of the textbook *Cryptography and Data Security* and was the first President of the International Association for Cryptologic Research. During the past two years, my research has focused on the impact of encryption and digital telephony on law enforcement's ability to conduct lawful wiretaps and on different approaches to encryption that accommodate the needs of law enforcement. I am one of the outside reviewers invited by the government to evaluate the Clipper Chip and its key escrow system, and a member of the Software Escrowed Encryption Working Group sponsored by NIST. I am pleased to have this opportunity to testify before the Subcommittee on Technology, Environment, and Aviation.

I will begin by giving my assessment of the Clipper Chip technology and associated key escrow system. I will then describe future options. My main conclusions are that the Clipper Chip is a technically sound approach for ensuring the security and privacy of electronic communications, that the more advanced Capstone Chip provides all the cryptographic functionality needed for information security on the National Information Infrastructure, and that the technology provides a starting point towards developing an international cryptography framework.

ASSESSMENT OF CLIPPER AND KEY ESCROW SYSTEM

The Clipper Chip is an implementation of the Escrowed Encryption Standard (EES), a voluntary government standard for encrypting sensitive but unclassified telephone communications, including voice, fax, and data.

The chip was designed with two main goals. The first is strong cryptographic protection for electronic communications. To meet this goal, Clipper uses the SKIPJACK encryption algorithm designed by the National Security Agency. The second goal is a mechanism that allows authorized law enforcement officials to decrypt Clipper encoded communications, while ensuring a high level of protection against unauthorized decryption. For this, Clipper transmits a Law Enforcement Access Field (LEAF) with all communications. The LEAF includes the encryption key for the communications, commonly called the "session key," encrypted under a special chip unique key. The chip unique key thereby provides access to the session key, which in turn provides access to the content of the communications. When conducting an authorized intercept, government officials obtain the chip unique key by getting two key components, which are encrypted and stored in escrow when the chip is manufactured, from two key escrow agents. These components are decrypted and combined inside a special key escrow decryption processor, which then decrypts the intercepted communications. Both SKIPJACK and the LEAF creation method are classified.

As one of the cryptographers invited by the government to evaluate Clipper, I had the opportunity to learn about NSA's design and evaluation of SKIPJACK, and to perform experiments on the algorithm to determine its ability to withstand particular attacks. As the result of this study, I concluded that SKIPJACK does not contain any "trapdoor" and is not vulnerable to any short-cut method of attack. The other four reviewers and myself issued a joint report stating that there was no significant risk that SKIPJACK could be broken by any short cut method of attack. In addition, we observed that because SKIPJACK's 80-bit keys are 24 bits longer than those used by the Data Encryption Standard (DES), under an assumption that the cost of processing power continues to be halved every year and a half, it will be 36 years before the cost of breaking SKIPJACK by trying all possible keys is comparable to the cost of breaking DES today. Thus, Clipper can be expected to provide strong cryptographic protection for several decades.

Although publication of SKIPJACK would have the advantage of giving more people the opportunity to review it and, therefore, foster greater public trust, publication would undermine the second goal of Clipper. In particular, it would enable someone to build a hardware or software product that used SKIPJACK without escrowing keys, thereby taking advantage of the government's strong algorithm in order to make communications immune from lawful interception and foreign intelligence operations. It is for this reason also that the EES specifies a tamper-resistant hardware implementation; there is no known way of reliably hiding the structure of an algorithm in software.

We also examined Clipper's classified LEAF creation method to make sure that chip unique keys and session keys are not vulnerable to exposure. We found no vulnerabilities.

Clipper's second goal of allowing authorized government access is implemented through a key escrow system, wherein keys are released upon receipt of certification of legal authority to wiretap. Of particular concern to users of Clipper is whether that system will adequately protect against unauthorized access by the government or anyone else.

We are currently in the process of reviewing the entire key escrow system, both as it is currently configured and as it will be configured in the final system. From what I have seen so far, I believe that the risk of unauthorized access will be acceptably low, and that any such occurrence will be detectable through auditing.

The key escrow system has been designed with extensive safeguards to ensure that no single individual or two individuals from the same organization can compromise the escrowed key components, and to ensure that any potential compromises are detectable. I would like to mention two of these safeguards here: "two person integrity" and auditing. Two person integrity has been used successfully for many years to protect top secret cryptographic material and other highly sensitive government information. It is used in the key escrow system for all operations that involve key escrow data. For example, it takes two people from each escrow agent to access that agent's escrowed key components, and representatives of both agents to supply law enforcement with the encrypted key components and information needed to decrypt those components.

Auditing is used extensively throughout the key escrow system. For example, detailed audit records are produced from the time the key components are generated, encrypted, and stored with the escrow agents through their release to law enforcement and ultimate deletion in the law enforcement decryption processor. Using these logs, it should be possible for an auditor to determine that a particular key released to the government was used only as authorized. If a key is used to decrypt communications not authorized to have been intercepted or used to decrypt communications not intercepted during the period when the authorization was in effect, this would be detected in the audit.

Some people have criticized Clipper's approach to key escrow for giving law enforcement access to the chip unique keys rather than the individual session keys on a per conversation basis. They are concerned that law enforcement will misuse the chip keys to decrypt traffic illegally intercepted prior to or following a court order. My assessment is that a key escrow system that would require law enforcement to go through the escrow agents for each individual conversation, which can be in the hundreds per day, not only would be excessively burdensome to the point of seriously jeopardizing many investigations, but also is unjustified and unnecessary given other legal, operational, and technical safeguards.

It is important to not make the key escrow more complicated or burdensome than required to make the risk of unauthorized use of Clipper keys acceptably low. I believe that with the current approach it will be extremely difficult if not impossible for anyone, including the government, to improperly access Clipper-encrypted communications, and that unauthorized use of Clipper keys will be detectable through auditing. Clipper will provide far greater protection against illegal wiretaps by the government that is presently available.

In addition to providing excellent protection, Clipper offers high speed encryption. Present chips encrypt at a rate of about 20 Mbits per second. As technology improves, we can expect corresponding improvements in the speed of Clipper.

Clipper is technically sound and inexpensive. In lots of 100,000 or more, a fully programmed chip is expected to cost $10.00 by fall. Clipper's implementation in commercial products such as the AT&T 3600 Telephone Security Device will give the government and public access to high quality, easy-to-use, and cryptographically strong encryption for telephone communications.

The Capstone Chip, which is an advanced version of Clipper, goes further and provides all the cryptographic functionality needed for information security within the National Information Infrastructure to support secure electronic commerce and other applications. In addition to implementing the specifications for the EES, Capstone implements the Digital Signature Algorithm, which provides a digital signature capability comparable in strength to the RSA digital signature system; the Secure Hash Algorithm, which provides integrity protection; a key exchange method; and various other functions. Capstone is embedded in the Tessera PCMCIA card, where it will be used in the government's Mosaic system to provide secure electronic mail for the Defense Messaging System.

FUTURE OPTIONS

Recent research suggests that the government's escrowed encryption approach can provide a starting point for developing an international cryptography framework that would support secure international communications while accommodating individual national cryptography policies. Such a framework would allow the U.S. computer and software industry to strengthen its leadership in the global market under existing export control policies.

Keith Klemba and Jim Schindler of Hewlett-Packard presented such a framework to NIST's Computer Systems Security and Privacy Advisory Board (CSSPAB) in March. Their approach is to standardize the service elements of national cryptography policies, which would be encoded in smart cards called "national flag cards." The U.S. flag card, for example, could include a Clipper or Capstone Chip. With a common standard, developers of software products could build applications that provide information security by interfacing with a national cryptographic module that satisfies the policy requirements of the country where the product is used. Since the applications themselves would not implement cryptographic functions, they would be exportable, addressing the main concern of the software industry regarding export controls.

Steve Walker, President of Trusted Information Systems, has proposed that a consortium of interested parties define preliminary standards for Cryptographic Application Programming Interfaces (CAPIs), and then experimentally test them out with cryptographic modules implemented in PCMCIA cards. Such CAPIs could build on NIST's draft set of Application Layer Cryptographic Service Calls, the interface specifications for the Tessera PCMCIA card, which uses the Capstone Chip and thus implements key escrow, and other publicly available specifications. A challenge will be to do this in a way that does not promote the proliferation of unescrowed encryption, thereby thwarting lawful access by the government.

Within an international cryptography framework, it might be possible to add a corporate key escrow system, wherein organizations and individuals could escrow keys with private sector agents, and then obtain access to those keys without a warrant. One of the concerns of many potential users of encryption, particularly organizations, is that encrypted information could become inaccessible if keys are accidentally lost, intentionally destroyed, or held for ransom. A corporate escrow system could help protect an organization's information assets and protect against liability problems by ensuring that keys are under the control of those accountable for the assets. Donn Parker at SRI International has been advocating such an approach, and Frank Sudia at Bankers Trust presented to the CSSPAB a proposal for an international corporate key escrow system, which could use escrow agents in different countries. The Bankers Trust system builds on an alternative approach to key escrow, which was developed by Professor Silvio Micali at MIT and ties in with public-key cryptography.

A corporate escrow system might be coupled with that used by the government for law enforcement and national security purposes, as in the Bankers Trust approach, but it also could be separate. Although many of the mechanisms would be similar, the goals are different. With a separate system, the keys escrowed under the corporate escrow system might be different from those escrowed for law enforcement.

Another possible option is a software-based approach to encryption and key escrow. The NIST-sponsored Software Escrowed Encryption Working Group, of which I am a member, is working towards requirements and specifications for an international software-based key escrow encryption system that would meet the needs of businesses, governments, and individuals for secure domestic and international communications and the needs of national governments for accessing communications under their legal authority. A challenge here is finding a way that does not allow the user to readily circumvent the key escrow process. At this point, it is too early to tell whether we will achieve our goal.

Both a corporate key escrow system and a software-based escrow system are likely to be substantially more complex than the current Clipper/Capstone key escrow system, and may depend on the implementation of a public key infrastructure Thus, they do not represent near-term alternatives to the Clipper approach. In addition to its simplicity, the Clipper system also has the advantage of guaranteeing key escrow without requiring any action on the part of users and of offering potentially greater privacy by escrowing keys by device rather than by user.

CONCLUSIONS

The Clipper Chip and associated key escrow system provides both strong communications security and lawful government access, while providing a very high level of protection against unauthorized access. Clipper offers strong encryption for electronic communications, while the more advanced Capstone Chip offers a full range of cryptographic functions to satisfy the requirements for secure electronic commerce and other applications on the NII.

As we move into an era of even greater electronic communications, we can and must design our telecommunications infrastructure and encryption systems to support our needs as a nation for secure communications, individual privacy, economic strength, effective law enforcement, and national security. The Clipper Chip is an important step towards meeting all our national needs, and the government should continue to move forward with the program.

The government needs an encryption standard to succeed DES. If in lieu of Clipper, the government were to adopt and promote a standard that provides strong encryption without government access, society could suffer severe economic and human losses resulting from a diminished capability of law enforcement to investigate and prosecute organized crime and terrorism, and from a diminished capability for foreign intelligence. Critics argue that unescrowed encryption will proliferate through the private sector anyway, undermining the government's efforts. Indeed, this is possible since some proponents of cryptography either actively oppose government wiretaps or dismiss law enforcement and national security needs as unessential. Nevertheless, the government rightly concluded that it would be irresponsible to promote a standard that foils law enforcement when technology is at hand to accommodate law enforcement needs without jeopardizing security and privacy. Moreover, through the Administration's commitment to Clipper or some other form of key escrow, escrowed encryption may dominate in the market, mitigating the impact of unescrowed encryption on law enforcement. Several researchers and industry leaders recognize the value of providing both secure communications and authorized government access, so escrowed encryption may gain in popularity, particularly as a framework for international cryptography evolves.

Clipper is also a good testbed for trying out key escrow. If key escrow encryption is successful, it might form the basis for a broader-based, more complex key escrow system, possibly managed by the private sector, which would allow individual and organizational access as well as access by the government. Such a system might support international key escrow and a variety of encryption standards and national policies. If the key escrow system for some reason fails to provide acceptable protection against unauthorized use of keys, then the escrowed keys can always be destroyed, leaving behind strong cryptographic protection. By contrast, it would be extremely difficult to go the other way and implement key escrow after some other form of strong encryption has come into widespread use.

Assuming efforts to develop an international key escrow framework prove successful, such a framework could support secure international communications while accommodating individual national policies governing cryptography. An international framework likely would be based on standard cryptographic application interfaces and national cryptographic modules, and could support Clipper and Capstone technology along with other forms of escrowed encryption. This approach would allow U.S. industry, under existing export control policies, to strengthen its leadership in the global market by developing and exporting software applications that meet the information security needs of government, industry, and individuals.

Just as encryption has threatened the government's ability to access communications intercepted under its legal authority, advances in telecommunications technology are already undermining the government's ability to intercept those communications in the first place and to obtain call setup information. While Clipper addresses the former problem, the proposed Digital Telephony legislation addresses the latter. Both are needed in order to ensure that as technology provides greater communications security, law enforcement agencies continue to have the tools they need to investigate major crimes and acts of terrorism.

Wiretaps for a Wireless Age*

David Gelernter

I'd be furious if my phone were tapped. Most people would. Americans have a long, proud history of low tolerance for Government snooping. Nonetheless, I strongly support the Government's ability to tap telephones when wiretapping serves a compelling law-enforcement end. Civilized life is a compromise, and wiretaps have proved their value beyond doubt: over the last decade, wiretaps have played a role in convicting tens of thousands of felons and solving (or preventing) large numbers of ghastly crimes. They seem particularly valuable in cases of large-scale drug trafficking and terrorist thuggery.

But in the age of high technology, the wiretap is a dead duck. In the old days, all conversations associated with a given phone number were funneled through one physical pathway, and by spying on that pathway you could hear it all. Nowadays, cellular phones and call forwarding make it much harder to find the right spot and to attach a tap. New techniques coming into use will make it harder still: when many conversations are squished together and sent barreling over a high-capacity glass fiber, it's hard for wiretappers to extract the one conversation they are after from the resulting mush.

Enter the Administration's Digital Telephony and Communications Privacy Improvement Act. Its goal is to save wiretapping. Congress will act on it soon. It is a good and an important bill. Congress should pass it.

The heart of the act requires phone companies to give law-enforcement agents the ability to execute "all court orders and lawful authorizations for the interception of wire and electronic communications" — whatever fancy new technology happens to be in vogue. It offers the phone companies $500 million to refit telephone equipment to allow compliance with the act. If the costs exceed $500 million, the Administration says, it will seek funds lo cover them.

Not everyone is happy with this bill. Some telephone companies argue that the required refitting is technically hard and does nothing for competitiveness or consumer satisfaction. Some civil libertarians argue that the bill poses a threat to privacy.

The bill does present a wide range of technical problems. In some cases, for example, it requires that the software controlling existing digital switches be modified; the phone companies are right when they argue that these changes would be a first-rate headache to carry out. Nor will the effort advance their competitiveness, or deliver anything exciting to the consumer. But, alas, not every civic duty is fun. And this bill sets a welcome precedent by honestly owning up to the costs and offering to pay them. The message I hope Congress will send to the phone companies is: stop whining and do it.

The more troublesome objection deals with privacy. Part of the opposition is based on simple misunderstanding. Some opponents behave that the act will give the Government new spying powers. In fact, the Government will be allowed to do exactly what it has always been allowed to do. The act is intended merely to make it technically possible for law enforcement to continue placing wiretaps.

Other opponents do understand the bill and are forthright about their intentions. If technical advances kill wiretapping, they will send flowers and have a party. They argue that wiretaps aren't terribly useful anyway. This argument is also being advanced in the context of the "clipper chip," another Administration initiative that lives right next door.

The clipper chip is a small piece of computer hardware designed to stave off encryption schemes that the Government can't crack. The chip would encode all information sent out into any computer network (the Internet, for example) so it can be read only by the intended recipient — and, if necessary, a court-authorized law-enforcement agent who has the key.

Because wiretapping is useless if all you can overhear is gibberish, the Administration would like every computer to come factory equipped with such a chip. Each chip would have its own key, and the keys would not be handed out like lollipops: each would be split in two, and each half would be lodged for safekeeping in its own Government vault somewhere.

Of course, the fact that some encryption scheme comes built in doesn't mean that you have to use it. You can throw out your factory disk drive and plug in another. You could plug in a different Government-proof encryption scheme just as easily. Hence, anti-clipperites gleefully conclude, the chip would be useless for law enforcement, because only a half-wit would discuss a crime using plain vanilla, straight-from-the-factory encryption. And after all, who ever heard of a stupid criminal?

It is impossible to take this kind of argument seriously. What kind of half-wit criminal would leave fingerprints, make calls on any home telephone or return a rental van that played a starring role in a big-budget terrorist spectacular? Many criminals *are* half-wits, many others are lazy or careless, and it's lucky they are. Clipper will make computer-based communication routinely safe and private, in a way that gives us a fighting chance of keeping our ability to spy on criminals. It is no cure-all, but it is a useful and intelligent step.

Whatever the details, opponents of initiatives like the clipper chip and the telephony act argue that they threaten the right to privacy. But in itself the right to privacy is no argument at all. We allow the Government to violate our privacy routinely for many purposes. The Internal Revenue Service makes a habit of violating it. Search warrants violate it. Privacy buffs are often big fans of gun control and the Endangered Species Act; some versions of gun control restrict the objects you may keep in your own home, and the species act has been interpreted in a way that drastically restricts the ways citizens may use their land. Whether the proposed legislation constitutes a potential invasion of privacy is immaterial. The question is, Is that a justifiable invasion? Experience suggests that it is eminently justifiable.

If Congress fails to pass the telephony bill there is every reason to believe that crime, particularly terrorist crime, will get worse. And when it happens we will shrug our shoulders, wonder vaguely how things got this way, build more prisons, tend our wounds, bury our dead — as is our wont.

All of this suggests a broader moral. A current project of mine involves a detailed study of the 1939 New York World's Fair. One of the questions I face again and again is: Over two generations during which our wealth and technical knowledge and medical expertise have all increased immeasurably, our laws have become more just and our human resources have expanded enormously — how can it be that our confidence in the future has all but collapsed? One part of the answer is that all too often we have allowed experts to come between us and our common sense.

Modern life is so complex that it often feels as if common sense can get no purchase on it. Common sense suggests that this is no time to abandon a useful weapon in the fight on crime. But if telecommunications experts tell us that we just don't understand modern phone systems well enough to make rules about them, if legal experts or would-be experts assure us that for reasons we don't fully understand, if we pass this bill we will regret it . . . who are we to object?

Nothing would do us more good as a nation than to reassert our right to tell the experts to get lost. I am a "technical expert," but don't take my word on this bill as an expert. I was seriously and permanently injured by a terrorist letter bomb last year, but don't take my word as a special pleader either. Take my word because common sense demands that wiretapping be preserved. This bill preserves it. Let's pass the bill.

Don't Worry Be Happy*

Stewart A. Baker

With all the enthusiasm of Baptist ministers turning their Sunday pulpits over to the Devil, the editors of WIRED have offered me the opportunity to respond to some of the urban folklore that has grown up around key escrow encryption—also known as the Clipper Chip.

Recently the Clinton administration has announced that federal agencies will be able to buy a new kind of encryption hardware that is sixteen million times stronger than the existing federal standard known as DES. But this new potency comes with a caveat. If one of these new encryption devices is used, for example, to encode a phone conversation that is subject to a lawful government wiretap, the government can get access to that device's encryption keys. Separate parts of each key are held by two independent "escrow agents," who will release keys only to authorized agencies under safeguards approved by the attorney general. Private use of the new encryption hardware is welcome but not required. That's a pretty modest proposal. Its critics, though, have generated at least seven myths about key escrow encryption that deserve answers.

Myth Number One. Key escrow encryption will create a brave new world of government intrusion into the privacy of Americans.

Opponents of key escrow encryption usually begin by talking about government invading the privacy of American citizens. None of us likes the idea of the government intruding willy-nilly on communications that are meant to be private.

But the key escrow proposal is not about increasing government's authority to invade the privacy of its citizens. All that key escrow does is preserve the government's current ability to conduct wiretaps under existing authorities. Even if key escrow were the only form of encryption available, the world would look only a little different from the one we live in now.

In fact, it's the proponents of widespread unbreakable encryption who want to create a brave new world, one in which all of us—crooks included—have a guarantee that the government can't tap our phones.

---

* Published in *WIRED*, June 1994.

Yet these proponents have done nothing to show us that the new world they seek will really be a better one.

In fact, even a civil libertarian might prefer a world where wiretaps are possible. If we want to catch and convict the leaders of criminal organizations, there are usually only two good ways to do it. We can "turn" a gang member—get him to testify against his leaders. Or we can wiretap the leaders as they plan the crime.

I once did a human rights report on the criminal justice system in El Salvador. I didn't expect the Salvadorans to teach me much about human rights. But I learned that, unlike the US, El Salvador greatly restricts the testimony of "turned" co-conspirators. Why? Because the co-conspirator is usually "turned" either by a threat of mistreatment or by an offer to reduce his punishment. Either way, the process raises moral questions—and creates an incentive for false accusations.

Wiretaps have no such potential for coercive use. The defendant is convicted or freed on the basis of his own, unarguable words.

In addition, the world will be a safer place if criminals cannot take advantage of a ubiquitous, standardized encryption infrastructure that is immune from any conceivable law enforcement wiretap. Even if you're worried about illegal government taps, key escrow reinforces the existing requirement that every wiretap and every decryption must be lawfully authorized. The key escrow system means that proof of authority to tap must be certified and audited, so that illegal wiretapping by a rogue prosecutor or police officer is, as a practical matter, impossible.

Myth Number Two. Unreadable encryption is the key to our future liberty.

Of course there are people who aren't prepared to trust the escrow agents, or the courts that issue warrants, or the officials who oversee the system, or anybody else for that matter. Rather than rely on laws to protect us, they say, let's make wiretapping impossible; then we'll be safe no matter who gets elected.

This sort of reasoning is the long-delayed revenge of people who couldn't go to Woodstock because they had too much trig homework. It reflects a wide—and kind of endearing—streak of romantic high-tech anarchism that crops up throughout the computer world.

The problem with all this romanticism is that its most likely beneficiaries are predators. Take for example the campaign to distribute PGP ("Pretty Good Privacy") encryption on the Internet. Some argue that widespread availability of this encryption will help Latvian freedom fighters today and American freedom fighters tomorrow. Well, not quite. Rather, one of the earliest users of PGP was a high-tech pedophile in Santa Clara, California. He used PGP to encrypt files that, police suspect, include a diary of his contacts with susceptible young boys using computer bulletin boards all over the country. "What really bothers me," says Detective Brian Kennedy of the Sacramento, California, Sheriff's Department, "is that there could be kids out there who need help badly, but thanks to this encryption, we'll never reach them."

If unescrowed encryption becomes ubiquitous, there will be many more stories like this. We can't afford as a society to protect pedophiles and criminals today just to keep alive the far-fetched notion that some future tyrant will be brought down by guerrillas wearing bandoleers and pocket protectors and sending PGP-encrypted messages to each other across cyberspace.

Myth Number Three. Encryption is the key to preserving privacy in a digital world.

Even people who don't believe that they are likely to be part of future resistance movements have nonetheless been persuaded that encryption is the key to preserving privacy in a networked, wireless world, and that we need strong encryption for this reason. This isn't completely wrong, but it is not an argument against Clipper.

If you want to keep your neighbors from listening in on your cordless phone, if you want to keep unscrupulous competitors from stealing your secrets, even if you want to keep foreign governments from knowing your business plans, key escrow encryption will provide all the security you need, and more.

But I can't help pointing out that encryption has been vastly oversold as a privacy protector. The biggest threats to our privacy in a digital world come not from what we keep secret but from what we reveal willingly. We lose privacy in a digital world because it becomes cheap and easy to collate and transmit data, so that information you willingly gave a bank to get a mortgage suddenly ends up in the hands of a business rival or your ex-spouse's lawyer. Restricting these invasions of privacy is a challenge, but it isn't a job for encryption. Encryption can't protect you from the misuse of data you surrendered willingly.

What about the rise of networks? Surely encryption can help prevent password attacks like the recent Internet virus, or the interception of credit card numbers as they're sent from one digital assistant to another? Well, maybe. In fact, encryption is, at best, a small part of network security.

The real key to network security is making sure that only the right people get access to particular data. That's why a digital signature is so much more important to future network security than encryption. If everyone on a net has a unique identifier that others cannot forge, there's no need to send credit card numbers—- and so nothing to intercept. And if everyone has a digital signature, stealing passwords off the Net is pointless. That's why the Clinton administration is determined to put digital signature technology in the public domain. It's part of a strategy to improve the security of the information infrastructure in ways that don't endanger government's ability to enforce the law.

Myth Number Four. Key escrow will never work. Crooks won't use it if it's voluntary. There must be a secret plan to make key escrow encryption mandatory.

This is probably the most common and frustrating of all the myths that abound about key escrow. The administration has said time and again that it will not force key escrow on manufacturers and companies in the private sector. In a Catch-22 response, critics then insist that if key escrow isn't mandated it won't work.

That misunderstands the nature of the problem we are trying to solve. Encryption is available today. But it isn't easy for criminals to use; especially in telecommunications. Why? Because as long as encryption is not standardized and ubiquitous, using encryption means buying and distributing expensive gear to all the key members of the conspiracy. Up to now only a few criminals have had the resources, sophistication, and discipline to use specialized encryption systems.

What worries law enforcement agencies—what should worry them—is a world where encryption is standardized and ubiquitous: a world where anyone who buys an US$80 phone gets an "encrypt" button that interoperates with everyone else's; a world where every fax machine and every modem automatically encodes its transmissions without asking whether that is necessary. In such a world, every criminal will gain a guaranteed refuge from the police without lifting a finger.

The purpose of the key escrow initiative is to provide an alternative form of encryption that can meet legitimate security concerns without building a web of standardized encryption that shuts law enforcement agencies out. If banks and corporations and government agencies buy key escrow encryption, criminals won't get a free ride. They'll have to build their own systems—as they do now. And their devices won't interact with the devices that much of the rest of society uses. As one of my friends in the FBI puts it, "Nobody will build secure phones just to sell to the Gambino family."

In short, as long as legitimate businesses use key escrow, we can stave off a future in which acts of terror and organized crime are planned with impunity on the public telecommunications system. Of course, whenever we say that, the critics of key escrow trot out their fifth myth:

Myth Number Five. The government is interfering with the free market by forcing key escrow on the private sector. Industry should be left alone to develop and sell whatever form of encryption succeeds in the market.

In fact, opponents of key escrow fear that businesses may actually prefer key escrow encryption. Why? Because the brave new world that unreadable encryption buffs want to create isn't just a world with communications immunity for crooks. It's a world of uncharted liability. What if a company supplies unreadable encryption to all its employees, and a couple of them use it to steal from customers or to encrypt customer data and hold it hostage? As a lawyer, I can say it's almost certain that the customers will sue the company that supplied the encryption to its employees. And that company in turn will sue the software and hardware firms that built a "security" system without safeguards against such an obvious abuse. The only encryption system that doesn't conjure up images of a lawyers' feeding frenzy is key escrow.

But there's a second and even more compelling reason why the key escrow initiative can't fairly be characterized as interfering with private enterprise: The encryption market has been more or less created and sustained by government. Much of the market for encryption devices is in the public sector, and much of the encryption technology now in widespread use in the private sector was funded, perfected, or endorsed by the federal government.

And not by accident, either. Good encryption is expensive. It isn't just a matter of coming up with a strong algorithm, although testing the strength of an algorithm can be enormously time-consuming. The entire system must be checked for bugs and weaknesses, a laborious and unglamorous process. Generally, only the federal government has been willing to pay what it costs to develop secure communications gear. That's because we can't afford to have our adversaries reading our military and diplomatic communications.

That's led to a common pattern. First, the government develops, tests, or perfects encryption systems for itself. Then the private sector drafts along behind the government, adopting government standards on the assumption that if it's good enough for the government's information, it's good enough to protect industry's.

As encryption technology gets cheaper and more common, though, we face the real prospect that the federal government's own research, its own standards, its own purchases will help create the future I described earlier—one in which criminals use ubiquitous encryption to hide their activities. How can anyone expect the standard-setting arms of government to use their power to destroy the capabilities of law enforcement—especially at a time when the threat of crime and terror seems to be rising dramatically?

By adopting key escrow encryption instead, the federal government has simply made the reasonable judgment that its own purchases will reflect all of society's values, not just the single-minded pursuit of total privacy.

So where does this leave industry, especially those companies that don't like either the 1970s-vintage DES or key escrow? It leaves them where they ought to be—standing on their own two feet. Companies that want to develop and sell new forms of unescrowed encryption won't be able to sell products that bear the federal seal of approval. They won't be able to ride piggyback on federal research efforts. And they won't be able to sell a single unreadable encryption product to both private and government customers.

Well, so what? If companies want to develop and sell competing, unescrowed systems to other Americans, if they insist on hastening a brave new world of criminal immunity, they can still do so—as long as they're willing to use their own money. That's what the free market is all about.

Of course, a free market in the US doesn't mean freedom to export encryption that may damage US national security. As our experience in World War II shows, encryption is the kind of technology that wins and loses wars. With that in mind, we must be careful about exports of encryption. This isn't the place for a detailed discussion of controls, but one thing should be clear: They don't limit the encryption that Americans can buy or use. The government allows Americans to take even the most sophisticated encryption abroad for their own protection. Nor do controls require that software or hardware companies "dumb down" their US products. Software firms have complained that it's inconvenient to develop a second encryption scheme for export, but they already have to make changes from one country to the next—in language, alphabet, date systems, and handwriting recognition, to take just a few examples. And they'd still have to develop multiple encryption programs even if the US abolished export controls, because a wide variety of national restrictions on encryption are already in place in countries from Europe to Asia.

Myth Number Six. The National Security Agency is a spy agency; it has no business worrying about domestic encryption policy.

Since the National Security Agency has an intelligence mission, its role in helping to develop key escrow encryption is usually treated as evidence that key escrow must be bad security. In reality, though, NSA has two missions. It does indeed gather intelligence, in part by breaking codes. But it has a second, and oddly complementary, mission. It develops the best possible encryption for the US government's classified information.

With code breakers and code makers all in the same agency, NSA has more expertise in cryptography than any other entity in the country, public or private. It should come as no surprise, therefore, that NSA had the know-how to develop an encryption technique that provides users great security without compromising law enforcement access. To say that NSA shouldn't be involved in this issue is to say the government should try to solve this difficult technical and social problem with both hands tied behind its back.

Myth Number Seven. This entire initiative was studied in secret and implemented without any opportunity for industry or the public to be heard.

This is an old objection, and one that had some force in April of 1993, when the introduction of a new AT&T telephone encryption device required that the government move more quickly than it otherwise would have. Key escrow was a new idea at that time, and it was reasonable for the public to want more details and a chance to be heard before policies were set in concrete. But since April 1993, the public and industry have had many opportunities to express their views. The government's computer security and privacy advisory board held several days of public hearings. The National Security Council met repeatedly with industry groups. The Justice Department held briefings for congressional staff on its plans for escrow procedures well in advance of its final decision. And the Commerce Department took public comment on the proposed key escrow standard for 60 days.

After all this consultation, the government went forward with key escrow, not because the key escrow proposal received a universally warm reception, but because none of the proposal's critics was able to suggest a better way to accommodate society's interests in both privacy and law enforcement. Unless somebody comes up with one, key escrow is likely to be around for quite a while. That's because the only alternative being proposed today is for the government to design or endorse encryption systems that will cripple law enforcement when the technology migrates—as it surely will—to the private sector. And that alternative is simply irresponsible.

Stewart A. Baker is the National Security Agency's top lawyer. He worked briefly as Deputy General Counsel of the Education Department under President Jimmy Carter, and he practiced international law at Steptoe & Johnson, in Washington, DC. He has been at the NSA since 1992. [He has now returned to Steptoe & Johnson.—Ed.]

5

*So, People, We Have a Fight on Our Hands**

Bruce Sterling

Since I'm the last guy to officially speak at CFP '94 [the Fourth Conference on Computers, Freedom, and Privacy—Ed.], I want to seize the chance to grandstand and do a kind of pontifical summation of the event. And get some irrepressible feelings off my chest.

What am I going to remember from CFP '94? I'm going to remember the chief counsel of the NSA and his impassioned insistence that key escrow cryptography represents normality and the status quo and that unlicensed hard cryptography is a rash and radical leap into unplumbed depths of lawlessness. He made a literary reference to *Brave New World*. What he said in so many words was, "We're not the Brave New World, Clipper's opponents are the Brave New World."

And I believe he meant that. As a professional science fiction writer I remember being immediately struck by the deep conviction that there was plenty of Brave New World to go around.

I've been to all four CFPs, and in my opinion this is the darkest one by far. I hear ancestral voices prophesying war. All previous CFPs had a weird kind of camaraderie about them. People from the most disparate groups found something useful to tell each other. But now that America's premiere spookocracy has arrived on stage and spoken up, I think the CFP community has finally found a group of outsiders that it cannot metabolize. The trenchworks are going up and I see nothing but confrontation ahead.

Senator Patrick Leahy (D-Vermont) at least had the elementary good sense to backpedal and temporize, as any politician would upon seeing the white-hot volcano of technological advance in the direct path of a Cold War glacier that has crushed everything in its way.

But that unlucky flak-catcher the White House sent down here— that guy was mousetrapped, basically. That was a debacle! The White House sent a representative to CFP who, in a fatal error of judgment, asked the audience whom they feared would abuse cryptography more: the American government or criminals? About three quarters of the audience voted against the government. He was later quoted as saying that he had demanded an extra year of retirement for every minute he stayed in the ring at CFP getting pummeled on Clipper. Who was briefing that guy? Are they utterly unaware? How on earth could they miss the fact that the Clipper Chip and Digital Telephony are violently detested by every element in this community—with the possible exception of one brave computer science professor? Dorothy Denning of Georgetown University is a noted Clipper proponent—noted not so much for her preeminence in debate as for her being one of the rare figures associated with this initiative who is actually willing to address the issue publicly at all. Don't they get it that everybody from Rush Limbaugh to Timothy Leary despises this initiative? Don't they read newspapers? *The Wall Street Journal, The New York Times*? I won't even ask if they read their e-mail.

That was bad politics. But that was nothing compared to the presentation by the gentleman from the National Security Agency. If I can do it without losing my temper, I want to talk to you a little bit about how radically unsatisfactory that was. (For a recap of the NSA position, see Stewart Baker's "Don't Worry, Be Happy," *Wired 2.06*, page 100 - *Eds.*). [See pp. 295–301 in this book—Ed.]

I've been waiting a long time for somebody from Fort Meade—the legendary Maryland home of the NSA—to come to the aid of Dorothy Denning in her heroic and heartbreaking solo struggle against the 12 million other people with e-mail addresses. And I listened very carefully and I took notes and—I swear to God—I even applauded at the end.

He had seven points: four were disingenuous, two were halftruths, and the other was the actual core of the problem.

Let me blow away some of the smoke and mirrors first, more for my own satisfaction than for the purpose of enlightening you people any. With your indulgence.

First, the kidporn thing. I am sick and tired of hearing this specious blackwash. Are American citizens really so neurotically uptight about deviant sexual behavior that we will allow our entire information infrastructure to be dictated by the existence of pedophiles? Are pedophiles that precious and important to us? Do the NSA and the FBI really believe that they can hide the structure of a telephone switch under a layer of camouflage called "child pornography"? Are we supposed to flinch so violently at the specter of child abuse that we somehow miss the fact that they're installing a Sony Walkman jack in our phones?

Look, there were pedophiles before the National Information Infrastructure and there will be pedophiles long after NII is just another dead acronym. Pedophiles don't jump out of BBSes like jack-in-the-boxes. You want to impress me with your deep concern for children? This is Chicago! Go down to the projects and rescue some children from being terrorized and recruited by crack gangs who wouldn't know a modem if it bit them on the ass! Stop pornkidding us around! Just knock it off with that crap, you're embarrassing yourselves.

But back to the speech by Mr. Baker of the NSA. Was it just me, ladies and gentlemen, or did anyone else catch that tone of truly intolerable arrogance? Did the guy have to make the remark about our having missed Woodstock because we were busy with our trigonometry? Do spook mathematicians—permanently cooped up inside Fort Meade—consider that a funny remark? I'd like to make an even more amusing observation—that I've seen scarier secret police agencies than his completely destroyed by one Czech hippie playwright with a manual typewriter.

Are people within the NSA unaware that the current President of the US once had a big bushel-basketful of hair? If they are, perhaps I can sell them my lapel button featuring a spectacularly hirsute Bill Clinton circa 1969 with the legend "My President." What does he expect from the computer community? Normality? Sorry, pal—we're fresh out! Who is it, exactly, that the NSA considers a level-headed, sober sort, someone to sit down with and talk to seriously? Jobs? Wozniak? Gates? Sculley? Perot? I hope to God it's not Perot. Bob Allen? OK, maybe Bob Allen, that brownshoe guy from AT&T Bob Allen seems to think that Clipper is a swell idea, at least he's somehow willing to merchandise it. Even though AT&T has, mysteriously, signed off on the Electronic Frontier Foundation's industrywide petition against Clipper. But Christ, Bob Allen just gave eight zillion dollars to a guy whose idea of a good time is Microsoft Windows for Spaceships also known as Teledesic, funded by Bill Gates and Craig McCaw.

When is the NSA going to realize that Kapor and his people (Electronic Frontier Foundation) and Rotenberg and his people (Computer Professionals for Social Responsibility) and the rest of the people here are as good as they get in this milieu? CFP includes people from just about every interest group in the world that knows and cares what a modem is. Yes, they are weird, and yes, they have weird friends (I'm one of them), but there isn't any normality left in this society, and when it comes to computers, when the going got weird the weird turned pro! The status quo is over! Wake up to it! Get used to it!

Where in hell does a crowd of spooks from Fort Meade get off playing "responsible adults" in this situation? This is a laugh and a half! Bobby Ray Inman, the legendary NSA leader, made a stab at computer entrepreneurism and rapidly sank with all hands. Then he got out of the shadows of espionage and into the bright lights of actual public service and immediately started gabbling like a daylight-stricken vampire. Is this the kind of responsive public official we're expected to trust blindly with the insides of our phones and computers? Who made him God? Harry Truman, apparently. By executive order. In the frenzy of McCarthyism that created the NSA.

You know, it's a difficult confession for a practiced cynic like me to make, but I actually trust EFF people. I do; I trust them. There, I've said it. But I wouldn't trust Bobby Ray Inman to go down to the corner store for a pack of cigarettes.

You know, I like FBI people. I even kind of trust them, sort of, kind of, a little bit. I'm sorry that they didn't catch Kevin Mitnick here. Rumors flew at CFP that Mitnick, a legendary computer intruder and phone phreak, was in attendance. A young attendee who reportedly resembled Mitnick was detained in handcuffs and fingerprinted at Chicago FBI headquarters. I'm even sorry that they didn't apprehend Robert Steele, who is about 100 times as smart as Mitnick and 10,000 times as dangerous.

Intelligence expert and underground hacker devotee Robert Steele was mistaken by FBI agents for sometime Mitnick accomplice, "Agent Steal." Steele was rousted from his CFP hotel bed by three FBI agents unsuccessfully pretending to be room service. When the agents saw that, unlike the actual "Agent Steal," Robert Steele does not possess an artificial leg, Steele was left in peace. Yet a third CFP attendee was accused by FBI agents, reportedly, of some nebulous involvement with the World Trade Center bombing. One would think that any connection, however tenuous, between Islamic zealot truck bombers and American hackers would be a cause for grave national alarm, but there has not been another peep from the FBI about this subject. CFP '94 was quite a busy event for the FBI.

But FBI people, I think your idea of Digital Telephony is a scarcely mitigated disaster, and I'll tell you why: because you're going to be filling out your paperwork in quintuplicate to get a tap, just like you always do, because you don't have your own pet court like the NSA does. And for you, it probably is going to seem pretty much like the status quo. But in the meantime, you will have armed the enemies of the United States around the world with a terrible weapon. Not your court-ordered, civilized Digital Telephony—their raw and tyrannical Digital Telephony.

You're gonna be using it to round up wise guys in street gangs, and people like Saddam Hussein are gonna be using it to round up democratic activists and national minorities. You're going to strengthen the hand of despotism around the world, and then you're going to have to deal with the hordes of state supported truck bombers these rogue governments are sending our way after annihilating their own internal opposition by using your tools. You want us to put an ax in your hand and you're promising to hit us with only the flat side of it. But the Chinese don't see it that way; they're already licensing fax machines and they're gonna need a lot of new hardware to gear up for Tiananmen II.

I've talked a long time, but I want to finish by saying something about the NSA guy's one real and actual argument: the terrors of the Brave New World of free individual encryption. When he called encryption enthusiasts "romantic" he was dead-on, and when he said the results of spreading encryption were unpredictable and dangerous he was also dead-on—because, people, encryption is not our friend. Encryption is a mathematical technique, and it has about as much concern for our human well-being as does the fact that 17 times 17 equals 289. It does, but that doesn't make us sleep any safer in our beds.

Encrypted networks worry the hell out of me, and they have since the mid-1980s. The effects are scary and unpredictable and could be very destabilizing. But even the Four Horsemen of Kidporn, Dope Dealers, Mafia, and Terrorists don't worry me as much as totalitarian governments. It's been a long century, and we've had enough of them.

Our battle this century against totalitarianism has left terrible scars all over our body politic, and the threat these people pose to us is entirely and utterly predictable. You can say that the devil we know is better than the devil we don't, but the devils we knew were ready to commit genocide, litter the earth with dead, and blow up the world. How much worse can that get? Let's not build chips and wiring for our police and spies when only their police and spies can reap the full benefit of them.

I don't expect my arguments to persuade anyone in the NSA. If you're NSA and I do somehow convince you, by some fluke, then I urge you to look at your conscience—I know you have one—and take the word to your superiors, and if they don't agree with you—resign. Leave the agency. If I'm right about what's coming down the line, you'll be glad you didn't wait.

But even though I have a good line of gab, I don't expect you to argue people out of their livelihood. That's notoriously difficult.

So CFP people, you have a fight on your hands. I'm sorry that a community this young should have to face a fight this savage, for such terribly high stakes, so soon. But what the heck; you're always bragging about how clever you are; here's your chance to prove to your fellow citizens that you're more than a crowd of Net-nattering Mensa dilettantes. In cyberspace one year is like seven dog years, and on the Internet nobody can tell you're a dog, so I figure that makes you CFP people 28 years old. And people, for the sake of our society and our children you had better learn to act your age.

## 6

*Jackboots on the Infobahn**

John Perry Barlow

> Clipper is a last ditch attempt by the United States, the last great power from the old Industrial Era, to establish imperial control over cyberspace.

On January 11, I managed to schmooze myself aboard Air Force 2. It was flying out of L.A., where its principal passenger had just outlined his vision of the information superhighway to a suited mob of television, show-biz, and cable types who fervently hoped to own it one day—if they could ever figure out what the hell it was.

From the standpoint of the Electronic Frontier Foundation the speech had been wildly encouraging. The administration's program, as announced by Vice President Al Gore, incorporated many of the concepts of open competition, universal access, and deregulated common carriage that we'd been pushing for the previous year.

But he had said nothing about the future of privacy, except to cite among the bounties of the NII its ability to "help law enforcement agencies thwart criminals and terrorists who might use advanced telecommunications to commit crimes."

On the plane I asked Gore what this implied about administration policy on cryptography. He became as noncommittal as a cigar-store Indian. "We'll be making some announcements. . . . I can't tell you anything more." He hurried to the front of the plane, leaving me to troubled speculation.

Despite its fundamental role in assuring privacy, transaction security, and reliable identity within the NII, the Clinton administration has not demonstrated an enlightenment about cryptography up to par with the rest of its digital vision.

The Clipper Chip—which threatens to be either the goofiest waste of federal dollars since President Gerald Ford's great Swine Flu program or, if actually deployed, a surveillance technology of profound malignancy—seemed at first an ugly legacy of the Reagan-Bush modus operandi. "This is going to be our Bay of Pigs," one Clinton White House official told me at the time Clipper was introduced, referring to

---

* Published in *WIRED*, April 1994.

the disastrous plan to invade Cuba that Kennedy inherited from Eisenhower.

(Clipper, in case you're just tuning in, is an encryption chip that the National Security Agency and FBI hope will someday be in every phone and computer in America. It scrambles your communications, making them unintelligible to all but their intended recipients. All, that is, but the government, which would hold the "key" to your chip. The key would separated into two pieces, held in escrow, and joined with the appropriate "legal authority.")

Of course, trusting the government with your privacy is like having a Peeping Tom install your window blinds. And, since the folks I've met in this White House seem like extremely smart, conscious freedom-lovers—hell, a lot of them are Deadheads—I was sure that after they were fully moved in, they'd face down the National Security Agency and the FBI, let Clipper die a natural death, and lower the export embargo on reliable encryption products.

Furthermore, the National Institutes of Standards and Technology and the National Security Council have been studying both Clipper and export embargoes since April. Given that the volumes of expert testimony they had collected overwhelmingly opposed both, I expected the final report would give the administration all the support it needed to do the right thing.

I was wrong. Instead, there would be no report. Apparently, they couldn't draft one that supported, on the evidence, what they had decided to do instead.

THE OTHER SHOE DROPS

On Friday, February 4, the other jackboot dropped. A series of announcements from the administration made it clear that cryptography would become their very own "Bosnia of telecommunications" (as one staffer put it). It wasn't just that the old Serbs in the National Security Agency and the FBI were still making the calls. The alarming new reality was that the invertebrates in the White House were only too happy to abide by them. Anything to avoid appearing soft on drugs or terrorism.

So, rather than ditching Clipper, they declared it a Federal Data Processing Standard, backing that up with an immediate government order for 50,000 Clipper devices. They appointed the National Institutes of Standards and Technology and the Department of Treasury as the "trusted" third parties that would hold the Clipper key pairs. (Treasury, by the way, is also home to such trustworthy agencies as the Secret Service and the Bureau of Alcohol, Tobacco, and Firearms.)

They reaffirmed the export embargo on robust encryption products, admitting for the first time that its purpose was to stifle competition to Clipper. And they outlined a very porous set of requirements under which the cops might get the keys to your chip. (They would not go into the procedure by which the National Security Agency could get them, though they assured us it was sufficient.)

They even signaled the impending return of the dread Digital Telephony, an FBI legislative initiative requiring fundamental reengineering of the information infrastructure; providing wiretapping ability to the FBI would then become the paramount design priority.

INVASION OF THE BODY SNATCHERS

Actually, by the time the announcements thudded down, I wasn't surprised by them. I had spent several days the previous week in and around the White House.

I felt like I was in another remake of The Invasion of the Body Snatchers. My friends in the administration had been transformed. They'd been subsumed by the vast mindfield on the other side of the security clearance membrane, where dwell the monstrous bureaucratic organisms that feed on fear. They'd been infected by the institutionally paranoid National Security Agency's Weltanschauung.

They used all the telltale phrases. Mike Nelson, the White House point man on the NII, told me, "If only I could tell you what I know, you'd feel the same way I do." I told him I'd been inoculated against that argument during Vietnam. (And it does seem to me that if you're going to initiate a process that might end freedom in America, you probably need an argument that isn't classified.)

Besides, how does he know what he knows? Where does he get his information? Why, the National Security Agency, of course. Which, given its strong interest in the outcome, seems hardly an unimpeachable source.

However they reached it, Clinton and Gore have an astonishingly simple bottom line, to which even the future of American liberty and prosperity is secondary: They believe that it is their responsibility to eliminate, by whatever means, the possibility that some terrorist might get a nuke and use it on, say, the World Trade Center. They have been convinced that such plots are more likely to ripen to hideous fruition behind a shield of encryption.

The staffers I talked to were unmoved by the argument that anyone smart enough to steal a nuclear device is probably smart enough to use PGP or some other uncompromised crypto standard. And never mind that the last people who popped a hooter in the World Trade Center were able to get it there without using any cryptography and while under FBI surveillance.

We are dealing with religion here. Though only ten American lives have been lost to terrorism in the last two years, the primacy of this threat has become as much an article of faith with these guys as the Catholic conviction that human life begins at conception or the Mormon belief that the Lost Tribe of Israel crossed the Atlantic in submarines.

In the spirit of openness and compromise, they invited the Electronic Frontier Foundation to submit other solutions to the "problem" of the nuclear-enabled terrorist than key escrow devices, but they would not admit into discussion the argument that such a threat might, in fact, be some kind of phantasm created by the spooks to ensure their lavish budgets into the post-Cold War era.

As to the possibility that good old-fashioned investigative techniques might be more valuable in preventing their show-case catastrophe (as it was after the fact in finding the alleged perpetrators of the last attack on the World Trade Center), they just hunkered down and said that when wiretaps were necessary, they were damned well necessary.

When I asked about the business that American companies lose because of their inability to export good encryption products, one staffer essentially dismissed the market, saying that total world trade in crypto goods was still less than a billion dollars. (Well, right. Thanks more to the diligent efforts of the National Security Agency than to dim sales potential.)

I suggested that a more immediate and costly real-world effect of their policies would be to reduce national security by isolating American commerce, owing to a lack of international confidence in the security of our data lines. I said that Bruce Sterling's fictional data-enclaves in places like the Turks and Caicos Islands were starting to look real-world inevitable.

They had a couple of answers to this, one unsatisfying and the other scary. The unsatisfying answer was that the international banking community could just go on using DES, which still seemed robust enough to them. (DES is the old federal Data Encryption Standard, thought by most cryptologists to be nearing the end of its credibility.)

More frightening was their willingness to counter the data-enclave future with one in which no data channels anywhere would be secure from examination by one government or another. Pointing to unnamed other countries that were developing their own mandatory standards and restrictions regarding cryptography, they said words to the effect of, "Hey, it's not like you can't outlaw the stuff. Look at France."

Of course, they have also said repeatedly—and for now I believe them—that they have absolutely no plans to outlaw non-Clipper crypto in the US. But that doesn't mean that such plans wouldn't develop in the presence of some pending "emergency." Then there is that White House briefing document, issued at the time Clipper was first announced, which asserts that no US citizen "as a matter of right, is entitled to an unbreakable commercial encryption product."

Now why, if it's an ability they have no intention of contesting, do they feel compelled to declare that it's not a right? Could it be that they are preparing us for the laws they'll pass after some bearded fanatic has gotten himself a surplus nuke and used something besides Clipper to conceal his plans for it?

If they are thinking about such an eventuality, we should be doing so as well. How will we respond? I believe there is a strong, though currently untested, argument that outlawing unregulated crypto would violate the First Amendment, which surely protects the manner of our speech as clearly as it protects the content.

But of course the First Amendment is, like the rest of the Constitution, only as good as the government's willingness to uphold it. And they are, as I say, in the mood to protect our safety over our liberty.

This is not a mind-frame against which any argument is going to be very effective. And it appeared that they had already heard and rejected every argument I could possibly offer.

In fact, when I drew what I thought was an original comparison between their stand against naturally proliferating crypto and the folly of King Canute (who placed his throne on the beach and commanded the tide to leave him dry), my government opposition looked pained and said he had heard that one almost as often as jokes about roadkill on the information superhighway.

I hate to go to war with them. War is always nastier among friends. Furthermore, unless they've decided to let the National Security Agency design the rest of the National Information Infrastructure as well, we need to go on working closely with them on the whole range of issues like access, competition, workplace privacy, common carriage, intellectual property, and such. Besides, the proliferation of strong crypto will probably happen eventually no matter what they do.

But then again, it might not. In which case we could shortly find ourselves under a government that would have the automated ability to log the time, origin and recipient of every call we made, could track our physical whereabouts continuously, could keep better account of our financial transactions than we do, and all without a warrant. Talk about crime prevention!

Worse, under some vaguely defined and surely mutable "legal authority," they also would be able to listen to our calls and read our email without having to do any backyard rewiring. They wouldn't need any permission at all to monitor overseas calls.

If there's going to be a fight, I'd rather it be with this government than the one we'd likely face on that hard day.

Hey, I've never been a paranoid before. It's always seemed to me that most governments are too incompetent to keep a good plot strung together all the way from coffee break to quitting time. But I am now very nervous about the government of the United States of America.

Because Bill 'n' Al, whatever their other new-paradigm virtues, have allowed the very old-paradigm trogs of the Guardian Class to define as their highest duty the defense of America against an enemy that exists primarily in the imagination—and is therefore capable of anything.

To assure absolute safety against such an enemy, there is no limit to the liberties we will eventually be asked to sacrifice. And, with a Clipper Chip in every phone, there will certainly be no technical limit on their ability to enforce those sacrifices.

WHAT YOU CAN DO

Get Congress to Lift the Crypto Embargo

The administration is trying to impose Clipper on us by manipulating market forces. By purchasing massive numbers of Clipper devices, they intend to induce an economy of scale which will make them cheap while the export embargo renders all competition either expensive or nonexistent.

We have to use the market to fight back. While it's unlikely that they'll back down on Clipper deployment, the Electronic Frontier Foundation believes that with sufficient public involvement, we can get Congress to eliminate the export embargo.

Rep. Maria Cantwell, D-Washington, has a bill (H.R. 3627) before the Economic Policy, Trade, and Environment Subcommittee of the House Committee on Foreign Affairs that would do exactly that. She will need a lot of help from the public. They may not care much about your privacy in DC, but they still care about your vote.

Please signal your support of H.R. 3627, either by writing her directly or e-mailing her at cantwell@eff.org. Messages sent to that address will be printed out and delivered to her office. In the subject header of your message, please include the words "support HR 3627." In the body of your message, express your reasons for supporting the bill. You may also express your sentiments to Rep. Lee Hamilton, D-Indiana, the House Committee on Foreign Affairs chair, by e-mailing hamilton@eff.org.

Furthermore, since there is nothing quite as powerful as a letter from a constituent, you should check the following list of subcommittee and committee members to see if your congressional representative is among them. If so, please copy them your letter to Rep. Cantwell.

- Economic Policy, Trade, and Environment Subcommittee: Democrats: Sam Gejdenson (Chair), D-Connecticut; James Oberstar, D-Minnesota; Cynthia McKinney, D-Georgia; Maria Cantwell, D-Washington; Eric Fingerhut, D-Ohio; Albert R. Wynn, D-Maryland; Harry Johnston, D-Florida; Eliot Engel, D-New York; Charles Schumer, D-New York. Republicans: Toby Roth (ranking), R-Wisconsin; Donald Manzullo, R-Illinois; Doug Bereuter, R-Nebraska; Jan Meyers, R-Kansas; Cass Ballenger, R-North Carolina; Dana Rohrabacher, R-California.
- House Committee on Foreign Affairs: Democrats: Lee Hamilton (Chair), D-Indiana; Tom Lantos, D-California; Robert Torricelli, D-New Jersey; Howard Berman, D-California; Gary Ackerman, D-New York; Eni Faleomavaega, D-Somoa; Matthew Martinez, D-California; Robert Borski, D-Pennsylvania; Donal Payne, D-New Jersey; Robert Andrews, D-New Jersey; Robert Menendez, D-New Jersey; Sherrod Brown, D-Ohio; Alcee Hastings, D-Florida; Peter Deutsch, D-Florida; Don Edwards, D-California; Frank McCloskey, D-Indiana; Thomas Sawyer, D-Ohio; Luis Gutierrez, D-Illinois. Republicans: Benjamin Gilman (ranking), R-New York; William Goodling, R-Pennsylvania; Jim Leach, R-Iowa; Olympia Snowe, R-Maine; Henry Hyde, R-Illinois; Christopher Smith, R-New Jersey; Dan Burton, R-Indiana; Elton Gallegly, R-California; Ileana Ros-Lehtinen, R-Florida; David Levy, R-New York; Lincoln Diaz-Balart, R-Florida; Ed Royce, R-California.

Boycott Clipper Devices and the Companies Which Make Them

Don't buy anything with a Clipper Chip in it. Don't buy any product from a company that manufactures devices with Big Brother inside. It is likely that the government will ask you to use Clipper for communications with the IRS or when doing business with federal agencies. They cannot, as yet, require you to do so. Just say no.

Learn about Encryption and Explain the Issues to Your UnWIRED Friends

The administration is banking on the likelihood that this stuff is too technically obscure to agitate anyone but nerds like us. Prove them wrong by patiently explaining what's going on to all the people you know who have never touched a computer and glaze over at the mention of words like "cryptography."

Maybe you glaze over yourself. Don't. It's not that hard. For some hands-on experience, download a copy of PGP—Pretty Good Privacy—a shareware encryption engine which uses the robust RSA encryption algorithm. And learn to use it.

Get Your Company to Think about Embedding Real Cryptography in Its Products

If you work for a company that makes software, computer hardware, or any kind of communications device, work from within to get them to incorporate RSA or some other strong encryption scheme into their products. If they say that they are afraid to violate the export embargo, ask them to consider manufacturing such products overseas and importing them back into the United States. There appears to be no law against that. Yet.

You might also lobby your company to join the Digital Privacy and Security Working Group, a coalition of companies and public interest groups—including IBM, Apple, Sun, Microsoft, and, interestingly, Clipper phone manufacturer AT&T—that is working to get the embargo lifted.

Enlist!

Self-serving as it sounds coming from me, you can do a lot to help by becoming a member of one of these organizations. In addition to giving you access to the latest information on this subject, every additional member strengthens our credibility with Congress:

- Join the Electronic Frontier Foundation by writing membership@eff.org.
- Join Computer Professionals for Social Responsibility by e-mailing cpsr.info@cpsr.org. CPSR is also organizing a protest, to which you can lend your support by sending e-mail to clipper.petition@cpsr.org with "I oppose Clipper" in the message body. Ftp/gopher/WAIS to cpsr.org /cpsr/privacy/crypto/clipper for more info.

In his LA speech, Gore called the development of the NII "a revolution." And it is a revolutionary war we are engaged in here. Clipper is a last ditch attempt by the United States, the last great power from the old Industrial Era, to establish imperial control over cyberspace. If they win, the most liberating development in the history of humankind could become, instead, the surveillance system which will monitor our grandchildren's morality. We can be better ancestors than that.

San Francisco, California

Wednesday, February 9, 1994

John Perry Barlow (barlow@eff.org) is co-founder and Vice-Chairman of the Electronic Frontier Foundation, a group which defends liberty, both in Cyberspace and the Physical World. He has three daughters.

## 7

'Secret' Agency Steps Over the Line*

Washington Technology

The Clinton administration's Feb. 4 policy statement on the Clipper chip is a wispy smokescreen for a number of troublesome issues, and so far it's provided enough cover to put off some tough questions.

What's emerging from Clinton's Clipper policy is a picture of yet another government agency filled with old Cold Warriors trying to hold onto their mortgages in Washington suburbs. The computer industry is justifiably outraged, and the average American ought to be scared. The truth is that the administration's Clipper policy and its hesitancy to relax trade restrictions on encryption technology are being driven solely by the National Security Agency, the secretive enclave of code-breakers in Fort Meade, Md. And the NSA is using the National Institute of Standards and Technology, which is ostensibly supposed to shepherd Clipper hardware, as a shield from the obvious charge the agency is breaking the law.

Consider: The 1987 Computer Security Act prohibits the NSA from having anything to do with non-classified information. So why did the administration allow it to come up with an algorithm for encryption— classified, of course—and intended for a national standard allowing the public comment in the process? NSA subsequently classified a report on Clipper produced by advisory and public interest groups.

Why is the NSA planning to send two of its top officials to Europe to peddle technology derived from Clipper's Skipjack algorithm—even after European governments said they aren't interested? (Germany, among others, is already making money by peddling encryption devices here that U.S. industry can't export, but that's another story.) The NSA is also trying to push key-escrow encryption domestically under a new name, "Tessera," and is handing out no-charge licenses to whatever vendor will let them in the door.

Isn't anybody disturbed by the idea of a $29 billion agency running around pushing a technology it has easy access to, even though the administration declared it a voluntary standard? Of course, this all gets

---

* February 10, 1994. Author of editorial and cartoon: Beau Brendler, editor; artist: Ralph Butler.

weirder when you factor in the unanswered questions about data security on the NII. If the NSA is successful in pushing its version of the puzzle, it could get a foot in the NII doorway impossible to dislodge.

## 8

A Closer Look on Wiretapping*

New York Times Editorial

The government's ability to tap private phone calls is under siege. Newly developed encryption systems allow callers to mathematically scramble their messages so that no one, including the government, can eavesdrop. And digital technology—from cellular phones to call-forwarding—makes wiretapping increasingly difficult.

The Clinton administration is running scared and proposes two fixes, neither satisfactory. Government needs to wiretap under legally restricted circumstances. Though used sparingly during the 1980s (1,000 a year), taps helped convict more than 20,000 felons. But before tampering with existing arrangements, the administration must show that its proposals are workable and will not trample on existing rights to conduct private phone conversations. So far it has cleared neither hurdle.

To overcome private encryption, the administration will encourage people who plan to encode calls to buy phones with a government-designed encryption system, known as Clipper, built into the hardware; the government, with judicial approval, would be able to unscramble the messages. But the policy is unlikely to work because Clipper phones are unlikely to dominate the market—leaving Washington the choice of admitting defeat or turning Big Brotherish and outlawing non-Clipper encryption systems.

To overcome technological barriers, the Federal Bureau of Investigation proposes a second fix: legislation that would require phone companies to adopt only those technologies that preserve the government's ability to wiretap. The problem with this plan is that its sweeping prohibitions threaten to stop telecommunication innovations before anyone calculates the consequences.

The administration would like to begin by encouraging the IRS and other agencies to buy Clipper phones; it might then require private parties that wish to send the government encoded messages to do so only with Clipper phones. The government hopes that in time Clipper phones would become standard equipment everywhere. Callers using other encryption systems would have to plan ahead and acquire compatible software, a big task for run-of-the-mill criminals.

But many experts predict that Clipper phones will not become standard. There are easy-to-use encryption systems that require no special phones, no shared secret passwords. And, unlike Clipper, they cannot be intercepted by the government. Because un-tappable systems will prove attractive the private market is likely to make them as readily available as Clipper.

Clipper uses a secret mathematical formula for scrambling calls. But there are flaws in the formula, as The New York Times recently revealed. The danger with secret formulas is that someone in or outside government could discover a new flaw and exploit it to tap encoded calls without a court order.

Another bad feature concerns the passwords (actually, numbers) the government needs to unscramble calls from Clipper phones. The passwords would be held in escrow by two federal agencies (and released to the FBI upon presentation of a court order). A better way to protect against government abuse would be to entrust passwords to the courts or designated non-government organizations.

The FBI's fix—requiring phone companies to build easily tappable systems—raises the unsettling image of forcing a phone company to design its "home" so that the police can easily enter. And the fix is unnecessarily blunt. The government could compel phone companies to solve specific problems, like making call-forwarding tappable.

The administration is right to worry about its ability to tap phones for legitimate law enforcement. So far, its suggestions for safeguarding that ability seem unworkable and potentially intrusive.

PART III

ASPECTS OF
CRYPTOGRAPHIC POLICY

## CHAPTER 5

LAW ENFORCEMENT

WHAT DOES IT COST TO COMMIT A PERFECT CRIME?

If the government can't obtain communications, it can't decrypt them. Thus, to maintain an effective surveillance capability, the government must be able to intercept the messages sent across telephone and computer networks. This is increasingly difficult as advances in telecommunications technology have begun to outrun law enforcement's ability to intercept communications. This chapter presents the latest proposed solution to this problem: legislation which requires telecommunications carriers to provide real-time remote access to the contents of communications data sought pursuant to a judicial warrant and to call setup and other transactional data sought in any lawful investigation.

It starts with the "Digital Telephony and Communications Privacy Improvement Act of 1994", which requires common carriers to (retrofit their systems to) provide a law enforcement agency in the possession of an appropriate warrant access to the communications and dialing information from the tappee's line. In Canada, the government is circulating an identical proposal.

Freeh argues for the need to preserve and improve the FBI's electronic surveillance capability in light of emerging new technological advances in communications. He provides several examples of past successes of FBI investigations conducted using electronic surveillance and outlines future negative scenarios which would result if electronic surveillance capability were not improved.

The Electronic Frontier Foundation is concerned that the act is overbroad and creates more problems than it will solve. It raises the concern that the cost of what the legislation mandates (in essence, a re-engineering of much of the U.S. phone system) may not be justified by the benefits. However, it succeeded in adding a number of privacy safeguards to the initial legislation, and describes these in its response to the passage of the bill.

The Electronic Privacy Information Center is not nearly as sanguine about the future of the National Information Infrastructure after the passage of the Act, and in its response vows to continue its aggressive monitoring of federal agencies charged with various responsibilities under the act.

One of the biggest complaints related to this legislation was that the FBI did not really present a cost-benefit analysis in its testimony delivered by Director Freeh. In fact, the government released the final documents in this chapter (related to cost-benefit analysis) only after a demand for them through a Freedom of Information Act (FOIA) request filed by Computer Professionals for Social Responsibility in December 1993.

The Department of Justice's Cost-Benefit Analysis admits up front that costs and benefits are "in many regards difficult to quantify". It then presents some numbers related to various benefits and costs which are informative. However, without further development, presentation, and justification of its underlying model, it is not surprising that the following three memoranda from Administration officials raise serious points concerning problems with the analysis. In these documents, Anderson and Buchholz from the White House, McIntosh and Gattuso from the Office of the Vice President, and Levy from the Treasury Department all voice concerns about the validity of the Justice Department analysis and point out additional questions in need of answers. In their individual memoranda, they request the details of how specific cost/benefit figures were computed. It is clear that more work is needed in this area.

Digital Telephony and Communications Privacy Improvement Act of 1994*

103rd Congress 8/9/94
2nd Session

H.R. 4922

IN THE SENATE
IN THE HOUSE OF REPRESENTATIVES

Mr. <u>Edwards of California</u> (for himself and Mr. Hyde) introduced
the following bill; which was referred to the
Committee on the Judiciary

A BILL

To amend title 18, United States Code, to make clear a
telecommunications carrier's duty to cooperate in the
interception of communications for law enforcement purposes,
and for other purposes.

*Be it enacted by the Senate and House of Representatives of the
United States of America in Congress assembled,*

SEC. 1.   INTERCEPTION OF DIGITAL AND OTHER COMMUNICATIONS.

(a) In General.--Part I of title 18, United States Code, is
amended by inserting after chapter 119 the following new chapter:

"CHAPTER   120-TELECOMMUNICATIONS   CARRIER   ASSISTANCE   TO   THE GOVERNMENT

---

* August 9, 1994.

&2601.   Definitions

(a) Definitions.--In this chapter--
the terms defined in section 2510 have, respectively, the meanings stated in that section.

'call-identifying information'--

(A) means all dialing or signalling information associated with the origin, direction, destination, or termination of each communication generated or received by the subscriber equipment, facility, or service of a telecommunications carrier that is the subject of a court order or lawful authorization; but

(B) does not include any information that may disclose the physical location of the subscriber (except to the extent that the location may be determined from the telephone number).

'Commission'   means   the   Federal   Communications Commission.

'government' means the government of the United States and any agency or instrumentality thereof, the District of Columbia, any commonwealth, territory, or possession of the United States, and any State or political subdivision thereof authorized by law to conduct electronic surveillance.

'information services'--

(A) means the offering of a capability for generating,   acquiring,   storing,   transforming, processing, retrieving, utilizing, or making available information via telecommunications; and

(B) includes electronic publishing and messaging services; but

(C) does not include any use of any such capability for the management, control, or operation of a telecommunications system or the management of a telecommunications service.

'provider of telecommunications support services' means a person or entity that provides a product, software, or service to a telecommunications carrier that is integral to such carrier's switching or transmission of wire or electronic communications.

'telecommunications carrier'--

(A) means a person or entity engaged in the transmission or switching of wire or electronic communications as a common carrier for hire (within the meaning of section 3(h) of the Communications Act of 1934 (47 U.S.C. 153(h))); and

(B) includes--

(i) a person or entity engaged in providing commercial mobile service (as defined in section 332(d) of the Communications Act of 1934 (47 U.S.C. 332(d))); and

(ii) a person or entity engaged in providing wire or electronic communication switching or transmission service to the extent that the Commission finds that such service is a replacement for a substantial portion of the local telephone exchange service and that it is in the public interest to deem such a person or entity to be a telecommunications carrier for purposes of this chapter; but

(C) does not include persons or entities insofar as they are engaged in providing information services.

ß2602.   Assistance capability requirements

(a) Capability Requirements.–Except as provided in subsections (b), (c), and (d) of this section, and subject to section 2607(c), a telecommunications carrier shall ensure that its services or facilities that provide a customer or subscriber with the ability to originate, terminate, or direct communications are capable of--

(1) expeditiously isolating and enabling the government to intercept, to the exclusion of any other communications, all wire and electronic communications carried by the carrier within a service area to or from equipment, facilities, or services of a subscriber of such carrier concurrently with their transmission to or from the subscriber's service, facility, or equipment or at such later time as may be acceptable to the government;

(2) expeditiously isolating and enabling the government to access call-identifying information that is reasonably available to the carrier--

(A) before, during, or immediately after the transmission of a wire or electronic communication (or at such later time as may be acceptable to the government); and

(B) in a manner that allows it to be associated with the communication to which it pertains, except that, with regard to information acquired solely pursuant to the authority for pen registers and trap and trace devices (as defined in section 3127), such call-identifying information shall not include any information that may disclose the physical location of the subscriber (except to the extent that the location may be determined from the telephone number);

(3) delivering intercepted communications and call-identifying information to the government in a format such that they may be transmitted by means of facilities or services procured by the government to a location other than the premises of the carrier; and

(4) facilitating authorized communications interceptions and access to call-identifying information unobtrusively and with a minimum of interference with any subscriber's telecommunications service and in a manner that protects--

(A) the privacy and security of communications and call-identifying information not authorized to be intercepted; and

(B) information regarding the government's interception of communications and access to call-identifying information.

(b) Limitations.--

(1) Design of features and systems configurations.--This chapter does not authorize any law enforcement agency or officer--

(A) to require any specific design of features or system configurations to be adopted by providers of wire or electronic communication service, manufacturers of telecommunications equipment, or providers of telecommunications support services; or

(B) to prohibit the adoption of any feature or service by providers of wire or electronic communication service, manufacturers of telecommunications equipment, or providers of telecommunications support services.

(2) Information services and interconnection services and facilities.--The requirements of subsection (a) do not apply to--

(A) information services; or

(B) services or facilities that support the transport or switching of communications for the sole purpose of interconnecting telecommunications carriers or private networks.

(3) Encryption.--A telecommunications carrier shall not be responsible for decrypting, or ensuring the government's ability to decrypt, any communication encrypted by a subscriber or customer, unless the encryption was provided by the carrier and the carrier possesses the information necessary to decrypt the communication.

(c) Emergency or Exigent Circumstances.--In emergency or exigent circumstances (including those described in sections 2518

(7) or (11) (b) and 3125 of this title and section 1805 (e) of title 50) , a carrier may fulfill its responsibilities under subsection (a) (3) by allowing monitoring at its premises if that is the only means of accomplishing the interception or access.

(d) Mobile Service Assistance Requirements.--A telecommunications carrier offering a feature or service that allows subscribers to redirect, hand off, or assign their wire or electronic communications to another service area or another service provider or to utilize facilities in another service area or of another service provider shall ensure that, when the carrier that had been providing assistance for the interception of wire or electronic communications or access to call-identifying information pursuant to a court order or lawful authorization no longer has access to the content of such communications or call-identifying information within the service area in which interception has been occurring as a result of the subscriber's use of such a feature or service, information is available to the government (before, during, or immediately after the transfer of such communications) identifying the provider of wire or electronic communication service that has acquired access to the communications.

§2603. Notices of capacity requirements

(a) Notices of Maximum and Initial Capacity Requirements.--

(1) In general.--Not later than 1 year after the date of enactment of this chapter, and after consulting with State and local law enforcement agencies, telecommunications carriers, providers of telecommunications support services, and manufacturers of telecommunications equipment, the Attorney General shall publish in the Federal Register and provide to appropriate telecommunications carrier associations, standard-setting organizations, and for a--

(A) notice of the maximum capacity required to accommodate all of the communication interceptions, pen registers, and trap and trace devices that the Attorney General estimates that government agencies authorized to conduct electronic surveillance may conduct and use simultaneously; and

(B) notice of the number of communication interceptions, pen registers, and trap and trace devices, representing a portion of the maximum capacity set forth under subparagraph (A), that the Attorney General estimates that government agencies authorized to conduct electronic surveillance may conduct and use simultaneously after the date that is 4 years after the date of enactment of this chapter.

(2) Basis of notices.--The notices issued under paragraph (1) may be based upon the type of equipment, type of service, number of subscribers, geographic location, or other measure.

(b) Compliance With Capacity Notices.--

(1) Initial capacity.--Within 3 years after the publication by the Attorney General of a notice of capacity requirements or within 4 years after the date of enactment of this chapter, whichever is longer, a telecommunications carrier shall ensure that its systems are capable of--

(A) expanding to the maximum capacity set forth in the notice under paragraph (1)(A); and

(B) accommodating simultaneously the number of interceptions, pen registers, and trap and trace devices set forth in the notice under paragraph (1)(B).

(2) Permanent capacity.--After the date described in paragraph (1), a telecommunications carrier shall ensure that it can accommodate expeditiously any increase in the number of communication interceptions, pen registers, and trap and trace devices that authorized agencies may seek to conduct and use, up to the maximum capacity requirement set forth in the notice under paragraph (1)(A).

(c) Notices of Increased Maximum Capacity Requirements.--

(1) The Attorney General shall periodically provide to telecommunications carriers written notice of any necessary increases in the maximum capacity requirement set forth in the notice under subsection (b)(1).

(2) Within 3 years after receiving written notice of increased capacity requirements under paragraph (1), or within such longer time period as the Attorney General may specify, a telecommunications carrier shall ensure that its systems are

capable of expanding to the increased maximum capacity set forth in the notice.

ß2604.   Systems security and integrity

A telecommunications carrier shall ensure that any court ordered or lawfully authorized interception of communications or access to call-identifying information effected within its switching premises can be activated only with the affirmative intervention of an individual officer or employee of the carrier.

ß2605.   Cooperation of equipment manufacturers and providers of telecommunications support services

(a)   Consultation.--A telecommunications carrier shall consult, as necessary, in a timely fashion with manufacturers of its telecommunications transmission and switching equipment and its providers of telecommunications support services for the purpose of identifying any service or equipment, including hardware and software, that may require modification so as to permit compliance with this chapter.

(b) Modification of Equipment and Services.--Subject to section 2607(c), a manufacturer of telecommunications transmission or switching equipment and a provider of telecommunications support services shall, on a reasonably timely basis and at a reasonable charge, make available to the telecommunications carriers using its equipment or services such modifications as are necessary to permit such carriers to comply with this chapter.

ß2606.   Technical requirements and standards; extension of compliance date

(a) Safe Harbor.--

(1) Consultation.--To ensure the efficient and industry-wide implementation of the assistance capability requirements under section 2602, the Attorney General, in coordination with other Federal, State, and local law enforcement agencies, shall consult with appropriate associations and standard-setting organizations of the telecommunications industry.

(2)   Compliance   under   accepted   standards.--A telecommunications carrier shall be found to be in compliance with the assistance capability requirements under section 2602,

and a manufacturer of telecommunications transmission or switching equipment or a provider of telecommunications support services shall be found to be in compliance with section 2605, if the carrier, manufacturer, or support service provider is in compliance with publicly available technical requirements or standards are adopted by an industry association or standard-setting organization or by the Commission under subsection (b) to meet the requirements of section 2602.

(3) Absence of standards.--The absence of technical requirements or standards for implementing the assistance capability requirements of section 2602 shall not--

(A) preclude a carrier, manufacturer, or services provider from deploying a technology or service; or

(B) relieve a carrier, manufacturer, or service provider of the obligations imposed by section 2602 or 2605, as applicable.

(b) FCC Authority.--

(1) In general.--If industry associations or standard-setting organizations fail to issue technical requirements or standards or if a government agency or any other person believes that such requirements or standards are deficient, the agency or person may petition the Commission to establish, by notice and comment rulemaking or such other proceedings as the Commission may be authorized to conduct, technical requirements or standards that--

(A) meet the assistance capability requirements of section 2602;

(B) protect the privacy and security of communications not authorized to be intercepted; and

(C) serve the policy of the United States to encourage the provision of new technologies and services to the public.

(2) Transition period.--If an industry technical requirement or standard is set aside or supplanted as a result of Commission action under this section, the Commission, after consultation with the Attorney General, shall establish a

reasonable time and conditions for compliance with and the transition to any new standard, including defining the obligations of telecommunications carriers under section 2602 during any transition period.

(c) Extension of Compliance Date for Features and Services.--

(1) Petition.--A telecommunications carrier proposing to deploy, or having deployed, a feature or service within 4 years after the date of enactment of this chapter may petition the Commission for 1 or more extensions of the deadline for complying with the assistance capability requirements under section 2602.

(2) Ground for extension.--The Commission may, after affording a full opportunity for hearing and after consultation with the Attorney General, grant an extension under this paragraph, if the Commission determines that compliance with the assistance capability requirements under section 2602 is not reasonably achievable through application of technology available within the compliance period.

(3) Length of extension.--An extension under this paragraph shall extend for no longer than the earlier of--

(A) the date determined by the Commission as necessary for the carrier to comply with the assistance capability requirements under section 2602; or

(B) the date that is 2 years after the date on which the extension is granted.

(4) Applicability of extension.--An extension under this subsection shall apply to only that part of the carrier's business on which the new feature or service is used.

§2607.   Enforcement orders

(a) Enforcement by Court Issuing Surveillance Order.--If a court authorizing an interception under chapter 119, a State statute, or the Foreign Intelligence Surveillance Act of 1978 (50 U.S.C. 1801 et seq.) or authorizing use of a pen register or a trap and trace device under chapter 206 or a State statute finds that a telecommunications carrier has failed to comply with the requirements in this chapter, the court may direct that the carrier comply forthwith and may direct that a provider of support services to the carrier or the manufacturer of the carrier's transmission or switching equipment furnish forthwith modifications necessary for the carrier to comply.

(b) Enforcement Upon Application by Attorney General.--The Attorney General may apply to the appropriate United States district court for, and the United States district courts shall have jurisdiction to issue, an order directing that a telecommunications carrier, a manufacturer of telecommunications transmission or switching equipment, or a provider of telecommunications support services comply with this chapter.

(c) Grounds for Issuance.--A court shall issue an order under subsections (a) or (b) only if the court finds that--

    (1) alternative technologies or capabilities or the facilities of another carrier are not reasonably available to law enforcement for implementing the interception of communications or access to call-identifying information; and

    (2) compliance with the requirements of this chapter is reasonably achievable through the application of available technology to the feature or service at issue or would have been reasonably achievable if timely action had been taken.

(d) Time for Compliance.--Upon issuance of an enforcement order under this section, the court shall specify a reasonable time and conditions for complying with its order, considering the good faith efforts to comply in a timely manner, any effect on the carrier's, manufacturer's, or service provider's ability to continue to do business, the degree of culpability or delay in undertaking efforts to comply, and such other matters as justice may require.

(e) Limitation.--An order under this section may not require a telecommunications carrier to meet the government's demand for interception of communications and acquisition of call-identifying information to any extent in excess of the capacity for which notice has been provided under section 2603.

(f) Civil Penalty.--

    (1) In general.--A court issuing an order under this section against a telecommunications carrier, a manufacturer of telecommunications transmission or switching equipment, or a provider of telecommunications support services may impose a civil penalty of up to $10,000 per day for each day in violation

after the issuance of the order or after such future date as the court may specify.

(2) Considerations.--In determining whether to impose a fine and in determining its amount, the court shall take into account--

(A) the nature, circumstances, and extent of the violation;

(B) the violator's ability to pay, the violator's good faith efforts to comply in a timely manner, any effect on the violator's ability to continue to do business, the degree of culpability, and the length of any delay in undertaking efforts to comply; and

(C) such other matters as justice may require.

(3) Civil action.-The Attorney General may file a civil action in the appropriate United States district court to collect, and the United States district courts shall have jurisdiction to impose, such fines.

§2608.   Reimbursement of telecommunications carriers

(a) In General.--The Attorney General shall, subject to the availability of appropriations, reimburse telecommunications carriers for all reasonable costs directly associated with--

(1) the modifications performed by carriers prior to the effective date of section 2602 or prior to the expiration of any extension granted under section 2606(c) to establish the capabilities necessary to comply with section 2602;

(2) meeting the maximum capacity requirements set forth in the notice under section 2603(a)(1)(A); and

(3) expanding existing facilities to accommodate simultaneously the number of interceptions, pen registers and trap and trace devices for which notice has been provided under section 2603(a)(1)(B).

(b) Procedures and Regulations.--Notwithstanding any other law, the Attorney General may establish any procedures and regulations deemed necessary to effectuate timely and cost-efficient reimbursement to telecommunications carriers for reimbursable costs incurred under this chapter, under chapters 119 and 121, and under the Foreign Intelligence Surveillance Act of 1978 (50 U.S.C. 1801 et seq.).

(c) Dispute Resolution.--If there is a dispute between the Attorney General and a telecommunications carrier regarding the amount of reasonable costs to be reimbursed under subsection (b), the dispute shall be resolved and the amount determined in a proceeding initiated at the Commission under section 2606(b) or by the court from which an enforcement order is sought under section 2607.

(d) Lack of Appropriated Funds.--The lack of appropriated funds sufficient to reimburse telecommunications carriers for modifications under subsection (a) shall be considered by the Commission or a court in determining whether compliance is reasonable under section 2607(c).".

(b) Technical Amendment.--The part analysis for part I of title 18, United States Code, is amended by inserting after the item relating to chapter 119 the following new item:

120. Telecommunications carrier assistance to the Government . . . . . . 2601".

SEC. 2.   AUTHORIZATION OF APPROPRIATIONS.

There are authorized to be appropriated to carry out section 2608 of title 18, United States Code, as added by section 1--

(1) a total of $500,000,000 for fiscal years 1995, 1996, 1997, and 1998; and

(2) such sums as are necessary for each fiscal year thereafter.

SEC. 3.   EFFECTIVE DATE.

(a) In General.--Except as provided in paragraph (2), chapter 120 of title 18, United States Code, as added by section 1, shall take effect on the date of enactment of this Act.

(b) Assistance Capability and Systems Security and Integrity Requirements.--Sections 2602 and 2604 of title 18, United States Code, as added by section 1, shall take effect on the date that is 4 years after the date of enactment of this Act.

SEC. 4.   REPORTS.

(a) Reports by the Attorney General.--

(1) In general.--On or before November 30, 1995, and on or before November 30 of each year for 5 years thereafter, the Attorney General shall submit to the Congress a report on the amounts paid during the preceding fiscal year in reimbursement to telecommunications carriers under section 2608 of title 18, United States Code, as added by section 1.

(2) Contents.--A report under paragraph (1) shall include-

(A) a detailed accounting of the amounts paid to each carrier and the technology, feature or service for which the amounts were paid; and

(B) projections of the amounts expected to be paid in the current fiscal year, the carriers to which reimbursement is expected to be paid, and the technologies, services, or features for which reimbursement is expected to be paid.

(b) Reports by the Comptroller General.--

(1) In general.--On or before April 1, 1996, and April 1, 1998, the Comptroller General of the United States, after consultation with the Attorney General and the telecommunications industry, shall submit to the Congress a report reflecting its audit of the sums paid by the Attorney General to carriers in reimbursement.

(2) Contents.--A report under paragraph (1) shall include the findings and conclusions of the Comptroller General on the costs to be incurred after the compliance date, including projections of the amounts expected to be incurred and the technologies, services, or features for which expenses are expected to be incurred.

SEC. 5.   CORDLESS TELEPHONES.

(a) Definitions.--Section 2510 of title 18, United States Code, is amended--

(1) in paragraph (1) by striking but such term does not include" and all that follows through base unit"; and

(2) in paragraph (12) by striking subparagraph (A) and redesignating subparagraphs (B), (C), and (D) as subparagraphs (A), (B), and (C), respectively.

(b) Penalty.--Section 2511 of title 18, United States Code, is amended--

(1) in subsection (4)(b)(i) by inserting a cordless telephone communication that is transmitted between the cordless telephone handset and the base unit," after cellular telephone communication,"; and

(2) in subsection (4)(b)(ii) by inserting a cordless telephone communication that is transmitted between the cordless telephone handset and the base unit," after cellular telephone communication,".

SEC. 6.   RADIO-BASED DATA COMMUNICATIONS.

Section 2510(16) of title 18, United States Code, is amended--

(1) by striking or" at the end of subparagraph (D);

(2) by inserting or" at the end of subparagraph (E); and

(3) by inserting after subparagraph (E) the following new subparagraph:

(F) an electronic communication;"

SEC. 7.   PENALTIES FOR MONITORING RADIO COMMUNICATIONS THAT ARE TRANSMITTED USING MODULATION TECHNIQUES WITH NONPUBLIC PARAMETERS.

Section 2511(4)(b) of title 18, United States Code, is amended by striking or encrypted, then" and inserting, encrypted, or transmitted using modulation techniques the essential parameters of which have been withheld from the public with the intention of preserving the privacy of such communication".

SEC. 8.   TECHNICAL CORRECTION.

Section 2511(2)(a)(i) of title 18, United States Code, is amended by striking used in the transmission of a wire communication" and inserting used in the transmission of a wire or electronic communication".

SEC. 9.   FRAUDULENT ALTERATION OF COMMERCIAL MOBILE RADIO INSTRUMENTS.

(a) Offense.--Section 1029(a) of title 18, United States Code, is amended--

(1) by striking or" at the end of paragraph (3); and

(2) by inserting after paragraph (4) the following new paragraphs:

(5) knowingly and with intent to defraud uses, produces, traffics in, has control or custody of, or possesses a telecommunications instrument that has been modified or altered to obtain unauthorized use of telecommunications services; or

(6) knowingly and with intent to defraud uses, produces, traffics in, has control or custody of, or possesses--

(A) a scanning receiver; or

(B) hardware or software used for altering or modifying telecommunications instruments to obtain unauthorized access to telecommunications services,".

(b) Penalty.--Section 1029(c)(2) of title 18, United States Code, is amended by striking (a)(1) or (a)(4)" and inserting (a)(1), (4), (5), or (6)".

(c) Definitions.--Section 1029(e) of title 18, United States Code, is amended--

(1) in paragraph (1) by inserting electronic serial number, mobile identification number, personal identification number, or other telecommunications service, equipment, or instrument identifier," after account number,";

(2) by striking and" at the end of paragraph (5);

(3) by striking the period at the end of paragraph (6) and inserting ; and"; and

(4) by adding at the end the following new paragraph:

(7) the term 'scanning receiver' means a device or apparatus that can be used to intercept a wire or electronic communication in violation of chapter 119.".

SEC. 10.   TRANSACTIONAL DATA.

(a) Disclosure of Records.--Section 2703 of title 18, United States Code, is amended--

(1) in subsection (c)--

(A) in subparagraph (B)--

(i) by striking clause (i); and

(ii) by redesignating clauses (ii), (iii), (iv) as clauses (i), (ii), and (iii), respectively; and

(B) by adding at the end the following new subparagraph:

(C) A provider of electronic communication service or remote computing service shall disclose to a governmental entity the name, billing address, and length of service of a subscriber to or customer of such service and the types of services the subscriber or customer utilized, when the governmental entity uses an administrative subpoena authorized by a Federal or State statute or a Federal or State grand jury or trial subpoena or any means available under subparagraph (B)."; and

(2) by amending the first sentence of subsection (d) to read as follows: A court order for disclosure under subsection (b) or (c) may be issued by any court that is a court of competent jurisdiction described in section 3126(2)(A) and shall issue only if the governmental entity offers specific and articulable facts showing that there are reasonable grounds to believe that the contents of a wire or electronic communication, or the

records or other information sought, are relevant and material to an ongoing criminal investigation.".

(b) Pen Registers and Trap and Trace Devices.--Section 3121 of title 18, United States Code, is amended--

(1) by redesignating subsection (c) as subsection (d); and

(2) by inserting after subsection (b) the following new subsection:

(c) Limitation.--A government agency authorized to install and use a pen register under this chapter or under State law, shall use technology reasonably available to it that restricts the recording or decoding of electronic or other impulses to the dialing and signalling information utilized in call processing.".

Summary Statement before the Subcommittee on Technology and the Law of the Committee on the Judiciary, United States Senate and the Subcommittee on Civil and Constitutional Rights of the Committee on the Judiciary, House of Representatives*

Louis J. Freeh
Director, Federal Bureau of Investigation

Mr. Chairmen, I appreciate the opportunity to appear before your Subcommittees.

The United States is facing a grave and growing problem.

New telecommunications technology is impeding or preventing law enforcement from conducting court-approved electronic surveillance— or wiretapping.

And the problems are just beginning.

Congress created a statute 25 years ago that allows wiretapping in the worst and most dangerous cases—cases where no other law enforcement tool can do the job.

Throughout that quarter-century, wiretapping has been invaluable in protecting our people and safeguarding the national security.

But the new technology in the nation's telephone systems is already thwarting some wiretap efforts.

It will be a disaster if this and other emerging telecommunications technology spread nationwide without needed law enforcement safeguards.

My plea to you today is for congressional passage of a statute that would require telecommunications companies to build into the new technology the capabilities that will allow law enforcement to conduct wiretapping with court approval.

We are not seeking any expansion of the authority congress gave to law enforcement when the wiretapping law was enacted 25 years ago.

With court approval, law enforcement is now technically able to wiretap on the *old* technology. We simply seek to insure a failsafe way

---

* March 18, 1994.

for law enforcement to conduct court-approved wiretapping on the recently deployed and emerging technology.

Unless Congress creates a new law, law enforcement's ability to protect the public against crime will be gravely eroded and the national security will be placed at risk.

Wiretapping is used on the most important, life-and-death cases: terrorism, espionage, drug trafficking, organized crime, kidnapping and a variety of other violent crimes.

Without a new statute, law enforcement at the federal, state, and local levels will be crippled. In all too many instances, an already-overburdened law enforcement system will then be fighting crime with **both** arms tied behind its back.

Members of your two Subcommittees surely know as experts that court-approved electronic surveillance is of incredible value—often the only way to prevent or solve the most ghastly crimes.

We need to reflect only for a moment for examples: one deadly terrorist incident that was solved; another terrorist incident prevented; and an arrest of an alleged spy in what is surely one of the major espionage cases of this or any decade.

Without wiretapping, those great victories for the cause of justice would never have occurred. If there is no new statute, law enforcement will be crippled. The costs to society will be staggering. Crime will claim untold victims who could otherwise be saved.

I am here today not just in my capacity as director of the FBI, but also as a spokesman for our nation's law enforcement and intelligence communities. I am here on behalf of the administration to urge you to solve a major threat to our ability to protect the American public, safeguard the national security, and effectively enforce the law. These new telephone impediments are the unintended side effects of advanced telecommunications technology which has been—and continues to be—deployed without consideration for the critical needs of law enforcement.

I am here to strongly assert what the administration and I believe is the only rational and viable means of removing this threat—the enactment of comprehensive legislation to address the digital telephony issue. Without it, one of our most effective weapons against national and international drug trafficking, terrorism, espionage, organized crime, and serious violent crimes will be severely harmed. The administration wants to work with the Congress to develop such comprehensive legislation. I have shared with each of you a legislative draft for favorable consideration.

The purpose of this legislation, quite simply, is to maintain technological capabilities commensurate with existing statutory authority—that is, to prevent advanced telecommunications technology from repealing *de facto* statutory authority already conferred by Congress.

The proposed legislation explicitly states that it does not alter the government's authority to conduct court-ordered electronic surveillance and use pen register or trap and trace devices. The essence of the legislation is to clarify and more fully define the nature and extent of the service provider's "assistance" requirement that was enacted by congress in 1970, which Congress imposed so that court orders would not be frustrated due to a provider's failure to furnish needed technological assistance and facilities. **The proposed legislation relates solely to advanced technology, not legal authority or privacy.**

We have not sought legislation lightly. For nearly four years, we have expended every reasonable effort to address this threat through numerous and ongoing meetings with the telecommunications industry. However, it is my judgement, and that of the administration, that dialogue alone, no matter how well intended, will not solve this serious threat to public safety. We have listened and learned, and the draft legislative proposal before you represents the only proper, balanced approach. It deals with the advanced telephony problem in an appropriately comprehensive fashion—it does not simply "bandaid-over" past problems; it also responsibly deals with new services and technologies (such as personal communications services) that soon will emerge. On the other hand, the legislation is narrowly focused on where the vast majority of the problems exist—the networks of common carriers, a segment of the industry which historically has been subject to regulation. The administration's draft proposal approaches the problem in a very rational fashion. It includes clearly-stated electronic surveillance requirements, systems security provisions, a reasonable deadline for compliance, requirements for equipment manufacturer and support service provider cooperation, proper enforcement and penalty provisions, ongoing government consultation to facilitate compliance, and, importantly, a commitment by the federal government to pay common carriers for reasonable charges associated with achieving compliance.

To appreciate fully the need for legislation, it is essential that Congress understand the critical importance of electronic surveillance and the severe harm that will result if this critical tool is lost or diminished.

The nation's phone networks are routinely used in the commission of serious criminal activities, including terrorism and espionage. Organized crime groups and drug trafficking organizations also rely heavily upon telecommunications to execute their crimes and hide their illegal profits.

In 1968, Congress passed the Omnibus Crime Control and Safe Streets Act, Title III, which contained comprehensive federal legislation regarding electronic surveillance. Title III established strict procedures for conducting electronic surveillance—procedures that are carefully adhered to by law enforcement and rigorously enforced by the courts. Thirty-seven states also have electronic surveillance laws. In 1992, a total of 919 Title III orders, as well as an estimated 9,000 pen register orders, were authorized for all federal, state, and local law enforcement agencies. Approximately two-thirds of the criminal-related electronic surveillance conducted in the United States is carried out by state and local law enforcement agencies. **As you are aware, Title III permits electronic surveillance only for serious felony offenses and only when other investigative techniques will not work or are too dangerous.**

Electronic surveillance is one of the most important investigative techniques—if not the most important. Frequently, criminality under investigation could never be detected, adequately investigated, or successfully prosecuted without this critical tool.

Though used sparingly, electronic surveillance has been *extremely* effective, leading to the convictions of thousands of dangerous criminals involved in drug trafficking, organized crime, violent crime, kidnaping, crimes against children, and public corruption. Its evidence has secured the convictions of more than 22,000 dangerous felons over the past decade.

Aside from its great importance as an investigative tool, electronic surveillance frequently has been essential in **preventing crimes** and in **saving human life,** such as preventing murders, saving numerous lives threatened by terrorist attacks, dismantling organized crime groups which prey on people through extortion and violence, and in attacking the national and international drug cartels whose illegal drugs so ravage society and cause incalculable personal injury.

Although I cannot discuss the details, I can assure you that court authorized electronic surveillance played a critical role in successfully resolving two recent, highly-publicized cases concerning terrorism and espionage. Electronic surveillance has been critical in numerous other cases. For example:

- The violent El Rukn gang in Chicago, acting as a surrogate for the Libyan Government and in support of terrorism, planned to shoot down a commercial airliner within the U.S. using a stolen military weapon. This act of terrorism was prevented **directly** through the use of electronic surveillance.
- The "Ill Wind" public corruption and Defense Department fraud investigation relied heavily on court-ordered electronic surveillance. To date, this investigation has resulted in the conviction of 65 individuals and **more than a quarter of a billion dollars in fines, restitutions and recoveries.**
- Numerous drug trafficking and money laundering investigations, such as the "Polar Cap" and "Pizza Connection" cases, utilized extensive electronic surveillance in the successful prosecution of

large scale national and international drug trafficking organizations. "Polar Cap" resulted in the arrest of thirty-three subjects and the recovery of fifty million dollars in assets seized. Additionally, in a 1992 Miami raid, which directly resulted from electronic surveillance, agents confiscated 15,000 pounds of cocaine and arrested twenty-two subjects.

- Finally, in a notable 1990 "sexual exploitation of children" investigation, the FBI relied heavily on electronic surveillance to prevent violent individuals from abducting, torturing, and murdering a child in order to make a "snuff murder" film.

I can assure you that a loss or diminishment of such surveillance will produce the following disastrous results:

- An increased loss of life, attributable to law enforcement's inability to prevent terrorist acts and murders.
- An increase in corruption and economic harm to business, industry, labor unions, and society generally, amounting to billions of dollars, caused by the growth of undetected and unprosecuted organized crime, public corruption, and governmental fraud.
- An increased availability of much cheaper narcotics and illegal drugs—along with the personal, societal, and economic harm brought about by increased drug use: that is, the numerous deaths, ravaged lives, increased health care costs, and the tremendous economic harm calculated in the billions of dollars.
- A substantial increase in undetected and unprosecuted violent crimes (bombings, murders, and other violent acts) along with the loss of hundreds of lives and millions of dollars in economic harm.

In enacting Title III, Congress carefully balanced the communications security and privacy rights of individuals with the legitimate needs of law enforcement to protect the public and effectively enforce the law. Congress required that electronic surveillance be used surgically: only as a last resort, only for serious felony offenses, and only for specific criminal communications. The acquisition of non-criminal, non-relevant communications is forbidden; such communications must be carefully minimized. **Contrary to what some vocal critics may believe, law enforcement cannot and does not conduct electronic surveillance against individuals who simply exercise their first amendment rights by engaging in political or anti-governmental discourse.**

Electronic surveillance has been conducted sparingly, judiciously, and **in compliance with the letter of the law and the spirit of Congress' intent.** As demonstrated by the lives saved and the important prosecutions successfully completed, Title III has served society extremely well. Indeed, after 25 years of usage, there is no evidence of significant abuse.

In 1970, Congress enacted an electronic surveillance "assistance" provision which mandates common carriers to furnish law enforcement with all the information, facilities, and technical assistance necessary to accomplish an interception. What is at issue today is the nature and extent of that requirement in light of new advanced technologies. **It is very important to understand that telephone companies historically have been extremely conservative, and often have declined to provide law enforcement with technical assistance, even when served with court orders, unless the statutory law is clear and their responsibilities explicitly set forth.** Attorneys analyzing the existing assistance provision believe that the current language does not explicitly mandate service providers to develop technical solutions in order to accommodate an electronic surveillance order issued by a court. Government and industry officials agree that requiring greater electronic surveillance technical assistance would not extend law enforcement's electronic surveillance *legal* authority to conduct electronic surveillance.

There is ample congressional and regulatory precedent for requiring telephone companies to assist law enforcement and provide for the public welfare. For example, they have been *required by regulation* to maintain telephone toll records longer than operationally necessary to assist law enforcement. *By legislation*, Congress has required then to assist the hearing-impaired and to restrict telephonically transmitted pornographic communications (so called "Dial-a-Porn"). Also, many localities *require by law* that phone companies provide "911" emergency service. Similarly, numerous other public safety/public welfare laws and regulations impose duties on industry such as sprinkler systems, smoke detectors, safety belts, and catalytic converters in vehicles. When electronic surveillance is viewed in terms of its critical utility in preventing and prosecuting crimes, **as a public safety requirement,** requiring technical assistance *through legislation* would be consistent with past legislative practice.

Since the divestiture of AT&T in 1984, the number of common carriers has grown to over 2,000 and telephone technology has become diverse and sophisticated. In the past, when law enforcement agencies conducted electronic surveillance or "wiretaps" on a subject's wires or "local loop," they were virtually assured of intercepting all of the content of communications as well as the associated dialing information. Now common carriers are deploying advanced technologies, including sophisticated services and features, permitting the transmission of multiple, simultaneous communications of different subscribers over fiber optic and wire facilities. Also, cellular telephones and features such as call forwarding permit mobility and the redirecting of calls anywhere. Likewise, "Follow-Me" features expand the call forwarding concept to national proportions. The deployment of the personal communications services (pcs) in the near future will further increase the problem of finding technical access points to effect a wiretap. **Industry representatives, in fact, acknowledge that existing networks offering these services and features, as well as networks planned for the future, in their current and planned configurations, often prevent, and will continue to prevent, common carriers from satisfying court orders and providing the needed access to all communications and dialing information.**

Over the last decade, it is estimated that several hundred court orders have been frustrated, in whole or in part, by various technological impediments. In 1993, the FBI, conducted an informal survey of federal and local law enforcement regarding *recent* technological problems which revealed 91 instances where law enforcement was precluded from implementing or fully implementing court orders. Two-thirds of them relate to cellular telephone systems or wireline communications that employed custom calling features. **It is important to note that many court orders have not been sought or served on carriers due to the awareness of pre-existing impediments, and thus could not be counted in this survey.** Other problems encountered include intercepting digital voice communications and high-speed data, and fiber optic lines. In 1992, one state law enforcement agency advised that 25% of its electronic surveillance interceptions were impeded by advanced systems features.

However, it would be a mistake to gauge this problem simply by attempting to count the number of court orders frustrated through some brief, informal survey. The indisputable fact is that **emerging technologies will have a much greater and more devastating impact on law enforcement and the public safety, unless the Congress acts now to ensure that old impediments are removed and new ones are not introduced.**

As I noted at the outset, for almost four years, we have attempted to resolve this problem with officials of the telecommunications industry at all corporate levels. Senior executives of major common carriers were briefed about the difficulties and the fact that future technologies would severely diminish, if not preclude, electronic surveillance. Although appearing supportive, several indicated that without some mandate, such as legislation, their companies could not *unilaterally* invest money or technical resources to develop and implement the solutions, especially if there were no assurance of competitors doing so.

In January 1992, then President Bush authorized the Justice Department to proceed with legislation. Shortly after Digital Telephony legislation was announced, industry responded by telling then Attorney General Barr **that the FBI had been talking to the wrong people in**

industry and that the solution to these problems rested with those upper/mid-level managers and engineers who oversee these technologies. The Attorney General agreed to an industry request that a technical working group consisting of the **"right industry people,"** picked by the CEOs, be created to identify technical solutions and to get the job done. For two full years, the working group has studied impediments in major technology areas, and the process has led to a better understanding of the problems; **nevertheless, no implementable solutions have been developed, let alone implemented.** These lengthy efforts clearly belie the loose talk of industry "lobbyists" and the Digital Privacy and Security Working Group that there are no current or future technological problems. I support continued dialogue between industry and law enforcement. However, the working group process and the standards body forum now being used is *voluntary* and is not equipped or chartered to solve the problem or ensure implementation of solutions. There is no mechanism, no resolution, short of legislation that can compel a timely, comprehensive, and binding solution. **Thus, the administration has concluded after an in-depth study conducted pursuant to a presidential review directive that this process is not, and cannot be, a substitute for comprehensive legislation.**

The draft legislation represents, in my estimation, the only rational, viable approach to solving this problem in a timely and comprehensive fashion. Legislation alone can assure that the impediments to electronic surveillance will be removed within a reasonable period of time.

The draft legislation includes law enforcement's requirements, which, by design, are generic in nature. The government purposely avoids setting "technical" standards because it does not desire to "dictate" technological solutions, believing that each carrier is best qualified to determine how it will satisfy these requirements in the most cost-effective way.

In brief, common carriers are required to provide the necessary capability and capacity to permit law enforcement access to the communications and dialing information occurring over the criminal subject's telephone; to do so concurrent with the communication in an unobtrusive fashion; to do so to the exclusion of other subscribers' communications; and to do so regardless of the mobile nature of the service or the features used. Systems security and privacy concerns will be enhanced because common carriers will be required to activate any interception within common carriers' premises. The proposal requires cooperation between common carriers, support services providers, and equipment manufacturers, and encourages the attorney general to consult with the FCC and industry associations and standards bodies to facilitate compliance. A reasonable compliance timeframe of three years is set forth and proper enforcement provisions are included. The federal government shall pay common carriers for reasonable charges directly associated with achieving compliance.

This legislation overcomes the 1970 amendment's major short-coming—lack of specificity as to what carriers must do and how quickly they must do it. It deals comprehensively with current and future telecommunications technologies and will preclude the need for much more costly legislation in the future. If we do not act now, the number and types of new impediments will mushroom and likely will preclude any prospect of removing them in the future because of the sheer complexity and prohibitive expense. **I must emphasize: any legislation that limits its application only to certain technological impediments or addresses technologies on a "piece-meal" basis would be disastrous and probably worse than no legislation at all.**

Much of the criticism of the administration's proposal has been misleading or incorrect. Contrary to some critics' allegations, the proposed legislation does not expand the current legal authority to conduct electronic surveillance or use pen registers. Rather, it maintains the status quo. With minor exception, the legislation does *not* address the issue of encryption. While encryption certainly poses a problem for law enforcement, the government's approach is to deal with encryption through nonlegislative market forces. This proposal does not restrict technology nor does it affect network security and reliability. Just as network maintenance and audit access can be accomplished with full regard for security, so also can electronic surveillance access be accomplished with a high regard for security and privacy. This proposal will not introduce systems' vulnerabilities. **Contrary to some statements, law enforcement is not building "back doors" into the common carriers' systems. The proposed legislation is not some dreaded Orwellian prophecy come true. Rather, this legislative proposal represents a recognition of legitimate law enforcement needs and a desire to protect the American people.**

We are unaware of any authoritative industry statement that these requirements would significantly delay development of new technologies. Legislation creates a "level playing field"
among all competitors; no carrier will be put at a competitive disadvantage. **In fact, industry has stated that without a statutory mandate any carrier that would pursue compliance on its own would be put at a competitive *disadvantage*.** Legislation will not adversely affect American competitiveness. If anything, this legislation would provide U.S. industry with a competitive edge since other democratic nations are telling us they need equipment that includes electronic surveillance capabilities for their domestic law enforcement agencies. Hence, U.S. manufacturers may see increasing foreign demands for their equipment and services.

The proposed legislation does not adversely impact privacy. To the contrary, privacy protection is extended, by conferring full legal protection for cordless telephone communications, radio-based electronic communications, and communications transmitted using privacy-enhancing modulation. **It distresses me that special interest groups are introducing false or unrelated privacy issues and rhetoric concerning this proposal. In this regard, allegations have been made that we are attempting to create** *new* **widespread tracing and surveillance capabilities. This is simply not true—we seek** *only* **to maintain technical capabilities commensurate with existing statutory authority.**

Mr. Chairmen and members of the subcommittees, I am pleased to announce that since this legislative proposal was circulated we have met with subcommittee staff and are supportive of language regarding a reporting and audit requirement for telephone companies that initiate interceptions within their switching facilities, and to include language regarding the term "call setup information" to make clear it does not include any tracking or surveillance information. We also have met recently with the telecommunications industry and provided a very important clarification that their responsibilities do not include communications transmitted by other secondary carriers when communications are "handed off" by them or dialing information they do not acquire. We are making progress in reaching closure on the important issue of compliance periods for various technologies, with the idea that perhaps some of the more complex technologies could be addressed beyond the three-year period. My sense is that in addressing these considerations most of the sting of the proposal has been removed.

In summary, this is the number one law enforcement, public safety, and national security issue facing us today. Maintaining an effective electronic surveillance capability is essential to fighting national and international drug-trafficking cartels, organized crime, terrorists, and violent criminals. Without this capability, we will not be able to protect the public or acquire the evidence needed to put society's most dangerous felons in jail. Recent efforts to ensure substantial jail time for violent, hardened criminals will be undercut if we in law enforcement first cannot identify them and obtain the compelling evidence required to secure their convictions. The administration has concluded that comprehensive federal legislation is the only viable means of solving this problem. Left unaddressed, this problem will soon grow to dangerous proportions. These impediments must not be allowed to stand.

Over the last four years, we have made every reasonable effort to resolve this problem with industry, including a two year effort with an industry technical group that was created by industry to **"solve the problem."** However, the unvarnished truth is that industry has no mechanism for assuring the timely, comprehensive development and implementation of the required solutions. The chairman of the industry technical working group has acknowledged this fundamental shortcoming in a letter which was provided to the subcommittees. Obtaining these solutions can no longer be left to chance. Federal legislation represents the only **realistic** solution to this problem.

We fully support the Vice President's initiative to create a national information superhighway to share information, educate Americans, and increase productivity. However, it would be wrong for us as public servants to knowingly allow this information superhighway to jeopardize the safety and economic well-being of law-abiding Americans by becoming an expressway and safe haven for terrorists, spies, drug dealers, murderers, and thugs.

I do not relish the thought of being the first FBI director to tell a father and mother that we were unable to save their son or daughter because advanced telecommunications technology precluded the telephone company from providing us with the information that would have prevented the death of that innocent child; nor should the President have to tell the American public that law enforcement could not prevent a violent terrorist act in a major metropolitan area solely because of advanced telecommunications technology.

It is imperative that Congress promptly enact the administration's proposed legislation. The longer this problem remains unsolved, the longer the safety and economic well-being of the American public will be unnecessarily put at risk.

I look forward to working with each one of you and this Congress in enacting this important legislation. Thank you Mr. Chairmen and the Members of these Subcommittees for providing me this opportunity to testify. At this time I will be happy to answer any questions you may have.

3

EFF Statement on and Analysis of Digital Telephony Act*

Electronic Frontier Foundation

Washington, DC—Congress late Friday (10/7) passed and sent to the President the Edwards/Leahy Digital Telephony Legislation (HR 4922/ S 2375). The bill places functional design requirements on telecommunications carriers in order to enable law enforcement to continue to conduct electronic surveillance pursuant to a court order, though the bill does not expand law enforcement authority to conduct wiretaps. Moreover, the design requirements do not apply to providers or operators of online services such as the Internet, BBS's, Compuserve, and others. The bill also contains significant new privacy protections, including increased protection for online personal information, and requirements prohibiting the use of pen registers to track the physical location of individuals.

Jerry Berman, EFF's Policy Director, said: "Although we remain unconvinced that this legislation is necessary, the bill draws a hard line around the Internet and other online networks. We have carved cyberspace out of this legislation".

Berman added, "The fact that the Internet, BBS's, Prodigy, and other online networks are not required to meet the surveillance capability requirements is a significant victory for all users of this important communications medium."

PRIVACY PROTECTIONS FOR ONLINE PERSONAL INFORMATION INCREASED

The bill adds a higher standard for law enforcement access to online transactional information. For maintenance and billing purposes, most online communications and information systems create detailed records of users' communication activities as well as lists of the information, services, or people that they have accessed or contacted. Under current law, the government can gain access to such transactional re-

---

* October 8, 1994.

cords with a mere subpoena, which can be obtained without the intervention of a court. To address this issue, EFF pushed for the addition of stronger protections against indiscriminate access to online transactional records.

Under the new protections, law enforcement must convince a court to issue an order based on a showing of "specific and articulable facts" which prove that the information sought would be relevant and material to an ongoing criminal investigation.

Berman said: "The new legal protections for transactional information are critical in that they recognize that these records are extremely sensitive and deserve a high degree of protection from casual law enforcement access. With these provisions, we have achieved for all online systems a significantly greater level of protection than exists today for any other form of electronic communication, including the telephone."

EFF to Continue to Monitor Implementation

Berman added: "There are numerous opportunities under this bill for public oversight and intervention to ensure that privacy is not short-changed. EFF will closely monitor the bill's implementation, and we stand ready to intervene if privacy is threatened."

In the first four years, the government is required to reimburse carriers for all costs associated with meeting the design requirements of the bill. After four years, the government is required to reimburse carriers for all costs for enhancements that are not "reasonably achievable", as determined in a proceeding before the FCC. The FCC will determine who bears the costs in terms of the impact on privacy, costs to consumers, national security and public safety, the development of technology, and other factors. If the FCC determines that compliance is not reasonably achievable, the government will either be required to reimburse the carrier or consider it to be in compliance without modification.

Berman said: "EFF is committed to making a case before the FCC, at the first possible opportunity, that government reimbursement is an essential back-stop against unnecessary or unwanted surveillance capabilities. If the government pays, it will have an incentive to prioritize, which will further enhance public accountability and protect privacy."

EFF Decision to Work on Legislation

Since 1992 EFF, in conjunction with the Digital Privacy and Security Working Group (a coalition of over 50 computer, communications, and public interest organizations and associations working on communications privacy issues, coordinated by EFF) has been successful at stopping a series of FBI Digital Telephony proposals, which would have forced communications companies to install wiretap capability into every communications medium. However, earlier this year, Senator Leahy and Rep. Edwards, who have helped to quash previous FBI proposals, concluded that passage of such a bill this year was inevitable. Leahy and Edwards stepped in to draft a narrow bill with strong privacy protections, and asked for EFF's help in the process.

"By engaging in this process for the last several months," Berman noted, "we have been successful in helping to craft a proposal that is significantly improved over the FBI's original bill in terms of privacy, technology policy, and civil liberties, and have, in the process, added significant new privacy protections for users of communications networks. We commend Representative Edwards, Senator Leahy, and Representatives Boucher and Markey for standing up for civil liberties and pushing for strong privacy protections."

The Electronic Frontier Foundation (EFF) is a non-profit public interest organization dedicated to achieving the democratic potential of new communications technology and works to protect civil liberties in new digital environments.

OTHER PRIVACY PROTECTIONS ADDED BY THE BILL

The bill also adds the following new privacy protections

- The standard for law enforcement access to online transactional records is raised to require a court order instead of a mere subpoena.
- No expansion of law enforcement authority to conduct electronic surveillance.
- The bill recognizes a citizen's right to use encryption.
- All authorized surveillance must be conducted with the affirmative intervention of the telecommunications carrier. Monitoring triggered remotely by law enforcement is prohibited.
- Privacy advocates will be able to track law enforcement requests for surveillance capability, and expenditures for all surveillance capability and capacity added under this bill will be open to public scrutiny.
- Privacy protections must be maintained in making new technologies conform to the requirements of the bill, and privacy advocates may intervene in the administrative standard setting process.

- Information gleaned from pen register devices is limited to dialed number information only. Law enforcement may not receive location information.

ANALYSIS OF AND COMMENTS ON MAJOR PROVISIONS OF THE BILL

A.   Key new privacy protections

1.   Expanded protection for transactional records sought by law enforcement

Senator Leahy and Rep. Edwards have agreed that law enforcement access to transactional records in online communication systems (everything from the Internet to AOL to hobbyist BBSs) threatens privacy rights because the records are personally identifiable, because they reveal the content of people's communications, and because the compilation of such records makes it easy for law enforcement to create a detailed picture of people's lives online. Based on this recognition, the draft bill contains the following provisions:

i.   Court order required for access to transactional records instead of mere subpoena

In order to gain access to transactional records, such as a list of to whom a subject sent email, which online discussion group one subscribes to, or which movies you request on a pay-per view channel, law enforcement will have to prove to a court, by the showing of "specific and articulable facts" that the records requested are relevant to an ongoing criminal investigation. This means that the government may not request volumes of transactional records merely to see what it can find through traffic analysis. Rather, law enforcement will have to prove to a court that it has reason to believe that it will find some specific information that is relevant to an ongoing criminal investigation in the records that it requests.

With these provisions, we have achieved for all online systems, a significantly greater level of protection than currently exists for telephone toll records. The lists of telephone calls that are kept by local and long distance phone companies are available to law enforcement without any judicial intervention at all. Law enforcement gains access to hundreds of thousands of such telephone records each year, without a warrant and without even notice to the citizens involved. Court order protection will make it much more difficult for law enforcement to go on "fishing expeditions" through online transactional records, hoping to find evidence of a crime by accident.

ii.   Standard of proof much greater than for telephone toll records, but below that for content

The most important change that these new provisions offer, is that law enforcement will (a) have to convince a judge that there is reason to look at a particular set of records, and (b) have to expend the time and energy necessary to have a US Attorney or DA actually present a case before a court. However, the burden or proof to be met by the government in such a proceeding is lower than required for access to the content of a communication.

2.   New protection for location-specific information available in cellular, PCS and other advanced networks

Much of the electronic surveillance conducted by law enforcement today involves gathering telephone dialing information through a device known as a pen register. Authority to attach pen registers is obtained merely by asserting that the information would be relevant to a criminal investigation. Courts have no authority to deny pen register requests. This legislation offers significant new limits on the use of pen register data.

Under this bill, when law enforcement seeks pen register information from a carrier, the carrier is forbidden to deliver to law enforcement any information which would disclose the location or movement of the calling or called party. Cellular phone networks, PCS systems, and so-called "follow-me" services all store location information in their networks. This new limitation is a major safeguard which will prevent law enforcement from casually using mobile and intelligent communications services as nation-wide tracking systems.

i.   New limitations on "pen register" authority

Law enforcement must use "technology reasonably available" to limit pen registers to the collection of calling number information only. Currently, law enforcement is able to capture not only the telephone number dialed, but also any other touch-tone digits dialed which reflect the user's interaction with an automated information service on the other end of the line, such as an automatic banking system or a voice-mail password.

3.   Bill does not preclude use of encryption

Unlike previous Digital Telephony proposals, this bill places no obligation on telecommunication carriers to decipher encrypted messages, unless the carrier actually holds the key. The bill in no way prohibits citizens from using encryption.

4.   Automated remote monitoring precluded

Law enforcement is specifically precluded from having automated, remote surveillance capability. Any electronic surveillance must be initiated by an employee of the telecommunications carrier.

5.   Privacy considerations essential to development of new technology

One of the requirements that telecommunications carriers must meet to be in compliance with the Act is that the wiretap access methods adopted must protect the privacy and security of each user's communication. If this requirement is not met, anyone may petition the FCC to have the wiretap access service be modified so that network security is maintained. So, the technology used to conduct wiretaps cannot also jeopardize the security of the network as a whole. If network-wide security problems arise because of wiretapping standards, then the standards can be overturned.

6.   Increased Public Accountability

All law enforcement requests for surveillance capability and capacity, as well as all expenditures paid by law enforcement to telecommunications carriers and all modifications made by carriers to comply with this bill, will be accountable to the public. The government is also required to pay for all upgrades, in both capability and capacity, in the first four years, and all costs after four years for incorporating the capability requirements in the costs for meeting those requirements are not 'reasonably achievable'. A determination of whether compliance after four years is reasonably achievable will be made by the FCC in an open and public proceeding. Government reimbursement for compliance costs will permit the public the opportunity to decide whether additional surveillance capability is necessary.

In all, the reimbursement requirements combined with the reporting requirements and the open processes built in to this bill, law enforcement surveillance capability, capacity, and expenditures will be more accountable to the public than ever before.

B.   Draconian provisions softened

In addition, the surveillance requirements imposed by the bill are not as far-reaching as the original FBI version. A number of procedural safeguards are added which seek to minimize the threatens to privacy, security, and innovation. Though the underlying premise of the Act is still cause for concern, these new limitations deserve attention:

1.   Narrow Scope

The bill explicitly excludes Internet providers, email systems, BBSs, and other online services. Unlike the bills previously proposed by the FBI, this bill is limited to local and long distance telephone companies, cellular and PCS providers, and other common carriers.

2.   Open process with public right of intervention

The public will have access to information about the implementation of the Act, including open access to all standards adopted in compliance with the Act, the details of how much wiretap capacity the government demands, and a detailed accounting of all federal money paid to carriers for modifications to their networks. Privacy groups, industry interests, and anyone else has a statutory right under this bill to challenge implementation steps taken by law enforcement if they threaten privacy or impede technology advancement.

3.   Technical requirements standards developed by industry instead of the Attorney General

All surveillance requirements are to be implemented according to standards developed by industry groups. The government is specifically precluded from forcing any particular technical standard, and all requirements are qualified by notions of economic and technical reasonableness.

4.   Right to deploy untappable services

Unlike the original FBI proposal, this bill recognizes that there may be services which are untappable, even with Herculean effort to accommodate surveillance needs. In provisions that still require some strengthening, the bill allows untappable services to be deployed if redesign is not economically or technically feasible.

BACKGROUND INFORMATION

- The Bill:
  ftp.eff.org, /pub/EFF/Policy/Digital_Telephony/digtel94.bill
  gopher.eff.org, 1/EFF/Policy/Digital_Telephony, digtel94.bill
  http.eff.org/pub/EFF/Policy/Digital_Telephony/digtel94.bill

  All other files available from
  ftp.eff.org, /pub/EFF/Policy/Digital_Telephony/Old/
  gopher.eff.org, 1/EFF/Policy/Digital_Telephony/Old
  http.eff.org/pub/EFF/Policy/Digital_Telephony/Old/
- EFF Analysis of Bill as Introduced: digtel94_analysis.eff
- EFF Statement on Earlier 1994 Draft of Bill:
  digtel94_old_statement.eff
- EFF Analysis of Earlier 1994 Draft: digtel94_draft_analysis.eff
- EFF Statement on Announcement of 1994 Draft:
  digtel94.announce
- EFF Statement on Announcement of 1993 Draft:
  digtel93.announce

- Late 1993/Early 1994 Draft: digtel94_bill.draft
- EFF Statement on 1992 Draft: digtel92_analysis.eff
- EFF Statement on 1992 Draft: digtel92_opposition.announce
- Late 1992 Draft: digtel92_bill.draft
- Original 1992 Draft: digtel92_old_bill.draft

For more information, contact Jerry Berman, Policy Director,
<jberman@eff.org>, or Jonah Seiger, Project Coordinator,
<jseiger@eff.org> (202-347-5400 [voice] 202-393-5509 [fax]).

4

EPIC Statement on Wiretap Bill*

Electronic Privacy Information Center

The passage of the FBI Wiretap Bill in the closing hours of the 103d Congress demonstrates the need for continued and aggressive advocacy in support of communications privacy. The legislation, which mandates the re-design of the nation's telecommunications infrastructure to facilitate government interception, was enacted with no floor debate and no resolution of the lingering questions concerning the need for such an unprecedented and far-reaching change in the law. The Electronic Privacy Information Center (EPIC) opposed passage of the bill and believes that its enactment could establish a dangerous precedent for the design and development of the National Information Infrastructure.

The grassroots campaign that emerged to oppose the wiretap legislation shows the potential of the Internet as a means of educating the public and promoting democratic participation in the policymaking process. In the two-month period between the introduction of the legislation and its enactment, grassroots efforts demonstrated that a measure initially touted as a "compromise" bill was, in fact, a highly controversial proposal. Numerous Congressional offices admitted to being astounded by the number of calls and faxes they received in opposition to the legislation as it moved to consideration in both houses. EPIC believes that the on-line campaign to defeat the wiretap bill can serve as a model for the Internet community to build upon in the future. We congratulate the thousands of individuals who participated in the process and wish to express our appreciation and admiration for the work of the Voters Telecomm Watch (VTW) in bridging the gap between Washington and activists around the country. EPIC looks forward to continuing to work with VTW, the American Civil Liberties Union, the Internet Business Association and the many other organizations that joined us in opposing the FBI Wiretap Bill.

Implementation of the newly enacted legislation must be closely monitored. EPIC is committed to continuing its efforts to obtain relevant government data under the Freedom of Information Act, including the aggressive pursuit of our pending litigation against the FBI for the

---

* October 8, 1994.

release of information cited in support of the wiretap legislation. EPIC also intends to monitor proceedings in the Federal Communications Commission pursuant to the new law and to participate in such proceedings to protect the privacy interests of network users. EPIC will also continue its research and advocacy activities in the areas of encryption policy, medical records privacy, transactional data privacy, proposed national identification systems, and other issues now emerging with the advent of the information superhighway.

Electronic Privacy Information Center
666 Pennsylvania Avenue, S.E.,
Suite 301 Washington, DC 20003

(202) 544-9240 (voice)
(202) 547-5482 (fax)
info@epic.org (e-mail)

5

Benefits and Costs of Legislation to Ensure the Government's Continued Capability to Investigate Crime with the Implementation of new Telecommunications Technologies*

Department of Justice

SUMMARY

The Nation's telecommunications systems and networks are often used in furtherance of serious criminal activities. Recent and continuing advances in telecommunications technology and the introduction of new technologies and transmission modes have made it increasingly difficult for Federal and state government agencies to enforce the criminal law through a key investigative technique: statutory-based, court-ordered electronic surveillance. The proposed legislation is intended to preserve the status quo for the criminal law enforcement community in terms of its current ability to carry out court-ordered or otherwise authorized electronic surveillance.

The societal and economic benefits derived from the effective enforcement of the criminal law are in many regards difficult to quantify. The use of electronic surveillance by State and Federal authorities has in a number of instances been essential in preventing murders, saving human life put at risk through planned terrorist attacks, dismantling entrenched organized crime groups which severely harm the economy through extortion, fraud, and corruption, and in attacking the major national and international drug importation and distribution cartels and networks whose activities cause incalculable personal and economic injury in our society. The economic benefit from the continued use of electronic surveillance that would be assured by the legislation easily could be billions of dollars per year.

The cost to the telecommunications industry of complying with the provisions and requirements of the legislation is not susceptible to precise measurement. Nonetheless, consultations with the industry have indicated that first order estimates of the cumulative costs suggest a

---

* Obtained from the FBI in December 1993, through a Freedom Of Information Act (FOIA) request by Computer Professionals for Social Responsibility. Department of Justice document C.A. 92–2117.

range from \$150–\$250 million. By way of context, the telecommunications industry, which has annual revenue exceeding \$190 billion, expends approximately \$22 billion each year in acquisition of systems equipment and components. The maximum developmental costs may be \$300 million, or approximately 1.5% of the industry's acquisition budget. Further, the total costs associated with compliance with the legislation would not necessarily be incurred in the first year after enactment of the legislation, but would likely be expended and amortized over several years concurrent with implementation of technologies.

Accordingly, the benefits of enactment of the proposed legislation far outweigh the associated costs.

BENEFITS AND COSTS OF LEGISLATION
TO ENSURE THE GOVERNMENT'S CONTINUED CAPABILITY
TO INVESTIGATE CRIME WITH THE
IMPLEMENTATION OF NEW TELECOMMUNICATIONS
TECHNOLOGIES

Pursuant to the President's directive to all heads of Federal departments and agencies, dated April 29, 1992, concerning the benefits and costs of legislative proposals, this analysis is submitted to provide the American public and the Congress with information necessary to make a full and fair evaluation of the benefits and costs, direct and indirect, of the instant legislation.

THE UNDERLYING PROBLEM

The Nation's telecommunications systems and networks are often used in furtherance of serious criminal activities. Recent and continuing advances in telecommunications technology and the introduction of new technologies and transmission modes have made it increasingly difficult for Federal and state government agencies to enforce the criminal law through a key investigative technique—statutory-based, court-ordered electronic surveillance. Without the assistance of the telecommunications industry and others, deployment of these new technologies will continue to erode the efficacy of this technique and, in time, will preclude it in many instances, thereby significantly impeding the ability of these agencies to enforce the criminal law and protect the national security. Although these technological developments are not intentionally being introduced to thwart effective criminal law enforcement, nevertheless such will be the effect, unless consideration and accommodation are given to the electronic surveillance needs of government agencies. Indeed, without remedial legislation which clarifies the responsibility of various service providers and operators, the continued and future introduction of these technologies will bring about a *de facto* repeal of the existing electronic surveillance authority conferred upon these criminal law enforcement agencies by the Congress.

THE PROPOSED LEGISLATION

The proposed legislation is intended to preserve the status quo for the criminal law enforcement community in terms of its current and past ability to carry out court-ordered or otherwise authorized electronic surveillance. The legislation does not, and is not intended to, enlarge the government's substantive legal authority to conduct electronic surveillance or to include any new types of communications not currently covered. Current electronic surveillance law requires that telecommunication service providers and others assist the criminal law enforcement community in effecting electronic surveillance orders. Indeed, whenever electronic surveillance is ordered by a court, a secondary "assistance" order is directed to the appropriate service provider mandating the assistance requested by the government agency. Historically, interceptions in the hardware, analog telecommunications world were not difficult to effect, and the minor assistance provided by services providers was sufficient to accommodate criminal law enforcement's needs. However, with the advent of cellular and various other types of wireless personal communications, sophisticated switching features supported by digital technology, digital subscriber services, and the introduction of fiber optic transmission lines, the ability of service providers to fully comply with the assistance orders and to readily provide to the criminal law enforcement agency the needed access for conducting interceptions of all the target's communications, without disrupting service or risking the disclosure of the wiretapping effort, has been put in doubt. To the extent that certain research, development, and system(s) modifications (software or hardware) would be required, many service providers have questioned whether the "assistance" language of the existing statutes explicitly compels their commitment to such engineering efforts or their expending of funds to satisfy criminal law enforcement's electronic surveillance needs.

In short, the proposed legislation is intended to clarify the responsibility of electronic communication service providers and private branch exchange operators (1) by putting them on notice of the continuing electronic surveillance needs of government and their responsibility to effectively respond thereto, and (2) by setting forth reasonable time frames for compliance. Although there should be little difficulty for the mainstream exchange carriers, interexchange carriers, and major cellular service providers to achieve timely compliance, the legislation recognizes that certain service providers and operators are less likely to be called upon to provide electronic surveillance assistance and that other technical or fiscal constraints may preclude timely compliance. Consequently, provision is made for the Attorney General to exempt certain classes and types of providers and operators or to grant waivers, where appropriate. Failure to comply without exemption or waiver would result in civil fines and/or injunctive sanctions.

BENEFITS

The societal and economic benefits derived from the effective enforcement of the criminal law are in many regards difficult to quantify. Fundamentally, a society which cannot adequately enforce its laws invites disrespect and disregard for law. Nevertheless, a number of available statistics and cases illustrate the critical importance of viable electronic surveillance to both government agencies and society. The use of electronic surveillance by State and Federal authorities has in a number of instances been essential in preventing murders, in saving human life put at risk through planned terrorist attacks, in dismantling entrenched organized crime groups which severely harm the economy through extortion, fraud, and corruption, and in attacking the major national and international drug importation and distribution cartels and networks whose activities cause incalculable personal and economic injury in our society.

For the purposes of this analysis, a more finite set of measures is used. First, the statistical analysis and the examples given all come from the operations of the Federal Bureau of Investigation, the agency that requests more authorizations than any other federal agency. Accordingly, the benefits discussed below reflect only a small portion of the total benefits within the criminal law enforcement community, i.e. only a portion of the approximately 350 *federal* authorizations reported by the Administrative Office of the United States Courts. This analysis does not reflect the benefits that are generated by other federal criminal law enforcement agencies, such as the Drug Enforcement Administration, the United States Secret Service, or other enforcement agencies. Nor does this analysis reflect benefits that are generated by State criminal law enforcement agencies in approximately 500 authorizations reported in 1991 by the Administrative Office of the United States Courts.

Second, the information provided must be provided in a circumspect fashion because of the ongoing nature of many investigations. Accordingly, only summaries of specific cases are given.

Organized Crime Investigations

In April, 1988, the importance of the electronic surveillance technique was uniformly recognized by all levels of criminal law enforcement during the U.S. Senate Permanent Subcommittee on Investigations' hearings on organized crime: "25 Years After Valachi." In particular, David C. Williams, Office of Special Investigations, General Accounting Office, testified that "Electronic Surveillance is another tool that has been of great value to the law enforcement community to combat the La Cosa Nostra (LCN) [organized crime families]. Evidence gathered through electronic surveillance . . . has had a devastating impact on organized crime."

To illustrate the impact of this extremely important investigative technique, during the period of 1985 to 1991, court-ordered electronic surveillance conducted by the FBI for all criminal investigations led to:

- 7,324 individuals convicted;
- $295,851,162 in fines being levied;
- $756,363,288 in court-ordered recoveries, restitutions and forfeitures; and
- $1,862,414,937 in prevented potential economic loss.

Further, numerous lives were saved through information gleaned from electronic surveillance. Court-Ordered electronic surveillance were essential to and/or substantially assisted in 3,348 investigations from 1985 to the present.

The loss or impairment of the ability to conduct court-ordered electronic surveillance would catastrophically inhibit the FBI's ability to investigate organized criminal groups. The consequent cost to society and industry would be dramatic. For example, in the President's Commission on Organized Crime 1986 report, *The Impact: Organized Crime Today*, the commission utilized the Wharton Business School's long-term model of the United States economy to estimate the cost of organized crime on the economy, in terms of sustained higher prices and the continued underpayment of taxes to the Federal Government. The Commission concluded that the estimated economy-wide impact of organized crime was as follows:

- U.S. output is reduced by 18.2 billion in 1986 dollars.
- U.S. employment is reduced by 414,000 jobs.
- Consumer prices are higher by 0.3 percent; and,
- Per capita personal income is lower by $77.22, measured in 1986 dollars.

Although no studies have been conducted to determine how the successes of Federal and state criminal law enforcement agencies against organized crime have reduced its negative impact on the U.S. economy, it is logical to postulate that an abatement in successful organized crime investigations, due to the loss or impairment of the court-ordered electronic surveillance technique, would allow the aforementioned impact on the U.S. economy to remain the same, if not become substantially more debilitating.

The President's Commission on Organized Crime stated the following conclusions in its report, *The Edge: Organized Crime, Business and Labor Unions*:

- If unchecked, organized crime can take over, own, and operate legitimate business. It can also control entire industries. The ways in which industry can be affected are by the increased price of items due to theft, bribery (kickbacks), price fixing and the control of trade.
- The control of the marketplace by organized crime is also obtained by the control of unions and by monopolizing power in specific industries.
- Through the control of unions, payoffs can be demanded to ensure labor peace. Businesses comply with the labor union's demands rather than lose profits or lose business. Another deleterious effect of organized crime control is through the illegal utilization of union funds. At the time of the report of the PCOC, union benefit funds had cumulative assets of over $51 billion. Influence in the unions on a local level, if strong enough, may lead to control of the union at the international level.
- The costs of labor racketeering are hard to trace. The Commission estimated that millions of dollars in workers' labor union dues were stolen from the unions through embezzlement, lost through illegal loans, and taken through extortionate and illegal fees paid to trust and service fund providers.

As a result, the U.S. public is forced to pay higher commodity costs because of organized crime's control. Examples cited by the Commission of the various types of economic loss are:

- Amalgamated Local 355, an independent union in Queens, New York, lost nearly $2 million in a kickback and embezzlement scheme in the mid-1970s. The scheme involved the union's secretary/treasurer and a well-known real estate developer.
- The control of the concrete industry by the LCN in New York, as brought out in the LCN Commission indictment, was demonstrated in evidence which showed that over the period 1981—1984, the 2% skim collected on the total cost of poured concrete, on the delivery of it to the job site, and on the attendant labor costs could range anywhere from $1.6 to $3.5 million. This figure was estimated on the control of the concrete industry alone. Increased construction costs then lead to higher overall building project costs and increased rental rates, etc. Essential evidence supporting this prosecution was derived from electronic surveillance.

Through the utilization of electronic surveillance, Federal and state investigations continue to have a significant impact upon organized crime groups. In Fiscal Year 1991, at the Federal level, there were 239 recorded convictions and 246 indictments of LCN members and associates. In addition, civil RICO complaints spawned by the criminal investigations were filed against 25 individuals and/or entities, and judgements were entered against 23. Aggressive use of the seizure and forfeiture provisions of the RICO statute yielded $17,554,865. Over $11,779,106 in fines were levied against convicted individuals; recoveries and restitutions totaling $22,881,539 were obtained; and $7,044,625 in potential economic losses were prevented. A few recent cases, wherein electronic surveillance played a critical role, illustrate the importance of maintaining the efficiency of this investigative technique.

■ *Commercial seafood and longshoremen dock-loading industries.* For over 70 years, organized crime, and particularly the Genovese LCN family, had dominated and controlled the Fulton Fish Market and its immediate environment in New York City. Through electronic surveillance which spanned over two years, the government acquired substantial evidence as to the influence and control of organized crime in the seafood industry and the labor unions related to it. As a result, in October 1987, a civil RICO complaint was filed against the Genovese LCN crime family, certain unions controlled by organized crime, and a number of LCN members and associates. In 1988, in a landmark RICO decree and judgment, the Fulton Fish Market was placed under the oversight of a court-appointed administrator. Judgments in this civil RICO action permanently bar the Genovese crime family and other defendants from having any future dealings in that seafood market.

Although it is difficult to quantify the impact of the government's intervention into this industry, the enormous economic and social costs associated with the LCN's control of this market have been significantly reduced. Illegal activities such as hijacking, gambling, robbery, burglary, loansharking, extortion, murder, narcotics trafficking, and labor racketeering flourished in the Market's environment while under the dominion of the LCN. These activities have dramatically abated with the imposition of the consent and default judgments. The court-appointed administrator and other independent sources of information, such as the media, report that the Fulton Fish Market has sales approximating two billion dollars annually. Seafood that passes through the market is bought and sold throughout the United States. Illegal activity at the Market has inflated seafood costs by $1—$2 dollars per pound and virtually every household in America has absorbed that cost. By a conservative estimate, the American public has been spared literally millions of dollars in increased seafood costs as a result of this investigation.

■ *International Longshoremen's Association.* This investigation focused primarily upon corruption on the New York and New Jersey waterfront, the second largest port in the world. The civil RICO complaint names as defendants the International Longshoremen's Association (ILA), their executive boards, six local labor unions, and 32 present or former officials of these ILA locals, 21 of whom are identified as members or associates of the Gambino and Genovese LCN crime families, and the "Westies" criminal gang. Twelve additional individuals are identified in the complaint as members or associates of the Gambino and Genovese LCN families and the Westies, and several employers in industries affecting waterfront commerce are named for purposes of obtaining adequate relief.

The complaint alleges that the LCN figures have used these locals and their various affiliated benefit funds to conduct a pattern of racketeering activity on the waterfront, which includes murder, extortion, embezzlement of union funds, illegal labor and benefit fund payments and mail fraud. To prove such wide-ranging conspiracies, the type of evidence needed typically requires substantial reliance upon electronic surveillance-based information.

These investigations, which heavily relied upon electronic surveillance, demonstrated an extraordinary breadth of control by the Genovese LCN family over waterfront activity that extended from the New York—New Jersey piers all the way to the Port of Miami. This pervasive control by organized crime over the waterfront extends back to the turn of the century. Organized crime obtained this control by its early recognition that to transport goods to the eastern seaboard, markets often required passage through the New York/New Jersey waterfront, and that this transportation terminal point presented a labor intensive bottleneck. To control waterfront labor, thus, was to exercise tremendous leverage over the entire shipping industry, effect the commerce of a huge section of the American economy, and ultimately to drive up prices of a myriad of commodities sold in the United States.

There are numerous other examples where, through the use of court-ordered electronic surveillance, major economic harm was abated. The nationwide investigation into organized crime-labor racketeering influence in the union health and dental care industry has resulted in the termination of frauds and kickbacks which cost unions and insurance companies millions of dollars. In one investigation, sixteen different FBI field offices were involved, eight of which conducted extensive electronic surveillance. At the conclusion of the investigation in September, 1988, seven separate Federal Grand Jury indictments were returned in Atlanta, Chicago, Baltimore, San Diego, and San Francisco, charging ten individuals and five corporations with numerous Federal violations including RICO, conspiracy, mail fraud, wire fraud, and labor racketeering. As a result of this investigation, ten health care executives were convicted, the U.S. Public Health Service changed its bidding procedures nationwide, SAFECO Insurance Company terminated its practice of paying double commissions to insurance agents nationwide, and spin-off investigations resulted in the conviction of a Federal judge and two labor-related organized crime leaders.

Electronic surveillance was extensively utilized in the landmark civil RICO investigation called "Liberatus" which resulted in the formal break up of LCN control over the nation's largest union, the International Brotherhood of Teamsters. The LCN's grip over this union had been intact since the 1950s. As a result, for the first time in decades the nation's largest union is free from organized crime control and corruption, and the continued pillage of union funds has ceased.

The loss of the ability to fully conduct court-ordered electronic surveillance would also have an extremely negative impact upon human safety in U.S. society. Many violent acts, including murder, have been prevented by law enforcement's "real time" response to, and preventive actions taken pursuant to, intercepted conversations. The following are specific examples of cases in which court-ordered electronic surveillance have saved lives or prevented violent acts from occurring:

- During the course of court-ordered electronic surveillance, members of the New England LCN Family discussed the murder of three individuals and discussed the details concerning six murders which had previously been committed by them or by other LCN members. Of the three planned murders discussed by the LCN, two were prevented by the FBI. The third could not be prevented due to the fugitive status of the victim and the inability to locate him prior to his murder.

- One of the most violent Asian Organized Crime (AOC) groups active in the New York City area is the Green Dragons. The gang is telephonically directed in its criminal activities by Kin Fei Wong from the People's Republic of China. The Green Dragons perpetrate murder, armed robberies, home invasions, extortion, drug trafficking, and are involved in the obstruction of justice. In November 1990, Kin Fei Wong and the Green Dragons were indicted in the Eastern District of New York. The indictment was based on evidence obtained during three months of court-ordered electronic surveillance and physical surveillance conducted by a Task Force composed of FBI Special Agents and New York City Police Officers.

The court-ordered electronic surveillance coverage also provided evidence that the Green Dragons were about to engage in a "shoot out" with a rival Asian gang. Immediately, the Task Force arrested 16 members of the group and prevented an imminent violent confrontation and loss of life. The subsequent simultaneous execution of search warrants resulted in the recovery of 36 firearms, including several Mac-10 sub-machine guns. On April 9, 1992, following a seven week trial, all defendants were found guilty of racketeering, racketeering conspiracy and numerous substantive counts which included murder, kidnapping, home invasions, armed robbery, extortion and bribery of a public official.

■ In a notable 1990 sexual exploitation of children case involving electronic surveillance, the FBI thwarted two individuals who were conspiring to abduct, torture, and kill a teenage boy for the purpose of making a "snuff murder" film.

During fiscal year 1991, Title III—based electronic surveillance involving wire communications was conducted by the FBI in a variety of life-threatening matters, including "murder-for-hire" kidnapping, armored car robbery, and "product tampering." Information obtained from the electronic surveillance (a) helped to prevent the death or physical injury of innocent victims, (b) thwarted future violent criminal activity, and (c) provided extremely credible and persuasive evidence in the prosecution of these cases.

In sum, the loss of the ability to conduct court-ordered electronic surveillance would destroy the FBI's ability to effectively conduct investigations of organized crime groups. Thirty odd years of successes would be reversed. The LCN would be permitted to regroup and regain a solid hold on its economic base and AOC and other International Organized Crime groups would be permitted to emerge as a threat on a par with the LCN. Additionally, individual acts of violence would not be effectively investigated or prevented.

Narcotics and Dangerous Drugs

The greatest single use of electronic surveillance relates to the government's war on drugs. Almost two thirds (62%) of all governmental electronic surveillance reported by the Administrative Office of the United States Courts is devoted to this serious national problem. Although figures abound with regard to the billions of dollars in seizures of drugs, illegal drug proceeds (cash and other assets), etc., the fundamental harm to society is incalculable. It would be impossible to fully identify the economic or societal harm brought about by drug dependency and addiction. The Public Health Service has estimated the health, labor, and crime costs of drug abuse at $58.3 billion in 1988, exclusive of the value of the drugs themselves. D. Rice, et al., U.S. Dept. of Health and Human Services, *The Economic Cost of Alcohol and Drug Abuse and Mental Illness: 1985*, Table 1, page 2 (1990). Those drugs which are responsible for this problem are essentially those (such as cocaine and heroin) which must be imported into the United States by organized crime groups, drug trafficking cartels, and other syndicates. Thus, electronic surveillance is critical in identifying and then dismantling those national and international drug trafficking organizations which rely heavily upon telecommunications. Further, information derived from electronic surveillance is essential for prosecuting the executive levels of the drug trade. Drug chieftains do not appear at drug buys or shipments; they send underlings and lieutenants to complete these transactions. Electronic surveillance is ordinarily the only reliable method of linking them to the importation and distribution chain. The recent April, 1992, raid in Miami, for instance, which netted 15,000 pounds of cocaine, was instigated by electronic surveillance. Evidence derived from electronic surveillance was instrumental in identifying the network's leader among the 22 defendants arrested. Similarly, the Herrara investigation in New York City last November resulted in the prosecution of 51 defendants, including key individuals linked to the Cali drug cartel. The economic harm brought about by lost productivity; employee absence; extensive and expensive health care; crime such as thefts, robberies, murders brought on by drug use and turf battles to control drug distribution; as well as the sad occurrence of a generation of drug dependent babies, etc., ultimately defy quantification economically or otherwise.

Government Corruption

Governmental fraud and corruption has also been a key target of court-ordered electronic surveillance. The "Ill Wind" investigation, jointly conducted by the Department of Justice and the Department of Defense, which was largely based upon 36 separate court-ordered electronic surveillances conducted across the United States, has had a tremendous impact upon fraud and abuse both within the government and within the industries which contract with the government. To date, the "Ill Wind" investigation has resulted in 56 convictions (including high-level Department of Defense officials), sanctions against contractors, and over a quarter-billion dollars ($239,577,000) in fines, restitutions, and recoveries ordered.

With regard to public corruption, electronic surveillance in several recent investigations has directly led to the conviction of two Federal District Court Judges and to the indictment of four Dade County, Florida state judges and several attorneys. Within the recent past, a major police corruption case was investigated and prosecuted based in part upon electronic surveillance evidence. This case which involved the police force of a large midwestern city included extortion and protection for gambling and narcotics distribution. As a result of the investigation, 30 police officers and 17 others were indicted. To date, 46 of the 47 have either pled or been found guilty.

Terrorism and Foreign Counterintelligence

The entire area of terrorism and foreign counterintelligence remains a highly sensitive subject. Electronic surveillance conducted in support of the prevention and investigation of terrorist acts is not reported by the Administrative Office of the United States Courts. This area of endeavor comes under the ambit of the Foreign Intelligence Surveillance Court.

A number of terrorist acts have been frustrated through the effective use of electronic surveillance. In one case, the bombing of a foreign consulate in the United States was prevented and the electronic surveillance evidence was used in the subsequent conviction of the principals. In another case, a terrorist rocket attack against a United States ally by a foreign-based terrorist group was thwarted, and the electronic surveillance-based investigation led to the arrest of the principals, and to the prevention of the loss of life of scores of persons. More recently, in 1990, foreign based terrorists were prevented from acquiring a Stinger surface-to-air missile which was to be employed in a terrorist act wherein numerous people would undoubtedly have been killed. Also, as a direct result of court-ordered electronic surveillance in a terrorist-related matter, information was obtained which resulted in the conviction of two individuals for the brutal homicide of their 16 year-old daughter.

Beyond these instances, numerous other terrorist-related investigations have utilized electronic surveillance to solve the murder of a United States Court of Appeals Judge, prevent a rocket attack against an FBI field office, prevent the destruction of a nuclear power facility, solve several murders and identify the perpetrators of a $7,000,000 armed robbery, and solve and prevent anti-Castro bombings in the Miami, Florida area.

Costs

The cost to the telecommunications industry of complying with the provisions and requirements of the legislation is not susceptible to precise measurement. Nonetheless, an effort has been made to analyze by category the various telecommunication areas wherein advanced telephony is employed, or will be employed in the near future, which pose problems for, or preclude, full effectuation of court orders for electronic surveillance or for dialed-number information.

This information is deemed sensitive. To provide information pursuant to the directive to develop benefit/cost analyses, it is necessary to identify specific areas of current and potential vulnerabilities.

Enhanced Features

Modern "enhanced" switch-based technology found both in analog and digital switching has supported a number of new commercial telecommunication features which, if utilized by the target of the electronic surveillance order, would frustrate or diminish the full interception as authorized. For example, features such as "call forwarding," "speed dialing," and "automatic re-dial," etc., result in the content of a target's calls (or the dialed number information associated with the call) bypassing the government agency's interception, regardless of whether the interceptions are carried out in the so called "local loop" or from the service provider's central office. Hence, the government's need to fully capture the content and the dialed number information associated with the communication will necessitate modifications to existing switch software which supports these features.

Of the approximately 22,000 switches currently found in the central offices within the public switched and private networks, approximately 40–45% of these support the new features either directly or through the intelligent network. Costs associated with needed modifications in this area are discussed below in connection with "Interception of digitized transmissions."

Digitized Transmissions

A second facet of conducting central office-based interceptions pertains to problems associated with Integrated Services Digital Network (ISDN) and other digital subscriber service technologies. For some time, telecommunication services providers (essentially local exchange carriers), have transmitted communications within the core of their network via digital technology, with communications to and from the caller/callee's premises (the so-called local loop) being transmitted in an analog mode or format. Historically, almost all criminal law enforcement wire interceptions have occurred within the local loop. In the near future, however, with the advent of new digital-based technologies, such as ISDN, and the increasing employment of multiplexing in lieu of dedicated wire pairs, and the transition to fiber optic transmission lines to the curb or to subscriber's home/office, traditional approaches to court-ordered electronic surveillance will largely be precluded. Industry figures found in recent trade journals indicate that there are approximately 350 ISDN-equipped switches embedded in the network. Consequently, electronic surveillance interceptions (that is, the initial acquisition of the communication signal carrying the content/dialed number information) will necessarily be forced to occur within the central office facilities of service providers. (Of course, the actual execution of the electronic surveillance search, i.e., the monitoring of the communications by government agencies, will occur remotely — away from the central office, at a government monitoring facility.) Such central office-based interceptions must of course, as alluded to above, be able to be implemented without impedance attributable to enhanced features being utilized by the subscriber.

The cost for the development of software to enable government agencies to fully effectuate electronic surveillance orders and to provide for the isolation and routing of a specific "call session" utilizing either analog or digital services, is difficult to estimate absent specific feasibility studies. However, discussions with industry experts indicate that the level of effort necessary to satisfy law enforcement's needs which affect enhanced features and digital transmissions and switching would require software development in four different series of central offices switches, to insure compliance for approximately 80–90% of the embedded switch base. Development costs for the foregoing embedded switch based solutions are estimated to range from $100-$150 million.

With regard to implementing the software modifications through switch software loading, the government indicates that compliance by each exchange carrier/interexchange carrier could be achieved by their having readily available the software modification, such that the loading of the software would only be required as needed, on an ad hoc basis, for a particular switch. Realistically, not every electronic surveillance interception involves a situation where these enhanced features or digital subscriber services would be encountered. Consequently, the number of switches which would be required to be loaded with the "software package" would be substantially less than the number of interceptions actually conducted. The cost for acquiring and loading this software would be dependent on the switch base population for which it was designed. For example, if a software solution was designed for a particular switch series at a cost of $25 million and the number of switches in the series was 2,000, the cost allocated over the total would be about $12,500 for each switch. Using 1991 figures, where some 800 "Title III" court orders for electronic surveillance were installed, a "worst case" scenario would suggest that, in the first years, 800 switches would need the software package installed at a cost of $10 million with regard to criminal investigation-based interceptions. Costs in subsequent years would presumably be less since at least some switches subject to surveillance orders in those years would already have been modified. Electronic surveillance conducted pursuant to the Foreign Intelligence Surveillance Act (FISA) would likely necessitate software loading with a cost of from $4-$8 million. Further, once the software is loaded into the switch, it is anticipated that future software loading costs in the outyears would fall significantly.

Industry may, after comparing the necessary attributes of electronic surveillance with available or planned network/system analysis and maintenance tools, formulate solutions for embedded and emerging systems that would require a much less extensive level of efforts, and a commensurate reduction in costs.

Wireless Services

Cellular and other wireless telecommunications services constitute a major growth area and can be expected to become an even more significant sector in the U.S. telecommunications systems in the future. Because of the mobility associated with this technology, criminal law enforcement agencies have for some time focused electronic surveillance efforts at the cellular service providers' Mobile Telephone Switching Office (MTSO). Most of the service providers have been cooperative with criminal law enforcement agencies in attempting to provide assistance pursuant to the electronic surveillance assistance orders issued by the courts. The most efficacious approach has been to isolate signal access through ports in the cellular switches. However, as this equipment was not designed with the needs of criminal law enforcement in mind, the number of ports available in these switches is extremely limited. The limited port capacity, over the past several years, has led to the frustration of numerous court orders for either electronic surveillance interception or for dialed number information (pen registers), both of which compete for the same switch facilities. For example, at one specific time, one criminal law enforcement agency was authorized by the courts to implement 60 pen register orders that were not executed due to the capacity problems associated with cellular switches. The Cellular Telephone Industry Association (CTIA) has been working with the Government to sensitize the cellular industry to the capacity issue. The Government's electronic surveillance needs will necessitate cellular providers to ensure that there is sufficient port capacity in their switches to accommodate the volume of electronic surveillance and dialed number information (pen register) requests. Segments of the cellular switch industry are currently developing modular units to extend the port capacity, consequently the cost associated with remedying this problem would be dependent upon the amount of deployment. With this approach, as capacity at a given switch is reached, the modular unit can be added as necessary. As an example, modular units which could accommodate an additional 24 lines are estimated to cost approximately $50,000–$75,000. (As a practical matter, current electronic surveillance needs would indicate that only ten Metropolitan Service Areas (MSAs) would require the expansion upgrades discussed here in the near term). Consequently, it would be expected that costs associated with providing additional switch port capacity would amount to approximately $1.5 million.

Because criminal law enforcement's needs include the ability to acquire the dialed number information of the called party contemporaneous with the communication, some cellular providers will be requested to examine their switches' capabilities. It is estimated that approximately five percent (5%) of the estimated 650 switches currently deployed will not comply with this existing requirement. There are indications that compliance could be reached by minimal software changes and through continued dialogue between the providers and the switch manufacturers.

Finally, as cellular roaming services are enhanced, there will need to be greater intercarrier/provider coordination in order to channel "roaming" communications to the original point of interception/monitoring. The costs associated with networks' software and architectural modifications are not currently identifiable. However, since this is an area which is largely in the developmental stages, the costs would be minimal if the modifications are incorporated into the design process in the near future.

Private Branch Exchanges

Because of cost savings achievable by obtaining telecommunication service independent of local exchange carriers (or partially so, through Centrex service), private branch exchange (PBX) systems have emerged as a significant part of Nation's telecommunications networks. The FCC has indicated, based upon its contacts with private sector sources, that there are currently between 234,000—400,000 PBXs in place. Each PBX typically is centered around an "in-house" switch. The FCC estimates that approximately 70% of the PBXs utilize analog technology which, as alluded to above, does not pose interception problems for criminal law enforcement. The remaining 30% would be digital based systems. Although criminal law enforcement has had rather limited experience in conducting interceptions within digital PBXs, these PBX systems have not impeded or precluded successful implementation for electronic surveillance, since access to the signal is centered at the PBX switch rather than in the "local loop" portion of the network which historically has been the point of access in the local exchange carrier's system. It is estimated that only a small number of existing PBX switches preclude successful electronic surveillance.

Unlike local exchange carriers and private service providers who would likely need to rewrite and modify existing switch software (at some cost) to deal with the "enhanced features" and certain digital transmission issues, this problem can be effectively dealt with in PBXs at *no* cost through ad hoc system reconfigurations within software applications already resident in the switch. (Once the Government agency acquires the signal, be it analog or digital, it will process the signal without any need for additional help from the PBX operator. Thus, no cost would be incurred by the PBX operators relative to digital signal processing.) Implementation for this capability should be generally limited to a documentation/explanation process by the PBX vendor. The legislative initiative will ensure that future PBX technology development will not preclude the government agencies' capability to conduct electronic surveillance.

With regard to the latter category of PBXs which utilize systems which may currently thwart electronic surveillance (typically the older generations of PBX systems) and which would not be susceptible to modification, the cost for replacement of the PBX system could be substantial (average 1992 estimated costs for a PBX is $70,000). Consequently, the Government would likely be inclined to grant relief through exemptions, waiver, or by extending compliance dates beyond the three years set for PBX system compliance. Without committing itself, the Government would likely view a significant number of the major PBX users as candidates for exemption and waiver, e.g. hospitals, urban school systems, libraries, and museums. It is anticipated that the Attorney General, through direction to the FBI engineering and research operations, would institute a process to identify for PBX operators and manufacturers those PBX systems that already provide for criminal law enforcement's electronic surveillance needs, to avoid confusion and expenditures for unnecessary modifications.

Personal Communications Services—PCS (Low Earth Orbit Satellites, CT-2, etc)

PCS technology is a concept of seamless worldwide personal communications which is largely in its incipient stages of development and deployment, wherein people can be contacted instantly regardless of their geographic location. The most cost efficient solution to providing for the government agencies' intercept capability in the PCS environment is to address these electronic surveillance needs during the development and pre-production phase. This would allow for court-ordered intercepts to be administered without interference or degradation to the systems or the users' communications. More importantly, no proprietary information such as software, protocols, or other signalling schemes need be disclosed by the manufacturer to the criminal law enforcement community. This solution could be accomplished by using a manufacturer's designed feature which would route identified targeted information to a specific switch where the court-ordered intercept can occur. The cost impact of such a feature would be minimal as long as the feature is accounted for during the design, development, and pre-production phase by each PCS manufacturer.

Cable TV–based Telecommunications

With the potential entry of the Cable TV industry into the telecommunications arena, a certain number of electronic surveillance interceptions would be expected to occur within such a system. To the extent that Cable TV utilizes existing network facilities found within the local exchange carrier's network, criminal law enforcement's needs would have already been addressed, as discussed above. If the Cable TV industry develops independent networks and switching capacity, it would be contemplated that it would "engineer in" criminal law enforcement's needs in the design stages of development. In either event, the costs associated with compliance would be minimal.

Data Networks

Data networks include systems such as electronic messaging (read and read-write services—Prodigy, COMPUSERVE), packet switched networks (Internet, X400, etc.), and broadcast networks (LANs, WANs, and MANs). These networks can utilize the public switched network and/or privately owned facilities for transmission and interconnections. Such providers are currently subject to the electronic surveillance laws since they are providers of electronic communication services. 18 U.S.C. §2510(14), (15). Broadcast networks, packet switched networks, and some electronic messaging networks are self-contained within a particular network architecture and are generally comprised of switching components to include hosts, servers, bridges, routers, and gateways. Discussion with industry consultants has indicated that by their very nature these systems read and route data traffic, and that based on this functionality, routing instructions could be performed on an ad hoc basis to allow-for authorized court-ordered monitoring of data communications. An example of this would be the Message Transfer Agents (MTA) or Network Management Centers that process traffic for "customer" of the systems. The current functionality of MTAs that "replicate and forward" messages could be utilized to allow authorized monitoring of selected communications traffic. It should also be recognized that every point or segment within a system does not need to allow law enforcement to have access to an individual's computer communications, but rather any point(s) that would be cost effective, technically feasible, and complies with the attributes of electronic interception specified in the legislation would suffice. These network functions are controlled by network operating systems software that often possess utilities that allow auditing of the system user's on-line activity. It is expected that these auditing functions in their current state, or with some level of augmentation would suffice in complying with the attributes of electronic interception contained in the legislation. Enhanced audit functions could be included in future operating system revisions or through after-market diagnostics/audit software packages, this providing this capability to service providers. The implementation of this capability would be, in essence, a no (negligible) cost educational process for the system's operator or administrator.

Many of these networks that provide such services as point-of-sale, inventory, banking, and brand name services such as Prodigy, etc., could be likely candidates for the Attorney General's exemptions.

Services such as COMPUSERVE and Prodigy are accessed by subscribers utilizing modems and the existing public switched network. In these instances, targeted communications would be subjected to interception through access within the public switched network, rather than through the data network.

Administrative Costs

In order to implement the administrative provisions of the legislation, particularly with regard to the Attorney General's authority to grant exemptions and waivers, the government will be required to dedicate sufficient administrative staffing. Based upon an estimate of a need for 8 professional and support staff of six to ten, the projected governmental cost in the first three years would be approximately $500,000–$1,000,000 per year. It would be expected that in the out years, the staffing requirements would likely decrease.

Private Sector Costs Associated with Seeking a Waiver

The legislation provides that the Attorney General may grant waivers from compliance with the provisions of the legislation. It is anticipated that with an early promulgation of a listing of the types and classes of service providers and operators who are exempt from compliance that the number of individual entities seeking relief through waiver will be relatively small. Since the government does not anticipate the waivers or waiver process as being grounded in hyper-technical considerations, the petitions for waiver should be relatively straightforward and relatively simple to prepare. If pursued by the service provider or systems operator, the costs associated with the effort should be negligible. If legal counsel is employed, the cost per waiver petition could typically range from $3,000–$5,000, according to FCC estimates (based upon FCC-related actions). At this point in time it is impossible to project the number of waivers likely to be sought.

Summary

The total costs to the industry are expected to be between $150 million and $250 million, for reconfiguration of the embedded base and engineering-in attributes to expected developments. The following table summarizes these costs.

COST SUMMARY		
CATEGORY	**LOW**	**HIGH**
A. Software R&D (Digital/Analog) Enhanced Features	$100,000,000	$150,000,000
B. Implementation/Software Loading for (a) (3 to 5 year cycle)	$42,000,000	$54,000,000
C. Cellular Port Capacity Modules (3 to 5 year cycle)	$1,500,000	$4,500,000
D. Cellular Software Modifications	$5,000,000	$15,000,000
E. Data Network Software Modifications	$3,000,000	$15,000,000
F. Government Administrative Costs	$1,500,000	$3,000,000
G. Private Sector Waiver Costs	$1,500,000	$5,000,000
Total	$154,500,000	$246,500,000

CONCLUSION

As previously discussed, estimating the exact costs associated with the legislative proposal are difficult because of the many variables, including the extent of industry cooperation, the degree to which research and development can be shared within the industry, the evolutionary status of specific emerging technologies, and the approaches to development and deployment of technical solutions. First order estimates of the cumulative costs suggest a range from $150-$250 million. By way of context, the telecommunications industry, which has annual revenue exceeding $190 billion, expends approximately $22 billion a year in acquisition of systems equipment and components. Further, the total costs associated with compliance with the legislation would not necessarily be incurred in the first year after enactment of the legislation, but would likely be expended and amortized over several years concurrent with implementation of technologies.

When the Administration compares the foregoing telecommunications industry costs with those societal and economic costs associated with failing to effectively protect human life, failing to aggressively enforce the Nation's laws and protect national security, and with failing to prevent the enormous economic harm caused by crime (estimated in the multibillion dollar range), it becomes clear that the legislation is needed and is cost effective. Additionally, it is worth noting that, although it has been deregulated in many areas, the telecommunications industry historically has been required to respond to public safety needs both at the state and Federal levels. We view the legislative proposal as being consistent with the need to ensure the public's safety through the effective enforcement of the law.

## 6

Digital Telephony—Cost-Benefit Analysis*

Betsy Anderson, Todd Buchholz

THE WHITE HOUSE
WASHINGTON
May 22, 1992

Memorandum for Jim Jukes

From: Betsy Anderson
           Todd Buchholz

Subject: Digital Telephony—Cost-Benefit Analysis

The draft DoJ cost-benefit analysis that has been circulated appears to be a good start toward providing to Congress a thorough and defensible estimate of the costs and benefits of this legislation. We do, however, have several concerns with the current draft:

- The analysis does not appear to address comprehensively on the *cost* side a number of assessments required by the President's memorandum of April 29, e.g., impact on consumers; effect on U.S. employment, inflation, international competitiveness and economic growth; and federal government outlays and revenues. It would appear that in order to address some of the issues, there will have to be a discussion of who bears the cost of this legislation.
- The benefits analysis assumes that, in the absence of this legislation, *no* electronic surveillance will be possible in the future and no convictions will be obtained in the absence of such surveillance. These assumptions are inconsistent with statements in the costs analysis, e.g., "Realistically, not every electronic surveillance interception involves a situation where these enhanced features of digital subscribes services would be encountered" (p. 13) and the discussion of PBX access in the third paragraph on p. 15.

---

* Obtained in December 1993, through a Freedom Of Information Act (FOIA) request by Computer Professionals for Social Responsibility.

The analysis should make consistent assumptions with respect to both costs and benefits. The benefits analysis should reflect clearly that only some cases involve electronic surveillance; that some surveillance could continue in the absence of this legislation (at least for some period of years); and that some convictions could probably still be obtained absent surveillance.

The paper needs a detailed analysis of the cost assumptions, including how fast the new technologies are coming on-line and the expected percentage of surveillance operations that would be obstructed by year.

- The analysis does not consider the existence of or the potential for other forms of surveillance that might compensate for the reduction in telephone wiretapping capabilities.
- No specific exemptions or waivers are provided in the draft bill. Nevertheless, the costs analysis assumes that:
  — Implementation costs will be diminished or stretched out over time because government officials will allow providers to download software modifications as needed. How does that square with the bill's requirements that all providers "shall comply" by the deadlines set forth in the bill? Is a drafting fix required?
  — Justice notes that it will likely grant waivers or exemptions to certain providers, but specifically declines to so in the legislation. It therefore seems that the cost analysis must attempt to estimate costs *absent* such exemptions or waivers since they are not guaranteed.
- On p. 4 and p. 6 certain figures representing "prevented potential economic loss" are cited. Please explain what losses are encompasses in those figures and how they are calculated.
- On p. 10 there is a statement that the economic harm due to drug use ultimately defies quantification. Just above that statement, an HHS estimate that purports to do precisely that is cited.
- It is unclear whether the administrative costs estimate on pp. 17–18 includes not only DoJ's costs, but also those to be incurred by DoC and FCC during the consultation process.
- On p. 16, the estimate of private sector costs for seeking waivers or exemptions says legal costs for waiver petitions could "typically range from $3,000 to $5,000 based on FCC-related actions." Given lawyers' fees, that would appear to be based on the assumption that it is a simple, uncontested waiver that was granted. What if appealed or based on technology development problems that are complex and require more extensive briefing, discussion with regulators and lawyer time? Is this an accurate estimate for costs of exemption petitions on behalf of an industry sector as well?

## 7

Digital Telephony—Cost-Benefit Analysis*

David McIntosh, James Gattuso

OFFICE OF THE VICE PRESIDENT
WASHINGTON
May 22, 1992

Memorandum for Jim Jukes

From: David McIntosh
          James Gattuso

Re: Digital Telephony

The draft **DOJ** cost-benefit analysis looks like a very good start toward getting the economic analysis we need to get this bill through. We don't see any reason to hold up this bill. There are several specific areas which we think need to be further explored in the RIA (some of which could be addressed by changes in the bill language):

1. The estimates of benefits seems to assume that without this legislation law enforcement agencies would have no ability to intercept communications. Yet, at least in the short term, new technologies would only partially reduce interception capabilities. Should the figures for benefits therefore be reduced, perhaps based on the amount of digital technology now in the system and the amount expected in the future?

2. The analysis assumes that new software would need to be loaded only in those switches for which a court order has been entered. This makes sense, but the language of the bill could be read to require all switches to be modified. Should the bill be amended to make clear that not all switches would need to be modified?

3. The analysis states that only a small number of **PBX** switches currently preclude surveillance, but provides no figures on how large this number may be. Because there is no guarantee that operators

---

* Obtained in December 1993, through a Freedom Of Information Act (FOIA) request by Computer Professionals for Social Responsibility.

of those systems will receive waivers, shouldn't these figures be included in an "upper bound" estimate of the cost of the bill? Alternatively, the language of the bill could be changed to make clearer the circumstances under which exemptions and waivers would be granted.

4. The analysis assumes little or no cost to emerging technologies, assuming that the necessary changes could be incorporated into the design process. However, there could be significant opportunity costs imposed if the new requirements delay the development process, or foreclose the use of other features. Could we determine whether such costs exist and what their magnitude could be?

5. In several places in the analysis, figures are cited without reference to their source or to how they were derived. For example, on p. 4 a figure of $1.8 billion is cited for potential economic loss. On p. 13 "industry consultants" are cited for the cost of loading new software into switches. Could more information be provided here?

6. Aside from the discussion of **PBX** costs, the draft includes no discussion of the cost to private telecommunications networks (private microwave networks, etc). Couldn't this be included in some way?

## 8

Digital Telephony—Cost-Benefit Analysis*

Ron Levy,
Treasury Department

May 26, 1992

Memorandum for	Doug Steiger, OMB Legislative Analyst
From:	Ron Levy, Treasury Attorney Adviser
Re:	DOJ's Cost Analysis, Digital Telephony

The following comments are from our Office of the Assistant Secretary for Economic Policy:

General Comment:

It is difficult at best to do a critical analysis of DOJ's cost benefit package without a full explanation of how DOJ arrived at its cost/benefit figures, and what costs and benefits were included in those figures. It is not clear that DOJ knows, or could know, all the costs and benefits involved, but this should be clearly stated.

Specific Comments:

Page 1, paragraph 3, line 5: Is "$150–$250 million" a total cost, or a one time cost. Both could be correct, but it should be stated.

Page 3, bottom, tick 2; Page 4, top, tick 1; and page 10, 4th line from the bottom: Is the "Illwind" figure ($584,502,243) on page 10 included in the total of tick 2 ($295,851,162) and tick 1($331,861,045) [pages 3 and 4 respectively]? If yes, then 90% of the fines and recoveries contemplated by the bill come from "Illwind." If no, should there be a

---

* Obtained in December 1993, through a Freedom Of Information Act (FOIA) request by Computer Professionals for Social Responsibility.

separate tick on either pages 3 or 4. In either event, a explanation is required.

Page 4, top, tick 2: How was the $1,862,414,937 figure arrived at? What, for example does it include? Is this net of the costs of preventing potential economic losses, *i.e.* have the costs of preventing economic losses been subtracted out? Here too a better explanation is required.

Ron

## CHAPTER 6

CIVIL LIBERTIES

SAFEGUARDING PRIVACY (AND MORE) IN A DIGITAL, TAPPABLE AGE

This chapter presents the civil liberties aspects of the encryption policy debate. Issues include who is empowered to develop and disseminate encryption technology and balancing between individual liberties and government effectiveness in a world where a perfect crime is mathematically possible through cryptography.

Diffie leads off this chapter with an analysis of the effect of a *secret* cryptographic standard on individual rights and technology development. He is concerned about the effect this has on innovation in the computer and communications industries, and claims that the public (not government) cryptographic community has been the principal source of innovation in cryptography; he does not want to hobble this innovation. He urges that all aspects of Clipper be made public, not only to expose them to public scrutiny but also to guarantee that once made available as standards they will not be prematurely withdrawn by an all-powerful agency. He observes that "law, technology, and economics . . . must all be kept in harmony if freedom is to be secure" and wants rights (such as that to have a private conversation) recognized by law to be supported rather than undermined by technology.

The second article, written by Bulkeley for the *Wall Street Journal*, describes the development of PGP and the legal implications for Phil Zimmermann, its author, who has come under pressure from the U. S. government for the unregulated distribution of strong encryption. It goes on to discuss the wide availability of cryptographic material in the world today and presents Zimmermann's attitudes towards this situation.

The extent of industry opposition to the Clipper proposal can be seen in the letter of the Digital Privacy and Security Working Group to

President Clinton. The signers represent a broad cross-section of the American computer community.

The American Civil Liberties Union (ACLU), in a position statement to the Computer System Security and Privacy Advisory Board in reaction to the announcement of the Clipper Chip proposal, expressed a concern that the rights protected under the First, Fourth, and Fifth Amendments of the U. S. Constitution may be violated. They implicitly call for an appropriate cost/benefit analysis, pointing out that "neither law enforcement or national security can be protected at any cost". They also assert that the present system of export controls on cryptography is unconstitutional, a point apparently agreed to by an assistant attorney general in a 1978 government memo (see page 537).

Froomkin sees the issue as less clear, however. As he points out, "the rights of private non-commercial users appear to be a distressingly close question given the current state of civil rights doctrine and the great importance that the courts give to law enforcement and national security." Following this paper, Chandler, Arrington, Gill, and Berkelhammer then examine the legal questions behind U. S. controls on encryption technology, and specifically export and import controls.

To show that the public welfare may indeed be threatened by too much and too good cryptography available to the general public, we present an example of the criminal sophistication that is possible with today's technology: Von Solms and Naccache provide a mathematical formulation of the undetectable electronic crime using cryptographic techniques. The reader, and the populace, will have to judge whether the scepter of enough of these is so likely and so threatening that diminution of some other civil liberties is warranted.

The Impact of a Secret Cryptographic Standard on Encryption, Privacy, Law Enforcement and Technology*

Whitfield Diffie

I'd like to begin by expressing my thanks to Congressman Boucher, the other members of the committee, and the committee staff for giving us the opportunity to appear before the committee and express our views.

On Friday, the 16th of April, a sweeping new proposal for both the promotion and control of cryptography was made public on the front page of the New York Times and in press releases from the White House and other organizations.

This proposal was to adopt a new cryptographic system as a federal standard, but at the same time to keep the system's functioning secret. The standard would call for the use of a tamper resistant chip, called Clipper, and embody a 'back door' that will allow the government to decrypt the traffic for law enforcement and national security purposes.

So far, available information about the chip is minimal and to some extent contradictory, but the essence appears to be this: When a Clipper chip prepares to encrypt a message, it generates a short preliminary signal rather candidly entitled the Law Enforcement Exploitation Field. Before another Clipper chip will decrypt the message, this signal must be fed into it. The Law Enforcement Exploitation Field or LEEF is tied to the key in use and the two must match for decryption to be successful. The LEEF in turn, when decrypted by a government held key that is unique to the chip, will reveal the key used to encrypt the message.

The effect is very much like that of the little keyhole in the back of the combination locks used on the lockers of school children. The children open the locks with the combinations, which is supposed to keep the other children out, but the teachers can always look in the lockers by using the key.

---

* 11 May 1993. Hearings before the Subcommittee on Telecommunications and Finance of the Committee on Energy and Commerce, House of Representatives, 103RD Congress, 1ST Sesion, April 29 and June 9, 1993, Serial No. 103–53, pp. 111–116.

In the month that has elapsed since the announcement, we have studied the Clipper chip proposal as carefully as the available information permits. We conclude that such a proposal is at best premature and at worst will have a damaging effect on both business security and civil rights without making any improvement in law enforcement.

To give you some idea of the importance of the issues this raises, I'd like to suggest that you think about what are the most essential security mechanisms in your daily life and work. I believe you will realize that the most important things any of you ever do by way of security have nothing to do with guards, fences, badges, or safes. Far and away the most important element of your security is that you recognize your family, your friends, and your colleagues. Probably second to that is that you sign your signature, which provides the people to whom you give letters, checks, or documents with a way of proving to third parties that you have said or promised something. Finally you engage in private conversations, saying things to your loved ones, your friends, or your staff that you do not wish to be overheard by anyone else.

These three mechanisms lean heavily on the physical: face to face contact between people or the exchange of written messages. At this moment in history, however, we are transferring our medium of social interaction from the physical to the electronic at a pace limited only by the development of our technology. Many of us spend half the day on the telephone talking to people we may visit in person at most a few times a year and the other half exchanging electronic mail with people we never meet in person.

Communication security has traditionally been seen as an arcane security technology of real concern only to the military and perhaps the banks and oil companies. Viewed in light of the observations above, however, it is revealed as nothing less than the transformation of fundamental social mechanisms from the world of face to face meetings and pen and ink communication into a world of electronic mail, video conferences, electronic funds transfers, electronic data interchange, and, in the not too distant future, digital money and electronic voting.

No right of private conversation was enumerated in the constitution. I don't suppose it occurred to anyone at the time that it could be prevented. Now, however, we are on the verge of a world in which electronic communication is both so good and so inexpensive that intimate business and personal relationships will flourish between parties who can at most occasionally afford the luxury of traveling to visit each other. If we do not accept the right of these people to protect the privacy of their communication, we take a long step in the direction of a world in which privacy will belong only to the rich.

The import of this is clear: The decisions we make about communication security today will determine the kind of society we live in tomorrow.

The objective of the administration's proposal can be simply stated:

They want to provide a high level of security to their friends, while being sure that the equipment cannot be used to prevent them from spying on their enemies.

Within a common society like the military, a mechanism of this sort that allows soldiers' communications to be protected from the enemy, but not necessarily from the Inspector General, is an entirely natural objective. Its imposition on a free society, however, is quite another matter.

Let us begin by examining the monitoring requirement and ask both whether it is essential to future law enforcement and what measures would be required to make it work as planned.

Eavesdropping, as its name reminds us, is not a new phenomenon. But in spite of the fact that police and spies have been doing it for a long time, it has acquired a whole new dimension since the invention of the telegraph. Prior to electronic communication, it was a hit or miss affair. Postal services as we know them today are a fairly new phenomenon and messages were carried by a variety of couriers, travelers, and merchants. Sensitive messages in particular did not necessarily go by standardized channels. Paul Revere, who is generally remembered for only one short ride, was the American Revolution's courier, traveling routinely from Boston to Philadelphia with his saddle bags full of political broadsides.

Even when a letter was intercepted, opened, and read, there was no guarantee, despite some people's great skill with flaps and seals, that the victim would not notice the intrusion.

The development of the telephone, telegraph, and radio have given the spies a systematic way of intercepting messages. The telephone provides a means of communication so effective and convenient that even people who are aware of the danger routinely put aside their caution and use it to convey sensitive information. Digital switching has helped eavesdroppers immensely in automating their activities and made it possible for them to do their listening a long way from the target with negligible chance of detection.

Police work was not born with the invention of wiretapping and at present the significance of wiretaps as an investigative tool is quite limited. Even if their phone calls were perfectly secure, criminals would still be vulnerable to bugs in their offices, body wires on agents, betrayal by co-conspirators who saw a brighter future in cooperating with the police, and ordinary forensic inquiry.

Moreover, cryptography, even without intentional back doors, will no more guarantee that a criminal's communications are secure than the Enigma guaranteed that German communications were secure in World War II. Traditionally, the richest source of success in communications intelligence is the ubiquity of busts: failures to use the equipment correctly.

Even if the best cryptographic equipment we know how to build is available to them, criminal communications will only be secure to the degree that the criminals energetically pursue that goal. The question thus becomes, "If criminals energetically pursue secure communications, will a government standard with a built in inspection port stop them?"

It goes without saying that unless unapproved cryptography is outlawed, and probably even if it is, users bent on not having their communications read by the state will implement their own encryption. If we require them to forgo a broad variety of approved products, it will be an expensive route taken only by the dedicated, but this sacrifice does not appear to be necessary.

The law enforcement function of the Clipper system, as it has been described, is not difficult to bypass. Users who have faith in the secret Skipjack algorithm and merely want to protect themselves from compromise via the Law Enforcement Exploitation Field, need only encrypt that one item at the start of transmission. In many systems, this would require very small changes to supporting programs already present. This makes it likely that if Clipper chips become as freely available as has been suggested, many products will employ them in ways that defeat a major objective of the plan.

What then is the alternative? In order to guarantee that the government can always read Clipper traffic when it feels the need, the construction of equipment will have to be carefully controlled to prevent non-conforming implementations. A major incentive that has been cited for industry to implement products using the new standard is that these will be required for communication with the government. If this strategy is successful, it is a club that few manufacturers will be able to resist. The program therefore threatens to bring communications manufacturers under an all encompassing regulatory regime.

It is noteworthy that such a regime already exists to govern the manufacture of equipment designed to protect unclassified but sensitive government information, the application for which Clipper is to be mandated. The program, called the Type II Commercial COMSEC Endorsement Program, requires facility clearances, memoranda of agreement with NSA, and access to secret 'Functional Security Requirements Specifications.' Under this program member companies submit designs to NSA and refine them in an iterative process before they are approved for manufacture.

The rationale for this onerous procedure has always been, and with much justification, that even though these manufacturers build equipment around approved tamper resistant modules analogous to the Clipper chip, the equipment must be carefully vetted to assure that it provides adequate security. One requirement that would likely be imposed on conforming Clipper applications is that they offer no alternative or additional encryption mechanisms.

Beyond the damaging effects that such regulation would have on innovation in the communications and computer industries, we must also consider the fact that the public cryptographic community has been the principal source of innovation in cryptography. Despite NSA's undocumented claim to have discovered public key cryptography, evidence suggests that, although they may have been aware of the mathematics, they entirely failed to understand the significance. The fact that public key is now widely used in government as well as commercial cryptographic equipment is a consequence of the public community being there to show the way.

Farsightedness continues to characterize public research in cryptography, with steady progress toward acceptable schemes for digital money, electronic voting, distributed contract negotiation, and other elements of the computer mediated infrastructure of the future.

Even in the absence of a draconian regulatory framework, the effect of a secret standard, available only in a tamper resistant chip, will be a profound increase in the prices of many computing devices. Cryptography is often embodied in microcode, mingled on chips with other functions, or implemented in dedicated, but standard, microprocessors at a tiny fraction of the tens of dollars per chip that Clipper is predicted to cost.

What will be the effect of giving one or a small number of companies a monopoly on tamper resistant parts? Will there come a time, as occurred with DES, when NSA wants the standard changed even though industry still finds it adequate for many applications? If that occurs will industry have any recourse but to do what it is told? And who will pay for the conversion?

One of the little noticed aspects of this proposal is the arrival of tamper resistant chips in the commercial arena. Is this tamper resistant part merely the precursor to many? Will the open competition to improve semiconductor computing that has characterized the past twenty-years give way to an era of trade secrecy? Is it perhaps tamper resistance technology rather than cryptography that should be regulated?

Recent years have seen a succession of technological developments that diminish the privacy available to the individual. Cameras watch us in the stores, x-ray machines search us at the airport, magnetometers look to see that we are not stealing from the merchants, and databases record our actions and transactions. Among the gems of this invasion is the British Rafter technology that enables observers to determine what station a radio or TV is receiving. Except for the continuing but ineffectual controversy surrounding databases, these technologies flourish without so much as talk of regulation.

Cryptography is perhaps alone in its promise to give us more privacy rather than less, but here we are told that we should forgo this technical benefit and accept a solution in which the government will retain the power to intercept our ever more valuable and intimate communications and will allow that power to be limited only by policy.

In discussion of the FBI's Digital Telephony Proposal—which would have required communication providers, at great expense to themselves, to build eavesdropping into their switches—it was continually emphasized that wiretaps were an exceptional investigative measure only authorized when other measures had failed. Absent was any sense that were the country to make the proposed quarter billion dollar investment in intercept equipment, courts could hardly fail to accept the police argument that a wiretap would save the people thousands of dollars over other options. As Don Cotter, at one time director of Sandia National Laboratories, said in respect to military strategy "Hardware makes policy."

Law, technology, and economics are three central elements of society that must all be kept in harmony if freedom is to be secure. An essential element of that freedom is the right to privacy, a right that cannot be expected to stand against unremitting technological attack. Where technology has the capacity to support individual rights, we must enlist that support rather than rejecting it on the grounds that rights can be abused by criminals. If we put the desires of the police ahead of the rights of the citizens often enough, we will shortly find that we are living in police state. We must instead assure that the rights recognized by law are supported rather than undermined by technology.

At NSA they believe in something they call 'security in depth.' Their most valuable secret may lie encrypted on a tamper resistant chip, inside a safe, within a locked office, in a guarded building, surrounded by barbed wire, on a military base. I submit to you that the most valuable secret in the world is the secret of democracy; that technology and policy should go hand in hand in guarding that secret; that it must be protected by security in depth.

RECOMMENDATIONS

There is a crying need for improved security in American communication and computing equipment and the Administration is largely correct when it blames the problem on a lack of standards. One essential standard that is missing is a more secure conventional algorithm to replace DES, an area of cryptography in which NSA's expertise is probably second to none.

I urge the committee to take what is good in the Administration's proposal and reject what is bad.

- The Skipjack algorithm and every other aspect of this proposal should be made public, not only to expose them to public scrutiny but to guarantee that once made available as standards they will not be prematurely withdrawn. Configuration control techniques pioneered by the public community can be used to verify that some pieces of equipment conform to government standards stricter than the commercial where that is appropriate.

- I likewise urge the committee to recognize that the right to private conversation must not be sacrificed as we move into a telecommunicated world and reject the Law Enforcement Exploitation Function and the draconian regulation that would necessarily come with it.

- I further urge the committee to press the Administration to accept the need for a sound international security technology appropriate to the increasingly international character of the world's economy.

Genie Is Out of the Bottle*

William M. Bulkeley

BOULDER, Colo.—During the battle between Boris Yeltsin and the Russian Parliament lat October, with Russian freedom hanging in the balance, software author Philip Zimmermann received an electronic-mail message from Latvia. "If dictatorship takes over Russia," it read, "your PGP is widespread from Baltic to Far East now and will help democratic people if necessary. Thanks."

PGP—for Pretty Good Privacy—is a program written by Mr. Zimmermann for scrambling computer messages. Dissidents around the world use it to protect their electronic communications from the prying eyes of secret police.

But PGP has a darker side. In Sacramento, Calif., police lament that last year PGP encryption blocked them from reading the computer diary of a convicted pedophile and finding critical links in a suspected child-pornography ring.

Admired by freedom lovers and criminals alike, PGP is one more thing: uncrackable, or as close to it as a secret code has ever been. Even U.S. government snoopers can't break it. And that places Mr. Zimmermann—a paunchy, bearded, 40-year old computer consultant who is fast becoming a folk hero on the information highway—in peril.

A federal grand jury in San Jose, Calif., is examining whether he broke laws against exporting encryption codes. The Federal Bureau of Investigation suspects that Mr. Zimmermann has a role in putting PGP on the Internet, the world-wide web of computer networks, making it easy for foreign governments and terrorists to use it and render their computer traffic impervious to U.S. spying.

Mr. Zimmermann's lawyer says his client could face charges carrying a prison sentence of up to 51 months.

The world-wide use of Mr. Zimmermann's software has altered forever notions of government surveillance, electronic privacy and export bans on cryptography. Until recently, difficult codes could always be deciphered by stealing the key that unraveled the encryption puzzle. During World War II, for example, the Allies captured a German encrypting Enigma machine, allowing them to crack Nazi communica-

---

tions. U.S. convoys taking munitions to Britain used it to elude German U-boats.

KEYS ARE THE KEY

But PGP, like a growing number of encryption programs, takes advantage of a new, mathematically sophisticated encrypting technology that requires two different keys, both of which are necessary to unlock the puzzle. The sender need only one to send a message. The receiver decodes the message with the second key—which never needs to leave his computer, where it can be protected by passwords from easy pilfering. Although the mathematics are daunting, the program makes the process quick and straightforward.

In an age when computers can whip up codes of devilish complexity and zip them around the globe for anyone with a personal computer, the lot of the encryption policeman is not a happy one. The Internet alone reaches 20 million people.

"The genie is out of the bottle," says Leonard Mikus, president of ViaCrypt, a Phoenix company that sells a $100 version of PGP in the U.S. "There's no way anybody can stop the technology."

THE PERSONAL TOUCH

The availability world-wide of encryption programs makes export controls "a farce," says Stephen Walker, a former top National Security Agency cryptographer who is now president of Trusted Information Systems Inc., a research firm in Glenwood, Md. He says he knows European government officials who use PGP for their personal e-mail. "We have to recognize what's out there."

Mr. Zimmermann, twice-arrested anti-nuclear-war activist, became an electronic-freedom fighter in 1990. At that time, the FBI and the NSA were pushing for a law that would ban certain forms of encryption, and force computer makers to build into their machines hardware that would allow law-enforcement agencies to decipher any code that was used. The proposal outrages confidentiality-minded corporations and computer users alike. Eventually, it was dropped.

But while the issue was still open, Mr. Zimmermann took it upon himself to thwart the government's purpose by working on what came to be PGP—an impenetrable code that could be used by virtually anyone. "I did it to inoculate the body politic" from the danger of government prying, he says.

Mr. Zimmermann stopped consulting and holed up in the computer-filled workroom in the back of a bungalow in Boulder, where he lives with his wife and two children. He says he spent six months of 12-hour days writing the program, drained his family's savings and missed five months of mortgage payments. He finished the program in June 1991, and named it Pretty Good Privacy—in deference to Ralph's Pretty Good Grocery in humorist Garrison Keillor's Prairie Home Companion radio show.

When Mr. Zimmermann was through, he gave the encryption program to friends. One of them, whom he won't identify, placed it on the Internet sometime around June or July 1991, he says. Once there, any computer user in the world with access to the Internet could download it. Almost immediately, many did.

But federal laws covering munitions prohibit exporting encryption software without a license. A year ago, U.S. Customs Service agents asked Mr. Zimmermann how his software went overseas. In September the U.S. Attorney's office in San Jose, which has expertise on computer crimes because of its proximity to Silicon Valley, told Mr. Zimmermann he was a target of an investigation. Mr. Zimmermann says he neither sent PGP overseas nor posted it on computer systems.

PATENTED MATH

RSA Data Security Inc. is also angry at Mr. Zimmermann. The computer-security firm says that in creating PGP, Mr. Zimmermann used one of its patented cryptographic algorithms with out permission, after RSA had denied him a free license.

"We sometimes joke that PGP stands for 'Pretty Good Piracy,'" says James Bidzos, president of the Redwood City, Calif., firm. "What he did was simple. In this business, you simply don't rip off people's intellectual property." RSA, which sells its technology to most of the major software makers and makes an encryption program called MailSafe, hasn't sued Mr. Zimmermann. But it has asserted its legal rights in letters to anyone it catches using PGP. As a result, few companies use PGP and many universities and commercial on-line services keep it off their computers.

Mr. Zimmermann says that technically he hasn't violated RSA patents because he didn't sell the software until he signed the deal with ViaCrypt, which does have a license to use the algorithm. He notes that the on-line documentation for PGP suggests that people who use the program should contact RSA about a license.

For many individuals, PGP has become something of a standard for encrypted e-mail on the Internet. A Glendale, Calif., college student who goes by the name of Monk on the Internet says, "It's free; it's solid; it promotes privacy. How can you argue with it?" While the NSA wants to keep control of encryption, "This teeny little company with a wonderful hero has changed that," says Thomas Lipscomb, president of InfoSafe Corp., a New York developer of security devices for CD-ROM publishers.

AN INTERNET CULT

Fear that hackers may intercept e-mail has spawned a grass-roots cult of PGP users in the Internet community. Craig McKie, a sociology professor at Carleton University in Ottawa, encrypts chapters of a new book with PGP as he sends them to his publisher, fearing that otherwise, "a gazillion copies would go flying off into the night." Lance Cottrell, an astronomer at the University of California at San Diego, says he uses PGP to share unpublished observations with collaborators to keep others from claim-jumping a discovery.

PGP also helps make the otherwise leaky Internet safe for commerce. Members of the Electronic Frontier Foundation, a group that advocates electronic free speech, can pay dues by sending PGP-encrypted credit-card numbers over computer networks. S. Soloway Inc., a Palo Alto, Calif., accounting firm, scrambles backup tapes with PGP, so that clients needn't worry about lost confidentiality if the tapes are lost or stolen. Kenneth Bass, a Washington lawyer, communicates with some clients and other attorneys in PGP code.

For human-rights advocates, the consequences of compromised sources can be devastating. Daniel Salcedo, who works for the Human Rights Project of the American Association for the Advancement of Science in Washington teaches activists in El Salvador and Guatemala to use PGP. "In this business, lots of people have been killed," Mr. Salcedo says.

Alan Dawson, a writer living in Thailand, says rebels opposing the regime in neighboring Burma are using PGP to encrypt information sent among rebel groups. Before use of PGP became widespread, Mr. Dawson wrote Mr. Zimmermann, "captured documents have resulted directly in arrests, including whole families, and their torture and death."

COMPUTER FORENSICS

But investigators say PGP and other encryption systems aid crime. William Spernow, a computer-crime specialist with Search Group, a federally funded police-training firm in Sacramento, Calif., predicts criminals will routinely encrypt information within two years. "This could signal the end of computer forensics before it even gets off the ground," he says.

Mr. Bidzos of RSA says he has had several calls from police in the Miami area asking for help in decrypting information on computers seized in drug raids. He says the encryption is unbreakable. Mr. Spernow studied one case where a criminal conducted a fraud by keeping a double set of books—the real set encrypted in PGP.

Mr. Zimmermann says he is disturbed by criminal use of encryption, but thinks the benefit of providing electronic privacy to everyone outweighs the costs. "It is impossible to obtain real privacy in the information age without good cryptography," he says.

Encryption also raises some eyebrows inside corporations. Mr. Bass, the Washington lawyer, notes that most companies assert a right to read employees' e-mail since it is composed on their computers and travels their networks. "What will they do when people start encrypting messages to each other?" he asks.

Without e-mail encryption, widespread surveillance would be easier. In theory, CIA, FBI and police computers could tap telephone cables and look for key words such as "missile" or "bomb" to find people who needed closer watching. Mr. Zimmermann says: "This is analogous to drift-net fishing."

Computerized encryption "is a technology that for a change benefits our civil liberties," he adds. "The government law-enforcement agencies have benefitted from many technologies," such as telephones that made wire-tapping undetectable. In fact, Mr. Zimmermann is currently seeking funding for a project to create a phone that uses a personal computer equipped with a microphone and a speaker, to encrypt voice conversations just as PGP encrypts data exchanges.

CHILDHOOD SECRETS

Mr. Zimmermann has been suspicious of the government for a long time. After growing up in Boca Raton, Fla., where a children's book on secret writing first interested him in codes, he moved to Boulder in 1978 and worked as a computer engineer. After he was laid off by Storage Technology Corp. in 1985, along with 3,000 others, he became a consultant specializing in telecommunications and data security.

In the 1980s he became worried about the nuclear-arms race. He and his wife investigated moving to New Zealand. But they stayed in Boulder, an antiwar hotbed, where he lectured on arms policy.

Mr. Zimmermann says he has not been active on the Internet and adds, "I'm not a cipherpunk—I wear a suit when I visit clients." But he says he agrees with the electronic free-speech ideals of the cipherpunks, the Internet habitues who fill cyberspace with blistering criticisms about the U.S. government's proposal to promote use of the so-called "Clipper chip." The chip would let companies and individuals encrypt sensitive communications, but the government would hold a key making it possible—with court permission—to decipher them for law-enforcement or national-security purposes.

Mr. Zimmermann thinks the Clipper project confirms the need for PGP by showing the government's desire to read electronic mail. "They're treating us like an enemy foreign population," he says.

## 3

DPSWG Letter to President Clinton on Clipper

Digital Privacy and Security Working Group

May 7, 1993

The President
The White House
Washington, D.C. 20500

Dear Mr. President:

On April 16 you initiated a broad industry/government review of privacy and cryptography policies. We applaud your efforts to develop a greater understanding of these complex issues. With the end of the Cold War and the rapid evolution of technology in the computer and communications industries, a comprehensive review of our communications security policies such as you have directed is sorely needed. As the world becomes linked by a myriad of interconnected digital networks, and computer and communications technologies converge, both government and the private sector need to evaluate information security and privacy issues. Of course, any overall policy must recognize the authorized law enforcement and national security needs, and must evaluate the impact on American competitiveness.

The Digital Privacy and Security Working Group—a coalition of communications and computer companies and associations, and consumer and privacy advocates—was formed almost a decade ago when Congress undertook a review of technology and security policy. That review led to the Electronic Communications Privacy Act of 1986. Subsequently, many members of the Working Group served on the Privacy and Technology Task Force that Senator Leahy charged with examining these and similar issues in 1991.

While we recognize the importance of authorized national security and law enforcement needs, we believe that there are fundamental privacy and other constitutional rights that must be taken into account when any domestic surveillance scheme is proposed. Moreover, it is unclear how your proposal and the overall review of cryptography policy will impact on U.S. export controls. Over the past two years, the Digital Privacy and Security Working Group has held numerous meetings at which both public and private sector representatives have exchanged technical and legal information with the law enforcement community on just such issues.

In the White House press release of April 16, the Press Secretary stated that you have "directed early and frequent consultations with affected industries . . . and groups that advocate the privacy rights of individuals . . ." Our group of over 50 members—from computer software and hardware firms, to telecommunications companies and energy companies, to the American Civil Liberties Union and the Electronic Frontier Foundation—requests the opportunity to participate in developing policy on the broad range of security and privacy issues being considered, including appropriate encryption techniques. We believe that our membership has the breadth and depth of expertise and experience that would allow us to provide an excellent forum for the development of new policies in these areas.

During the past few weeks, the Working Group has met several times to identify issues that need to be addressed. Several aspects of the Administration's encryption proposal warrant further discussion, including, but not limited to:

- whether a key escrow system will produce the desired law enforcement results
- the level of strength and integrity of the algorithm and the security of the key escrow system;
- the advisability of a government-developed and classified algorithm;
- its practicality and commercial acceptability;
- the effect of the proposal on American competitiveness and the balance of trade;
- possible implications for the development of digital communications; and,
- the effect on the right to privacy and other constitutional rights.

A detailed list of our questions relating to this subject is being prepared to facilitate this dialogue.

We are making our views known to officials within your Administration and Members of Congress as the review begins. We would welcome the opportunity to participate in the review process and look forward to working with you and your Administration on this important issue in the coming months. Representatives of the Digital Privacy and Security Working Group are anxious to meet with your staff at their earliest convenience to establish a consultation process.

Sincerely,

abcd, The Microcomputer Industry Association
Hewlett-Packard Company
Advanced Network & Services, Inc.
IBM
American Civil Liberties Union
Electronic Frontier Foundation
Information Technology Association of America
Apple Computer, Inc.
Information Industry Association
AT&T
Iris Associates
Business Software Alliance
Lotus Development Corporation
Cavanagh Associates, Inc.
McCaw Cellular Communications
Cellular Telephone Industry Association
MCI
Computer Professionals for Social Responsibility
Microsoft Corporation
Computer & Business Equipment Manufacturers Association
RSA Data Security, Inc.
Computer & Communications Industry Association
Software Publishers Association
Crest Industries, Inc.
Sun Microsystems, Inc.
Digital Equipment Corporation
Toolmaker, Inc.
EDUCOM
Trusted Information Systems
Electronic Mail Association
United States Telephone Association

Cryptographic Issue Statements: Letter to the Computer System Security and Privacy Advisory Board*

American Civil Liberties Union

The American Civil Liberties Union (ACLU) submits the following comments to the Computer System Security and Privacy Advisory Board in response to its pre-publication notice of comments dated May 13, 1993, regarding the Administration's "Clipper Chip" proposal.

The ACLU is a non-profit, private organization with over 275,000 members dedicated to the preservation of the Bill of Rights. The ACLU has long worked to protect civil rights and civil liberties, including the rights of privacy and free speech.

The following comments are not exhaustive, but were prepared in the very short time period between the solicitation for these comments and their due date. The issues raised are both numerous and complex and thus the comments that follow outline our concerns but do not address them in detail. However, we are in the process of working with the Digital Privacy and Security Coalition, comprised of industry and advocacy groups preparing a more thorough, in-depth discussion of the constitutional, legal and policy issues posed by the proposal.

The ACLU is concerned that government policies related to public key encryption in general and to its recently announced Clipper Chip initiative raise serious constitutional problems under the First, Fourth and Fifth Amendments that have been insufficiently addressed in the past. We believe the constitutional questions must be addressed before the initiative goes forward. Further, there are legal issues under the Electronic Communications Privacy Act (ECPA) and public policy concerns to address as well. We start with some basic and perhaps obvious premises that bear repeating.

Recent technological advances permit individuals to communicate faster and more frequently and provide access to enormous amounts of information quickly and cheaply. Such communications and information sharing are fundamental free speech activities protected by the First Amendment whether they take place over new telecommunica-

---

* May 28, 1993.

tions and computer technologies or in code. At the same time, these new technologies threaten to erode individuals' privacy by making possible the rapid and inexpensive amassing of vast amounts of personal information on others that would not have been so easily accessible in the past.

The most simple example is private communications on both computer networks and telephones. While those technologies are vulnerable to interception or overhearing by third parties without the consent of the parties to the communication, it is essential to recognize that the privacy interests in the communications and information are the same and must be equally protected as if the communications were in person or by written letters. In fact, both the U.S. Supreme Court and the Congress has recognized that people do have a reasonable expectation of privacy in most electronic communications (see, *U.S. v. Katz* and the Electronic Communications Privacy Act of 1986).

Indeed, while technology makes such invasions of privacy possible, new technology can also be used to protect such speech and privacy. One of the major ways in which this has been done is through the development of encryption technology that permits individuals to protect the privacy and property of their communications.

We are greatly concerned that the present Clipper Chip initiative does not give adequate recognition to the important constitutional principles at stake, but instead erodes them. As we understand it, the government's objective here is to hold the key to unlock any encrypted voice or data communication. (It appears that the Clipper Chip and Capstone chips together are designed for all voice and data communication.) The Administration defends the proposal as necessary for law enforcement and national security purposes, because otherwise it may find itself in the position of executing a warrant to intercept a communication but being unable to decode encrypted communications on a real time bases or perhaps ever. The Administration presently describes the proposal as "voluntary," claiming that it does not presently seek to outlaw domestic use of encryption where it does not hold the key, but rather intends to use its overwhelming market power to drive out any alternatives.

Nevertheless, the ACLU believes that there are important unresolved issues concerning the degree of government coercion involved in this proposal. It is clear that the government's stated law enforcement objective can only be achieved if it ends up holding the key to substantially all encrypted communications. Otherwise, the government will have access to decipherable communications, but serious law breakers will use other encryption devices to which the government does not hold the keys. Any scheme that is either mandatory or leads to a "de facto" universal standard has constitutional implications. But even the proposal as presently described contains legal restrictions in the form of export controls that would seem to be essential to the government's scheme, as well as the coercive use of overwhelming market power (i.e., through the use of government contracts).

First, the ACLU is disturbed about the process put in place by the Administration by announcing a major new policy initiative which it has already begun to implement without soliciting any prior public comment or review. The timetable that the Administration has announced for fully implementing its proposal is so short as to preclude adequate public study and comment.

Second, while the proposal is described as providing for "escrowed" key systems, in fact, it appears that the "escrow" holders will be either government agencies or agents and therefore, the traditional legal notions of independent escrow agents with fiduciary obligations to both parties will not apply. The term "escrow" would seem to obscure rather than illuminate the government's role here.

Third, while the ACLU recognizes the importance of both effective law enforcement and protecting true national security interests, we have long pointed out that one of the costs of living in a free and democratic society is that neither law enforcement nor national security can be protected at any cost. Some balance must be struck between the two. We do not believe that the government has yet established a sufficient justification for its unprecedented key escrow scheme on either law enforcement or technical grounds. It has not shown that its present inability to decrypt encoded communications or data has had a serious deleterious effect on either law enforcement or national security interests. Nor has it established that this system is the only technical solution: that relying on traditional warrant procedures it would not be able to obtain most of the evidence that it requires.

Fourth, any prohibition on encrypted communications, including one that restricts such communications unless the government holds the key, raises substantial First Amendment problems. Such a prohibition on encrypted speech is a direct restriction on speech and we do not believe that the government may, in effect, ban all encrypted speech, because encrypted speech that is evidence of crime may be unobtainable. There are other First Amendment problems including the issues regarding export controls outlined below as well as the propriety of classifying the algorithm used for the Clipper Chip.

Fifth, there are serious Fourth and Fifth Amendment problems in requiring disclosure of the key to the government in advance of there being probable cause sufficient to entitle the government to seize an encrypted communication and to search and seize the key to such communication. In this connection, we believe that a case has not yet been made about why traditional warrant procedures will be insufficient to obtain evidence of criminal activity when such evidence is encrypted.

We also note that a crucial distinction must be made between sei-zure of encrypted conversations and seizure of encrypted documents or papers. The Fourth Amendment prohibits secret searches of an in-dividual's papers. This means that the government, through the war-rant procedure, must give an individual notice that her papers are to be searched or seized. The law has approved only one exception to the prohibition on secret searches, namely the real-time seizure of conver-sations without notifying the parties that their conversations are being overheard. Even then, under Title III of the U.S. code, they must usually be given subsequent notification. The rationale for this exception is the ephemeral nature of conversations—if the parties knew they were be-ing overheard, they would not have the conversations in the first place. Thus, it is important in evaluating the government's asserted need for a pre-warrant code-breaking ability, to recognize that it has no right to the secret seizure of "papers" or electronically stored documents, but must notify the owner that documents are being seized at the time.

Sixth, the ACLU asserts that the present system of export controls on cryptography is unconstitutional. The government has imposed ex-port controls on cryptography software and algorithms, even when those exist in the public domain and were in no way developed by the government. This technology must meet strict First Amendment stan-dards before imposing such a licensing scheme, which is essentially a prior restraint that operates as censorship. We do not believe those standards have been met.

Moreover, we are distressed that the government appears to take the position that because such speech can be encoded onto a computer disk, it somehow loses First Amendment protection, and can be regu-lated in the same fashion as weapons hardware. The present export system is objectionable on its own and, as an essential element of the Clipper Chip initiative, makes that proposal even more problematic.

Finally, there is the broader aspect of individual privacy rights. The Administration describes the initiative as an effort to protect individual privacy, when in fact its sole purpose is to make sure that all commu-nications are accessible to the government and cannot remain private outside the scope of government decryption.

We appreciate the opportunity to submit these comments. We urge the Advisory Board to recommend to the Administration that the Clip-per Chip initiative be delayed until a serious examination of the legal and policy issues is undertaken and the critical questions resolved. In this regard, we believe it is imperative that the Administration involve the Digital Privacy and Security Coalition in this process. We look for-ward to providing you with more detailed comments in the near future.

5

The Constitutionality of Mandatory Key Escrow—A First Look*

A. Michael Froomkin

Imagine a law requiring a license to use strong cryptography to communicate by electronic means. Licensed users of cryptography must either escrow all session keys or use a LEAF-equivalent to so that the government is able to determine the session key without informing the parties to the communication that an investigation is in progress. Mandatory key escrow could use a hardwired chip key like Clipper, or it could be implemented by software designed to resist tampering by the user.[1] Would such a statute be constitutional?[2]

In an attempt to provide a first approximation of the answer to that question, this essay offers a whirlwind survey of relevant First, Fourth and Fifth amendment doctrines as well as evolving conceptions of the

* Copyright © A. Michael Froomkin, 1994. All rights reserved. Associate Professor, University of Miami School of Law. M.Phil. (Cantab) 1984, J.D. 1987, Yale Law School. Internet: Mfroomki@Umiami.ir.miami.edu. Research for the article of which this extract forms a part was supported by a summer research grant from the University of Miami School of Law. SueAnn Campbell, Nora de la Garza, Yolanda Jones and Brian Williams provided superb library support and Julie Owen provided indefatigable research assistance. I am grateful to Stuart Baker, Tom Baker, Caroline Bradley, Dorothy Denning, Steve Fishbein, Lance Hoffman, Mark Lemly, Jonathan Simon, David Sobel, Cleveland Thorton, Lee Tien, and Eugene Volokh for their comments, corrections, and suggestions.

[1] Trusted Information Systems have proposed a software key escrow protocol to NIST. Telephone Interview with David Balenson, Trusted Information Systems (June 10, 1994). Some of the constitutional questions discussed below arguably might be avoided by saying that since the chip (or commercial software) is produced by a corporation, and it is the corporation which is required to give the government the keys, the ultimate user lacks standing to complain (and, in some cases, the corporation lacks the rights enjoyed by natural persons). Since, however, much encryption takes place in software rather than hardware, and software typically generates new session keys for each communication, the discussion in the text assumes that the end-user, be it a person or a corporation, is the one who will have to give the government the information it seeks. For ease of exposition, the text uses the phrase "chip key" to refer to *any* unique identifying key which allows LEAF-like access to a session key, whether the "chip key" is implemented in hardware or software.

[2] Mandatory key escrow would require federal legislation. *See* Robert D. Poling, Congressional Research Service American Law Division, *Current Legal Authority to Mandate Adoption of "Clipper Chip" Standards By Private Parties* (Oct. 4, 1994). The Computer Security Act applies only to federal computer systems, which are defined to exclude civilian systems (other than those operated by federal contractors for the government's benefit) which contain no classified information.

constitutional right to privacy. The focus of this essay is analytic and predictive rather than prescriptive; it attempts to sketch what, given the current state of the law, the courts would likely make of a mandatory key escrow statute.

FIRST AMENDMENT ISSUES

The First Amendment states that "Congress shall make no law . . . abridging the freedom of speech, or of the press; or the right of the people peaceably to assemble."[3] Scholars debate whether the First Amendment is a means or an end, and if means then to what end.[4] Whether understood as protecting self-realization as an end in itself, or political expression as a means of preserving the political process, conventional First Amendment doctrine offers numerous obstacles to mandatory key escrow. None, strangely, is insurmountable.

Mandatory key escrow affects public debate in three ways. Mandatory key escrow forces users of cryptography to disclose something that they would prefer to keep secret, which amounts to compelled speech. Second, it chills speech by persons who seek to remain either secure or anonymous when speaking, whether for fear of retribution or other reasons. Third, it chills the associational freedom of persons who wish to band together but do not wish to call attention to the fact of their association, or to their participation in a known association.

Compelled Speech

Mandatory disclosure of keys can be viewed as compelled speech, akin to laws requiring disclosure of financial records by charities, and market-sensitive information by publicly traded companies.[5] The U.S. Supreme Court treats compelled disclosure of non-commercial information as akin to a content-based restriction on speech, demanding the

---

[3] U.S. CONST. amend. I.

[4] See generally LAURENCE H. TRIBE, AMERICAN CONSTITUTIONAL LAW § 12–1 (2d ed. 1988). For the view that the most important function of the First Amendment is to promote and protect democracy, see A. MEIKLEJOHN, FREE SPEECH AND ITS RELATION TO SELF-GOVERNMENT (1972).

[5] Whether mandatory key escrow is compelled speech does not turn on how the government gets the keys. Although in the Escrowed Encryption System (EES), Approval of Federal Information Processing Standards Publication 185, Escrowed Encryption Standard (EES), 59 Fed. Reg. 5997 (1994), the keys are provided to the government before the user buys the product, the user is still forced to send a LEAF to use the encryption. Similarly, in software encryption, users will be required to communicate the session key to the government in some fashion.

strictest scrutiny.[6] To pass this test, a regulation must be motivated by a compelling state interest, avoid undue burdens, and be narrowly tailored.[7] Thus, in *Wooley v. Maynard* the Supreme Court struck down a New Hampshire law requiring that automobiles display licence plates bearing the state motto "Live Free or Die."[8] The statute was unconstitutional because the state required citizens to use their private property as mobile billboards for the state's message, even though the state, by allowing cars to carry disclaimers too, compelled no affirmation of belief.[9]

Mandatory key escrow differs from the leading mandatory disclosure cases[10] because the disclosure is not public. Instead, the government says it will keep the chip key secret and will decrypt the LEAF only for good cause. The Supreme Court has stated that mandatory disclosure laws will be sustained only if there is "a 'relevant correlation' or 'substantial relation' between a substantial government interest and the information required to be disclosed."[11] If the state interest in telling donors how charities use their contributions is sufficient to justify a mandatory disclosure statute,[12] then the state interest in crime-fighting and national security should be sufficiently compelling too.[13] Since the government keeps the key in escrow, the rule is more narrowly tailored than a public disclosure rule.[14] The critical question therefore is whether the burdens—forcing the user to utter a LEAF or the equiv-

---

[6] *See* Riley v. National Fed. of the Blind, 487 U.S. 781, 795 (1988). Thus compelled disclosures of fact enjoy the same protection as the compelled expressions of opinion in Wooley v. Maynard, 430 U.S. 705 (1977) and West Virginia State Bd. of Ed. v. Barnette, 319 U.S. 624 (1943). *But see* R. George Wright, *Free Speech and the Mandated Disclosure of Information*, 25 U. RICH. L. REV. 475, 496 (1991) (arguing that a less stringent standard would have been more appropriate in *Riley*).

[7] *Riley*, 487 U.S. at 798.

[8] 430 U.S. 705 (1977).

[9] *Id.* at 720 (Rehnquist, J., dissenting).

[10] In addition to *Wooley, supra*, these include West Virginia State Bd. of Ed. v. Barnette, 319 U.S. 624 (1943) (compulsory flag salute and recital of pledge of allegiance unconstitutional); Miami Herald Publishing Co. v. Tornillo, 418 U.S. 241 (1974) (state law requiring newspaper provide right of reply to political candidates unconstitutional).

[11] Buckley v. Valeo, 424 U.S. 1, 64 (1976); *see also* Gibson v. Florida Legislative Investigation Comm., 372 U.S. 539 (1963).

[12] This was the issue in *Riley*, 487 U.S. 781 (1989).

[13] The Supreme Court described the protection of national security as a compelling state interest in Aptheker v. Secretary of State, 378 U.S. 500, 509 (1964). *See generally* Developments in the Law, *The National Security Interest and Civil Liberties*, 85 HARV. L. REV. 1130 (1972); *but see* National Fed'n of Fed. Employees v. Greenberg, 789 F. Supp. 430, 436 (D.D.C. 1992) ("[S]ecurity concerns do not, under the American system of ordered liberty, ipso facto override all constitutional and privacy considerations. The purpose of national security is to protect American citizens, not to overwhelm their rights."), *vacated*, 983 F.2d 286 (D.C. Cir. 1993).

[14] *See* Ward v. Rock Against Racism, 491 U.S. 781, 799 (1989) (regulation is not narrowly tailored when substantial portion of burden on speech does not advance state's content-neutral goals).

alent and introducing doubt as to the security of what might otherwise be a completely secure system—are worth the gain to national security and law enforcement. This is a value judgment, not one that can easily be settled by doctrinal argument, yet it is one that the courts would have to make to resolve the issue. As with many value judgments, reasonable people may differ on the outcome; the less speculative the claim that harms will flow from allowing promiscuous unescrowed encryption (i.e. the more terrorists who have managed to blow things up because they used secure telephones), the more likely the courts would find that the measure passed strict scrutiny insofar as it compels speech.[15]

Chilling Effect on Speech

Since mandatory key escrow applies to all who use strong encryption, regardless of what they say, it can be considered a content-neutral regulation of speech and association.[16] As such it is subject to an intermediate level of scrutiny involving balancing of interests.[17] Since mandatory key escrow directly regulates a mode of speech, the review will be more searching than it would be if the statute had only an incidental effect on speech.[18]

In practice, the factors that the Supreme Court balances are the extent to which speech is likely to be chilled, the degree to which the prohibition falls unevenly on a particular group as opposed to society at large, and whether there are alternate channels of communication available.[19] It seems evident that speech will be chilled, although ex-

---

[15] *See* TRIBE, *supra* note , at § 12–24.

[16] *See* Turner Broadcasting Sys., Inc. v. FCC, 114 S. Ct. 2445, 2459–61 (1994) (holding that must-carry provision which distinguished between speakers solely by technical means used to carry speech is not a content-based restriction); Clark v. Community for Creative Non-Violence, 468 U.S. 288, 293 (1984); City Council of Los Angeles v. Taxpayers for Vincent, 466 U.S. 789, 804 (1984) (describing anti-sign ordinance as content-neutral); Heffron v. International Soc. for Krishna Consciousness, Inc., 452 U.S. 640, 649 (1981) (holding time, place and manner regulation on all solicitations at state fair to be content-neutral).

[17] The Supreme Court's practice of balancing constitutional rights against public needs has attracted considerable criticism. For a survey of the issues see Symposium, *When is a Line as Long as a Rock is Heavy?: Reconciling Public Values and Individual Rights in Constitutional Adjudication*, 45 HASTINGS L.J. 707 (1994).

[18] *See* David S. Day, *The Incidental Regulation of Free Speech*, 42 U. MIAMI L. REV. 491 (1988); Ned Greenberg, Note, Mendelsohn v. Meese: *A First Amendment Challenge to the Anti-Terrorism Act of 1987*, 39 AM. U. L. REV. 355 (1990); Geoffrey R. Stone, *Content-Neutral Restrictions*, 54 U. CHI. L. REV. 46 (1987).

[19] *See* City of Ladue v. Gilleo, 114 S. Ct. 2038, 2046 (1994); Clark v. Community for Creative Non-Violence, 468 U.S. 288, 293 (1984); Consolidated Edison Co. v. Public Serv. Comm'n, 447 U.S. 530, 535 (1980); TRIBE, *supra* note , § 12–23. The discussion in the text assumes that a court would not find that mandatory key escrow shut down a traditional public forum. Although mandatory key escrow most severely affects private con-

actly how much is uncertain.[20] To the extent that the prohibition falls unevenly on society, it will tend to affect those with access to computers and scrambler telephones. This is not the group whose speech the Court traditionally takes the most care to protect, since wealthy and well-educated people have the greatest access to alternative channels of communication.[21] The critical issue is likely to be whether mandatory key escrow "unduly constricts the opportunities for free expression."[22] Since a mandatory key escrow scheme promises to release keys only with just cause, the Court would likely find the constricting effect to be relatively minor. Ultimately, however, the standard collapses to a balancing test in which distinguishing "due" from "undue" content-neutral restrictions requires highly contextual judgments.

Anonymity and the Freedom of Association

Anonymity is essential for the survival of some dissident movements.[23] Identification requirements "extend beyond restrictions on time and

---

versation, it also affects USENET, which may be a public forum or (in universities, at least) a series of linked public fora, and other bulletin-board services (private fora, *cf.* Allen S. Hammond, IV, *Regulating Broadband Communications Networks*, 9 YALE J. ON REG. 181 (1992)) by making anonymous posting of messages less secure. If a court were to find that mandatory key escrow seriously inhibited a traditional public forum, the court would be likely to find the statute unconstitutional. *See* TRIBE, *supra* note , at § 12–?4

[20] On the use of computers for political speech, see Eric C. Jensen, Comment, *An Electronic Soapbox: Computer Bulletin Boards and the First Amendment*, 39 FED. COMM. L.J. 217 (1987). Leaving aside the special case of anonymous speech, discussed below, the extent to which encrypted speech (e.g. on Clipper telephones) is likely to be chilled is a an empirical question on which it would be difficult to collect evidence. It is hard to measure the number of people who will not use encrypted telephones or email if they are not confident the system is secure; and harder still to measure how their speech changes as a result. A court considering this issue is likely to assume that the government will act legally and decrypt EES communications only when authorized. Courts are unlikely to accept that reasonable people might disagree, although whether they would, and how much, is the central empirical question.

[21] *See* TRIBE, *supra* note , at 979–80 (describing how Court seeks to avoid upholding communicative limits with disproportionate impact on poor, since poor have fewest alternative communication channels).

[22] City of Ladue v. Gilleo, 114 S. Ct. 2038, 2045 n.13 (1994) (quoting Stone, *Content-Neutral Restrictions*, 54 U. CHI. L. REV. 46, 57–58 (1987)); Wayte v. United States, 470 U.S. 598, 611, (1985) (part of test is whether an incidental restriction on alleged First Amendment freedoms is no greater than is essential to the furtherance of that interest); United States v. O'Brien, 391 U.S. 367, 377 (1968) (same).

[23] Talley v. California, 362 U.S. 600 (1960) (striking down statute forbidding distribution of anonymous handbills); TRIBE, *supra* note , at 1019; *see also* Gilmore v. City of Montgomery, 417 U.S. 556, 575 (1974); NAACP v. Alabama *ex rel.* Patterson, 357 U.S. 449, 462 (1958); NAACP v. Button, 371 U.S. 415, 431 (1963); Brown v. Socialist Workers Party, 459 U.S. 87, 91 (1982).
On October 12, 1994, the Supreme Court heard arguments in *McIntyre v. Ohio Elections Commission*, *cert. granted* 63 U.S.L.W. 302 (U.S. July 19, 1994) (No. 93–986). Like *Talley*, the *McIntyre* case concerns the validity of a state statute that imposes flat ban on distribution of anonymous political campaign leaflets. The reader is cautioned that the decision in *McIntyre*, which had not been handed down at press time, may have a very significant impact on the law surveyed in this sub-section.

place—they chill discussion itself."[24] They also can infringe the right of assembly.[25] Cryptography allows unprecedented anonymity both to groups who communicate in complete secrecy and to individuals who, by sending electronic mail through anonymizing remailers, can hide all traces of their identity when they send mail to other persons. Combined with the ability to broadcast messages widely using services such as the Internet, anonymous email may become the modern equivalent of the anonymous handbill.[26] Cryptography thus enhances communicative privacy and anonymity. Key escrow threatens this anonymity in two ways. First, and of greater significance, it makes it possible for eavesdroppers armed with the escrowed key to identify the ultimate source and actual content of encrypted e-mail messages being sent out to anonymous remailers. Second, key escrow makes it possible for eavesdroppers armed with the escrowed key to identify the person to whom the target of a wiretap is speaking; without the key, the only information gleaned would be call setup information, which identifies the telephone on the other end of the conversation.

In the last thirty years, the Supreme Court has struck down several statutes requiring public disclosure of the names of members of dissident groups,[27] stating that "[i]nviolability of privacy in group association may in many circumstances be indispensable to preservation of freedom of association."[28] Nevertheless, the right to privacy in one's political associations and beliefs can be overcome by a compelling state interest.[29] Thus, the Court held that associational freedoms do not

---

[24] Hynes v. Mayor of Oradell, 425 U.S. 610, 626 (1976) (Brennan, J., concurring in part).

[25] *See* Bates v. City of Little Rock, 361 U.S. 516, 522–24 (1960) (holding, on freedom of assembly grounds, that NAACP did not have to disclose membership lists).

[26] A challenge to mandatory key escrow as an infringement of the freedom of association would increase its chances of success if the challengers could demonstrate that mandatory key escrow closes off a channel of anonymous communication that has no true alternative. City of Ladue v. Gilleo, 114 S. Ct. 2038 (1994) (holding that flyers are not a substitute for cheap and convenient signs in front of house). There appears to be no substitute for the anonymous remailer: unlike anonymous leaflets, no one can see an e-mail being created, and thanks to the anonymous remailer, no one can see it being distributed either.

[27] *E.g.*, Talley v. California, 362 U.S. 600 (1960); NAACP v. Alabama *ex rel.* Patterson, 357 U.S. 449 (1958); Shelton v. Tucker, 364 U.S. 479 (1960); Brown v. Socialist Workers Party, 459 U.S. 87 (1982); Hynes v. Mayor of Oradell (Brennan, J., concurring in part) (ID requirement puts impermissible burden on political expression). "[I]t is hardly a novel perception that compelled disclosure of affiliation with groups engaged in advocacy may constitute . . . restraint on freedom of association. "Joint Anti-Fascist Refugee Comm. v. McGrath, 341 U.S. 123, 145 (1951) (Black, J., concurring). *But see* Communist Party of the United States v. SACB, 367 U.S. 1 (1961); New York *ex rel.* Bryant v. Zimmerman, 278 U.S. 63 (1928).

[28] *NAACP*, 357 U.S. at 462.

[29] Brown v. Socialist Workers Party, 459 U.S. at 91–92. The Supreme Court has recently granted certiorari on McIntyre v. Ohio Elections Comm., 618 N.E.2d 152 (Ohio 1993), *cert. granted*, 114 S.Ct. 1047 (1994), in which the Ohio Supreme Court let stand a state statute forbidding the circulation of anonymous leaflets pertaining to the adoption or defeat of a ballot issue.

trump the application of statutes forbidding discrimination in places of public accommodation. In so doing, however, the Court reiterated that the Constitution protects against unjustified government interference with an individual's choice to enter into and maintain intimate or private relationships.[30] As the Court stated in *Rotary International*, two key issues affecting the degree of constitutional protection to be afforded to an association are the degree of intimacy and whether the relationship is conducted "in an atmosphere of privacy" or one where the group seeks to "keep their 'windows and doors open to the whole world.' "[31] Impediments to the right to choose one's associates, including presumably publicity, can violate the First Amendment.[32]

A requirement that group members communicate in a fashion that is accessible to lawful government wiretaps is less intrusive than a requirement that groups publish their membership lists, but some similarity remains. And, a national security/law-enforcement justification for a narrowly tailored limit on associational privacy is likely to be at least as compelling as the state's legitimate desire to root out invidious discrimination. Nevertheless, groups seeking to change the social order in ways likely to be resented by police and others in positions of power will have reason to fear that state actors will find ways to access their keys. Indeed, in *Buckley v. Valeo*[33] and again in *Brown v. Socialist Workers Party*[34] the Supreme Court recognized that minor political parties may be able to show a "reasonable probability" that disclosure of membership information will subject those identified to "threats, harassment, or reprisals"—- including harassment from the government.[35] Ultimately, therefore, the courts again will be left with an essentially non-legal value judgment: whether the interests supporting mandatory key escrow are sufficiently great to justify the increased risk of harassment to political dissidents.

FOURTH AMENDMENT ISSUES

The Fourth Amendment guarantees "[t]he right of the people to be secure in their houses, papers and effects, against unreasonable

---

[30] *See* New York State Club Ass'n, Inc. v. City of New York, 487 U.S. 1 (1988); Board of Dirs. of Rotary Int'l v. Rotary Club of Duarte, 481 U.S. 537 (1987); Roberts v. United States Jaycees, 468 U.S. 609 (1984); Moore v. City of East Cleveland, 431 U.S. 494, 503–04 (1977) (plurality op.) (intimate association).

[31] 481 U.S. at 544–45, 547.

[32] *See id.* at 548; *see also* Citizens Against Rent Control/Coalition for Fair Housing v. City of Berkeley, 454 U.S. 290, 294 (1981).

[33] 424 U.S. 1, 74 (1976).

[34] 459 U.S. 87, 88 (1982).

[35] *Brown*, 459 U.S. at 99–100 (describing "massive" harassment of SWP by FBI).

searches and seizures." It also states that "no Warrants shall issue but upon probable cause ... particularly describing the place to be searched, and the persons or things to be seized."[36]

Americans already acquiesce to substantial invasions of privacy by government fiat, which occurs without a warrant. We disclose personal details of our lives on tax returns. We consent to having our belongings X-rayed, opened, and searched, while our persons are scanned for metal (sometimes followed by a pat-down) as a condition of being allowed to board an airplane or enter some public buildings. The law says the government may paw through a citizen's garbage without a warrant,[37] and she lacks a reasonable expectation of privacy in relation to telephone numbers dialed.[38] The police may overfly her house in a helicopter at 400 feet,[39] and use special cameras to photograph everything below.[40] The government may use satellites to spy in her windows[41]; it may use heat-detection gear to detect excess heat emanations from her chimneys;[42] it may use dogs to sniff her luggage and her per-

---

[36] U.S. CONST. amend. IV.

[37] California v. Greenwood, 486 U.S. 35 (1988); *see also* United States v. Scott, 975 F.2d 927 (1st Cir. 1992) (warrantless seizure and reconstruction of 5/32 inch pieces of shredded documents in trash did not violate Fourth Amendment), *cert. denied sub nom.* Scott v. United States, 113 S. Ct. 1877 (1993); United States v. Comeaux, 955 F.2d 586, 589 (8th Cir.) (warrantless search of garbage within the curtilage of the home permissible because the garbage was readily accessible to the public), *cert. denied sub nom.* Comeaux v. United States, 113 S. Ct. 135 (1992); United States v. Hedrick, 922 F.2d 396 (7th Cir.) (same), *cert. denied sub nom.* Hendrick v. United States, 112 S. Ct. 147 (1991).

[38] *See* Smith v. Maryland, 442 U.S. 735 (1979). The rationale is that the telephone company keeps this information for billing purposes. This is neither necessarily true, nor timelessly true, nor beyond the ability of persons and service providers to change by contract, but it is still the rule.

[39] Florida v. Riley, 488 U.S. 445, 451–52 (1989) (plurality op.); *see also* California v. Ciraolo, 476 U.S. 207, 215 (1986) (warrantless aerial surveillance of yard enclosed by 10 foot fence held valid).

[40] Dow Chem. Co. v. United States, 476 U.S. 227, 239 (1986) (taking aerial photographs of factory with stereoscopic camera from navigable airspace held valid).

[41] *See* Lisa J. Steele, Comment, *The View From on High: Satellite Remote Sensing Technology and the Fourth Amendment*, 6 HIGH TECH. L.J. 317 (1991).

[42] *See* United States v. Pinson, 24 F.3d 1056 (8th Cir. 1994) (holding warrantless use of infrared sensing device did not violate Fourth Amendment because defendant's subjective expectation of privacy in heat emanating from his house was not one that society would find objectively reasonable); United States v. Penny-Feeney, 773 F. Supp. 220 (D. Haw. 1991) (no warrant required for use of infrared sensing device; heat considered a sign that marijuana may be growing within), *aff'd on other grounds sub nom.* United States v. Feeney, 984 F.2d 1053 (9th Cir. 1993); United States v. Kerr, 876 F.2d 1440, 1443–44 (9th Cir. 1989) (not ruling on warrant requirement; absence of heat considered sign of suspiciously good insulation); U.S. v. Domitrovich, 852 F. Supp. 1460 (E.D. Wash. 1994) (no warrant required); United States v. Kyllo, 809 F. Supp. 787 (D. Or. 1992) (infrared sensing is not a "search"); United States v. Deaner, No. 92–0090–01, 1992 U.S. Dist. Lexis 13046 (M.D. Pa. July 27, 1992), *aff'd on other grounds*, 1 F.3d 192 (3d Cir. 1993) (same). *But see* State v. Young, 867 P.2d 593 (Wash. 1994) (holding use of infrared thermal detection device to perform warrantless, surveillance of defendant's home violated Washington Constitution's protection of defendant's private affairs, ban on warrantless invasion of home; and U.S. Constitution Fourth Amendment); United States v.

son.[43] Once the government has arranged for an informant to plant a beeper on a citzen, the government may use the signal to track the citizen's movements.[44] When national security is at risk, many procedural protections that are required in the ordinary course of an investigation go out the window. For example, the government may break into some premises without a warrant to plant a bug on national security grounds, although a warrant would be required in an ordinary criminal investigation.[45] National security wiretap requests go to a secret court which meets in camera and never issues opinions.[46]

On the other hand, mandatory key escrow differs from each of these examples in significant ways, especially when it affects private non-commercial use. Absent exigent circumstances such as fires, hot pursuit or the like, the Supreme Court has yet to approve of a warrantless intrusion into a home occupied by an ordinary taxpayer much less one which has made efforts to shield itself from detection.[47] Except

---

Ishmael, 843 F. Supp. 205, 209–10 (E.D. Tex. 1994) (defendants had reasonable expectation of privacy in building and surrounding property). *Cf.* Lisa J. Steele, *Waste Heat and Garbage: The Legalization of Warrantless Infrared Searches*, 29 CRIM. L. BULL. 19 (1993) (arguing warrant required for use of infrared to determine activity within dwelling).

[43] United States v. Place, 462 U.S. 696 (1983).

[44] United States v. Karo, 468 U.S. 705 (1984); *see also* United States v. Knotts, 460 U.S. 276 (1983) (monitoring signals is not a search); Note, *Tying Privacy in Knotts: Beeper Monitoring and Collective Fourth Amendment Rights*, 71 VA. L. REV. 297 (1985) (criticizing *Knotts* and *Karo* decisions).

[45] *See* In re Application of the United States for an Order Authorizing the Physical Search of Nonresidential Premises and Personal Property (D. FISA), *reprinted in* S. REP. No. 280, 97th Cong., 1st Sess. 16 (1981) (FISA decision). Warrantless wiretaps are authorized by the Foreign Intelligence Surveillance Act, 50 U.S.C.A. § 1802(a) (1991). The President, acting through the Attorney General, may authorize electronic surveillance for up to one year if the surveillance is directed solely at the communications exclusively between or among foreign powers, there is no substantial likelihood of acquiring communication of U.S. citizens, and minimization procedures have been followed. *Id.* 18 U.S.C.A. § 2518(7) (1970 & West Supp. 1994), also permits unwarranted surveillance in an emergency situation involving immediate danger or death or serious physical injury to any persons, conspiratorial activities threatening the national interest, or conspiratorial activities characteristic of organized crime.

[46] All of the court's activities are classified. It is widely believed, however, that the FISA Court, as it is known, has yet to turn down a wiretap request. It is known that not one of the more than 4200 FISA wiretap requests was turned down during the Court's first ten years. The Court did turn down a request for authorization for a break-in, denying it on the dual jurisdictional grounds that the Court lacked the statutory authority to issue such an order and that the President has the inherent authority to order domestic national security surveillance without need of a court order. Americo R. Cinquegrana, *The Walls (and Wires) Have Ears: The Background and First Ten Years of the Foreign Intelligence Surveillance Act of 1978*, 137 U. PA. L. REV. 793, 814, 823 (1989); *see also* SUSAN LANDAU ET AL., ASSOCIATION FOR COMPUTING MACHINERY, CODES, KEYS AND CONFLICTS: ISSUES IN U.S. CRYPTO POLICY 18 (1994) [hereinafter ACM REPORT].

[47] The Supreme Court *has* allowed warrantless searches of homes occupied by parolees, probationers, or welfare recipients. *See infra* text accompanying note . Lower courts have sanctioned two additional exceptions to this rule. First, some courts have approved warrantless national security break-ins (presumably, however, the

for consent to X-rays and searches at airports and public buildings, none of the examples above require the target of the probe to take any action to aid the prober, much less to ensure that the probe is successful; and this exception does not reach into the home.

In principle, warrants are required for all domestic security wiretaps.[48] The next sections describe how the Fourth Amendment also prohibits warrantless mandatory key escrow for private, non-commercial, users of encryption.[49] Commercial and corporate use, however, presents a more difficult question. These uses may not be entitled to Fourth Amendment protection against mandatory key escrow.

The Fourth Amendment Does Not Give the Government an Affirmative Right to an Effective Search

The government's residual prerogative under the Fourth Amendment to make reasonable searches does not give it the power to require that people help it to create the conditions that would make such searches effective, even if the government has valid grounds for the search. The Fourth Amendment does not create rights for the government. It creates rights for the people.[50] Congress's power to criminalize conduct and the Executive's power to enforce the criminal laws of the United States stem from the grants of power in Articles I and II of the Constitution, such as the Commerce Clause and the Necessary and Proper Clause.[51] Those powers are in turn limited by the Bill of Rights, of which the Fourth Amendment is a part.

The absence in the Fourth Amendment of an affirmative grant of power to make effective searches does not, however, determine

---

premises were not specifically designed to resist such break-ins). Second, as described *supra* note , several lower courts have allowed warrantless infra-red inspections of properties, including at least one property that was carefully insulated.

[48] United States v. United States District Court [*Keith*], 407 U.S. 297 (1972) (holding warrantless wiretap violated both Fourth and First Amendment rights).

[49] Fourth Amendment privacy in this context begins with the premise that people have control over who knows what about them, and the right to shape the 'self' that is presented to the world. This control is protected by the Fourth Amendment freedom from unwarranted searches and seizures. TRIBE, *supra* note , at § 15–16, p. 1389–90.

[50] "[T]he purpose of the Fourth Amendment was to protect the people of the United States against arbitrary action by their own Government." United States v. Verdugo-Urquidez, 494 U.S. 259, 266 (1990). *See also* Warden v. Hayden, 387 U.S. 294, 303–04 (1967) (stating that Fourth Amendment serves primarily to protect the right of privacy); O'Connor v. Ortega, 480 U.S. 709, 730 (1987) (Scalia, J., concurring) (same).

[51] Technically, federal courts are involved solely in the adjudication of criminal cases, since they lack jurisdiction to define common law crimes. United States v. Hudson & Goodwin, 11 U.S. (7 Cranch) 32 (1812). Note that Article II is also involved in a different type of enforcement because some searches, at least those against agents of foreign powers operating both in the U.S. and abroad, can be conducted pursuant to the President's national security powers. *See* 18 U.S.C.A. § 2511(3) (1970), *repealed by* Foreign Intelligence Surveillance Act of 1978, 50 U.S.C.A. §§ 1801–11 (1991).

whether the affirmative grants in Articles I and II give the government the power to require that communications be searchable. It simply means that from the Fourth Amendment perspective mandatory key escrow poses strictly traditional problems: Is mandatory key escrow, which takes place without a warrant, a search and seizure?[52] And if so, is it a reasonable warrantless search and seizure, or would a warrant be required?

Mandatory Escrow of a Key Is a "Search or Seizure"

A search is a governmental invasion of a legitimate expectation of personal privacy.[53] Non-consensual searches by the government into matters for which individuals have a (subjectively and objectively) reasonable expectation of privacy ordinarily require a search warrant.[54]

Not every acquisition of information by the government from sources reasonably expected to be private is necessarily a search. For example, the Supreme Court has held that unintrusive means of piercing personal privacy, such as overflights[55] or the use of dogs to sniff for contraband[56] are not searches for Fourth Amendment purposes. Although wiretapping is also unobtrusive, since Olmstead[57] was overturned,[58] there has not been any question that wiretapping is a search or seizure for Fourth Amendment purposes.

Not every search affecting matters reasonably expected to be private necessarily requires a warrant. Examples of legitimate warrantless searches include "administrative searches,"[59] searches incident to valid arrests,[60] exigent circumstances such as the likely destruction of evidence,[61] and border searches.[62] However, absent a specific national se-

---

[52] For an argument that a mandatory key escrow scheme is a search, and thus would violate the particularity requirement of the Fourth Amendment, see Mark I. Koffsky, Comment, *Choppy Waters in the Surveillance Data Stream: The Clipper Scheme and the Particularity Clause*, 9 HIGH TECH. L.J. 131 (1994).

[53] Oliver v. United States, 466 U.S. 170, 177–78 (1984); Katz v. United States 389 U.S. 347, 361 (1967). Items in plain view are not considered private. *See* Horton v. California, 496 U.S. 128, 136–37 (1990); Coolidge v. New Hampshire, 403 U.S. 443 (1971) (plurality op.); *see also* Minnesota v. Dickerson, 113 S. Ct. 2130 (1993) (extending *Horton* rationale to items in "plain touch").

[54] Katz v. United States, 389 U.S. at 357.

[55] Florida v. Riley, 488 U.S. 445, 451–52 (1989) (plurality op.); *see also* California v. Ciraolo, 476 U.S. 207, 215 (1986).

[56] United States v. Place 462 U.S. 696, 707 (1983).

[57] Olmstead v. United States, 277 U.S. 438 (1928).

[58] *See* Katz v. United States; *see also* Berger v. New York, 388 U.S. 41 (1967).

[59] See *infra* text accompanying note .

[60] *See, e.g.*, New York v. Belton, 453 U.S. 454 (1981).

[61] *E.g.*, Cupp v. Murphy, 412 U.S. 291, 294–96 (1973); Schmerber v. California, 384 U.S. 757, 761–77 (1966).

[62] United States v. Montoya de Hernandez, 473 U.S. 531, 537–38 (1985) (entering); California Bankers Ass'n v. Schultz, 416 U.S. 21, 62–63 (1974) (dictum) (leaving); United States v. Martinez-Fuerte, 428 U.S. 543 (1976) (border checkpoints).

curity rationale directly related to the conversation or the speaker, or exigent circumstances, a warrant is required for a wiretap both under the Fourth Amendment and under Title III.

A key is not itself a conversation, however, but the means to decrypt it. Despite this, there should be no doubt that absent government action to force disclosure, a properly guarded key to a cryptographic system would be an item of information for which the user would have both a subjective and objectively reasonable expectation of privacy.[63] Indeed, the entire point of having a cryptographic system is to increase or create privacy. This is especially true in a public-key cryptographic system, where the private key is never disclosed. A requirement that keys (or the means to decrypt them) be turned over to the government is thus clearly a search or seizure for Fourth Amendment purposes. The question then becomes whether it falls into any of the classes of exception to the warrant requirement.

Mandatory Key Escrow as a "Regulatory Search"

Only the regulatory search exception to the warrant and particularity requirements of the Fourth Amendment seems at all likely to apply to mandatory key escrow, but one exception is enough. The requirement that all users of strong cryptography escrow their chip keys or other means to decrypt their session keys closely resembles routinized searches, such as employee drug testing, for which the Supreme Court no longer requires a warrant. Unlike traditional law-enforcement searches, which are designed to find evidence of a crime, regulatory searches are "aimed at deterrence of wrongdoing through fear of detection."[64] Like the warrantless, wide-ranging, regulatory searches approved by the Supreme Court, the government's acquisition of keys will not provide evidence of anything criminal. Rather, by requiring the disclosure of keys the government seeks to remove the shield of strong cryptography from what it believes would otherwise be socially undesirable uses.

The leading regulatory search case is *National Treasury Employees Union v. Von Raab*,[65] in which the Supreme Court endorsed a Customs Service program of mandatory employee drug testing. The Court stated

---

[63] [The full paper describes some reasons to doubt expectations of privacy.]

[64] Craig M. Cornish & Donald B. Louria, *Drug Testing in the Workplace: Employment Drug Testing, Preventive Searches, and the Future of Privacy*, 33 WM. & MARY L. REV. 95, 97–98 (1991).

[65] 489 U.S. 656, 665 (1989). *See also* Skinner v. Railway Labor Executives' Ass'n, 489 U.S. 602 (1989); Florida v. Bostick, 501 U.S. 429 (1991) (random approaches to passengers in buses); Michigan Dep't of State Police v. Sitz, 496 U.S. 444 (1990) (suspicionless sobriety checkpoints to deter drunk driving); Marshall v. Barlow's, Inc., 429 U.S. 1347 (1977) (requiring warrant); Camara v. Municipal Court, 387 U.S. 523 (1967).

that "neither a warrant nor probable cause, nor, indeed, any measure of individualized suspicion, is an indispensable component of reasonableness in every circumstance."[66] Instead, "where a Fourth Amendment intrusion serves special governmental needs, beyond the normal need for law enforcement," one should "balance the individual's privacy expectations against the Government's interests to determine whether it is impractical to require a warrant or some level of individualized suspicion in the particular context."[67]

It is difficult to imagine a case where the government would find it easier to plead "special needs," such as a need to prevent the development of "hidden conditions" and the impracticality of warrants for every key,[68] than in its attempt to compile a database of chip keys or session keys.[69] Mandatory key escrow fits several of the criteria enunciated in *Von Raab*. In particular, mandatory key escrow is not designed to produce evidence for criminal prosecutions (the actual wiretaps do that, but they require warrants or other authorization) but to deter crimes that might otherwise be furthered by the use of encryption.[70] The key's owner knows that the key is being escrowed. And, if encryption becomes widespread, a more particularized approach would be difficult if not impossible.[71] Furthermore, since the government only plans to use the key segments for legitimate searches, it can argue that the cost to personal privacy is low.[72]

On the other hand, although the courts have allowed warrantless regulatory searches in the workplace, at airports, in prisons, at the border and in schools, none of the leading regulatory search cases has involved a search that entered into the home, unless the home was the scene of a fire or was occupied by a parolee, probationer, or welfare recipient.[73] Indeed, in *Camara v. Municipal Court* the Supreme Court

---

[66] National Treasury Employees Union v. Von Raab, 489 U.S. 656, 665 (1989).

[67] *Von Raab*, 489 U.S. at 665–66.

[68] *See* Skinner v. Railway Labor Executives' Assn., 489 U.S. 602, 624 (1989) (giving these as examples of persuasive special needs).

[69] The special needs standard has received strong criticism from academic commentators. *See* William J. Stuntz, *Implicit Bargains, Government Power, and the Fourth Amendment*, 44 STAN. L. REV. 553, 554 n.10 (1992) (collecting criticisms).

[70] *See Von Raab*, 489 U.S. at 667.

[71] *Cf.* United States v. Martinez-Fuerte, 428 U.S. 543, 557 (1976) (requiring particularized suspicion before routine stops on major highways near the Mexican border "would be impractical because the flow of traffic tends to be too heavy to allow the particularized study of a given car that would enable it to be identified as a possible carrier of illegal aliens").

[72] "A determination of the standard of reasonableness applicable to a particular class of searches requires 'balanc[ing] the nature and quality of the intrusion on the individual's Fourth Amendment interests against the importance of the governmental interests alleged to justify the intrusion.' " (citations omitted). O'Connor v. Ortega, 480 U.S. 709, 719 (1987).

[73] *See* WAYNE R. LAFAVE & JEROLD H. ISRAEL, CRIMINAL PROCEDURE § 3.9 (2d ed. 1992).

refused to eliminate the warrant requirement for routine searches that penetrated residential property in search of violations of the city's housing code. The Court characterized the housing inspectors' intrusions into the home as too "significant" to be allowed without a warrant—although the same Court then went on to balance the interests at stake and concluded that warrants could be issued with a lesser showing of need than that traditionally required for probable cause.[74]

Mandatory key escrow would affect many different types of users, including both business and personal users sending messages both commercial and political. The regulatory search precedents, particularly *Von Raab*, suggest that Congress might be able to require mandatory key escrow for businesses and other commercial users without infringing the Fourth Amendment as it is currently understood. The broad sweep of the special needs justification, however, is not easily confined to the market sector of society and there is nothing in the logic of *Von Raab* that requires it remain there, particularly when one considers the means by which the Court permitted warrantless intrusions into welfare recipients' homes in *Wyman v. James*.[75]

Although the Court decided *Wyman* after *Camara*, to date the Court has not extended the special needs justification of *Von Raab* to reach into the home. This suggests that private, non-commercial users of encryption might not fall within any of the currently specified special needs categories of the regulatory search exception to the Fourth Amendment. As currently understood, therefore, the Fourth Amendment probably prohibits warrantless mandatory key escrow for at least private, non-commercial users of encryption.[76]

FIFTH AMENDMENT ISSUES

The Fifth Amendment guarantees that "[n]o person . . . shall be compelled in any criminal case to be a witness against himself."[77] The "historic function" of this part of the Fifth Amendment is to protect a "natural individual from compulsory incrimination through his own

---

[74] Camara v. Municipal Court, 387 U.S. 523 (1967). The Court relied on several factors absent from the mandatory key escrow scenario for its holding, among them the "long history of judicial and public acceptance" of housing code inspections.

[75] 400 U.S. 309 (1971).

[76] Given the plasticity of the special needs doctrine, it is possible that the Court would extend the regulatory search exception to the home user of encryption. Extending the logic of *Von Raab* to the home would gut much of what remains of the Fourth Amendment, and is a result to be avoided at all costs.

[77] U.S. CONST. amend. V.

testimony or personal records."[78] Currently, there is a tension in the Supreme Court's treatment of the reach of the Fifth Amendment. On the one hand, the Court interprets the right narrowly, to apply to criminal defendants only.[79] While "[i]t is true that the Court has often stated" that the Fifth Amendment protects personal privacy, the "Court has never suggested that every invasion of privacy violates the privilege" and "the Court has never on any ground, personal privacy included, applied the Fifth Amendment to prevent the otherwise proper acquisition or use of evidence which, in the Court's view, did not involve compelled testimonial self-incrimination of some sort."[80] On the other hand, the Court continues to recognize the special nature of some private non-commercial personal papers such as diaries and to give them Fifth as well as Fourth Amendment protection.[81]

With one exception, neither the Fourth nor Fifth Amendments have ever been understood to allow the government to require civilians, in peacetime, to structure their lives to make hypothetical future searches by law enforcement easy. That exception, the required records doctrine, is inapposite to mandatory key escrow.[82] Instead, the Fifth Amendment is potentially relevant to mandatory key escrow in two ways. The required disclosure of the chip key resembles the required disclosure of a private paper, which may have some Fifth Amendment protection, and the forced utterance of a LEAF may be the type of incriminating testimony proscribed by the Fifth Amendment.

The Chip Key as a Private Paper

In *Boyd v. United States*, the Supreme Court stated that private papers are an owner's "dearest property." Relying on both the Fourth and Fifth

---

[78] Anderson v. Maryland, 427 U.S. 463, 470–71 (1976) (holding that "business records" are outside privilege).

[79] "Although conduct by law enforcement officials prior to trial may ultimately impair that right, a constitutional violation occurs only at trial." United States v. Verdugo-Urquidez, 494 U.S. 259, 264 (1990) (citations omitted).

[80] Fisher v. United States, 425 U.S. 391, 399 (1976).

[81] *See* Nixon v. Administrator of Gen. Servs., 433 U.S. 425 (1977). The protection is agains subpoenas only and does not protect them from search warrants.

[82] The required records doctrine came into full flower in *Shapiro v. United States*, 335 U.S. 1 (1948), which upheld a subpoena for incriminatory records that were required under a wartime price control statute. Later cases made clear, however, that there are limits to the government's power to define records as 'required' and hence outside the Fifth Amendment. *See* Marchetti v. United States 390 U.S. 39 (1968) (registration requirement held to violate fifth amendment because it materially increased chances of prosecution); Grosso v. United States, 390 U.S. 62 (1968), although other cases have cast doubt on the firmness of these limits. *See, e.g.*, California v. Byers, 402 U.S. 424 (1971) (plurality op.) (requiring hit and run motorist to identify self). One thing which is beyond dispute, however, is that the government requires a court order to get access to required records. Since the point of a mandatory key escrow scheme would be to get access to the keys without a court order, the required records exception is irrelevant.

Amendments, the Court found that allowing the state to compel production of that property would be "abhorrent to the instincts" of an American and "contrary to the principles of a free government."[83] As recently as *Bellis v. United States,* the Supreme Court allowed that the Fifth Amendment protects " 'a private inner sanctum of individual feeling and thought'—an inner sanctum which necessarily includes an individual's papers and effects to the extent that the privilege bars their compulsory production and authentication."[84] Nevertheless, the rule found "abhorrent" in 1886 is now practically the law.[85]

The Supreme Court has eliminated most Fifth Amendment protections for incriminating documentary evidence sought by compulsion. First, the Supreme Court narrowed the privilege so that it applies only if the act of producing papers or records, by itself, has a self-incriminatory communicative or testimonial aspect. If the act of handing over the papers is non-communicative, that is if it neither reveals the existence of the document nor authenticates it, then the Fifth Amendment ordinarily does not apply.[86] Second, only natural persons can shelter under the Fifth Amendment, and only for papers they both own and control. Thus, corporations can never claim the privilege, and neither can natural persons with regard to corporate records, even if they created and control those records.[87] Third, once papers are handed to another, the legitimate expectation of privacy needed to maintain a claim under either the Fourth or Fifth Amendments disappears.[88] Fourth, records required to be kept for legal or regulatory purposes are outside the privilege.[89]

---

[83] Boyd v. United States, 116 U.S. 616 (1886). Judge Friendly criticized this statement as "ringing but vacuous" because it "tells us almost everything, except why." Henry J. Friendly, *The Fifth Amendment Tomorrow: The Case for Constitutional Change,* 37 U. CIN. L. REV. 671, 682 (1968).

[84] 417 US 85, 91 (1974).

[85] *See* Samuel A. Alito, Jr., *Documents and the Privilege Against Self-Incrimination,* 48 U. PITT. L. REV. 27 (1986); Note, *Formalism, Legal Realism, and Constitutionally Protected Privacy Under the Fourth and Fifth Amendments,* 90 HARV. L. REV. 945 (1977).

[86] Fisher v. United States, 425 U.S. 391 (1976); United States v. Doe, 465 U.S. 605 (1984). *See also id.* at 618 (O'Connor, J., concurring) ("the Fifth Amendment provides absolutely no protection for the contents of private papers of any kind.").

In Baltimore City Dept. of Social Servs. v. Bouknight, 493 U.S. 549 (1990) (holding that mother could not invoke Fifth amendment privilege against court order to produce child she had allegedly abused), the Supreme Court held that producing a child was not testimonial, and that the Fifth Amendment did not apply. The Court analogized the mother's care of the child to a required record. *Id.* at 556–60. In light of this decision it is fair to ask whether the Fifth Amendment applies to anything other than oral testimony.

[87] *See, e.g.,* Braswell v. United States, 487 U.S. 99, 109–10 (1988); Bellis v. United States, 417 US 85 (1974); Anderson v. Maryland, 427 U.S. 463 (1976); United States v. White, 322 U.S. 694 (1944); Hale v. Henkel, 201 U.S. 43 (1906).

[88] *See* Couch v. United States, 409 U.S. 322, 330 (1973) (papers handed to accountant); Bellis v. United States, 417 U.S. at 92 (papers handed to partner in small law firm). The attorney-client privilege is an exception to this general rule.

[89] *See supra* note . Fifth, and only tangentially related to documents, the Supreme

Nevertheless, *Boyd* has a residual vitality for non-business, non-financial private papers and documents which are kept in the home, if only because the Supreme Court has yet to compel production of such a document.[90]

Is a Chip Key or a Session Key "Incriminating"?

The hornbook rule is that testimony must be incriminating when uttered in order to be entitled to protection under the Fifth Amendment. It must relate to past conduct and, if it does not directly incriminate ("Yes, I did it") must at least create a "substantial" and "real" hazard of prosecution for the Fifth Amendment to apply.[91]

The Fifth Amendment does not protect testimony that might become incriminating through future conduct. In *United States v. Freed*, the Supreme Court upheld a National Firearms Act registration requirement against a Fifth Amendment claim that the disclosed information might be used against the defendant if he committed an offence with a firearm in the future.[92]

Forced disclosure of a chip key and a session key fit uneasily into this framework. The forced discloser of a chip key[93] before the chip has ever been used to communicate cannot be incriminating, since nothing has happened yet. Thus, mandatory key escrow itself fits squarely within the *Freed* rationale. In contrast, the LEAF raises a more delicate problem. Since the LEAF precedes the actual conversation, forced utterance of a LEAF could be said to fall within the *Freed* rationale also. But this is really too facile to be credible. The encrypted session key within the LEAF is unique, and directly tied to the conversation which follows it. In any case, whether the LEAF is part of the conversation or not, it is an utterance which creates a "substantial" and "real" hazard of prosecution if the conversation that follows the LEAF is an incrim-

---

Court held that persons can be forced to perform non-testimonial acts such giving writing samples, Gilbert v. California, 388 U.S. 263 (1967), or voice samples, Untied States v. Wade, 388 U.S. 218 (1967), and must submit to non-testimonial procedures such as blood tests, Schmerber v. California, 384 U.S. 757 (1966).

Sixth, aliens outside the sovereign territory of the United States do not enjoy Fifth Amendment rights, Johnson v. Eisentrager, 339 U.S. 763 (1950). But, United States citizens abroad have Fifth Amendment rights, Reid v. Covert, 354 U.S. 1 (1957).

[90] *See* LaFave & Israel, *supra* note , at § 8.12.

[91] *See* Marcheti v. United States, 390 U.S. 39 (1968) (holding that reporting of illegal gambling income by frequent gambler was reasonable basis for fear of incrimination).

[92] 401 U.S. 601, 606 (1971).

[93] Recall that for the purposes of this discussion "chip key" means either the hardwired chip unique key in a Clipper Chip which can lead the government to the encrypted session key buried in a LEAF, or the information needed to decrypt the equivalent information generated by a software package.

inating one and a public servant happens to be listening.[94] On the other hand, the Supreme Court has emphasized that non-testimonial compelled disclosures (and the LEAF itself is not testimonial, save insofar as it ties a particular conversation to a particular pair of chips) are not privileged.[95]

In summary, the Fifth Amendment may not protect disclosure of a chip key against mandatory key escrow, but it protects individuals against the routine warrantless *use* of that key to decrypt the LEAF and, especially, to decrypt an incriminating communication. Since the stated purpose of escrowed encryption is to allow the government to retain the abilities it currently has, and the government accepts that a warrant is required to conduct a wiretap, the Fifth Amendment imposes no significant restriction on a mandatory key escrow proposal of the type hypothesized.

PRIVACY ISSUES

The constitutional right to privacy derives from the First, Third, Fourth, Fifth, Ninth and Fourteenth Amendments, but exceeds the sum of its parts.[96] The right to privacy has at least three components: a right to be left alone, a right to autonomous choice regarding intimate matters, and a right to autonomous choice regarding other personal matters.[97] There is no question that mandatory key escrow would infringe each of these component rights. The question, already partly canvassed above, is whether the courts would consider the intrusions reasonably related to a sufficiently compelling state interest to justify the intrusion. As might be expected, the limitations on mandatory key escrow deriving from the right to privacy conform closely to those derived from the First, Fourth and Fifth amendments on which the privacy right partly relies. Privacy jurisprudence is in some turmoil, however, and it is possible that privacy will prove to be the most fertile area for legal adap-

---

[94] *See* Hoffman v. United States, 341 U.S. 479 (1951) (witness' response is incriminating if it might furnish a link in the chain of evidence needed to prosecute).

[95] *See, e.g.,* Doe v. United States, 487 U.S. 201, 208 n.6 (1988) (communication doesn't become privileged just because "it will lead to incriminating evidence").

[96] That at least was Justice Harlan's view in Griswold v. Connecticut, 381 U.S. 479, 499–500 (1965) (Harlan, J., concurring) (privacy derives not from penumbras in the Bill of Rights, but from fundamental ideas of ordered liberty); *see also* Roe v. Wade, 410 U.S. 113, 152 (1973) (relying on penumbras of Bill of Rights).

[97] For a taxonomy of taxonomies, see TRIBE, *supra* note , at § 15–1 and Ken Gormley, *One Hundred Years of Privacy*, 1992 WIS. L. REV. 1335. For an argument that the three strands described below are actually inimical to each other, at least in the eyes of their advocates on the Supreme Court, see David M. Smolin, Essay, *The Jurisprudence of Privacy in a Splintered Supreme Court*, 75 MARQ. L. REV. 975 (1992).

tation to the new challenges posed by increasing state surveillance power and compensating private responses such as cryptography.

The Right to Autonomous Choice Regarding Non-Intimate Matters

The right to autonomous choice regarding non-intimate personal matters is the most general component of the right to privacy. More outward-looking than the right to be left alone, but more wide-ranging than the right to autonomous choice regarding intimate matters, this component relates to those important individual personal decisions which are fundamental without being intimate, such as the choice of friends, political party, vocation, and other allegiances.[98] Disputes concerning this category, such as alleged infringements of associational freedom, tend to be adjudicated directly under the rubric of one or more amendments in the Bill of Rights rather than by appeal to privacy principles. These aspects of privacy law were canvassed above,[99] and will not be repeated here.

The Right to Be Left Alone

The right to privacy includes a generalized "right to be left alone,"[100] which includes "the individual interest in avoiding disclosure of personal matters."[101] This strand forms the basis for many claims to a right to informational privacy.[102] Informational privacy is the area in which a right to privacy most easily translates into a right to secrecy. In *Whalen v. Roe*[103] the Court allowed New York state to keep a computerized list of prescription records for dangerous drugs, and allowed the

---

[98] *See, e.g.*, Hampton v. Mow Sun Wong, 426 U.S. 88 (1976) (federal government's denial of resident alien's right to work unconstitutional); Lamont v. Postmaster General, 381 U.S. 301 (1965) (invalidating statutory requirement that persons wishing to receive "communist propaganda" identify selves to post office); Shelton v. Tucker, 364 U.S. 479 (1960) (striking down statute requiring teachers to list every organization joined during prior five years); NAACP *ex rel.* Patterson v. Alabama, 357 U.S. 449 (1958); *see also, e.g.*, John Hart Ely, *Democracy and the Right to be Different*, 56 N.Y.U. L. REV. 397 (1981).

[99] *See supra* part .

[100] Olmstead v. United States, 277 U.S. 438, 478 (1928) (Brandeis, J., dissenting); *see also* Stanley v. Georgia, 394 U.S. 557 (1969).

[101] Whalen v. Roe, 429 U.S. 589, 599–600 (1977) (acknowledging existence of right, but finding it could be overcome by narrowly tailored program designed to serve state's "vital interest in controlling the distribution of dangerous [prescription] drugs"); Gary R. Clouse, Note, *The Constitutional Right to Withhold Private Information*, 77 NW. L. REV. 536, 547–557 (1982) (collecting, and dissecting, inconsistent cases from circuit courts). However, the right to be left alone is insufficiently compelling to prevent a large number of physical intrusions to bodily integrity when the police seek forensic evidence relating to a criminal investigation. *See supra* note ; TRIBE, *supra* note , at 1331 (collecting cases).

[102] *See, e.g.*, Francis S. Chlapowski, Note, *The Constitutional Protection of Informational Privacy*, 71 B.U. L. REV. 133 (1991); Clouse, *supra* note .

[103] 429 U.S. 589 (1977).

state to require physicians to disclose the names of patients to whom they prescribed those drugs. The decision balanced the social interest in informational privacy against the state's "vital interest in controlling the distribution of dangerous drugs."[104] Finding New York's program to be narrowly tailored, and replete with security provisions designed to reduce the danger of unauthorized disclosure, the Supreme Court held that the constitutional balance tilted in favor of the statute.[105]

Mandatory key escrow appears comparable in its intrusive effects to the regulatory scheme upheld in *Whalen,* so long as the courts hold the government to its promise that keys will remain secret and will be released only pursuant to a warrant or to a very limited number of other lawful orders. Without that proviso, mandatory key escrow would verge upon unjustified data collection.[106] The warning in *Whalen* that the Court is "not unaware of the threat to privacy implicit in the accumulation of vast amounts of personal information in computerized data banks or other massive government files"[107] suggests, however, that informational privacy rights may grow in response to new technological threats to privacy.

The Right to Autonomous Choice Regarding Intimate Matters

A second component of the right to privacy is a narrow individual right to make intensely personal decisions about (some) intimate associations without state interference. The Court has described certain decisions about intimate association and family- and sex-related decisions as falling within a special privacy zone for "marriage, procreation, contraception, family relationships, and child rearing and education."[108] The contours of this zone have always been fuzzy, in part

---

[104] *Id.* at 598.

[105] *Id.* at 601–04.

[106] An extreme statute, requiring broad data collection combined with a requirement that reports be available to the public, was held unconstitutional in Thornburgh v. American College of Obstetricians and Gynecologists, 476 U.S. 747 (1986).

What limits there might be to data collection and the safeguards required against disclosure were issues left open in *Whalen*: "We .. do not[] decide any question which might be presented by the unwarranted disclosure of accumulated private data—whether intentional or unintentional—or by a system that did not contain comparable security provisions." 429 U.S. at 606–06.

[107] 429 U.S. at 605.

[108] Paul v. Davis, 424 U.S. 693, 713 (1976); *see also* Roberts v. United States Jaycees, 468 U.S. 609, 615–20 (1984) (describing types of "personal bonds" and relationships entitled to heightened constitutional protection); Roe v. Wade, 410 U.S. 113 (1973) (reproductive decisions of women); Eisenstadt v. Baird, 405 U.S. 438 (1972) (procreative decisions of unmarried opposite-sex couple); Griswold v. Connecticut, 381 U.S. 479 (1965) (procreative decisions of married opposite-sex couple); Moore v. City of East Cleveland, 431 U.S. 494 (1977) (plurality op.) (right to choose which relatives to live with); Poe v. Ullman, 367 U.S. 497, 551 (1961) (Harlan, J., dissenting); Doe v. Bolton, 410 U.S. 179 (1973); Loving v. Virginia, 388 U.S. 1 (1967) (interracial marriage); Skinner v. Okla-

because of long-standing decisions forbidding minority marriage practices[109] which would logically appear to belong within the zone of privacy described by cases such as *Griswold, Baird, Davis* and *Roe*.[110] The fuzziness currently is at an all-time high due to *Bowers v. Hardwick*,[111] and the continuing controversy concerning the right to abortion.[112]

As applied, this second strand of privacy jurisprudence is primarily directed at the preservation of personal autonomy,[113] and especially autonomy relating to the sexual and reproductive practices and values of the traditional family and the "traditional unmarried couple."[114] Secrecy has a role to play here too, since sometimes secrecy is a prerequisite to the exercise of autonomy even (or especially) within the family.[115]

Furthermore, electronic communications will increasingly become a critical part of intimate association. In a world in which the commuter marriage is increasingly common, electronic communications such as the telephone, fax and especially e-mail (which is cheaper and

---

homa, 316 U.S. 535 (1942) (right not to be sterilized); Pierce v. Society of Sisters, 268 U.S. 510 (1925) (parental right to determine schooling of children); Meyer v. Nebraska, 262 U.S. 390 (1923) (parental right to determine language spoken by children); Kenneth L. Karst, *The Freedom of Intimate Association*, 89 YALE L.J. 624 (1980) (arguing that divorce—the freedom of disassociation—is a fundamental privacy right).

[109] *E.g.* Reynolds v. United States, 98 U.S. 145 (1878) (rejecting First Amendment challenge to statute forbidding polygamy), remains good law. *See* Cleveland v. United States, 329 U.S. 14 (1946).

[110] In addition, many states have laws prohibiting adultery that remain on the books. These laws are not currently enforced, but there is reason to believe that if they were enforced they could survive a constitutional challenge based on privacy principles. *See* Commonwealth v. Stowell, 449 N.E.2d 357 (Mass. 1983) (rejecting constitutional attack against a Massachusetts adultery statute); *but see* Martin J. Siegel, *For Better or for Worse: Adultery, Crime & the Constitution*, 30 J. FAM. L. 45 (1991/1992) (arguing laws criminalizing adultery are unconstitutional).

[111] The Supreme Court refused to extend the vision of privacy set out in the cases above to protect the sexual choices of an unmarried same-sex couple in Bowers v. Hardwick, 478 U.S. 186 (1986), and did so in a way that casts doubt on the entire strand of privacy protection for intensely personal and intimate associations. Professor Tribe describes the decision in *Bowers* as erroneous and unprincipled, and predicts that it will not be followed. TRIBE, *supra* note , at § 15–21. For a thoughtful reformulation of privacy doctrines after *Bowers* see Jed Rubenfeld, *The Right of Privacy*, 102 HARV. L. REV. 737, 737 (1989).

[112] *See* Planned Parenthood v. Casey, 112 S. Ct. 2791 (1992); Rust v. Sullivan, 500 U.S. 173 (1991).

[113] On the psychological and moral importance of allowing individuals to make voluntary choices in matters vitally affecting them see Bruce J. Winick, *On Autonomy: Legal and Psychological Perspectives*, 37 VILL. L. REV. 1705 (1992); *see also* Steven A. Bercu, *Toward Universal Surveillance in an Information Age Economy: Can We Handle Treasury's New Police Technology?*, 34 JURIMETRICS J. 383, 402–03 (1994).

[114] TRIBE, *supra* note , at § 15–21.

[115] *See, e.g.*, Planned Parenthood v. Casey, 112 S. Ct. 2791 (1992) (striking down statute requiring spousal notification prior to abortion); Thornburg v. American College of Obstetricians and Gynecologists, 4766 U.S. 747 (1986) (judicial by-pass provisions of abortion statutes relating to minors).

less intrusive than a telephone, more private than a fax, and often instantaneous) are increasingly becoming the glue that holds marriages and other intimate relationships together.[116] The current rule, which provides much greater privacy protection to the bedroom than the intimate inter-spousal trans-continental e-mail,[117] may soon need revision.[118] The collapse of the distinction between home and office, fueled in part by the growth of telecommuting, will place a further strain on existing rules that attempt to distinguish between private, non-commercial activities whose classical locus is the home, and less private more commercial activities whose classical location was the office. If the courts further erode the zone of privacy that still surrounds the home, the growth in freedom to work at home will have come at a high price.

SUMMARY

On balance, as the law stands today private non-commercial users of encryption probably have a Fourth Amendment right to resist mandatory key escrow. Whether commercial users or corporations would have such a right under current doctrines is less clear. Even the rights of private non-commercial users appear to be a distressingly close question given the current state of civil rights doctrine, and the great importance that the courts give to law enforcement and national security. While these precedents form a basis for any discussion of the constitutionality of mandatory key escrow, they are only a starting point for any discussion. The law in this area has undergone great change in the past two decades, and there is no reason to believe that the evolution has stopped.

---

[116] E-mail also allows people to meet and exchange ideas, increasing their chances of forming lasting relationships. Steve Lohr, *Therapy on a Virtual Couch*, N.Y. TIMES, Aug. 28, 1994, at C7 (interview with psychiatrist and novelist Avodah Offit). Indeed, in a few cases e-mail apparently has become a *substitute* for sex, as some of Dr. Offit's patients have consulted her about their "E-mail love relationships". *Id.*

[117] *But see* Lovisi v. Slayton, 539 F.2d 349 (4th Cir.) (en banc), *cert. denied sub nom.* Lovisi v. Zahradnick, 429 U.S. 977 (1976) (holding that marital couple's right to bring privacy challenge to conviction under Virginia sodomy statute was waived due to presence of invited third party but would not have been waived if they had spoken or written about their activities to third parties).

[118] The even thornier problem of the intimate international inter-spousal e-mail is beyond the scope of this Article. The question is complex because it will turn on the citizenship of the parties, their location, and other factors.

## 6

Review and Analysis of U.S. Laws, Regulations, and Case Laws Pertaining to the Use of Commercial Encryption Products for Voice and Data Communications*

James Chandler, Diana Arrington, Lamarris Gill, and Donna Berkelhammer

CONSTITUTIONAL ISSUES REGARDING USE OF ENCRYPTION TECHNOLOGY

U.S. CONTROLS ON ENCRYPTION TECHNOLOGY

Domestic Controls

Computer Security Act of 1987

The Computer Security Act requires federal agencies to identify and develop security plans for computer systems that hold sensitive information. The Act intended to prevent persons from illegally tapping into government computer systems and altering or destroying records.[254] The Act gives the National Institute of Standards and Technology (NIST) responsibility for promulgating guidelines to protect the security of sensitive but unclassified computer information.[255] The term "sensitive information" means any nonsecret information that could adversely affect the national interest, the conduct of federal programs, or rights created under the Privacy Act.[256]

Brooks Act

The Brooks Act was enacted to ensure the "economic and efficient" procurement of automated data processing and telecommunications

---

* Excerpted from *Review and Analysis of U.S. Laws, Regulations, and Case Laws pertaining to the use of Commercial Encryption Products for Voice and Data Communications.* January 1994, Martin Marietta report no. K/DSRD/SUB/93-RF105/2.

[254] Note, *Nineteenth Annual Administrative Law Issue: Developments under the Freedom of Information Act,* 1988 Duke L.J. 566 (1987).

[255] *Id.*

[256] H.R. 145, 100th Cong., 1st Sess. § 3(c)(4), 133 Cong. Rec H5340 (daily ed. June 22, 1987).

equipment (ADPTE) by federal agencies. All computer supplies and services as well as telecommunications equipment fall into the ADPTE category.[257] The General Services Administration is responsible for providing ADPTE to federal agencies either directly or under a delegation of procurement authority.

Over the Act's 25-year history, the most important development involved the ability for certain agencies to exempt themselves from ADPTE purchasing requirements. The Warner Amendment passed in 1981 exempted certain Defense Department purchases from the Brooks Act provisions.[258] These purchases included any Defense Department procurements "critical to the direct fulfillment of military or intelligence missions" of the United States or in which the ADPTE exists as an "integral part of a weapon or weapons system;" these purchases also included "cryptologic activities related to national security."[259]

NIST provides cryptographic technology for unclassified government information primarily pursuant to the Brooks Act.[260] The Act explicitly grants control over national security information data processing needs to the President, who in turn has delegated that task to the NSA or other military agencies.[261]

Export Controls

Arms Export Control Act, 22 U.S.C. § 2778

The AECA is the statutory authority that governs export controls of defense articles and services to foreign countries. The purpose of the AECA is to control the export of defense articles that may contribute to an arms race, support international terrorism, increase the possibility of outbreak or escalation of conflict, or prejudice the development of bilateral or multilateral arms control arrangements.[262] Thus, "[i]n furtherance of world peace and the security and foreign policy of the United States, the President is authorized to control the import and the export of defense articles and defense services. . . . The President is authorized to designate those items which shall be considered as de-

---

[257] Marshall, Robert C., Michael J. Meurer, Jean-Francois Richard, *The Privacy Attorney General Meets Public Contract Law: Procurement Oversight by Protest*, 20 Hofstra L. Rev. 1, 34 (1991).

[258] Department of Defense Authorization Act of 1982 (Warner Amendment), Pub. L. No. 97–86, § 908(a)(1), 95 Stat. 1099, 1117 (1981) (amended 1982), codified as 10 U.S.C. § 2314 (1988).

[259] *Id.* at § 2315(a); see Marshall, *supra*, at 35.

[260] Franks, Renae A., Note, *The National Security Agency and Its Interference with the Private Sector Computer Security*, 72 Iowa L. Rev. 1015, 1019 (1987).

[261] *Id.*; see *U.S. v. Curtiss-Wright*, 299 U.S. 304, 319 (1936) (the President's power over national security is based on his constitutional authority in foreign relations).

[262] 22 U.S.C. § 2778 (a)(2).

fense articles and defense services for the purposes of this section and to promulgate regulations for the import and export of such articles and services."[263]

International Traffic in Arms Regulations The ITAR, 22 C.F.R. §§ 120–130, promulgates the policies set forth in the AECA. The State Department is given exclusive regulatory authority to carry out the ITAR by the President.

U.S. Munitions List. Items considered defense articles and services appear in the U.S. Munitions List,[264] and individual validated export licenses must be approved for these items. The designation of items to appear on the Munitions List is handled by the State Department in concurrence with the Defense Department. Designations of articles to the Munitions List is based primarily on whether the article or service is deemed to be inherently military in character. Whether an item is used for both military and civilian purposes does not determine whether it will be placed on the list. Also, the intended use of the article is not relevant in determining whether an item will be subject to restrictions.[265]

The determination of items to be placed on the Munitions List is not judicially reviewable.[266] However, the AECA provides for periodic review of items appearing on the Munitions List to determine which items no longer warrant export restrictions under the AECA and ITAR. For an item on the Munitions List to be decontrolled, a request to remove the item from the list must be received by the State Department. The State Department reviews the item with the appropriate agencies and determines whether the item should be decontrolled. Items decontrolled by the State Department may be placed on the Commerce Control List, and control of these items accordingly shifts to the Commerce Department.[267]

Export Licenses. Defense items appearing on the Munitions List are under the exclusive jurisdiction of the State Department. Those wishing to export items on the Munitions List must be registered with the State Department prior to submitting an export license application. Any person intending to export a defense article must obtain an individually validated license from the State Department prior to each export. An application for the permanent export of defense articles sold commercially must be accompanied by a purchaser order, letter of in-

---

[263] 22 U.S.C. § 2778 (a)(1).
[264] 22 C.F.R. § 121.1.
[265] 22 C.F.R. § 120.3.
[266] 22 U.S.C. § 2778 (h).
[267] 22 U.S.C. § 2778(f).

tent, or any other appropriate documentation.[268] With respect to distribution warehouses, the initial agreement for warehousing and distributing defense articles must be approved by the State Department before they enter into force. The agreement must contain conditions for special distribution, end-use, and reporting and must specify the terms and conditions in which the article will be exported, the duration of the agreement, and the countries involved in the distribution territory.[269] Licenses for exports pursuant to a distribution agreement must be approved prior to export.

An export license is required for the export of unclassified technical data. A license must be obtained for any oral, visual, or documentary disclosure of technical data to foreign nationals during visits to foreign countries by U.S. persons, visits by a foreign national to the United States, or any other situation. A license is required regardless of the manner in which the technical data are transmitted, whether the transfer be in person, by telephone, through correspondence, or electronically.[270] However, information which is in the public domain[271] is not subject to the controls for technical data.

In determining whether to issue an export license, consideration must be given to whether an article will contribute to the arms race, support international terrorism, increase the possibility of outbreak or escalation of conflict, or prejudice the development of bilateral arms control arrangements. When considering applications, recommendations from other agencies may be sought. These recommendations are used to aid in determining whether to grant export licenses.

Violations and penalties. The export or attempt to export any defense article or technical data or to furnish any defense service for which a license is required without obtaining the required license or violating any of the terms or conditions of a granted license is prohibited under the ITAR.[272] Persons granted export licenses are responsible for the acts of their employees, agents, and all persons entrusted with the operation, use, possession, transportation, and handling of licensed defense articles or technical data abroad.[273]

It is also a violation for a person to knowingly apply for a license, or order, buy, receive, use, sell, deliver, store, dispose of, forward transport, finance, or otherwise participate in any transaction involving a defense article or technical data, for the benefit directly or indirectly

---

[268] 22 C.F.R. § 123.1.
[269] 22 C.F.R. § 124.14 (a)–(b).
[270] 22 C.F.R. § 125.2 (c).
[271] 22 C.F.R. § 120.18.
[272] 22 C.F.R. § 127.1 (a)(1), (3).
[273] 22 C.F.R. § 127.1 (b).

of a person facing debarment or suspension.[274] In addition, it is unlawful for a person to willfully aid, abet, cause, counsel, demand, induce, procure, or permit the commission of any act prohibited by the ITAR.[275] It is also unlawful to use any export control document containing false statements, misrepresentations, or omissions of material facts for the exporting of any defense article or technical data or the furnishing of any defense service for which a license is needed.[276]

Any person willfully violating any part of the AECA or the ITAR or, in a registration, license application, or report, willfully making untrue statements of a material fact, omitting a material fact, or making misleading statements shall, upon conviction, be subject to fine, imprisonment, or both.[277] For criminal offenses, the fine shall be not more than $1,000,000 or imprisonment not more than 10 years, or both, for each violation.[278] Civil penalties shall be in accordance with those set forth in the Export Administration Act, 50 U.S.C.S. App. 2410 (c), which may not exceed $500,000 for each violation.[279] Civil penalties may be in addition to or in lieu of any other liability or penalty which may be imposed.

U.S. Customs may take the appropriate steps to enforce the regulations set forth in the ITAR. U.S. Customs may inspect the loading or unloading of any vessel, aircraft, or vehicle or order the production of any relevant documents or information pertaining to a particular export.[280]

ITAR Controls on Encryption Technology Category XIII(b)(1) of the Munitions List covers cryptographic equipment. Originally section (b)(1) of the category consisted of "[s]peech scramblers, privacy devices, cryptographic devices and software (encoding and decoding), and components specifically designed or modified therefore, ancillary equipment, and protective apparatus specifically designed or modified for such devices, components, and equipment." Recent amendments to the ITAR have decontrolled specific categories of cryptographic equipment. These amendments removed cryptographic technology involving message authentication, access control devices, television descramblers, automatic teller machines, virus protection, and "smart cards," and placed these items under Commerce Department jurisdiction. Also,

---

[274] 22 C.F.R. § 127.1 (c)(1)–(2).
[275] 22 C.F.R. § 127.1 (d).
[276] 22 C.F.R. § 127.2 (a).
[277] 22 C.F.R. § 127.3.
[278] 22 U.S.C. § 2778(c).
[279] 22 C.F.R. § 127.9(a).
[280] 22 C.F.R. § 127.4.

certain (but not all) types of mass-market software have been decontrolled. All other items remain under State Department jurisdiction.[281]

Export applications involving cryptography are reviewed by the State Department and then reviewed by the Defense Technology Security Agency, the Energy Department, the appropriate Military Services, and the NSA. The application must include the proposed use of the item and the end user of the item. Recommendations from the aforementioned agencies to approve or reject the application are then sent to the State Department, and the State Department makes the final decision on the license.

Certain types of mass market software still under State Department control may be approved on an expedited basis. Software involving RC2/RC4 algorithms may be approved in 7 days, whereas other software may be approved in 15 days. Also, other less powerful algorithms may appear on an "automatic" list, which is a list of commonly approved noncritical items still under the control of the State Department which are immediately approved. The Data Encryption Standard (DES) and other strong algorithms are not eligible for approval under this schedule. DES may be approved for financial institutions and U.S. subsidiaries through the normal approval process. However, generally cryptographic technology used to encrypt data is not approved. Only those used for message authentication and access control are approved.

The Export Administration Act of 1979, 50 U.S.C.S. app. §§ 2401–2420
The EEA of 1979 and its subsequent amendments are designed to strengthen the international commercial commerce position of the United States. This Act implements policies designed to "minimize uncertainties in export control policy and to encourage trade with all countries with which the United States has diplomatic or trading relations, except those countries with which such trade has been determined by the president to be against the national interest."[282] This policy was based on the findings of Congress that "[e]xports contribute significantly to the economic well-being of the United States and the stability of the world economy by increasing employment and production in the United States, and by earning foreign exchange, thereby contributing favorably to the trade balance. . . . It is important for the national interest of the United States that both private sector and the Federal Government place a high priority on exports, consistent with the economic, security, and foreign policy objectives of the United States."[283]

---

[281] See Interim Final Rule, amendments to ITAR, 57 Fed. Reg. 32148, July 20, 1992; Final Rule, amendments to ITAR, 57 Fed. Reg. 15227, April 27, 1992.

[282] 50 U.S.C. app. § 2402.

[283] 50 U.S.C. app. § 2401.

As a result of these and other findings and policy considerations, the EEA declares that restrictions on exports may be used

only after full consideration of the impact on the economy of the United States and only to the extent necessary—

(A) to restrict the export of goods and technology which would make a significant contribution to the military potential of any other country or combination of countries which would prove detrimental to the national security of the United States;

(B) to restrict the export of goods and technology where necessary to further significantly the foreign policy of the United States or to fulfill its declared international obligations; and

(C) to restrict the export of goods where necessary to protect the domestic economy from the excessive drain of scarce materials and to reduce the serious inflationary impact of foreign demand.[284]

Export Administration Regulations The EARs, 15 C.F.R. parts 768–799, promulgate the policies set forth by the EEA. The Commerce Department is given regulatory authority over the export control of commodities.

Commerce Control List. Commodities under the control of the Commerce Department appear on the Commerce Control List (CCL). The Commerce Department requires export licenses for the export of goods or technologies that appear on the CCL. Licenses that may be required include (1) a validated license for a specific export; (2) a validated license for multiple exports, which include distribution licenses, comprehensive operations licenses, project licenses, and service supply licenses (see 50 U.S.C.S. app. 2403); (3) a general license; and (4) other licenses as required under the EEA.

The following groups of items are not controlled under the EARs and do not appear on the CCL:

- U.S. Munitions List,
- narcotics and dangerous drugs,
- commodities subject to Atomic Energy Act,
- watercraft,
- natural gas and electric energy,
- tobacco seeds and plants,
- endangered fish and wildlife, and
- patent applications (secrecy orders).

Export Licenses. The export of all commodities appearing on the CCL and technical data[285] requires a general license (if established) or

---

[284] 50 U.S.C. app. § 2402.
[285] As defined in 15 C.F.R. § 779.1.

a validated license or other authorization for export granted by the Office of Export Licensing, except for the following:

- any export to Canada for consumption in Canada, unless an individual validated license is required;
- exports for the official use of or consumption by the U.S. Armed Forces; and
- exports of commodities and technical data controlled by another U.S. agency.[286]

A general license is one for which no application is required and for which no document is granted or issued. It is available for use by all persons, except by those specifically prohibited from exporting commodities.[287] These general licenses are only applicable to exports under the licensing authority of the Commerce Department.[288]

A validated license is a document issued by, or under the authority of, the Commerce Department authorizing a specific export.[289] Types of validated licenses include (1) individual license, (2) project license, (3) distribution license, (4) service supply license, and (5) special chemical license.[290]

The Commerce Department will, when applicable, consult with other appropriate agencies before approving an export application requesting a validated license. Foreign policy concerns (which involve restrictions of certain exports to certain countries) and national security concerns will be taken into consideration when an application is being evaluated.[291] If an application is denied, notification will be provided within 5 days to the applicant. The notice will state the statutory basis for the denial, the policies that will be furthered by the denial, the specific considerations which led to the denial, and the availability of appeal procedures.[292] The EARs provide procedures for appeals of denied applications.

The Commerce Department reviews items on the CCL at least every 3 years for multilateral controls and every year for all other controlled commodities. In the review, commodities presently under the validated license control are reviewed to determine whether such a control is still warranted, and commodities that may be exported under general license to most destinations are examined to ascertain whether controls should be extended or expanded.[293]

---

[286] 15 C.F.R. § 770.3(a).
[287] Table of Denial Orders Currently in Effect, 15 C.F.R. § 788, Supplement 1.
[288] Definition of General License, 15 C.F.R. § 770.2.
[289] 15 C.F.R. § 772.2(a).
[290] For definitions see 15 C.F.R. § 772.2(b)(1)–(5).
[291] 15 C.F.R. § 770.13(i)(1).
[292] 15 C.F.R. § 770.13(j)(1)–(2).
[293] 15 C.F.R. § 770.1(b)(1).

Violations. Anyone who willfully violates or conspires to or attempts to violate any provision of the EEA with knowledge that the exports involved will be used for the benefit of, or that the destination or intended destination of the goods or technology involved is to, any controlled country or any country to which exports are controlled for national security or foreign policy purposes, shall be subject to penalties. Except in the case of an individual, the violator shall be fined not more than 5 times the value of the exports involved or $1,000,000, whichever is greater; or, in the case of an individual, the violator shall be fined not more than $250,000, or imprisoned not more than 10 years, or both.[294]

Any person who is issued a validated license under this Act for the export of any goods or technology to a controlled country and who, with knowledge that such goods or technology is being used by such controlled country for military or intelligence gathering purposes contrary to the conditions under which the license was issued, willfully fails to report such use to the Secretary of Defense shall be subject to penalties. Except in the case of an individual, a violator shall be fined not more than five times the value of the exports involved or $1,000,000, whichever is greater, or, in the case of an individual, shall be fined not more than $250,000, or imprisoned not more than 5 years, or both.[295]

Civil penalties may be enforced and may not exceed $500,000 for each violation. Civil penalties may be in addition to or in lieu of any other liability or penalty which may be imposed.[296]

Encryption Technology on the Commerce Control List Requirements for licenses of encryption technology appear in Category 5, Part II—Telecommunications, Information Security, in Supplement No. 1 of the CCL. All items with encryption capabilities that are controlled by the Commerce Department appear in this section. All encryption technology, with a few exceptions, require a validated license.[297]

Initially, all encryption technology appeared in the ITAR and was controlled by the State Department, but recent amendments moved some of these items to the CCL. Cryptographic items now controlled by the Commerce Department are those involving message authentication, access control devices, television descramblers, automatic teller machines, virus protection, and "smart cards." Also, certain (but not all) types of mass-market software have been decontrolled by the State

---

[294] 50 U.S.C. App. § 2410(b)(1)(A)–(B).
[295] 50 U.S.C. App. § 2410(b)(2)(A)–(B).
[296] 50 U.S.C. App. § 2410(c).
[297] See 15 C.F.R. § 799.1, Supp. 1, Cat. 5, pt. II, n.1–5.

Department. Mass market software not decontrolled remains under the control of the State Department.[298]

Invention Secrecy Act, 35 U.S.C. §§181–188

The Invention Secrecy Act prevents the disclosure of patent applications filed in the Patent and Trademark Office for inventions made in the United States. Patent applications containing subject matter that may be detrimental to the national security if disclosed are subject to secrecy orders.

Regulations issued by the Patent and Trademark Office govern the export to foreign countries unclassified technical data in the form of a patent application or an amendment, modification, or supplement. These regulations are found under 37 C.F.R. part 5.

Secrecy orders. Patent applications containing subject matter that may be detrimental to national security interests if disclosed are made available for inspection by defense agencies.[299] If it is determined that the disclosure or publication of the invention by granting a patent would in fact be detrimental to the national security, the Commissioner, upon request from the defense agency, will issue an order that the invention be kept secret.[300] The secrecy order is directed to the subject matter of the patent application.[301] The secrecy order is enforced against the applicant, successors, any and all assignees, and any legal representatives.[302]

Petitions for rescission of secrecy order. A petition to rescind or remove a secrecy order may be filed by the applicant, assignees, or legal representatives.[303] The petition must include all facts that support a showing that the order is ineffectual or futile, or it may show where other applications not subject to a secrecy order disclose a significant part of the subject matter of the application under secrecy order.[304]

Petitions to export. Generally, if a secrecy order has been issued, an application cannot be exported to or filed in a foreign country.[305] However, a permit to disclose or modification of a secrecy order may be granted upon petition. The petition must fully recite the reason or purpose for the disclosure and all countries in which the petitioner wishes to file as well as all attorneys, agents, and others to whom the material will be consigned before filing in a foreign patent office.[306] The permit

---

[298] See Interim Final Rule, amendments to ITAR, 57 Fed. Reg. 32148, July 20, 1992.
[299] 37 C.F.R. § 5.1 (b).
[300] 37 C.F.R. § 5.2(a).
[301] 37 C.F.R. § 5.2(d).
[302] 37 C.F.R. § 5.2(b).
[303] 37 C.F.R. § 5.4(a).
[304] 37 C.F.R. § 5.4(b); 37 C.F.R. § 5.2(d).
[305] 37 C.F.R. § 5.11(d).
[306] 37 C.F.R. § 5.5(b),(c).

or modification may contain conditions and limitations on disclosure or filing.[307]

Import Controls

Temporary Imports (Intransit)

Items imported into the United States which may subsequently be reexported to another country are considered temporary imports. These items may be items that are intransit or merely passing through the United States from one country to another, or the item may be one that is sent to the United States for repairs, maintenance, etc. These items which are imported may be items that require export licenses from the State or Commerce Department. A temporary import license will allow the reexport of those items, even though such a license for a regular export may not be granted.

Import Jurisdiction The State Department regulates the temporary import of defense articles which appear on the U.S. Munitions List. Permanent imports of defense articles into the United States are regulated by the Treasury Department[308] (see 27 C.F.R. parts 47, 178, and 179).

Temporary Import Licenses A temporary import license is required for the temporary import and subsequent export of unclassified defense articles, unless exempted in accordance with 22 C.F.R. 123.4. Licenses from the State Department are required for (1) temporary imports of unclassified defense articles that are to be returned directly to the country from which they were shipped to the United States, and (2) temporary imports of unclassified defense articles in transit to a third country.[309]

Encryption Technology Controls The encryption devices that appear in Category XIII of the U.S. Munitions List are regulated by the State Department for temporary importation.

Permanent Imports

Items that are imported into the United States as a final destination for use or consumption are considered permanent imports. Typically, the Bureau of Alcohol, Tobacco and Firearms (Treasury Department) regulates the import of defense articles. The FCC also regulates a few items

---

[307] 37 C.F.R. § 5.5(e).
[308] 22 C.F.R. § 123.2.
[309] 22 C.F.R. § 123.3(a)(1)–(2).

pertaining to communications. These two agencies may affect the import of encryption technology if the item falls within its jurisdiction.

Treasury Department, Bureau of Alcohol, Firearms and Tobacco Controls
The Treasury Department regulates the permanent importation of defense articles which appear on the U.S. Munitions Import List.[310] This list was developed from the U.S. Munitions List, minus items not subject to controls. Category XIII, consisting of encryption technology, has been deleted from the U.S. Munitions Import List, and those items are not controlled by the Treasury Department.

Federal Communications Commission Controls Pursuant to the Communications Act, 47 U.S.C.S. §302a, the FCC has regulations prohibiting the importation of scanning devices equipped with decoders that convert digital cellular transmissions to analog voice audio or scanning devices that may receive transmissions allocated to cellular radio telecommunications service. The control of the import of these items may involve items using encryption technology.

Commerce Department Controls
Regulation. The Commerce Department will receive from the importers in the United States the representations regarding the intended destination of commodities.[311] An importer will certify to the exporting country that he will import specific commodities into the economy of the United States and will not reexport such commodities except in accordance with the export regulations of the United States.[312]

Violations and sanctions. A maximum fine of $10,000 or imprisonment for 5 years, or both, may be imposed for those making willfully false statements or concealing material fact or knowingly using a document containing a false statement in any matter.

BIBLIOGRAPHY

Citations Applicable to the First Amendment, Freedom of Speech (Sect. 1.1.1)

Citations Applicable to the U.S. Controls on Encryption Technology (Chap. 2)

Statutes
1. Arms Export Control Act, 22 U.S.C.S. § 2778, Pub. L. No. 90–629.

---

[310] 22 C.F.R. § 47.21.
[311] 15 C.F.R. § 768.1(a)(2)(i).
[312] 15 C.F.R. § 768.1(a)(1).

2. 40 U.S.C.S. § 759(a), Pub. L. No. 89–306, 79 Stat. 1127.

3. Communications Act, 47 U.S.C.S. § 302a, Pub. L. No. 90–379.

4. Computer Security Act, 40 U.S.C.S. § 759, Pub. L. No. 100–235, 101 Stat. 1724

5. Export Administration Act, 50 U.S.C.S. app. §§ 2401–2420, Pub. L. No. 96–72.

6. Invention Secrecy Act, 35 U.S.C.S. §§ 181–188, 66 Stat. 805.

Regulations

1. Export Administration Regulations, 15 C.F.R. pts. 768–799. Supplement No. 1 to § 799.1, Commerce Control List; Supplement No. 2 to § 799.1, General Software Note.

2. International Traffic in Arms Regulations (ITAR), 22 C.F.R. pts. 120–130. Final Rule, amendments to ITAR (57 Fed. Reg 15227, April 27, 1992); General—The U.S. Munitions List, 22 C.F.R. § 121.1. Interim Final Rule, amendments to ITAR (57 Fed. Reg. 32148, July 20, 1992); the U.S. Munitions List, 22 C.F.R. § 121.1, note added to Category XIII(b)(1). Final Rule, amendments to the ITAR (58 Fed. Reg. 39280, July 22, 1993).

3. Importation of Arms, Ammunitions and Implements of War, 27 C.F.R. pt. 47.

4. Secrecy of Certain Inventions and Licenses to Export and File, 37 C.F.R. pt. 5.

Law Review Articles

1. Franks, Renae Angeroth, *The National Security Agency and Its Interference with Private Sector Computer Security*, 72 Iowa L. Rev. 1015 (May 1987).

2. Pierce, Kenneth J., *Public Cryptography, Arms Export Controls, and the First Amendment: A Need for Legislation*, 17 Cornell Int'l L.J. 197 (1984).

3. Shinn, Allen M. Jr., *The First Amendment and the Export Laws: Free Speech On Scientific and Technical Matters*, 58 Geo. Wash. L. Rev. 368 (November 1989).

Other Publications

1. Browning, Graeme, *Software Hardball*, 24 Nat'l J. 2062, Sept. 12, 1992.

2. Groner, Jonathan, *U.S. Export Limits Split Software Makers, NSA; Sales vs. Cold War Mentality*, Legal Times, December 7, 1992, at 1.

3. Peterson, Ivars, *A Fierce Debate Erupts Over Cryptography and Privacy*, 143 Science News 394, June 19, 1993.

4. Rarog, Bob, *Statement by Bob Rarog, Export Policy Manager, Digital Equipment Corporation, to the Computer Systems Security and Privacy Advisory Board*, June 3, 1993.

5. Smoot, Ollie, *Statement of the Computer and Business Equipment Manufacturers Association (CBEMA)*, May 27, 1993.

6. Daily Report For Executives, 1991 DER 112 A9, *Export Controls, Restrictions Will Weaken Communications Security Technology, Conference Says*, June 11, 1991.

7. Daily Report For Executives, 1992 DER 140 d2, *Today's Summaries*, July 21, 1992.

8. Daily Report For Executives, 1992 DER 140 d5, *Export Controls, U.S. Sets Procedures for Easing Controls on Exports of Encoding-Capable Software*, July 21, 1992.

9. Daily Report For Executives, 1993 DER 82 d25, *Communications, Communications Policy Must Address Security, Fraud Issue*, April 30, 1993.

10. Daily Report For Executives, 1993 DER 88 d22, *Communications, Group Calls For Attention to Network Privacy in Administration Policy Review*, May 10, 1993.

11. Daily Report For Executives, 1993 DER 105 d22, *Communications, Commerce Advisory Board Faces Doubts About 'Clipper Chip' Initiative*, June 3, 1993.

12. Daily Report For Executives, 1993 DER 106 d27, *Communications, Industry Criticizes 'Clipper Chip'; Calls for Review of Other Systems*, June 4, 1993.

13. Daily Report For Executives, 1993 DER 107 d23, *Communications, Further Review Needed For Clipper Chip, Says Commerce Department Advisory Board*, June 7, 1993.

14. Daily Report For Executives, 1993 DER 110 d24, *Communications, House Subcommittee Skeptical of Proposed Communications Coding Device*, June 10, 1993.

## 7

On Blind Signatures and Perfect Crimes*

Sebastiaan von Solms and David Naccache

David Chaum has introduced the idea of blind signatures, an extension of the concept of digital signatures, as a way to protect the identity and privacy of a user in electronic payment and service networks. Blind signatures also prevent so-called "dossier creation" about users by organizations.

While the concept of blind signatures still allows authorities to distinguish between valid and false data, it prevents these authorities from connecting specific data or actions to specific users.

With the growing emphasis on the protection of the privacy of user data and user actions in electronic systems, blind signatures seem to be a perfect solution. This paper however, discusses a problematic aspect of blind signatures, showing that this perfect solution can potentially lead to perfect crime.

We use a real crime case as an example.

INTRODUCTION

Blind signatures can be used when a user wants to create legal electronic money, i.e. electronic money authorized by the bank. Once this money is created, it can be spent by the user without anybody anywhere being able to trace the money back to the user. This idea is described in detail in refs. 1 and 2.

The big (potential) benefit of the data is that individual surveillance (traceability) becomes impossible since it is not possible to determine who spends the electronic money.

Very much simplified, the concept works as follows. Assume the public existence of a one-way function f and an RSA modulus n.

Step 1.   The user requests electronic money from the bank.

* Computers and Security, Vol. 11, No. 6. Copyright 1992, Elsevier Science Publishers Ltd.

1.1. The user chooses two random numbers: a so-called blinding factor r, and x, and computes

$$B = r^3 f(x) \bmod n$$

B is sent to the bank.

1.2. The bank computes:

$$D = \sqrt[3]{B} \bmod n$$

and withdraws one "money unit" from the user's bank account, putting this "money unit" into a money pool. The bank sends D back to the user.

1.3. The user divides D by $r \pmod n$, and keeps $C = \sqrt[3]{f(X)} \bmod n$, the result of the division. $\{x, \sqrt[3]{f(X)} \bmod n\}$ now represents one legal authorized "money unit" $\{x, C\}$. Note that, although the bank knows it sent D back to the specific user, once D is divided by r, with only r known to the user, the resultant $\{x, C\}$ is in no way traceable to the specific user.

Step 2. The user spends his electronic money.

2.1. The user now offers $\{x, C\}$ as payment for one "money unit's" purchase to the shopkeeper/cash delivery machine/service selling entity.

2.2. The shopkeeper checks that $f(x) = C^3$ and if so, checks with the bank that $\{x, C\}$ has not been used previously.

2.3. The shopkeeper offers $\{x, C\}$ to the bank, who pays him one "money unit" from the money pool. It is totally impossible to trace this "money unit" back to our original user (in step 1).

Note that the user will, of course, use a smart card or similar technology to do the necessary calculations but for allowing the users to get convinced that the system is really blind, all such technological details are assumed to be public and only the factoring of the modulus n is kept secret by the authority.

THE KOBAYASHI CREDIT CARD CASE

In his book *Dossiers d'Interpol 2*, Pierre Bellemare [3] reports the following criminal case. In the early 1970s, a man opens bank account # 1326387 in the Shinjubu branch of the First Kangyo Bank (Tokyo) and, after he has deposited ¥15,000 the bank supplies him with a credit card. About a month later the baby of Mashahito Tsugawa, a famous Japanese TV actor, is kidnapped and a so-called "Kobayashi" threatens to kill the baby if an amount of 5 million Yen is not immediately accredited on the bank account # 1326387. A short enquiry shows that Kobayashi is a false identity. The police identify the program of the central computer to trace ATM operations in real-time. Policemen are placed near each machine and all withdrawal operations are filtered. Some days later, Kobayashi is caught while trying to withdraw money with his card.

THE KOBAYASHI BLIND SIGNATURE CASE

Suppose the First Kangyo Bank used a blind signature system, and Kobayashi decided to use it. If he used the following strategy, he could have committed the perfect crime (as far as the financial aspect is concerned!).

Step 1.   Open a bank account, receive the smartcard and kidnap the baby.

Step 2.

2.1.   Choose a set of xs $(x_1, x_2, \ldots, x_p)$ and a set of rs $(r_1, r_2, \ldots, r_p)$.

2.2.   Compute the set B_j where $B_j = r_j^3 f(x_j) \bmod n$ and mail the set B_j to the authorities with the threat to kill the baby if the following instructions are not complied with:

2.2.1.   For all j, compute the set $D_j = \sqrt[3]{B_j} \bmod n$

2.2.2.   Publish the set D_j in a newspaper.

2.3.   Buy the newspaper and compute the set $C_j = D_j/r_j \bmod n$. $\{(x_j, C_j)\}$ now represents legal authorized money which can in no way be traced to Kobayashi.

Step 3.   Free the baby.

Kobayashi can now freely spend all this money without any danger of ever being identified.

DISCUSSION

Note that Kobayashi's first attempt failed because the credit card was an identity token which linked him to the bank account where the money was deposited. Withdrawing the money could therefore be traced back to him. In the second attempt this was impossible.

CONCLUSION

In this paper we tried to show that, while blind signatures can protect individuals from the "big brother is watching" situation, it may on the other hand create the situation where these same individuals may be deprived of some other type of protection.

Blind signatures can therefore provide potential problems for law enforcement of some types of crimes.

For the discussion above it is clear that blind signatures can be employed for successful criminal purposes that could not have been achieved without blind signatures.

On the other hand, blind signatures have beautiful properties which can be used to benefit mankind in general, and one should be careful not to throw out the baby with the bath water.

Maybe the moral of the story is, specifically in the area of information security research, to try to develop more formal ways in which new mechanisms and protocols can be proved to be sound, or at least analyzed to determine if any conflicting conditions or situations do exist.

Promising work on these issues is being done, e.g. ref. 4.

REFERENCES

[1] D. Chaum, A. Fiat and M. Naor, Untraceable electronic cash. In S. Goldwasser (ed.), *Lecture Notes in Computer Science # 403, Proc. Crypto '88*, Springer-Verlag, Berlin, 1990, pp. 319–327.

[2] D. Chaum, Security without identification: Transaction systems to make big brother obsolete, *CACM 28/10*, 1985, pp. 1030–1044.

[3] P. Bellemare and J. Antoine, *Dossiers d'Interpol 2*, Editions N1, 1976, pp. 301–308.

[4] S. H. von Solms and N. Edwards, Designing and implementing a new security model, Int. J. Comp. Math., 29 (1989) 139–149.

## CHAPTER 7

EXPORT POLICY

PRUDENT CONTROLS IN A RISKY WORLD OR MAKING THE WORLD SAFE FOR FOREIGN COMPETITION?

The United States Government continues to impose rigid controls on the export of encryption software and hardware products, despite evidence that the policies governing the issuing of export licenses inhibit U.S. businesses' ability to compete in the foreign marketplace—a marketplace that already offers encryption software and hardware that incorporates the very standards that U.S. businesses cannot export because of export controls.

As Bernstein describes, exports of cryptographic software and hardware are controlled by the U.S. Department of State and the U.S. Department of Commerce. The State Department uses the International Traffic in Arms Regulations (ITAR) which include the "Munitions List"; this list enumerates munitions material for which export licensing is required; encryption materials are included in Category XIII. Commerce Department requirements are set forth in the Export Administration Regulations and the Commerce Control List. The National Security Agency (NSA) has a very strong voice in these decisions.

Turner discusses how U.S. firms and multinationals with U.S. operations have to increasingly be aware of electronic espionage, in some cases by intelligence agencies of foreign powers who have a broader definition of "national security" than they once did, expanding it now to include "economic security". Good encryption is, of course, a prime weapon against this kind of espionage. Turner argues that export controls inhibit the employment of encryption technology by U.S.-based multinational corporations at a time when cryptography is becoming increasingly indispensable to securing sensitive business information.

453

He asserts that the position of the U.S. government does not reflect the realities of international business needs in today's global markets, and presents action items for a policy agenda for the U.S. Government to help U.S. corporations in the face of the increased threat from economic espionage. He also notes that as cryptographic products become increasingly embedded in general purpose products, the old cryptographic export policy becomes increasingly unworkable. [Note that references to COCOM are dated—it no longer exists.]

Walker presents data gathered in conjunction with the Software Publishers Association which shows numerous hardware and software encryption products available around the world. Roughly half of these use DES; they are available in the United States and 22 other countries (see Exhibit 1). He describes importing several DES products and notes the "frustrating and somewhat humorous" incident in which NIST

EXHIBIT 1. *Countries from Which Encryption Products were Obtained*

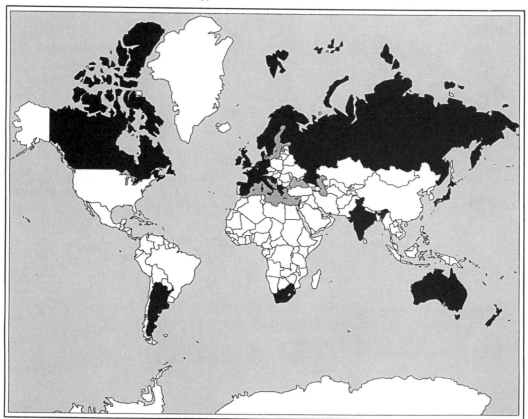

Software Publishers Association, 1994

posted source code for DES to the Internet without an export restriction notice and it was immediately copied by computers in Denmark, the United Kingdom, and Taiwan. As he points out, FIPS 181 (which contains the DES source code) now "is available from hosts throughout the world along with the notice that export from the U. S. is in violation of U.S. export controls."

Walker, drawing upon information from others, relates a large number of lost sales opportunities for U. S. firms due to crypto export controls, with probable losses in the millions of dollars. He supports treating export of crypto products as normal commodities, rather than munitions. At this writing, the federal government is currently studying that situtation [see the Gore-Cantwell letter on pp. 236–238.] Walker's testimony includes two appendices: cryptographic products available around the world, and companies manufacturing and/or distributing cryptographic products around the world.

Christensen provides a summary of the recent structure of the Export Administration Regulations as they apply to software and technology transfers. I challenge anyone to understand these in less than three detailed readings! Complying with these regulations is daunting, and his paper illustrates that a manufacturer who is exporting software or having foreign nationals develop it could unwittingly run afoul of U. S. law.

We then present two conflicting U.S. government rulings on the legality of exporting cryptographic software. In the first, the Department of State contents that export of a diskette with source code for high quality cryptography is prohibited, even though export of the same source code printed in a book is allowed (even in this day of inexpensive scanners!). The second, written by Harmon in a Justice Department memorandum to the Science Advisor to the President, states that "the present ITAR licensing scheme does not meet constitutional standards". He gives detailed arguments to support this, and makes some suggestions to remedy some of the problems. Specifically, he concludes that "a prepublication review requirement for cryptographic information might meet First Amendment standards if it provided necessary proecedural safeguards and precisely drawn guidelines."

1

Encryption's International Labyrinth*

David S. Bernstein

Companies conducting business put their proprietary information at risk with every transmission. To shield their secrets from individual spies, foreign intelligence operators and other snoops, many multinational enterprises are increasingly relying on encryption.

"There's a feeling that information is not secure, especially from foreign governments themselves," says James Wegman, manager of security for Philip Morris Companies Inc. in New York City. "If you're moving into a country where you haven't been before, you must have an information protection program, including encryption."

However, there are risks to using encryption technology as a result of the myriad regulations that restrict precisely who may scramble messages and how, when, and where the technology can be used.

International use of encryption plunges the user headfirst into a legal morass of import, export and privacy regulations that are often obscure and sometimes contradictory. "A company doing business in Denmark, Germany, Belgium and France might find itself in a position where it cannot encrypt messages while satisfying all the [governmental] requirements," says Ralph Spencer Poore, director, information security services for New York-based Coopers & Lybrand. "There are corporations that are clearly violating the law, often unintentionally," he says. They could wake up to substantial liabilities."

"It is very difficult to standardize your products" in this atmosphere adds Douglas Miller, government affairs representative for the Software Publishers Association (SPA) in Washington, D.C. "You have to spend huge amounts of billable legal hours trying to figure out what you can do."

Only a lawyer can sort out the potential liabilities of international encryption, but awareness of the following issues should keep an organization safe, or at least looking in the right places.

ENCRYPTION IS A WEAPON

The United States classifies encryption products as munitions, and is wary of allowing such products out of the country. This accounts for

---

* January/February 1994. Infosecurity News.

the near-impossibility, according to many security experts, of obtaining export licenses for products featuring the tougher encryption algorithms.

Export restrictions also apply to all products that contain cryptography, such as electronic mail, databases and data-compression products. An "export-controlled sticker on any of those probably means that the purchaser cannot legally send a copy to any overseas office, even its own, without proper licensing.

The United States has relaxed export controls on encryption using RC2 or RC4 algorithms, but critics contend that these proprietary 40-bit keys are too easy to crack compared to the 56-bit Data Encryption Standard (DES) algorithm. In addition, with DES a *de facto* standard in many application, RC2, RC4, and other relatively weak encryptors may be simply incompatible for some uses. Still, they may be perfectly adequate for many purposes. "Not everybody needs to drive around in a tank," notes Lance Hoffman, professor of computer science at George Washington University and director of the GWU Computer and Telecommunications Systems Policy Institute in Washington, D.C.

Organizations can always apply to the State Department and the National Security Agency (NSA) for licenses to export more robust products, a process that typically takes six to eight weeks. The government professes that those licenses are obtainable for legitimate reasons. Others claim that only the weakest algorithms are given the go-ahead. "It's a Catch-22," says Poore. "If you get permission from the U.S. to use it, that probably means it's too easy to decrypt."

"Getting an export license is a lot of work," adds Richard Heffernan, president of R.J. Heffernan Associates, Inc., a security consultant based in Branford, Connecticut. "Say the wrong thing and you'll never get that license."

Others disagree. "The system isn't there to be unnecessarily restrictive," argues William Ferguson, vice president of sales and marketing at Semaphore Communications Corp., a Santa Clara, Calif. manufacturer of encryption products. Ferguson says that requests to export DES-based and other encryption products are almost always approved for legitimate business use to overseas subsidiaries with at least 50.1 percent U.S. ownership.

"For use within our sites in 60 or 70 countries, I'm confident that we could get a license to implement any security we wanted to," says Fred Mailman, export manager for Hewlett-Packard Co., based in Palo Alto, California. "Of course, a big company like HP can hire a guy like me to be on the phone to bug the NSA day in and day out.

Ferguson recommends asking the encryption vendor to process the organization's export-license request, which will ensure that all proper steps are taken through the bureaucratic maze. Mailman agrees. "For the uninitiated it's overwhelming to go through these regulations," he says.

Another alternative is to purchase foreign-made encryption products, which are proliferating, according to an SPA study. The SPA has identified more than 200 foreign encryption products, including many that use the DES algorithm.

The Clinton administration may yet relax the export restrictions on encryption, as it recently did on multiprocessor RISC computers. But as of now, the U.S. takes its munitions control seriously. Poore relates one instance of a company that received permission to send an encryption hardware product to its Middle East office, with the stipulation that it keep a blender next to the machine. In the event of a security breach in the office, the security officer is required to remove the algorithm-embedded chip and pulverize it in the blender.

Differing National Laws

Encryption products are not on the Coordinating Committee (CoCom) International Munitions List, so the type of encryption an organization uses may affect its acceptance by other countries. Encryption for the purposes of message authentication is widely allowed, whereas encryption for the purposes of keeping information private raises eyebrows. Financial institutions, for example, routinely use encryption on all transactions. In most instances the text of these transmissions is readable; the cryptography serves only to validate that the message is legitimate and has not been altered.

Another potentially troublesome technology is high-security devices that support frequent regeneration of encryption keys. This technology may be incompatible with a country's key-registration requirements and lead to trouble. "You can register your master key, but within seconds that key is history," explains Ralph Spencer Poore, director, information security services for New York-based Coopers & Lybrand. If a government for any reason wants to read an encrypted message, the old registered key would do nothing—and the company might be unable to replicate the key. "It could create a horrible liability," Poore says. "They could take your inability to cooperate as a contempt of court."

All of the problems associated with international use of data encryption will apply equally to voice and video encryption, which more organizations are adding to their security repertoire. "Now that we have the capability to transmit [voice and data] digitally, you can store that transmission and manipulate it any way you want," says James P. Chandler, President of the National Intellectual Property Law Institute in Washington, D.C. "It can be modified as easily as text."

Products that automate key management and password updating will be a boon to crypto users. But users may have to obtain licenses to send those products to every needed international location, which may not be easy.

Also unanswered is how encryption will keep pace as companies use more and more high-speed digital-transmission technologies. Current DES encryption tops out at about 9 Mbps, according to William Ferguson, vice president of sales and marketing at Semaphore Communications Corp., a Santa Clara, Calif. manufacturer of encryption products. While this adequately covers T1 (1.544 Mbps) and European E1 (2.048 Mbps) link speeds, it will fall woefully behind future asynchronous-transfer mode link speeds exceeding 100 Mbps.

2

Federal Policy Impact on U.S. Corporate Vulnerability to Economic Espionage*

Geoffrey W. Turner

My name is Geoffrey Turner. I am a senior consultant in the Information Security program at SRI International. I have been involved in both sides of the economic espionage issue, first as a U.S. Naval intelligence officer, and then as a vice president at Bank of America responsible for communications security. For the last four years, I have been supporting SRI's International Information Integrity Institute, which has been assisting over 60 large multinational corporations to establish and sustain the security of their sensitive information in the international environment. I have also been involved in the debate surrounding the cryptographic policy issues that I discuss below for over seven years, and I welcome the opportunity to assist the committee in assessing these policies in the context of the increasingly serious threat of economic espionage.

ECONOMIC ESPIONAGE AND U.S. CORPORATIONS

With the end of the Cold War has come both an increased incidence of economic espionage targeted against U.S. corporations, as well as an increased awareness of the existence of this activity. This espionage is aimed at acquiring U.S. corporate trade secrets, advanced technology, product information business plans and all types of proprietary information which can provide competitors with an advantage. Business has long experienced this type of activity originating from competing businesses, but what is new is that foreign national intelligence services are now conducting such espionage against U.S. corporations, employing resources of much greater scale and sophistication. Intrusion into corporate information systems and interception of business messages in commercial and private networks by these intelligence services is a real and ongoing threat of which many U.S. corporations are unaware and vulnerable.

---

* Statement Before the Subcommittee on Economic and Commercial Law, Committee on the Judiciary, United States House of Representatives. May 7, 1992.

In the case of the former Soviet-bloc nations, it is becoming clear that the intelligence services that operated under the control of past communist governments continue operations under postcommunist governments. Since these nations see themselves at severe relative disadvantage to the highly competitive market economies of the West, it is obvious that they will place high national priorities on becoming more effective competitors in business affairs. In the past, this same situation applied to the balance of military technology between East and West, and the response of the Eastern Bloc intelligence services was to acquire Western technology and duplicate it in their own systems to remain competitive militarily. It is reasonable to assume that the intelligence services will continue to use this strategy that was previously effective and apply it to meeting economic objectives rather than military ones. Since the technology and information of strategic interest has now expanded to all types of U.S. business, and not just defense contractors, sectors of U.S. business that have not been prepared by U.S. counterintelligence programs are now subject to the same level of espionage as was previously directed at defense targets.

An additional problem is that the operations of the former East Bloc intelligence services may not be under effective control of their present governments. Some intelligence collection operations, such as that uncovered in Belgium recently, appear to have continued out of the sheer momentum of the long-standing targeting of Western nations and the immense resources applied to those targets. Such incidents lend credence to the concerns that the new governments have not yet gained full control of their intelligence services, and that the economic espionage that is beginning to intensify may exceed the constraints that their governments would like to have applied to preserve good relations with both U.S. businesses and the government.

Further, there is an additional concern that there are large numbers of former intelligence service agents with advanced capabilities in espionage techniques that are no longer employed by their national governments and whose services may be available on the open market. This could lead to the increase in the economic espionage threat from Third World nations that had not previously had access to more sophisticated espionage resources, as well as to non-government organizations such as terrorist groups and foreign businesses not constrained by ethics to legal methods in business competition. An early indicator that this may become a problem in the future is the appearance of former KGB agents in Hollywood selling the story of their past exploits. The resulting movie projects may well serve as either intentional or unintentional advertising campaigns for their new commercial availability as freelance espionage agents.

The end of the Cold War has, in addition to creating new problems for U.S. corporations with former Eastern Bloc national intelligence resources, shifted the focus of international attention on national competition from military to economic contexts. As a result of the increasing decline of the threat of a catastrophic nuclear war, there is a concurrent increase in the realization of the importance of economic competitiveness in the definition of national security. National relationships previously defined in terms of military alliances change significantly when viewed instead in terms of economic competition. Allies become competitors in economic terms. And to the extent that intelligence services support the current definition of national security, as economic objectives rise in priority in our allies' definition of national security so does the interest of allied nations' intelligence services in economic espionage.

Several cases of economic espionage directed against U.S. business by the intelligence services of our allies have been exposed in the media in the last few years, which raises serious concerns about the extent of cases which are known but not exposed in the media or are never discovered at all. Non-defense contractor U.S. corporations are ill-prepared to recognize the scope, scale or intensity of the threat of economic espionage directed against them, and are even less prepared to defend their trade secrets, proprietary technology and information, and consequently retain their international competitiveness.

The U.S. government has just begun to assess the potential seriousness of the impact this new threat of economic espionage has on U.S. national security. There are a few early initiatives to address the issue, such as that by the State Department's Overseas Security Advisory Committee, however, much more needs to be done and done in a much more comprehensive context. Not only do we need to assess the extent of the threat, and what specifically can be done to counter it, we also urgently need to identify what we are presently doing that is counter-productive to defending U.S. corporations against economic espionage.

Changing current government policy and programs to be more effective counters to economic espionage provides a much needed immediate and cost-effective response to the urgent needs of U.S. business. Several areas of government policy towards cryptography that can be adjusted to address some of the more important defensive requirements of U.S. corporations include:

- Export controls on commercial cryptography—such as the restrictions on DES
- NIST's role in developing civil and commercial information and communications security capabilities—such as the current problems with the proposed Digital Signature Standard

COMMERCIAL CRYPTOGRAPHY

Commercial cryptography has recently arrived at several critical junctures in its evolution. It has matured technically to the point where it is now widely available for implementation in many different architectures and has been incorporated into many different types of products. More importantly, business has begun to recognize the tremendous utility of applying cryptography to many different commercial information security problems. The net result is that the use of cryptography in the commercial environment has finally matured into a generally accepted mainstay of information security. This maturity is very timely, since the technical threat to sensitive information in distributed processing networks is rising dramatically as more national intelligence agencies increasingly target proprietary business information in the post-bipolar world.

However, even though cryptography is becoming increasingly indispensable to securing sensitive business information, a major impediment to full realization of cryptography's benefits to international business operations remains which could severely hamper or deny the effective use of cryptography to protect business information. Export controls on cryptographic technology continue to unduly restrict the movement of cryptographic technology across national borders to the international locations where multi-national enterprises need them.

BACKGROUND

Over the last ten years, there has been rapid and widespread growth in the commercial sector's dependence on computers and data networks to accomplish business objectives vital to the functioning of national economies. As this dependency continues to expand, the health of national economies must rely on the ability of these systems to continue operations unimpeded. A primary factor in ensuring this is the availability and use of systems security technology to protect these systems and the critical business data they contain.

In much of modern international business information processing, such as with Electronic Funds Transfer or Electronic Data Interchange, vital information with very high dollar value is resident within computers and networks in electronic form. This information, in order to benefit business and the economy, must flow securely across networks, national borders and through multiple computer systems. In this fluid environment, the information must be protected by a mechanism that can flow with that information, regardless of its position in any system or network. Increasingly, business is depending upon commercial cryptography to provide this protection.

The pre-eminent cryptographic algorithm used for this purpose has been that in the Data Encryption Standard, which is commonly referred to as DES. Established as a federal government standard in the United States in the late 1970's, it is being adopted by the international banking industry as the primary means of protecting electronic funds transfers. DES has been established in a number of banking industry national and international standards for security, and it is now being extended into non-financial industry standards, such as EDI. DES is also increasingly being used by multinational corporations to protect sensitive information transmitted between internal units in different countries. The demand for DES technology is growing rapidly, and is consequently being imbedded by manufacturers into many computer systems products.

The DES algorithm is unique in that it has been publicly available, world-wide, since its development. The security provided by the algorithm does not depend upon keeping the algorithm secret. On the contrary, the fact that it has been published widely and yet not broken over the space of more than fifteen years indicates a high degree of security strength. It is because of this security strength and the wide availability of the algorithm, that DES has become so prevalent in the commercial sector.

THE ERODING BASIS FOR EXISTING EXPORT POLICY

Prior to the Computer Age, the primary users of cryptography were those involved in the traditional national security disciplines: the military, intelligence agencies and the diplomatic corps. In this context, nations were concerned that their cryptographic technology not fall into the hands of those whose interests were inimical to their national interests. Such an event could jeopardize sensitive government information protected by the same technology, and could also make it more difficult for the national intelligence agencies to collect intelligence against such technological protection. Consequently, national export controls were emplaced to restrict the export of all cryptographic technology and techniques.

The export of cryptographic technology for commercial use continues to be strictly controlled by national governments, with the rationale for this continuing to be based upon "national security" considerations. Several years ago in I-4, we discussed how the changing nature of international relations was rapidly weakening the case for controlling cryptographic export for stereotypical national security reasons. We also made the point that as national competition increasingly shifts from the military sphere to the economic, the threat to a country's national security comes more from threats to its business sector than from military adventurism. While this was quite true two years ago, it is an even more forceful argument today.

In the last two years, we have witnessed the bipolar world of the Cold War disintegrating with shocking suddenness. First, Eastern Europe became truly independent and then came the stunning events in the Soviet Union that lead to its continuing breakup as a superpower. The significant military threat that the West had been defending against for more than four decades has largely evaporated, and continues to decline further with successive new disarmament agreements. Military threats to national security have now devolved to potential disruptions of regional stability, as in the recent conflict with Iraq, rather than questions of national or global survival in the face of massive strategic nuclear threats. Yet the old national security rationale still dominates cryptography export control policy; intelligence agencies insist on maximizing the ability to freely collect intelligence on potential enemies at the expense of any other national priorities.

That the intensity of the military threat to world stability is receding should by itself prompt a review of the severity of national policy on cryptographic export for commercial purposes. But adding to the urgency for such review is the other major influence, the increasing intensity of national economic competition. As discussed in I-4 before, the potential damage to national security from trade imbalances and lack of economic competitiveness is today much more imminent than military threats. Intelligence agencies are beginning to awaken to this new intelligence collection mission area, as much out of bureaucratic self-interest and for maintaining a justification for continued existence, as for reasons of deliberate national policy. We are beginning to see indications that they are now targeting the proprietary information of commercial enterprises, as exemplified in the recent media reports about the French secret service operations.

Cryptographic export policy should also be reviewed in the context of each nation ensuring that its business sector has available to it the security resources necessary to protect proprietary information against theft by foreign intelligence services or other commercial competitors. National security, in the form of damage to the national economy, can be severely affected by the loss of a competitive advantage in a critical industry due to the theft of leading edge technology or manufacturing processes by competing nations. National governments do not appear to have yet adequately considered this aspect of cryptographic export policy. The responsible government agencies generally retain their orientation towards traditional national security definitions and are unfamiliar with the implications of international economic competition on national security since such concerns in the past had been outside their policy jurisdiction. And those government agencies with responsibility for national economic well-being have either been slow to recognize the growing problem with export controls on cryptography, or have not had the bureaucratic power to bring the issue up for national review.

In many cases, it is the same government agency that is responsible for both intelligence collection and for providing for the security of its own nation's communications, as well as establishing the basis for cryptography export policy. This conflict of interest has led to abuses of authority in the past, which has hampered the development of commercial cryptography. One basis for restricting export of commercial cryptographic technology is the possibility that the technology could fall into the hands of organizations against which the nation is trying to collect intelligence. In the past, the most commonly cited example was a terrorist organization. But now in the context of the above discussion, potential intelligence targets include the commercial businesses trying to export the cryptography technology to protect their proprietary information. This is clearly a case of the fox guarding the henhouse, and a review of a nation's cryptographic export policy needs to take this institutional bias and conflict of interest into account.

The export policy of the U.S. remains basically unchanged from two years ago. Export of DES technology is under the control of the Department of Commerce for the following types of cryptographic products:

- Message authentication
- Access control (password or PIN encryption only)
- Software protection (encryption of the code only)
- ATM

All other types of cryptography remain under the procedural control of the State Department, and the policy control of the National Security Agency (NSA). The NSA has not published its own policy guidelines on what it will allow to be exported, but has informally indicated to the business community that it will issue export licenses for DES technology:

- For financial industry use—use by a financial institution for financial purposes. This includes but is not limited to funds transfer applications, automated teller controllers, point-of-sale or other bank-customer devices, if the financial institution holds title to the equipment.
- Computer access control applications—Authentication, PIN and password protection, proprietary software protection, and other uses designed to prevent access to the computational facilities of computers. This does not include file encryption or other transmission security features.

■ Use by a U.S. company—A U.S. company may export DES for the protection of its own information.

The guidelines for export of non-DES cryptographic products are not publicly known and are basically decided on a case by case basis. The NSA has not identified what constitutes "financial use" or how they define a company to be U.S.-owned. Thus while they presently appear to be flexible in approving export licenses for DES technology under these guidelines, this flexibility can disappear without notice, as can the guidelines themselves. The U.S. policy generally is most flexible for all uses of cryptography except data encryption, which is consistent with the concern about intelligence collection discussed above. This was not a major problem for businesses in the past, because previously the major concern of commercial information security was with information integrity, rather than information confidentiality. Yet we have also just discussed the growing threat of government-sponsored spying on business communications, which is increasing the requirement for businesses to have data encryption capabilities to meet the rising priority of data confidentiality. It is in the area of data encryption that U.S. export policy is most restrictive, and this policy is generated by the NSA, which now has a large potential interest in collecting economic intelligence from multinational commercial business enterprises.

CONSEQUENCES OF THESE CONSTRAINTS

Such positions, taken on the grounds of national security, do not reflect the realities of international business needs in today's global markets. For users of DES technology, these limited views of national security have reduced the ability of companies to protect their critical business information in computer systems and data networks around the world. For manufacturers of computer and network technology, global markets are increasingly demanding imbedded security capabilities, such as DES cryptography. Manufacturers in less export restrictive nations are able to incorporate DES technology in their products, while more restrictive nations, such as the U.S., prevent manufacturers from exporting competitive products to international markets.

In fact the existing U.S. export controls on commercial cryptography are not completely effective, as many companies are either unaware of the export controls or are unaware that cryptography has been imbedded in such ordinary processors and software products as personal computers and file management software. As a consequence, cryptographic capabilities are being exported in contravention to the existing controls, making ludicrous the arguments that the controls are effective in preventing this cryptography from falling into the hands of international terrorists and criminals. What the controls are effective in doing, however, is preventing widespread international business use of this cryptography, including more effective use by U.S businesses. In fact the actual goal of the intelligence services is to use the export controls to keep the level of international communications encrypted by commercial cryptography to levels low enough to be manageable by their code-breaking resources.

However, since DES technology is widely available internationally, restrictive DES export policies cannot provide the national security benefits they are intended to provide: prevent DES technology from being widely used internationally. The effect that such policy does have is to force affected companies to either risk lower levels of protection of their business information internationally, or to buy foreign-made information technology for international use, which can have DES technology incorporated into it.

The net effect of this policy is to make U.S. corporations less competitive in foreign markets, with consequential impact on the balance of trade. This is not a small impact, considering that the industry most impaired by this export policy is the computer manufacturing industry. That industry provides most of this nation's competitive edge in advanced technology innovation, and has substantial impact on the nation's exports and trade balance. Reduced international competitiveness in the U.S. computer manufacturing industry would have serious long term effects on the economy of the nation.

From an international market perspective, manufacturers in less export restrictive nations have more open access to foreign markets than manufacturers from more highly export restrictive nations. This artificial segmentation of international markets for information technology has been less problematic in the early stages of development of security technology. But now DES technology is becoming more widely used internationally and will increasingly be imbedded in mainstream computer products. Export restrictions will become a significant obstacle both to free competition amongst international information technology manufacturers and to the wide availability of secure cryptographic products for international use. Should some of the more export restrictive nations reduce or eliminate export restrictions on DES technology, it will motivate other governments to do the same in order to preserve the competitiveness of their own computer manufacturing industries. The resulting unrestricted access to international markets will benefit the economies of both provider and user nations.

An additional consideration in evaluating the impact of these policies on commercial information security is that they are designed to allow export of cryptography that is good enough to discourage most unsophisticated attackers, but not so good as to unduly complicate the intelligence collection mission of intelligence agencies. This policy context was basically acceptable to businesses when they were primarily concerned about relatively unsophisticated attacks on their information by hackers, competitors or casual insider browsers. But now that the threat has been expanded to include a new interest by intelligence agencies in proprietary business information, cryptography that is "good enough but not too good," is no longer acceptable. Thus export policies that restrict the transnational movement of strong commercial cryptography such as DES or RSA (the pre-eminent public key cryptographic algorithm in commercial use) encryption are becoming increasingly serious threats to the trade secrets and therefore the international competitiveness of U.S. business.

The cryptographic export policies of most western nations capable of producing sophisticated hardware implementations of cryptography are generally consistent with those of the U.S. described above. This consistency of policy derives from bilateral treaties between the nations, separate from the COCOM agreements. Thus while COCOM export restrictions are increasingly being eased in light of post-bipolar developments, this does not mean the same will occur in the area of cryptography export controls. Cryptography export policy changes will have to occur as the result of decisions by individual national governments taken outside the context of COCOM, and hopefully with consideration of the issues discussed above.

RISING COMMERCIAL PRESSURES FOR CHANGE

Commercial cryptography has matured in a number of ways, one of the most important of which is the increasing ubiquity of the function in information technology products. There continue to be products that are solely cryptographic in nature, both software and hardware, and these are being more widely implemented. Much more important though, is the increasingly widespread imbedding of cryptographic functions within other information technology architectures and products:

- IBM has announced a Common Cryptographic Architecture, Integrated Cryptographic Facility, Transaction Security System, all of which provide for the integration of DES cryptographic functions as utilities functions in processors such as the ES /390.
- DEC has announced the Distributed Systems Security Architecture that employs both DES and RSA cryptography in providing security in a distributed environment.
- Motorola, Microsoft, Lotus, Apple and others have announced the incorporation of the RSA algorithm into their products, initially

for software integrity protection, but most likely ultimately as a utility function for digital signatures and other data security functions.

- Kerberos and SESAME are distributed processing security architectures which depend on the use of cryptography to establish and maintain a consistent level of security.
- Electronic Funds Transfer and Electronic Data Interchange security are dependent upon cryptographic standards to provide the security functionality necessary to operate these systems.

This trend is certain to accelerate as more users become accustomed to having security functions based upon cryptography as an integral part of their systems, and come to expect these security functions to be a normal utility. The information technology market is certainly moving in this direction, which means that an increasingly large proportion of general purpose information technology products are going to contain an imbedded cryptographic capability. This also means that these general purpose products will fall under the aegis of the national cryptographic export laws. If export policies are not changed then many general purpose products will not be exportable, putting information technology manufacturers, vendors and users in a dilemma.

If they want to use the state of the art information technology in support of their international business objectives, they will either have to procure all products with imbedded cryptography from each country in which they intend to use it, or they will have to forego the effective security inherent in imbedded cryptographics. In the former case interoperability of disparate cryptographic systems becomes a problem, in addition to the problems of finding adequate products in all of the international locations where it is necessary to do business securely. In the latter case, the security risks of doing business without cryptographic protection for proprietary information may be too high, and the business opportunity in that location is lost.

Present cryptographic export policy was developed when cryptographic products were specialized, dedicated products which had no other functions than performing cryptographic functions. Now that the information technology marketplace has evolved towards cryptographic functions imbedded in operating systems, applications programs, network operating systems, mainframes, microcomputers, and a multitude of other mainstream commercial information technology products, the old cryptographic export policy becomes increasingly unworkable.

If the existing policies remain unchanged, each country with these policies will begin to experience a loss of competitiveness in the information technology market as their products with imbedded cryptography are restricted from full competition in international markets.

Their user businesses may also begin to suffer due to lost opportunities or loss of proprietary information to international competitors. Reportedly, there are large Japanese electronics and computer manufacturers which are not subject to comparable restrictions by their government on the export of commercial cryptography, creating a potentially serious competitive imbalance between U.S. and Japanese corporations in the market for secure information and communications systems for international businesses.

Clearly this is unacceptable to most countries, and the likelihood is that in the next few years the pressure from both manufacturers and users of information technology will force a change in the current restrictive export policies. Because these policies are national and only consistent internationally due to a web of bilateral treaties, liberalization will likely not be implemented collectively, but rather by individual nations independently. The countries experiencing the most economic pain from current export policies towards cryptography will also likely be the first to change these policies, creating an unequal playing ground for information technology products. Once the first one or two nations liberalize cryptography export policy, the others will be forced to follow suit by economic realities. The present stalemate in export policy is awaiting the first nation to break ranks, and the pressure to do so is rapidly rising.

While no changes to U.S. export policies on cryptography appear imminent, there is some apparent movement in that direction in Europe. The Department of Trade and Industry (DTI) has recognized that current cryptography export policies are an issue with U.K. industry. DTI has indicated that if U.K. industry believes that the current policy is restrictive to the point of putting U.K. companies at a competitive disadvantage internationally, DTI would be receptive to a collective statement from industry to that effect. They would be willing to accept such a statement from industry and carry it to the U.K. government policy-making bodies for consideration. This discussion is taking place and has advanced to the stage of identifying alternative approaches to export controls for meeting the information security needs of U.K. business and the traditional national security needs of the U.K. defense and intelligence organizations.

The recent call in the U.S. by the NIST Computer System Security and Privacy Advisory Board for a review of U.S. national policy on commercial cryptography appears to be a hopeful indication that the NSA is open to constructive discussions with U.S. corporations with the objective of better meeting their legitimate security needs. Congress should encourage and stimulate this dialog by providing the opportunity to incorporate the results of this dialog into legislation which modifies the structures of U.S. policy-making in areas which provide support for and create obstacles to improving the security of U.S. corporations in the face of an increasing economic espionage threat.

NIST's NATIONAL ROLE AND THE DIGITAL SIGNATURE STANDARD ISSUE

Digital signatures are created by using cryptographic techniques to "sign" electronic documents such as e-mail and electronic data interchange documents so that the authenticity of the sender and the integrity of the documents content can be proven. This is accomplished by calculating a number that represents the contents of the message, and then creating a digital signature by encrypting that number in a way that can be checked again when the message is received. The most well-known such digital signature process uses the encryption method called RSA, and it is in widespread commercial use world-wide. The U.S. government identified the need for a federal government standard for digital signatures, and a federal digital signature standard was proposed in October. Unfortunately, the standard won't use the already widely accepted RSA, and also contained several major flaws which made the standard's security weaker than that required for effective use in generating digital signatures.

The National Institute of Science and Technology's proposed federal Digital Signature Standard (DSS) has been the subject of controversy since it was introduced. The DSS was proposed to provide a digital signature integrity and authenticity mechanism for U.S. federal sensitive but unclassified information, and to serve as the business sector integrity mechanisms as well. Initially much of the debate centered around the fact that it employs a different algorithm, rather than the widely used RSA. After cryptographers analyzed the proposed algorithm, they also identified a significant number of shortcomings in it which indicate it is too weak to effectively produce unforgeable digital signatures. There has been widespread condemnation of the DSS from the commercial sector and from security experts. Given the serious flaws in the DSS that have been identified thus far, it now appears increasingly likely that the proposed DSS will not be approved as a U.S. federal standard.

Two researchers at Bellcore, Stuart Haber and Arjen Lenstra, have reportedly determined that it is possible to build a trapdoor into the proposed NIST Digital Signature Standard, allowing for forging apparently valid digital signatures. NIST acknowledged the existence of this potential vulnerability, but notes that it was not pointed out by NSA during the DSS design process. As a result of this discovery, Bellcore has decided not to distribute software implementing the DSS and has written strongly negative comments on DSS to the federal government.

There was widespread suspicion expressed publicly about the U.S. National Security Agency's specific role in developing the DSS algorithm, and it seems clear that the NSA was the driving force behind the specific cryptographic design of the DSS. A major reason for selecting the specific DSS algorithm, El Gamal, is that unlike the RSA algorithm, it cannot be used to encrypt information and thus complicate the NSA's intelligence collection mission. But once NSA had made this design choice for DSS, why did NSA then design a digital signature algorithm that had an obvious security flaw that made it too weak for its intended purpose?

Earlier this year, Senate Bill 266 was introduced in the U.S. Senate containing language that indicated that unnamed federal agencies wanted to ensure that they had the ability to circumvent commercial cryptographic security systems. The first federal cryptographic standard to be issued after this intent was expressed in fact does have a potential for trapdoor vulnerabilities. DSS appears to have been designed with a known vulnerability to trapdoors, meeting the intent of the language expressed in SB 266 for having such vulnerabilities exploitable by unnamed federal agencies. Subsequently this same basic trapdoor approach, requiring the inclusion of planned security vulnerabilities in the design of commercial systems, has been extended to commercial telecommunications systems in the legislation being suggested by the FBI under the Digital Telephony Amendment.

As a result of these objectives which are not directed at improving the security of commercial information systems, we are presented with proposed cryptographic standards that meet intelligence and law enforcement agency objectives for security mechanisms that can be defeated by those U.S. agencies. Unfortunately for U.S. corporations, it also makes these systems implementing these standards vulnerable to foreign intelligence agencies targeting them in economic espionage. Consequently such standards completely fail to meet the security objectives of the civil and business sectors for sound security mechanisms. Further, even if the DSS were established as a federal standard, it would not supplant RSA in the business sector, particularly internationally, where RSA is already the de facto digital signature standard.

U.S. corporate managers should strongly oppose the proposed DSS, but it is such a technical issue that the senior management of far too few corporations have become aware of the potential significance of the issue and the need to provide comment to government. Congress should also be aware that the current structure for carrying out the mandate of the Computer Security Act is not effective in meeting the real information security needs of the civil government and U.S. business.

Congress should amend the Computer Security Act to allow NIST sufficient independence from the NSA to be able to act as an uninhibited proponent of the valid and critical information security needs of civil government and the business sector. And Congress should appropriate sufficient funds for NIST to more effectively support both civil government and more importantly, U.S. corporations, in protecting their information against economic espionage. The defense-oriented approaches to security offered by the NSA are either not available for international use by U.S. corporations, are incompatible with acceptable business practices, or do not provide the level of security required to defend against economic espionage. When effective security technology is made available by the NSA, it too often comes with preconditions on its use that are incompatible with the real-world requirements for international operations by U.S. corporations.

BROADER NATIONAL SECURITY DEFINITION

From the preceding discussion, it becomes apparent that a national security policy, and its derivative national policies such as export controls, that focuses solely on military and intelligence objectives does not really serve the true national interests. Loss of U.S. corporate proprietary information and trade secrets to economic espionage by foreign intelligence services and non-availability of effective commercial information security countermeasures, will increasingly be the consequences of government policy and programs which adhere to an outdated definition of national security. The impact of these problems on U.S. corporate competitiveness in the international economy will become an increasingly serious concern to the U.S. national security that can be measured in financial terms. The degree to which national security, in a military or intelligence sense, is affected by the export of strong commercial cryptographic technology cannot be so precisely measured but is very likely to be far less significant due to the already widespread international availability of this technology.

Threats to the national security that are as severe and far-ranging as those raised by trade imbalances are unlikely to derive from inimical use of commercial cryptographic technology. There are far more powerful cryptographic and other security technologies available to those entities inimical to the interests of the U.S. who wish to evade monitoring by U.S. intelligence agencies. The only real damage to national security inflicted by increased use of commercial cryptographic technology, is that caused to U.S. commercial competitiveness by restrictive export policies.

A significant component of a nation's security is its continued economic well-being, which depends in large part on its ability to compete in global markets. Economic competitiveness must be more carefully balanced with traditional military and intelligence concerns in determining policy to protect the national security. In the case of export policy for commercial cryptography, the need for this balance has not been generally recognized, and the national security of the U.S. and its corporations are suffering as a result.

REQUIREMENTS FOR CHANGE

In the context of the above discussion, it is clear that at present the U.S. government is not effective in assisting U.S. corporations to effectively defend themselves against economic espionage by foreign intelligence services. One area of current U.S. government policy, export controls of commercial cryptography, are in fact operating contrary to the true U.S. national security interest by impeding access of U.S. corporations to effective use of cryptography in international commerce. At the same time, these policies place U.S. computer manufacturers at a competitive disadvantage in international markets by preventing them from fielding competitive products with imbedded cryptography as the market demands. As other nations begin to liberalize their own export controls in this area, the disadvantage to U.S. business on both counts deepens, and the requirement for change in U.S. export control policy deepens.

Therefore, there are several action items on the policy agenda of the U.S. government to help U.S. corporations in the face of the increased threat from economic espionage:

- At very senior policy levels within Congress and the Administration, review the past assumptions of what policy areas constitute definitions of national security, to free government policy from outdated Cold War assumptions that are increasingly damaging the economic national security of the United States.
- Conduct an honest and open review of national policies on commercial cryptography closely involving NIST, NSA, Congress and the Business sector with the goal of adapting policy to the valid needs of U.S. citizens and corporations, as well as law enforcement and intelligence agencies.
- Eliminate the export control restrictions on the two most important commercial cryptographic algorithms which are already widely available internationally, DES and RSA. It helps U.S. economic national security far more than it hinders military national security.
- Provide adequate funds and legislative authority for NIST to operate more independently of NSA influence in providing more ef-

fective assistance to U.S. corporations in developing and support-ing the information and communications security tools and programs that work effectively in competitive international com-merce.

- Re-affirm the Data Encryption Standard in 1993 as a federal stan-dard for the protection of sensitive but unclassified information. It remains one of the most effective commercial cryptographic sys-tems available to U.S. business and its reaffirmation as a federal standard is important to its continued effective use by business.

- Reject the proposed Digital Signature Standard (DSS) for being incompatible with the de facto digital signature standard in use world-wide, RSA. The DSS has less capability and is perceived as less secure than RSA, and will not be widely adopted by business, and for those who do adopt it, it provides a lesser degree of security.

3

Testimony Before the Committee on the Judiciary Subcommittee on Technology and the Law of the United States Senate*

Stephen T. Walker

EXPORT CONTROL OF CRYPTOGRAPHY

And there are other examples of how the government's dominant concern for national security and law enforcement capabilities has driven the U.S. down paths that harm our national economic interests.

Since the publication of the DES as a U.S. Federal Information Processing Standard (FIPS) in 1977, cryptography has shifted from the exclusive domain of governments to that of individuals and businesses. DES in both hardware and software implementations is a defacto international standard against which all other cryptographic algorithms are measured.

The controversy that arose as soon as DES was published concerning whether it had weaknesses that intelligence organizations could exploit fostered the highly fruitful academic research into public key cryptography in the late 1970s. Public key algorithms have the major advantage that the sender does not need to have established a previous secret key with the recipient for communications to begin. Public key algorithms, such as RSA, have become as popular and widely used as DES throughout the world for integrity, confidentiality, and key management.

Software Publishers Association Study

The Administration has asserted that export controls are not harming U.S. economic interests because there are no foreign cryptographic products and programs commercially available. Implementations of DES, RSA, and newer algorithms, such as the International Data Encryption Algorithm (IDEA), are available routinely on the Internet from sites all over the world. But according to the Administration, these do not count as commercial products.

---

* Extract from Testimony. May 3, 1994.

In order to understand just how widespread cryptography is in the world, in May of 1993, the Software Publishers Association (SPA) commissioned a study of products employing cryptography within and outside the U.S. There was a significant amount of knowledge about specific products here and there, but no one had ever tried to assemble a comprehensive database with, where possible, verification of product availability. I reported the results of this survey in hearings before the Subcommittee on Economic Policy, Trade and Environment, Committee on Foreign Affairs, U.S. House of Representatives last October.

Information on new products continues to flow in daily. As of today:

- We have identified 340 foreign hardware, software, and combination products for text, file, and data encryption from 22 foreign countries: Argentina, Australia, Belgium, Canada, Denmark, Finland, France, Germany, Hong Kong, India, Ireland, Israel, Japan, the Netherlands, New Zealand, Norway, Russia, South Africa, Spain, Sweden, Switzerland, and the United Kingdom.
- Of these, 155 employ DES either in hardware or software.
- We have confirmed the availability of 70 foreign encryption software programs and kits that employ the DES algorithm. These are published by companies in Australia, Belgium, Canada, Denmark, Finland, Germany, Israel, the Netherlands, Russia, Sweden, Switzerland, and the United Kingdom.
- Some of these companies have distributors throughout the world, including in the U.S. One German company has distributors in 14 countries. One U.K. company has distributors in at least 13 countries.
- The programs for these DES software products are installed by the users inserting a floppy diskette; the kits enable encryption capabilities to be easily programmed into a variety of applications.

A complete listing of all confirmed products in the database is identified in Attachment 1.

As part of this survey, we have ordered and taken delivery on products containing DES software from the following countries: Australia, Denmark, Finland, Germany, Israel, Russia, and the United Kingdom.

Foreign customers increasingly recognize and are responding to the need to provide software only encryption solutions. Although the foreign encryption market is still heavily weighted towards encryption hardware and hardware/software combinations, the market trend is towards software for reasons of cost, convenience, and space.

- On the domestic front, we have identified 423 products, of which 245 employ DES. Thus, at least 245 products are unable to be exported, except in very limited circumstances, to compete with the many available foreign products.

- In total, we have identified to date 763 cryptographic products, developed or distributed by a total of 366 companies (211 foreign, 155 domestic) in at least 33 countries.

DES is also widely available on the Internet, and the recently popularized Pretty Good Privacy encryption software program, which implements the IDEA encryption algorithm, also is widely available throughout the world.

The ineffectiveness of export controls is also evident in their inability to stop the spread of technology through piracy. The software industry has a multibillion dollar worldwide problem with software piracy. Mass market software is easy to duplicate and easy to ship via modem, suitcase, laptop, etc. Accordingly, domestic software products with encryption are easily available for export—through illegal but pervasive software piracy—to anyone who desires them.

Foreign customers who need data security now turn to foreign rather than U.S. sources to fulfill that need. As a result, the U.S. Government is succeeding only in crippling a vital American industry's exporting ability.

Frequently Heard Arguments

There are a series of arguments frequently heard to justify continued export control of cryptographic products.

The first argument is that such products are not available outside the U.S., so U.S. software and hardware developers are not hurt by export controls. The statistics from the SPA survey prove that this argument is false!

A second argument is that even if products are available, they cannot be purchased worldwide. Our experience with purchasing products indicates that this also is not true. We have found 462 companies in 33 foreign countries and the U.S. that are manufacturing, marketing, and/or distributing cryptographic products, most on a worldwide basis. The names of these companies are listed in Attachment 2.

All the products we ordered were shipped to us in the U.S. within a few days. The German products were sent to us directly from their U.S. distributors in Virginia and Connecticut, respectively. Our experience has been that if there is paperwork required by the governments in which these companies operate to approve cryptographic exports, it is minimal and results in essentially immediate approval for shipping to friendly countries.

A third argument frequently heard is that the products sold in other parts of the world are inferior to those available in the U.S. We have purchased products from several sources throughout the world. We ordered DES-based PC file encryption programs for shipment using routine channels from:

- Algorithmic Research Limited (ARL), Israel
- Sophos Ltd., UK
- Cryptomathic A/S, Denmark
- CEInfosys GmbH, Germany
- uti-maco, Germany
- Elias Ltd., Russia (distributed through EngRus Software International, UK)

The products we obtained from these manufacturers and distributors were in every case first-rate implementations of DES. To better understand if foreign products are somehow inferior, we have examined several of these products to see if we can detect flaws or inherent weaknesses.

What we have found in our limited examination is that while these products generally use fully compliant DES implementations, they sometimes do not make use of all the facilities that might be available to them. The result is a full-strength DES product that is fully adequate for protecting commercial sensitive information but would not meet the strict requirements of a full national security product review.

Two examples of facilities that these products do not fully utilize are:

- Initialization Vector (IV) (data added to the beginning of text to be encrypted to ensure synchronization with the decryption process)

    Frequently, these simple file encryption products use the same IV everytime. A product designed for protecting national security information would vary the IV each time.
- Key Generation

    Frequently, these products use an encryption key derived from a string of text that is typed in by the user. Users may tend to use the same simple alphanumeric text strings to encrypt multiple files. A product designed for protecting national security information would generate a truly random encryption key, usually with each use.

It is important to note that there appears to be no difference between foreign and U.S. commercial products in the use of these simplifications.

A fourth frequently heard argument is that many countries have import restrictions that would prevent U.S. exports even if the U.S. relaxed its export controls. While our survey has focused on the ease of importing products into the U.S., we have noted that many of the companies in our survey have distributors throughout the world. There may be countries that restrict imports of cryptography just as there may be those that restrict internal use of cryptography. But we are unaware of any countries in this category.

Other Countries Have Relaxed Export Controls

Our survey results also point to a much more ominous finding! Apparently the controls imposed by the U.S. Government on export of cryptographic products from the U.S. are far more restrictive than those imposed by most other countries, including our major allies. The effect of this most unfortunate situation is to cripple U.S. industry while our friends overseas appear to be free to export as they wish.

The U.S. imposes very strict rules on the export of cryptographic products. In general, applications for the export of products that use DES will be denied even to friendly countries unless they are for financial uses or for U.S. subsidiaries. We have been told repeatedly by the U.S. Government that other countries such as the United Kingdom and Germany have the same export restrictions that the U.S. does.

But our experiences with the actual purchases of cryptographic products show a very different picture.

We know that companies in Australia, Denmark, Germany, Israel, South Africa, Sweden, Switzerland, and the United Kingdom are freely shipping DES products to the U.S. and presumably elsewhere in the world with no more then a few days of government export control delay, if any. Sometimes the claim is that they have to "fill out some papers," but it's no big problem. In Australia, we are told, the exporting company must get a certificate that the destination country does not repress its citizens. Many countries allow shipment so long as it is not to former CoCom restricted countries (the former Soviet block and countries that support terrorism).

Our experience with these purchases has demonstrated conclusively that U.S. business is at a severe disadvantage in attempting to sell products to the world market. If our competitors overseas can routinely ship to most places in the world within days and we must go though time consuming and onerous procedures with the most likely outcome being denial of the export request, we might as well not even try. And that is exactly what many U.S. companies have decided.

And please be certain to understand that we are not talking about a few isolated products involving encryption. More and more we are talking about major information processing applications like word processors, databases, electronic mail packages, and integrated software systems that must use cryptography to provide even the most basic level of security being demanded by multinational companies.

Demonstrations of Available Cryptographic Products

[Material related to demonstrations omitted—Ed.]

Export Control of Information in the Public Domain

The U.S. International Trade in Arms Regulations (ITAR) govern what products can and cannot be subjected to export controls. These regulations clearly define a set of conditions in which information considered to be in the "public domain" can not be subject to controls. In the ITAR itself, public domain is defined as information that is published and that is generally accessible or available to the public:

- through sales at bookstores,
- at libraries,
- through patents available at the patent office, and
- through public release in any form after approval by the cognizant U.S. Government department or agency.

The Data Encryption Standard has been openly published as a Federal Information Processing Standard by the U.S. Government since 1977. Implementations of it in hardware and software are routinely available in the U.S. and throughout the world. Publication of software programs containing DES in paper form are permitted because of the First Amendment in the Bill of Rights. But the export of DES as hardware or software remains subject to export control despite its clearly being in the public domain.

One frustrating and somewhat humorous result of this situation occurred recently when NIST published a FIPS that contained source code for DES. In paper form, the Automated Password Generation Standard, FIPS 181, is acceptable for worldwide dissemination. But when NIST made the FIPS available over the Internet without an export restriction notice, it was immediately copied by computers in Denmark, the UK, and Taiwan. When it was pointed out that NIST's actions were in apparent violation of the ITAR, they quickly moved the file to a new directory with an appropriate export prohibition notice. Now FIPS 181 is available from hosts throughout the world along with the notice that export from the U.S. is in violation of U.S. export control.

NIST "exported" source code for DES with apparent immunity. Phil Zimmerman is still being investigated by the U.S. government and facing a four year imprisonment for allegedly doing nothing more.

Unfortunately, U.S. companies are not allowed to treat the export of DES in quite so simple a manner. As discussed earlier, DES is routinely available anywhere in the world. It meets the definition of "in the public domain" on numerous levels. And yet U.S. companies are prevented from exporting it other than to Canada. This situation is yet another example of the inconsistencies of U.S. export control policies.

Industrywide Experiences

Some companies do try to compete and offer excellent DES-based products in the U.S. But because of the export restrictions, they must develop weaker versions for export if they wish to pursue foreign markets. Many companies forgo the business rather than spend extra money to develop another inferior product that cannot compete with products widely available in the market.

The government already has a measure of lost sales and dissatisfied customers in the number of State Department/NSA export license applications denied, modified, or withdrawn. However, it is impossible to estimate accurately the full extent of lost sales. Many potential customers know that U.S. companies cannot meet their demand and thus no longer inquire. Conversely, most major companies have given up even trying to get export approvals for DES to meet customer demand.

One U.S. company, Semaphore Communications Corporation, that makes products using DES encryption has provided the following comments on their recent experiences (quoted from a letter dated 4/20/94 to Stephen T. Walker from William Ferguson of Semaphore):

> As a small company with limited resources, we have chosen to get an assessment directly from the NSA prior to investing too many resources in pursuing the situations, as the NSA Export Office is the ultimate authority on whether any export license will be granted; or the U.S. companies with familiarity of the export regulations have advised us of their position before we invested too many resources.
>
> The recent short-list of opportunities include:
>
> 1. NATO: order placed by SHAPE Technical Centre in 11/93 as precursor of NATO-wide security plan; pre-order query to State Dept. gave verbal approval as shipment was to an APO address: on submitting license application, NSA denied permission to ship. NATO officials are currently trying to get permission from NSA, but have thus far been denied.
> 2. Hong Kong Immigration Department: project to secure network communications for all department sites with fully redundant scheme: sought ruling before bidding in partnership with AT&T; denied 4/93. All competitors bid Racal; as a British company they had no restrictions.
> 3. Norway Telecom: planning secure network for government and financial users using single solution: sought ruling before bidding: told use sounded too general and export office would have difficulty approving, 10/93.
> 4. Dutch National Police computer network: application to secure entire national data network: advised would not be granted permission when

seeking pre-bid ruling, 11/93. Attempted to have our application viewed in same context as open license granted to DEC and IBM for similar equipment, but advised would need letters from all Dutch government agency department heads for any consideration. This effort would have required more than three months of effort by company executive located in Holland. Deemed too expensive for only one project.

5. Michelin: seeking solution to secure global network including all US-based, ex-Firestone facilities: when advised of export restrictions, Michelin rejected US-based technology to seek other solution; 4/93.

6. Volkswagen: in planning of security strategy for global networks; solicited bid: rejected US-based technology when informed of export regulations, 2/93.

7. Boeing: one of largest global users of secure communications: advised Boeing didn't want to have to deal with export regulations for meeting needs: continues to buy Racal products to avoid U.S. regulations. Continue to try to sell, but have met with resistance for procurements 10/92, 4/93, 11/93. Volume would be very high as Boeing took delivery of 800 routers in 1993, and our equipment would have 1:1 relationship. Boeing now in another review cycle.

8. GE: has major program in planning to secure global networks: diverse ownership in many locations has GE seeking foreign solutions for global uniformity.

9. Swiss National Justice and Police Department: project to connect all police and court locations in country: advised by NSA that approval would be hard to justify based on fact that it was Switzerland, 4/94.

10. Thomsen CSF: seeking technology partner for next generation of Thomsen products: sought out Semaphore as Thomsen technology group finds our technology to be far ahead of any other global options, and wanted to have fast time-to-market: NSA suggested we discontinue further discussions. 4/94.

11. Sikorsky: advised permission would not be granted for equipment at foreign joint-venture partners for new commercial helicopter venture, 3/94. Revisited with another NSA export official in 4/94, and advised that license might be granted if use was to principal benefit of a USA company. No firm commitment until license application is submitted as one location is in Japan.

12. Glaxo Pharmaceutical: world's largest pharmaceutical company has global requirement to secure testing and development data: will seek other solutions as Semaphore cannot deliver to other global locations. 2/94 .

13. Pillsbury: has strategy to secure global networks: as owned by UK-based Grand Metropolitan, will seek other solutions which can be shipped to all global locations, 11/93.

The total value for all of these opportunities are estimated to be in the range of $30 to $50 million based on the preliminary estimates of the projects.

You have Semaphore's permission to submit this information with your testimony before the Congress.

Gauging the extent of economic harm industrywide is what is an inherently difficult task because most companies do not want to reveal that sort of information. Consequently what exists, with the exception of statements like that from Semaphore, is mostly anecdotal information. But the accumulation of anecdotal information collected by the SPA paints a picture of three ways in which the export controls on cryptographic products are hurting American high-tech industry.

(1) Loss of business directly related to cryptographic products: First, for many data security companies, every sale is vital, and the loss of contracts smaller than $1 million can often mean the difference between life and death for these companies. The confusion and uncertainty associated with export controls on encryption generate severe problems for small firms, but not as severe as the loss of business they suffer from anti-competitive export controls. Examples abound:

■ One U.S. company reported loss of revenues equal to a third of its current total revenues because export controls on DES-based encryption closed off a market when its customer, a foreign government, privatized the function for which the encryption was used, and the U.S. company was not permitted to sell to the private foreign firm. The company estimates it loses millions of dollars a year because it receives substantial orders every month from various European customers but cannot fill them because of export controls.

■ One small firm could not sell to a European company because that company sold to clients other than financial institutions (for which export controls grant an exception). Later, the software firm received reports of sales of pirated copies of its software. This constituted the loss of a $400,000 contract for the small U.S. software firm.

■ Because of existing export restrictions, an American company recently found itself unable to export a mass market software program that provided encryption using Canadian technology based on a Japanese algorithm. Yet other European and Japanese companies are selling competing products worldwide using the same Canadian technology.

■ An SPA member's product manager in Europe reported the likely loss of at least 50% of its business among European financial institutions, defense industries, telecommunications companies, and government agencies if present restrictions on key size are not lifted.

■ Yet another SPA member company reported the potential loss of a substantial portion of its international business if it cannot commit to provide DES in its programs.

- A German firm that opened a subsidiary in the U.S. sought a single source encryption software product for both its German and U.S. sites. A U.S. data security firm that bid for the contract lost the business because U.S. export controls required that the German firm would have to wait approximately six months while a license was processed to sell them software with encryption for foreign application. The license could only be for one to three years, the three year license being more expensive. Consequently, the German firm ended up purchasing a DES-based system from another German company, and the U.S. firm lost the business.
- A foreign government selected one software company's data security product as that government's security standard. The company's application to export the DES version was denied, and as a consequence the order was lost. This cost the company a $400,000 order and untold millions in future business.

(2) Loss of business from U.S. companies with international concerns: Second, multinational corporations (MNCs) are a prime source of business in the expanding international market for encryption products. Many U.S.-based firms have foreign subsidiaries or operations that do not meet export requirements. While U.S. products may be competitive in the U.S., many MNCs obtain from foreign sources encryption systems that will be compatible with the company's worldwide operations. Moreover, foreign MNCs cannot rely on the availability of U.S. products and have been known to import foreign cryptography for use in their U.S. operations.

- One U.S. firm reports the loss of business from foreign MNCs that will not integrate the company's products into their U.S. operations because of the export restrictions that would prevent them from being compatible with their domestic operations.
- The Computer Business Equipment Manufacturers Association reports that one of its members was denied an export license and lost a $60 million sale of network controllers and software for encryption of financial transactions when the Western European customer could not ensure that encryption would be limited to financial transactions.

(3) Loss of business where cryptography is part of a system: Third, encryption systems are frequently sold as a component of a larger system. These "leveraged" sales offer encryption as a vital component of a broad system. Yet the encryption feature is the primary feature for determining exportability. Because of the export restrictions, U.S. firms are losing the business not just for the encryption product but for the entire system because of the restrictions on one component of it.

- One data security firm has estimated that export restrictions constrain its market opportunities by two-thirds. Despite its superior system, it has been unable to respond to requests from NATO, the Swedish PTT, and British telecommunications companies because it cannot export the encryption they demand. This has cost the company millions in foregone business.
- One major computer company lost two sales in Western Europe within the last 12 months totaling approximately $80 million because the file and data encryption in the integrated system was not exportable.

One possible solution to the problem of export controls may be for U.S. companies to relocate overseas. Some U.S. firms have considered moving their operations overseas and developing their technology there to avoid U.S. export restrictions. Thus, when a U.S. company with technology that is clearly in demand is kept from exporting that technology, it may be forced to export jobs instead.

How Are U.S. Citizens and Businesses Being Affected by All This?

The answer to this question is painfully simple. When U.S. industry forgoes the opportunity to produce products that integrate good security practices, such as cryptography, into their products because they cannot export those products to their overseas markets, U.S. users (individuals, companies, and government agencies) are denied access to the basic tools they need to protect their own sensitive information.

The U.S. Government does not have the authority to regulate the use of cryptography within this country. But if through strict control of exports they can deter industry from building products that effectively employ cryptography, then they have achieved a very effective form of internal use control. You and I do not have good cryptography available to us in the word processors and data base management and spreadsheet systems even though there is no law against our use of cryptography. If we want to encrypt our sensitive information, we must search out special products that usually must be used separately from our main workstation applications. This is a very effective form of internal use control, and it makes all levels of U.S. industry vulnerable to foreign and domestic industrial espionage.

And Clipper, as presently being implemented, does nothing to help this problem.

What Should Congress Do?

In this case, Congress is already doing something! Last November, Representative Maria Cantwell introduced HR3627, a bill that would shift export control of mass market software products including those with cryptography, for the Department of State to the Department of Commerce, thus allowing them to be treated as normal commodities instead of munitions. This bill should be considered as part of Chairman Gejdenson's overall bill to reform export controls. In the Senate, the Murray-Bennett initiative, S 1846, to reform export controls has a similar objective.

Legislation such as HR3627 and S1846 must be passed as soon as possible to balance the national economic interests against those of law enforcement and national security.

SUMMARY

On Export Control of Cryptography

The widespread availability of cryptography throughout the world and the ease with which other countries, including our closest allies, allow the export of cryptography to the U.S. and elsewhere make it imperative that our U.S. Government's regulation of cryptographic exports move out of the Cold War. Export controls have been relaxed on every other form of high tech computer and communications technology. Continuation of cryptography export controls is only hurting American citizens and businesses.

Law enforcement and national security interests will continue to encounter ever-growing amounts of encrypted communications no matter how many restrictive steps the Administration attempts to take. We must realize this basic fact of technology advancement and stop hamstringing U.S. national economic interests in the hope that we are helping our national security interests.

It is evident from the Administration's refusal to relax cryptographic export policies during the Clipper Interagency Review that the Executive Branch is going to continue to emphasize the interests of national security and law enforcement over our national economic interests until we become a third-rate economic power.

Only the Congress can take the steps to balance the interests of American citizens and businesses against that immovable force. I strongly support the Cantwell Bill, HR 3627, and the Murray—Bennett initiative, S1846.

ATTACHMENT 1. Foreign Text, File, and Data Encryption Programs and Products Identified by the SPA as of March 22, 1994 [Updated information is available online from nttp://www.tis.com/crypto/crypto-survey.html.].

Company	Country	Product	Type	DES
CNET		RSA chip	HW	No
Queen's University		RSA chip	HW	No
Newnet S.A.	Argentina	DSD 9612 Data Security Device	NW	Yes
Cybanim Pty Ltd.	Australia	DES32 v1.02	SW	Yes
Cybanim Pty Ltd.	Australia	DESF v1.4	SW	Yes
Cybanim Pty Ltd.	Australia	LUC 2.03	SW	No
Cybanim Pty Ltd.	Australia	RSAx 1.20	SW	No
Cybanim Pty Ltd	Australia	SIFR v2.0	SW	No
Eracom Pty Ltd.	Australia	ERA 2007 Line Encryptor	HW	Yes
Eracom Pty Ltd.	Australia	ERA 4007 Line Encryptor	HW	Yes
Eracom Pty Ltd.	Australia	Eracom Security Module (ESM)	HW	Yes
Eracom Pty Ltd	Australia	Micro Channel Slave Encryptor (MCSE 16)	HW	Yes
Eracom Pty Ltd.	Australia	Micro Channel Slave Encryptor (MCSE-8)	HW	Yes
Eracom Pty Ltd.	Australia	PC Encryptor (PCE-16)	HW	Yes
Eracom Pty Ltd.	Australia	PC Encryptor (PCE-8)	HW	Yes
Eracom Pty Ltd	Australia	ProtectSNA	SW/HW	Yes
Eracom Pty Ltd.	Australia	Secure Access System Software (SAS)	SW	Yes
Eracom Pty Ltd.	Australia	Series 90 ESM	HW	Yes
Eracom Pty Ltd.	Australia	Windows Application Security Program (WASP)	SW	Yes
Eric Young	Australia	Icrypt	SW	Yes
Eric Young	Australia	libdes	SW	Yes
News Datacom	Australia	N-Sure Access 1000	HW	Yes
Randata	Australia	FAXSAFE	HW	No
Randata	Australia	GSA1000 Duplex Mini Scrambler	HW	No
Randata	Australia	GSA 1300	HW	No
Randata	Australia	Guardian-E Data Encryptor	HW	Yes
Randata	Australia	Guardian-EM Encryptor Modem	HW	Yes
Randata	Australia	Guardian-EMP Data Encryptor	HW	Yes
Randata	Australia	Guardian-EP Data Encryptor	HW	Yes
Randata	Australia	Megecrypt High Speed Data Encryptor	HW	Yes
Randata	Australia	RD185 Fax	HW	No
Randata	Australia	RD187 Data Encryptor	HW	Yes
Randata	Australia	SecurLAN Network Encryption Unit-Router (NEU-RT)	HW	Yes
Randata	Australia	SecurPAC EM Encryptor Modem	HW	Yes
Randata	Australia	SecurPac PEM Data Encryptor	HW	Yes
Randata	Australia	Securlink Data Encryptor	HW	Yes
Robust Software	Australia	Block-It		No
Ross Williams	Australia	Veracity	SW	No
Cryptech NV/SA	Belgium	Crypto Administrator	SW/HW	No
Cryptech NV/SA	Belgium	DES Software Toolkit	SW	Yes
Cryptech NV/SA	Belgium	DES-CHIP	HW	Yes
Cryptech NV/SA	Belgium	PC-Crypto Toolkit	HW	Yes
Cryptech NV/SA	Belgium	PC-RSA Processor	HW	No
Cryptech NV/SA	Belgium	RSA Processor	HW	No

ATTACHMENT 1. *Continued*

Company	Country	Product	Type	DES
GSA Ran Data Europe	Belgium	MARTLET		No
Highware, Inc.	Belgium	Fileguard		No
A.B. Data Sales, Inc.	Canada	HardDrive Lockup	SW	No
Isolation Systems	Canada	ISAC 1100	HW	Yes
Isolation Systems	Canada	ISAC 1500	SW/HW	Yes
Isolation Systems	Canada	ISAC 2200	HW	Yes
Isolation Systems	Canada	ISAC 2400	HW	Yes
Isolation Systems	Canada	ISAC 2500	HW	Yes
Isolation Systems	Canada	ISAC 3200	HW	Yes
Isolation Systems	Canada	ISAC 3500	HW	Yes
Isolation Systems	Canada	ISAC 4200	HW	Yes
Isolation Systems	Canada	ISE 2100	HW	Yes
Mobius Encryption Technologies	Canada	FaxSecrets	HW	No
Mobius Encryption Technologies	Canada	TradeSecrets 1000	HW	Yes
Mobius Encryption Technologies	Canada	TradeSecrets 2000	HW	Yes
Newbridge Microsystems	Canada	CA20C03A	HW	Yes
Northern Telecom Canada Limited	Canada	Packet Data Security Overlay (PDSO)	HW	Yes
Okiok Data	Canada	Data Encryption Board (DEB)	HW	Yes
Okiok Data	Canada	FAS-PACK	SW	Yes
Okiok Data	Canada	RAC/M 3.0	SW/HW	Yes
Okiok Data	Canada	RAC/M II 3.0	SW/HW	Yes
Secured Communication Canada 93 Inc.	Canada	PCMCIA	HW	Yes
Secured Communication Canada 93 Inc.	Canada	Session Key	HW	Yes
Aarhus University, Computer Science Department	Denmark	VICTOR	HW	No
Cryptomathic	Denmark	6303 SIS	SW	No
Cryptomathic	Denmark	8051 DES	SW	Yes
Cryptomathic	Denmark	DES Kemel	SW	Yes
Cryptomathic	Denmark	DES Security Mechanisms	SW	Yes
Cryptomathic	Denmark	DSP 56000 DES	SW	Yes
Cryptomathic	Denmark	DSP 56000 RSA	SW	No
Cryptomathic	Denmark	F2F (File-to-File)	SW	Yes
Cryptomathic	Denmark	FRAS-File RSA	SW	No
Cryptomathic	Denmark	Hash Security Mechanisms	SW	Yes
Cryptomathic	Denmark	Multiprecision Kemel	HW	No
Cryptomathic	Denmark	PIC16C57 SIS	SW	No
Cryptomathic	Denmark	RSA Security Mechanisms	SW	No
GN Datacom	Denmark	safeMatic Security Module	HW	Yes
LSI Logic/Dataco AS	Denmark	DATACO LSA4043 2030025402	HW	Yes
LSI Logic/Dataco AS	Denmark	Dataco L5A4043 2030025402	HW	Yes
Antti Louko	Finland	AloDES	SW	Yes
Digital Equipment Corp. (DEC) Paris Research Lab	France	RSA chip	HW	No
LAAS	France	RSA implementations		No
Philips Communication Systems	France	P83C852 Smart Card Crypto Controller	HW	No
Rast Electronics	France	Crypt It		No
Smart Diskette	France	Very Smart Disk	HW	Yes
CE Infosys GmbH	Germany	CryptCard	HW	Yes
CE Infosys GmbH	Germany	MiniCrypt	HW	Yes

Attachment 1. *Continued*

Company	Country	Product	Type	DES
CE Infosys GmbH	Germany	SC8810 AT Design Kit	HW	Yes
CE Infosys GmbH	Germany	SC8820 MCA Design Kit	HW	Yes
CE Infosys GmbH	Germany	SoftCrypt	SW	Yes
CE Infosys GmbH	Germany	SuperCrypt	HW	Yes
CE Infosys GmbH	Germany	cryptLine Controller	HW	Yes
DataSafe	Germany	ENCRYPT-IT v3.06	SW	Yes
DataSafe	Germany	WINDEX! v2.01 for DOS	SW	No
DataSafe	Germany	WINDEX! v2.01 for Windows	SW	No
GMD	Germany	SecuDE PEM	SW	Yes
GMD	Germany	SecuDE-4.2 (Security Development Environment)	SW	Yes
Tele Security Timmann GmbH & Co.	Germany	TST 3010 High Performance Mil-Spec Cipher Terminal	HW	No
Tele Security Timmann GmbH & Co.	Germany	TST 3550 Handy Crypt	HW	No
Tele Security Timmann GmbH & Co.	Germany	TST 3570 Pocketcrypt	HW	No
Tele Security Timmann GmbH & Co.	Germany	TST 3677 VDU/Screen-Oriented Headquarter Cipher	HW	No
Tele Security Timmann GmbH & Co.	Germany	TST 4043 HF Slow Speed Modem with encryption	HW	No
Tele Security Timmann GmbH & Co	Germany	TST 4045 HF Modem 2.4Kbps with encryption	HW	No
Tele Security Timmann GmbH & Co.	Germany	TST 5500 Crypto Modem	SW/HW	No
Tele Security Timmann GmbH & Co.	Germany	TST 5560 DataCipher Set	HW	No
Tele Security Timmann GmbH & Co.	Germany	TST 5573 C Data Encryptor	HW	No
Tele Security Timmann GmbH & Co.	Germany	TST 5573 F/C	HW	No
Tele Security Timmann GmbH & Co.	Germany	TST 5573 H/C	HW	No
Tele Security Timmann GmbH & Co.	Germany	TST 5573 PC	HW	No
Tele Security Timmann GmbH & Co.	Germany	TST 5573 X/C	HW	No
Tele Security Timmann GmbH & Co.	Germany	TST 7595 HF voice encryption	HW	No
Tele Security Timmann GmbH & Co.	Germany	TST 7610 Secure Office Telephone	HW	No
Tele Security Timmann GmbH & Co.	Germany	TST 7698 Miniature Military Voice Coder	HW	No
Tele Security Timmann GmbH & Co.	Germany	TST 7700 Telephone Vocoder and Modem	HW	No
Tele Security Timmann GmbH & Co.	Germany	TST 8010 Spreadspectrum Radio	HW	No
Tele Security Timmann GmbH & Co.	Germany	TST 9669 Telex Cipher Module	HW	No
Tele Security Timmann GmbH & Co.	Germany	TST 9700 INMARSAT "C" encryptor	SW/HW	No
Telenet Kommunication	Germany	File Transfer		No
Tulip Computers	Germany	Disk Encryption Unit		No
UTI-MACO GmbH	Germany	BACK-Guard	SW	Yes
UTI-MACO GmbH	Germany	C:Crypt	SW	Yes
UTI-MACO GmbH	Germany	SAFE-Board I	HW	No
UTI-MACO GmbH	Germany	SAFE-Board II	HW	Yes
UTI-MACO GmbH	Germany	SAFE-Board III	HW	Yes
UTI-MACO GmbH	Germany	SAFE-Guard EZ	SW	Yes
UTI-MACO GmbH	Germany	SAFE-Guard OS/2 3.0	SW	Yes
UTI-MACO GmbH	Germany	SAFE-Guard Professional 3.2C	SW	Yes
UTI-MACO GmbH	Germany	SIGN-Guard	SW	Yes
Triple D Ltd.	Hong Kong	P-8 Security Master Card	SW/HW	Yes
Chenab Info Technology	India	Cryptic		No

ATTACHMENT 1. *Continued*

Company	Country	Product	Type	DES
Eurologic Systems, Ltd.	Ireland	Datacrypt	HW	No
Algorithmic Research Ltd.	Israel	AR Crypto3270-E	SW	Yes
Algorithmic Research Ltd.	Israel	AR Crypto3270-P	SW/HW	Yes
Algorithmic Research Ltd.	Israel	AR CryptoBIOS	SW	Yes
Algorithmic Research Ltd.	Israel	AR CryptoCODE	SW/HW	Yes
Algorithmic Research Ltd.	Israel	AR CryptoCOM	SW	Yes
Algorithmic Research Ltd.	Israel	AR CryptoMAC	SW	No
Algorithmic Research Ltd.	Israel	AR CryptoMAIN	SW	Yes
Algorithmic Research Ltd.	Israel	AR CryptoPAD	HW	Yes
Algorithmic Research Ltd.	Israel	AR CryptoPC	SW	Yes
Algorithmic Research Ltd.	Israel	AR CryptoSAT	HW	Yes
Algorithmic Research Ltd.	Israel	AR CryptoSafe	HW	Yes
Algorithmic Research Ltd.	Israel	AR DISKrete	SW	Yes
Fujitsu Labs Ltd.	Japan	FJPEM ver 1.0	SW	Yes
Yokohama National University	Japan	KPS L1CARD		No
Ad Infinitum Programs (AIP-NL)	Netherlands	UltraCompressor II	SW	Yes
Concord Eracom Nederland BV	Netherlands	DEA Crypto Toolkit	SW	Yes
Concord Eracom Nederland BV	Netherlands	Multi-Functional PC Security (MFPS) Card	HW	Yes
Concord Eracom Nederland BV	Netherlands	SCORE	SW	Yes
Concord Eracom Nederland BV	Netherlands	SECNET (FCM)	SW/HW	Yes
Concord Eracom Nederland BV	Netherlands	SECNET (HCM)	HW	Yes
Concord Eracom Nederland BV	Netherlands	SECNET (SCM)	SW	Yes
Concord Eracom Nederland BV	Netherlands	SECNET FBI-Encryptor	HW	Yes
Concord Eracom Nederland BV	Netherlands	SECNET MFPS	SW/HW	Yes
Concord Eracom Nederland BV	Netherlands	SECNET PC Soft-Lock		No
DigiCash	Netherlands	Electronic cash systems		No
DigiCash	Netherlands	Electronic toll payment systems		No
DigiCash	Netherlands	Kryptor Board	SW/HW	Yes
Incaa Datacom BV	Netherlands	AUTHORIZER	HW	No
Verspeck & Soeters b.v.	Netherlands	SecuriO	HW	Yes
Verspeck & Soeters b.v.	Netherlands	SecuriO I	HW	Yes
Verspeck & Soeters b.v.	Netherlands	SecuriO II	HW	No
Verspeck & Soeters b.v.	Netherlands	SecuriO III	HW	Yes
LUC Encryption Technology, Ltd. (LUCENT)	New Zealand	LUC Implementation	SW	No
Peter Gutmann	New Zealand	HPACK Archiver	SW	No
Askri	Russia	Cryptos	SW	Yes
DKL Ltd., Moscow Department	Russia	Absolute Cryptographer	SW	No
Elias Ltd.	Russia	Excellence for DOS	SW	No
LAN Crypto	Russia	ATHENA	SW	No
LAN Crypto	Russia	Notary	SW	No
LAN Crypto	Russia	VESTA-1	SW	Yes
LAN Crypto	Russia	VESTA-2	SW	Yes
ScanTech	Russia	Krypton	HW	No
TELECRYPT, Ltd.	Russia	TELECRYPT	SW	Yes
Infoplan—Division of Denel P/L	South Africa	IWATCH	SW	No
Siemens Ltd.	South Africa	SESAM		No
Technetics	South Africa	N3000M		No
Ardy Electronics	Sweden	SLF 2000	HW	No

ATTACHMENT 1. *Continued*

Company	Country	Product	Type	DES
Ardy Electronics	Sweden	SLP 2000	HW	No
Ardy Electronics	Sweden	SLD/OUS-200	HW	No
COST Computer Security Technologies International	Sweden	COST-Development Tools (GSL/SCL)	SW	Yes
COST Computer Security Technologies International	Sweden	COST-EDI	SW	Yes
COST Computer Security Technologies International	Sweden	COST-LAN	SW	Yes
COST Computer Security Technologies International	Sweden	COST-PEM	SW	Yes
COST Computer Security Technologies International	Sweden	COST-SC	SW/HW	Yes
DynaSoft	Sweden	BoKS 4.1.X	SW/HW	Yes
SONNOR Crypto AB	Sweden	HR&S	SW	No
SONNOR Crypto AB	Sweden	PCrypt	SW	No
SecuriCrypto AB	Sweden	SecuriCrypto V.24	HW	No
SecuriCrypto AB	Sweden	SecuriCrypto V.248	HW	No
SecuriCrypto AB	Sweden	SecuriCrypto V.35	HW	No
SecuriCrypto AB	Sweden	SecuriCrypto V.36	HW	No
SecuriCrypto AB	Sweden	SecuriCrypto X.21	HW	No
SecuriCrypto AB	Sweden	SecuriCrypto X.25	HW	No
SecuriCrypto AB	Sweden	SecuriCrypto X.26	HW	No
SecuriCrypto AB	Sweden	SecuriFax	HW	No
SecuriCrypto AB	Sweden	SecuriVoice	HW	No
SecuriCrypto AB	Sweden	X.25 Advanced Key System	HW	No
Stig Ostholm	Sweden	DES Implementation 2.0	SW	Yes
Stig Ostholm	Sweden	DES Implementation 2.2	SW	Yes
ASCOM Tech AG	Switzerland	VINCI	HW	No
Gretag Data Systems AG	Switzerland	Gretacoder 519	HW	No
Gretag Data Systems AG	Switzerland	Gretacoder 522	HW	Yes
Gretag Data Systems AG	Switzerland	Gretacoder 524	HW	Yes
Gretag Data Systems AG	Switzerland	Gretacoder 526	HW	Yes
Gretag Data Systems AG	Switzerland	Gretacoder 545	HW	Yes
Gretag Data Systems AG	Switzerland	Gretacoder 605	HW	Yes
Gretag Data Systems AG	Switzerland	Gretacoder 705 Authenticator	HW	Yes
Gretag Data Systems AG	Switzerland	Gretacoder 710 Authenticator	HW	Yes
Info Guard AG	Switzerland	I-1100	HW	Yes
Info Guard AG	Switzerland	I-1200	SW/HW	Yes
Info Guard AG	Switzerland	I-1200 DES Software	SW	Yes
Info Guard AG	Switzerland	I-2010	HW	Yes
Info Guard AG	Switzerland	I-3010	HW	No
Omnisec AG	Switzerland	Omnisec 211	HW	No
Omnisec AG	Switzerland	Omnisec 510	HW	No
Omnisec AG	Switzerland	Omnisec 520	HW	No
Omnisec AG	Switzerland	Omnisec 610	HW	No
Omnisec AG	Switzerland	Omnisec 620	HW	No
Omnisec AG	Switzerland	Omnisec 630	HW	No
Omnisec AG	Switzerland	Omnisec 640	HW	No
Organa	Switzerland	mProtect		No

ATTACHMENT 1. *Continued*

Company	Country	Product	Type	DES
Airtech Computer Security	UK	PC Guard Professional		No
British Telecom	UK	RSA chip	HW	No
Business Simulations	UK	Ultralock		No
Compserve Ltd.	UK	Softlock 10	SW	Yes
Compserve Ltd.	UK	X-LOCK 10	SW	Yes
Compserve Ltd.	UK	X-LOCK 50	SW	Yes
Computer Associates	UK	ACF2		No
Computer Associates	UK	Cortana		No
Computer Associates	UK	Top Secret		No
Computer Security Ltd.	UK	Safe Guard Systems		No
Data Innovation Ltd.	UK	CG500	HW	Yes
Data Innovation Ltd.	UK	DG510-VSM	HW	No
Data Innovation Ltd.	UK	ED2048	HW	Yes
Data Innovation Ltd.	UK	ED500	HW	Yes
Data Innovation Ltd.	UK	ED600	HW	No
Data Innovation Ltd.	UK	ED600R	HW	No
Data Innovation Ltd.	UK	Network Security Workstation (NSW)	SW/HW	Yes
Data Innovation Ltd.	UK	PSP400	HW	Yes
DataSoft International Ltd.	UK	DataCode	SW	No
DataSoft International Ltd.	UK	DataTalk	SW	No
Digital Crypto	UK	OS2-IRIS	SW	Yes
Digital Crypto	UK	PC-IRIS V4.0-2	SW	Yes
Digital Crypto	UK	PC-MERLIN V2.0-1	SW	Yes
Digital Crypto	UK	VMS-IRIS	SW	Yes
Dynatech Communications Ltd.	UK	Cipher 2200	HW	No
Dynatech Communications Ltd.	UK	Cryptopad	HW	Yes
Dynatech Communications Ltd.	UK	Cybercrypt LE	HW	Yes
Dynatech Communications Ltd.	UK	Multicrypt	HW	Yes
GEC-Marconi Secure Systems	UK	DATALOK H	HW	No
GEC-Marconi Secure Systems	UK	DATALOK L	HW	No
GEC-Marconi Secure Systems	UK	FAXLOK	HW	No
GEC-Marconi Secure Systems	UK	IC-H10SR	HW	No
GEC-Marconi Secure Systems	UK	IC-RP1510SB	HW	No
GEC-Marconi Secure Systems	UK	IC-V200SR	HW	No
GEC-Marconi Secure Systems	UK	MASC	HW	No
GEC-Marconi Secure Systems	UK	MASC Crypto Management System	SW	No
GEC-Marconi Secure Systems	UK	Marcrypt	HW	No
GEC-Marconi Secure Systems	UK	SDT-100	HW	No
Global CIS Ltd.	UK	Safeguard Security System	SW	No
IT Security International	UK	Secure LAN		No
International Data Security	UK	DataSave-ABA		No
J.R. Ward Computes Ltd.	UK	Code-It	SW	No
JPY Associates, Ltd.	UK	DataLock CIPHER Procedure	SW	Yes
JPY Associates, Ltd.	UK	DataLock Editor (DLE)	SW	Yes
JPY Associates, Ltd.	UK	DataLock, Version 3.1	SW	Yes
Jaguar Communications Ltd.	UK	ZCODA-A	HW	No
Jaguar Communications Ltd.	UK	ZCODA-X	HW	No
Janus Sovereign	UK	Padlock		No
Microft Technology Ltd.	UK	CLAM	SW	No

ATTACHMENT 1. *Continued*

Company	Country	Product	Type	DES
Micronyx UK Ltd.	UK	Trispan	SW	No
Micronyx UK Ltd.	UK	Triumph! V2	SW	Yes
Network Systems	UK	Data Delivery/Management System		No
PC Security Ltd.	UK	CP8-AuthentICC	HW	No
PC Security Ltd.	UK	LapGUARD	SW	No
PC Security Ltd.	UK	Stoplock III	SW	No
PC Security Ltd.	UK	Stoplock IV	SW	Yes
Plessey Crypto	UK	Datalok-H	HW	No
Plessey Crypto	UK	Datalok-L	HW	No
Plessey Crypto	UK	FAXLOK		No
Plessey Crypto	UK	FTSM100		No
Plessey Crypto	UK	NC100		No
Plessey Crypto	UK	RSA chip	HW	No
Plessey Crypto	UK	Voicelok 100		No
Plus 5 Engineering Ltd.	UK	Policeman	SW	No
Protection Systems Ltd.	UK	Guardian Angel Plus	SW	Yes
Racal-Milgo	UK	Datacryptor Key Management Center	HW	No
S&S International	UK	Dr. Solomon's PC Armour	SW	No
S&S International	UK	SAVEDIR	SW	No
Shareware plc	UK	DES	SW	Yes
Shareware plc	UK	PC-IRIS	SW	Yes
Shareware plc	UK	PC-Merlin	SW	Yes
Sophos Ltd.	UK	CRYPTO-JET	HW	Yes
Sophos Ltd.	UK	DES Toolkit	SW	Yes
Sophos Ltd.	UK	EDS	SW	Yes
Sophos Ltd.	UK	PUBLIC	SW	Yes
Sophos Ltd.	UK	RSA Toolkit	SW	No
Sophos Ltd.	UK	SHRED	SW	No
Sophos Ltd.	UK	SPA Toolkit	SW	No
Sophos Ltd.	UK	T-SAFE		No
Stralfors Data	UK	PS3		No
The Software Forge Ltd.	UK	Data Jumbler	SW	Yes
Time & Data Systems	UK	Microstop		No
University College London	UK	OSISEC	SW	Yes
University College London	UK	UK DRA-PEM	SW	Yes
Zergo	UK	CP400		No
Zeta Communications Ltd.	UK	Zetacoda A	HW	No
Zeta Communications Ltd.	UK	Zetacoda X	HW	No

ATTACHMENT 2. *Companies Manufacturing and/or Distributing Cryptographic Products Worldwide (From the Software Publishers Association survey of cryptographic products as of April 25, 1994).*

ARGENTINA	Newnet S.A.
AUSTRALIA	Cybarnim Pty Ltd. Datamatic Pty Ltd. Eracom Pty Ltd. Eric Young Loadplan Austlalasia Pty Ltd. LUCENT News Datacom Randata Robust Software Ross Williams Sagem Australasia Pty Ltd. TRAC Systems Tracom
AUSTRIA	Schrack-Dat
BAHRAIN	International Information Systems
BELGIUM	Cryptech NV/SA GSA Ran Data Europe Highware, Inc. Unina SA Vector
CANADA	A.B. Data Sales, Inc. Concord-Eracom Computer Ltd. Isolation Systems Mobius Encryption Technologies Newbridge Microsystems Northern Telecom Canada Limited Okiok Data Paradyne Canada Ltd. Secured Communication Canada 93, Inc.
DENMARK	Aarhus University, Computer Science Department CryptoMathic GN Datacom Iversen & Martens A/S LSI Logic/Dataco AS Swanholm Computing A/S
FINLAND	Antti Louko Ascom Fintel OY Instrumentoiti OY
FRANCE	Atlantis

ATTACHMENT 2. *Continued*

	CCETT
	CSEE—Division Communication et Informatique
	CSIL
	Cryptech France
	Dassault Automatismes et Telecommunications
	Digital Equipment Corporation (DEC), Paris Research Lab
	Incaa France S.A.R.L.
	LAAS
	Philips Communication Systems
	Rast Electronics
	S.A. Gretag
	Sagem
	Smart Diskette
	Societe Sagem
GERMANY	AR Datensicherungssysteme GmbH
	CCI
	CE Infosys GmbH
	Concord-Eracom Computer GmbH
	Controlware GmbH
	Data Safe
	Dynatech-Gesellschaft fiur Datenverarbeitung GmbH
	EuroCom EDV
	FAST Electronic
	Gliss & Herweg
	GMD
	Gretag Elektronik GmbH
	KryptoKom
	Markt & Technik SoRware Partners Intl. GmbH
	Paradyne GmbH
	Siemens
	Smart Diskette GmbH
	Tela Versicherung
	Tele Security Timmann
	Telenet Kommunikation
	The Compatibility Box GmbH
	Tulip Computers
	UTI-MACO GmbH
GREECE	G.J.Messaritis & Co. Ltd.
	ORCO Ltd.
HONG KONG	News Datacom
	Triple D Ltd.
INDIA	Chenab Info Technology
IRELAND	Eurologic Systems, Ltd.
	Renaissance Contingency Services, Ltd.

ATTACHMENT 2. *Continued*

	Shamus Softare Ltd.
ISRAEL	Algorithmic Research Ltd.
	ELYASIM
	News Datacom
	TADIRAN
ITALY	Incaa SRL
	Olivetti
	Ratio Srl
	Telvox s.a.s.
	Uniautomation
JAPAN	Fujitsu Labs Ltd.
	Japan's National Defense Academy
	Paradyne Japan, KK
	Yokohama National University
LUXEMBORG	Telindus SA
MALTA	Shireburn Co. Ltd.
NETHERLANDS	Ad Infinitum Programs (AIP-NL)
	CRYPSYS Data Security
	Concord Eracom Nederland BV
	Cryptech Nederland
	DigiCash
	DSP International
	Geveke Electronics BV
	Incaa Datacom BV
	Incaa Nederland BV
	Repko BV Datacomms
	Verspeck & Soeters BV
NEW ZEALAND	LUC Encryption Technology, Ltd. (LUCENT)
	Peter Gutmann
	Peter Smith and Michael Lermon
NORWAY	BDC Bergen Data Consulting A/S
	Ericcson Semafor
	PDI
	Scand PC Sys/Sectla
	Skanditek A/S
	UMI SA
POLAND	SOFT-u.1.
PORTUGAL	Infomova
	Redislogar SA
RUSSIA	Askri
	DKL Ltd.

ATTACHMENT 2. *Continued*

	Elias Ltd. LAN Crypto RESCrypto ScanTech TELECRYPT, Ltd.
SAUDI ARABIA	Info Guard Saudi Arabia
SINGAPORE	Communications Systems Engineering Pty. Ltd. Digitus Computer Systems
SOUTH AFRICA	BSS (Pty) Ltd. Computer Security Associates EFT InfoPlan—Division of Denel P/L Intelligent Nanoteq Net One Siemens Ltd. Spescom Technetics
SPAIN	Asociacion Española de Empresas de Informatica Asociacion Nacional de Industrias Electronics Redislogar Comminicaciones SA SECARTYS Sinutec Tecnitrade Int. SA
SWEDEN	AV System Infocard Ardy Elektronics Au·System Infocard AB COST Computer Security TechnoloPies International DynaSoft QA Infommatik AB SONOR Crypto AB SecunCrypto AB Stig Ostholm Tomas Tesch AB
SWITZERLAND	ASCOM Tech AG Brown-Boveri Crypto AG ETH Zurich Ete·Hager AG Gretag AG Incaa Datacom AG Info Guard AG

ATTACHMENT 2. *Continued*

	Omnisec AG
	Organa
	Safeware
UK	Airtech Computer Security
	British Telecom
	Business Simulations
	Cambridge Electric Industnes
	Codepoint Systems Ltd.
	Compserve Ltd. Compserve Ltd.
	Computer Associates
	Computer Security Ltd.
	Cylink Ltd.
	Data Innovation Ltd.
	DataSoR International Ltd.
	Datamedia Corporation, Ltd.
	Digital Crypto
	Dynatech Cormnuncations Ltd.-(Northem office)
	Dynatech Communication Ltd.
	EngRus
	Fulcrum Communications
	GEC-Marconi Secure Systems
	Gelosia
	Global CIS Ltd.
	Gretag Ltd.
	Honeywell
	IT Security International
	ITV
	Incaa UK
	Interconnections
	Intemational Data Security
	Intemational Soflware Management
	J.R.Ward Computers Ltd.
	JPY Associates
	Jaguar Commnunications Ltd.
	Janus Sovereign
	Loadplan
	Logica
	Marcon
	Microft Technology Inc.
	Micronyx UK Ltd.
	Micronyx UK Ltd.
	Network Systems
	News Datacom
	Northem Telecom Europe Limited
	PC Security Ltd.
	PPCP

ATTACHMENT 2. *Continued*

	Paradyne European Headquarters
	Plessy Crypto
	Plus 5 Engineering Ltd.
	Prosoft Ltd.
	Protection Systems Ltd.
	Racal
	Racal Milgo
	Radius
	S&S International
	Shareware plc
	Sington Associates
	Smart Diskette UK
	Smith's Associates
	SoRdiskette
	Sophos Ltd.
	Stralfors Data
	Sygnus Data Communications
	The Software Forge Ltd.
	Time & Data Systems
	Tricom
	University College London
	Widney Ash
	Zergo
	Zeta Communications Ltd.
USA	3COM Corp.
	ADT Security Systems
	AO Electronics
	AOS
	ASC Systems
	ASD SoRware Inc.
	ASP
	AST Research
	AT&T
	AT&T Bell Laboratories
	AT&T Datotek Inc.
	Access Data Recovery
	Advanced Computer Security Concepts
	Advanced Encryption Systems
	Advanced Information Systems
	Advanced Micro Devices, Inc. (AMD)
	Aladdin Software Security
	American Computer Security
	Anagram Laboratories
	Applied Software Inc.
	Arkansas Systems, Inc.
	Ashton Tate

ATTACHMENT 2. *Continued*

BCC
BLOC Development Corporation
Banyan
Bi-Hex Co.
Borland
Braintree Technology
Burroughs
CE Infosys of America, Inc.
Casady and Greene
Centel Federal Systems Inc.
Central Point Software
Certus International
Cettlan Corp.
Chase Manhattan Bank, N.A.
Clarion
Codex Corp.
Collins Telecommunications Products Division
Command SW Systems
Commcrypt
Communication Devices Inc.
Complan
Computer Associates International, Inc.
Contemporary Cybernetics
Cryptall
Cryptech
Cryptex/Gretag Ltd.
Cylink Corp.
Cypher Comms Technology
DSC Communications
DataEase International
Datakey Inc.
Datamedia Corporation
Datamedia Corp. (DC Area)
Datawatch, Triangle Software Division
Datotek, Inc.
Dell Computer
Digital Delivery, Inc.
Digital Enterprises Inc.
Digital Equipment Corporation (DEC)
Digital Pathways
Docutel/Olivetti Corp.
Dolphin Software
Dowty Network Systems
ELIASHIM Microcomputers Inc.
EMUCOM
Enigma Logic, Inc.

ATTACHMENT 2. *Continued*

Enterprise Solutions Ltd.
Fairchild Seminconductor
Fifth Generation Systems, Inc.
Fischer International
Front Line Software
GN Telematic Inc.
GTE Sylvania
Gemplus Card International
General Electric Company
Glenco Engineering
HYDELCO, Inc.
Hawk Technologies Inc.
Hawkeye Grafix, Inc.
Hilgraeve, Inc.
Hughes Aircraft Company
Hughes Data Systems Inc.
Hughes Network Systems—California
Hughes Network Systems—Maryland
Hybrid Communicatior .
INFOSAFE
Incaa Inc.
Info Resource Engineering
Info Security Systems
Information Conversion Sevices
Information Security Associates, Inc.
Information Security Corp.
Innovative Communications Technologies, Inc.
Intel
International Business Machines (IBM)
Inter-Tech Corp.
Isolation Systems, Inc.
Isolation Systems, Inc.
John E. Holt and Associates
Jones Futurex, Inc.
Kensington Microware Ltd.
Kent Marsh Ltd.
Key Concepts
Kinetic Corp.
LUCENT
Lassen Software, Inc.
Lattice Inc.
Lexicon, ICOT Corporation
Litronic Industries (Information Systems Division)
Litronic Industries (Virginia)
Lotus
MCTel

ATTACHMENT 2. *Continued*

Maedae Enterprises
Magna
Mark Riordan
Massachusetts Institute of Technology
Matsushita Electronic Components Co.
Mergent International
Micanopy MicroSystems Inc.
Micro Card Technologies, Inc.
Micro Security Systems Inc.
MicroFrame Inc.
Microcom Inc. (Utilities Product Group)
MicroLink Technologies Inc.
Micronyx
Microrim
Microsoft
Mika, L.P.
Mike Ingle
Morning Star Technologies
Morse Security Group, Inc.
Motorola
NEC Technologies
National Semiconductor
Network-1, Inc.
Networking Dynamics Corp.
Nixdorf Computer Corporation
Northern Telecom Inc.
Norton
Novell
OnLine SW International
Ontrak Computer Systems Inc.
Optimum Electronics, Inc.
Otocom Systems Inc.
PC Access Control Inc.
PC Dynamics Inc.
PC Guardian
PC Plus Inc.
Paradyne Caribbean, Inc.
Paradyne Corporation
Paralon Technologies
Personal Computer Card Corp.
Pinon Engineering, Inc.
Prime Factors
RSA Data Security, Inc.
RSA Laboratories
Racal Datacom
Racal-Guardata

ATTACHMENT 2. *Continued*

Racal-Milgo USA
Rainbow Technology
Raxco
Rothenbuhler Engineering
S Squared Electronics
SCO
SVC
Safetynet
Samna Corp
Scrambler Systems Corp.
Sector Technology
Secur-Data Systems, Inc.
Secura Technologies
Secure Systems Group Internationl, Inc.
Security Dynamics
Security Microsystems Inc.
Semaphore Communications
Sentry Systems, Inc.
Silver Oak Systems
SmartDisk Security Corp.
Software Directions, Inc.
Solid Oak Sofware
SophCo, Inc.
Sota Miltope
Stellar Systems Inc.
Sterling Softare Inc. (Dylakor Division)
Sterling Software Inc. (System SW Marketing Division)
SunSoR
Symantec
TRW, Electronic Product Ltd.
Techmar Computer Products, Inc.
Techmatics, Inc.
Technical Communications Corp. (TCC)
Telequip Corp.
Terry Ritter
Texas Instruments, Inc.
The Exchange
Thumbscan, Inc.
Tracor Ultron
Trigram Systems
Tritron Sytems
Trusted Information Systems, Inc.
UNIVAC
UTI-MACO Safeguard Systems
UUNet Technologies, Inc.

ATTACHMENT 2. *Continued*

	United Software Security
	Uptronics, Inc.
	VLSI Technology, Inc.
	Verdix Corp. (Secure Products Division)
	ViaCrypt
	Visionary Electronics
	Wang Laboratories
	Wells Fargo Security Products
	Westem DataCom Co. Inc.
	Western Digital Corporation
	Westinghouse Electric Corp.
	WordPerfect
	XTree
	Xetron Corp.
	Yeargin Engineering
	Zenith Data Systems
	hDC
	usrESZ Software, Inc.
YUGOSLAVIA	Sophos Yu d.o.o.

4

Technology and Software Controls*

Larry E. Christensen

This article is a review of the controls for technology (also referred to as "technical data") and software under the Export Administration Regulations ("EAR"). The topics in this article include:

1. A recent history of the structure of technology and software controls;
2. A decision tree or checklist for determining the appropriate general or validated license;
3. The structure of technical data and software controls after the September 1, 1991 Commerce Control List ("CCL") amendments and after the Conforming Regulation of February 6, 1992[1];
4. The General Technology Note;
5. The General Software Note;
6. Operation technical data and software;
7. Sales technical data;
8. General License GTDA; and
9. Disclosures to foreign nationals.

A RECENT HISTORY OF THE STRUCTURE OF TECHNOLOGY AND SOFTWARE CONTROLS

In early 1988, the U.S. Department of Commerce ("Commerce") began an extensive review of the technology and software controls of the EAR.[2] As part of this review, Commerce invited papers for presentation at an open forum. On February 11, 1988, approximately twenty such papers were delivered to a panel of Commerce representatives during a forum attended by approximately 300 people. Commerce then organized the review in an interagency Working Group at the staff level and

---

* Law and policy of export controls: recent essays on key export issues. Washington DC: Section of International Law and Practice, American Bar Association, Copyright 1993. Reprinted by permission.

[1] 57 Fed. Reg. 4553 (February 6, 1992).

[2] Hereafter, citations to the EAR shall be to section or part numbers at 15 C.F.R. 768 *et seq*

a Steering Committee at the political level. Both groups included private sector representation by distinguished export control managers. On October 13, 1988, Commerce published a proposed rule to amend Part 779.[3]

During the review and after consideration of the comments submitted in response to the proposed rule, five major objectives evolved:

1. Create a mass-market software exclusion from controls.
2. Integrate technology and software license requirements into the CCL.
3. Clarify the scope of General License GTDA.
4. Eliminate unilateral national security controls both as a matter of law and on the face of the regulations.
5. Make Part 779 clear and user-friendly.

The extent to which the current regulations have achieved these objectives is as follows.

Mass-Market Software

Mass-market software was first excluded from validated license requirements to destinations controlled by the Coordinating Committee[4] ("COCOM") with the addition of note 6 to then-Supplement 3 to Part 779 of the EAR. This also provided for the export of such software under General License GTDR without a written assurance. This reflected a COCOM decision several years before to exclude "standard commercial software" from most COCOM controls. The principle of exclusion of mass-market software from controls was continued by the implementation of the General Software Note, which became effective on September 1, 1991, and is discussed further below.

Technology and Software in the CCL

Implementation of the so-called Core List exercise decisions by CO-COM integrated technology and software licensing requirements into the CCL effective September 1, 1991. All software is now in the CCL and appears under Export Control Classification Numbers ("ECCNs") with a second character of "D." (*See* for example ECCN 3D01A and ECCN 3D96G).[5] All technology is now in the CCL and appears under ECCNs with a second character of "E." (*See* for example ECCN 3E01A and ECCN 3E96G).[6]

---

[3] 53 Fed. Reg. 40074.
[4] 770.2.
[5] 56 Fed. Reg. 42824, 42861–62 (August 29, 1991).
[6] *Id.* at 42862–63.

The integration of technology and software descriptions and licensing requirements into the CCL has several impacts. First, it makes the task of finding the licensing requirement easier. Previously, licensing requirements were scattered throughout the various provisions of Part 779. This goes far towards making Part 779 clearer and more user friendly. Secondly, it shows the reader that unilateral national security controls no longer exist for technology and software. Thirdly, it permits and requires the classification of technology and software as the key first step in complying with the EAR as they apply to technology and software. Fourthly, policy makers can now implement more precise controls for specific reasons targeted at specific destinations. This will prove a valuable asset as the various non-proliferation controls evolve under the Enhanced Proliferation Control Initiative ("EPCI").

The integration of technical data and software into the CCL proved to be the most difficult hurdle to comprehensive reform of technical data and software controls. From time to time, other regulations had higher priority or Commerce did not have the scarce resources necessary both to revise the text of Part 779 and to put all software and technical data into the CCL. Therefore, in 1991, Commerce decided to split the revision of the technology and software controls into two distinct regulatory amendments: (1) the integration of technical data and software into the CCL; and (2) the revision of the text of Part 779.

The opportunity to integrate technology and software into the CCL presented itself in the Core List exercise, which was a COCOM review of Industrial List controls starting with a blank sheet of paper ("Core List"). During the negotiations on the Core List, the technical working groups were directed to structure each category to include separate entries for both technology and software. As a result of the COCOM Industrial List negotiations, there was a consensus within the United States Government to publish the new CCL with technology and software in the CCL. However, publishing the new CCL before the COCOM effective date required an enormous amount of work with only a few weeks to accomplish the task by the effective date of September 1, 1991, agreed to in COCOM. Of course, the most challenging part of this task was to write product descriptions and licensing requirements for the non-proliferation controls and other foreign policy controls that were not encompassed in the Core List.

General License GTDA (Technical Data Available)

General License GTDA ("GTDA") is the first, and perhaps most important, general license for technology. Prior to the Fall of 1989, the scope of GTDA was not readily apparent to the reader of Part 779 of the EAR. In the early 1980s, managers of a technical conference on bubble memory technology unwittingly triggered a years-long review of GTDA when they excluded foreign nationals from attending their conference. What followed this controversial bubble memory conference was an outcry from the academic community and an interagency review of GTDA by the National Science Foundation, Commerce, and the Department of Defense. During the general technical data review, it became obvious that no effort to revise technology and software controls would be complete without redrafting GTDA.

Commerce published the clarified GTDA in the Fall of 1989. The most significant contribution to the clearer GTDA was the publication of a Supplement 5 to Part 779. This is a long list of examples that illustrate the application of GTDA. The substance of GTDA is discussed further later in this article.

Elimination of Unilateral National Security Controls

Before February 23, 1989, the EAR prohibited the export of all trade secrets to the former Soviet Bloc and China. In other words, the controls applied to all technology except GTDA-eligible technology. The scope of this control was well in excess of the COCOM controls. And there was no policy that necessarily favored the export of non-COCOM technology. For example, in the middle 1980s, the agencies hotly debated the export to the former Soviet Bloc of technology for the production of items such as roofing shingles, women's sanitary napkins, and furniture. In the era following the demise of the Warsaw Pact and the Soviet Union, it is difficult to conceive of such debates; but they did, in fact, occur. Congress grew weary of unilateral national security controls and amended section 5(c)(6) in 1988 to end such controls effective February 23, 1989.

As announced in the preamble to a commodity rule published in the Federal Register of February 28, 1989[7], unilateral national security controls on technology and software expired by operation of law on February 23, 1989. Unfortunately, the CCL did not describe technology and software multilaterally controlled at the time. Therefore, the reader did not know what unilateral controls had expired. Commerce interpreted the statutory mandate to be self-executing. The regulations remained unchanged. Unwary exporters who did not consult the statute but relied only upon the regulations may have been unaware of the decontrol. Between February 23, 1989, and September 1, 1991, exporters often consulted the British control list to determine whether their technology was COCOM controlled. During that period, the only certain method for the exporter to determine whether his technology

---

[7] 54 Fed. Reg. 8281, 8281–82.

was COCOM controlled was to consult with the Office of Technology and Policy Analysis to obtain a classification.

Make Part 779 Clear and User-Friendly

The objective of clarifying Part 779 is not fully met. On the positive side, the licensing requirements are now primarily in the CCL and exporters determine those requirements by first classifying their technical data and software just as they have done with commodities for years. As a consequence of placing such requirements on the CCL, the validated license subparagraphs of old section 779.4(c) and (d) and Supplements 3 and 4 have been eliminated pursuant to the so-called Conforming Regulation.[8] Moreover, the Conforming Regulation makes clear that if GTDU (the equivalent of GDTR without written assurance) is not authorized by the CCL, the exporter may nonetheless attempt to qualify for operation technical data authority (779.4(b)(1)), sales technical data authority (779.4(b)(2)), and software updates authority (779.4(b)(3)).[9] For software, the exporter may nonetheless attempt to qualify for so-called mass-market treatment under the General Software Note at Supplement 2 of the CCL.[10] Commerce intends that such software may be exported GTDU to all destinations except Country Groups S and Z and the South African police and military; however, the country scope of GTDU for mass-market software requires clarification on the face of the regulations.

Exporters now also have the option to use the term "General License GTDU" to describe General License GTDR without written assurance. The Conforming Regulation amended section 779.4(b)(4) to provide in part:

> Exporters have the option of using the term "GTDU" to describe General License GTDR without written assurance for all purposes, including information requirements on the Shipper's Export Declaration.[11]

On the other hand, Part 779 continues to use the term "technical data" to mean both "technology" and "software." In addition, Part 779 continues to use the term "GTDR without written assurance" even though the term "GTDU" means exactly the same general license and even though the EAR clearly allows an exporter to use the "GTDU" in all the circumstances where GTDR without written assurance is authorized. In other words, there is now one general license with two acceptable names. As described at section 779.4(b), this one general

---

[8] *See* 57 Fed. Reg. 4553 at p. 4564 and p. 4567 (February 6, 1992).
[9] *Id.* at 4565.
[10] 56 Fed. Reg. 42824, 42903 (August 29, 1991).
[11] *Id*

license consists of four distinct and separate authorities. In addition, this one general license authorizes the export of mass-market software. Also on the negative side, there is no clarification of the application of the rules regarding the disclosure of technology to foreign nationals, no clarification or relief from the commingled rule, and no relief from the foreign-produced direct product controls for items made in cooperating countries.

Other objectives established during the technical data review included clarification of the scope of operation and sales technical data authority. As discussed below, operation technical data authority was clarified by publication of the third paragraph of the General Technology Note, which now appears in Supplement 2 to the CCL, and the Conforming Regulation. Sales technical data authority was clarified in the Conforrning Regulation and is also discussed below.

At this writing, it is quite clear that the complete redrafting of Part 779 as proposed in 1988[12] will not be made a final rule despite the strong public support reflected in comments. Some agencies seek substantive changes in technical data and software control policy as a precondition to approve the further clarification of Part 779. Ironically, the integration of technical data and software into the CCL accomplished 95% of the objectives sought in the technical data review. Now the need to achieve the last 5% of the task is simply not important enough to cause either side to yield in the ongoing policy debates.

For those who seek the maximum clarity for exporters and the maximum enforceability for prosecutors, perhaps the best strategy now is to declare victory and move on to the new policy issues that are already upon us and those sure to arrive in the uncertain future that lies ahead. As a result of the technical data review and COCOM's recent efforts, we can be optimistic that future multilateral negotiations regarding non-proliferation controls and future policy making within the United States will no longer treat technology and software controls as after thoughts to commodity controls. We can also be optimistic that technology and software controls will be clear and that these controls will no longer be the sole domain of those few who would spend weeks, months, even years to understand the old Part 779. The rest of this article is dedicated to that end.

Decision Tree for Technology and Software Controls

The following steps should be taken in descending order to determine the appropriate general or validated license for the export of technology

---

[12] 53 Fed. Reg. 40,074 (October 13, 1988).

or software. Follow these steps until you identify a general license available to you and then go no further. If these questions are answered out of order, or if you go down the decision tree beyond the first available general license, you may reach erroneous conclusions that no general license is available or that you must use an unduly restricted general license. If you choose to go further down the decision tree than is necessary because you have business reasons to use a more restrictive authorization, you may do so; but you are not required to:

1. *Classification.* Classify your technology and software. All technology and all software is on the CCL in some entry.[13]
2. *GTDA.* Determine the applicability of General License GTDA at 779.3.
3. *List-driven GTDU.*[14] From the proper ECCN entry on the CCL, determine the availability of General License GTDU. (General License GTDR without written assurance).
4. *Mass-market software GTDU.* For software, determine the availability of mass-market software authority at the General Software Note in Supplement 2 of the CCL.
5. *Sales technical data GTDU.* Determine the availability of sales technical data authority at 779.4(b)(2).
6. *Operation technical data GTDU.* Determine the availability of operation technical data and software authority at 779.4(b)(1) and the third paragraph of the General Technology Note at Supplement 2 to Part 779.
7. *Software updates GTDU.* Determine the availability of software update authority at 779.4(b)(3).
8. *G-TEMP.* Determine the availability of General License G-TEMP for software at 771.22.
9. *GTDR with written assurance.* Determine the availability of GTDR with written assurance at the proper entry on the CCL.
10. *Validated license.* If no general license is available, obtain a validated license before you make the physical export or disclose the technology or source code to a foreign national.[15]

---

[13] Certain technology and software is properly under the jurisdiction of other federal agendes. See 770.10 and Supplement Nos. 2, 3 and 4 to Part 770 of the EAR.

[14] General Licenses GTDR with written assurance, GTDR without written assurance (GTDU), and validated licenses may not be used contrary to the provisions of 778.7(c) and 778.8(c), which prohibit exports for end-uses related to the design, development, production, or use of certain missiles and end-uses related to the design, development, production, stockpiling, or use of chemical or biological weapons respectively. Such prohibitions do not apply to General License GTDA.

[15] A single page version of the above decision tree appears at Attachment A for ease of use.

Explanation of the Decision Tree

With the publication of the Commerce Control List ("CCL") on August 29, 1991, technology and software license requirements are described on the CCL for the first time. The first step in determining licensing requirements is to classify your technology or software by finding it on the CCL. This is the classification process familiar to exporters of commodities. There is one exception to this rule.

If you prefer, you may determine the availability of General License GTDA before classifying your technical data or software. Under a few limited circumstances, it will be easier to determine the availability of General License GTDA than to classify the technical data. For example, a published book is clearly eligible for General License GTDA and yet classifying all the technology in that book may prove difficult and time consuming. General License GTDA is the only general license that may be considered before classifying an item (technology, software, or commodities). GTDA is the only general license that is available to all destinations, all end users, and all end uses.

If you have first classified your technology or software, your next step is to examine GTDA. Two serious mistakes are (1) ignoring the full scope of General License GTDA or (2) failing to take steps to determine whether your technology or software are "publicly available." Unfortunately, such mistakes are made frequently.

"General License GTDU: Yes"

If the ECCN for your technology or software indicates "General License GTDU: Yes," then you may export this technology and software to all countries except Country Groups S and Z, police and military entities in South Africa, and (under the relevant Treasury regulations) Iraq, Haiti, and Yugoslavia (Serbia and Montenegro). You may do so without a validated license and without obtaining a written assurance of the type referred to at section 779.4(f). Eligibility for GTDU is thus driven by the CCL license provisions. It is imperative to realize there are five different authorities or means to qualify under General License GTDU. The authority discussed above is granted on the face of the ECCN. I refer to this authority as the "list-driven" GTDU. The other four authorities or means to qualify under General License GTDU are operation technology, sales technology, software updates, and mass-market software. These are discussed below. Remember, there are five distinct and separate means to qualify for General License GTDU. Therefore, there are five distinct and separate authorities to export under GTDU: list-driven GTDU, GTDU for sales technical data and software, GTDU for operation technical data and software, GTDU for software updates, and GTDU for mass-market software. Remember the distinctions between these five different authorities under GTDU when using the above decision tree.

If your software or technology enjoys the "list-driven" GTDU, then you may use this general license. You should not go on to examine operation technology or sales technology authority. This is true regardless of the nature of your export transaction. For example, under ECCN 4E96G, technical data may be exported under GTDU. Assume you plan to disclose this technology to a foreign firm during a sales presentation but the technology does not qualify for sales technical data authority because you are providing detailed information that you do not customarily provide to potential domestic customers. Under these circumstances, "list-driven" GTDU is available regardless of the fact that the disclosure of the technology would not qualify for sales technical data authority, which is a separate distinct authority or means of qualifying for General License GTDU. Even though the export will take place within the context of a sales presentation, you need not qualify for sales technical data authority. This is a rational result because GTDU is available for an outright sale of the technology and an export in the context of a sales presentation should not be subject to more restrictive export treatment. Exporters occasionally reach the opposite, incorrect conclusion. Such an incorrect conclusion will be avoided by going down the decision tree until a general license is established and then going no further.

"General License GTDU: No"

If the ECCN for your technology or software indicates "General License GTDU: No," then you may not export this technology and software under the list-driven authority of GTDU. However, you may then go on to determine whether your export qualifies for GTDU or GTDR without written assurance for sales technical data (779.4(b)(2)), operation technical data (779.4(b)(1)), software updates (779.4(b)(3)), or mass-market software (General Software Note at Supplement 2 of the CCL).[16] Commerce intends that such mass-market software may be exported GTDU to all destinations except Country Groups S and Z and the South African police and military; however, the country scope of GTDU for mass-market software requires clarification on the face of the regulations. All these conclusions would be clearer if only there were a separate general license for each separate authority. In fact, one major corporation has recommended this. Unfortunately, this outcome is unlikely because some exporters have criticized the proliferation of general licenses. Nonetheless, these five different authorities under GTDU

---

[16] 56 Fed. Reg. 42824, 42903 (August 29, 1991).

and GTDR without written assurance are each separate and distinct authorizations to export, and exporters must view them as such to take full advantage of their rights under the EAR and to develop proper compliance programs.

General License G-TEMP is the only general license currently available for both commodities and software. For that reason, exporters may overlook G-TEMP when planning compliance programs for the marketing of software. G-TEMP can be an effective general license for software marketing and other purposes. It should not be overlooked.

This author sees no reason other commodity general licenses should not be used for software and technology. General Licenses GCT, GLV, and others might be appropriate for software and technology; but, at this time, such general licenses are not available for technology and software.

THE STRUCTURE OF TECHNICAL DATA AND SOFTWARE CONTROLS AFTER THE SEPTEMBER 1, 1991, CCL AMENDMENTS AND AFTER THE CONFORMING REGULATION OF FEBRUARY 6, 1992

The structure of the technical data and software controls is now almost identical to the structure for commodity controls. The licensing requirements for technical data and software were included in the CCL effective September 1, 1991.[17] Exporters may classify their items themselves without requesting a classification from the Bureau of Export Administration ("BXA"). However, exporters who classify their own items take the responsibility to do so correctly.

All technology, software, and commodities are on the CCL. The CCL covers the entire economy except those items properly within the export control jurisdiction of another Federal agency. The proper CCL entry or ECCN for your item may be a general entry for items not elsewhere specified ("n.e.s."), such as those ECCNs ending with the letter "G." Exporters and government personnel may casually state that a given item is "not on the CCL." Such a statement is not legally correct and is a mere unfortunate, short hand description of an item that does not require a validated license to any destination except Country Groups S and Z. Every item is on the CCL, and if you have not found our technology, software, or commodity on the CCL, you simply have not looked hard enough.

The General Technology Note and the General Software Note at supplement 2 to the CCL explain the scope of technology and software

---

[17] See 56 Fed. Reg. 42824 (August 29, 1991).

controls for all control reasons. Each note is discussed below. For purposes of explaining the structure of the technology and software controls, it is important to recognize one fundamental difference between these two notes. The first paragraph of the General Technology Note provides that technology is controlled "according to the provisions in each category." Therefore, the provisions of the category and each entry prevail and determine the scope of the technology control. In this respect, the first paragraph of the General Technology Notes serves primarily to introduce definitions of terms used throughout the CCL to describe the scope of technology controls. For example, ECCN 4E01A controls the technology for the *"development" and "production" and "use"* of equipment, materials, or software in ECCNs beginning with 4A, 4B, or 4C. By contrast, ECCN 1E01A controls certain *"development" and "production"* technology but does not capture *"use"* technology. This is not a typographical error or style difference. Rather, it reflects a substantive decision not to include "use" technology within the scope of ECCN 1E01A.

On the other hand, the General Software Note prevails over the language of the CCL entries. Thus, if software meets the so-called mass-market standards of the General Software Note, it is eligible for export under GTDR without written assurance or GTDU, regardless of the licensing requirements found in each software entry of the CCL. For example, ECCN 3D03A controls certain computer-aided-design software and authorizes GTDR with written assurance to Country Groups T and V except Iran, Syria, and the PRC. All other destinations require a validated license and list-driven GTDU is not available. However, if your software meets the standards of the General Software Note as so-called mass-market software, then your software may be exported under mass-market GTDU authority regardless of the terms of the ECCN.

Validated license requirements are provided in each ECCN. This requires some explanation concerning the relationship between the entries for "Validated License Required" and "GTDR." Take, for example, ECCN 3E01A for certain computer technology:

> Validated License Required: QSWYZ, Iran, Syria, PRC, South Africa military and police.
> GTDR: yes, except MT (see note).

First, a validated license is required to Country Groups T and V if the importer does not provide the required written assurance. (Section 779.4(f)). Secondly, GTDR as described in the CCL always requires a written assurance. In the regulation on how to use the CCL, section 799.1(d)(1)(iv) provides in relevant part:

> For software and technical data, the descriptions of eligibility for general licenses are set forth as GTDR, which means General License GTDR with

written assurance, and GTDU which is used to indicate General License GTDR without written assurance.[18]

Thirdly, GTDR with written assurance is not available for exports to Country Groups QSWYZ, Iran, Syria, the PRC, and the South Africa police or military by reason of the limits in Part 779. In the view of this author, that result should be underscored by a GTDR entry that might read:

> Yes for Country Groups T and V, except the PRC, Iran, Syria, South Africa police or military, and MT (see note).

Currently, the reader must still refer to the country limitations of GTDR at section 779.4 in order to know the true scope of the GTDR authority. The drafting of the entries differs somewhat in style because the small amount of time allowed to all the new ECCNs required writing by several different drafters. This, too, may be a source of confusion if you do not take care to recognize the country limitations for General License GTDR with written assurance. For example, ECCN 2E01A controls certain technology required for items controlled under the materials processing category:

> Validated License Required: QSTVWYZ
> GTDR: yes, except MT (see Note) and exports to Iran and Syria.

First, a validated license is required to Country Groups T and V if the consignee does not provide a written assurance. (Section 779.4(f)). Secondly, GTDR as described in the CCL always requires a written assurance. Thirdly, GTDR with written assurance is not available for exports to Country Groups QSWYZ, Iran, Syria, the PRC, or the South Africa police or military, by reason of the limits in Part 779. In the view of this author, Country Groups Q, W, Y, S, and Z should be excepted from eligibility for GTDR with written assurance just as Iran and Syria are excepted on the face of this ECCN. This is the correct legal conclusion one will reach by reading all the applicable regulations. It would simply be easier for the reader if the complete set of country exclusions were spelled out in each ECCN rather than making the reader refer back to Part 779.

As noted above in the discussion of the decision tree, an entry that reads "GTDU: No" merely means that the list-driven GTDU authority is not available. However, you may then go on to determine whether your export qualifies for GTDU or GTDR without written assurance for sales technical data (779.4(b)(2)), operation technical data (779.4(b)(1)), software updates (779.4(b)(3)), and mass-market software. Thus, there

---

[18] *Id.* at 42827.

are six authorities or authorizations to export technology or software not specified in each ECCN on the CCL. Those are:

1. General License GTDA,
2. Sales technical data GTDU,
3. Operation technical data and software GTDU,
4. Software updates GTDU,
5. Mass-market software under GTDU, and
6. General License G-TEMP.

Certain basket categories in the CCL are important because they show the reader that Commerce has eliminated unilateral national security controls and because they implement the embargo on Cuba, North Korea, Viet Nam, Cambodia, and Libya. For example, ECCN 4E96G describes certain technology required for certain G-DEST commodities and software in the "n.e.s." entries, which stands for "not elsewhere specified":

> Validated license required: SZ, South Africa Military and Police.
> GTDR: No.
> GTDU: Yes.

Keep in mind that there are end-use and end-user limitations on the use of General License GTDR with written assurance and GTDU. For example, many of the proliferation controls prohibit the use of all items for particular purposes. These limitations would apply to General Licenses GTDR with written assurance and GTDU. In the opinion of this author, such limitations do not extend to General License GTDA.

THE GENERAL TECHNOLOGY NOTE

For years COCOM relied upon a General Technology Note ("GTN") that was not published in the EAR. For the most part, COCOM used the GTN to control technology related to commodities described on the various COCOM lists until September 1, 1991. There were, however, exceptions in COCOM to the general rule and those were described in various entries. During the Core List exercise COCOM redrafted the GTN as it applies to the Industrial List and agreed that all COCOM members should publish it along with the list of items controlled.[19]

---

[19] The complete GTN for the COCOM Industrial List is as follows:

The export of "technology" which is "required" for the "development" "production" or "use" of products embargoed in the International Industrial List is controlled according to the provisions in each Category.

"Technology" "required" for the "development" "production" or "use" of a product under embargo remains under embargo even when applicable to any unembargoed product.

COCOM also negotiated and redrafted certain definitions that are essential to an understanding of the scope of the COCOM controls. This GTN is implemented in the CCL. It is applicable thus far to all entries on the CCL regardless of the reason for control. The GTN as implemented in Supplement 2 to the CCL provides in relevant part:

> 1. General Technology Note
>   The export of "technology" that is "required" for the "development" "production" or "use" of products on the Commerce Control List is controlled according to the provisions in each Category.
>   "Technology" "required" for the "development" "production" or "use" of a controlled product remains controlled even when applicable to a product controlled at a lower level.

General License GTDR, without written assurance, is available for "technology" that is the minimum necessary for the installation, operation, maintenance (checking), and repair of those products that are eligible for General Licenses or that are exported under a validated export license.[20]

> N.B.: This does not allow release under a general license of the repair "technology" controlled by 1E02.e, 1E02.f, 7E03, or 8E02.a.
> N.B.: The "minimum necessary" excludes "development" or "production" technology and permits "use" technology only to the extent "required" to ensure safe and efficient use of the product. Individual ECCNs may further restrict export of "minimum necessary" information.

The GTN provides that technology is controlled "according to the provisions of each Category." This means that a given ECCN may incorporate all or a portion of the potential scope of technology controls captured by the terms used in the GTN. Therefore, the definitions of the terms are important. The most important of those terms is the word "required."

> "Required" as applied to technology, refers to only that portion of "technology" which is peculiarly responsible for achieving or exceeding the embargoed performance levels, characteristics or functions. Such "required" "technology" may be shared by different products.

Controls do not apply to that "technology" which is the minimum necessary for the installation, operation, maintenance (checking) and repair of those products which are unembargoed or whose export has been authorized. N.B.: This does not release the repair technology embargoed by Category 8E2a.

Controls do not apply to "technology" "in the public domain" or to "basic scientific research."

[20] Note the modification made at 56 Fed. Reg. 67171, 67174 (December 30, 1991) to extend this authority for operation technical data related to a product, including software, exported under any general license.

COCOM adopted the term "required" to more precisely define the scope of know-how subject to the controls. In effect, the term captures individual items of know-how that are both necessary and sufficient to achieve the performance parameter of the commodity used to define the scope of the technology entry. COCOM specifically recognizes that controlled technology remains controlled even if it can be used and is used to develop or produce uncontrolled items.

> "Technology" "required" for the "development" "production" or "use" of a controlled product remains controlled even when applicable to a product controlled at a lower level.

Examples will illustrate the various points:

Example of Technologies "Required"

Assume product "X" is under controls if it operates at or above 400 Mhz, and is free from controls if it operates below 400 Mhz. If production technologies "A" "B" and "C" allow production of products that operated at no more than 399 Mhz, then technologies "A" "B" and "C" are not "required" to produce the controlled product "X." If technologies "A" "B" "C" "D" and "E" are used together, a manufacturer can produce a product "X" which does operate at or above 400 Mhz. In this example, technologies "D" and "E" are "required" to make the controlled product and are themselves controlled under the General Technology Note.

Example of Technologies "Required" for More Than One Product

Assume that product "X" is under controls if it operates at or above 400 Mhz. Assume product "Y" is under controls if it operates at a CTP of 12.5 or faster. If technologies "D" and "E" are "required" to produce product "X" (operating above 400 Mhz) and technologies "B" and "C" are "required" to produce product "Y" (operating above 12.5 CTP), then technologies "B" "C" "D" and "E" are controlled under the General Technology Note regardless of the product the consignee intends to produce; i.e., even if the consignee intends to produce product "X" operating at 200 Mhz.

Example of One Technology "Required" for Both a Controlled and an Uncontrolled Commodity

Assume that one item of know-how is used to process an ore to make an uncontrolled material. Assume further that the same item of know-how is used to process an ore to make a controlled material. In this example, the know-how is "required" to produce the controlled material. The know-how is controlled for export regardless of its actual end use.

The terms "development" "production" and "use" as defined in COCOM and in Supplement 3 to section 799.1 are significant for the purpose of defining the scope of controls.[21] The definition of the term "technology" is not.

The third paragraph of the GTN is the COCOM equivalent to operation technical data authority. It prevails over the terms of ECCN entries on the CCL. This paragraph excludes such operation technical data from validated license controls; and it is identical, redundant authority to that found in 779.4(b)(1). Note that certain repair technology is excluded from this authority.

THE GENERAL SOFTWARE NOTE

The General Software Note ("GSN") in COCOM was also negotiated during the Core List exercise. It applies to all categories in the COCOM Industrial List. As implemented in Supplement 2 to section 799.1 of the CCL, it prevails over all entries on the CCL and provides as follows:

> General License GTDR, without written assurance, is available for release of software that is generally available to the public by being:
>
> a. Sold from stock at retail selling points, without restriction, by means of:
>   1. Over the counter transactions;
>   2. Mail order transactions; or

---

[21] *"Development"* is related to all stages prior to serial production, such as: design, design research, design analyses, design concepts, assembly and testing of prototypes, pilot production schemes, design data, process of transforming design data into a product, configuration design, integration design, layouts.

"Production" means all production stages, such as: product engineering, manufacture, integration, assembly (mounting), inspection, testing, quality assurance.

"Use"—operation, installation (including on-site installation), maintenance (checking), repair, overhaul and refurbishing.

"Technology"—specific information necessary for the "development" "production" or use" of a product. The information takes the form of "technical data" or "technical assistance". Embargoed "technology" is defined in the General Technology Note and in the International Industrial List.

"Technical assistance" may take forms, such as: instruction, skills, training, working knowledge, consulting services. *N.B.* "Technical assistance" may involve transfer of technical data.

"Technical data" may take forms such as blueprints, plans, diagrams, models, formulae, tables, engineering designs and specifications, manuals and instructions written or recorded other media or devices such as disk, tape, read-only memories.

    3. Telephone call transactions; and

b. Designed for installation by the user without further substantial support by the supplier.

General License GTDA is available for software that is publicly available.

The theory underlying the GSN is that there is a subset of software that is so widely available to the general public that it is uncontrollable and therefore the COCOM governments should not impose an unmanageable control burden on the firms subject to such controls. To qualify for GSN treatment, software must be generally available to the public, and this is one of the three key limitations on eligibility for GSN exclusion from controls. The software must be held out to the public as available. This element is not satisfied if software is marketed only through a system that prequalifies the customer or provides advice and assistance in the form of systems configuration.

Exporters should be wary of the trap that stems from giving too much weight to the provisions regarding channels of distribution. For example, a given firm might negotiate a $1,000,000 software development and licensing agreement over several years and then close the sale or license by an exchange of letters. Of course, that is not a mail order transaction within the meaning of the GSN. Similarly, firms engage in a wide variety of negotiations for sales or licenses that are concluded via telephone or FAX. Such contracts are not all of the type referred to in the GSN as "telephone call transactions." A firm may qualify for GSN treatment if it has its own telephone mail order system with telephones answered by persons who merely take orders and fill them. If a firm has a group of engineers who answer the telephone and help configure systems of controlled products for the caller, this does not qualify for GSN reatrnent.

The second key limitation for GSN treatment is that the software must be sold "from stock." For this reason, software customized for an individual customer does not qualify.

The third key limitation is that the software must be designed for user installation. This provision raises a question. Who is the user that is the installer? In this author's opinion, the user is not the head of a large management information system in a large company. Rather, the user is that person in the firm who will sit at a terminal and use the software not as a computer or software expert or specialist but as a consumer of the functions delivered by the software. For example, the user of computer-aided design software is the design engineer and not the head of the computer systems department.

Application of the GSN will raise issues that are appropriate for resolution in the classification system.

Operation Technical Data and Software

The publication of the Core List corrected two problems with the prior rule on operation technical data. The third paragraph of the General Technology Note excludes from controls certain maintenance repair, and operating know-how. (Section 799.1, Supplement 2). This superseded and eliminated the single shipment and one-year limitations that previously existed at 779.4(b)(1). The publication of the Conforming Regulation also made these changes explicit on the face of 779.4(b)(1), which now states:

(i) For definitions and conditions for use of General License GTDR without written assurance for operation technical data, refer to the third paragraph of the General Technology Note as listed in Supplement No. 2 to 799.1 of this subchapter. As defined in that Note, "operation technical data" is the minimum necessary for the installation, operation, maintenance (checking), and repair of those products that are eligible for general licenses, or that are exported under a validated export license. The "minimum necessary" excludes from operation technical data development or production technical data and indudes use technology only to the extent required to ensure safe and efficient use of the product. Individual entries in the software and technology subcategories of the CCL may further restrict export of "minimum necessary" technical data. *(See Supplement Nos. 2 and 3 to 799.1 of this subchapter for further information and definitions of the terms "development" "production" "use" and "required.")*

(ii) Operation software may be exported under GTDR without assurance, provided that:
   (A) The operation software is the minimum necessary to operate the equipment authorized for export; and
   (B) The operation software is in object code.

9. Exporters of digital computer equipment must describe on their license applications any software, including that shipped under General License GTDR, to be used with the equipment.[22]

The COCOM exclusion from controls for operation technical data provides for one exception for repair technology described at ECCN 8E02.a. The GTN in the EAR provides for three additional exceptions to the relief from controls: repair "technology" controlled by 1E02.e, 1E02.f, and 7E03. Note that repair "technology" is a subset of "use" technology as the term is defined in COCOM and for the CCL at section 799.1, Supplement 3:

Use (General Technology Note)—Operation, installation (including on-site installation), maintenance (checking), repair, overhaul and refurbishing.[23]

---

[22] Fed. Reg. at 4564–65.
[23] 23. Fed. Reg. at 42902.

The three additional exceptions to the relief from controls are now the subject of USG proposals to COCOM and are therefore not precluded by reason of the prohibitions on unilateral controls. The theory behind these exclusions is that certain repair know-how is identical to the know-how to produce and item. Policy makers feel they should have an opportunity to condition the export of know-how to repair an item previously authorized for export and in this way assure that such know-how is not disclosed to foreign nationals, who could then use it to produce an unlimited quantity of such end products or use the technology to make other controlled end products.

Arguably, this exclusion of certain items is redundant given that the further qualification on operation technical data in section 779.4(b)(1) provides in part:

> The "minimum necessary" excludes from operation technical data development or production technical data and includes use technology only to the extent required to ensure safe and efficient use of the product.

This paragraph of the EAR is not a part of COCOM's GTN. In addition, the same result could be achieved by COCOM placing limitations or conditions on validated licenses for the export of related commodities. Of course, this strategy would not be effective in those few cases where COCOM has decontrolled a commodity but maintained controls on technology required to design or produce such a commodity.

It is important to remember that the provisions of the GTN apply to all entries on the CCL and are not limited to the implementation of COCOM controls. This is a significant feature because it permits the same definitions and procedures to apply regardless of the reasons for control. Any other approach could prove to be hopelessly confusing. It is also appropriate and likely that solutions found in COCOM will be applied to similar issues that inevitably face other, newer, evolving multilateral regimes such as the Missile Technology Control Regime, the Australia Group,[24] and the Nuclear Supplier Group.

In addition, section 779.4(b)(1) clarifies an existing Commerce practice or interpretation regarding software. This provides general license treatment for the "minimum necessary" software to operate a commodity authorized for export by either a general or validated li-

---

[24] The Australia Group, chaired by the Australian Government, was formed in 1984 to address the growing concern over chemical weapons proliferation and use. The Group is an informal body that operates on the basis of consensus. The participating governments represent supplier or producer countries. The member governments of the Australia Group are Australia, Austria, Belgium, Canada, Denmark, France, Germany, Greece, Ireland, Italy, Japan, Luxembourg, the Netherlands, New Zealand, Norway, Portugal, Spain, Switzerland, the United Kingdom, and the United States. Finland and Sweden recently joined the Australia Group.

cense. In the judgment of this author, the operating software authority extends beyond computer operating systems and also authorizes software that is the minimum necessary to operate other commodities. Such authority does not permit the export of software that increases the performance levels of the related products beyond those authorized in the relevant validated or general license for the related product.

Furthermore, the amendment to 779.4(b)(1) now permits the export of operation technical data by a party other than the exporter of the related commodity. Thus, if you can establish that the related commodity was exported lawfully, you may compete for maintenance and training business for such commodities and rely upon operation technical data authority under GTDU.

It is important to recognize here that, in practice, some information provided to support repair and maintenance is publicly available and therefore eligible for General License GTDA. For example, some firms put their maintenance manuals in public libraries or make them available to anyone for the asking at no more than the cost of reproduction and distribution. Such technology is eligible for General License GTDA. (See section 779.3 and Supplement 5 to Part 779). For this reason, it is imperative that exporters follow the logic of the decision tree described above in this Part II of this article. Exporters should not reach the incorrect conclusion that, for technology disclosed to support repair and maintenance, the only potential general license is GTDU for operation technical data.

SALES TECHNICAL DATA AND SOFTWARE

Historically, the prohibition of the use of sales technical data authority when the technology was "related" to a COCOM controlled product represented the major barrier to the use of such authority. The publication of the Conforming Regulation solved that problem. Section 779.4(b)(2) reads:

> (2) *Sales technical data.*
>   (i) "Sales technical data" is defined as data supporting a prospective or actual quotation, bid, or offer to sell, lease, or otherwise supply any item controlled by the EAR.
>   (ii) Sales technical data may be exported under GTDR, without written assurances, provided that:
>   (A) The technical data is a type customarily transmitted with a prospective or actual quotation, bid, or offer in accordance with established business practice; and
>   (B) The export will not disclose the detailed design, production, or manufacture, or the means of reconstruction, of either the quoted item or its product. The purpose of this limitation is

to prevent disclosure of technical data so detailed that the consignee could use the technical data in production.

NOTE: Neither this authorization nor its use means that the U.S. Government intends, or is committed, to approve an export license application for any commodity, plant, or technical data that may be the subject of the transaction to which such quotation, bid, or offer relates. Exporters are advised to include in any quotations, bids, or offers, and in any contracts entered into pursuant to such quotations, bids, or offers, a provision relieving themselves of liability in the event that an export license (when required) is not approved by the Bureau of Export Administration.[25]

The important safeguards for sales technical data authority remain. The technology cannot be so detailed that "the consignee could use the technical data in production." In effect, this underscores the natural business incentive of the vast majority of exporters, at the marketing stage, to refrain from disclosing know-how so detailed that the potential technology customer can reduce the know-how to production before paying for it. This provision is consistent with the implementation of the COCOM controls by other COCOM members. Such members probably do not consider general information (information that is not "detailed") to be subject to the COCOM controls.

It is important to note again that, in practice, much information provided to support bids is publicly available and therefore eligible for General License GTDA. For example, information given away at trade shows and information available to anyone for the asking at no more than the cost of reproduction and distribution is eligible for General License GTDA. (See section 779.3 and Supplement 5 to Part 779). For this reason, it is imperative that exporters follow the logic of the decision tree described above in Part II of this article. Exporters should not incorrectly conclude that GTDU sales technical data authority is the *only* potential general license for exporting technology in the marketing context. In addition, exporters often fail to properly classify the information they provide in a marketing context or in contract negotiations. Such information might be only performance data for the product to be sold, and this information may or may not constitute "design" "production" or "use" technology controlled under an ECCN that requires a validated license or written assurance.

GENERAL LICENSE GTDA

A complete discussion of GTDA is beyond the scope of this article. For a complete discussion, see section 779.3 and the questions and answers

---

[25] 57 Fed. Reg. at 4565.

at Supplement 5 to Part 779. Nonetheless, some observations are important. First, GTDA is the only general license that is in no way limited by technical limitations, country restrictions, end use restrictions, or end user restrictions. This is because GTDA is driven by the First Amendment. Secondly, there are several different means to qualify for GTDA, and you need only qualify under one of those options to benefit from GTDA. Thirdly, GTDA runs to the technology and not to the transaction. Therefore, under GTDA, you may export information published by someone else even though your transaction would not itself qualify the technology for GTDA.

Technology published or placed in libraries accessible to the public is GTDA-eligible because it is publicly available. (Sections 779.3(b)(1) and (2)). This is a broad category. However, only that which is public is GTDA-eligible. For example, if five production processes are published, each is publicly available. But if your firm is the first to find the combination of these five processes is useful and you chose not to publish the idea of combining the five processes, the combination is not GTDA-eligible. The whole is greater than the sum of the parts; and your trade secret cannot be exported or disclosed to foreign nationals by authority of GTDA.

Know-how in public records open to the public is also publicly available. This too is a broad authority because it includes the public records of any patent and copyright office. (Section 779.3(b)(3)). Of course, such information is subject to proprietary rights as intellectual property. However, in the export control context, such information is lost to potential adversaries with its publication. Publication of such information in the patent system serves two fundamental purposes: it puts the public on notice not to infringe these intellectual property rights, and it tells inventors the state-of-the-art so they do not reinvent such know-how but go on to advance the state-of-the-art. There is no practical way to advance these public policies and at the same time deny the know-how to adversaries. This is why the U.S. Government has a so-called secrecy order system to prevent the publication of certain technology even under the patent system. This element of TDA eligibility is separate and distinct from the authority to make foreign patent filings under section 779.3(e) and 37 C.F.R. Part 5.

In addition, technology is publicly available and therefore eligible for GTDA when it is made available to the public or "a community of persons, such as those in a scientific or engineering discipline" free or at no more than the cost of reproduction and distribution. (Section 779.3(b)(1)). Such information must be available to all comers within such a community, including your toughest competitors.

Finally, technology is GTDA-eligible if it is educational information released by "instruction in catalog courses and associated teaching laboratories of academic institutions." (Section 779.3(a)(3) and (d)). This too is a broad element of GTDA eligibility and is often overlooked by exporters. For persons interested in exporting certain fundamental research that will be published, refer to sections 779.3(a)(2) and (c) and Supplement 5 to Part 779.

DISCLOSURE TO FOREIGN NATIONALS

Section 779.1(b) provides that an export of technical data includes not only the physical export of technology but also any release in the U.S. with "knowledge or intent" that the data will be exported from the United States. Section 779.1(c) contains a comparable provisions regarding reexports.

Does release of data to a foreign national constitute such "knowledge or intent" regardless of the circumstances surrounding the disclosure? For years, the Office of Technology and Policy Analysis has concluded that it does.

As currently interpreted by the Office of Technology and Policy Analysis, this rule means that disclosure or release of technical data to a foreign national is a deemed export to his home country(ies). The rationale behind this interpretation is that after a foreign national receives controlled technology, he is free to leave the U.S. In fact, he may be required to leave the U.S. by reason of the immigration laws. When a foreign national does leave the country, export control enforcement officials cannot drain such know-how from his mind. Therefore, the ability to control such technology is lost at the moment of disclosure to him.

Currently, the deemed export interpretation does not apply to permanent resident aliens. However, there is no explicit provision for this on the face of the regulation. Probably the best justification for this element of the interpretation is that a permanent resident alien has virtually the same the same rights as a citizen to remain in the U.S. and that a foreign national is subject to at least some level of scrutiny by the U.S. Government before he is accorded permanent resident alien status.

Commerce has proposed that the deemed export prohibition be made explicit and that it be narrowed so as not to apply to intending citizens under the amnesty program and intending citizens with political asylum. This is the position now taken by the State Department in the implementation of the International Traffic in Arms Regulations. However, a consensus has not been reached on this proposal, and clarification of the deemed export interpretation under sections 779.1(b) and (c) remains unfinished business. Other proposals to limit the application of the deemed export interpretation are beyond the scope of this article.

The hiring of foreign nationals is not prohibited by the EAR. However, the disclosure of trade secrets to a foreign national is a deemed export under the above interpretation unless the foreign national is a permanent resident alien. This presents challenges for export control managers who must implement personnel policies necessary to comply with the EAR. The justification for such a policy is that there is no more effective means of conveying detailed information about design and production techniques than to work side-by-side in a laboratory or on the shop floor.

The same general licenses that would authorize the physical export of technology to a particular country also authorize release of such technology to foreign nationals of that country. For example, if GTDR with written assurance authorizes the export of your technology to country X, then a national of country X may receive your technology once he has given you the required written assurance. For this reason many firms obtain written assurances from employees at the time they are hired.

Of course, some technology requires a validated license to all destinations; and many firms seek to hire nationals from controlled countries or countries that are the target of non-proliferation and other foreign policy controls. For applications to disclose such technology, I suggest you provide the following types of information to the Office of Export Licensing in addition to the letter of explanation described at section 779.5(d):

1. The nationality of the individual.
2. The visa status of the individual.
3. The length of time the individual has been in the U.S.
4. The employment status of the individual, for example part-time versus full-time status and permanent versus temporary status.
5. Whether the employer intends to maintain employment of employee (visa status and work performance permitting). Note: this is not a representation from the employee, who might lose his visa if he makes an impermissible representation regarding his intent to remain in the U.S.
6. The nature of the non-disclosure agreement the individual has or will provide the employer.
7. Any other facts that may be relevant to the likelihood the individual will return to his home country and release the information you propose to disclose to him.

Section 779.1(b) provides that an export of technical data includes not only the physical export of technology but also any release in the U.S. with "knowledge or intent" that the data will be exported from the United States. Section 779.1(c) contains comparable provisions regarding reexports. These provisions apply to releases to U.S. citizens and permanent resident aliens, as well as other foreign nationals. However, such releases to U.S. citizens and permanent resident aliens are not deemed exports without more. Rather, these regulations create a duty of care in making releases to U.S. citizens and permanent resident aliens. This is the same duty of care required by section 787.4, which provides that no person may engage in any transaction with reason to know a violation is about to occur. For information on this standard of care, see the BXA paper entitled *"Know Your Customer" Guidance* set forth as Attachment B to this article.

The application of the deemed export interpretation also has a bearing on software controls. OTPA currently takes the position that access to source code is a release and deemed an export of the software to the home country of a foreign national other than a permanent resident alien. Access to software to use it without the ability to see the source code is not deemed an export of the software, and access to technical data loaded on software is a release and deemed export when the software is used by a foreign national, even if the source code is not seen by the foreign national. Of course, release of the machine code with reason to know an unauthorized export is about to occur is also prohibited by section 787.4.

CONCLUSION

Frequent changes in the scope of substantive controls over technology and software have been and likely will continue to be an ever-present feature of the EAR. The only constant in export control policy is change; and this will no doubt continue given the demise of the Soviet Union, the aftermath of Tiananmen Square, the race to multilateralize non-proliferation controls, progress towards the elimination of apartheid in South Africa, and the continued legislative debates regarding export controls. However, the structure for implementing software and technical data controls should now be stable and will always be a ready tool for the purpose of implementing technology and software control policy in a way that is clear to the exporter, manageable for the policy maker, and enforceable by the prosecutor.

Attachment A

Decision Tree for Technology and Software Controls

The following steps should be taken in descending order to determine the appropriate general or validated license for the export of technology or software. Follow these steps until you identify a general license available to you and then go no further. If these questions are answered out of order, or if you go down the decision tree beyond the first available general license, you may reach erroneous conclusions that no general license is available or that you must use an unduly restricted general license. If you choose to go further down the decision tree than is necessary because you have business reasons to use a more restrictive authorization, you may do so; but you are not required to:

1. *Classification.* Classify your technology and software. All technology and all software are on the CCL in some entry.*
2. *GTDA.* Determine the applicability of General License GTDA at 779.3.
3. *List-driven GTDU.*** From the proper ECCN entry on the CCL, determine the availability of General License GTDU. (General License GTDR without written assurance).
4. *Mass-market software GTDU.* For software, determine the availability of mass-market software authority at the General Software Note in Supplement 2 of the CCL.
5. *Sales technical data GTDU.* Determine the availability of sales technical data authority at 779.4(b)(2).
6. *Operation technical data GTDU.* Determine the availability of operation technical data and software authority at 779.4(b)(1) and the third paragraph of the General Technology Note at Supplement 2 to Part 779.
7. *Software updates GTDU.* Determine the availability of software update authority at 779.4(b)(3).
8. *G-TEMP.* Determine the availability of General License G-TEMP for software at 771.22.
9. *GTDR with written assurance.* Determine the availability of GTDR with written assurance at the proper entry on the CCL.
10. *Validated license.* If no general license is available, obtain a validated license before you make the physical export or disclose the technology or source code to a foreign national.

* Certain technology and software is properly under the jurisdiction of other federal agencies. See 770.10 and Supplement Nos. 2, 3, and 4 to Part 770 of the EAR.

** General Licenses GTDR with written assurance, GTDR without written assurance (GTDU), and validated licenses may not be used contrary to the provisions of 778.7(c) and 778.8(c), which prohibit exports for end-uses related to the design, development, production, or use of certain missiles and end-uses related to the design, development, production, stockpiling, or use of chemical or biological weapons respectively. Such prohibitions do not apply to General License GTDA.

Attachment B
BXA's "Know Your Customer" Guidance

Recent amendments to the Export Administration Regulations (EAR) require an exporter to obtain an individual validated license if the exporter "knows" that any export otherwise eligible for general license is destined for facilities or activities involving nuclear, chemical, or biological weapons, or related missile delivery systems, in named countries or regions.

In response to many requests, BXA offers some guidance here as to how individuals and firms should act under this knowledge standard. This guidance does not change or interpret the EAR.

- *Decide whether there are "red flags."* Take into account any abnormal circumstances in a transaction that indicate that the export may be destined for an inappropriate end-use, end-user, or destination. Such circumstances are referred to as "red flags." Included among examples of red flags are orders for items that are inconsistent with the needs of the purchaser, a customer declining installation and testing when included in the sales price or when normally requested, or requests for equipment configurations which are incompatible with the stated destination (e.g., 120 volts in a country with 220 volts). Commerce has developed lists of such red flags that are not all-inclusive but are intended to illustrate the types of circumstances that should cause reasonable suspicion that a transaction will violate the EAR. BXA is working on updating "red flags" which will apply more directly to weapons proliferation concerns.
- *If there are "red flags," inquire.* If there are no "red flags" in the information that comes to your firm, you should be able to proceed with a transaction in reliance on information you have received. That is, absent "red flags" (or an express requirement in the EAR), there is no affirmative duty upon exporters to inquire, verify, or otherwise "go behind" the customer's representations. However, when "red flags" are raised in information that comes to your firm, check out the suspicious circumstances and inquire about the end-use, end-user, or ultimate country of destination.

The duty to check out "red flags" is not confined to the use of general licenses affected by the "know" or "reason to know" language in the EAR. Applicants for validated licenses are required by EAR 772.6 to obtain documentary evidence concerning the transaction, and misrepresentation or concealment of material facts is prohibited, both in the licensing process and in all export control documents. You can rely upon representations from your customer and repeat them in the documents you file unless red flags oblige you to take verification steps.

- *Do not self-blind.* Do not cut off the flow of information that comes to your firm in the normal course of business. For example, do not instruct the sales force to tell potential customers to refrain from discussing the actual end-use, end-user, and ultimate country of destination for the product your firm is seeking to sell. Do not put on blinders that prevent the learning of relevant information. An affirmative policy of steps to avoid "bad" information would not insulate a company from liability, and it would usually be considered an aggravating factor in an enforcement proceeding.
- *Employees need to know how to handle "red flags."* Knowledge possessed by an employee of a company can be imputed to a firm so as to make it liable for a violation. This makes it important for firms to establish clear policies and effective compliance procedures to ensure that such knowledge about transactions can be evaluated by responsible senior officials. Failure to do so could be regarded as a form of self-blinding.

REEVALUATE ALL THE INFORMATION AFTER THE INQUIRY. The purpose of this inquiry and reevaluation is to determine whether the "red flags" can be explained or justified. If they can, you may proceed with the transaction. If the "red flags" cannot be explained or justified and you proceed, you run the risk of having had "knowledge" that would make your action a violation of the EAR.

REFRAIN FROM THE TRANSACTION OR ADVISE BXA AND WAIT. If you continue to have reasons for concern after your inquiry, then you should either refrain from the transaction or submit all the relevant information to BXA in the form of an application for a validated license or in such other manner as BXA may advise.

Industry has an important role to play in preventing exports and reexports contrary to the national security and foreign policy interests of the United States. BXA will continue to work in partnership with industry to make this front line of defense effective, while minimizing the regulatory burden on exporters. Your comments and questions are always welcome. *Write to: "Know Your Customer Guidance," P.O. Box 273, Washington, DC 20044.*

5

State Department Ruling on Cryptographic Export Media

United States Department of State

United States Department of State
Washington, DC 20520

October 7, 1994

Philip R. Karn, Jr.
[Home address deleted—Ed.]

Dear Mr. Karn:

I have now completed consideration of your appeal of CJ case 081-94, concerning your "applied cryptography source code disk." Pursuant to section 120.4(g) of the International Traffic in Arms Regulations (ITAR), I hereby reaffirm the determination by the Office of Defense Trade Controls that the disk you submitted is designated as a defense article under Category XIII(b)(1) of the United States Munitions List.

As you know, ITAR section 120.4, which sets forth the commodity jurisdiction procedure, states that the procedure may be used "if doubt exists as to whether an article or service is covered by the U.S. Munitions List" or "for consideration of a redesignation of an article or service currently covered by the U.S. Munitions List."

We have concluded that your disk is covered by Category XIII(b)(1) of the U.S. Munitions List as currently written, since it is [c]ryptographic . . . software with the capability of maintaining secrecy or confidentiality of information or information systems . . . ." You state in your March 9 letter that "[t]he software on this diskette is provided for those who wish to incorporate encryption into their applications." In your June 7 letter, you refer to the disk as an example of "cryptographic software".

You contend in your June 7 letter that the disk is not covered by the U.S. Munitions List because the disk qualifies for the ITAR "public domain" exemption. However, the ITAR's "public domain" exemption applies only to technical data meeting the "public domain" criteria, and cryptographic software does not come within the meaning of technical data as defined by the ITAR. The ITAR's software definition, at section 121.8(f), specifically excludes cryptographic software from the software for which an exporter should apply for a technical data license.

Having determined that your disk is covered by the U.S. Munitions List as currently written, I went on to consider whether your disk should remain covered by the List.

My conclusion that your disk should remain covered by the U.S. Munitions List rests on several considerations. Among these are a determination that the source code on the disk you submitted is of such a strategic level as to warrant continued State Department licensing. We have also reviewed your statement that the export of your disk is protected by the First Amendment to the Constitution, and have concluded that continued control over the export of such material is consistent with the protections of the First Amendment.

Please be assured that I reviewed your appeal with great care. The review process engaged attorneys, technical experts, and others both within the State Department and at various other government agencies. I personally spent a significant amount of time wrestling with the important and difficult issues raised by your request. Indeed, as I indicated to you in my letter of September 20, it was necessary to extend the normal period for consideration of such an appeal in order to ensure that the various legal and policy issues raised by your appeal were satisfactorily addressed.

As you know, section 120.4(g) of the ITAR provides that, if you so desire, an appeal of my determination may be made to the Assistant Secretary for Politico-Military Affairs.

Thank you again for the patience with this process that you and your attorneys have shown.

Sincerely,
[signed]
Martha C. Harris
Deputy Assistant Secretary
for Export Controls

## 6

Constitutionality Under the First Amendment of ITAR Restrictions on Public Cryptography*

John M. Harmon
Assistant Attorney General, Office of Legal Counsel

The purpose of this memorandum is to discuss the constitutionality under the First Amendment of restrictions imposed by the International Traffic in Arms Regulation (ITAR), 22 C.F.R. § 121 et seq. (1977), the regulation implementing § 38 of the Arms Export Control Act, 22 U.S.C.A. § 2778 (1977), on dissemination of cryptographic information developed independent of government supervision or support by sci entists and mathematicians in the private sector.[1] Our discussion is confined to the applicability of the regulation to the speech elements of public cryptography, and does not address the validity of the general regulatory controls over exports of arms and related items. We have undertaken our review of the First Amendment issues raised by the ITAR as an outgrowth of our role in implementing Presidential Directive NSC-24.[2]

ITAR PROVISIONS AND STATUTORY AUTHORITY

Under the ITAR, exports of articles designated on the United States Munitions List as "arms, ammunition, and implements of war" must be licensed by the Department of State 22 C.F.R. §§ 123, 125. Cryptographic devices are included on the list, 22 C.F.R. § 121.01, Category XIII, as are related classified and unclassified technical data, Category XVII, Category XVIII. It is this control over the export of unclassified

---

* Memorandum to Dr. Frank Press, Science Advisor to the President. May 11, 1978.

[1] The cryptographic research and development of scientists and mathematicians in the private sector is known as "public cryptography." As you know, the serious concern expressed by the academic community over government controls of public cryptography, see, *e.g.*, 197 Science 1345 (Sept. 30, 1977), led the Senate Select Committee on Intelligence to conduct a recently concluded study of certain aspects of the field.

[2] Our research into the First Amendment issues raised by government regulation of public cryptography led tangentially into broader issues of governmental control over dissemination of technical data. Those questions are numerous, complex, and deserving of extensive study, but are beyond the scope of this memorandum.

technical data which raises the principal constitutional questions under the ITAR.[3]

The broad definition of the term technical data in the ITAR includes:

> Any unclassified information that can be used, or be adapted for use, in
> the design, production, manufacture, repair, overhaul, processing, engi-
> neering, development, operation, maintenance, or reconstruction of arms,
> ammunition and implements of war on the U.S. Munitions List.

22 C.F.R. § 125.01. The definition of the term "export" is equally broad.
Under § 125.03 of the ITAR an export of technical data takes place:

> Whenever technical data is inter alia, mailed or shipped outside the United
> States, carried by hand outside the United States, disclosed through visits
> abroad by American citizens (including participation in briefings and sym-
> posia) and disclosed to foreign nationals in the United States (including
> plant visits and participation in briefings and symposia).

Thus ITAR requires licensing of any communication of cryptographic
information,[4] whether developed by the government or by private researchers, which reaches a foreign national.[5]

The standards governing license denial are set out in § 123.05. The
Department of State may deny, revoke, suspend or amend a license:

> whenever the Department deems such act advisable in furtherance of (1)
> world peace; (2) the security of the United-States; (3) the foreign policy of
> the United States; or (4) whenever the Department has reason to believe
> that section 414 of the Mutual Security Act of 1954, as amended, or any
> regulation contained in this subchapter shall have been violated.

---

[3] Unclassified technical data would generally encompass only privately developed,
nongovernmental cryptographic research. It is our understanding that government-sponsored cryptographic research traditionally has been classified. The only unclassified government cryptographic information of which we are aware is the Data Encryption Standard (DES) algorithm. The DES was developed for public use by IBM with National
Security Agency assistance and published in the Federal Register by the National Bureau
of Standards.

[4] The ITAR does exempt from the licensing requirement unclassified technical data
available in published form. 22 C.F.R. § 125.11(a). The scope of that exemption is somewhat unclear, although it does appear that the burden of ascertaining the ITAR status of
possibly exempt information is on the individual seeking publication. See 22 C.F.R. § 125
n.3. In order to claim the exemption, an "exporter" must comply with certain certification
procedures. 22 C.F.R. § 125.22.

[5] For example, in one instance the Office of Munitions Control, the office in the State
Department which administers the ITAR, refused to issue licenses to a group of scientists
preparing to address a conference on space technology in Madrid. The scientists, who
had already arrived in Spain, were refused permission to deliver papers at the symposium
on the subject of rocket propulsion and re-entry problems of space vehicles. Note, *Arms
Control-State Department Regulation of Exports of Technical Data Relating to Munitions
Held to Encompass General Knowledge and Experience*, 9 N.I.U. Int'l Law J. 91, 101 (1976).

Upon any adverse decision, the applicant may present additional information and obtain a review of the case by the Department. § 123.05(c). No further review is provided.

Nearly all of the present provisions of the ITAR were originally promulgated under § 414 of the Mutual Security Act of 1954 (former 22 U.S.C. § 1934). That statute gave the President broad authority to identify and control the export of arms, ammunition, and implements of war, including related technical data, in the interest of the security and foreign policy of the United States. Congress recently substituted for that statute a new § 38 of the Arms Export Control Act, 22 U.S.C.A. § 2778 (1977), *as amended*, 22 U.S.C.A. § 2778 (Supp. 3 1977). This statute substitutes the term "defense articles and defense services" for the term "arms, ammunition, and implements of war."[6] The President delegated his authority under both statutes to the Secretary of State and Secretary of Defense. Exec. Order No. 11,958, 42 Fed. Reg. 4311 (1977), *reprinted in* 22 U.S.C.A. § 2778 (Supp. 1 1977); Exec. Order No. 10,973, 3 C.F.R. 493 (Supp. 1964). A willful violation of § 38 of the Arms Export Control Act or any regulation thereunder is punishable by a fine up to $100,000, imprisonment up to two years, or both. 22 U.S.C.A. § 2778(c).[7]

THE FIRST AMENDMENT ISSUES

The ITAR requirement of a license as a prerequisite to "exports" of cryptographic information clearly raises First Amendment questions of prior restraint.[8] As far as we have been able to determine, the First Amendment implications of the ITAR have received scant judicial attention.

---

[6] The ITAR has not yet been amended to reflect the statutory change. We understand, however, that the Department of State has nearly completed a draft revision of the ITAR. It is our understanding that the revision is not intended to make any major substantive changes in the ITAR, but rather to update and clarify the regulatory language.

[7] Although the focus of this memorandum is on the First Amendment issues raised by the ITAR, we feel that one comment about the breadth of the two statutes is in order. It is by no means clear from the language or legislative history of either statute that Congress intended that the President regulate noncommercial dissemination of information, or considered the problems such regulation would engender. We therefore have some doubt whether § 38 of the Arms Export Control Act provides adequate authorization for the broad controls over public cryptography which the ITAR imposes.

[8] In addition, the regulatory provisions present questions of overbreadth and vagueness. "Overbreadth" is a First Amendment doctrine invalidating statutes which encompass, in a substantial number of their applications, both protected and unprotected activity. The "vagueness" concept, on the other hand, originally derives from the due process guarantee, and applies where language of a statute is insufficiently clear to provide notice of the activity prohibited. The same statute or regulation may raise overlapping questions under both doctrines.

The Ninth Circuit presently has a case under consideration which squarely presents a First Amendment challenge to the ITAR and could serve as a vehicle for the first comprehensive judicial analysis of its constitutionality. In that case, *United States* v. *Edler*, No. 76-3370, the defendants, Edler Industries, Inc. and Vernon Edler its president, were charged with exporting without a license technical data and assistance relating to the fabrication of missile components. Although the State Department had denied defendants an export license to provide technical data and assistance to a French aerospace firm, the government alleged that defendants nonetheless delivered data and information to the French during meetings in both France and the United States. Defendants were tried before a jury and found guilty. The trial court, the United States District Court for the Central District of California, did not issue an opinion in the case. On appeal, the defendants contend that the ITAR is both overbroad and establishes an unconstitutional prior restraint. The government's rejoinder to those claims is that the ITAR licensing provisions involve conduct not speech and that any effect upon First Amendment freedoms is merely incidental and therefore valid. We anticipate that the resolution of these issues by the Ninth Circuit may provide substantial guidance as to the First Amendment implications of the ITAR.[9]

The only published decision addressing a First Amendment challenge to the ITAR of which we are aware is *United States* v. *Donas-Botto*, 363 F.Supp. 191 (E.D. Mich. 1973), *aff'd sub nom. United States* v. *Van Hee*, 531 F.2d 352 (6th Cir. 1976). The defendants in that case were charged with conspiracy to export technical data concerning a Munitions List item without first obtaining an export license or written State Department approval. The exports by the defendants both of blueprints and of their technical knowledge concerning an armored amphibious vehicle were alleged to be in violation of § 414 of the Mutual Security Act and the ITAR. In a motion to dismiss the indictments, defendants contended that inclusion of technical knowledge within the Statute violated the First Amendment. The trial court disposed of that contention summarily, stating:

> [W]hen matters of foreign policy are involved the government has the constitutional authority to prohibit individuals from divulging "technical data" related to implements of war to foreign governments.

363 F. Supp. at 194. The Sixth Circuit upheld the conviction of one of the defendants without reaching any First Amendment questions since none was presented on appeal.[10]

---

[9] We understand that the case was argued this past March.

[10] The court did agree with the trial judge that the ample scope of the term "technical data" in the ITAR encompassed unwritten technical knowledge. 531 F.2d at 537.

The First Amendment analysis of the ITAR in the case thus is limited to a paragraph in the district court's opinion. In reaching the conclusion that the prosecutions did not violate the First Amendment, that court relied upon two Espionage Act decisions, *Gorin v. United States*, 312 U.S. 19 (1941), and *United States v. Rosenberg*, 195 F.2d 583 (2d Cir.), *cert. denied*, 344 U.S. 838 (1952). While those cases establish that the First Amendment does not bar prosecutions for disclosing national defense information to a foreign country, they by no means resolve the prior restraint question.[11]

A decision in a somewhat analogous area, the use of secrecy agreements by government agencies as a means of protecting against the unauthorized disclosure of information by present or former employees, while not directly applicable to the First Amendment questions we confront under the ITAR, is helpful for its discussion of government's power to control the dissemination of government information. That case, *United States v. Marchetti*, 466 F.2d 1309 (4th Cir.), *cert. denied*, 409 U.S. 1063 (1972), after remand, *Alfred A. Knopf, Inc. v. Colby*, 509 F.2d 1362 (4th Cir.), *cert. denied*, 421 U.S. 992 (1975), involved an action for an injunction brought by the United States to prevent a former CIA agent from publishing certain information he had obtained as a result of his CIA employment. The court held that the particular secrecy agreement was valid and enforceable in spite of Marchetti's First Amendment objections, but observed that:

> The First Amendment limits the extent to which the United States, contractually or otherwise, may impose secrecy agreements upon its employees and enforce them with a system of prior censorship. It precludes such restraints with respect to information which is unclassified or officially disclosed.

Id. at 1313. The general principle we derive from the case is that a prior restraint on disclosure of information generated by or obtained from the government is justifiable under the First Amendment only to the extent that the information is properly classified or classifiable.

Our research into areas in which the government has restricted disclosure of nongovernmental information provided little additional guidance. Perhaps the closest analogy to controls over public cryptography are the controls over atomic energy research.[12] Under the Atomic

---

[11] It is not clear from reading the district court's opinion on what First Amendment ground or grounds the defendants based their unsuccessful motion to dismiss.

[12] Atomic energy research is similar in a number of ways to cryptographic research. Development in both fields has been dominated by government. The results of government created or sponsored research in both fields have been automatically classified because of the imminent danger to national security flowing from disclosure. Yet meaningful research in the fields may be done without access to government information. The results of both atomic energy and cryptographic research have significant nongovern-

Energy Act of 1954, 42 U.S.C. § 2011 et seq. (1970), all atomic energy information, whether developed by the government or by private researchers, is automatically classified at its creation and subjected to strict nondisclosure controls.[13] Although neither the Atomic Energy Act nor its accompanying regulations establish formal procedures for prior review of proposed atomic energy publications, the Atomic Energy Commission (whose functions are now divided between the Nuclear Regulatory Commission and the Department of Energy) has been empowered to maintain control over publications through threat of injunction or of heavy criminal penalties, two potent enforcement tools provided under the Act. 42 U.S.C. §§ 2271–2277, 2280. It does not seem, however, that the broad information controls of the Atomic Energy Act have ever been challenged on First Amendment grounds. Our search for judicial decisions in other areas in which the government has imposed controls over the flow of privately generated information was equally unavailing.[14]

In assessing the constitutionality of the ITAR restrictions on the speech elements of public cryptography we therefore have turned to Supreme Court decisions enunciating general First Amendment principles. It is well established that prior restraints on publication are permissible only in extremely narrow circumstances and that the burden on the government of sustaining any such restraint is a heavy one. See, *e.g.*, *Nebraska Press Association* v. *Stuart*, 427 U.S. 539 (1976); *New York Times Co.* v. *United States*, 403 U.S. 713 (1971); *Organization for a Better Austin* v. *Keefe*, 402 U.S. 415 (1971); *Carroll* v. *Princess Anne*, 393 U.S. 175 (1968); *Near* v. *Minnesota*, 283 U.S. 697 (1931). Even in those limited circumstances in which prior restraints have been deemed constitutionally permissible, they have been circumscribed by specific, narrowly drawn standards for deciding whether to prohibit disclosure and by substantial procedural protections. *Erznoznik* v. *City*

---

mental uses in addition to military use. The principal difference between the fields is that many atomic energy researchers must depend upon the government to obtain the radioactive source materials necessary in their research. Cryptographers, however, need only obtain access to an adequate computer.

[13] See Green, *Information Control and Atomic Power Development*, 21 Law and Contemporary Problems 91 (1956); Newman, *Control of Information Related to Atomic Energy*, 56 Yale L.J. 769 (1947). The Atomic Energy Act uses the term "Restricted Data" to describe information which the government believes requires protection in the interest of national security. "Restricted data" is defined in 42 U.S.C. § 2014(4). The information control provisions of the Act are set out at 42 U.S.C. § 2161–2164.

[14] For example, it does not appear that the broad controls over exports of technical data and related information under the Export Administration Act of 1969, 50 U.S.C. App. § 2401 et seq. (1970), and accompanying regulations have been judicially tested on First Amendment grounds. Nor have the provisions of the patent laws restricting patentability of inventions affecting national security, 35 U.S.C. § 181 et seq. (1970), nor governmental restrictions on communications with Rhodesia, 22 U.S.C. § 287c (1970); Exec. Order No. 11,322.

of Jacksonville, 422 U.S. 205 (1975); *Blount* v. *Rizzi*, 400 U.S. 410 (1971); *Freedman* v. *Maryland*, 380 U.S. 51 (1965); *Niemotko* v. *Maryland*, 340 U.S. 268 (1951); *Kunz* v. *New York*, 340 U.S. 290 (1951) *Hague* v. *C.I.O.*, 307 U.S. 496 (1939).[15]

Even if it is assumed that the government's interest in regulating the flow of cryptographic information is sufficient to justify some form of prior review process, the existing ITAR provisions we think fall short of satisfying the strictures necessary to survive close scrutiny under the First Amendment. There are at least two fundamental flaws in the regulation as it is now drawn: first, the standards governing the issuance or denial of licenses are not sufficiently precise to guard against arbitrary and inconsistent administrative action; second, there is no mechanism established to provide prompt judicial review of State Department decisions barring disclosure. *See, e.g., Blount* v. *Rizzi, supra*; *Freedman* v. *Maryland, supra*; *Hague* v. *C.I.O., supra*. The cases make clear that before any restraint upon protected expression may become final it must be subjected to prompt judicial review in a proceeding in which the government will bear the burden of justifying its decisions. The burden of bringing a judicial proceeding cannot be imposed upon those desiring export licenses in these circumstances. The ITAR as presently written fails to contemplate this requirement.[16]

For these reasons it is our conclusion that the present ITAR licensing scheme does not meet constitutional standards. There remains the more difficult question whether a licensing scheme covering either exports of or even purely domestic publications of cryptographic information might be devised consistent with the First Amendment. Recent Supreme Court decisions certainly suggest that the showing necessary to sustain a prior restraint on protected expression is an onerous one.

---

[15] In *Freedman*, 380 U.S. at 58–59, the Court summarized the procedural protections necessary to sustain a scheme of prior review:
1. A valid final restraint may be imposed only upon a judicial determination;
2. The administrator of a licensing scheme must act within a specified brief period of time;
3. The administrator must be required either to issue a license or go to court to seek a restraint;
4. Any restraint imposed in advance of a final judicial determination on the merits must be limited to preservation of the status quo for the shortest period compatible with sound judicial resolution;
5. The licensing scheme must assure a prompt final judicial decision reviewing any interim and possibly erroneous denial of a license.

[16] The government's argument to the Ninth Circuit in *Edler*, that the impact of the ITAR upon protected communications is merely incidental, and that the ITAR should be viewed as a regulation of conduct not speech, deserves note. According to that argument, the less rigorous constitutional standard of *United States* v. *O'Brien*, 391 U.S. 367 (1968), would govern the validity of the ITAR. Although that may be true with respect to certain portions of the ITAR, even a cursory reading of the technical data provisions reveals that those portions of the ITAR are directed at communication. A more stringent constitutional analysis than the *O'Brien* test is therefore mandated.

The Court held in the *Pentagon Papers* case that the government's allegations of grave danger to the national security provided an insufficient foundation for enjoining disclosure by the *Washington Post* and the *New York Times* of classified documents concerning United States activities in Vietnam. *New York Times Co.* v. *United States, supra.*[17] The Court also invalidated prior restraints when justified by such strong interests as the right to fair trial, *Nebraska Press Ass'n, supra*, and the right of a homeowner to privacy, *Organization for a Better Austin* v. *Keefe, supra.* Such decisions raise a question whether a generalized claim of threat to national security from publication of cryptographic information would constitute an adequate basis for establishing a prior restraint. Nonetheless, it is important to keep in mind that the Court has consistently rejected the proposition that prior restraints can never be employed. See, *e.g., Nebraska Press Ass'n, supra* at 570. For example, at least where properly classified government information is involved, a prior review requirement may be permissible. *United States* v. *Marchetti, supra.*

In evaluating the conflicting First Amendment and national security interests presented by prior restraints on public cryptography, we have focused on the basic values which the First Amendment guarantees. At the core of the First Amendment is the right of individuals freely to express political opinions and beliefs and to criticize the operations of government. See, *e.g., Landmark Communications* v. *Virginia*, 46 U.S.L.W. 4389, 4392 (May 1, 1978); *Buckley* v. *Valeo*, 424 U.S. 1, 14 (1976); *Mills* v. *Alabama*, 384 U.S. 214, 218 (1966). Adoption of the Amendment reflected a "profound national commitment to the principle that debate on public issues should be uninhibited, robust, and wide-open," *New York Times* v. *Sullivan*, 376 U.S. 254, 270 (1964), and was intended in part to prevent use of seditious libel laws to stifle discussion of information embarrassing to the government. *New York Times Co.* v. *United States, supra* at 724 (concurring opinion of Mr. Justice Douglas).

---

[17] The Pentagon Papers case produced a total of ten opinions from the Court, a per curiam and nine separate opinions. All but Justices Black and Douglas appeared willing to accept prior restraints on the basis of danger to the national security in some circumstances. There was, however, no agreement among the Justices on the appropriate standard. Justice Brennan stated his view that a prior restraint on publication was justified only upon:

> "proof that publication must inevitably, directly, and immediately cause the occurrence of an event kindred to imperiling the safety of a transport already at sea. . . ."

403 U.S. at 726–27. Justice Stewart, with whom Justice White concurred, suggested that a prior restraint would be permissible only if disclosure would "surely result in direct, immediate and irreparable damage to our Nation or its people." *Id.* at 730. Several other Justices declined, given the facts and procedural posture of the case, to formulate a standard.

Prior restraints pose special and very serious threats to open discussion of questions of public interest. "If it can be said that a threat of criminal or civil sanctions after publication 'chills' speech, prior restraint 'freezes' it at least for the time." *Nebraska Press Ass'n, supra* at 559.

Since views on governmental operations or decisions often must be aired promptly to have any real effect, even a temporary delay in communication may have the effect of severely diluting "uninhibited, robust, and wide-open" debate. And protection of any governmental interest may usually be accomplished by less restrictive means. One avenue generally available to the government, and cited by Supreme Court as the most appropriate antidote, is to counter public disclosures or criticisms with publication of its own views. *See, e.g.,* *Whitney* v. *California,* 274 U.S. 357, 375 (1927) (concurring opinion of Mr. Justice Brandeis).

The effect of a prior restraint on cryptographic information, however, differs significantly from classic restraints on political speech. Cryptography is a highly specialized field with an audience limited to a fairly select group of scientists and mathematicians. The concepts and techniques which public cryptographers seek to express in connection with their research would not appear to have the same topical content as ideas about political, economic or social issues. A temporary delay in communicating the results of or ideas about cryptographic research therefore would probably not deprive the subsequent publication of its full impact.

Cryptographic information is, moreover, a category of matter "which is both vital and vulnerable to an almost unique degree."[18] Once cryptographic information is disclosed, the damage to the government's interest in protecting national security is done and may not be cured. Publication of cryptographic information thus may present the rare situation in which "more speech" is not an alternative remedy to silence.[19] See *Whitney* v. *California, supra* at 376 (concurring opinion of Mr. Justice Brandeis).

---

[18] *New York Times Co.* v. *United States,* 403 U.S. 713, 736 n.7 *quoting* H.R. Rep. No. 1895, 81st Cong., 2d Sess., 1 (1950). That report pertains to the bill which became 18 U.S.C. § 798, the criminal statute prohibiting disclosure of information concerning the cryptographic systems and communications intelligence activities of the United States. Section 798 does not reach disclosure of information published by public cryptographers, as its coverage is restricted to classified information. Classified information by definition is information in which the government has some proprietary interest. See § 1(b) of the May 3, 1978 draft of the Executive Order on national security proposed to replace Executive Order 11,652; *cf.* 22 C.F.R. § 125.02.

[19] In stressing the differences between cryptographic information and other forms of expression we do not mean to imply that the protections of the First Amendment are not applicable to cryptographic information or that they are confined to the exposition of ideas. See *Winters* v. *New York,* 333 U.S. 507, 510 (1948). We recognize that the scope

Given the highly specialized nature of cryptographic formation and its potential for seriously and irremediably impairing the national security, it is our opinion that a licensing scheme requiring prepublication submission of cryptographic information might overcome the strong constitutional presumption against prior restraints. Any such scheme must, as we have said, provide clear, narrowly defined standards and procedural safeguards to prevent abuse.

While a detailed discussion of the specific provisions and procedures of a valid scheme of prior review of cryptographic information or of its practical and political feasibility is beyond the scope of this memorandum, some general observations are in order. First, we wish to emphasize our doubts that the executive branch may validly provide for licensing or prior review of exports of cryptographic information without more explicit Congressional authorization. The scope of the existing delegation of authority from Congress to the President, as we note above, is somewhat unclear. Before imposing a prior restraint on exports of public cryptographic information, we believe that a more clear cut indication of Congressional judgment concerning the need for such a measure is in order. *See United States* v. *Robel*, 389 U.S. 248, 269 (1967) (concurring opinion of Mr. Justice Brennan); *cf. Yakus* v. *United States*. 321 U.S. 414 (1944).

Second, further Congressional authorization would obviously be necessary in order to extend governmental controls to domestic as well as foreign disclosures of public cryptographic information. Such an extension might well be necessary to protect valuable cryptographic information effectively. Indeed, limiting controls to exports while permitting unregulated domestic publication of cryptographic research would appear to undermine substantially the government's position that disclosure of cryptographic information presents a serious and irremediable threat to national security.[20]

---

of the amendment is broad. It encompasses, for example, purely commercial speech, *Virginia State Board of Pharmacy* v. *Virginia Citizens Consumer Council, Inc.* 425 U.S. 748 (1976), and communicative conduct, *Cohen* v. *California* 403 U.S. 15 (1971). We believe, however, that the extent of First Amendment protection may vary depending upon the nature of communication at issue. It is established in the area of commercial speech that greater governmental regulation may be tolerated due to the special attributes of that form of speech. *Virginia State Board of Pharmacy* v. *Virginia Citizens Consumer Council, supra* at 770–71 and n.24. Speech in the labor context also presents special First Amendment considerations. *See, e.g., N.L.R.B.* v. *Gissel Packing Co.*, 395 U.S. 575 (1969). And obscene communications have received specialized treatment from the courts. *See, e.g., Roth* v. *United States*, 354 U.S. 476 (1957).

[20] A question which would arise from complete governmental control over cryptographic information is whether the government would be required under the Fifth Amendment to pay just compensation for the ideas it had effectively "condemned." For example, the patent and invention provisions of the Atomic Energy Act require the government to pay for patents which it revokes or declares to be affected with the public interest. 42 U.S.C. §§ 2181–2190. A cryptographic algorithm, however, would not appear

Third, no final restraint on disclosure may be imposed without a judicial determination. We recognize that a requirement of judicial review presents substantial problems. The proof necessary in order to demonstrate to a judge that highly technical cryptographic information must be withheld from publication because of the overriding danger to national security might be burdensome and might itself endanger the secrecy of that information. It is our opinion, however, that any system which failed to impose the burden on government of seeking judicial review would not be constitutional.[21] See, e.g., *Blount* v. *Rizzi, supra.*

Finally, any scheme for prior review of cryptographic information should define as narrowly and precisely as possible both the class of information which the government must review to identify serious threats to the national security and the class of information which the government must withhold.[22] The scheme clearly should exempt from a submission requirement any information, such as that which is publicly available or which poses no substantial security threat, that the government has no legitimate interest in keeping secret.[23] Failure to draft provisions narrowly might well invite overbreadth challenges for inclusion of protected communication. See, e.g., *NAACP* v. *Alabama,* 357 U.S. 449 (1958). And a precisely drawn scheme is also necessary to avoid objections of vagueness. See, e.g., *Smith* v. *Goguen,* 415 U.S. 566 (1974).[24]

---

to be a patentable process. See *Gottschalk* v. *Benson,* 409 U.S. 63 (1972). And it is unresolved whether copyright protection is available for computer software. See *Nimmer on Copyright,* § 13.1 (Supp. 1976). We are therefore uncertain as to the status of cryptographic ideas under the Fifth Amendment.

[21] The threat to national security posed by a judicial review procedure could be reduced substantially by conducting the review in camera. See *Alfred A. Knopf, Inc.* v. *Colby,* 509 F.2d 1362 (4th Cir.), *cert.* denied 421 U.S. 992 (1975); *cf.* § U.S.C. 552(a)(4)(B) (Supp. 1975) (in camera review provision of the Freedom of Information Act). The Supreme Court, in any event, has been unimpressed by arguments that disclosure of sensitive national security information to a court raises such serious problems of public dissemination that exemption from constitutional requirements is appropriate. See *United States* v. *U.S. District Court,* 407 U.S. 297 (1972).

[22] In other words, we assume that the information submitted under the scheme would not be coextensive with the information withheld. We note, however, that the authority of the government to require prepublication submission of information which is neither classified nor classifiable is unsettled. That issue is posed in the suit recently filed by the Department of Justice in the United States District Court for the Eastern District of Virginia against former CIA employee Frank Snepp for breach of his secrecy agreement. *United States* v. *Snepp,* Civil Action No. 78–92-A.

[23] As we noted above, at n.4, *supra,* the present ITAR provisions attempt to exempt publicly available information. But the scope of that exemption and the procedures for invoking it, particularly with respect to oral communications, are somewhat clear.

[24] Although we mention questions of overbreadth and vagueness raised by the technical data provisions of the ITAR previously in this memorandum, we have not attempted to identify and analyze particular problems for several reasons. First, our opinion that a prior restraint on public cryptography might survive First Amendment scrutiny is a lim-

In conclusion, it is our view that the existing provisions of the ITAR are unconstitutional insofar as they establish a prior restraint on disclosure of cryptographic ideas and information developed by scientists and mathematicians in the private sector. We believe, however, that a prepublication review requirement for cryptographic information might meet First Amendment standards if it provided necessary procedural safeguards and precisely drawn guidelines.

---

ited one and does not purport to apply to the many other types of technical data covered by the ITAR. Second, we believe that public cryptography presents special considerations warranting separate treatment from other forms of technical data, and that a precise and narrow regulation or statute limited to cryptography would be more likely to receive considered judicial attention. Finally, we are uncertain whether the present legislative authority for the technical data provisions of the ITAR is adequate.

Afterword

Charles A. Hawkins, Jr., Acting Assistant Secretary of Defense (C3I) summarized the encryption policy issue very well in a memo for the U.S. Deputy Secretary of Defense on May 3, 1993[1]:

> Advances in telecommunications have created the opportunity for public use of encryption to ensure the privacy and integrity of business and personal communications. These same advances threaten the capabilities of law enforcement and national security operations that intercept the communications of narcotraffickers, organized criminals, terrorists, espionage agents of foreign powers and a broad range of SIGINT targets. Diverse interests are in diametric opposition with regard to industry's right to sell and the public's right to use such capabilities. A highly-emotional, spirited public debate is likely.
>
> The law enforcement and national security communities argue that if the public's right to privacy prevails and free use of cryptography is allowed, criminals and spies will avoid wiretaps and other intercepts. They propose that cryptography be made available to the public which contains a "trapdoor" that would allow law enforcement and national security officials, under proper supervision, to decrypt enciphered communications. Such cryptography exists, and while there are many practical problems to be solved, this proposal is technically possible to implement.
>
> Opponents of the proposal argue that the public has a right to and expectation of privacy, that such a system would be prone to misuse and abuse, and that the proposed solution would not work in any practical sense. They assert that criminals and spies will not hesitate to use secure cryptography supplied by offshore companies. Thus, the loss of privacy would outweigh any advantages to law enforcement or national security.
>
> The computer industry points out that it has one of the few remaining positive trade balances and that it is vital that the dominance of the American computer industry in world markets be preserved. The industry fears that this will be lost if offshore developers incorporate high-quality cryptography into their products while U.S. industry either cannot do so or suffers higher costs or delays due to requirements for export licenses because of strict controls of export of cryptography. The industry argues persuasively that overseas markets (much less drug lords or spies) will not look with favor on U.S. products which have known trapdoors when offshore products which do not have them are available.

He also correctly observed that encryption policy is not a technological issue:

> Trapdoor encryption technology is not essential to the debate since a system that required the escrow of keys by users of cryptographic tech-

---

[1] Obtained through a Freedom Of Information Act (FOIA) request by John Gilmore.

nologies could be established even if the trapdoor chips did not exist. Proposed use of trapdoor technology does raise a further complication: neither the academic community nor private industry is comfortable with encryption algorithms that are kept secret, as will be the case with the trapdoor chip. It has been suggested that an independent panel of cryptography experts will be invited to evaluate the algorithm. This will not reassure the community at large that there are no unrecognized vulnerabilities, since the panel will be perceived as captive and tainted.

The essence of the cryptographic policy debate was captured by a speech delivered well before the personal computer was ever invented. In 1968, Thomas J. Watson Jr., Chairman of the Board of IBM, was discussing privacy in computer systems[2].

> ". . . the problem of privacy in the end is nothing more and nothing less than the root problem of the relation of each one of us to our fellow men.
> What belongs to the citizen alone?
> What belongs to society?
> Those, at bottom, are the questions we face—timeless questions on the nature and place and destiny of man. . . ."

These same questions work equally well for cryptography.

Unfortunately, the body charged by the Computer Security Act of 1987 with advising the U. S. government on computer security was systematically frozen out by the Bush and Clinton administrations. Willis Ware, Chairman of the Computer System Security and Privacy Advisory Board, in his May 3, 1994 testimony before the Subcommittee on Technology, Environment, and Aviation of the Science and Technology Committee of the U. S. House of Representatives, described in detail how the Board passed its initial resolution on cryptography policy in March 1992, calling for a national public review. A number of their concerns were ignored by the Administration, and the April 16, 1993 Clipper announcement was a complete surprise to the Board. As Ware pointed out, "such a broad examination of a subject that had never been widely discussed publicly would be difficult to conduct, primarily because of the conflicting interests of so many stakeholders inherent in cryptography. [It] found no one within government willing to accept the challenge and, eventually, we realized that NIST could not do it either. . . ."

Information Security and Privacy in Network Environments, an excellent report by the U.S. Congress Ofice of Technology Assessment, recently observed that

---

[2] Watson, Thomas J., Jr. "Technology and Privacy" Address to the Commonwealth Club of California, U.S.A., 5 April 1968. Reported in "The Considerations of Data Security in a Computer Environment" International Business Machines Corp. (IBM), U.S.A. Publication No. G520-2169-0, July 1970.

"The escrowed-encryption initiative in general and the EES in particular have been met with intense public criticism and concern: the EES has not yet been embraced within government and is largely unpopular outside of government. The controversy and unpopularity stem in large part from privacy concerns and the fact that users' cryptographic keys will be held by government-designated "escrow agents" (currently, within the Departments of Commerce and Treasury). Other concerns regarding the EES and its implementation include the role of NSA in the escrowed-encryption initiative and in NIST's standards development, the use of a classified algorithm in the standard, the requirement that the standard be implemented in hardware (not software), the possibility of key-escrow encryption being made mandatory in the future, and the general secrecy and closed processes surrounding the Clinton Administration's escrowed-encryption initiative.

Recognizing the importance of cryptography and the policies that govern the development, dissemination, and use of the technology, Congress has asked the National Research Council (NRC) to conduct a major study that would support a broad review of cryptography. The OTA report presents several options for congressional consideration in the course of a strategic policy review. Because information to support a congressional review of cryptography is out of phase with the government's implementation of key-escrow encryption (the NRC report is expected to be completed in 1996), one option would be to place a hold on further deployment of key-escrow encryption, pending a congressional policy review.

An important outcome of a broad review of national cryptography policy would be the development of more open processes to determine how cryptography will be deployed throughout society in support of electronic delivery of government services, copyright management, and digital commerce. More open processes would build trust and confidence in government operations and leadership, as well as allow for public consensus-building, providing better information for use in congressional oversight of agency activities. As part of a broad national cryptography policy, Congress could also periodically examine export controls on cryptography to ensure that these continue to reflect an appropriate balance between the needs of signals intelligence and law enforcement and the needs of the public and business communities."

Further it noted that

"Congress may also wish to address the working relationship of NIST and the National Security Agency in implementing the Computer Security Act of 1987 (P.L. 100-235). The act gives NIST (then the National Bureau of Standards) final authority for developing government-wide standards and guidelines for safeguarding unclassified, sensitive information, and for developing government-wide security training programs. Implementation of the Computer Security Act has been controversial, particularly regarding the roles of NIST and NSA in standards development; a 1989 memorandum of understanding between the two agencies appears to cede more authority to NSA than the act had granted or envisioned.

The OTA report offers a range of options for dealing with privacy issues in the public and private sectors, ranging from continuing to allow federal agencies to manage privacy on an individual basis to establishing a Federal Privacy Commission."

The NRC study had its kickoff meeting on October 5, 1994, and its results are not expected until late 1995 at the earliest.

List of Acronyms

ACLU	*American Civil Liberties Union*
ANSI	*American National Standards Institute*
CIA	*Central Intelligence Agency*
COCOM	*Coordinating Committee*
CPSR	*Computer Professionals for Social Responsibility*
CSSPAB	*Computer System Security and Privacy Advisory Board*
DES	*Data Encryption Standard*
DPSWG	*Digital Privacy and Security Working Group*
DSS	*Digital Signature Standard*
EES	*Escrowed Encryption Standard*
EFF	*Electronic Frontier Foundation*
FBI	*Federal Bureau of Investigation*
IDEA	*International Data Encryption Algorithm*
IITF	*Information Infrastructure Task Force*
ISO	*International Standards Organization*
ITAR	*International Traffic in Arms Regulations*
LEAF	*Law Enforcement Access Field*
NII	*National Information Infrastructure*
NIST	*National Institute of Standards and Technology*
NSA	*National Security Agency*
NSC	*National Security Council*
OMB	*Office of Management and Budget*
PGP	*Pretty Good Privacy*
RSA	*RSA encryption algorithm developed by Rivest, Shamir and Adleman; also RSA Data Security, Inc.*

Index